# HANDBOOK OF CHILDREN, CULTURE, AND VIOLENCE

*To Myrtle Sweet, Alice Fretwell, and*
*Glen R. W. Wilson II for being such wonderful examples.*

—Robin

*To Jerry, with gratitude for all your support.*

—Dorothy

*To Zoe and Zack.*

—Nancy

# HANDBOOK OF CHILDREN, CULTURE, AND VIOLENCE

EDITED BY

Nancy E. Dowd

*University of Florida, Levin College of Law*

Dorothy G. Singer

*Yale University*

Robin Fretwell Wilson

*University of Maryland, School of Law*

*For information:*

Sage Publications, Inc.
2455 Teller Road
Thousand Oaks, California 91320
E-mail: order@sagepub.com

Sage Publications Ltd.
1 Oliver's Yard
55 City Road
London EC1Y 1SP
United Kingdom

Sage Publications India Pvt. Ltd.
B-42, Panchsheel Enclave
Post Box 4109
New Delhi 110 017 India

Printed in the United States of America

**Library of Congress Cataloging-in-Publication Data**

Handbook of children, culture, and violence / edited by Nancy E. Dowd, Dorothy G. Singer, Robin Fretwell Wilson.
p. cm.
Includes bibliographical references and indexes.
ISBN 1–4129–1369–1 (cloth)
1. Children and violence. 2. Children—Crimes against. 3. Violence in children. 4. Violence in popular culture. I. Dowd, Nancy E., 1949– II. Singer, Dorothy G. III. Wilson, Robin Fretwell.
HQ784.V55H34 2006
362.76—dc22

2005018302

This book is printed on acid-free paper.

05 06 07 08 09 10 9 8 7 6 5 4 3 2 1

| | |
|---|---|
| *Acquisitions Editor:* | Jim Brace-Thompson |
| *Editorial Assistant:* | Karen Ehrmann |
| *Production Editor:* | Kristen Gibson |
| *Copy Editor:* | Teresa Herlinger |
| *Typesetter:* | C&M Digitals (P) Ltd. |
| *Cover Designer:* | Michelle Lee |

# Contents

# *Tables and Figures*

# Introduction

Nancy E. Dowd

Every day, 9 children are homicide victims and 20 die from firearms. Every day, nearly 8,000 children are reported as abused or neglected. Every day, over 4,000 children are arrested, 180 for violent crimes, and 367 children for drug abuse. Over 17,000 children are suspended each day from school. Every day, Black and Hispanic children are disproportionately more of the victims and more of the perpetrators (Children's Defense Fund, 2004).

Children are the victims of violence, and the perpetrators of violence, in staggering numbers. Violence in the lives of children is so pervasive that it might even be conceived of as a kind of terrorism. Unlike the difficulties that face us in combating foreign or domestic terrorism, however, violence that victimizes children, or that children engage in, is a problem that can more easily be confronted, and it is a problem that adults and society must solve. This volume is an effort to bring multidisciplinary expertise to bear on the complex issues involved in the intersection between children, culture, and violence, and to suggest directions for public policy.

Violence pierces the lives of all of our children, sometimes in multiple ways. Children and young adults are more at risk of victimization from violence than any other age group. Gun-related deaths are the second leading cause of death for persons age 15 to 19; they are the leading cause of death of African American and Hispanic youth of all ages under 18. Over 90% of known juvenile homicide offenders are male (America's Children, 2001; Rennison, 2001; Snyder & Sickmund, 1999, as cited in Center for Substance Abuse Prevention, n.d.). The U.S. homicide rate for males age 15 to 24 is the highest among developed countries, and is 8 times higher than the rate of the next-highest country (Glicklich-Rosenberg, 1996). While gun deaths are the most dramatic form of victimization, the most common forms of personal violence come from family and peers. This includes adult abuse and neglect as well as adult assaults; sibling assaults; and peer intimidation, bullying, harassment, and assaults (Lewit & Baker, 1996). Victimization is not limited to being the victim of direct or indirect physical threat or harm. Violence in children's lives also includes witnessing violence to others and witnessing or experiencing violence in our culture, particularly from television and other media (Brown & Bzostek, 2003).

Children are especially vulnerable in their homes. The place that should be a sanctuary, where children are the most dependent and which is most private and hidden from public view, is a common place where children are physically victimized. Younger children are particularly at risk. Child abuse and neglect is more frequent than one might imagine. Nearly a million children are abused by their parents each year; in 2002, the estimated number was 896,000 children (United States Department of Health and Human

Services, 2004). Double that number are victims of neglect (Hill, Rugs, & Young, 2004, as cited in National Center on Addiction and Substance Abuse Prevention, 1999). The data on victimization are disputed by some, but there is no doubt that children's victimization from abuse and neglect can be fatal: in 2000, there were 1,137 child fatalities from abuse and neglect nationally (Child Welfare League of America, 2001). Over half a million children are in foster care, a number that continues to rise, and one-fifth of those children at any time are waiting for a permanent adoptive placement and hoping for a home free of direct violence toward them (Child Welfare League of America, 2001).

The rate of less direct violence is also high. Annually, an estimated 3.3 million children witness domestic violence in their homes (Edelson, as cited in Carlson, 1984). If a child's mother or father is being battered, the child is more likely to be hurt as well, or to be a victim of neglect (Edelson, 1999). Not only do children suffer physically, they also suffer higher alcohol and drug abuse problems, juvenile delinquency, cognitive and developmental problems, and speech and language problems (Edelson, 1997). Tragically, as adults, those who witnessed domestic violence as children may commit domestic violence themselves, repeating the pattern they have experienced. Boys are more likely to be batterers if they have grown up with a man who batters, and girls are more likely to be victimized when they have seen their mothers battered (A Safe Place, n.d.).

Children are also subject to violence in their schools. Children are targets for racial and sexual harassment, homophobic harassment and violence toward gay and lesbian youth, and bullying. Bullying is widespread: one survey given to children in Grades 3 through 8 found that 75% of the children reported being bullied in the past month (Walls, 1998). Sexual harassment is also commonplace. According to a 2001 American Association of University Women (AAUW) study, four of every five students in eighth through eleventh grades report some kind of sexual harassment in school (defined in the AAUW study as "unwanted and unwelcome sexual behavior that interferes with your life. Sexual harassment is not behavior that you like or want, for example, wanted kissing, touching, or flirting"), with the percentages for boys (79%) nearly as high as that for girls (83%) (AAUW, 2001). Half of the surveyed students admit to being harassers as well (AAUW, 2001). Gay and lesbian students suffer even more pervasively from bullying and harassment (Human Rights Watch, 2001). Racism continues to pervade our schools 50 years after *Brown v. Board of Education* was decided. The rate of residential segregation is as high or higher than 50 years ago, which is closely linked to ongoing de facto racial segregation as well as educational inequality (Dowd, 2005). Racial harassment, including racial slurs but also physical acts of violence, varies significantly by race, with rates as high as 50% among children of color (Anderson, Attwood & Howard, 2004; Reis, Mendoza & Takamura, n.d.; Rosenbloom, 2004). "Everyday racism" (meaning daily acts of micro-aggression and devaluation), that may not be considered racial harassment but which strongly affects children's well-being, continues to be part of the culture in which children must function (Feagin, Early, & McKinney, 2001).

In its most extreme manifestation, school violence can lead to eruptions of vengeance like Columbine and other school shootings. Violence in schools has shifted from primarily urban settings, linked to gang-related disputes and disputes between individual students, to more severe and widespread violence that involves urban, suburban, and rural schools. Victims remain predominantly male but no longer disproportionately involve young men of color ("Youth Violence," 2001).

Some children are also victimized on the streets in their communities. Although children age 12–19 constitute only 14% of the population, they are victims in 3 of 10 crimes, and 1 in 4 thefts (Finkelhor, Paschall, & Hasinma, 2001; Snyder & Sickmund, 1999). Some children live in communities with higher rates of violence, where drive-by shootings and other acts of street violence are commonplace, drug selling is omnipresent, and life expectancy for the young is short (Stop the Violence, n.d.). Street gangs exist in nearly all communities with a population of over 100,000, and their presence directly raises the homicide risk for the children in those communities. Membership in a gang increases one's risk of homicide by 60% (Hixon, 1999).

It is not an accident that children are disproportionately victimized by violence—it is precisely *because* they are children that they are victims. Their very status makes them targets. For example, child homicide victims most commonly are either very young or are adolescents. The highest rate of homicides is among very young children, particularly infants. Very young children most frequently die at the hands of family members, while adolescents are most commonly killed by acquaintances (Federal Bureau of Investigation, 1995, as cited in Lewit & Baker, 1996). Within children as a group, moreover, certain children are more likely to be victims than others, reflecting inequalities of gender, race, and class. Females are more likely at any age to be the victim of sexual abuse and assault (Wilson, this volume). For most other kinds of violence, males are at much higher risk. Black children are at greater risk for homicide, abuse, and neglect; they are also more likely than children of other races to be victims of assault or robbery. Black children watch considerably more television than other children and therefore are exposed to more media violence. "Among 8th graders in 2001, 62% of black students watched four or more hours of TV on an average weekday, compared to 22% of white students. Similarly, large differences are evident for 10th and 11th grade students, though the levels are lower" (Brown & Bzostek, 2003).

Children are also perpetrators of violence at an alarming rate. Young persons between the ages of 12 and 17 are responsible for approximately 20 to 25% of serious violent crime ("Youth Victims and Perpetrators," n.d.). Children, including those under age 12, sexually assault other children at a high rate. In 2001, according to the FBI Uniform Crime Report, 4,600 juveniles were arrested for forcible rape and 18,000 for other sexual offenses, representing 17% and 20%, respectively, of all arrests in those categories (Snyder, 2003). The link between juvenile sex offenses and adult sex offenses is strong: the majority of adult offenders report a history of sex offenses before age 18 (Shaw, 1999). The other strong link is between offenders and their own victimization as children: sexual abuse was present for 92–95% of adult sexual offenders, with 100% of female offenders reporting abuse, and 50–75% of male offenders. This abuse was predominantly by family members, most commonly fathers (Araji, 1997, as cited in Concepcion, 2004).

The level of child-to-child violence is reflected in the number of children and youth who carry lethal weapons. In a 1999 study, almost 20% of students had carried a weapon during the prior 30 days, and males were far more likely to do so than females (Kann, Kinchen, Williams, et al., 2000, as cited in Center for Substance Abuse Prevention, n.d.). One study of juvenile arrestees found that more than two thirds claimed their primary reason for carrying a weapon was self-protection (Decker, Pennell, & Caldwell, 1997).

Those who enter the juvenile justice system most often, and who receive the most serious sanctions, are Black males. One in three Black males is in the juvenile system. Although Black youth make up approximately 25% of the juveniles arrested, they are roughly half of those tried as adults and also half of those housed in state prisons (Jacobs, 2004).

The data concerning juvenile violence must be linked to the record of child victimization. Particularly disheartening is the link between childhood victimization and violent acts by these victims. The same children who are brutally harmed frequently use violence as the way to feel empowered, becoming child or adult perpetrators. The failure to deal with childhood victimization by redirecting early violent acts has the predictable consequence of continuing the cycle of violence against children. The victimization of children and their acts of violence also are linked to cultural messages about violence that are part of children's socialization. Children are victimized not solely by physical violence, or even verbal, emotional, or psychological abuse. They also are harmed by a popular culture saturated with violence that contributes to the possibility of physical or other forms of direct victimization. The role of culture in socializing both children and adults to accept and participate in violent acts rather than peaceful resolutions is among the most troubling aspects of the relationship between children and violence. Violent culture can be another form of victimization because of its direct negative effect on children as they develop. Our culture may contribute to children being violent, either as children or when they become adults.

Children on average watch 3 to 4 hours of television daily (American Academy of Child and Adolescent Psychiatry, 2001). Some surveys find an even higher average of up to 6.5 hours daily (Woodard & Gridina, 2000). According to one study, there are on average 20 violent incidents per hour of children's programming (American Psychological Association, n.d.). In addition, there is considerable racial and sexual stereotyping. Extensive research indicates a link between viewing television violence and increased aggressiveness in children (Kunkel & Zwarun, this volume). In addition, studies show that children become desensitized to violence, accept it as a way to solve problems, imitate the violence that they watch, and identify with particular characters who may be victims or victimizers (American Academy of Child and Adolescent Psychiatry, 2001; American Psychological Association, n.d.). Children spend more time watching media than they do attending school. The cumulative effect is staggering. Based on an assumption of 28 hours of television per week, the average American child "by the age of 18 will have seen 16,000 simulated murders and 200,000 acts of violence" (American Psychiatric Association, n.d).

If children are not watching television, they may be spending their time on computers, watching videotaped movies, playing video games, or surfing the Internet. The average time spent on these alternate forms of media, in addition to television, is 4 hours per child per day (Youth Violence, 2001). While children ages 2–18 overall "consume" 5.5 hours daily of some form of media (including television, video games, the Internet, or other forms), the highest rates of consumption are found among children ages 8–13 (Kaiser Foundation, 1999). Even children under age 6 average 2 hours daily (Kaiser Foundation, 2005). First introduced in the 1970s, video games are now a fixture in our culture. They are also another source of violence directed at children. Studies show that those who play prefer violent games over nonviolent games, and that the level of violence in games has increased (Anderson & Bushman, 2001). The impact of gaming is similar to that of television, particularly the fact that it increases aggressiveness (Anderson & Bushman, 2001; Cesarone, 1994). The average child plays 90 minutes of video games every day. Boys game more than girls do, and games have a strong gender message that is attached to stereotypical gender roles

(Children Now, 2000). Women are victims, with Black women victimized twice as often as White women (Children Now, 2001). The games are infused with racial stereotypes: the majority of heroes are White males, while men of color are limited to sports competitors or villains.

The presence of violence in culture is a delicate and difficult subject. It is delicate because it quickly generates concerns about free speech. Music can be a powerful language of protest and criticism, while it can also celebrate subordination and objectification. Protest can be voiced in ugly, profane, offensive language as a tool to gain attention and provoke, or such language may be used purely for shock value for commercial gain. Political protest can be commingled with misogynist, racist, or homophobic speech. Similarly, the Internet is the epitome of the free marketplace of ideas. It provides vast amounts of information and creative opportunity to children. It permits the articulation of ideas and the organization of citizens from the grass roots. But that same freedom can permit rampant racism and sexism, and predatory acts intended to victimize children. It is difficult to deal with these aspects of our culture because we may either assume conclusions or ignore contradictions between the presence of violence and the link to children as victims or as perpetrators. Culture is a constantly evolving, created piece of society. Arguably the solutions to cultural problems lie within society, not in laws or regulations. It is essential to explore mediating influences to the presence of violence as well as the difficult question of how to change culture without inhibiting it.

Culture can become an easy scapegoat for concerns about children as perpetrators of violence, when there are other explanations that would require a different or additional focus of policy. Poverty is powerfully associated with a range of factors that contribute to violence and which in turn perpetuate poverty. In 2002, the federal poverty guideline was $18,100 for a family of four (United States Department of Health and Human Services, 2002). That year, one in six American children were poor; by race, nearly one third of Black and Hispanic children and 10% of White children were poor (Children's Defense Fund, 2004). Racism is a powerful generator of violence and has had catastrophic effects, particularly on Black boys and men. Similar roles are played by sexism and homophobia. Both poverty and hatred can justifiably be seen as forms of violence as well as factors that contribute to violence toward children or the violent behavior of children. Our focus in this collection on culture is not intended to deny the powerful impact of these and other factors, but rather to focus more specifically on the link between culture and violence.

The challenge that this volume seeks to address is the interlocking nature of violence, culture, and children, in order to suggest short-term and long-term ways to combat violence. Understanding the nexus between violence and culture is critical to better addressing the policy issues in this area. It is also critical to ground policy in empirical data and to draw on a multidisciplinary approach as essential to effective problem solving. Legal approaches may be tempting in many instances, but as this book reveals, they often are a shortsighted, inadequate response. What is needed is far more comprehensive if children are not to be permanently scarred by violence.

Children's dependency on adults makes them vulnerable. Society is obligated to do better for its children, for their own sake and for the sake of the larger society. The elimination of violence or its reduction in the lives of children is a high priority, a precondition for many other essential needs. It has a direct impact on both the future of children and the future of society.

## PLAN OF THE BOOK

This handbook is representative of the range of ways that children intersect with violence and culture. It presents empirical data, theoretical grounding, and policy recommendations. A multidisciplinary approach is critical to effective public policy in this area.

The book is divided into three parts that consider children as victims, as consumers, and as perpetrators of violence. Dorothy Singer's Prologue is an essential context for all that follows because it reminds us that children must be considered in a developmental context. What is frightening to a 4-year-old may have an entirely different effect on a 10-year-old or an adolescent. How we understand the impact of direct or indirect violence, of various cultural modes, and violent acts by children, mandates that we understand children's basic developmental stages and capabilities. Developmental differences may inform the construction of policy differently for preschoolers than high school students. It can also frame expectations of veracity and reliability when children testify in legal proceedings, whether they are victims of or eyewitnesses to violence. Singer discusses children's intellectual, social, and emotional development in the preschool, elementary school, middle school, and high school years.

Part I, Children as the Victims of Violence, explores the experiences of children as victims, in the context of domestic violence, sexual abuse, and child abuse. Naomi Cahn begins with an exploration of the implications of children witnessing domestic violence. Only in the last decade have courts and researchers focused on witnessing; previously only direct victimization was considered harmful. Cahn details the empirical evidence that children who witness domestic violence may suffer significant short-term and long-term cognitive, emotional, and physical effects. Courts have begun to respond to these harms to children by considering the implications for custody, visitation, and other relevant legal issues. After critically evaluating recent legislative efforts and the application of existing statutes to deal with the harms of witnessing, Cahn suggests that four critical principles must guide policy and practice in this area. First, the harms from witnessing domestic violence must be taken seriously. Second, the relationships that children have with the battered adult should be fostered and supported. Direct victims should not be subjected to blame and separation from their children. Third, the safety of children and the adult victim should be the most important consideration in any proceeding. Finally, batterers should be held to account for the harm of children witnessing violence to another family member. Implementation of these principles would require statutory reform as well as changes in the application of the law, which Cahn suggests in the conclusion of her chapter.

The powerful arguments raised by domestic violence advocates may lead, however, to unintended consequences for children. Tom Lyon and Mindy Mechanic examine the contradictory forces that may treat victims of domestic violence as inadequate parents from whom children should be removed, as an unintended result of persuasive data used to justify limiting the custody rights of batterers. The cogency of the arguments like those raised by Cahn and others might logically be extended, in other words, to justify greater intervention in the family in dependency actions to prevent actual harms or potential risks to children. The correlation between battering of adults and abuse of children is high, suggesting significant risk for children when battering of adults occurs. Moreover, as Cahn's chapter demonstrates, witnessing alone is harmful. Finally, the underlying dynamic of battering is a poor foundation for parenting. Yet as Lyon and Mechanic point out, automatic intervention is unjustified. Such intervention blames the victim and fails to recognize the difficult choices facing adult victims of domestic violence and the consequences for children. The policy issue is whether intervention should mean removal or some alternative, effective system of support for children as well as the adult victim. Fundamentally, Lyon and Mechanic raise the question of how the cycle of violence can be broken or avoided within the context of legal and social institutions that are arguably inadequate for adults but are even worse for children.

Robin Wilson discusses a related issue of intervention and policy in the context of child sexual abuse. Wilson argues for stronger state intervention in the context of incest. Based on the empirical data about offenders, Wilson contends the evidence of potential risk for other children in the household is so overwhelming that as a matter of policy, an adult who commits incest should be removed from the household. Wilson documents the evidence that parents who commit incest rarely stop with one child. Courts, however, frequently ignore this evidence, she points out, and fail to adequately protect other siblings from parents who are sexual predators. In particular, courts sometimes disagree about whether a sex offender will victimize biological children as much as stepchildren, and whether they will victimize sons as well as daughters. The data indicate, however, that these distinctions are irrelevant: once one child is victimized, others are at significant risk. Wilson argues that the policy of dealing with this problem simply by engaging in risk assessment is an incomplete solution, because all other children *are* at risk. She advocates a more radical, fundamental response that would exclude the offender from the household. This approach is widespread in the United Kingdom, providing a template for the United States. Wilson evaluates this approach and urges its adoption on a wide scale in the United States.

Diana Russell and Natalie Purcell explore the very definition of what constitutes child sexual abuse in their chapter on child pornography. Russell and Purcell argue that non-computer-generated pornographic photographs of children are a form of child sexual abuse because the impact of viewing child pornography is demonstrably likely to support acts of child sexual abuse by juvenile and adult males. The social science data that substantiate the effect of child pornography should, they argue, be the basis for prosecution of child abuse. According to Russell and Purcell, the data demonstrate that when males view child pornography, it has three effects that victimize children. First, it predisposes some males to want to sexually abuse children, or intensifies previously existing predispositions in some males. Second, child pornography undermines some males' internal inhibitions against their desire to sexually abuse children. Third, child pornography undermines some males' *social* inhibition against their desire to sexually abuse children. While all of these effects are significant, Russell and Purcell especially underscore the harm of child pornography in reorienting boys and men to victimize children when they previously had no inclination to sexually abuse children. The logical implication of these effects would be to link this data to redraft child abuse statutes or consider whether in their current form they could be applied to child pornography.

Whether the state effectively uses statutory rape to deal with sexual crimes against children is the focus of the chapter by Ross Cheit and Laura Braslow. Statutory rape has been a controversial subject because of the historically strongly gendered construction of the criminal prohibition. Originally devised to protect only girls, statutes are now gender neutral but nonetheless are disproportionately applied when the victims are girls. Some have argued that imposing strict liability for sex with young girls imposes the state's views of sexuality on young women and, indirectly, young men. In addition, some would contend that modern sexual mores among teenagers makes prosecution for statutory rape an ineffective weapon to prevent "young love." On the other hand, others argue that the statutes are necessary to protect against sexual predators and, in particular, the victimization of young girls by older teenagers or adult men. Cheit and Braslow examine these conflicting views by evaluating the data on statutory rape in Rhode Island for an 18-year period from 1985 to 2002 against the backdrop of existing studies on teen sexuality, teen pregnancy, and statutory rape. Their data strongly contradict the view that statutory rape prosecutions are aimed at "young lovers" who simply violate social norms. To the contrary, they found that statutory rape arrests and prosecutions are relatively rare, sentences are lenient, and the relationships at issue do not appear to be good, positive relationships. They suggest that criminal prosecution of statutory rape is underutilized for the real harm it was intended to prevent, while substituting for other harms when prosecution for child abuse or rape would be more appropriate. One set of data presented in this chapter suggests that the crime is not taken seriously, as the cases frequently are not referred for prosecution and, for those that are, offenders rarely do time. A second set of data suggests that the relationships involved commonly have large age differences and are not dating relationships, undermining the idea that prosecutions are intrusions into healthy adolescent relationships. Collectively the data support the view that the sexual crimes against children that statutory rape was intended to sanction are serious, but that prosecution under existing statutes is not taken seriously.

In a wide range of contexts where children are victims, their participation in the criminal justice system should generate special solicitude. In the concluding chapter to Part I, Charles Putnam and David Finkelhor argue for uniform laws to protect the identities of child victims and witnesses from public disclosure and publicity. The range of situations in which children can be victimized, as well as the developmental context that must be considered in order to help children, are essential when evaluating children's privacy interests. As Putnam and Finkehor point out, children and adolescents are frequent crime victims. In fact, children and adolescents are twice as likely as adults to be crime victims. With respect to sex offenses, they are 75% of the victims that come to the attention of police. If the perpetrator of the crime is a juvenile, then the perpetrator and victim are shielded from public view. If the perpetrator is an adult, however, we value public scrutiny, and that exposes children to such scrutiny, including media attention. The identity of the child and details of the crime may be disclosed, whether the child is the victim or a witness. Putnam and Finkelhor explore the data on the effects of publicity on children; the history of our legal traditions shielding certain participants in the legal system; current statutory approaches to protecting the privacy interests of children; and non-statutory means to protect children. They conclude that the most effective response to protecting children from identified harm is through the adoption of strong, uniform statutory protection to shield the identity of child victims and witnesses. In the conclusion of their chapter, Putnam and Finkelhor set forth detailed specifications of what such legislation should include.

Part II, Children as Consumers of Violence, moves from considering children as direct victims of violence to examining the interaction of children with culture. Claims of harm may be grounded on the impact of violence on children in the process of their development, fostering violent tendencies or violent problem solving. Harm may also be based on the argument that violence in our culture fosters violent acts in adults who then victimize children *because* they are children. This section examines violence in the cultural forms to which children are most frequently exposed. It is a picture of complexity and even contradiction, rather than one of easy analysis.

John Cech begins by reminding us that when considering violent speech or violent culture, we tend to think of movies, television, the Internet, and video games, but we should also think about children's literature. As Cech points out, violence is a staple of children's literature, including the most famous and classic children's stories—Aesop's Fables, Mother Goose, the Brothers Grimm—as well as contemporary adolescent novels. In his well-known study of fairy tales, Bruno Bettelheim argues that violent endings in fairy tales clarify the consequences of good and evil: good is rewarded and evil is harshly punished. Cech provides us both with perspective and challenge, pointing out the persistent presence of violence in literature. He therefore suggests the impact of regulation would affect this form of culture as well. His work also raises the issue of what purpose violence serves in literature, and other cultural realms.

Nancy Signorielli's examination of violence in prime-time television echoes Cech's point that violence can have many different purposes in narrative. Signorielli focuses on the role and purpose of violence in context. Rather than simply looking to see if violence is present in a program, Signorielli focuses on violence as a plot element. She examines who does the hurting or killing, and who gets hurt or killed, particularly from the perspectives of gender, age, race, and occupation. Her concern is not merely with the presence of violence but also with what else it might communicate about power and victimization, threat and protection. Her analysis of the effects of violence on children is therefore a more nuanced, sophisticated examination of the messages about self conveyed by violence. She finds that more men than women, more Whites than minorities, and more middle-aged than younger characters are involved in violence. Although men formerly outnumbered women in television violence, women now have parity in their association with violent programming. Those who watch more television tend to see the world as more violent than it actually is; they also get messages about the distribution of power and the place of people who look like them in the pecking order. Children, who are consistently among the victimized, get the message of their powerlessness. Very young children, under 7, may see the way out of their powerlessness as being like certain cartoon characters, who commit "sanitized" violence that has little real effects and is defended as morally justified.

Joanne Cantor redirects our attention to the *effects* on children of violence in the media, particularly television, and suggests strategies for coping with those effects that maximize the role of parents while casting media and community in supportive roles. Cantor focuses on the well-established data showing that exposure to violence in the media increases anxiety, and links that to data establishing a general increase in anxiety levels of children and adults in the last half of the 20th century. While media violence is not the only cause of that increased anxiety, it is nevertheless a significant one. The combination of real and media violence has lasting effects on young people. Regulating media violence continues to be controversial. Cantor advocates providing essential information about violence to parents and others so that the effects can be better mediated. Cantor sees parents and other caregivers as critical educators of children, to regulate programming and help children cope with psychological effects. Media can be helpful by supporting parents' role with information regarding programming well in advance. Cantor also suggests that the media need to be better advised about child-friendly strategies. She outlines a mandated universal content-rating system for all media as a helpful strategy, as well as regulation of children's access to adult-rated video games. She also advocates the inclusion in custody decisions of consideration of a parent's media access practices. Her goal is at a minimum to better inform parents so that they can provide basic media education for their children.

Just as controversial as some television programming, and sometimes included on television in the form of music videos, are some forms of music and the lyrics of certain songs. Barbara Wilson and Nicole Martins examine the violence in popular music, especially rap and hip-hop, genres that have broad appeal among youth. They detail the listening habits of youth as well as the content of what they listen to. Music is a pervasive part of children's lives, both as a primary and a background activity. Indeed, for adolescents it may be the most important form of media. Wilson and Martins explore the differences by gender that emerge by the end of elementary school in the content of what children listen to, but they also point out that a far stronger basis of differentiation in content is race and ethnicity. Black youth listen primarily to "Black" music, White youth listen to "White" and "Black" music, and Latino youth listen to "Black," "White," and "Latin" music. Rap/hip-hop, however, is a genre popular across racial lines. Wilson and Martins examine the reasons why children listen to music and the messages within music and music videos. Content analysis is less developed with music than with music videos. Wilson and Martins also point out, however, that content analysis alone does not tell us how children process music lyrics. In some sense, younger children may be somewhat "protected" because they do not understand the lyrics. As the authors point out, the symbolism and use of metaphor in music makes it more difficult to comprehend, and therefore many preteen children literally will not understand lyrics. In addition, no single meaning may emerge because of the nature of the language and the music. On the other hand, devoted fans of particular music are more likely to know and understand the lyrics. Although there is far less research on the effects of violent music or music videos, Wilson and Martins conclude that the available research plus learning theory suggest that the same connection exists between violent music and greater aggressiveness as has been established between television violence and aggression. Wilson and Martins conclude that further research is needed to explore effects, including the impact of music on younger children, particularly as they are developing their social and dating roles in preadolescence and adolescence.

Dale Kunkel and Lara Zwarun present a comprehensive look at research on violence in television. Kunkel and Zwarun point out that violence contributes to three main negative psychological effects for children: learning and encouraging aggressiveness; desensitization to real violence; and an exaggerated fear of being attacked. They caution that not all violence in media has the same effect in terms of fostering these psychological effects. Context and consequences have a significant impact in terms of how children understand and are affected by violence in media. Nevertheless, the violence present in television is widespread, with much of it in a form that is most harmful to children. Kunkel and Zwarun's work suggests a more nuanced approach to regulation, whether by law, parents, or voluntary media self-regulation. At the same time, their research suggests several cautions. Of the regulations that have been attempted, few have been successful due to First Amendment issues. One notable exception is the V-chip, but they find parents use it far less than what might be expected. A second caution that emerges from prior attempts at regulation is its limitation to broadcast channels, leaving unregulated cable channels, which now dominate television programming.

Craig Anderson and Doug Gentile shift the focus to video games. Video games are among the more recent additions to children's culture, but are powerfully attractive to children. Anderson and Gentile review the empirical research on the effects of exposure to violent video games on children, as well as relating it to the research literature on television and film violence. While there is far less research on games than on television, the available research suggests that the effects of violence in games is just as negative for children as the research on television violence concludes. Anderson and Gentile document the evolution of violent games, the emergence of a voluntary rating system, and the development of ever more violent games with more sophisticated graphics. They outline the different types of studies needed on this type of media, and the results from available studies. While some studies demonstrate the positive effects of video games, the studies that focus on the effect of violence in games demonstrate negative outcomes: increased aggressiveness, although this outcome depends on both frequency of play and content of the games. While there are other risk factors for aggressiveness, they point out that playing video games can be controlled, while other risk factors (for instance poverty, drug use, psychological disorders) are far more challenging to deal with. They suggest three responsibilities of the game industry: to clearly label what is in the games; to market appropriately and not lure children into games that pose significant risks for them; and to educate and encourage parents to use a meaningful ratings system. Parents have equivalent responsibilities to be informed and to limit both the amount and content of games. Retailers and rental companies can support parents by making it more difficult for children to get access to adult games. Gentile and Anderson consider an array of possible public policy options. Like Cantor, they support a universal, and improved, ratings system for all media to assist parents.

While the negative effects of violent video games appear to be documented in the available research, Laurie Taylor encourages consideration of the positive effects of video games, even violent games. She cautions us to evaluate the positive effects, especially for particular children, when considering regulation. How children play games, including video games, is the basis for her evaluation of positive effects. Taylor emphasizes that the reason the games are played is not solely because of their violent content, but because they are enjoyable and rewarding. Creativity (such as changing the rules) and cooperation (playing with one or more other children, with defined expectations of sharing and fairness) are part of gaming. In addition, she points out that video games also provide the benefit of safe play in a social context where some children lack a safe environment for other kinds of play. Children in single-family or latchkey homes, or in dangerous neighborhoods, may use video games to enjoy and learn social rules without risk. Taylor suggests video games can provide other benefits including learning cultural and community rules, problem and puzzle solving, strategic and critical thinking skills, spatial exploration, stories, and more. Video games can provide positives as well as negatives, and Taylor suggests how to balance these effects to insure children in need of the positives are not disproportionately hurt by policies that seek to eliminate or dissipate the negatives in a simplistic way.

Brendesha Tynes examines similar issues of violence on the Internet, particularly the presence of racism and other stereotypical attitudes in chat rooms on the Internet. Tynes explores the use of the Internet by hate groups to spread their views about race, and the impact of these sites for children. Although much of the research on Internet hate groups has focused on adults, Tynes's research monitored Web sites, chat rooms, and discussion boards specifically geared to youth, that engage in racist or anti-Semitic hate speech. Tynes reminds us that nearly all children have Internet access. The nature of the Internet permits the availability of information that would be less accessible, if not totally absent, from other forms of media, with far fewer controls. Tynes details how hate groups use persuasive rhetoric to attract children to their message. At the same time, Tynes points out that children also are active perpetrators of hate messages on the Internet. Children as young as 11, alone or with the help of others, use the anonymity of cyberspace to engage in hate speech. As Tynes points out, these developments pose several harms for children. First, hate speech has direct harmful effects on its victims. Second, this fosters racism in our culture in a new, disturbing, and more virulent form. Third, hate speech has the potential to inspire other kinds of violence, including harms to both property and persons. She suggests a number of policy implications from this data. First, regulation of hate speech runs into difficult First Amendment problems, which make it virtually impossible to regulate the speech itself. Filters to deal with content are both inadequate and overly broad. Tynes advocates a far-reaching, community-based response to Internet hate speech. She recommends monitoring the problem online similar to the way hate speech is monitored offline. Second, she contends that online hate crimes should be vigorously prosecuted. Third, and most significant, she advocates a counter-discourse of tolerance, broadly supported by the community. Legal and regulatory approaches, she contends, ultimately are not a solution; rather, the solution lies in the values we embrace as our social norms.

This section closes by examining the core legal issues under the First Amendment that arise when these various forms of media are challenged as harmful to children because of their violent content. Catherine Ross cautions that a simplistic call to regulate is likely to trigger serious First Amendment concerns. Her chapter considers the quintessential First Amendment issues that arise when trying to regulate violence because of its harms to children. She examines whether the state has a more compelling interest, sufficient to withstand constitutional scrutiny, in regulating violent speech than in regulating sexually oriented (though not obscene) speech. One of the most challenging difficulties is defining how "violence" would be defined for purposes of regulation. In addition, it is difficult to regulate for the benefit of children without restricting the speech available to adults. Ross also concludes that despite the significant social science data on violence in the culture and its harms, the evidence is still insufficient to meet the demanding standard that must be satisfied for regulation to pass constitutional scrutiny. She ultimately determines that regulation is not the answer and that parents, supported by the media, are best suited to regulate children's exposure to inappropriate or harmful materials. She concludes that it is difficult to imagine effective regulation that would pass constitutional muster. Ross's chapter suggests the challenges that must be confronted in effectively dealing with children's exposure to violence in our culture.

The necessity for broad-based, multidisciplinary approaches that link parents, communities, and policy makers to issues of children and violence in our culture, to construct effective solutions rather than to blame, is also essential in dealing with children when they are the perpetrators of violence. Children as the victimizers are the focus of Part III, Children as Perpetrators of Violence.

While only a small portion of children may engage in hate speech on the Internet, many children engage in bullying and teasing at school. Susan Limber and Ellen deLara offer two valuable chapters that present concrete policy recommendations for confronting this commonplace form of violence committed by children.

Susan Limber's overview of current research reminds us that it has only been since the high-profile Columbine incident in 1999 that research and prevention have become a priority. The prevalence of bullying is widespread and disturbing. Limber summarizes the intersections with age, developmental stage, gender, and race, and also emphasizes that this is just as common in suburban as urban settings. The highest prevalence of bullying is among elementary-aged children. Victims may either be passive victims or bully-victims—children who are both bullies and victims of bullies. Certain children, such as disabled children and obese children, are particularly likely to be bullied. Those who bully frequently are not loners or social misfits, but rather are popular and social leaders. Limber also outlines family characteristics of bullies, which links family abuse to bullying behavior. The author emphasizes that bullying is rarely an act done in isolation, but rather commonly involves an audience of other students. It is action taken in a context and culture that either supports or accepts bullying. Limber explores the social ecology of bullying, including school characteristics and community or social influences. She suggests taking a social-ecological approach to devising programs to prevent bullying, utilizing known risk and protective factors to devise strategies for prevention that link families to schools and take a comprehensive, schoolwide approach.

Ellen deLara is critical of adult approaches to bullying that either minimize or misunderstand the problem. She points out that our very naming of these acts of violence tends to diminish its seriousness, treating them as a rite of passage of childhood. By accepting the behaviors as normal, adults condone them and to a great extent, she argues, leave children to their own devices to deal with peer violence. Particularly chilling is her description of the ways in which children cope with bullying because of their perception that adults will do nothing about this violence. Indeed, frequently adults even blame the victims for being bullied. The harm of bullying, which includes both in-school conduct and the newer cyberbullying, is both its direct effects on victims and its link to retaliatory violence. As deLara points out, many children fear a "Columbine" could happen at their schools because of the pervasiveness of bullying and the targeting of unpopular youth. DeLara characterizes school as our children's workplace, and argues that behavior that would be intolerable in the adult workplace under a range of laws and employer policies is nevertheless tolerated in schools. The victims of that toleration, moreover, have little or no power to confront this violence, in comparison to adults in the workplace. DeLara argues that the responsibility for ending these violent behaviors rests with adults and their control of the school environment. Family and community beliefs and behavior support and enable bullying; it is adults, then, who must act to prevent it. DeLara points out convincingly, however, that the ways in which this can be accomplished must come from the children who experience this violence. She focuses on adolescents' perception of the problem and solutions, which reflects much greater sophistication and pragmatic problem solving than the dismissive or paternalistic approaches of adults or school administrators. Rather than placing the responsibility on children to intervene on their own behalf, her recommendations place the onus on adults to address the underlying issues, by engaging in communication and partnership with children. She outlines the characteristics of successful interventions to deal with bullying that requires a community-based model of involvement by adults, mirroring the policy recommendations of Tynes with respect to Internet hate speech.

Bullying is not the only form of violence committed by children. Children commit criminal acts outside of school against persons and property that may bring them within the criminal justice system or family courts. A separate juvenile justice system, together with family courts, is justified based on children's developmental differences that distinguish their culpability and consequences from that of adults. Most significantly, the justice system ideally aims to rehabilitate children so that they may still become productive adults. In the process, the system should also treat juveniles fairly and insure that racial, ethnic, or gender bias does not taint the system.

Structuring the juvenile justice system based on sound behavioral science research is the focus of Mark Fondacaro and Lauren Fasig's chapter. Ecological jurisprudence brings legal assumptions into line with modern behavioral science research. Fondacaro and Fasig argue that the system has been narrowly premised on issues of development and psychological culpability, when broader contextual factors are essential to understanding juvenile behavior. These include family, school, peer, neighborhood, and media influences. The authors discuss empirical data that demonstrate the importance of situational influences, in sharp contrast to the assumption of autonomous individualism that underlies imposition of criminal responsibility for juveniles and adults. The social ecological approach sees no decision as made in a vacuum; rather, psychological ability interacts with context. The most critical contextual factor for children is their family. Peers, in addition, have a strong impact on children's behavior, and Fondacaro and Fasig note that criminal conduct more often happens when a child is in a group rather than when a child acts alone. Low socioeconomic status, poverty, and poor schools as well as poor academic achievement are also strongly linked to juvenile crime, as are social norms and situational factors. Fondacaro and Fasig propose a risk-management model designed not to allocate blame but to prevent recidivism. In addition, they argue against the movement toward harsher punishment and treating children more the way adults are treated in the adult criminal justice system.

Richard Redding also critiques the movement toward a more punitive approach to juvenile crime, particularly the movement to transfer juveniles to the adult criminal justice system. In his chapter, he focuses on the fundamental question of whether trying and punishing children as adults prevents crime. Redding documents the movement toward adjudicating serious and chronic juvenile offenders as adults, either by giving them adult-like sentences in juvenile court, or transferring juveniles for trial and incarceration in adult facilities. This movement has been based on the assumption that harsher treatment will act as a deterrent to serious juvenile crime. Redding argues that there is little empirical data to support this assumption, and therefore concludes that adult punishment does not reduce juvenile crime. His analysis yields two interlocking conclusions that suggest a rethinking of the approach to juvenile crime that complements the analysis of Fondacaro and Fasig. First, he finds the rehabilitative goal of the juvenile justice system to be fundamentally sound, as a goal that is most successful in helping children and preventing further crime. Redding also finds, however, that earlier, stronger consequences within the system may be more effective for offenders. In other words, the necessity that a "message" be sent to juvenile offenders, in the form of meaningful sanctions instead of a slap on the wrist, has validity, but needs to be accomplished earlier in their interface with the courts and within the rehabilitative model of the juvenile justice system. Second, Redding points out that the available evidence suggests transfer to the adult system is counterproductive. Rather than reducing crime, it *increases* recidivism as compared to trying and sentencing juveniles in the juvenile system. The reasons for this outcome are tied to juveniles being labeled as convicted felons, a sense of abandonment and resentment toward the system and society, and the lack of emphasis on rehabilitation and family support. Because the adult system is focused on punishment, children get the message that there is no hope for them. In addition, in the adult system they enter a culture that teaches them to be criminals. Redding documents public support for a system that works, rather than a system that punishes. He recommends well-calibrated consequences for first-time serious offenders. He also suggests that a very small number of adolescents commit a disproportionate amount of juvenile crime, and the risk factors for these chronic offenders is well-known: early and serious offending, trouble in school, drug problems, family problems, and gang involvement or running away from home. Policy makers must be attentive to the data on the lack of effectiveness of punitive models for most juveniles, and should also be made aware that the public supports an effective rehabilitative approach. All participants in the system, moreover, must be cognizant of the data in order to craft a response that is most effective to rehabilitate those who commit serious crimes.

The distinctive problems of the chronic offenders that Redding discusses are the focus of Matthew Howard and his coauthors, Michael Dayton, Kirk Foster, Michael Vaughn, and John Zelner. Because the chronic offenders present such distinctive issues, Howard et al. argue it is essential to include psychopathy within the mental health evaluation of juvenile offenders. Although psychopathy is a long-recognized serious psychiatric disorder, it has been included only recently in juvenile evaluations. This chapter reviews contemporary approaches to assessment and theories of psychopathy, empirical findings of the disorder, and effects of the diagnoses on criminal proceedings. The challenge they articulate for including psychopathy is how to do so without stigmatizing and marginalizing offenders, and insure that they will receive appropriate treatment and rehabilitation. Howard et al. detail the taxonomies for evaluating psychopathy, developed with adults. They also summarize the research concerning the characteristics of psychopathic youth, finding little research to support simplistic presumed correlations other than between psychopathy and violent offending. They advocate a detailed research agenda as essential to dealing with this group of children who commit serious crimes. Just as important, they argue, is insuring that further information is used to help, rather than "write off," these children.

In the final chapter of the handbook, we come full circle, from the developmental context with which we began to a comprehensive reorientation of how we should construct public policy responses, and especially legal responses, to the issues of children, culture, and violence. Barbara Bennett Woodhouse argues for an EcoGenerist paradigm, based on ecological principles developed in the environmental arena, informed by the principle of *generism,* or the primacy of supporting and nurturing the next generation. She analogizes the violence in culture, with its known negative effects on children, to a toxic substance in children's environment, and calls upon us to learn from environmentalists how to think about and address the toxic qualities of children's cultural and social environment. Traditional legal approaches, she maintains, tend to classify and categorize in a way that ignores the broader context as well as the interconnections that foster violence, and serve only to harm children rather than to help them. She argues for the benefits of a multidisciplinary approach that would identify the threats posed by toxic exposure of violence, and develop appropriate regulatory responses. Woodhouse shows how a variety of ecological concepts, including deep ecology, sustainable development, ecofeminism, and bioregionalism, are tools that can be used to address the intersections of complex factors in producing and reproducing violence to the detriment of children. Applying an ecogenerist paradigm would permit a range of responses that would be measured by their effectiveness in reducing the violence toxins and outcomes in children's environment. Woodhouse provides two examples of how this might work, applying the ecogenerist paradigm to violence on the Internet and to juveniles who commit acts of violence. Her challenge to accepted legal analysis incorporates the complexity and necessary multidiciplinarity to address this issue, as well as the need for provisional responses in order to respond to new challenges. By placing children's welfare at the center of analysis, broad change in children's environment, reducing the presence of violence in their world and ours, would become the goal of policy and the measure of its success.

## REFERENCES

American Academy of Child and Adolescent Psychiatry. (1999). *Children and TV violence*. Retrieved October 21, 2004, from http://www.aacap.org/publications/factsfam/violence.htm

American Academy of Child and Adolescent Psychiatry. (2001). *Children and watching TV*. Retrieved February 28, 2005, from http://www.aacap.org/publications/factsfam

American Association of University Women (AAUW). (2001). *Hostile hallways: Bullying, teasing, and sexual harassment in schools*. Retrieved October13, 2004, from http://www.aauw.org/member_center/HostileHallways/hostilehallways.pdf

American Psychiatric Association. (n.d.). *Psychiatric effects of media violence*. Retrieved February 28, 2005, from www.psych.org/public_info/media_violence.cfm

American Psychological Association. (n.d.). *Violence on television: What do children learn? What can parents do?* Retrieved October 21, 2004, from http://www.apa.org/pubinfo/violence.html

America's Children. (2001). *Key indicators of well-being*. Bethesda, MD: National Institute of Child Health and Human Development.

Anderson, C. A., & Bushman, B. J. (2001). Effects of violent video games on aggressive behavior, aggressive cognition, aggressive affect, physiological arousal, and prosocial behavior: A meta-analytic review of the scientific literature [Electronic version]. *Psychological Science, 12* (5) 353–358.

Anderson, S. L., Attwood, P. F., & Howard, L. C. (Eds.). (2004). *Facing racism in education* (3rd ed.). Cambridge, MA: Harvard Education Publishing Group.

Araji, S. K. (Ed). (1997). *Sexually aggressive children: Coming to understand them*. Thousand Oaks, CA: Sage.

Brown, B., & Bzostek, S. (2003, August). Violence in the lives of children. *Cross Currents, 1,* 1–13. Retrieved October 12, 2004, from http://www.childtrends databank.org/PDF/Violence.pdf

Carlson, B. E. (1984). Children's observations of interparental violence. In A. R. Roberts (Ed.), *Battered women and their families* (pp.147-167). New York: Springer.

Center for Substance Abuse Prevention, Substance Abuse and Mental Health Service Administration. (n.d.). *Youth and firearms*. Retrieved October 12, 2004, from http://www.preventionpathways.samhsa.gov/res/_fact_yfirearms.htm

Cesarone, B. (1994). *Video Games and children*. Urbana, IL: ERIC Clearinghouse on Elementary and Early Childhood Education. (ERIC Document Reproduction Service No. ED365477). Retrieved October 21, 2004, from http://www.ericdigests.org/1994/video.htm

Child Welfare League of America, National Data Analysis System. (2001). *Number of child abuse and neglect fatalities, by history with the child welfare system (CWLA survey)*. Accessed July 15, 2005, from http://ndas.cwla.org/data_stats/access/predefined/home.asp?MainTopicID=2&SubTopicID=25

Children Now. (2000). *Girls and gaming: Gender and race in video games*. Los Angeles: Author.

Children Now. (2001). *Fair Play? Violence, gender, and race in video games*. Los Angeles: Author.

Children's Defense Fund. (2004). *Each day in America*. Retrieved October 12, 2004, from http://www.childrensdefense.org/data/eachday.asp

Concepcion, J. I. (2004). Understanding preadolescent sexual offenders. *Florida Bar Journal*, *78*, 30–37.

Decker, S. H., Pennell, S., & Caldwell, A. (1997). *Illegal firearms: Access and use by arrestees*. Retrieved October 19, 2004, from http//www.ncjrs.org/pdffiles/163496.pdf

Dowd, N. (2005). Bringing the margin to the center: Comprehensive strategies for work/family policies. University of Cincinnati Law Review *73*, 433–455).

Edelson, J. L. (1997). *Problems associated with children's witnessing of domestic violence*. Retrieved October 13, 2004, from http://www.vaw.umn.edu/documents/vawnet/witness/witness.html

Edelson, J. L. (1999). Children's witnessing of adult domestic violence. *Journal of Interpersonal Violence*, *14* (8), 839–870.

Feagin, J. R., Early, D. E., & McKinney, K. D. (2001). *The Many Costs of discrimination: The Case of middle class African Americans*. Indiana Law Review, *34*, 1313–1360.

Federal Bureau of Investigation. United States Department of Justice. (1995). *Uniform crime reports for the United States*. Washington, DC U.S. Government Printing Office.

Finkelhor, D., Paschall, M. J., & Hasinma, P. Y. (2001). Juvenile crime victims in the justice system. In S. O. White (Ed.), *Law and social science perspectives on youth and justice*. New York: Plenum.

Glicklich-Rosenberg, L. (1996). Violence and children: A public health issue [Electronic version]. *Psychiatric Times*, *13* (3). Retrieved November 30, 2004, from http://www.pyschiatrictimes.com/p960345.html

Hill, H. A., Rugs, D., & Young, M. S. (2004). The impact of substance use disorders on women involved in dependency court [Electronic version]. *Washington University Journal of Law and Policy*, *14*, 359–384.

Hixon, A. L. (1999). Preventing street gang violence. *American Family Physician*. Retrieved November 30, 2004, from http://www.aafp.org/afp/990415ap/medicine.html

Human Rights Watch. (2001). *Hatred in the hallways: Violence and discrimination against lesbian, gay, and transgender students in U.S. schools*. Retrieved October 13, 2004, from http://www.hrw.org/reports/2001/uslgbt

Jacobs, M. S. (2004). Piercing the prison uniform of invisibility for black female inmates. *The Journal of Criminal Law and Criminology*, *94* (3), 795–818.

Kann, L., Kinchen, S. A., Williams, B. I., et al. (2000). Youth risk behavior surveillance: United States, 1999. *Morbidity and Morality Report 49* (SS05), 1–96.

Kaiser Foundation. (1999). *Kids and the media at the new millennium.* Retrieved February 28, 2005, from http://kff.org.entmedia

Kaiser Foundation. (2005). *The effects of electronic media on children ages zero to six: History of research—issue brief.* Retrieved February 28, 2005, from http://www.kff.org/entmedia

Lewit, E. M., & Baker, L. S. (1996). Child indicators: Children as victims of domestic violence [Electronic version]. *The Future of the Children, The Juvenile Court, 6*(3), 147–156. Retrieved October 16, 2004, from htpp://www.futureofchildren.org/usr_doc/vol6no3ART13.pdf

National Center on Addiction and Substance Abuse Prevention at Columbia University. (1999). *No safe haven: Children of substance abusing parents.* New York: Author.

Reis, B., Mendoza, M., & Takamura, F. (n.d.). *If these were racial slurs, teachers would be stopping them: Three activists object.* Retrieved February 10, 2005, from www.youth resource.com

Rennison, C. M. (2001). *Criminal victimization 2000: Changes 1999–2000 with trends 1993–2000.* Publication No. NCJ 187007. Washington, DC: Bureau of Justice Statistics.

Rosenbloom, S. R. (2004). Experiences of discrimination among African American, Asian American, and Latino Adolescents in an urban high school. *Youth & Society, 35*(4), 420–451.

A Safe Place, Lake County (IL) Crisis Center. (n.d.). *Effects of domestic violence on children: Part 1.* Retrieved November 30, 2004, from http://www.asafeplaceforhelp.org/childrendomesticviolence.html

Shaw, J. A. (1999). Practice parameters for the assessment and treatment of children and adolescents who are sexually abusive of others. *Journal of the American Academy of Child and Adolescent Psychiatry, 38,* 555–765.

Singer, D. G., & Singer, J. L. (Eds.). (2001). *Handbook of children and the media.* Thousand Oaks, CA: Sage.

Snyder, H. N. (2003). *Juvenile arrests 2001.* Retrieved October 19, 2004, from htttp://www.ncjrs.org/html/ojjdp/201370/page1.html

Snyder, H. N., & Sickmund, M. (1999). *Juvenile offenders and victims: 1999 National Report.* Washington, DC: Office of Juvenile Justice and Delinquency Prevention.

Stop the Violence, Face the Music. (n.d.). *Teens and the streets.* Retrieved October 13, 2004, from http://www.stv.net/teens_streets.htm

United States Department of Health and Human Services. (2002). *The 2002 HHS poverty guidelines.* Retrieved November 30, 2004, from http://aspe.hhs.gov/poverty/02poverty.htm

United States Department of Health and Human Services. Administration on Children, Youth and Families. (2004). *Child maltreatment: 2002 reports from the states to the national child abuse and neglect data system.* Washington, DC: U.S. Government Printing Office.

Walls, L. (1998). *Bullying and sexual harassment in schools.* Retrieved October 13, 2004, from http://www.cfchildren.org/articlef/walls1f/walls1_print

Woodard, E. H. IV, & Gridina, N. (2000). Media in the home 2000: The fifth annual survey of parents and children. *The Annenberg Public Policy Center of the University of Pennsylvania. Survey Series No. 7.* Accessed on the Web at: www.appcpenn.org/mediainhome/survey/survey7.pdf

*Youth victims and perpetrators of serious violent crime.* (n.d.). Retrieved October 19, 2004, from http://www.childstats.gov/ac2003/indicators.asp?IID=136&id=5

*Youth violence: A report of the Surgeon General.* (2001). Retrieved October 13, 2004, from http://www.surgeongeneral.gov/library/youthviolence/chapter2/sec12.html

# Prologue

## *Developmental Variations Among Children and Adolescents—An Overview of the Research and Policy Implications*

DOROTHY G. SINGER

> *Development is not simply the acquisition of information about a given world. Rather, it involves becoming grounded in an uncertain world that is beyond understanding. This is achieved thorough enculturation into the myths, rituals, social practices, and assumptions that order, orient, and organize individuals in common ways and provide a sense of reality that allows for confident action in the world.*
>
> —(Vandenberg, 2004, p. 52)

A "sense of reality" and "confident action in the world" is achieved when parents or other caregivers offer their children, from birth on, what the psychoanalyst Erik Erikson (1968) called basic trust—"an essential trustfulness of others as well as a fundamental sense of one's own trustworthiness" (p. 96). Trust implies expectations about the response of others to one's actions, and about opportunities for affection as well as for experiences of certainty and security. Unfortunately, as many court cases indicate, trust and confidence in children's caregivers are often violated through physical or sexual abuse, neglect, abandonment, or through the verbal and behavioral concomitants of a contentious divorce.

To better understand how children process information related to legal issues, it is useful to review the various stages of child development, and how children change physically, cognitively, socially, emotionally, and morally from birth to adolescence. Child-rearing practices do not happen in a vacuum. Parental influences on development may be limited to some degree if the customs, beliefs, and mores are significantly different from a broader surrounding culture, or from the information available through education and the media.

The first part of this book touches on issues of domestic violence and particularly the effects of physical and sexual violence directed toward children. How does a child comprehend this betrayal of parental behavior? How can a child deal with this abhorrent behavior while it is going on, and what are the long-term effects on a child's self-concept and self-esteem? It is helpful for members of the legal profession to be aware of how differently the child or adolescent victim processes the information related to such acts as they occur, and later, during an investigation, or in a courtroom during testimony.

The young child may comply with the parent's sexual advances because he or she needs the love of the parent and may think this is a way a parent is demonstrating this love. The older child continues to comply, thinking she or he is protecting the other parent from learning about the spouse's behavior, or because the adolescent may even fear the abusive parent. Facing an abusive parent or an abusive stranger in court is terrifying for the young child, and in some cases, a child may even lie out of fear of the parent or stranger, or may lie in order to protect the parent. A child who has witnessed abusive behavior toward another person, in the form of either physical violence or sexual attacks, may also be traumatized by such acts, and as a consequence, may disassociate himself or herself by complete denial or repression.

The second part of the book addresses the impact of media on children. Television, of all electronic media including video games and computers, is still the most favored among young children (Rideout, Vandewater, & Wartella, 2003). Children interpret information gleaned from films, television, video games, computers, and even from books in ways commensurate with their cognitive level. A very young child may be frightened by a violent or sexually provocative scene on television that does not affect an adolescent in the same way. Adolescents are able to distinguish the difference between reality and fantasy more clearly than younger children.

While most Western countries have boards of overseers who control television input for children, the United States has no such group of individuals who rule on what a children's program may show. The Children's Television Act (1990) required television broadcasters to address the needs of children through educational and informational programming. In 1996 the law adopted more stringent rules and mandated a minimum of 3 hours per week of educational programs for children up to age 16 that were to be aired on network channels (Federal Communications Commission [FCC], 1996). The FCC is the closest we have to a ruling body concerning the media, but it offers no guidance on when children's programs must be aired, nor does it specify how much educational content each station is expected to provide. It is important that legislators and policy makers understand how children's thinking processes are affected by the media depending on their age, and how the media influences their emotions and social mores. There have been a number of court cases where defense attorneys have attempted to blame television for a crime committed by a young person, but the First Amendment has been used to protect the rights of the broadcasters to air programs that they deem inoffensive (Liebert & Sprafkin, 1988). The introduction of legislation to require a V-chip, the electronic filtering device that parents can use to block out potentially harmful or sensitive material, was endorsed by President Clinton in 1996 and became part of the Telecommunications Act of 1996 (FCC, 1996).

The last part of the book discusses children as perpetrators of violence and touches on fundamental issues of children's social conduct. Why does a child bully another child? Why does a child commit a violent crime? Are there genetic or environmental factors, or a combination of biological, cultural, and social influences that cause some children to become deviant? Understanding the normal stages of development hopefully sheds some light on why a child relinquishes values and moral precepts and becomes aggressive, and in some cases violent or even psychopathic. Should children be treated as adults in the courts? It is clear that legislators in many states should consider the age and the cognitive capabilities of a minor when meting out verdicts and in sentencing.

Wherever possible, in the following discussion of children's development, examples are drawn from research and actual court cases to demonstrate how important it is for the legal sector of society to understand how these differences in children may impact evidence and court decisions, and how these decisions in turn affect the child depending on age and cognitive level. Later chapters in this book concerning particular legal issues involving children go into greater detail than presented here.

## THE BRAIN

It seems logical to begin with a brief review of the brain since the way in which children and adolescents process material depends on how advanced they are in their ability to attend, perceive, think, remember, problem solve, and use language to communicate. In any situation where testimony is needed, or where a person stands trial, aspects of competence are usually considered. In some cases, the possibility of neurological damage may also be a factor.

Brain development begins after the first month of conception. Nearly all of the brain's billions of nerve cells have been created by the sixth month of prenatal development with new neurons being generated at an average rate of 250,000 per minute (Thompson, 2004). At birth, most researchers believe that the brain has all the neurons or nerve cells it will have for life. Eighty billion serve as hard wiring and handle information. The first area of the brain to evolve is called the reptilian brain, which is responsible for breathing, digestion, and regulation of metabolism, consciousness, and alertness. The second area of the brain is the paleomammalian, which is concerned with emotions, scent, taste, sexual behavior, and memory. One part of this area of the brain important to memory functions is the hippocampus, which usually matures by age 5. A third area of the brain is the cortex, divided into the left and right hemispheres and connected by the corpus callosum, a band of fibers. The left hemisphere in humans is concerned with language, attention, working memory, speech, and mathematics, while the right hemisphere is concerned with music, rhythm and other non-speech sounds, negative emotions, and spatial understanding. To be more specific about brain functioning, the frontal lobe of the cortex is involved in involuntary movements and thinking, the occipital lobe controls vision, the temporal lobe is involved in hearing, and finally, the parietal lobe processes information about the body and sensations such as touch.

Neurons are serviced by 100 billion glial cells that nourish and activate them; glial cells are necessary for the development of a fatty substance called myelin that coats and protects the neural fibers. Most of the myelination is completed by the first 2 years of an infant's life, but some myelination occurs even up to early adolescence. A neuron consists of the cell body, the nucleus, the axon (encased by the myelin sheath), and dendrites. The dendrites receive incoming information. At the end of the dendrites is a gap called the synapse, which receives information from the neurotransmitters. Neurons come to assume specialized roles; they form connections or synapses with other neurons to enable them to communicate and to store information.

Plasticity refers to the fact that the brain has the capacity to "bloom," or to produce new synapses. In addition to blooming, there is a process called "pruning." The infant by the age of 3 has so many synapses competing in the brain for space, that the brain sheds some of these in order to function more efficiently. About 40% of the cortical synapses present in infancy are eliminated by childhood. Those that are used are strengthened and survive. Synapses may grow in parts of the brain even without the trigger of stimulation and according to different timetables. Brain development also varies by region. Thus, the sensory regions that govern sight, touch and hearing, and other sensations undergo their most rapid development early in life, while higher forms of thinking and reasoning continue to bloom and prune well into early adolescence. Although one might expect the adolescent to process material more accurately than a young child because of blooming, the experiences of adolescents may actually interfere with their ability to separate their thoughts about "what they perceived from the perceptions themselves" as found in some testimonies of children in this adolescent period (Perry & Wrightsman, 1991, p. 61). Data indicate that the mature adult brain can generate new neurons (Thompson, 2004). This controversial information contradicts the earlier assumption that all nerve cells are present at birth and that the brain cannot generate new ones if neurons die.

There are two forms of brain development that occur. *Experience-expectant* involves the common experiences of an infant and child that provide the essential stimulation for normal brain development such as early visual stimulation, exposure to hearing, language, coordinating vision, and movement. The brain expects and requires these human experiences for growth. *Experience-dependent* refers to the individual experiences that continue throughout our lives and that refine our existing brain structures. These are not typical experiences of all persons, but rather are individualized. A musician who plays an instrument early in life, an artist who paints early in life, or a poet who uses many words early in life will all have had experiences that account for new learning and the development of particular skills (Greenough & Black, 1992; Thompson, 2004).

In addition to the genetic makeup of the individual, it is important to acknowledge the role of the environment in the development of the healthy child. For example, some of the issues include (1) physical opportunities for the child to explore, learn, and play in a safe area; (2) biological inputs such as early good nutrition, good health care, immunizations, sensory screening, and protection from dangerous drugs, viruses, and environmental toxins; (3) social interactions with adults, using verbal and nonverbal communication with the infant including play, and later peer play, affording practice in social skills—sharing, taking turns, cooperating, and exposure to music and the arts; (4) emotional support and sensitivity to a child's needs, comforting, stability, disciplining as appropriate, handling of aggression and negative moods; and (5) cognitive opportunities for learning, language development, imagination and creativity, and later, opportunities for emergent literacy, reading, and telling stories to a child from infancy on.

In the discussion that follows, Table P.1 is useful in tracking the developmental expectations and the personality implications at each stage, from infancy to late adolescence. Some researchers have suggested that at particular ages the very nature of physical and mental development, as well as society, demands of us the performance of certain tasks (Havighurst, 1953; Tryon & Lillienthal, 1950). The table presents a lifespan model incorporating Erikson's psychosocial theory of development, and a restructuring of Erikson's model along with the listing of the developmental tasks (Erikson, 1962; Franz & White, 1985).

**Table P.1** Developmental Tasks and Their Personality Implications

| *Approximate age when task or social expectation first appears or is critical* | *Developmental task life-crisis or social expectation* | *Personality Implication* | |
|---|---|---|---|
| | | *Individuation pathway* | *Attachment pathway* |
| Infancy (to 18 mos.) | Achieving secure attachment; giving and receiving affection; learning to walk and beginning to talk | Trust vs. mistrust | Trust vs. mistrust |
| Early childhood | Developing self-control; beginnings of sense of right and wrong; communication skills | Autonomy vs. shame | Object and self-constancy vs. loneliness and helplessness |
| | Developing capacity for play and imagination | Developing private personality; initiative vs. guilt | Beginning to play with others and to "show off"; vs. passivity or aggression |
| Middle childhood (7–12) | Relating to social peers, school groups, forming close friendships, learning new motor skills; developing cognitive skills, accepting or adjusting to one's changing body | Industry vs. inferiority | Empathy and collaboration vs. excessive power or caution |
| Puberty and early adolescence (12–15) | Learning psychobiological and social sex roles; developing specific sexual "appetites (hetero- or homosexual attractions); confronting issues of group membership, "popularity"; specific athletic, artistic, or academic skill development | Identity vs. identity diffusion | Mutuality interdependence vs. alienation |
| Late adolescence (16–19) | Learning to understand and control the physical world and the broader social milieu; developing an appropriate symbol system and conceptual abilities; learning creative expression | Identity vs. identity diffusion | Mutuality interdependence vs. alienation |

*Source:* Adapted and reprinted with permission of the publishers from *The House of Make-Believe: Children's Play and the Developing Imagination* by Dorothy G. Singer and Jerome L. Singer, pp. 35–36, Cambridge, MA: Harvard University Press, copyright © 1990 by Dorothy G. Singer and Jerome L. Singer.

## BIRTH TO TWO YEARS

### *Physical Development*

Newborns sleep about 70% of the time. Sleep may occur in seven or eight segments in the course of a day. The healthy baby is born with a number of reflexes including sucking, rooting for the nipple, the Babinski reflex (flexing the big toe dorsally and fanning out the other toes), grasping an object with fingers, the Moro reflex (extending arms and legs and then bringing them toward each other as a response to a loud noise), a swimming reflex, a knee jerk reflex, and blinking. When you observe infants, their movements are global and undifferentiated as if they are using their legs and arms at the same time. Gradually, fine motor movements occur, with the hands learning to separate the thumb from the rest of the fingers, and by the end of 1 year, most babies are able to grasp an object quite firmly much as an adult will. Babies are generally able to sit up alone by 6 months, crawl at about 9 months, and from about 12 months to 18 months begin to walk.

From the time they are born, babies can perceive the difference between dark and light, but discriminating among colors usually takes place at around 3 months. Babies are able to track an object. If you hold a bright rattle over their face, they will follow the path with their eyes as you move it from side to side. In terms of their attention to the human face, eyes and mouth are gazed at first, and then gradually babies focus on the nose and the rest of the face. They tend to focus on parts of objects that are moving, objects that are the largest, or objects that have the greatest contrast. Babies can hear at birth and by about 1 to 2 weeks, can discriminate between loud and soft and high and low sounds, and are able to detect differences among musical notes on a scale. By 2 weeks, babies can detect the difference between a human voice and other sounds. Babies are great explorers, trying to make sense of their environment through tasting, touching, hearing, seeing, and smelling. They like to grasp objects, put them into their mouths, feel and stroke things, focus on colorful toys or pictures, push and pull, and later as they walk and enter the toddler stage, they become more mobile, climb, and try to jump and hop.

### *Intellectual Development*

Perhaps the most systematic study of the development of intelligence stems from the work of the Swiss psychologist Jean Piaget (1952), who kept detailed diaries about the day-to-day experiences of his three young children. Intellectually, a baby, by the end of year 1, is performing many cause-and-effect experiments (Gopnik, Meltzoff, & Kuhl, 1999). Dropping clothespins in a box and turning it over to empty it, stacking rings on a pole, building a nest of blocks, hitting a xylophone to hear the different sounds, are all experiments by the baby to make sense of the world. As the baby matures, she depends less on trial and error and more on intent. By the end of 1 year, the baby uses what Piaget (1968) called "invention of new means" to produce a result. At times, babies' actions may appear funny to us, as when a baby uses a pail as a hat instead of as a container for sand.

### *Social/Emotional Development*

Socially, the baby evidences a true smile at approximately 6 weeks, although a parent may detect a slightly crooked smile earlier than that—the neonatal smile that is present shortly after birth. The reaction of a parent to the true smile is one of joy and it is the impetus for the "love dance" or bonding between the two. As mother smiles and talks, baby responds with a smile and a gurgle. Actually, in terms of adoption issues, as well as what has relevance for the legal profession, it is best to adopt a baby as early as possible, before the bonding takes place between birth mother and child. If loving parents adopt babies, there is usually no difficulty for the baby to make a new adjustment and a new bond. However, the baby who is put into an institution after it has bonded with a caregiver experiences what is called anaclitic depression, or the listlessness that we see in overcrowded settings where there is not enough staff to hold a baby and offer the baby the sense of trust described above. These babies may engage in head banging, rocking motions, and autoerotic activity in order to self-stimulate. Witness the actions of babies who were tragically left during the war in the Bosnian orphan asylums. It takes many years of patience, affection, and skill on the part of the adoptive parents to overcome the trauma of early deprivation.

As the baby approaches the last part of year 1, he has more awareness that objects exist apart from the self. For example, if the rattle falls on the floor, baby will now look for it, whereas before, anything out of sight was out of mind. This important concept, *object permanency,* suggests that two separate ideas become joined or coordinated. The baby can retain images of people and objects in its head even when they are not present. Hearing the mother's voice outside the room signifies to the baby that mother is there, even though baby cannot see her. This is the beginning of representational thought—the ability to keep a picture in one's head of an absent object—and the beginning of imagination, the human being's unique intellectual gift.

Below the age of 2, it is rare that such a young child would be interviewed in a court proceeding. This is mainly because of the lack of verbal ability to describe or even draw an event with any accuracy. One particular child I treated in my practice was 13 months old at the time his father strangled his mother in a room next door to where the infant slept in a crib. It was difficult to ascertain if he knew anything that had happened in the adjoining room. He was referred to me because of the custody struggle between the brother of the convicted murderer, the parents of both brothers who also wanted to raise the child, and the new wife of the murderer who married him in prison and who wanted to adopt the child. My task was not to unearth any memory of the murder incident, but to treat the child for the anxiety he was experiencing as a result of being moved from home to home during the custody proceedings. When I did see him for therapy a year after the murder incident, his play was that of a child who was frightened, insecure, and anxious. He generally put a miniature doll in a dollhouse room and barricaded it with all the toy furniture. As the therapy progressed, as he grew to trust me, and as the custody issues were resolved, his play became more of that of a normal child. Whether there remains some unconscious memory of the incident is something we will probably never know, but certainly, there appears to be no reliable way of recovering these memories for use in such legal proceedings.

## AGES TWO TO SIX

### *Physical Development*

The growth rate for children is faster during their first few years than at any other time except during a spurt of growth in adolescence. Between 2 and 6, coordination increases so that by kindergarten children run, skip, jump, climb, throw, dance, and pedal a tricycle. Some by age 6 can ski, skate, and swim. Children's fine motor movements enable them to hold a pencil correctly, do puzzles, tie shoes, cut their own food, manipulate stringing beads, draw, use scissors, and paste. Children's exuberance and energy often lead to accidents. At every age boys tend to have more accidents than do girls. On the other hand, not all injuries to children at this age are the result of accidents. There are parents who claim a child has been in an accident, when beatings, inflicted burns, and even starvation account for their injuries. In 1974, Congress passed the Child Abuse Prevention and Treatment Act (1974), which requires physicians, teachers, and other persons aware of any suspected injury to a child to report it to public authorities.

### *Intellectual Development*

Children at these ages learn primarily through their actions and senses. They are attempting to master many cognitive skills such as learning to attend and concentrate, to associate words and symbols with objects, and to perceive and discriminate. They are also learning how to identify similarities and differences among objects and how to classify these objects. For example, preschoolers begin to see that animals, vehicles, and fruits and vegetables belong in specific categories. They are uncertain about concepts such as space, shape, time, and size, and do not recognize age differences. Therefore, they may distort facts because of their inability to process information as correctly as an older child would. A taller person, for example, would be described by preschoolers as older than a shorter person. Children also have trouble recognizing unfamiliar people, which may affect their testimony. In the classic book, *Eyewitness Testimony,* by Elizabeth Loftus (1979), she summarizes experiments where children were asked to remember information after exposure to films or to pictures and found that children are "relatively inaccurate" and "highly suggestible" (p. 160). They can be influenced by subtle changes in the questions posed to them and may feel frightened about entering the court system. Similarly, Goodman found that in following a group of 218 children through criminal court and collecting data on them, younger children had a more difficult time answering the attorney's questions and testified in less detail than did older children (Goodman et al., 1992).

Preschoolers are curious and love to explore. Reasoning at these ages is intuitive rather than logical and accounts for their delightful expressions. They are concerned more with "why" rather than "how." For example, most children at this age do not understand how things in nature are formed. One child, in a daycare center where we were conducting a study, explained that a giant made big footsteps in the ground, and then when it rained, a lake appeared. She also believed that the rain was caused by a person in the sky turning on faucets.

Language development increases gradually in the use of complex and compound elaborations. We hear children engage in *echolalia,* the repetition of other people's words and phrases. Until about age 3, "conversation" takes the form of a monologue—just continuous talking without truly listening to another person's point of view—or a child may engage in collective monologue where a child talks alongside another child at the same time, but is not truly responsive to the other child's conversation. Social speech with actual listening and replying to the other person comes later. Preschoolers are developing a sense of humor and enjoy talking nonsense, using words that shock, making scatological jokes, and enjoying slapstick and tricks. They reach a plateau of sentence length at about age 4 1/2 years. By age 5, children can master most of the grammatical structure of adult speech. The advance in language development will be advantageous when a child is asked to offer testimony in cases where the child witnessed a heinous crime.

In terms of legal issues, it behooves an attorney to be aware that in cases involving children as eyewitnesses, the child below the age of 6 will have difficulty with recalling particular facts. A young child may also have difficulty in understanding that another person's thoughts are not the same as his or her own. The conception of a child's distinguishing his or her mental expectations or experiences from others has opened an exciting and challenging area of research (Harris, 2000; Wellman, 1990). As the British psychologist Alan Leslie (1987) pointed out some years ago, a child's "theory of mind" (the awareness that "I have thoughts and they are different from other people's thoughts"), may well depend on experiences garnered in pretend play. At Yale, we have directed studies that have shown how children engaging together in make-believe play demonstrate advances in recognizing others' thoughts or in differentiating fantasy representations from reality (Rosen, Schwebel, & Singer, 1997; Schwebel, Rosen, & Singer, 1999).

Astute questioning is needed to enable a child to retrieve information that may have been stored through images or witnessed under traumatic circumstances. Anne Graffam Walker, a forensic linguist, suggests that in questioning children below the age of 6 who have been abused, it is a good idea to tell children that you need their help and that they should tell all, even if they think the attorney, or psychologist, or social worker already knows everything. She suggests being specific, repeating proper names and places to lessen confusion. Walker states that it is important, wherever possible, to avoid the use of complex words or negatives like "no" and "not" in questions. Finally, she believes that because it takes a child 1.9 times as long as an adult to process information, one should wait as long as 10 seconds after a child finishes an answer before asking another question because a child may provide additional information (Greer, 2004).

Young children can deal with the present and remember things in the immediate past and even some events that may have occurred a year ago, but the future is more difficult for them to comprehend. If you say that we will go on a trip next week on Sunday, each day until that day, the preschooler asks, "Is this Sunday?" This difficulty in understanding time sequence is one more impediment to the accuracy of a preschooler's testimony in court. Goldstein, Freud, and Solnit (1973) in their seminal book, *Beyond the Best Interests of the Child,* were cognizant of the time dimension in adoption proceedings. They state, "The courts, social agencies, and all adults concerned with child placement must greatly reduce the time they take for decision[s]" about placement (p. 42). They suggest that "irreparable damage" will occur the longer courts delay the placement. They argue, too, for placement with a parent who meets the psychological needs of a child. This parental role can be "fulfilled either by a biological parent or by an adoptive parent or by any other caring adult—but never by an absent, inactive adult, whatever his biological or legal relationship to the child may be" (p. 19).

Preschoolers believe that wishes can influence reality and are dismayed when a wish does not come true. How often do we hear of a child who believes that such a wish will make his or her parents reconcile after a divorce? Children at this age are capable of increased symbolic thought, meaning that they are now able to substitute objects in their mind for those that are not present. This accounts for the tremendous involvement in play and make-believe. In my psychotherapy practice, I have witnessed children of divorce playacting the reconciliation of parents in their use of puppets and then learning through therapy how to cope with the inevitability that this reconciliation may not occur.

Two of the many researchers studying the effects of divorce on children have reached different conclusions about its impact. Wallerstein (2000) reported on a sample of 131 children, whom she followed over a 25-year period. She found that divorce was an extremely traumatic experience. The children she tracked experienced more depression, greater learning difficulties, and more aggression toward parents and teachers. The greatest toll on their lives was during early adulthood. On the other hand, Hetherington (2002), in a study of 2,500 children over a 30-year period, found that only about 25% of the children she studied had serious social and emotional problems that appeared to require professional attention as a result of divorce. Variables to consider in any study of divorce are the temperaments and resiliency of the children and the nature of the divorce—whether the divorce is a disruptive one or an amicable one—and of course the degree of positive involvement by the custodial or noncustodial parent with the children.

All states have gender-neutral child custody laws, which have replaced laws and precedents that generally gave preference to mothers in custody decisions. A study by Stamps (2002) found that in a questionnaire given to 149 judges, they still indicated preference for maternal custody. Fraser (2001) reported similar results examining 455 legal and mental health responses to a questionnaire regarding decision making for children in Los Angeles County. A case of spouse brutality in Wisconsin led to a new law overturning joint custody in situations of abuse, asserting that it is against a child's best interest to give custody to a parent who has committed a serious act of spouse abuse or who is engaged in a pattern of abuse (Pommer, 2004). This decision is important in terms of visitation rights. Children who are forced to visit abusive parents may believe that the judge accepts and even approves of their parent's abusive behavior (Bancroft & Silverman, 2002).

On another note, many parents argue about visitation rights when one of the parents moves to another state. This issue of relocation is one of the most contentious in custody cases. Mothers, who generally have physical custody of the children in about 80% of cases, often find that they cannot move out of state because the father refuses to allow the children to relocate. In a recent ruling, the California Supreme Court decided that the parent with physical custody has the right to choose the child's residence unless the other parent can demonstrate some detriment to the child that would result (Eaton, 2004). This ruling may eventually affect other states. A child is affected by the decisions made by each parent concerning the child's welfare and one wonders what is the "best interest" rule here. At times it is useful to have the court appoint a guardian ad litem for a juvenile when a conflict of interest exists between the parents and the juvenile. This guardian acts as the supporting parent to the child.

### *Social Development*

Dramatic play, a feature of play in general, is most evident for 3- to 5-year-olds. This play becomes increasingly more social and complex. Dramatic play is one important way to help children begin to distinguish between reality and fantasy. You hear children say "Let's pretend," or "Let's make-believe" before they start their play. They begin to appreciate the social differences among their peers and enjoy communicating with them although there may be frequent, but brief, arguments. Playgroups are loose and easily disbanded; although children begin to choose a best friend, these choices may not last long at this age. Self-reliance is evidenced in terms of clothing choice, eating, cleaning their rooms, and helping to do simple chores in preschool and around the house. Parents are still the most important adults in children's lives, but children begin to form attachments to other adults during this period of development.

### *Emotional Development*

The emotions of preschoolers are fairly fluid with rapid changes of mood, from independence to clinging, affection to hostility or anger, security to feelings of insecurity. Children at these ages like to win at games and are devastated if they lose. Jealousy, the fear of loss of possessions, loss of love from caregivers, and fear of physical vulnerability are fairly common among preschoolers. Electronic media present an additional challenge for these young children. Because they have a difficult time separating reality from fantasy, television programs that feature violence seem very real and may be frightening to them (Cantor, 2001).

Preschoolers begin to worry about physical harm and death at around age 5, but do not fully understand what death means. Cartoons suggest that when a character is hurt he can reappear whole again. There is some concern about being left alone and about the loss of a parent. Studies by psychologists on the adjustment of children after a parent's death suggest that children need considerable support during their grieving and recovery period (Garbarino, 1992). Preschoolers tend to translate thoughts and feelings into words and actions immediately. Some children, however, cannot express their concerns through the use of words, and they react to anxiety through various regressive acts such as thumb-sucking, bed-wetting, clinging, nightmares, and other physical signs of distress. Imaginative or sociodramatic play is important in furthering emotional well-being. Through these kinds of play the child can try out various roles of persons, real and fantastical—teacher, doctor, fireperson, police officer, king or queen, evil witch, or monster—and express feelings of anger, sadness, fear, and joy. Through play, the child learns to socialize, share, take turns, and cooperate.

### *Moral Development*

Until age 4, there is no sense of obligations to rules. Behavior is governed by fear of punishment or submission to wishes of adults. Toddlers also believe in what Piaget (1965) calls "immanent justice," that objects have within them the power to punish. If, for example, children play with matches and are burned, they believe that the "burn" was their punishment because they disobeyed. Gradually, the young child develops a conscience and has a rigid idea of right and wrong. It is important for preschoolers to focus on telling the truth, but they may seem to tell lies. This is often a consequence of their inability to distinguish clearly between reality and fantasy. They are also susceptible to bribes and threats. In the famous McMartin Preschool case, caregivers were wrongfully accused of child abuse because children had difficulty remembering facts, but also because they were suggestible during questioning by parents, and by the psychologist who tested them (Perry & Wrightsman, 1991). In a meta-analysis examining numerous studies of research involving children as expert witnesses, Demmie (1999) found that young children are the most vulnerable and at the greatest risk for suggestibility. Paul Ekman (1989), a psychologist who studies emotions, indicates that it is not always easy to detect liars through their facial expressions, voice, or body movements. When very young children, however, have extended discussions about the difference between truth and lying (Huffman, Warren, & Larson, 1999), or when 4-year-olds are taught to say "I don't know" when uncertain (Nesbitt, 1999), or promise to tell the truth (Talwar, Lee, & Bala, 2002), lying is significantly reduced.

## AGES SIX TO NINE

### *Physical Development*

This period from ages 6 to 9, in general, is one of good health, but these school-aged children are concerned about gaining physical competence. They are interested in active and energetic games and sports, although block play, play with trains, and even dollhouse and puppet play may continue for the 6- and 7-year-olds. Up to 8 years, boys are heavier and taller than girls, and then girls begin to catch up in weight and height. Until about age 9, large-muscle control is superior to small-muscle control for both sexes. Most girls, however, will engage less in rough-and-tumble games than boys. Games of skill are important, but children below age 9 often overestimate their capacities. They enjoy climbing, running, jumping, swimming, skating, and become more daring on the playground—trying to climb higher or riding a bike with no hands; girls skip rope with more complicated jumps. The improvement in large motor skills and coordination by both sexes enables them to engage more in competitive sports and they may begin to join organized leagues.

Children now gain better control over fine motor skills so that using pencil, pen, and arts and crafts materials is easier. There is a general decrease in errors of judgment, and perspective in drawing begins. Some children study a musical instrument using their small motor skills for correct fingering. This involvement in learning an instrument may continue as children grow older. As children improve in musical performance, they acquire skills in timing and in mathematical awareness.

### *Intellectual Development*

Children ages 6 to 9 can now think out rather than act out solutions to problems, but they still think concretely and are less able to deal with abstractions. They look at the world naturalistically rather than just magically. They are able to think more logically about things in distant time and space and are curious about how things work. Other symbol systems besides language are learned such as numbers, maps, signs, and graphs. Children of these ages use television as a main source of entertainment more than any other group (Rideout, Vandewater, & Wartella, 2003). They also are challenged by the computer and use it for games as well as communications with friends. Because children are vulnerable to the advertisements on the various Web sites, the Children's Online Privacy Protection Act (1998) requires that commercial Web sites aimed at children under 13 must give parents notice about their data collection practices and obtain verifiable parental consent before collecting information about their children. Commercial Web sites must also provide parents with access to the collected information and the opportunity to curtail any further uses of this collected information (Turow, 2001).

Parents also need to be aware of how computers play a role in their lives in terms of chat rooms and possible communication with predatory adults or children's access to online pornography. Although there are arguments for filtering information on the Internet, the American Library Association (2003) maintains reasonably that parents have the right to decide which materials are appropriate for a child, and that teaching children to think critically about the materials they read and view helps them to make positive choices.

Language skills are more advanced at this stage than previously, with a growth in vocabulary, both oral and written, and an increase in speed and extension of vocabulary with more complex use of language. Children take pleasure in role-playing; making up rhymes, songs, and stories; tongue twisters; secret codes; and riddles and jokes. Children are able to control their behaviors through covert speech. The ground rules of conversation are now more advanced and the child can realize the position of the listener. Memory is increasing. As mentioned above, children in this early–elementary school period think concretely. Many children become great collectors. They do jump from subject to subject and this enables them to sample and develop their own interests rather than adult-imposed ideas. Reading plays a major role in this period and is of paramount importance in order to master a variety of school subjects. There is constant improvement in communication skills through using opportunities to talk, listen, read, and write. These language skills enable children to express their needs more clearly and have some bearing on children's expression of preferences in custody disputes.

### *Social Development*

There is a growing sense of independence at these ages, along with a sense of industry in construction and planning (Erikson, 1968). There is an energy and eagerness to try to do new things and to watch and imitate people around them who are engaged in various occupations. Identification is mainly with family figures, teachers, religious leaders, and media-related characters. Individuation in relation to the family begins and peers are now important, replacing adults as major source of behavior standards and recognition of achievement. Self-esteem is dependant on what friends think of one. Children are selective about close friends and may seek a permanent friend or even make an enemy. Quarrels and boasting are frequent. There is some defiance of adult authority and conflict between adult and peer codes. Peers dictate dress that may cause some strain with parents. Self is seen more in terms of social roles or labels such as age, sex, race, religion, and class. The self-concept is gradually forming through a growing self-evaluation according to parent and teacher criteria. Television and other electronic media influence children at these ages in terms of role models and heroes. Interest in video and computer games is prevalent and boys, especially, tend to be attracted to the more action-oriented and violent forms of games (Singer & Singer, 2005). Special skills are now manifested through an interest in music, art, sports, science, and crafts. Sex-related division of interests is developing in terms of play styles and hobbies. Contrary to the notion of Sigmund Freud (1905/1962), who labeled this time in the 6- to 9-year-old's life as "latency" characterized by a delay of physical sexual maturation, no interest in sexual matters, and a repression of sexual thoughts, a child in this period is indeed curious about sex, and as Erikson (1962) points out, is accepting and adjusting to bodily changes.

### *Emotional Development*

Children gain a sense of competency during this period. They become less egocentric and can be more empathic. They can see themselves with some objectivity. A love of ritual still remains with incantation and repetition for its own sake as a part of the process of warding off danger and fear. As part of forming group identity, children may join clubs at this age with secret passwords. Fears are still present, and children are still vulnerable to the negative effects of violent television and violent video games. Magic and make-believe become increasingly private activities and may take the form of poetry, prose, making up simple plays, and music preferences. There is enjoyment of fantasy as evidenced by the widespread popularity of Harry Potter and Lord of the Rings books and films.

### *Moral Development*

Morally, until about age 8, the sense of right still lies in literal obedience to rules. There is a sense of obligation still based on submission to authority and fear of punishment. By 9 years, children are more aware of the purposes of rules and what the consequences are if rules are violated. The concepts of right and wrong, however, are still rather rigid. Children at these ages tend to judge themselves and peers more harshly than adults and if they break rules, they will create elaborate rationales and self-justifications for having done so.

Morality, by and large, is imposed from without by significant authority figures such as God, parents, teachers, or law enforcers. In a sampling of studies comparing preschoolers with early elementary-aged children concerning their understanding of a lie, it was found that the older children ages 7 and 10 rated truths more positively than lies more often than younger ones, aged 4 (Bussey & Grimbeck, 2000); 4-year-olds were more suggestible than 8-year-olds (Shapiro, 2002); and 4-year-olds exhibited less accuracy in response to direct questions compared to children aged 8 (Poole, 2001).

## AGES NINE TO TWELVE

### *Physical Development*

By about age 9, fine motor stills are improved such as writing, drawing, tying of knots and laces, and use of tools and gadgets. Motor skills, using large-muscle movements, are also evident in such activities as bicycle riding, scooters, trampolines, ice skating, roller skating, hockey, swimming, skiing, and soccer. There is even greater skill, strength, and coordination for the 12-year-olds. Hand–eye coordination and perception are much improved, as is demonstrated by building complicated constructions of various objects using arts and crafts materials, making intricate puzzles, model building, sewing, and knitting. There is a continued interest in video and computer games. This period continues to be, in general, one of good health. Girls are generally taller and heavier than the boys aged 9 to 12. Secondary sex characteristics appear for some girls in this 11- to 12-year-old range.

### *Intellectual Development*

Children are still in the concrete-thinking stage of development and abstract thinking will emerge more fully as they approach adolescence. They may just begin to attempt to construct theories and make logical deductions. They are less reliant on visual modes of representations. Curiosity is on the increase and there is a growth of individual cognitive interests, and they are more likely to pursue a subject in depth than previously. They remain collectors but with more avid interest in staying with one collection of objects than earlier.

Language skills continue to grow with further opportunities to talk, listen, read, and write. Memory capacity is still increasing. Nine- to 12-year-olds gradually begin to construct theories and make logical deductions. They are less reliant on visual modes of representations. Children can tell more complicated jokes than before and a sense of humor is apparent for many children. There is further growth in vocabulary both oral and written, with more complex use of language. There is a continuation of role-playing, making up rhymes and songs, and writing poetry and stories. Reading speed increases and children expand their choices of reading material.

### *Social Development*

The peer group continues to replace adults as the major source of behavior standards and recognition of achievement. Children increase their friendship circles and they become more outgoing, but there are more social fears emerging, evidenced by the strong concern about how others will regard them.

Children at these ages are becoming part of a subculture with its own values, rules, codes, superstitions, and rituals. There is a continued defiance of adult authority and conflict between adult and peer codes. Music is extremely important in the lives of this age group, with many girls developing crushes on rock stars or movie stars. Boys, too, become interested in music with more involvement with rap or heavy metal groups than girls, who tend to prefer the more romantic songs, rhythm and blues, and even some of the "oldies." Television and video games remain an important part of the entertainment life of this age group and there is particular enjoyment among girls of teen movies. By ages 9 or 10, children develop a sense of humor with appreciation of satire, sarcasm, and putting down of adult pomposity. Thus, many children are great fans of *MAD* magazine.

### *Emotional Development*

At these ages, there is a concern and curiosity about sex, and some crushes may develop, particularly for children who observe older siblings dating or who become engrossed in viewing soap operas or particular situation comedies where there are many sexual innuendoes. Hero worship continues as in previous years. A best friend is still essential in a child's life. There is an increasing movement toward independence or separateness as evidenced through exploration of unknown places around their home, school, and if they can, their town. Mood swings may be in evidence so that many parents feel that this is a difficult time for them in terms of communicating with their children. Although these children feel independent, they still seek and want parental guidance and support. This may be evidenced by ambivalence and unpredictable behavior. Children may also feel frustrated or guilty because they cannot live up to a set of standards required by family or school.

### *Moral Development*

Morally, these preteens are capable of understanding that rules and codes are suggested courses of action rather than absolutes. By 10 years, children look more to intention. They express the fairness sentiment by taking into account moderating circumstances. A noble sense of justice is coming to the fore with a clearer understanding of what is right and what is wrong. The 9- to 12-year-olds take into account the personal circumstances of each situation when considering a person who lies.

## AGES TWELVE TO FIFTEEN

### *Physical Development*

Rapid growth follows puberty in both boys and girls after age 12 with primary and secondary sex characteristics appearing. There is great variation, so that some 13-year-old girls may still have some of the 10-year-old's characteristics and this may affect self-esteem. They worry about the appearance of their skin, height, and weight. Girls more often than boys may develop anorexia or bulimia, trying desperately to look as thin as the role models with whom they identify on television or in film. The early bloomers in terms of physical characteristics may become more popular in school. For girls, this may lead to early sexual activity, and in some cases teen pregnancy. The late bloomers among boys find this period especially difficult. They feel somewhat inferior to the boys who are now growing more rapidly, developing their secondary sex characteristics, and who may become the popular sports heroes. Because of the use of growth hormones as a treatment technique with short youths, a study of 956 students of both genders in Grades 6 through 12 was conducted by Sandberg and colleagues (Sandberg, Bukowski, Fund, & Noll, 2004).

Contrary to earlier research concerning negative stereotypes regarding adjustment of short youths (Karpati, Rubin, Kieszak, Marcus, & Troiano, 2002), the researchers found that there were no significant relationships between height and measures of friendship, popularity, or reputation with peers. They concluded that extremes of stature have a "minimal detectable impact on peer perceptions of social behavior, friendship, or acceptance" (Sandberg et al., 2004, p. 744). These data, however, still do not preclude giving serious consideration to the boy or girl who expresses anxiety about his or her height.

Diet and sleep habits tend to be poor for the 13- and 14-year-olds. Nevertheless, teenagers have greater skill, strength, and coordination that is now helpful in the sports arena. Unfortunately, teenagers experiment with cigarette smoking, alcohol, and drugs at these ages, as well. In a sample of 48,500 students from Grades 8 to 12, more than 54% of U.S. youth by 12th grade have tried smoking, with about a quarter of 12th graders still smoking (Johnston, O'Malley, Bachman, & Schulenberg, 2003). Alcohol remains extremely widespread among today's youth. The report found that nearly four out of every five students (77%) have consumed alcohol by the end of high school; nearly 50% have done so by 8th grade. The only drugs showing an increase among 8th graders were inhalants. Other drug use such as marijuana, tranquillizers, and amphetamines showed some decline in 2003 compared to previous years, but hallucinogens other than LSD showed no decline. Obviously, the anti-drug campaigns on MTV and other sources such as pamphlets, school curricula, and church groups have helped with the lessening of some drug usage, but there is still a problem with drinking and smoking among young people. In terms of aggression, sex differences have been examined in a meta-analytic review (Archer, 2004), and it was found that physical aggression was more common in males than in females across cultures and at all ages sampled, occurring from early childhood on with the peak between 20 and 30 years. Anger showed no differences between the sexes.

### *Intellectual Development*

These young teenagers can think more abstractly and have the ability to construct theories and mentally test them out. There is much questioning about existing ideas, especially where authority is concerned. Teens question how choices are made and the logic behind these choices, and they acknowledge that there are many ways to solve problems and that solutions are not always evident or to their liking. They are curious about politics and community organizations, and they may take an interest in school government. They are learning how to be sensitive to another's viewpoint and have lost some of their egocentricity. They are learning how to negotiate in varying contexts and debating is often an outlet for expressing their ideas. Language skills are increasing through a growing vocabulary, through the use of more complex syntax, and through the increased ability to use similes and metaphors. They can engage in more sophisticated discussions with parents, peers, and teachers.

### *Social Development*

One of the most important aspects of the social life of the teenager is to be accepted by the peer group. The loner suffers in high school and may often be bullied. It is important for teens to have a sense of belonging either to same-sex or mixed-sex groups. Peer pressure is strong in terms of behavior patterns, concerning the use of drugs, alcohol, and whether to engage in sex. Cliques are fairly common in this age group, with strong pressure to conform to peer society. Fads are often changing in terms of music preferences, hair style, clothing, and language (use of slang and common expressions that only teens seem to understand). Peers continue to dictate dress and this may cause further strain with parents, especially since some youths at this age ask for tattoos or body piercing. Subcultures develop, as expressed in meeting places where these young people hang out, and by their choice of magazines, music, Internet favorites, and use of chat rooms. Studies of teen magazine readers found that girls who are socialized to be feminine look to magazines as much as they do to friends for advice on fashion, beauty and how to deal with relationships with males (Duke & Kreshel, 1998; Greer, 2004). Electronic media continue to be used mainly for viewing sports by boys, while girls tend to prefer to watch MTV and soaps. Both boys and girls generally enjoy reality shows on television.

Studying and reading for school take much of the teenager's time. An interest in being a scout, participating in a Big Brother or Big Sister program, or doing some other volunteer work such as a candystriper in a hospital, appeals to some teenagers. Socially, girls are more advanced than boys at this age. Both sexes are vulnerable to criticism and wear a façade or mask of "cool" for protection; they feel that the opinion of others is very important. Teens are restless, and need frequent changes of pace and breaks for relaxation, but if interested in a subject, they can pursue it with intense concentration. Family values are still important, but they question these and consider alternatives as far as religion and politics are concerned. Thus, they are susceptible to the influence of radical sects, ideas, and lifestyles. In some extreme cases, teens who are rebellious may even consider emancipation. Only a few states allow minors to file for emancipation ("Emancipation of a Minor," 2004). Most states only consider a child legally emancipated after age 18. If the court grants emancipation to a minor, it may only be because there is some action on the part of the parent such as abuse or neglect, or because the minor has received permission from the parent because of a marriage or joining the military (Maryland Legal Assistance Network, 2004). There are some children who are runaways and seek help through friends, underground newspapers, or hotlines. They generally do not move too far from home, and try to find shelter in churches, centers set up to aid runaways, or in crash pads. Because of their lack of funds they may sell drugs, or engage in prostitution.

### *Emotional Development*

The teenager asks the question, "Who am I to be"? Erikson calls this stage in life "identity confusion" where young persons question their religious, ethnic, and sexual identity. With genital maturation and the uncertainty about making choices about their future, they need "a moratorium for the integration of the identity elements" (Erikson, 1968, p. 128) that have taken place in the earlier stages of development. Thus, there is a good deal of stress and conflict that is family- and school-related. Friendships are intense, but so are the quarrels. There is a strong desire for independence and at the same time the young person unconsciously seeks controls and limits set by parents and other adults—teachers, coaches, and religious leaders. There is an increased interest in sex-related issues and temptation to explore many sexual relationships. In addition, there are great fluctuations of mood along with a tendency to daydream and to fantasize.

### *Moral Development*

Young people in this age group can now consider a variety of perspectives in making moral choices. They begin to develop their own code of ethics and moral principles aside from the authority of the groups of persons who advocate them. They are in the autonomous stage of moral thinking according to Piaget (1965). They accept the moral principle that "right" is defined by laws, but for some more thoughtful adolescents, there is also a belief that right is defined by individual conscience in agreement with one's own ethical code or principles. There is the dilemma of how to accept an adult code when one's own sense of fairness is in conflict with this code. In Mark Twain's *The Adventures of Huckleberry Finn,* Huck's sense of morality prevented him from betraying Jim, the runaway slave, to his would-be captors. Huck cannot accept the prejudices of the adult community and thus he tells a lie to save Jim. Nevertheless, teenagers generally develop a sense of responsibility to the social system as a whole. They believe that "they must be good in order to keep the system from disintegrating and in order to maintain self-respect by meeting personal obligations" (Perry & Wrightsman, 1991, p. 85). If they are involved in court trials at this age, it is relatively easy to explain what is expected of them in terms of telling the truth.

## IMPLICATIONS AND RECOMMENDATIONS

The issues raised by this developmental summary suggest how members of the legal profession may need to work together with psychologists to meet the needs of young children who are involved in testimony in the courts, or in other matters related to law. Attorneys, social workers, and others involved with the court system could benefit from either a formal course in developmental theory, or at the very least, becoming familiar with the literature in this area.

Increasingly, children are brought into court to testify in cases of child abuse and neglect, child custody disputes, and to bear witness to a serious crime. Young children are more apt to make errors in memory, especially if they testify long after an event has occurred. In addition, language skills are often not well developed in younger children, and therefore may impede the ability of a child to express him- or herself in a coherent manner. Children also may often agree with the examiner in order to please, even though they have not actually witnessed a detail in an event related to a crime. Young children are suggestible, and leading questions may result in a child answering the examiner incorrectly. Preschoolers are especially poor in their ability to tell the examiner exactly where they obtained their information (Berk, 2005).

Young children may be fearful of the physical appearance of the courtroom and its imposing surroundings. Some of the procedures commonly used by the courts to elicit testimony from a child call for modification based on whether a child is able to handle questions in direct examination, or in cross-examination. Should there be limits placed on such examinations? Questions posed to children need to be simple and without the use of complex clauses or ambiguities. Difficult vocabulary must be avoided. In cases of sexual abuse, should the use of anatomical dolls be permitted in order to obtain evidence? How valid is this as a technique for uncovering instances of sexual abuse? Should a child be forced to face the accused? Should videotaped testimony or a screen be allowed, rather than having a child confront the accused?

Child witnesses are able to understand more easily what occurs in a courtroom and what to expect if they are carefully prepared. There are "court schools" where children are taken through the procedures step by step and given an opportunity to actually visit a courtroom, sit in the witness chair, and practice answering questions about unrelated events. Children can also testify over closed-circuit television so that they do not have to face the offender. This reduces the stress for a child and at the same time protects the defendant's constitutional rights (Berk, 2005; Perry & Wrightsman, 1991).

To shed some light on the subject, legal and mental health professionals met together at the 11th National Conference on Children and the Law in Washington, D.C., from June 3 to June 5, 2004, to discuss numerous issues relating to both fields (Bailey, 2004). Social scientists explained how research involving children and adolescents' development could inform the legal process. Topics such as privacy issues, placement of children, eyewitness testimony, preparing a child for testimony, how to ask questions relating to child abuse, and how to deal with a client's emotions in high-conflict divorce and child-maltreatment cases were among the many topics presented at the conference (Bailey, 2004; Murray, 2004).

Research concerning brain functioning also was presented, specifically noting the research that indicates that brains do not develop fully until age 25 and what the ramifications are for teenage testimony (Kersting, 2004a). Special education issues were also discussed in terms of children's rights and the need for an advocate for a child if rights are not being upheld (Kersting, 2004b).

Conferences such as this one can surely pave the way for a more integrated use of social science literature in the legal system and lead to outcomes that are truly in the best interests of the child.

## REFERENCES


American Library Association (2003). *Libraries and the Internet tool kit.* Chicago: Author.

Archer, J. (2004). Sex differences in aggression in real-world settings: A meta-analytic review. *Review of General Psychology, Vol. 8,* No. 4, pp. 291–322.

Bailey, D. S. (2004, July/August). Joining together for children's interests. *Monitor on Psychology,* p. 78.

Bancroft, L., & Silverman, J. G. (2002). *Batterer as parent: Addressing the impact of domestic violence on family dynamics.* Thousand Oaks, CA: Sage.

Berk, L. E. (2005). *Infants, children, and adolescents* (5th ed.). Boston: Allyn & Bacon.

Bussey, K., & Grimbeck, E. J. (2000). Children's conceptions of lying and truth-telling: Implications for child witness. *Legal & Criminal Psychology, Vol. 5* (Part 2), pp. 187–199.

Cantor, J. (2001). The media and children's fears, anxieties, and perceptions of danger. In D. G. Singer & J. L. Singer (Eds.), *Handbook of children and the media* (pp. 207–221). Thousand Oaks, CA: Sage.

Child Abuse Prevention and Treatment Act (CAPTA) Pub.L. 93–247, § 88 Stat. 4 (1974).

Children's Online Privacy Protection Act, S.2326, 105th Cong. 2d Session (1998).

Children's Television Act, P.L. 101–437, § 103 (1990).

Demmie, H. M. (1999, March). Suggestability of children's recollections: A meta-analysis. *Dissertation Abstracts International: Section B: The Sciences and Engineering, Vol. 59* (9–13), 5134. Ann Arbor, MI: University Microfilms International.

Duke, L., & Kreshel, P. (1998). Negotiating femininity: Girls in early adolescence read teen magazines. *Journal of Communication Inquiry, 22,* No. 1, 48–72.

Eaton, L. (2004, August 8). Divorced parents move, and custody gets trickier. *The New York Times*, p. A-1.

Ekman, P. (1989). *Why kids lie*. New York: Scribner.

Erikson, E. (1962). *Childhood and society*. New York: Norton.

Erikson, E. (1968). Identity: Youth and crisis. New York: Norton.

*Emancipation of a minor* (2004). Retrieved August 7, 2004, from http://www.peopleslaw.org/children/emancipation/emanciption%20home.htm

Federal Communications Commission (FCC). (1996). In the matter of policies and rules concerning children's television programming: Report and order. *Federal Communications Record 11*, 10660–10778.

Franz, C. E., & White, K. M. (1985). Individuation and attachment in personality development: Extending Erikson's theory. *Journal of Personality, 53*, pp. 224–256.

Fraser, R. A. (2001, April). Decision making in child custody: A comparison of legal and mental health professionals. *Dissertation Abstracts International, Vol. 61* (9-A), 3786. Ann Arbor, MI: University Microfilms International.

Freud, S. (1962). Three essays on sexuality. In J. Strachey (Ed.), *The standard edition of the complete psychological works of Sigmund Freud* (pp. 135–231). London: Hogarth Press. (Original work published 1905)

Garbarino, J. (1992). *What children can tell us*. San Francisco: Jossey-Bass.

Goldstein, J., Freud, A., & Solnit, A. J. (1973). *Beyond the best interests of the child*. New York: The Free Press.

Goodman, G. S., Taub, E. P., Jones, D. P. H., England, P., Port, L. K., Rudy, L., et al. (1992). Testifying in criminal court. *Monographs of the Society for Research in Child Development, 57*(5), pp. 1–142.

Gopnik, A., Meltzoff, A. N., & Kuhl, P. K. (1999). *The scientist in the crib: Minds, brains, and how children learn*. New York: Morrow.

Greenough, W. T., & Black, J. E. (1992). Induction of brain structure by experience: Substrates for cognitive development. In M. Gunnar & C. A. Nelson (Eds.), *Minnesota symposia on child psychology* (pp. 155–200). Hillsdale, NJ: Lawrence Erlbaum.

Greer, M. (2004, July/August). A look at limitations of studies on child suggestibility. *Monitor on Psychology*, p. 79.

Harris, P. (2000). *The work of the imagination*. Malden, MA: Blackwell.

Havighurst, R. J. (1953). *Human development and education*. New York: Longmans and Green.

Hetherington, E. M. (2002). *For better or worse: Divorce reconsidered*. New York: Norton.

Huffman, M. L., Warren, A. R., & Larson, S. M. (1999). Discussing truth and lies in interviews with children: Whether, why, and how? *Applied Developmental Science, Vol. 3* (1) pp. 6–15.

Johnston, L. D., O'Malley, P. M., Bachman, J. C., & Schulenberg, J. E. (2003). *Monitoring the future: National results on adolescent drug use*. Washington, DC: U.S. Department of Health and Human Services, National Institute on Drug Abuse.

Karpati, A. M., Rubin, C. H., Kieszak, S. M., Marcus, M., & Troiano, R. P. (2002). Stature and pubertal stage assessment in American boys: The 1988–1994 Third National Health and Nutrition Examination Survey. *Journal of Adolescent Health, 30*, pp. 205–212.

Kersting, K. (2004a, July/August). Brain research advances help elucidate teen behavior. *Monitor on Psychology, 80.*

Kersting, K. (2004b, July/August). Meeting children's special education needs. *Monitor on Psychology, 80.*

Leslie, A. (1987). Pretense and representations: The origin of theory of mind. *Psychological Review, 94,* 412–426.

Liebert, R. M., & Sprafkin, J. N. (1988). *The early window: Effects of television on children and youth.* New York: Pergamon Press.

Loftus, E. (1979). *Eyewitness testimony.* Cambridge, MA: Harvard University Press.

Maryland Legal Assistance Network (2004). www.mdjustice.org/public/mlan.html

Murray, B. (2004, July/August). Determining the best place for maltreated children: A call for help. *Monitor on Psychology, 78.*

Nesbitt, M. (1999). Improving young children's accuracy of recall for an eyewitness event. *Journal of Applied Developmental Psychology, Vol. 20* (3), pp. 449–459.

Perry, N. W., & Wrightsman, L. S. (1991). *The child witness: Legal issues and dilemmas.* Newbury Park: Sage.

Piaget, J. (1952). *The origins of intelligence in children.* New York: International Universities Press.

Piaget, J. (1965). *The moral judgment of the child.* New York: The Free Press.

Piaget, J. (1968). *The psychology of intelligence.* New Jersey: Littlefield, Adams.

Pommer, M. (2004, February 28). Law makes abuse top custody matter. *The Capital Times,* Madison, WI.

Poole, D. A. (2001). Children's eyewitness reports after exposure to misinformation from parents. *Journal of Experimental Psychology: Applied,* 7(1), pp. 27–50.

Rideout, V. J., Vandewater, E. A., & Wartella, E. A. (2003). *Zero to six: Electronic media in the lives of infants, toddlers, and preschoolers* (A Kaiser Family Foundation Report). Menlo Park, CA: The Henry J. Kaiser Family Foundation.

Rosen, C., Schwebel, D., & Singer, J. L. (1997). Preschoolers' attributions of mental states in pretense. *Child Development, 66,* 1133–1142.

Sandberg, D.E., Bukowski, W. M, Fung, C. M., & Noll, R. B. (2004). Height and social adjustment: Are extremes a cause for concern and action? *Pediatrics, Vol. 114* (3), pp. 744–750.

Schwebel, D., Rosen, C., & Singer, J. L. (1999). Preschoolers' pretend play and theory of mind: The role of jointly-conducted pretense. *British Journal of Developmental Psychology, 17,* 333–348.

Shapiro, T. F. (2002). Suggestibility in children's eyewitness testimony: Cognitive and social influences. *Dissertation Abstracts International: Section B: The Sciences & Engineering, Vol. 63* (4–B). Ann Arbor, MI: University Microfilms International, p. 2086.

Singer, D. G., & Singer, J. L. (2005). Imagination and play in the electronic age. Cambridge, MA: Harvard University Press.

Stamps, L. E. (2002). Maternal preference in child custody decisions. *Journal of Divorce & Remarriage, Vol. 37* (1–2), pp. 1–11.

Talwar, V., Lee, K., & Bala, N. (2002). Children's conceptual knowledge of lying and its relations to their actual behaviors: Implications for court competence examinations. *Law & Human Behavior, Vol. 26* (4), pp. 395–415.

Thompson, R. A. (2004). Development in the first years of life. In E. F. Zigler, D. G. Singer, & S. J. Bishop (Eds.), *Children's play: The roots of reading* (pp. 15–31). Washington, DC: Zero to Three Press.

Tryon, C., & Lillienthal, J. (1950). *Fostering mental health in our schools.* Washington, DC: National Education Association.

Turow, J. (2001). *Primary policies on children's websites: Do they play by the rules?* Washington, DC: Annenberg Public Policy Center of the University of Pennsylvania.

Vandenberg, B. (2004). Real and not real: A vital developmental dichotomy. In E. F. Zigler, D. G. Singer, & S. J. Bishop (Eds.), *Children's play: The roots of reading* (pp. 49–58). Washington, DC: Zero to Three Press.

Wallerstein, S. (2000). *Unexpected legacy of divorce: A 25 year landmark study.* New York: Hyperion.

Wellman, H. M. (1990). *The child's theory of mind.* Cambridge: Massachusetts Institute of Technology Press.

# Acknowledgments

This volume grew out of the second annual conference of the Center for Children and Families (CCF) at the University of Florida Fredric G. Levin College of Law, entitled "Children, Culture, and Violence," held March 20–21, 2003, co-sponsored by the Center for the Study of Children's Literature and Culture (CSCLC), also at the University of Florida. Barbara Bennett Woodhouse, the Director of CCF, and John Cech, the Director of CSCLC, were instrumental in organizing a multidisciplinary conference that drew together an amazing group of scholars collectively engaged in confronting this important topic. It was immediately apparent that finding a way to publish findings and to include other noted scholars unable to participate in the conference was a primary goal. Two of the conference presenters, Dorothy Singer and Robin Wilson, committed early on to be part of this effort, and were instrumental in gathering the outstanding authors represented in this volume, and were joined by Nancy Dowd, Co-Director of CCF. The University of Florida College of Law and the University of Maryland School of Law generously supported this project, with research support, outstanding librarians, and ongoing support for the book at all stages. We would particularly like to thank Jon Mills, who was then Dean of the University of Florida College of Law, as well as Florida's current Dean, Robert Jerry, for their generous support.

Nancy Dowd would like to thank Teris Meija, who provided research support that was invaluable to her work on the book. All of us lean on our families when we do this kind of work. Nancy would like to thank her children, Zoe and Zack Dowd, who once again have been incredibly understanding when Mom has been working on "the book."

Dorothy Singer would like to thank Jane Erickson and Brittania M. Weatherspoon at Yale University for their assistance with clerical matters. Dorothy thanks her husband, Dr. Jerome L. Singer, for his understanding and moral support throughout this undertaking.

Robin Wilson thanks her 10-year-old son, Glen, for believing in Mom and feigning interest in "Mom's book." Pamela Melton, John Duncan, Yvonne McMorris, Michael Clisham, and Kenneth Wilkinson provided endless assistance and encouragement in everything from the concept for the volume through its completion.

Rosemary Howard has been an incredible research assistant, editorial manager, and project leader. She has been tireless in her efforts for all three editors and this book could not have been done without her amazing work.

We all thank Jim Brace-Thompson, our Senior Editor, for his continual encouragement and careful reading of the book, and Karen Ehrmann, Teresa Herlinger, and Kristen Gibson for their editorial help and support and attention to the many details involved in the preparation of this volume.

In addition, the following people reviewed this book:

Elizabeth D. Hutchison
Social Work
Virginia Commonwealth University

Amy Nathanson
Department of Communication
Ohio State University

James Howell
Senior Research Associate
National Youth Gang Center
Tallahassee, Florida

Brad Bushman
Department of Psychology
University of Michigan

Barbara Wilson
University of Illinois

Charles Garvin
Professor Emeritus of Social Work
The University of Michigan

# Part I

# CHILDREN AS VICTIMS

CHAPTER 1

# *Child Witnessing of Domestic Violence*

NAOMI CAHN

What happens to children when they see violence between their parents? Is there any impact on children when they see their mother or father with bruises inflicted by a partner? Discussions of family violence frequently distinguish between neglect or violence directed at children and violence directed at adults while children are present. Violence against children is legally considered either child abuse or child neglect. Witnessing violence directed at adults has generally not been treated as harmful to children.

Historically, courts deciding custody and visitation questions were inclined to dismiss the idea that witnessing partner abuse resulted in any relevant impact on children (Cahn, 1991). There is increasing sociological and psychological research that documents the detrimental effects on children of exposure to violence, regardless of the child's own direct victimization. The existence of violence in the family, even when not directed toward children, shapes children's behavior both in the short- and long term. Between 10 and 20% of all children are at risk for exposure to domestic violence (National Clearinghouse, 2003), and estimates are that 3.3 to 10 million children are exposed to domestic violence in their homes annually (Bernard, 2003). For many children, this exposure results in behavioral, emotional, and psychological problems.

Courts in virtually all states now consider domestic violence in custody decision making, and this can even result in a rebuttable presumption against giving custody to the batterer. Similarly, in domestic violence proceedings for civil protection orders, courts may impose protections for children who have been exposed to domestic violence, and may also allow these children to bring such proceedings themselves (Lemon, 1999). Child exposure to domestic violence is also important in child protection proceedings. As part of a plan to keep the child safe, the mother's relationship with her batterer may be important. Mothers may also be held accountable for failing to protect their children who have been exposed to domestic violence (Dunlap, 2004). Other legal actions to which child exposure may also be relevant include tort suits based on domestic violence exposure and criminal sentencing.

This chapter discusses the sociological and psychological studies showing the impact on children of exposure to domestic violence, describes some of the available treatment options, and reviews the legal system's approach to these issues. A total of 85% (or almost 600,000 victimizations) of all domestic violence each year occurs against women, and the remaining 15% occurs against men (Rennison, 2003). Thus, although this chapter will generally refer to male batterers and female victims, it is important to note that children also witness battering by same-sex partners and by women against men.

Based on this analysis, there are four principles that should guide legal approaches to child exposure. First, child witnessing of domestic violence must be a critical component of any legal proceeding that affects children. Second, the adult victims of domestic violence should be supported, not penalized, in their continuing relationship with their children. Third, the safety of the adult victim and the child should be of paramount importance. Finally, the batterer's exposure of children to domestic violence should be a consideration in other legal proceedings relating to the batterer.

## IMPACT ON CHILDREN: GENERAL THEMES

Although they may be the third parties within a battering relationship between intimate partners, children are victims. Even when they are not themselves the target of the abuse, children are affected cognitively, emotionally, and physically by their parents' violence. Children can be exposed to domestic violence in several different ways (Fantuzzo & Mohr, 1999). They may actually witness or hear the abuse. "Hiding in their bedrooms out of fear, the children may hear repeated threats of injury, verbal assaults on their mother's character, objects hurled across the room, suicide attempts, beatings, and threats to kill" (Field, 1998, p. 3). They may also be involved in the immediate aftermath of the violence by, for example, dialing 911, talking to the police, or visiting their parent in the hospital (Fantuzzo & Mohr, 1999). And they may be exposed to more long-term consequences of the violence through seeing the bruises on their mother or seeing her crying and depressed. One recent study found that more than 80% of battered mothers believed that their children overheard the abuse, and more than 75% reported that their children saw evidence of the abuse (Edleson, Mbilinyi, Beeman, & Hagemeister, 2003).

While research on the effect of domestic violence on children is still comparatively new, three major themes have emerged from the data. First, the existence of domestic violence in a family often translates into a direct risk of physical harm for children (Lyon, this volume, Chap. 2). The children of fathers who are abusive to their partners are 30 to 60% more likely to be physically abused as well. It is still not clear whether abused mothers are more likely to be physically abusive toward their children than are nonabused mothers (National Clearinghouse, 2003; Stark, 2002). Child witnessing and direct child victimization are strongly interconnected (Huth-Bocks, Levendosky, & Semel, 2001). One researcher has described the co-occurrence of witnessing domestic violence and being a victim of child maltreatment as the "double whammy" for children (Edleson et al., 2003).

Second, apart from possible physical abuse, children who witness abuse are at risk for severe behavioral and other psychological problems. Studies carried out over the last 25 years consistently agree that child witnesses to violence are at a higher risk for a wide range of behavioral, emotional, and intellectual problems than are children who have not been exposed to violence (Huth-Bocks et al., 2001). In fact, child witnesses of domestic violence suffer from some of the same consequences as do children who are direct victims of child maltreatment (Bernard, 2003). The effects of exposure to domestic violence may continue into adulthood (Edleson, 2004), although not all children experience such long-term effects.

Seeing one parent attack another may traumatize children in a variety of ways, ranging from interference with the parent–child bond to destroying a child's sense of security. Because children learn behaviors from their parents, they may ultimately imitate the abuser's actions toward the victim-parent or resort to violence in their own relationships. Studies that compare children of battering relationships who have not themselves been subject to abuse to children who have neither witnessed nor been subject to abuse, find that the children of the battering relationship show more aggression, exhibit impaired cognitive and motor abilities, and are delayed in verbal development. Other studies, as discussed below, further confirm that parental violence has negative behavioral and emotional effects on children who witness it.

Third, not all children who witness domestic violence will exhibit these problems nor be subject to direct physical abuse (Bernard, 2003; Stiles, 2002). Some children exposed to domestic violence show no greater problems than those who have not been exposed (Edleson, 2004). Some children who are exposed to violence face no greater risks than children who live in "distressed" relationships without abuse (Stark, 2002). A number of factors may influence the degree to which child witnesses are affected. They include: the age of the child witness, gender, intellectual ability, socioeconomic status, level of social support, the quality of the child's relationship with the parents, and the amount of time that has passed since the child's exposure to violence (Stiles, 2002). For example, younger children are more vulnerable to effects from exposure (National Clearinghouse, 2003). A good relationship with the child's victim-parent or another trusted person can help the child to handle the trauma (Bernard, 2003).

Direct abuse of the child also significantly affects a child's resilience. Children who are direct victims of domestic violence appear to experience the most severe effects (Bernard, 2003; Huth-Bocks et al., 2001). The most careful studies indicate that abused children who also witness domestic violence exhibit the most problematic behavior, while witnessing alone leads to "moderate" problems (Judicial Council of California, 2003). Unfortunately, however, many studies fail to distinguish between witnessing domestic violence and direct victimization of the child. While child abuse in the general population is present in only an estimated 6% of families, child abuse occurs in approximately 40% of families where partner abuse has occurred (Judicial Council of California, 2003).

## SPECIFIC EFFECTS ON CHILDREN

This section provides an overview of the available data, and develops the themes articulated above concerning the impact on children of witnessing partner abuse.

### *Psychological Impact*

On a psychological level, child witnesses tend to exhibit higher levels of anxiety and depression than do children who have not witnessed violence (Edleson, 1999; Stiles, 2002). Feelings of fear, anger, grief, shame, distrust, and powerlessness are among the host of emotional reactions that child witnesses may suffer (Bernard, 2003). Given these reactions, not surprisingly child witnesses also have a higher risk of suicide (Bernard, 2003). Some research has found that adolescent witnesses "are more likely to have a fatalistic view of the future resulting in an increased rate of risk taking and antisocial behavior, such as school truancy, early sexual activity, substance abuse, and delinquency" (Stiles, 2002, p. 12).

### *Behavioral Impact*

Children's behavior may be impacted in many ways when they are exposed to domestic violence.

#### *School Performance*

Many children's school performance suffers following exposure to domestic violence. Poor performance in school appears to have at least three aspects. First, there is some evidence that child witnesses have poorer intellectual functioning than non-witnesses, coupled with an increased risk of learning difficulties (Miller et al., 1989, as cited in Bernard, 2003). Second, witnesses tend to have obedience problems and are at higher risk of lying and cheating (Stiles, 2002). Finally, these children may develop social problems, manifesting in an inability to develop relationships with others (Stiles, 2002).

#### *Aggressiveness*

Aggressiveness is one of the most widely discussed behaviors exhibited by children who have witnessed domestic violence. It is important to remember that not every child that is exposed to domestic violence will respond with aggressive behaviors and that many additional factors play a role in affecting an individual child's response. Nevertheless, child witnesses are more likely to respond to conflict in an aggressive manner (Bernard, 2003; Edleson, 1999; Stiles, 2002). This aggressiveness results in an increased risk of fighting and bullying (Stiles, 2002). In addition to aggression, child witnesses may exhibit more anger and temperament problems than non-witnessing children (Edleson, 1999). Child witnesses exhibit both signs of aggression and signs of fearfulness and inhibition. In a carefully controlled study of 167 children in Seattle, Washington, the authors found that children exposed to domestic violence were 1.6 times more likely than other children to score in the borderline area of disturbance to the more clinically disturbed range for externalizing behaviors, such as aggressiveness. The authors found little differences in social competence or internalizing behaviors, such as depression (Kernic et al., 2003).

Some research suggests child witnesses are also more likely to end up in juvenile court. Child witnesses become involved in the justice system, not only for violent crimes, but also for sexual crimes and involvement with drugs and alcohol. Some studies have found that a child's exposure to violence within the home was significant in predicting the child's behavior outside of the home, and that child witnesses were more likely to try to commit suicide, abuse both alcohol and drugs, and engage in other delinquent acts (Edleson, 2004; National Resource Center on Domestic Violence, 2002).

Child witnesses come to view violence as an acceptable way to resolve problems. Even more frightening, some child witnesses accept violence as part of a normal relationship. These attitudes can lead to child witnesses growing up to be abusers or victims of abuse. Boys are significantly more likely to approve of violence than girls (Edleson, 1999).

### *Relationship With Each Parent and Siblings*

The existence of domestic violence in the home may result in the "children's paradox": children may feel loyal to one or both of their parents, and yet be fearful because of the existence of the violence (Wolfe, 2002).

Children who have been exposed to domestic violence are more likely to be disobedient at home, and adolescent witnesses have higher rates of interpersonal problems with other family members, especially interparental conflict (Stiles, 2002).

Battered women seem to share many of the same beliefs about parenting styles and behaviors with non-battered women (Judicial Council of California, 2003). One study found that the existence of domestic violence in the family did not negatively affect the intellectual quality of the home environment for preschoolers, although maternal depression, which is linked to domestic violence, did predict a less intellectually stimulating home environment (Huth-Bocks et al., 2001).

### *Long-Term Effects*

In addition to these immediate effects, children who witness domestic violence may also suffer from troubling long-term effects. Some scholars have suggested that child witnesses, males in particular, are likely to become abusers in their own relationships. While daughters may be less likely than sons to become involved in a violent relationship as an adult, women who have been exposed to domestic violence as children are more likely to tolerate abuse when they do experience it (Wolfe, 2002). In addition, emotional problems such as depression may carry through to adulthood. A study in 1995 of undergraduate students indicated that witnessing violence as a child was associated with adult depression and trauma-related symptoms for both men and women, and with low self-esteem for women (Bancroft & Silverman, 2002, as cited in Judicial Council of California, 2003). Thus, for children who live with a batterer, the continuing violence reinforces the lesson that violence is acceptable and puts them at risk for becoming abusers themselves.

### *Risks From Continuing Contact With the Batterer*

Given the potential damage to children who witness domestic violence, significant questions arise as to whether children should continue to have contact with the batterer. Perpetrators pose risks to children even if the children are no longer living with them. These risks include the obvious ones of neglectful or abusive parenting or exposure to additional domestic violence in the perpetrator's new relationship. In addition, perpetrators may undermine the mother's parenting and use the child as a pawn against the mother by trying to discover the mother's location or using visits as occasions for further violence against her (American Bar Association, 2004).

## TREATMENT OPTIONS

Because of the growing awareness in the mental health community that exposure of children to domestic violence constitutes a widespread public health concern, more post-treatment programs now serve child witnesses. Courts, social workers, shelters, and community-based organizations have begun to develop programs responding to children. These interventions focus on providing services to children, to their primary caretakers, and to the batterers. Children may participate in individual counseling or group programs that provide social support to help children feel less isolated (Judicial Council of California, 2003). There are a variety of different interventions, ranging from programs that are offered to target specific behaviors, such as reducing aggression, to programs focused on young children, offered by shelters or within the community; there also may be mentors or group therapy available. (Graham-Bermann, 2001).

Programs generally focus on helping children to deal with the trauma of witnessing violence as well as helping them to mend relationships with other family members (Bancroft & Silverman, 2002). Boston Medical Center has established a counseling, advocacy, and outreach program focusing on children who have witnessed violence both in their community and in their homes. The staff includes social workers, psychologists, an attorney, and both a child psychiatrist and a pediatrician. Counseling is provided on both a group and individual basis, with a focus on group interventions (Child Witness to Violence Project, 2004). The University of California Medical Center in San Francisco also has implemented a program to identify exposed children and to provide a parent–child treatment intervention (Violence Prevention Project, 2000).

There has, unfortunately, been comparatively little research on therapeutic models and approaches for children exposed to domestic violence (Groves, 1999, p. 127). Studies do show that children who have participated in group treatment or treatment that is focused on mother–child interactions experience a reduction in aggressive and depressive behaviors, as well as other positive outcomes, although these studies are limited in nature (Judicial Council of California, 2003, p. 21).

Programs that focus on battered women also aid battered children (Bancroft & Silverman, 2002). Battered parents have often had their parenting undermined by the batterer: the batterer's behavior may teach children not to respect their mother and the battering itself may affect their mother's parenting abilities (Bancroft & Silverman, 2002). Many battered women's shelters provide programs and support groups as well as parenting classes to help battered women break the cycle of violence and aid them in their own parenting skills (Judicial Council of California, 2003). The majority of these programs consist of group therapy that meets weekly, on average for four to eight weeks. In order to improve her parenting, the battered mother needs to feel safe.

Batterer programs are the primary option for the perpetrators. Some states require perpetrators to attend these programs. California requires that the perpetrator of domestic violence attend a 52-week batterer program that includes discussing the effects of abuse on children (Cal. Penal Code, § 1203.97, 2004). The program often consists of education about violence and the personal attitudes and beliefs that support abusive behavior in the home, and may include therapy (Emerge, 2003). Although many traditional programs have not focused on the effect of violence on children in their home, increasing numbers of batterer programs are stressing the importance of parenting and the effect of violence on the family in their curricula (Judicial Council of California, 2003). While some studies have questioned whether batterer programs reduce recidivism, a recent study of 633 batterers in three programs found that in the 15-month follow-up period, batterers who completed a full program were one-third less likely to re-assault their partners than batterers who exited the programs early (Jones, D'Agostino, Gondolf, & Heckert, 2004).

## LEGAL APPROACHES TO CHILD EXPOSURE TO DOMESTIC VIOLENCE

In child custody and visitation proceedings, witnessing is relevant to the initial custody determination, restrictions on visitation, and the appropriateness of joint custody (Matthews, 1999). Child exposure may also be a factor considered in child abuse and neglect proceedings, in tort suits, and in criminal actions.

### *Custody and Visitation*

In most families today, the mother is still the primary caretaker of the children.

However, a battered mother often can be manipulated into relinquishing custody when the parents separate. Given the consequences of domestic violence for children, abuse of the mother should be an important factor in determining custody and visitation arrangements. Domestic violence can explain a strained relationship between the abuser and the children, it can explain a mother's parenting, and it can support a judge's decision to protect the children and the victim from further abuse. Even after separation from the mother, many abusers continue their harassment and violence against her, and may abuse the children directly in order to punish the mother (Meier, 2003).

### *Custody*

In deciding between parents, virtually all states now have statutes suggesting or requiring that courts consider domestic violence as one factor in a custody award (Lemon, 1999). States have enacted other statutes recognizing the interrelationship between domestic violence and custody determinations. The custody-oriented legislation can be divided into three categories. First, some statutes require courts to consider domestic violence before joint or sole custody is awarded. For example, the Indiana statute directs that the court consider a series of factors in deciding on child custody, including "[e]vidence of a pattern of domestic or family violence by either parent" (Ind. Code Ann. § 31-17-2-8 (7), 2004). Second, some statutes create a presumption against awarding custody to a batterer. For example, Massachusetts provides the following:

> A probate and family court's finding, by a preponderance of the evidence, that a pattern or serious incident of abuse has occurred shall create a rebuttable presumption that it is not in the best interests of the child to be placed in sole custody, shared legal custody or shared physical custody with the abusive parent. Such presumption may be rebutted by a preponderance of the evidence that such custody award is in the best interests of the child. (Mass. Ann. Laws ch. 208 § 31A, 2004)

A third set of statutes direct that domestic violence be taken into account when making other decisions, such as determining whether a parent has abandoned her, or his, children by fleeing domestic violence, or (as discussed below) requiring that visitation arrangements take into account the violence. For example, Rhode Island's custody statute provides that a court can condition visitation or custody on a domestic violence perpetrator's completion of a batterer's program and also requires that if there has been a finding of domestic violence, the court must "consider as primary the safety and well-being of the child and the parent who is the victim of domestic violence" (RI Gen. Laws § 15-5-16 (g)(2)–(3), 2004). In Alabama, new legislation specifies that the rebuttable presumption against relocation of the custodial parent does not apply if the party objecting to the relocation has been found to have committed domestic violence (Ala. Code § 30-3-169.4, 2004).

Because parents are presumed fit, there is a presumption that their custodial rights trump those of all third parties. Only a few statutes prevent an abusive father who has killed the mother from prevailing in a custody battle against a third party such as the grandparents. For example, in Pennsylvania, a parent who has been convicted of first-degree murder of the child's other parent shall not be awarded custody (American Bar Association, 2004). In Nevada, conviction of first-degree murder of the other parent results in a presumption against custody and visitation (American Bar Association, 2004).

The statutes that take domestic violence into account in rendering custody decisions vary as to the type of evidence of domestic violence that must be presented to trigger this consideration. Florida and Delaware both require criminal domestic violence convictions, while Minnesota only requires "'evidence of domestic violence'" (Jaffe, Crooks, & Wolfe, 2003, pp. 65–66). Notwithstanding the increased sensitivity to domestic violence, Professor Joan Meier recently concluded that trial courts are granting custody to batterers "more often than not" (Meier, 2003, p. 662). Some courts exclude evidence of domestic violence, while others find that, even where there is proof, the violence does not rise to the level of abuse established by the relevant statute (Meier, 2003).

### *Visitation*

In most states it is difficult to deny visitation completely to the noncustodial parent, absent extraordinary circumstance. The existence of violence between the adults is rarely a sufficient basis. Based on misconceptions regarding the effects of witnessing domestic violence on children, courts may make judgments that may not be in the child's best interest. Even if the courts award custody to a battered woman, they may not adequately protect her with visitation provisions. Nonetheless, because of the potential for abuse inherent in transferring children between parents, many courts consider ordering supervised visitation or other conditions on visitation when there are allegations of domestic violence. In states with legislation requiring that visitation arrangements take into account the custodial parent's safety, and even in states without such legislation, a judge who hears testimony on the custodial parent's fear of further violence can order restrictions on visitation to ensure the safety of the child and the victim. Examples of the types of conditions that courts might impose include the following:

- Specifying the hours and days of visitation and prohibiting contact, either in person or via telephone, at other times;
- Conditioning visitation upon participation in batterer's counseling;
- Specifying monetary penalties for violating the time restrictions by picking up or returning a child late or by failing to appear altogether (Field, 1998).

In the alternative, courts can order supervised visitation. Several states have court-related supervised visitation and visitation exchange centers in which trained staff can supervise visitation and the transfer of children between the parents (Lemon, 1999). California has developed a standard supervised visitation court form, and has promulgated Standards of Practice for Providers of Supervised Visitation. These standards require that centers establish written security procedures, inform their clients of these procedures, and obtain copies of all relevant court documents, including protection orders (Cal. Rules of Court, 2004). Notwithstanding the reasonableness of supervised visitation, such conditions will be set only if the victim has made clear the link between the children and the violence, or if the judge seeks to prevent the abuser from continuing harassment through access to the children.

In some states, courts are directed, through "friendly parent" provisions, to consider which parent is more likely to encourage contact between the children and the other parent. In Minnesota, the friendly parent provision does not apply if there has been a finding of domestic violence (Minn. Stat. § 518.17, 2003).

### *Court-Ordered Mediation*

In many states, the parties are required to attend mediation sessions to resolve custody and visitation disputes. In domestic violence cases, however, mediation may not be appropriate for a variety of reasons, particularly because it requires the parties to cooperate in developing a parenting plan. Some jurisdictions prohibit mediation in domestic violence cases (Lemon, 2001). The Model Code of the National Council on Juvenile and Family Court Judges (1994, § 408) recommends that states not allow mediation when there is a restraining order in effect or, if it is allowed, then only under certain conditions, such as when the mediator is specially trained in domestic violence.

## *Child Abuse and Neglect*

When a child witnesses domestic violence, the family may become involved with the civil child abuse and neglect system even if there is no direct harm to the child. The abuse and neglect system focuses on protecting children from harmful parental conduct. Once children have been adjudicated abused or neglected under a state child abuse statute, they may be removed from their homes and placed in foster care, or the family may be required to participate in mandated services, including treatment that addresses safety and domestic violence. Abuse and neglect can also be the basis for criminal charges.

Abuse and neglect statutes are premised on the concept that parents' basic rights become attenuated as soon as the fitness of the parent(s) becomes questionable. In 2000, in *Troxel v. Granville,* the Supreme Court reiterated that parents have a basic right to raise their children, and that the decisions of fit parents should receive great deference (*Troxel v. Granville,* 2000). While courts give deference to the notion of parental prerogatives, the state can remove children from their parents for abuse and neglect. Moreover, when it comes to children's rights to receive adequate services to prevent abuse and neglect, courts have generally reinforced the state's decision-making process rather than parents and children's rights.

Child witnessing of domestic violence may form the basis for a "failure to protect" petition before the juvenile court that hears dependency cases. Battered mothers' parental rights may be affected or, in extreme circumstances, terminated based on a severe risk to the child due to continued exposure to the battering (Lemon, 1999). In fact, the intimate battering may affect the victim's parenting by causing her to be less attentive to her children because she is appeasing the batterer to prevent additional violence (National Clearinghouse, 2002). While children's advocates and battered women's advocates often see these issues differently, the two systems are, in some jurisdictions, developing methods to coordinate their efforts to protect vulnerable family members (Greenbook Initiative, 1999; Meier, 2003; Ross, 2004). The next section briefly discusses failure to protect in abuse and neglect cases.

### *Failure to Protect*

A common response of the child protective system in the United States has been to blame mothers for any harm to their children (Meier, 2003). When their partners batter them, women may be accused of neglect or failing to protect their children from witnessing the abuse. The child protective services agency may threaten the women with removal of their children unless they comply with mandated action, or the children may actually be removed from the household.

A recent decision challenging the practices of New York's child protective services system found that the system was disproportionately and inappropriately removing children from the custody of battered women; the women were being blamed for their victimization, and their children were placed in foster care (Meier, 2003; *Nicholson v. Williams,* 2002; Ross, 2004). New York City's Administration for Children's Services claimed that battered women were responsible for "engaging" in the abuse, and for exposing their children to it (*Nicholson v. Williams,* 2002). Consequently, they removed the children from their mother's care. None of the plaintiffs had physically abused their child; most of the children were removed from their mothers' care because the mother had either remained with the abuser, or had extricated herself from the battering situation but had not found a stable environment in which to live. Notwithstanding the mothers' care for their children, the City generally sought to remove the child before seeking removal of the batterer (*Nicholson v. Williams,* 2002). As numerous experts testified at the trial, however, removing the child is ill-advised and a dangerous disruption of the mother–child relationship (*Nicholson v. Williams,* 2002; Ross, 2004). As Robin Wilson points out, it is important to remove perpetrators, not children (Wilson, this volume, Chap. 3); focusing on the safety of the child does not require removal from a non-abusive mother.

### *Child Abuse*

There is a trend to define exposing a child to domestic violence as a distinct form of abuse and neglect that is sufficient, in and of itself, to activate the intervention of child protective services. As a practical matter, many child protection agencies define neglect to include child exposure to domestic violence (Edleson, 2004). In addition, some states, including Alaska, Florida, and Montana, have enacted statutes that characterize exposing a child to domestic violence as a type of child maltreatment (Stone & Falk, 1997). In Alaska, for example, a court may take jurisdiction over a child based on "conduct by or conditions created by the parent . . . [that have] placed the child at substantial risk of mental injury as a result of . . . repeated exposure to conduct by a household member . . . [that is a domestic violence crime] against another household member" (Alaska Stat. § 47.10.011, 2004). In Montana, legislation provides that committing violent acts against another resident of the same household may constitute psychological abuse or neglect but, unlike Alaska, the legislation explicitly protects the victim of violence by specifying that she will not be held responsible for failing to prevent the crime against her (Mont. Code Ann. § 41-3-102(19)(a)–(b), 2004).

Several courts have used similar statutes to terminate parental rights when children witness violence in the home. For example, an Alaska court found children abused and neglected and then terminated a father's parental rights based on, among other findings, his exposure of his children to two incidents of domestic violence (*A.H. v. State Dept. of Health & Social Services,* 2000). Such statutes are controversial because they are so broad, they may cause unnecessary removal of children from their battered mothers, and they presume a harm that does not exist for every child exposed to domestic violence (Edleson, 2004; Weithorn, 2001). Moreover, they may force a child to testify against the perpetrator and, unless the statutes are carefully drafted, they may be used against a victim who is acting in self-defense (Kent, 2001). In Minnesota, a statute that defined a child's exposure to domestic violence as requiring a child abuse report was repealed because it overwhelmed the resources of the child protective services system (Jaffe et al., 2003; Weithorn, 2001). To the extent that these statutes prove useful, they must focus on the batterer's actions and on holding him accountable, rather than holding the victim responsible for the batterer's actions (Weithorn, 2001).

## *Other Legal Actions for Children Who Witness Domestic Violence*

Outside of family court, there have been other legal developments recognizing the significance of children's exposure to domestic violence. In Wyoming, a tort lawsuit alleging intentional infliction of emotional distress was brought against an abuser on behalf of the two children who witnessed his physical abuse of their mother. The trial court granted summary judgment to the abuser, but the Supreme Court of Wyoming reversed (*Bevan v. Fix,* 2002).

State criminal statutes, which can be used to prosecute batterers for child exposure to domestic violence, may also define a new crime or provide for enhanced penalties in cases of child exposure. In Delaware, criminal endangerment of a child's welfare explicitly includes the commission of a violent felony with the knowledge that a child family member witnessed the crime (Del. Code Ann. tit. 11 § 1102(a)(4), 2004). In several states, including New York and California, batterers have been prosecuted under the child endangerment statutes based on children witnessing the adult violence (Stone & Falk, 1997). In some criminal proceedings, there are mandatory enhanced penalties for domestic violence defendants if they committed their crimes "in the presence of a child" (Hagemeister, 2003). States have, for example, doubled the penalty when the act is committed in a child's presence, defined witnessing as an "aggravating circumstance," or even established new categories of crimes. For example, in Washington, a crime involving domestic violence that is committed within the presence or hearing of either the perpetrator's or the victim's children can justify an increased sentence.

## FOUR PRINCIPLES TO GUIDE DECISIONS IN THE FUTURE

As this chapter shows, there has been a dramatic increase in the sociological analysis of child exposure to domestic violence as well as the legal recognition of its significance. Yet there are still many legal reforms that remain to be implemented to protect children and their families. Four guiding principles, at a minimum, should be applied when a child has been exposed to domestic violence, regardless of the legal or familial context (Spears, 2000). First, legal proceedings affecting children must consider the impact (if any) on each individual child of witnessing domestic violence, including how it affects self-esteem as well as relationships with both parents, and laws must be developed and administered to implement conclusions based on this individualized assessment. Second, the law should protect the parenting relationship between the victim and child. Third, priority should be placed on protecting the child and the victim from the perpetrator. Finally, the batterer should be held accountable for his or her actions.

The first principle, focusing on the impact of domestic violence on the particular child, reflects the research that shows exposure to domestic violence affects each child differently and depends on a series of factors. While assessment tools are difficult to develop, one curriculum for mental health practitioners suggests that an assessment should include a review of the violence, the child's current symptoms, a detailed history of the child's development, and the reactions of significant adults to the violence (Judicial Council of California, 2003). Assessment tools have also been developed to estimate the risk to children from continuing contact with the batterer, including a review of the abuser's history of abuse toward his partner, of using the children against his partner, and his substance abuse history (Bancroft & Silverman, 2002).

This assessment should be used in child custody and visitation decisions, as well as abuse and neglect procedures. In order to do so, reforms are necessary to these legal requirements. First, with respect to custody and visitation, custody reform must focus on the effects of domestic violence on the child. Severe acts of domestic violence should call into question the fitness of the parent to care for the child. Second, all states should require admission of evidence of abuse and should train judges to understand the psychological and sociological dimensions of violence for children. Third, custody awards should be modified if abuse continues between the parents.

Domestic violence is relevant to the custody decision to rebut any charges that the mother has abandoned her children by leaving her husband, an act that otherwise might show that she should not be the custodial parent (Weithorn, 2001, p. 495). Judges often view a woman's flight from battering without the children as evidence that the mother does not care about the children. Instead, leaving without the children could, and generally should, be viewed as a somewhat rational decision to save her life in the midst of her abuser's violence. Otherwise, women face an extremely difficult choice: endure the beating to stay with the children or flee the beating and leave the children while trying to get help. Several states have already recognized this difficulty, but more states need legislation addressing this issue. While children may feel temporarily abandoned when their mother flees the violence, her ability to return and remove the children to a safer environment will provide them with better protection.

Domestic violence should similarly be a factor in modification of custody awards. Courts currently use one of two standards to decide whether custody should be modified: (1) a material change in circumstances so that the best interest of the child requires a change in custody; or (2) regardless of any changes, the best interest of the child requires modification. Courts consider various factors under each standard, much like they do in the initial child custody decision. In some states, an act of domestic violence will constitute changed circumstances (American Law Institute, 2002).

Improved policies would provide that domestic violence should influence requests for, and decisions on, modification of custody and visitation orders. A custody award may encourage one parent to harass the other parent. For example, an award of reasonable visitation rights that does not explicitly set out the hours and times of visitation may cause the noncustodial parent to visit with the custodial parent at any time. When a joint custody award permits one parent to badger and abuse the other, the abused parent should be able to petition for a custody modification based on the continued harassment and abuse. Because domestic abuse has deleterious effects on children, if the parents' separation and a custody award do not prevent the abuse, the children will suffer.

In determining an appropriate modification to a visitation or custody arrangement, the court should weigh the abuser's behavior toward the victim, rather than focusing exclusively on whether the behavior has been directed toward the child, or even on whether the child has directly observed it. If abusers know that courts may take action against them if they harass the other parent about their visitation rights, then children will not become pawns who are used as an excuse by the batterer to continue the abuse of the other parent. In addition, victims will be protected from further abuse caused by arrangements for visitation and joint custody.

While adding another reason to permit modification may detract from the desired stability and permanence of a custody order, continued abuse between the parents does not provide stability for the child. Rather than allowing the child to remain exposed to the abuse and perhaps causing more harm, courts should permit modification upon a showing of the continuation of the pattern of violence between the parents.

With respect to abuse and neglect proceedings, some have proposed treating any exposure to domestic violence as a form of abuse or neglect (Edleson, 2004). While the recognition that child exposure may result in harm is a significant step toward accepting the ramifications of domestic violence, such a broad-brush approach is highly problematic. Children are affected differently by their exposure. Focusing on the impact of the violence on the particular child will indicate whether the exposure has resulted in abuse or neglect. When there is a finding of abuse or neglect based on a batterer's actions, failure-to-protect or neglect proceedings against the victim are certainly inappropriate, as some states have begun to recognize explicitly in their statutes. Failure-to-protect charges against the batterer become moot if the batterer has been removed from the situation. Moreover, because of the variability in children's response to exposure, state involvement is not prudent in every case; instead, providing community services for children who need help is the better solution (Edleson, 2004). Nonetheless, there may be a paradox here: parents are constitutionally protected against unwarranted state intervention, and because "many of the child problems associated with exposure to adult domestic violence do not rise to the level requiring public intervention, yet one wonders if these families are left without any intervention whether their situations will worsen" (Edleson, 2004, p. 12). Families could voluntarily seek services, of course.

While most child abuse and neglect statutes require some finding against the custodial parent before child protective services becomes involved, the child protective system could use strategies designed to reduce blame against the battered parent. These strategies would keep the children with the victim-parent, help keep the parent safe, and remove the risks presented by the batterer (Greenbook Initiative, 1999). For example, the Montana abuse and neglect statute specifies that if a child is in danger because of adult domestic violence in the household, the social service agency should protect the child, but may also prevent the child's removal from the victim, make reasonable efforts to remove the perpetrator, and protect the child from unsupervised visitation with the perpetrator (Mont. Code Ann. § 41-3-301(2), 2005). Creating a safe parenting situation can be done with a set of strategies designed to remove the abuser from the home or change the behavior, such as through arrest and prosecution, civil stay away orders, or requirements that the batterer participate in counseling (Greenbook Initiative, 1999).

The second principle suggests strategies that support the rest of the family unit by, for example, providing affordable housing, food, and child care so that the family can afford to stay away from the batterer. This can be done through removing the batterer and/or prosecuting him. Blaming the woman for not leaving her batterer or for allowing her children to see the violence committed against her does not help the children. For example, when a battered woman allows the perpetrator to return to her home, this must not be viewed as evidence of further neglect on her part; instead, the child protective system should examine why she permitted the abuser to return. The reason may be financial necessity (Spears, 2000), coercion, or fear, and the agency can then work with her on strategies that will protect her and the child. While removal to protect children should always be an option, this would be appropriate only after the agency has pursued safety planning and assessed the risks associated with removal rather than remaining within the family setting (Stark, 2002).

Another alternative is for child protective services to intervene in private litigation to support claims of risk to children from the batterer's behavior (Meier, 2003). Although such an intervention could help keep the victim and child together and safe, the problem, as with many of the other supportive services that could be offered to these families, is that protection services are "notoriously under-funded, overwhelmed, bureaucratically dysfunctional, and . . . fairly universally conditioned to see mothers as the problem" (Meier, 2003, p. 719).

Third, making the safety of the victim and child paramount may involve additional steps beyond mandating various protections during custody and visitation. In some jurisdictions, the address of the child and victim of domestic violence is confidential in child custody proceedings (Ga. Code Ann. § 19-9-7(b), 2000). In its newly promulgated Principles of the Law of Family Dissolution, the American Law Institute similarly provides for the confidentiality of information relating to child custody, such as the residential address and the child's schedule, where there is a "reasonable fear" of domestic violence and disclosure "would increase safety risks" (American Law Institute, 2002, § 2.05(2)). In some serious cases, if protection orders and visitation conditions have failed and the victim and child remain at grave risk of continuing harm, then it may be appropriate to consider other measures, such as temporarily suspending visitation or terminating the batterer's parental rights (Meier, 2003).

The fourth principle focuses on the perpetrator's accountability and involves wide-ranging changes that both support potential continuing contact with the child, and yet also ensure that the batterer is held responsible. This could involve prosecution for the domestic violence, but also require batterer intervention programs so that batterers understand the consequences of their behavior for themselves and their children (Spears, 2000). It might also include substance abuse assessment since batterers are more likely to be substance abusers than non-batterers. States might consider mandatory batterer treatment programs in both the civil and criminal justice systems because such programs can be an important aspect in keeping other family members safe (Kent, 2001). Batterers could also be required to participate in parent education programs, so long as the educators have been trained in dealing with domestic violence (Lutz & Grady, 2004).

In the custody area, an abuser who has killed the other parent should not be considered a fit parent, absent clear and convincing evidence to the contrary. This presumption would apply regardless of whether the abusive parent is convicted of voluntary manslaughter or first-degree murder; the fact of the killing rather than the nature of the conviction would be prima facie evidence of unfitness. To protect victims who kill in self-defense, this presumption would be irrelevant when a parent who has experienced a history of abuse kills the other parent.

To effectuate these principles will require changes within the legal system. In many states, there are already special unified courts for family law cases that generally attempt to assign one judge to handle all issues involving one family, such as domestic violence, child custody, juvenile delinquency, divorce, and child abuse. There are trainings for family law judges on the link between domestic violence and custody decisions (National Council of Juvenile and Family Court Judges, 2004). Such trainings should cover the legal, sociological, and psychological implications of domestic violence, including such topics as: (1) civil and criminal remedies for domestic violence, such as civil order of protection statutes and law enforcement procedures (mandatory arrest laws or prosecutor policies on domestic cases); (2) results of studies on the effect of spouse abuse on children and the relationship between spouse and child abuse; (3) counseling programs available for abusers and their families, including alcohol and drug rehabilitation; (4) an overview of family violence; and (5) the impact of gender bias. With this background, judges can be more effective both at identifying domestic violence and at ordering trial procedures and custody arrangements that are in the child's best interest, while also protecting the abused parent when necessary.

## CONCLUSION

Ultimately, domestic violence requires more fundamental reform to judicial decision making about children and violence. To overcome existing prejudices and images, domestic violence must be seen as a problem affecting the best interest of the child and, in cases of severe abuse, parental fitness. Domestic violence reveals parenting skills. It shows that at least one parent has taken actions that are diametrically opposed to the best interest of the child. Indeed, battering should be understood as a "parenting decision" on the abuser's part (Bancroft & Silverman, 2002). Instead of segregating abuse from custody or other issues concerning the child, there must be systemic recognition that violence is bad for the family. A narrow focus on actions that directly affect the child prevents courts from considering abuse between parents unless it is directed at a child. Because domestic violence has identifiable and deleterious effects on children, there must be a shift in the custodial standard to include this aspect of the parents' relationship.

## REFERENCES


*A.H. v. State Dept. of Health and Social Services,* 10 P.3d 1156 (Alaska 2000).

Ala. Code § 30-3-169.4 (2004).

Alaska Stat. § 47.10.011 (2003).

American Bar Association. (2004). *Custody decisions in cases with domestic violence allegations.* Retrieved October 5, 2004, from http://www.abanet.org/legal services/probono/childcustody/domestic_violence_chart1.pdf

American Law Institute (2002). *Principles of the Law of Family Dissolution: Analysis and recommendations.* Newark, NJ: Matthew Bender.

Bancroft, L., & Silverman, J. (2002). *The batterer as parent: Addressing the impact of domestic violence on family dynamics*. Thousand Oaks, CA: Sage.

Bernard, M. (2003). Domestic violence's impact on children. *The Maryland Bar Journal, 36,* 10–17.

Bevan v. Fix, 42 P.3d 1013 (Wyo. S. Ct. 2002).

Cahn, N. R. (1991). Civil images of battered women: The impact of domestic violence on child custody decisions. *Vanderbilt Law Review, 44,* 1041–1097.

Cal. Penal Code § 1203.097 (2004).

Cal. Rules of Court §26.2 (2004).

Child Witness to Violence Project at Boston Medical Center. (n.d.). Retrieved July 15, 2004, from http://www.athealth.com/practioner/ceduc/dv_children.html

Del. Code Ann. tit. 11 § 1102 (a)(4)(2004).

Dunlap, J. (2004). Sometimes I feel like a motherless child: The error of pursuing battered mothers for failure to protect. *Loyola Law Review* (50), 565.

Edleson, J. L. (1999). *Problems associated with children's witnessing of domestic violence* (revised Apr. 1999). Retrieved from http://www.vaw.umn.edu/documents/vawnet/witness/witness.html

Edleson, J. L. (2004). Should child exposure to domestic violence be defined as child maltreatment under the law? In P. G. Jaffe, L. L. Baker, & A. Cunningham

(Eds.), *Protecting children from domestic violence: Strategies for community intervention.* New York: Guilford Press. Retrieved October 5, 2004, from http://www.mincava.umn.edu/link/documents/shouldch/shouldch.shtml

Edleson, J. L., Mbilinyi, L. F., Beeman, S. K., & Hagemeister, A. K. (2003). How children are involved in domestic violence: Results from a four-city telephone survey. *Journal of Interpersonal Violence, 18*(1), 18–32.

Emerge: Counseling and Education to Stop Domestic Violence (2003). Retrieved from http://www.emergedv.com

Fantuzzo, J. W, & Mohr, W. K. (1999). Prevalence and effects of child exposure to domestic violence. *The Future of Children, 9,* 21–32.

Field, J. (1998). Visits in cases marked by violence: Judicial actions that can help keep children and victims safe. *Journal of the American Judges Association, 35*(3). Retrieved October 5, 2004, from http://www.omsys.com/fivers/visits.htm

Ga. Code Ann. § 19-9-7(b) (2000).

Graham-Bermann, S. (2001). Critical issues in research on social networks and social supports of children exposed to domestic violence. In S. Graham-Bermann & J. Edleson, *Domestic violence in the lives of children: The future of research, intervention, and social policy*, 203–218.

Greenbook Initiative. (1999). Retrieved October 4, 2004, from http://www.thegreenbook.info/init.htm

Groves, B. (1999). mental health services for children who witness domestic violence. *The Future of Children, 9,* 122–132.

Hagemeister, A. (2003). *Overlap of domestic violence and child maltreatment in USA state civil and criminal statutes.* Retrieved October 5, 2004, from http://www.mincava.umn.edu/link/documents/statutes/statutes.shtml

Huth-Bocks, A, Levendosky, A., & Semel, M. (2001). The direct and indirect effects of domestic violence on young children's intellectual functioning. *Journal of Family Violence, 16*(3), 269–290.

Ind. Code Ann. § 31-17-2-8 (7) (2004).

Jaffe, P. G., Crooks, C. V., & Wolfe, D. A. (2003). Legal and policy responses to children exposed to domestic violence: The need to educate intended and unintended consequences. *Clinical Child and Family Psychology Review, 6*(3), 205–213.

Jones, A. S., D'Agostino, Jr., R. B., Gondolf, E. W., & Heckert, A. (2004). Assessing the effect of batter program completion on reassault using propensity scores (2004). *Journal of Interpersonal Violence, 19,* 1002–1020.

Judicial Council of California. (2003, March). Parenting in the context of domestic violence. Retrieved October 5, 2004, from http://www.courtinfo.ca.gov.programs/cfcc/resources/publications/

Kent, L. (2001). Comment: Addressing the impact of domestic violence on children: Alternatives to laws criminalizing the commission of domestic violence in the presence of a child. *Wisconsin Law Review,* 2001, 1337–1369.

Kernic, M., Wolf, M., Holt, V., McKnight, B., Huebner, C., & Rivara, F. (2003). Behavioral problems among children whose mothers are abused by an intimate partner. *Child Abuse & Neglect, 27,* 1231–1246.

Lemon, N. K. D. (1999). The legal system's response to children exposed to domestic violence. *The Future of Children, 9,* 67–93.

Lemon, N. K. D. (2001). *Domestic violence law.* St. Paul, MN: West Group.

Lutz, V., & Grady, C. (2004). Necessary measures and logistics to maximize the safety of victims of domestic violence attending parent education programs. *Family Court Review, 42,* 363–371.

Mass. Gen. Laws Ann. ch. 208 § 31A (2004).

Matthews, M. (1999). The impact of federal and state laws on children exposed to domestic violence. *The Future of Children, 9,* 50–66.

Meier, J. (2003). Domestic violence, child custody, and child protection: Understanding judicial resistance and imagining the solutions. *American University Journal of Gender, Social Policy & the Law, 11,* 657–725.

Minn. Stat. § 518.17 (2003).

Mont. Code Ann. §41-3-301(2) (2005).

National Clearinghouse on Child Abuse and Neglect Information. (2002). *In harm's way: Domestic violence and child maltreatment.* Retrieved October 1, 2004, from http://www.calib.com/dvcps/facts/harm.htm

National Clearinghouse on Child Abuse and Neglect Information. (2003). *Children and domestic violence: A bulletin for professionals.* Retrieved October 4, 2004, from http://nccanch.acf.hhs.gov/pubs/factsheets/domesticviolence.cfm

National Council of Juvenile and Family Court Judges. (1994). *Model code on domestic and family violence.* Retrieved September 23, 2004, from http://www.ncjfcj.org/dept/fvd/publications/

National Council of Juvenile and Family Court Judges. (2004). *Current projects: The family violence department's current project overview.* Retrieved October 7, 2004, from http://www.ncjfcj.org/dept/fvd/aboutfvd/main.cfm?Action= CURRPROJ

National Resource Center on Domestic Violence. (2002). Children Exposed to Intimate Partner Violence. Retrieved from http://www.vawnet.org/NRCDV Publications/

*Nicholson v. Williams,* 203 F. Supp. 2d 153 (E.D.N.Y. 2002), *remanded sub nom Nicholson v. Scoppetta,* No. 02–7079, 2004 WL 2712425 (2d Cir. Nov. 30, 2004).

RI Gen. Laws § 15-5-16(g)(2)(3)(2004).

Rennison, C. (2003). *Intimate partner violence, 1993–2001.* Washington, DC: Bureau of Justice Statistics, U.S. Department of Justice; 2003. Publication No. NCJ197838.

Ross, C. J. (2004). The tyranny of time: Vulnerable children, "bad" mothers, and statutory deadlines in parental termination proceedings. *Virginia Journal of Social Policy and the Law, 11,* 176–228.

Spears, L. (2000). *Building bridges between domestic violence organizations and child protective services.* Retrieved October 1, 2004, from http://www.vaw.umn.edu/documents/dvcps/dvcps.html#id2636653

Stark, E. (2002). The battered mother in the child protection services caseload: Developing an appropriate response. *Women's Rights Law Reporter, 23,* 107–131.

Stiles, M. (2002). Witnessing domestic violence: The effect on children. *American Family Physician, 66,* 2052–2058.

Stone, A. E., & Falk, R. J. (1997). Recent developments: Criminalizing the exposure of children to family violence: Breaking the cycle of abuse. *Harvard Women's Law Journal, 20,* 205–227.

*Troxel v. Granville,* 530 U.S. 57 (S. Ct. 2000).

The Violence Prevention Project at UCSF Medical Center at Mount Zion. (2000). Retrieved July 16, 2004, from www.ucsfhealth.org/childrens/health_library/news/2000/04/11590.html

Weithorn, L. A. (2001). Protecting children from exposure to domestic violence: The use and abuse of child maltreatment. *Hastings Law Journal, 53,* 1–156.

Wolfe, D. (2002). *Consequences workshop on children exposed to domestic violence: Current status, gaps, and research priorities* 6–7. Retrieved October 1, 2004, from http://www.ed.gov/rschstat/research/pubs/cev-final-report.doc

# CHAPTER 2

# *Domestic Violence and Child Protection*

## *Confronting the Dilemmas in Moving From Family Court to Dependency Court*

THOMAS D. LYON AND MINDY B. MECHANIC

The overlap between domestic violence and child maltreatment has received an enormous amount of attention from domestic violence advocates, child advocates, policy makers, and researchers. The goals of empowering victims of domestic violence, usually women, and protecting children from abuse and neglect, usually by men, are theoretically compatible and mutually reinforcing. However, advocacy for battered mothers and protection for maltreated children have developed along different paths, leading to conflict and distrust (Edleson, 1999).

In dependency court, in which children may be removed from their parents' custody due to child maltreatment, battered women sometimes find themselves accused of child neglect because of their alleged failure to protect their children from exposure to domestic violence. At the extreme are child protection policies that remove children from their abused mother's custody with little consideration of the efforts the mother has made to remove herself and her children from her abusive partner, and no case-by-case analysis of the costs and benefits of family preservation versus removal (Magen, 1999; *Nicholson v. Williams,* 2002). Much has been written about the failure of child protective services and dependency courts to understand the difficulties faced by battered mothers, and the mother-blaming that commonly occurs (Lyon, 1999; Weithorn, 2001).

In this chapter we explore another cause of battered women's difficulties in dependency court. Ironically, the belief that domestic violence constitutes child neglect stems in part from arguments made by family court advocates on behalf of battered women. Confronted with judicial blindness to the effects of domestic violence on children, advocates successfully lobbied for legislative reforms limiting the custodial and visitation rights of batterers. Advocates succeeded by painting a hopeless picture of battering in which violence almost inevitably escalates, spreads to the children, and does not cease upon separation. In such a scenario, a home in which the mother is battered is also dangerous for children, and the prospects for escape are remote. From this perspective, removal and foster placement does not seem so extreme.

On the other hand, in New York, the federal courts have held that social service agencies cannot remove children from battered mothers solely on the basis of domestic violence (*Nicholson v. Williams,* 2002). The decision is generally regarded as a victory for battered women (Dunlap, 2003). The reasoning underlying the decision is double-edged. The decision downplays the negative effects of domestic violence on children and the difficulties battered women have in escaping from abusive relationships. Just as family court arguments about the harms of domestic violence have influenced child protection, this latest development may undermine the efforts made by advocates in family court. Family courts may conclude that exposure to domestic violence is really not that detrimental to children. Moreover, the highest state court's reaction to the decision hints that in the long run, the number of children removed from violent homes may not decline.

In this chapter we review the tensions between the treatment of battered women in family court and in dependency court. We first explore the arguments made on behalf of battered women in family court, namely, that the harms of domestic violence justify limiting batterers' custody and visitation rights. We then describe how these arguments justify concerns among child protection workers that children cannot be left in homes in which there is domestic violence. We analyze the federal litigation challenging the removal of children in New York due to domestic violence, and discuss how the federal district court opinion minimizes the negative effects of domestic violence on children and understates the difficulties in providing safety to mothers and their children. Finally, we consider the New York Court of Appeals' reaction to the federal litigation, and demonstrate that it leaves open the possibility that removal can be justified in many cases. Our conclusion is that the tensions between family court and dependency court have not been resolved, requiring further work to sort out the conditions under which removal of children from abusive homes is necessary to ensure their safety.

## ADVOCACY FOR BATTERED WOMEN AND CHILDREN IN FAMILY COURT

With the advent of no-fault divorce, family courts generally viewed spouse abuse as irrelevant in custody decisions. The purpose of child custody was not to punish or reward parents for their behavior during the marriage, but to ensure the future health and happiness of the child. Custody decisions are based on the "best interests of the child," and made without regard to the reasons for the divorce, unless those reasons can be linked to the child's welfare (Kurtz, 1997). Applying these general principles, batterers argue that their poor relationship with the child's mother is separable from their relationship with the child. Consequently, batterers have successfully won custody of their children even after murdering the mother, on the grounds that their motherless children need them more than ever (Jaffe, Lemon, & Poisson, 2003).

Domestic violence advocates, on the other hand, emphasize that exposure to domestic violence is harmful to children. Children may be physically injured in the course of domestic violence. Younger children may be injured because they are in the mother's arms during an assault. Older children may actively intervene during abuse and be injured in the process (Goodmark, 1999). Because batterers sometimes argue that their children were never physically harmed, advocates also emphasize the psychological harms from witnessing domestic violence (Cahn, this volume; Kurtz, 1997; Lemon, 2001; Meier, 2003). Witnessing any kind of violence can be traumatic; it is even more traumatic to see one's caretakers—upon whom one relies for one's safety and security—acting violently toward each other. Children see and hear far more than their parents realize (Goodmark, 1999). Moreover, even witnessing the aftereffects of abuse can traumatize children. Advocates for victims of domestic violence also emphasize the risk of other harms to children, pointing to the high rates of overlap among domestic violence, physical abuse, and sexual abuse (Goodmark, 1999; Kurtz, 1997; Meier, 2003).

Batterers argue that the harms of domestic violence are overstated because the abuse was only temporary or not severe, and in any event, that separation and divorce end the violence. Advocates for victims, on the other hand, emphasize that minimization and denial are common among abuse victims (Meier, 2003), and that abuse tends to escalate over time, even after separation (Jaffe et al., 2003; Kurtz, 1997; Weiner, 1999). Moreover, advocates argue that batterers tend to be poor parents whose parenting deficiencies will continue (Cahn, this volume; Lemon, 2001). Batterers may claim their problems have been cured by participating in a batterers' intervention program, whereas victims' advocates emphasize the programs' lack of efficacy (Evans, 2004; Meier, 2003).

Family court advocates have thus pushed for expanding the notion of what is detrimental to children in two ways. First, they have argued that the courts should take into account psychological harm, and not just physical injury. Second, they have emphasized the importance of considering risks of harm, including both undetected abuse and injury and the likelihood of future harm.

As a result of family court advocates' hard work, most states now require family courts to consider spousal abuse when making custody decisions (Lemon, 2001). Despite these statutory reforms, however, courts may defeat their purpose by paying lip service to the statute while awarding custody to a batterer (Meier, 2003). Moreover, batterers may argue that even if their spousal abuse is relevant, it ought not trump the non-abusive spouse's failings, such as substance abuse or harsh parenting practices.

In order to ensure that the courts take domestic violence seriously, advocates for victims have lobbied for two further changes in the law. First, they have argued that there should be a presumption against giving the batterer joint or sole custody of the children, a change enacted by some states (Lemon, 2001). A presumption implies that battering should be given more weight than other parental deficiencies. The presumption is justified by the seriousness of the effects, the substantial risk that children are being harmed even if there are no apparent ill effects, and the belief that many parental failings of battered mothers—such as depression and substance abuse—are attributable to abuse (Meier, 2003). Second, advocates have lobbied successfully for legislative determinations that domestic violence is "detrimental" to the child, which increases its importance in custody decision making (e.g., Cal. Family Code § 3020(a)). A finding of "detriment" enables the state to interfere with a parent's custodial rights. Hence, it empowers non-parents (such as grandparents) to take custody away from batterers when the mother has died or is unable to take the child (Baron, 2003).

Advocates for victims of domestic violence have also argued for stronger criminal action against batterers. Many states have adopted mandatory arrest provisions for domestic violence and for violations of protective orders (Zorza, 1992). Some states have sought to prosecute batterers for child endangerment (Whitcomb, 2002). The effects of domestic violence on children are thus used to justify criminal liability. In order to do so, prosecutors must overcome two obstacles. The first is similar to that confronted by the family courts: Batterers will argue that they are not liable for child endangerment because they injured their wives, not their children. Second, batterers will argue that they should not be held criminally responsible for harm when their intent was solely to harm their spouses. Prosecutors counter that parents have moral and legal responsibilities to prevent harm to their children. A parent who harms the other parent, and knows or should know that this will also harm the child, can be held criminally responsible.

In sum, advocates for victims of domestic violence have presented a strong argument for presuming that domestic violence is detrimental to children. Children are at risk of being injured in the cross fire between adults, and of being physically and sexually abused. They are subjected to the psychological harms of witnessing violence between adults they love and upon whom they depend for safety and security. They are also sometimes subjected to poor parenting, because men who beat their wives tend not to be sensitive caretakers, and because women abused by their husbands often suffer psychologically and may turn to drugs and alcohol as a means of coping with the consequences of abuse.

## HOW ADVOCACY CAN BACKFIRE: DOMESTIC VIOLENCE IN DEPENDENCY COURT

Domestic violence issues come up as frequently (if not more frequently) in dependency court, which is designed to protect abused and neglected children. In dependency proceedings, the state takes action against the parents on behalf of the child. If only one parent is abusing the child, that parent may be ordered out of the home as a precondition for allowing the child to remain with the non-abusive parent (Wilson, this volume). If both parents are abusing or neglecting the child, however, the state may remove the child and place him or her with a relative or in foster care. In order to regain custody, the parents may be ordered to complete treatment while demonstrating their interest in maintaining a relationship with the child. In less extreme cases, the state may allow the child to remain in the home while ordering the parents into treatment (e.g., Cal. Welf. & Inst. Code Sections 360–361).

A finding that domestic violence exposure is detrimental to children need not interfere with a woman's rights to her children, because the preferred solution in many cases is to separate the batterer from the children. Unfortunately, this is more easily said than done. The batterer may not cooperate. He may ignore restraining orders and other legal threats. He may resist all attempts at removal, making it necessary to arrest and incarcerate him. He may come looking for his spouse and children when he gets out of jail. Indeed, efforts to remove him may simply incite him to work harder to keep control, triggering separation assault. Second, the victim may not cooperate. She may not want the batterer to leave. She may deny that the abuse is occurring at all, minimize its severity or frequency, or state that the man is getting better. Minimization is likely accentuated by her fears that the social worker is there to take her children. She may believe that the benefits of the relationship outweigh the costs of abuse. These benefits include her love for the man, his other positive qualities (including the economic support he provides), and her lack of alternatives (Rusbult & Martz,

1995; Strube, 1988). Alternatively, she might like the idea of separation in the abstract, but understand that it is impractical in her case, and may only make matters worse. She is likely to understand the risks of separation assault, and the inability of the police, her family, and other players to protect her.

Perhaps the victim wants the batterer to leave, but cannot keep him out of the home. Suggesting she leave with the child raises new problems only too familiar to advocates working with battered women (Browne, 1987). First, she may feel unable to leave. Where is she going to go? Battered women's shelters, assuming they have room, are not viable long-term solutions. Staying with friends and relatives is inconvenient at best and unsafe at worst, because the batterer is likely to know where to find them, and staying with others puts those people at risk. Finding a new place takes time and money. Even if she secures new housing, he can look for her at her workplace or her child's school. To be truly safe, she may need to change her job and pull her child out of school. Second, she may not want to leave. She may legitimately ask, "Why shouldn't *he* leave?"

Even if the victim has left the batterer, it is likely that he will catch up with her or that she will return to him. It frequently takes several attempts before permanent separation is possible (Picker, 1993). Although few women who leave a shelter expect to reunite with their abuser, almost half do so within one year (Rusbult & Martz, 1995; Strube, 1988). This statistic is particularly powerful evidence of the pulls that abusive relationships exert on victims. Even taking refuge in a shelter does not usually signal the end of the relationship.

Assume that a social worker who understands the dynamics of domestic violence assesses a home in which the mother has been abused. Assume also that the children show minor signs of abuse and neglect that, by themselves, do not justify removal. Should the worker be concerned for the safety of the children? Recall the arguments put forward by domestic violence advocates in family court about the minimization of abuse; its escalation over time; and its overlap with other, often undetectable abuse. Should the worker offer services short of removal? If the batterer refuses services, the mother may be unwilling or afraid to accept them because acknowledging a need for help may be perceived as a confession of inadequacy. Without services, removal seems the only viable option. Ironically, even if services are accepted, the worker may worry that separation often incites more serious violence and that batterers' treatment is likely to be ineffective, making removal seem necessary.

## CASE STUDY: NEW YORK DEPENDENCY INTERVENTION DUE TO DOMESTIC VIOLENCE

The case of *Lonell J.* illustrates how removal of children from their mothers has been justified by arguments originally advanced by advocates seeking to limit the custodial rights of batterers (*In re Lonell J.*, 1998; *Matter of Latisha J. and Lonell J.*, 1997). In *Lonell J.*, the parents were living in a state-funded studio apartment with their two children, Latisha, 2-½ years old, and Lonell Jr., 6 months, when their children were removed by social services and placed in foster care. Social services filed a dependency petition alleging medical neglect and neglect based on exposure to domestic violence. The petition also alleged that the parents had failed to attend recommended counseling.

The first social worker to assess the family testified that "the children smelled of urine, Lonell Jr. was feverish and vomiting and Latisha was wearing a diaper that needed changing" (*In re Lonell J.*, 1998, p. 116). The second social worker, having learned that the parents had taken Lonell Jr. to the hospital, visited the home and found Lonell Jr. "lying in his crib covered with vomit" (*In re Lonell J.*, 1998, p. 117). The parents explained that the first social worker visited early in the morning, before they had had a chance to change Latisha's diaper, and that they had taken Lonell Jr. to the doctor several times for an illness that made it hard for him to keep food down.

The trial court dismissed the allegations of medical neglect as unfounded. It referred to the first caseworker, the agency's main witness, as "officious, confused, and misinformed," noting that the worker had falsely asserted in the petition that the mother had attempted suicide "based on the flimsiest of hearsay" (*Matter of Latisha J. & Lonell J.*, 1997, p. 28). The appellate court did not discuss these allegations, nor the credibility of the caseworker. It did not state whether it believed the parents' assertions that they had been taking Lonell Jr. to the doctor. It is unclear whether it believed that the allegations based on medical neglect should be sustained.

Both the trial court and the appellate court, however, believed that removal was justified when the children's physical condition was considered in light of the domestic violence in the home. The mother complained to the first social worker of physical abuse and rape, but refused to follow the worker's advice to go to a battered women's shelter. The social worker then "ceased working with the family due to the father's objections" (*In re Lonell J.*, 1998, p. 117). The second social worker learned that the father had been arrested for abusing the mother, that a protective order had been issued against him, and that the police had been called on five previous occasions. Moreover, the mother at one point left the family to live with her mother, but later returned. Whereas the trial court refrained from finding neglect on this basis, believing that expert testimony was necessary to establish a risk of emotional harm under the dependency statute, the appellate court reversed. It held that even without expert testimony, the children's ill-kempt condition justified a finding of emotional neglect due to the effects of domestic violence on the children.

The sources to which the trial court and appellate court refer illustrate the way in which arguments on behalf of battered women in family court turn into arguments in dependency court for taking children away from battered mothers. Believing it could not take jurisdiction on the basis of domestic violence, but wishing it could, the trial court asked the legislature to proclaim that domestic violence, standing alone, constitutes neglect due to the risk of emotional harm. It cited legislative findings that "[a]buse of a parent is detrimental to children whether or not they are physically abused themselves" (*Matter of Latisha J. & Lonell J.*, 1997, p. 28). These findings had been used to justify a mandate that domestic violence be considered in making custody decisions in *family* court, as well as to justify creation of a statewide registry for protective orders issued in family court and criminal court but, ironically, not in *dependency* court.

Both the trial court and appellate court believed that mothers in dependency court were less sympathetic than mothers in family court, making domestic violence an even more serious threat to children's safety. The trial court stated, "[I]t is tragic that many persons who are victims of domestic violence are unable or unwilling to make any attempt to break its invidious cycle. Nonetheless, they should be found neglectful if they fail to take some initiative, however meager or ineffectual to protect their children" (*Matter of Latisha J. &

*Lonell J.*, 1997, p. 28). The quotation contrasts women in family court, who are taking action to end the abuse through a divorce or custody proceeding, with women in dependency court who have not successfully separated from their abusers. The appellate court emphasized this distinction even more strongly, citing a family law case denying custody to an abuser but adding that, "[u]nlike the respondent mother here, the mother in [the custody case] was willing to take the child away from the abusive father" (*In re Lonell J.*, 1998, p. 118).

The trial court's reference to victims who are "unable or unwilling" to take action makes a second, and equally important, point. Dependency jurisdiction is premised on the *inability,* and not just the *unwillingness,* of a parent to protect his or her child. It is in this respect that dependency jurisdiction can properly be called "no-fault," focusing on the harms to the child rather than the fault of the parent. Of course, practically speaking, the parent experiences the state's intervention as punitive, and social workers routinely behave in a punitive fashion. The point is, however, that a parent's defense that she suffers from inabilities or incapacities beyond her control does not eliminate the grounds for intervening to protect the child. Thus, quibbling with the appellate court's assertion that the mother was truly unwilling, rather than unable, to escape the abuser does not undermine the legal basis for a finding of neglect.

The appellate court found support for its position in law review notes that had argued battered mothers should have greater rights to custody. Citing two law review notes describing the effects of domestic violence on children, the appellate court concluded that Lonell Jr.'s "fever, repeated vomiting and soiled bedding" (*In re Lonell J.*, 1998, p. 118) were attributable to the violence in the home. The court thus rejected the trial court's holding that expert testimony on the effects of domestic violence was required. Kurtz (1997), calling for a presumption against awarding custody to batterers, was cited for the proposition that younger children exposed to domestic violence are likely to suffer from somatic complaints, such as diarrhea and enuresis (*In re Lonell J.*, 1998). Haddix (1996), advocating the termination of batterers' parental rights, was cited for the proposition that "infants exposed to domestic violence often experience poor health and eating problems" (*In re Lonell J.*, 1998, p. 118). A review of other cases citing Kurtz (1997) and Haddix (1996) reveals that they have been most influential in cases limiting the parental rights of battered women, and less persuasive in cases seeking to limit the rights of abusive men (*In re Daphne J.*, 2003 [dissent]; *In re Estate of Thomas,* 2004 [dissent]; *McEvoy v. Brewer,* 2003).

### *The Federal Courts Step In: The Nicholson Opinions*

Two years after *Lonell. J.* was decided, a group of mothers brought a federal civil rights class action challenging New York City's Administration for Children's Services' (ACS) policy of intervening in homes experiencing domestic violence (*Nicholson v. Williams,* 2002). Sharwline Nicholson, the lead named plaintiff, had a young son and an infant daughter. Her daughter's father, who lived in another state, visited on a monthly basis. On one visit, Nicholson told the father that she was breaking off their relationship. He then attacked her, breaking her arm, fracturing her ribs, and bloodying her head. Although ACS had once substantiated an allegation against him for hitting his son, he had never assaulted Ms. Nicholson before. While Nicholson was in the hospital recovering from her injuries, ACS informed her that they had placed her children in foster care. They refused to tell her where the children were located and did not file a dependency petition for another five days because "after a few days of the children being in foster care, the mother will usually agree to ACS's conditions for their return without the matter ever going to court" (*Nicholson v. Williams,* 2002, p. 170).

The ACS worker was misinformed regarding the children's safety. Not knowing that the father lived in another state and did not have a key to the apartment, he believed that Nicholson could not safely return to her apartment with her children. He also believed that Ms. Nicholson had failed to request a restraining order, when in fact she had attempted to do so without success because the father lived out of state and she did not know his address.

One week after their removal, the dependency court ordered that the children could be returned to her, but only if she found a different place to stay. When Nicholson saw her children for the first time, eight days after their removal, her son had a swollen eye from being slapped by the foster mother and her daughter had a rash, a runny nose, and scratches. The children were not returned until 21 days after their removal because ACS did not think that the children had adequate bedding at Nicholson's cousin's home, where Nicholson was forced to stay. The other named plaintiffs experienced similar situations, losing their children to foster care because of exaggerated fears that they were unable to protect their children against abusive men.

Judge Weinstein of the federal district court granted a preliminary injunction prohibiting ACS from removing children "solely because the mother is a victim of domestic violence" (*Nicholson v. Williams,* 2002, p. 250). The Second Circuit Court of Appeals agreed that the removals raised serious questions of federal constitutional law, but hesitated to address those questions, instead asking the highest state court in New York whether, under state law, exposure to domestic violence is sufficient to presume that the risk of emotional injury justifies dependency jurisdiction (*Nicholson v. Scoppetta,* 2003). The federal district court had failed to cite New York state cases on dependency jurisdiction. New York's highest court, the New York Court of Appeals, answered that, "[p]lainly more is required for a showing of neglect under New York law than the fact that a child was exposed to domestic abuse against the caretaker" (*Nicholson v. Scoppetta,* 2004, p. 368). Consequently, the mothers and their children settled the case, agreeing that the case would be dismissed unless the mothers and their children could demonstrate, within one year, that ACS had "failed to act, on a systemic basis, consistent with the decision of the Court of Appeals in *Nicholson*" (*Nicholson v. Williams,* Stipulation and Order of Settlement, 2004, at 3).

### *Nicholson's Rationale: "Domestic Violence Isn't So Bad After All"*

The *Nicholson* litigation has been portrayed as a victory for battered women (Dunlap, 2003), and it is likely that it will reduce the number of removals of children from abusive homes, both in New York and in other jurisdictions influenced by the potential for future lawsuits. However, the possible effects of the litigation on custody decision making in family court have not been explored. Ironically, the decision was founded largely on a conclusion that the harms of domestic violence on children have been exaggerated, in contrast to the arguments advocates have made on behalf of battered mothers in family court.

## *The Effects of Witnessing on Children*

In the *Nicholson* opinion, Judge Weinstein heavily relied on Professor Evan Stark's "lengthy and well-substantiated opinion that children rarely experience long-term effects from witnessing domestic violence" (*Nicholson v. Williams,* 2002, p. 198). Dr. Stark is an associate professor in the Department of Public

Administration at Rutgers University and has written extensively on domestic violence. In his testimony for the plaintiffs, Stark "cited studies which demonstrated that, among children exposed to the most severe domestic violence, well over 80 percent, and sometimes over 90 percent, tested psychologically normal, were self-confident, had positive images of themselves, and were emotionally well off" (*Nicholson v. Williams,* 2002, p. 198). Stark's written report to the court (Stark, 2002) acknowledged that exposure "has been linked to a range of physical, psychological, and behavioral problems," but argued that,

> Despite these claims, several carefully designed studies have shown that children who witness violence are at no greater risk than children in distressed relationships where no violence occurs. Other studies, meanwhile, suggest that the vast majority of children who witness domestic violence show no mental health or behavioral effects whatsoever, or, conversely, that over 80% of children exposed retain their overall psychological integrity. (p. 116)

For the claim that 80 to 90% of exposed children are psychologically normal, Stark cited two sources. One study of eighty 7–12-year-olds in a battered women's shelter (Sullivan, Hguyen, Allen, Bybee, & Juras, 2000) found that "children reported being happy with themselves (83%), liking their physical appearance (83%), and feeling as if they often do the right thing (73%)" (p. 593). However, the other paper Stark referenced, a review of interventions for children exposed to domestic violence (Graham-Bermann, 2001), cited studies finding that "heightened levels of internalizing problems, such as depression and anxiety, characterize 33–75% of the children of batterers" (p. 253), and that 38% of children in one study exhibited symptoms in the "clinical range" on the Child Behavior Checklist (Hughes & Luke, 1998).

There is burgeoning research on the effects of domestic violence on children, which includes both qualitative reviews of the literature (e.g., Margolin & Gordis, 2000; Mohr, Lutz, Fantuzzo, & Perry, 2000) and quantitative meta-analyses (Kitzmann, Gaylord, Holt, & Kenny, 2003; Wolfe, Crooks, Lee, McIntyre-Smith, & Jaffe, 2003). Suffice it to say that the negative effects on children are likely more far-reaching than the *Nicholson* court recognized. For example, Kitzmann and colleagues (2003) conducted a meta-analysis of 118 studies examining the psychosocial outcomes of children exposed to domestic violence, including studies comparing such children to children exposed to other forms of interparental conduct (such as the one study cited by Stark, Hershorn & Rosenbaum, 1985). They estimated that "63% of child witnesses were faring more poorly than the average child who had not been exposed to interparental violence" (Kitzmann et al., 2003, p. 345). Moreover, witnesses to domestic violence were experiencing "significantly worse outcomes than those who witness other forms of destructive interparental conflict" (Kitzmann et al., 2003, p. 346). Children exposed to domestic violence experienced effects as serious as children who were physically abused. Hence, although it may be accurate to say that in most research a majority of children exposed to domestic violence do not exhibit symptoms triggering a need for professional intervention, a substantial minority do exhibit such symptoms and, based on the most thorough meta-analysis to date, most fare worse than non- exposed children or children in distressed relationships.

### The Overlap Between Domestic Violence and Child Abuse

The fact that domestic violence often co-occurs with physical and sexual child abuse is also well documented. One review of 31 studies spanning over two decades found a median co-occurrence of 40% between domestic violence and child physical abuse (Appel & Holden, 1998; see also Edleson, 1999). Some of the research also finds a high rate of overlap between domestic violence and child sexual abuse (Sas & Cunningham, 1995; Rumm, Cummings, Krauss, Bell, & Rivara, 2000). Children who are physically or sexually abused typically delay reporting, if they report at all, and often deny abuse when questioned (Lyon, 2002; Lyon, in press). Hence, domestic violence in a family is a risk factor for undetected child abuse.

The *Nicholson* decision recognized the overlap between domestic violence and child abuse, citing the Appel and Holden (1998) paper, but quoted Dr. Stark for the proposition that, "in the vast majority of cases [the] man who battered the mother was also the source of child abuse or neglect. In other words, the "man hits wife, wife hits child" scenario is rare; abuse tends to flow from a single source" (*Nicholson v. Williams,* 2002, p. 198). The problem with this proposition, as Stark (2002) acknowledged in his written report, is that "it has been widely reported that battered women are more likely to abuse their children than non-battered mothers" (p. 115, citing Giles-Sims, 1985; Straus & Gelles, 1990; Walker, 1979). Other research has similarly found elevated rates of physical abuse of children among battered women (Kruttschnitt & Dornfeld, 1992; O'Keefe, 1994; Walker, 1984). Moreover, there is evidence that battered mothers suffer from deficits in parenting (Jouriles & LeCompte, 1991; Levendosky & Graham-Bermann, 1998; McCloskey, Figueredo, & Koss, 1995; Margolin, Gordis, Medina, & Oliver, 2003), although the results are mixed (e.g., Holden & Ritchie, 1991; Holden, Stein, Ritchie, Harris, & Jouriles, 1998; Sullivan et al., 2000).

Identifying parenting deficiencies in battered mothers may sound like victim-blaming. However, it merely reflects awareness of the myriad negative effects of domestic violence on families. Indeed, if deficiencies in a battered woman's parenting are attributable to domestic violence, as many advocates argue (Meier, 2003), then it almost certainly follows that domestic violence will lead to parenting deficiencies. Appel and Holden (1998) note a number of possible explanations for why battered mothers may be more abusive than mothers who are not being abused. Battered mothers' stress from abuse may impair their parenting; there may be a spillover of negative marital interactions into the mother–child relationship; abusive fathers may coerce mothers into abusing their children; battered mothers may "engage in harsh parenting to preempt the father's even harsher punishments" and battered mothers may have learned through negative marital interactions that aggression is an effective means of control (Appel & Holden, 1998, pp. 589–590).

Criticizing the research on overlap, Stark (2002) points out that the definitions of child abuse in this research are "highly subjective and imprecise" (p. 116) and often include acts "that many parents consider normal discipline" (p. 115, n. 59). As one narrows one's definition of abuse, men increasingly predominate as the abusers (Stark, 2002). These points have been acknowledged by other reviews (Appel & Holden, 1998; Edleson, 1999). Nevertheless, Appel and Holden (1998) asserted that the 40% rate of overlap is based on a "conservative definition of child abuse" (p. 578). Stark (2002), in contrast, suggests that the definition of physical abuse should be limited to injuries requiring medical attention, and found that "the rate of harm that rises to the level of 'abuse' in domestic violence cases" occurs only 3–4% of the time (p. 115).

Taken at face value, the arguments advanced by Stark (2002) and the court in *Nicholson v. Williams* (2002) undermine many of the arguments advocates make in family court on behalf of battered women. A presumption against awarding custody to abusive spouses on the grounds that domestic violence exposure harms children is hard to justify if children from "distressed relationships"—which are likely to predominate among divorcing couples battling over custody—are just as likely to experience such harms. If the overlap between domestic violence and child abuse is less than 5%, it is hard to argue that the presumption of custody is justified by the risks of child abuse. On the other hand, if one acknowledges that substantial percentages of children in violent homes are both psychologically traumatized and at risk of abuse, the presumption maintains its viability. Much of the factual basis for the *Nicholson* opinion, however, is called into question.

### *The Efficacy of Restraining Orders*

At several points in the *Nicholson* opinions, restraining orders against the batterers are mentioned as a potential basis for allowing children to remain in the home (*Nicholson v. Williams,* 2002; *Nicholson v. Scoppetta,* 2004). The assumption that restraining orders are effective underlay the district court's claims regarding the relative harms of foster care placement. Judge Weinstein argued that foster care "can be much more dangerous and debilitating than the home situation," citing Stark's testimony that "foster homes are rarely screened for the presence of domestic violence, and . . . the incidence of abuse and child fatality in foster homes in New York City is double that in the general population" (*Nicholson v. Williams,* 2002, p. 249). Comparing foster care to the general population—rather than the homes from which children are removed—is an unreasonable means of balancing the costs and benefits of removal, unless one assumes that services can make children's homes free from violence.

If restraining orders are a viable alternative to removal of children from violent homes, then one can maintain that domestic violence exposure is indeed as harmful as family court advocates claim, without increasing the likelihood that battered mothers will lose their children. Stark testified in *Nicholson* that the negative effects on children have been observed to "abate after a relatively short period of safety . . . and security [is] provided" (*Nicholson v. Williams,* 2002, p. 198). Moreover, to the extent that any parenting deficiencies of battered women are caused by battering, many of those deficiencies should abate once the abuse has ended. There is some evidence that battered women's parenting improves after separation (Holden et al., 1998).

However, the *Nicholson* opinions failed to cite any research on the efficacy of restraining orders. Restraining orders are fully enforceable only with the cooperation of the mother, the police, and the prosecutors (if a restraining order is violated). Harrell and Smith (1996) interviewed 355 women who had filed petitions for temporary restraining orders due to domestic violence. Almost half did not return to court three weeks later to request a permanent order, and the severity of abuse did not predict whether they returned. Most had contact with the batterer in violation of the order within the first 3 months, and almost a third reported acts of severe violence within the first year, including kicking, strangling, beating, forced sex, threats with weapons, and threats to kill. Most failed to report violations to the police, many of them indicating that they were too afraid or that the police would not help. Despite a mandatory arrest statute for restraining order violations, 80% of the calls to the police failed to result in an arrest. Other research has found that the batterer usually flees before police arrive, making arrest unlikely (Feder, 1996; Kane, 2000). Kane (2000), studying the Boston Police's enforcement of 818 restraining order violations, found that even if the batterer remained on the scene, the police usually ignored the mandatory arrest statute unless there were threats of violence. In the "highest risk" situation, in which the batterer used a weapon and remained at the scene, the police still failed to make an arrest 25% of the time.

The police's failure to take proper action against restraining order violations is perhaps best illustrated by the experience of one of the named plaintiffs in the *Nicholson* case. Michelle Norris had a 2-year-old child and was living with the child's father, Angel Figueroa. ACS investigated a report of possible domestic violence and drug abuse but did not find reasons to intervene. Later that month, Ms. Norris decided to end the relationship and move out of the apartment, and Mr. Figueroa attacked her, dragging her by her hair, throwing her into the wall, and hitting her in the face. Ms. Norris showed the police her injuries, Mr. Figueroa was arrested, and she was granted a restraining order. She moved in with a friend, but went back the next month to obtain her possessions while Mr. Figueroa was gone. Mr. Figueroa arrived, attacked her again, breaking her phone and hitting her in the face.

> The police were called, and when they appeared Mr. Figueroa took the child to the bathroom and locked the door. The police informed Ms. Norris that, because of the order of protection, either she or Mr. Figueroa would have to leave the apartment or both would be placed under arrest. Ms. Norris explained to the police that she was trying to leave, but that she wanted her son back first. Mr. Figueroa refused to leave the bathroom, and the police escorted Ms. Norris out of the apartment without helping her to take her son back from Mr. Figueroa. The next day, Mr. Figueroa left the boy with a baby-sitter, and Ms. Norris returned to take the child (*Nicholson v. Williams,* 2002, p. 186).

If Ms. Norris had continued to live in the apartment, and obtained a restraining order to remove Mr. Figueroa from the home, then a social worker assessing the safety of the child would confront a difficult situation. What protection would the restraining order truly afford?

## DEPENDENCY INTERVENTION AFTER *NICHOLSON*

We have suggested that the effect of the *Nicholson* litigation will be to reduce the likelihood that children will be removed from their mother's custody because of domestic violence. At the same time, however, we have argued that the district court understated the effects of domestic violence on children and was over-optimistic regarding the prospects for restraining orders to protect children adequately. It is important to consider what guidelines the decisions establish for the future, once the immediate effects of the litigation have dissipated and the day-to-day difficulties of assessing safety in individual cases return.

Unfortunately, the decisions provide little guidance. The courts emphasized the wrongfulness of dependency jurisdiction and removal "solely" on the basis of domestic violence (*Nicholson v. Williams,* 2002, p. 257; *Nicholson v. Scoppetta,* 2003, p. 164; *Nicholson v. Scoppetta,* 2004, p. 366). In several of the named plaintiffs' cases, one could argue that the "only real basis for neglect was that the mother had been beaten" (*Nicholson v. Scoppetta,* 2003, p. 163). Either the workers failed to investigate adequately or there was no history of domestic violence and virtually no risk of future violence, making the workers' actions unsupportable.

Focusing on cases in which removal occurs "solely" because of domestic violence simplifies the otherwise difficult issues confronting the courts and dramatically limits the impact of their holdings. First, the courts need not confront the legitimacy of intervention when a parent is unable (rather than unwilling) to protect her children against domestic violence. Judge Weinstein found that ACS was inferring "from the fact that a woman has been beaten and humiliated that she permitted or encouraged her own mistreatment," concluding that "it desecrates fundamental precepts of justice to blame a crime on the victim" (*Nicholson v. Williams,* 2002, p. 252). We would agree that equating victimization with an unwillingness to protect one's children is clearly illegitimate. It sidesteps the issue, however, of how social services should respond when a battered mother has found herself repeatedly incapable of protecting her children against an abusive spouse. Dependency intervention founded on an inability to protect does not assume that the parent permitted or encouraged the abuse to occur.

Second, by disallowing only a small subset of cases in which removal was based "solely" on domestic violence, the courts did not have to draw lines between permissible and impermissible intervention. Although the Second Circuit Court of Appeals referenced several cases among the plaintiffs in which "the batterer had not only assaulted the mother but also in some way threatened the physical safety of the child," (*Nicholson v. Scoppetta,* 2003, p. 163), it did not discuss whether intervention in those cases would have been warranted. Similarly, the New York Court of Appeals, in holding that the definition of a "neglected" child under state dependency law did not include cases in which the "sole" allegation is that one parent allowed the child to witness domestic violence, specifically declined to apply its holding to the named plaintiffs, "recognizing that in the inordinately complex human dilemma presented by domestic violence involving children, the law may be easier to state than apply" (*Nicholson v. Scoppetta,* 2004, p. 367, n. 5). The court went on to approve of cases finding battered mothers neglectful when there was "repeated" domestic violence, when the children appeared fearful and distressed, and when the mother had failed to take action (e.g., "allowed [the batterer] several times to return to her home") (*Nicholson v. Scoppetta,* 2004, p. 371).

Although the New York Court of Appeals refused to consider the facts of the named plaintiffs' cases, it is instructive to do so. Consider Xiomara C., who had two children, aged four and five, with Justin C. In March of 2000, Justin

> violently attacked Xiomara. He punched her head, shoulders, and both eyes. He took two knives, put them against her eyes and told her that if she moved, he would kill her. Then he pushed her to the ground. When she tried to get up, he pushed her down again. He dragged her into the bathroom and forced her into a bathtub full of ice cold water until her skin was numb. Then he used the shower nozzle to hose her with scalding water. (*Nicholson v. Williams,* 2002, p. 190)

ACS removed the children the next day and filed a dependency petition that solely alleged domestic violence against both parents.

On the surface, the petition appears legally deficient because it describes nothing more than domestic violence. However, the facts of the case suggest additional factors that the New York Court of Appeals would consider relevant in justifying dependency jurisdiction. ACS had received previous reports of domestic violence in the household, and had provided Xiomara and Justin referrals for "domestic violence counseling and preventive services, but neither participated" (*Nicholson v. Williams,* 2002, p. 190). Xiomara acknowledged to the investigating social worker that Justin had been physically and verbally abusive for 6 years. Finally, after abusing Xiomara on the occasion in question, Justin kicked her out of the bathroom and locked himself in with their son. Xiomara called the police, and they knocked down the bathroom door. The son emerged, having "suffered bruises and cuts to his face while he had been locked in the bathroom with the father" (*Nicholson v. Williams,* 2002, p. 190).

It is unknown whether the mother was offered assistance in attempting to leave Justin, to seek temporary shelter, or to seek a restraining order. Nevertheless, in the New York Court of Appeals' analysis, the long history of abuse and the physical injuries suffered by her son suggest that removal could be justified. Although Judge Weinstein emphasized that "no allegations were made that Xiomara committed or threatened to commit any violence against Justin or her son" (*Nicholson v. Williams,* 2002, p. 190), the legally relevant factors do not require that the mother be violent, only that she be unable to protect the child.

What is most remarkable about the New York Court of Appeals opinion is its treatment of *Lonell J.* The reader will recall that the trial court was unable to find that the children in *Lonell J.* were medically neglected, leading it to ask the legislature to make exposure to domestic violence per se neglectful (*Matter of Latisha J. and Lonell J.*, 1997). The appellate court held that dependency jurisdiction was justified without any legislation, because the infant's illness (and, perhaps, the toddler's unchanged diaper) justified a finding that the children were suffering from the psychosomatic effects of domestic violence exposure (*In re Lonell J.*, 1998).

The New York Court of Appeals' analysis of the facts of *Lonell J.* highlights the limited impact of the holding that dependency court intervention and removal of children should not be predicated solely on domestic violence in the home. The court did not read *Lonell J.* as presuming that domestic violence justifies removal, because "multiple factors formed the basis for intervention and determinations of neglect," namely, "the unsanitary condition of the home and the children's poor health" (*Nicholson v. Scoppetta,* 2004, p. 383). Hence, problems in the home that do not justify intervention or removal become jurisdictional when coupled with domestic violence exposure. Moreover, the court accepted the assumptions of a causal link between the infant's physical illness and domestic violence exposure, noting that "[t]he tragic reality is, as the facts of Lonell J. show, that emotional injury may be only one of the harms attributable to the chaos of domestic violence" (*Nicholson v. Scoppetta,* 2004, p. 383). The court's acceptance of the tenuous link between domestic violence and the child's physical condition exposes the limited effects of the court's otherwise strong language that emotional harm would rarely justify removal.

## CONCLUSION

It is perhaps inevitable that arguments made for granting battered women custody in family court will conflict with arguments made against denying battered women custody in dependency court. In every dependency case in which a battered mother remains with the batterer, arguments emerging from family court will undermine her efforts to prove that she can be a good parent. Family court advocates' pessimism about future violence teaches that the only solution to domestic violence is permanent separation from the abuser.

There are three possible ways to resolve the conflict, none of them very appealing. One is to have more faith in the future safety for mothers and their children who remain in abusive homes. We have not critically examined the assumptions about future danger in this chapter, but a full understanding of the issues requires recognition of cases in which batterers can be rehabilitated. A second approach is to acknowledge the negative effects of domestic violence on children but to argue that taking custody away from the battered mother violates her parental rights. Taking this approach elevates parental rights above children's safety. A third approach is to put more emphasis on the harms of removal and foster care. Taking this approach undermines our efforts to protect children against other dangers in the home, because it calls into question the difficult choices we make in protecting children against physical and sexual abuse.

Given the dangers, there will be occasions in which child protective workers must conclude that even with a restraining order, children and their mothers face an imminent threat because of domestic violence. If the mother will not or cannot obtain shelter where the batterer cannot find her and her children, placement will be necessary. One can imagine a social services system in which foster placements are designed to take children and their non-abusive parents. That system, however, does not exist, making removal of children a necessary evil. The issue for policy makers and researchers is to better identify the conditions under which children are best served by our clumsy and imperfect methods for keeping them safe.

## REFERENCES


Appel, A. E., & Holden, G. W. (1998). The co-occurrence of spouse and physical child abuse: A review and appraisal. *Journal of Family Psychology, 12,* 578–599.

Baron, S. (2003). The scope of family court intervention. *Journal of the Center for Families, Children, and the Courts, 4,* 115–127.

Browne, A. (1987). *When battered women kill.* New York: Free Press.

Cal. Family Code Section 3020(a) (West Group, 2005).

Cal. Welf. & Inst. Code Sections 360–361 (West Group, 2005).

Dunlap, J. A. (2003). The "pitiless double abuse" of battered mothers. *American University Journal of Social Policy and the Law, 11,* 523.

Edleson, J. L. (1999). The overlap between child maltreatment and woman battering. *Violence Against Women, 5,* 134–154.

Evans, K. C. (2004). Can a leopard change his spots? Child custody and batterer's intervention. *Duke Journal of Gender Law & Policy, 11,* 121–139.

Feder, L. (1996). Police handling of domestic calls: The importance of offender's presence in the arrest decision. *Journal of Criminal Justice, 24,* 481–490.

Giles-Sims, J. (1985). A longitudinal study of battered children of battered wives. *Family Relations, 34,* 205–210.

Goodmark, L. (1999). From property to personhood: What the legal system should do for children in family violence cases. *West Virginia Law Review, 102,* 237–338.

Graham-Bermann, S. A. (2001). Designing intervention evaluations for children exposed to domestic violence: Applications of research and theory. In S. A. Graham-Bermann & J. L. Edleson (Eds.), *Domestic violence in the lives of children: The future of research, intervention, and social policy* (pp. 237–267). Washington, DC: American Psychological Association.

Haddix, A. (1996). Unseen victims: Acknowledging the effects of domestic violence on children through statutory termination of parental rights. *California Law Review, 84,* 757–815.

Harrell, A., & Smith, B. E. (1996). Effects of restraining orders on domestic violence victims. In E.S. Buzawa & C.G. Buzawa (Eds.), *Do arrests and restraining orders work?* (pp. 214–265). Thousand Oaks, CA: Sage.

Hershorn, M., & Rosenbaum, A. (1985). Children of marital violence: A closer look at the unintended victims. *American Journal of Orthopsychiatry, 55,* 260–266.

Holden, G. W., & Ritchie, K. L. (1991). Linking extreme marital discord, child rearing, and child behavior problems: Evidence from battered women. *Child Development, 62,* 311–327.

Holden, G. W., Stein, J. D., Ritchie, K. L., Harris, S. D., & Jouriles, E. N. (1998). Parenting behaviors and beliefs of battered women. In G. W. Holden, R. Geffner, & E. N. Jouriles (Eds.), *Children exposed to marital violence: Theory, research, and applied issues* (pp. 289–336). Washington, DC: American Psychological Association.

Hughes, H. M., & Luke, D. A. (1998). Hetereogeneity in adjustment among children of battered women. In G. W. Holden, R. Geffner, & E. N. Jouriles, (Eds.), *Children exposed to domestic violence: Theory, research, and applied issues* (pp. 185–221). Washington, DC: American Psychological Association.

In re Daphne G., 763 N.Y.S.2d 583 (Sup. Ct. App. Div. 2003).

In re Estate of Thomas, 2004 WL 943629 (N.J. Super. App. Div. 2004).

In re Lonell J., 673 N.Y.S.2d 116 (Sup. Ct. App. Div. 1998).

Jaffe, P. G., Lemon, N. K. D., & Poisson, S. E. (2003). *Child custody and domestic violence: A call for safety and accountability.* Thousand Oaks, CA: Sage.

Jouriles, E. N., & LeCompte, S. H. (1991). Husbands' aggression toward wives and mothers and fathers' aggression toward children: Moderating effects of child gender. *Journal of Consulting and Clinical Psychology, 59,* 190–192.

Kane, R. J. (2000). Police responses to restraining orders in domestic violence incidents: Identifying the custody-threshold thesis. *Criminal Justice & Behavior, 27,* 561-580.

Kitzmann, K. M., Gaylord, N. K., Holt, A. R., & Kenny, E. D. (2003). Child witnesses to domestic violence: A meta-analytic review. *Journal of Consulting and Clinical Psychology, 71,* 339–352.

Kruttschnitt, C., & Dornfeld, M. (1992). Will they tell? Assessing preadolescents' reports of family violence. *Journal of Research in Crime and Delinquency, 29,* 136–147.

Kurtz, L. R. (1997). Protecting New York's children: An argument for the creation of a rebuttable presumption against awarding a spouse abuser custody of a child. *Albany Law Review, 60,* 1345–1375.

Lemon, N. K. D. (2001). Statutes creating rebuttable presumptions against custody to batterers: How effective are they? *William Mitchell Law Review, 28,* 601–676.

Levendosky, A. A., & Graham-Bermann, S. A. (1998). The moderating effects of parenting stress in woman-abusing families. *Journal of Interpersonal Violence, 13,* 383–397.

Lyon, T. D. (1999). Are battered women bad mothers? Rethinking the termination of abused women's parental rights for failure to protect. In H. Dubowitz (Ed.), *Neglected children: Research, practice, and policy* (pp. 237–260). Thousand Oaks, CA: Sage.

Lyon, T. D. (2002). Scientific support for expert testimony on child sexual abuse accommodation. In J. R. Conte (Ed.), *Critical issues in child sexual abuse* (pp. 107–138). Thousand Oaks, CA: Sage.

Lyon, T. D. (in press). False denials: Overcoming methodological biases in abuse disclosure research. In M.E. Pipe, M. E. Lamb, Y. Orbach, and A. C. Cederborg (Eds.), *Disclosing abuse: Delays, denials, retractions and incomplete accounts.* Mahwah, NJ: Lawrence Erlbaum.

Magen, R. H. (1999). In the best interests of battered women: Reconceptualizing allegations of failure to protect. *Child Maltreatment, 4,* 127–135.

Margolin, G., & Gordis, E. B. (2000). The effects of family and community violence on children. *Annual Review of Psychology, 51,* 445–479.

Margolin, G., Gordis, E. B., Medina, A. M., & Oliver, P. H. (2003). The co-occurrence of husband-to-wife aggression, family-of-origin aggression, and child abuse potential in a community sample. *Journal of Interpersonal Violence, 18,* 413–440.

Matter of Latisha J. and Lonell J., 217 N.Y.L.J. 28 (April 16, 1997) (Bronx County Family Court 1997).

McCloskey, L. A., Figueredo, A. J., & Koss, M. P. (1995). The effects of systemic family violence on children's mental health. *Child Development, 66,* 1239–1261.

McEvoy v. Brewer, 2003 WL 22794521 (Tenn. Ct. App. 2003).

Meier, J. S. (2003). Domestic violence, child custody, and child protection: Understanding judicial resistance and imagining the solutions. *American University Journal of Gender, Social Policy, and the Law, 11,* 657–724.

Mohr, W. K., Lutz, M. J. M., Fantuzzo, J. W., & Perry, M. A. (2000). Children exposed to family violence: A review of research from an ecological-developmental perspective. *Trauma, Violence and Abuse, 1,* 264–283.

Nicholson v. Scoppetta, 344 F.2d 154 (2d Cir. 2003).

Nicholson v. Scoppetta, 3 N.Y.3d 357 (N.Y. 2004).

Nicholson v. Williams, 203 F.Supp.2d 153 (E.D.N.Y. 2002).

Nicholson v. Williams, Stipulation and Order of Settlement (E.D.N.Y. 2004).

O'Keefe, M. (1994). Linking marital violence, mother–child/father–child aggression, and child behavior problems. *Journal of Family Violence, 9,* 63–78.

Picker, C. A. (1993). The intersection of domestic violence and child abuse: Ethical considerations and tort issues for attorneys who represent battered women with abused children. *Saint Louis University Public Law Review, 12,* 69–112.

Rumm, P. D., Cummings, P., Krauss, M. R., Bell, M. A., & Rivara, F. P. (2000). Identified spouse abuse as a risk factor for child abuse. *Child Abuse & Neglect, 24,* 1375–1381.

Rusbult, C. E., & Martz, J. M. (1995). Remaining in an abusive relationship: An investment model analysis of nonvoluntary dependence. *Personality and Social Psychology Bulletin, 21,* 558–571.

Sas, L. D., & Cunningham, A. H. (1995). *Tipping the balance to tell the secret: The public discovery of child sexual abuse.* London, Ontario: London Family Court Clinic.

Stark, E. (2002). The battered mother in the child protective service caseload: Developing an appropriate response. *Women's Rights Law Reporter, 23,* 107-131.

Straus, M. A., & Gelles, R. J. (1990). *Physical violence in American families.* New Brunswick, NJ: Transaction.

Strube, M. J. (1988). The decision to leave an abusive relationship: Empirical evidence and theoretical issues. *Psychological Bulletin, 104,* 236–250.

Sullivan, C. M., Hguyen, H., Allen, N., Bybee, D., & Juras, J. (2000). Beyond searching for deficits: Evidence that physically and emotionally abused women are nurturing parents. *Journal of Emotional Abuse, 2,* 51–71.

Walker, L. E. (1979). *The battered woman.* New York: Harper.
Walker, L. E. (1984). *The battered woman syndrome.* New York: Springer.
Weiner, M. H. (1999). Domestic violence and custody: Importing the American Law Institute's principles of the law of family dissolution into Oregon law. *Willamette Law Review, 35,* 643–715.
Weithorn, L. A. (2001). Protecting children from exposure to domestic violence: The use and abuse of child maltreatment statutes. *Hastings Law Journal, 53,* 1–153.
Whitcomb, D. (October, 2002). Prosecutors, kids, and domestic violence cases. *Prosecutor, 36,* 32–34.
Wolfe, D. A., Crooks, C. V., Lee, V., McIntyre-Smith, A., & Jaffe, P. G. (2003). The effects of children's exposure to domestic violence: A meta-analysis and critique. *Clinical Child and Family Psychology Review, 6,* 171–187.
Zorza, J. (1992). The criminal law of misdemeanor domestic violence, 1970–1990. *Journal of Criminal Law & Criminology, 46,* 63–72.

CHAPTER 3

# *Sexually Predatory Parents and the Children in Their Care*

## *Remove the Threat, Not the Child*

ROBIN FRETWELL WILSON

Myths surrounding child sexual abuse hinder the ability of judges and others to protect children from real threats they face. One particularly deep-rooted and damaging myth maintains that incest with one child is an isolated event that a parent is not likely to repeat with another child. This chapter argues that the perpetrator who commits incest rarely stops with the first victim. To the contrary, incest is a predictably recurring event that could largely be avoided if child protective services (CPS) agencies would remove the alleged perpetrator from the home, rather than removing the victim while leaving other children in the home.

The choice to remove the child rather than the threat is driven largely by misunderstandings about the legality of excluding alleged offenders from their home, compounded by the equally entrenched, but wrong-headed view that a non-abusing parent who fails to protect once will do so again. CPS legally can, however, and should, place the burden of homelessness on the alleged offender rather than compromising children's safety.

### CLOUDED JUDGMENT

When a parent sexually abuses a child in his or her care, a question frequently arises regarding the safety of other children in the household. Because child sexual abuse by women occurs very rarely (Wilson, 2002), this chapter will consider only incest at the hands of fathers and father-substitutes. The state may intervene to protect the victim because he or she has already been harmed. For the state to intervene to protect the victim's sibling, however, the state must show that the sibling "more probably than not" faces substantial risk of imminent harm. Once the state proves that further incest is probable, it may act to protect additional children in a variety of ways, including removing the child, supervising the family, or mandating "voluntary" treatment of the perpetrator (Fla. Stat. Ann. § 39.52(1)(b), 2003; Goldstein, 1999).

Perhaps because judges believe the isolated act myth, they reach wildly different judgments regarding the risk to children left in the perpetrator's care. Courts in the United States generally react in one of three ways.

### *No Clear Risk*

Some courts see no clear risk to the victim's siblings. A New York family court in *In re Cindy B.* (1983) refused to protect the siblings of an incest victim, finding that the state produced no evidence "that the physical . . . condition of any [sibling] . . . is in imminent danger of becoming impaired" (p. 195). The father admitted sexual intercourse with his oldest daughter, Cindy. The New York Court of Appeals validated this approach in a case where the 12-year-old victim, Starr, was digitally penetrated by her mother's live-in boyfriend while he "instructed her to lick his penis 'like an ice cream cone'" (*In re Starr H.*, 1989, p. 767). The state CPS agency petitioned to protect Starr and her siblings, but the family court dismissed the petition without explanation. On appeal, the court found that while Starr was an abused child, her sexual abuse—standing alone—was insufficient to find that her siblings were at substantial risk. New York courts are not alone in refusing to protect a victim's siblings. Texas courts have reached similar conclusions in family court proceedings to terminate parental rights (*Lane v. Jefferson County Child Welfare Unit,* 1978). Rather than perceiving a threat to other children, these courts see sex with one child as an isolated instance—a fluke—as opposed to critical evidence of a larger and foreseeable pattern of predation.

### *Obvious Risk to the Victim's Siblings*

Other courts treat the risk to siblings as self-evident. The Ohio Court of Appeals in *In re Burchfield* (1988) held that "a child should not have to endure the inevitable to its great detriment and harm in order to give the [parent] an opportunity to prove [his] suitability" (p. 333). The father had inserted his finger into the vagina of his five-year-old daughter on two separate occasions and the court concluded "in light of [the daughter's sexual abuse], it follows that so long as the father was in the home with [her siblings] the environment of these children was such as to warrant the state to assume guardianship" (p. 333). As the court explained, "The law does not require the court to experiment with the child's welfare to see if he will suffer great detriment or harm" (p. 333). A number of other courts also see this risk as a "no-brainer," including courts in Arizona, California, Oregon, Rhode Island, Nebraska, and South Dakota (*In re Appeal in Pima County Juvenile Dependency Action No. 118537,* 1994; *In re Daniel B.*, 1994; *In re Dorothy I.*, 1984; In re J.A.H, 1993; *In re M.B, 1992*; *State ex rel. Juvenile Department v. Smith,* 1993).

### *Prior Victimization Is Merely a Factor in Deciding Risk to Siblings*

A third set of courts view the victim's violation as a relevant, but not sufficient, factor in determining whether siblings face a substantial risk of harm. The Florida Supreme Court adopted this approach where a father had intercourse with his stepdaughter who was under 12 at the time (*In re M.F.,* 2000, p. 1191). Following his incarceration, the state CPS agency sought to remove the father's two biological children from their mother's care based in part on the possibility of future abuse by the father. In a sharply divided opinion, the Florida Supreme Court announced that a parent's commission of a sex act with one child was, by itself, insufficient to support a ruling of dependency as to the victim's siblings.

Even when judges agree about the risk to the victim's siblings, they often sharply differ regarding whether a sibling's gender, age, ordinal position, and genetic relatedness mute the risk to him or her (Wilson, 2002). For example, courts disagree about whether a father who molests a daughter poses a threat to his sons. Some courts have concluded that a father who molests a daughter will confine his attentions to other daughters and poses no threat to his sons, while others reach exactly the opposite result (*In re Burchfield,* 1988; *In re Rubisella E.,* 2000). Courts also clash over whether a male parent who molests his stepchild is equally likely to victimize his own flesh and blood (*In re S.G.,* 1990; *State ex. rel. Juvenile Department v. Rhoades,* 1985).

## EMPIRICAL DATA SUPPORTING REMOVAL OF THE THREAT

Despite these conflicting views on the risk of future offenses, all courts can call on considerable social science data regarding incest to better protect the victim and the victim's siblings.

### *Unmistakable Evidence of Risk to Siblings*

The evidence of serial offending is overwhelming and chilling. Herman and Hirschman (1981) conducted a study of 40 families containing allegations of father–daughter incest. Victims in 53% of the families reported another victim or "strongly suspected" that incest with a sibling also occurred (p. 94). Forty-seven percent said there was no indication of other victims. However, in one-third of the families studied, there were no other possible female victims in the household. Similarly, in Russell's (1986) landmark study of 930 women in San Francisco, she found that one-half of the children abused by a stepfather reported at least one other victimized sibling, while one-third of the women abused by a father reported other sibling-victims. Although alarming, these figures may actually underestimate the incidence of serial predation due to the intense secrecy surrounding incest and the common assumption by victims that they are alone in being molested (Russell, 1986). Farber, Showers, Johnson, Joseph, and Oshins' (1984) study of medical records in 162 molestation cases yielded a lower rate of repeat incest with another child, 28%. While 72% of the records examined gave no indication of additional incest, in 41% no one asked the victim whether others may have also fallen prey.

The pattern of multiple victims in the same household is hauntingly familiar. De Francis (1969) studied 250 sexual abuse cases and found that in 22% of the cases, perpetrators victimized between two and five children. Faller (1990) analyzed 196 paternal caretakers whom she classified in two ways: biological father-offenders and father-substitutes, including stepfathers, mother's cohabitants, and mother's boyfriends. Faller indicated that four-fifths of the biological fathers abused more than one child in the household, as did two-thirds of father-substitutes. In many cases, every child in the household had experienced incest. Phelan (1986) found similar results in her study of 102 cases of father–daughter incest. Of the offenders, biological fathers molested 85% of all daughters available to them, while stepfathers molested 70%.

In fact, incest perpetrators have been found to frequently assault several children in their care. In a study of 373 incest offenders, Ballard et al. (1990) constructed a profile of perpetrators that included abuse history. They found 33.9% had at least one additional incestuous relationship after the first. Although frightening on the surface, perhaps more terrifying is how this number breaks down. The largest subgroup, 12.8%, had one additional incestuous relationship; but the second-largest category, 8.4%, represented perpetrators who admitted five or more additional incestuous relationships. Not surprisingly, Ballard concluded that incest offenders "often have histories of large numbers of victims" (p. 46).

Although the risk to siblings is clear, not all children face identical risks. The picture of risk is complex and depends on a number of factors, including the gender of the victim and the siblings, as well as the age of onset of the victim's abuse (Wilson, 2002). Certain children face only a slim chance of becoming victims. Specifically, there is minimal risk following father–daughter incest that began in the daughter's teenage years, when the family contains only one other child, a son. Absent other indicators of risk, the male child in this household is not likely to be victimized (Wilson, 2002).

Given the numerous studies of serial victimization, it would seem that the risk to siblings would be obvious. Nonetheless, some early studies of recidivism among incest offenders suggested that an offender, once caught, would just stop (Finkelhor, 1986). These studies predicted that only 4 to 10% of incest offenders would be recidivists (Quinsey, Lalumière, Rice, & Harris, 1995). New studies now suggest that incest offenders remain a continuing threat. Before assessing this new research, it is important to review the early studies as they offer important glimpses of sibling risk that have been overlooked.

In the early studies, incest offenders appeared at first to be much less threatening than sexual offenders who struck outside the home. Sturgeon and Taylor's (1980) study of 260 mentally disturbed sex offenders, for example, compared the reconviction rates of heterosexual pedophiles; homosexual pedophiles; and incestuous offenders, whether heterosexual or homosexual. Reconvictions for sexual crimes were 20% among heterosexual pedophiles, compared to 15% for homosexual pedophiles, and 5% for incest offenders. According to this comparison, incest offenders appeared to present only modest risks of reoffending. Yet, other evidence in the same study undercuts the incest perpetrator's image of relative safety. Specifically, 19% of incest offenders had prior convictions for sexual crimes. Although prior convictions for incest offenders fell significantly short of heterosexual pedophiles (43%) and homosexual pedophiles (53%), the findings nonetheless confirm that significant numbers of incest perpetrators do indeed engage in a pattern of repeat offenses against children.

Even before new studies emerged showing serial offenses, researchers faulted these early findings. Larson, Terman, Gomby, Quinn, and Behrman (1994) noted that recidivism is "extremely difficult to measure because many sex crimes may not result in arrest or conviction [and because] . . . official data are often inaccurate or outdated" (p. 10). Recidivism studies yield misleading appraisals of risk because they typically follow incarcerated offenders. Yet we know that incest offenders generally are not incarcerated (Bolen, 2003; Finkelhor, 1986). Finally, the early studies tracked subjects for short periods and simply missed new offenses occurring many years later, which frequently occur with child molesters (Meyer & Romero, 1980).

Recent studies directly take issue with the old thinking that incest offenders will not reoffend. Studer, Clelland, Aylwin, Reddon, and Monro (2000) grouped 220 patients who participated in an Alberta, Canada, treatment program for sex offenders into those whose index victim was related (incestuous offenders), and those who had abused an unrelated child (extrafamilial abusers). The authors compared the rates at which each reported offending occurred against other children within and outside the home. Contrary to conventional wisdom, they found "22% of the incestuous group had prior offenses against a related child," suggesting that "repeat offenses may not be so rare" (p. 18). By comparison, only 12.9% of offenders who victimized an unrelated child reported violations against related children, making incest offenders nearly twice as likely to report other related victims. As Studer et al. note:

> [I]f the "dogma" [of the incest offender's low propensity to reoffend] were theoretically and clinically sound (incest offenders being an entirely separate and discrete group), the [reported rate of other related victims among incest offenders] should approach 0%. . . . The fact that [0%] is so far from [the reported value] says as much as any real differences [between incest offenders and non-incestuous ones]. (Wilson, 2002, p. 261)

Studer et al.'s findings of continuing risk are mirrored in a raft of recent studies attacking the early distinction between incest offenders and other child molesters. These studies have found that incest offenders and child molesters who strike outside the family have "very similar arousal patterns" (Barsetti, Earls, Lalumière, & Bélanger, 1998, p. 283), indistinguishable erotic preferences (Studer, Aylwin, Clelland, Reddon, & Frenzel, 2002), and "disturbingly high" deviant sexual arousal from children (Firestone et al., 1999, pp. 512–513). Many child abuse researchers now question the extent to which "different categories of offenders, particularly intrafamilial and extrafamilial, are different from each other" (Salter, 1988, p. 49) and argue that the classification of sex offenders into two groups, incest offenders and pedophiles, was "prematurely disseminated as [it does] not appear to be valid" (Conte, 1999, p. 25). In the face of this evidence, the antiquated view that incest offenders are a special category who will not reoffend must be discarded.

While it is true that some fathers who victimize one child will not go on to victimize another in the household, the state may act to protect additional children if they face a substantial risk of imminent harm. The studies presented here suggest that the state can readily make this showing. More fundamentally, however, if the father's act of abuse with the first child is substantiated, the consequences of that abuse—homelessness—should fall on the father rather than the victim and other children, as this chapter argues more fully below.

## *Distrust of the Non-Abusing Parent*

Another factor that drives the policy of removing children rather than the threat is the belief that the non-abusing parent is complicit in the abuse. Removing the children would make sense in this instance because leaving them with a parent who failed to protect the victim might result in more harm. The belief that mothers are complicit is widespread among social workers, yet the available empirical data fail to support that belief. In addition, there are mechanisms to evaluate the non-abusing parent's ability to protect that are far superior to the solution of removing the child rather than the threat.

Numerous studies show that most caseworkers fiercely believe mothers share blame for incest. A series of studies in the 1990s found that 70 to 86% of all CPS professionals placed some responsibility on mothers, both for incest and for extrafamilial sexual abuse (Johnson, Owens, Dewery, & Eisenberg, 1990; Kelley, 1990; Reidy & Hochstadt, 1993). Some studies asked caseworkers to assign relative responsibility for the abuse. In several of these, the mothers' perceived responsibility for the abuse ranged from 11% to 21% (Kalichman, Craig, & Follingstad, 1990; Kelly, 1990). In Australia, Breckenridge and Baldry (1997) found that 61% of CPS workers felt that some mothers knew of the abuse. One in ten believed that most mothers actually knew about the abuse.

In the United States, Ryan, Warren, and Weincek (1991) found that in 82.3% of the case reports from five state, county, and private welfare agencies, caseworkers believed the mothers knew about the abuse before it was reported.

These suppositions of "maternal culpability" (Bolen, 2001, p. 193) translate directly into the choice to remove the child. In Ryan et al.'s (1991) study, assessments of "mother's ability and willingness to protect her child (1) before and (2) after the report of abuse . . . best explain[ed] the pattern of removal" (p. 132).

Yet, there is little support for this belief. As Ryan et al. (1991) flatly observes, "Although the myth has been widely held that [the non-abusing mother] is usually aware of the abuse and may contrive in setting it up, this is infrequently the case" (p. 124). In a study of 65 cases of paternal incest, Faller (1990) found that a mere 5% of mothers knew about the daughter's abuse, but "felt powerless to stop it" (p. 67). A study of grandfather incest found that 87% of mothers never knew. (Margolin, 1992). In 1985, Myer (1985) found that 75% or more of mothers did not know of their partner's abuse.

Many child victims never tell anyone of the abuse, especially when incest is involved. Mian, Wehrspann, Klajner-Diamond, LeBaron, and Winder (1986) found that the rate of purposeful disclosure by children decreased significantly when the perpetrator was intrafamilial. In fact, a greater proportion of children victimized by family never tell anyone of the abuse (17.7%), as compared to children who are the victims of extrafamilial abuse (10.9%) (Fischer & McDonald, 1998).

While a child's disclosure may not be not the only clue that abuse is occurring, other cues one might expect are also frequently absent. A third of sexually abused children have no apparent symptoms (Kendall-Tackett, Williams, & Finkelhor, 1993). Roughly half fail to display the classic, most characteristic symptom of child sexual abuse: "sexualized" behavior (p. 167). As disquieting as it is, "the more severe cases [are] the ones most likely to remain secret" (Russell, 1986, p. 373). Russell reports that in 72% of the cases in which mothers were unaware of the abuse, more severe abuse had occurred. All of this makes one wonder how precisely mothers could have ferreted out their children's abuse. Clearly, "[m]others cannot report what they do not know" (Bolen, 2001, p. 190). This is not to say that mothers can never be complicit in a child's abuse. They can. Nonetheless, absent specific indications of a mother's complicity, caseworkers should generally assume that mothers did not simply go along.

Nor is there any reason to believe that non-abusing mothers are not protective after the abuse. Most are "very" or "mostly" protective once they find out. Ninety-one percent of non-abusing mothers in a 2005 study were "supportive" following the disclosure of child sexual abuse (Alexander et al., 2005). Pellegrin and Wagner (1990) found that 74% of non-abusing mothers "either totally or largely believed the child's account of abuse" (p. 57), while caseworkers rated 67% of mothers as having average or better compliance with the caseworker's recommended treatment plan. Even Ryan et al.'s 1991 study, in which caseworkers harshly assessed mothers' knowledge, found that over half the mothers (50.8%) acted "mostly" or "very" protective following the report. Importantly, most mothers believed the disclosure. Sirles and Franke (1989) discovered that 78% believed the child's report of alleged abuse. Although there are studies showing that only one in four non-offending mothers were "very supportive" (Adams-Tucker, 1982, p. 1252), such studies are in a distinct minority (Bolen, 2002). One meta-analysis concluded that "75% of nonoffending guardians are partially or fully supportive after disclosure" (Bolen, 2002, p. 40).

In any event, if an unspoken concern that a "mother who failed once will fail again" is informing the decision to remove children, caseworkers should assess the likelihood of a failure prospectively, on the basis of validated assessment tools, rather than the fact of the child's past abuse. Such tools exist (Bolen, 2002, p. 40) and are widely used elsewhere and in some U.S. jurisdictions (New Zealand Child, Youth and Family Services, 2004; M. Testa, personal communication, Oct. 29, 2004). Caseworkers should also realize that if the alleged abuser is gone, it lessens significantly the burden on the mother, making the question of whether she will do the right thing less of an issue.

## CONSTRUCTING A SAFER PATH

These studies alone justify a presumption that a perpetrator who strikes once within the family will strike again. The studies affirm, moreover, that most non-offending mothers did not know and could not have known about the abuse before it was disclosed, and that they act protectively of their children following disclosure.

In addition to this evidence, there are a number of sound public policy reasons for presuming risk to other children in the family. First, a presumption of risk sanctions the efforts of CPS caseworkers who, without clear guidance, may be slow to react or may not act at all. In addition, a presumption places the burden on the offender to prove the sibling's safety, erring on the side of additional protection for other children. After all, the offender chose to sexualize his relationship with one child in his care and he is the primary determinant of repeat performances. Finally, presuming risk gives courts discretion to reject the rebuttal if they sense risk to the siblings rather than requiring additional harm before acting.

Beyond shifting burdens of proof, or improving judicial predictions of risk outlined elsewhere (Wilson, 2002), we should embrace fundamental change: The alleged offender should be removed from the home, pending a full investigation, rather than plucking the victim and other children from their homes. The next section explores why this seemingly radical shift in our default position at the inception of a child abuse investigation is rarely made, but eminently achievable and well within the mainstream of governing legal precedent (Wilson, 2005).

### *Understanding Decisions to Remove Children*

Questions of safety drive the impulse to remove the victim first and sort things out later. Prosecution rates for those who victimize children are abysmal—"93% or more of all offenders are allowed to remain within the child's environment or to return within the year" (Bolen, 2001, p. 258). Less than 2% of all suspected offenders are convicted, while only 7% of all offenders whose abuse is substantiated ever spend more than a year in jail (Bolen, 2001). This failure to prosecute and convict creates a perceived need to protect children by removing them from their home rather than removing the threat.

In a study of factors influencing the state's decision to remove a child, Cross, Martell, McDonald, and Ahl (1999) found that "the decision not to prosecute was the strongest predictor of child placement" (p. 41) outside the home. As the authors note, "[i]f cases are not accepted for prosecution . . . the child's removal from the home . . . may be the only way to protect the child" (p. 41). In this instance, child placement is seen "as the lesser of the two evils" (p. 42).

This Hobson's choice grows out of a deep-seated belief that offenders cannot legally be excluded from their homes absent prosecution—despite the fact that states can, and do, remove children from their homes every day (American Prosecutors Research

Institute, 2004, p. 279). Bagley and King (1990) have argued that "[a] proper legal framework which would enable the child to remain with her mother while the alleged offender is removed, still has to be established" (p. 101). Another child abuse researcher, Rebecca Bolen (2003), observes:

> Removing the alleged offender instead of the victim from the child's environment . . . may be one of the most difficult policy changes because it conflicts with society's presumption that the accused is innocent until proven guilty. (p. 1358)

The experience of other countries, coupled with the experiences of some U.S. jurisdictions, supports presumptive removal of the alleged offender. Authorities in Great Britain, for example, are explicitly authorized during an investigation to require the accused parent "to leave a dwelling-house in which he is living with the child" (Children Act 1989, c. 41 § 38A (3)). Indeed, this is the "preferred course of action" (Wickham & West, 2002, p. 153) when a child is at risk from someone living in the home.

Seven American jurisdictions explicitly authorize CPS agencies to obtain protective orders directing an alleged offender to vacate the home, including Hawaii, Kentucky, Maine, New York, Tennessee, and Texas, as well as Guam (19 Guam Code Ann. § 13316, 2004; Haw. Rev. Stat. Ann. § 587-53(f), 1999; Ky. R. Jefferson Fam. Ct. Rule 6 app., 2003; Me. Rev. Stat. Ann. tit. 19A §§ 4005(1) & 4006(5), 1998; Me. Rev. Stat. Ann. tit. 22 § 4036(1)(F-1), 1998; Morgan & Gaither, 1999; N.Y. Fam. Ct. Act § 842, 2004; Tenn. Code Ann. § 37-1-152, 2001).

### *Statutes Authorizing Removal of the Alleged Offender*

These new statutes do not rely on a household member (like the child or mother) to ask for assistance; instead they permit judges and caseworkers unilaterally to remove the offender. Thus, for instance, Maine authorizes its Department of Human Services to petition for a protective order on behalf of a child who has been abused by a family member and allows the court, without the parties present, temporarily to enjoin the alleged abuser from "[e]ntering the family residence" (Me. Rev. Stat. Ann. tit. 19A, §§ 4005(1) & 4006(5), 1998). After a hearing, this order may be made permanent for up to 2 years (Me. Rev. Stat. Ann. tit. 19A, §§ 4005(1) & 4007, 1998). Tennessee authorizes its CPS agency to apply for a "no contact order" removing the alleged perpetrator from the child's home if there is probable cause that the adult sexually abused the child (Tenn. Code Ann. § 37-1-152, 2001). Other states also authorize state agencies to take such steps (Haw. Rev. Stat. Ann. § 586-3(b)(2), 1999; Morgan & Gaither, 1999).

In several states and territories, removal of the child can occur only after the court first gives "due consideration to ordering the removal . . . of the alleged perpetrator from the child's family home" (19 Guam Code Ann. § 13316, 2004). In both Hawaii and Guam, the "burden of establishing that it is not in the best interests of the child that the alleged perpetrator be removed from the family's home" (19 Guam Code Ann. § 13316; see also Haw. Rev. Stat. Ann. § 587-53(f), 1999) falls on the child's family, not the state CPS agency. In Texas, if the state CPS agency determines that "the child would be protected in the child's home by the removal of the alleged perpetrator," it "must file a petition" to exclude the alleged offender (Morgan & Gaither, 1999). The court then has no choice but to exclude the parent if it finds that the child has been sexually abused and "there is substantial risk" he or she will be abused again if the parent remains in the residence (Morgan & Gaither, 1999).

These emerging statutes do not simply duplicate the protection already available under domestic violence statutes, although many of the latter would also be available to protect children (Klein & Orloff, 1993, p. 820). Domestic violence statutes generally require that someone says "protect me" (Ky. Rev. Stat. Ann. § 403.725, 2003; Klein & Orloff, 1993; W. Va. Code Ann. §§ 48-27-305 & 48-27-204, 2004). In contrast, these statutes permit CPS agencies unilaterally to act to protect children from the threat in their home.

Domestic violence statutes are also intended "[t]o allow family and household members who are victims of domestic abuse to obtain expeditious and effective protection against further abuse" (Me. Rev. Stat. Ann. tit. 19A, § 4001(2), 1998). Any protective order issued under such a statute is granted for a limited time only (*Cooke v. Naylor,* 1990, p. 379; Me. Rev. Stat. Ann. tit. 19A, § 4007(2), 1998). In *Cooke,* the court took an opportunity to explain the difference. It cautioned counsel that protective orders are "not the most efficient use of litigation resources for the final resolution of the controversy" (p. 379) over access to the child. As the court explained, "once a temporary order safeguarded the child from immediate harm" (p. 379), proceedings to assure the child's safety permanently—as CPS proceedings do—should have followed.

## *Immunity Doctrines*

Even without specific statutory authorization, caseworkers outside these seven jurisdictions also may take steps to remove the alleged offender. A pragmatic barrier, however, might be the risk of liability for social workers from parents if removal is not justified (Pearson, 1998). Courts' treatment of social workers, however, does not substantiate this risk. To the contrary, case law indicates courts will defer to the decisions of social workers absent egregious circumstances and generally insulate caseworkers from liability when removal is ordered.

One way courts protect social workers is through the application of immunity doctrines. Some courts have accorded absolute immunity similar to that given to judges, to social workers in the performance of certain duties, largely so that they are "free to exercise their discretion without fear of personal consequences" (English, 1995, p. 768). Without such insulation, "[i]ndividual caseworkers and supervisors facing the possibility of losing their life savings in a law suit might allow fear to influence their decisions, intentionally or otherwise" (*Gottlieb v. Orange County,* 1994, p. 629).

Other courts provide a more limited form of immunity, known as qualified immunity. State officials acting under this more limited form of protection still enjoy broad protection from civil liability. Under this framework, a social worker receives qualified immunity when he or she acts, in the words of one court, on the basis of "some reasonable and articulable evidence giving rise to a reasonable suspicion that a child has been abused or is in imminent danger of abuse" (*Croft v. Westmoreland County Children and Youth Services,* 1997, p. 1126) or, in the words of another, upon "an objectively reasonable suspicion of abuse" (*Puricelli v. Houston,* 2000, p. 19). If such a basis exists, CPS will be justified in removing either a child or a parent from the home, "even where later investigation proves no abuse occurred" (*Croft v. Westmoreland,* 1997, p. 1126). The basis for this immunity lies in the balancing of parental and children's rights:

> The due process clause of the Fourteenth Amendment prohibits the government from interfering in familial relationships unless the government adheres to the requirements of procedural and substantive due process:
>
> In determining whether [a parent's] constitutionally protected interests were violated, we must balance the fundamental liberty interests of the family unit with the compelling interests of the state in

> protecting children from abuse. (*Croft v. Westmoreland,* 1997, pp. 1125–1126)

The rights of parents with respect to their children, although fundamental, are not without bounds. Instead they are

> limited by the compelling governmental interests in the protection of children—particularly where the children need to be protected from their own parents. . . . The right to familial integrity, in other words, does not include a right to remain free from child abuse investigations. . . . Whatever disruption or disintegration of family life [a parent] may have suffered as a result of [a] child abuse investigation does not, in and of itself, constitute a constitutional deprivation. (*Croft v. Westmoreland,* pp. 1125–1126)

Some courts appear to ratchet up the level of protection further, with an articulated standard that exceeds the "reasonable suspicion" qualified immunity standard:

> [A] social worker acting to separate parent and child rarely will have the luxury of proceeding in a deliberate fashion, as prison medical officials can. As a result, in order for liability to attach, *a social worker need not have acted with the "purpose to cause harm," but the standard of culpability for substantive due process purposes must exceed both negligence and deliberate indifference, and reach a level of gross negligence or arbitrariness that indeed "shocks the conscience.* (*Miller v. City of Philadelphia,* 1999, pp. 375–376, emphasis supplied)

Importantly, in analyzing claims of due process violations by "excluded" parents, courts give equal weight to the interests of parents and children. These courts have *not* crafted heightened, stringent tests to protect parents from removal.

### *Application of Immunity Doctrines: CPS Agencies Enjoy Wide Latitude*

Of course, tests like these are abstractions. It is their application to specific facts that illustrates just how much latitude courts have given caseworkers. Courts have typically been generous in the application of immunity. For example, in *Gottlieb v. Orange County* (1994), caseworkers for the county and CPS directed a father to either leave his home because of his alleged abuse of his daughter or face her removal. The father exited for approximately 1 month and later sued, alleging violations of his civil rights. The court began its analysis with the father's claims against the caseworkers. It found the caseworkers had an objectively reasonable basis for acting, and were therefore immune from suit, even though they made a number of significant missteps: They never investigated the anonymous informant's background or motives; failed to question the daughter in a neutral, nondirective manner; and asked "neither the daughter's teacher nor the school nurse, if the child exhibited any behavioral oddities" (*Gottlieb v. Orange County,* 1994, p. 630). The court refused to fault the workers because they had not been trained in less suggestive means of interviewing.

The father also sued the county and its Department of Social Services ("Department"). While the lower court initially denied their requests for dismissal (*Gottlieb v. Orange County,* 1994, p. 630), the court ultimately granted the county summary judgment in a later round of litigation, based on undisputed evidence that the county adequately trained its caseworkers (*Gottlieb v. Orange County,* 1995, p. 73). The Department also acted reasonably, the court found, in issuing an ultimatum to exit without "pausing to obtain a court order" since their source reported ongoing abuse, and since the daughter herself described repeated molestations at her father's hands, said that her father did not like tattletales, and said that she expected to be punished for talking about it outside her home (*Gottlieb v. Orange County,* 1996, p. 520). In the final analysis, the father did not prevail against any defendant (*Gottlieb v. Orange County,* 1996).

Consider also the decision of the United States Court of Appeals for the Third Circuit (which encompasses Delaware, New Jersey, Pennsylvania, and the Virgin Islands) in *Miller v. City of Philadelphia* (1999), a case of alleged physical abuse by a mother that led to the temporary removal of her three children. There, in a shoddy investigation, the CPS investigator asked the children leading questions, requested that the mother produce all three children for a physical exam even though the abuse allegation pertained to only one child, met secretly with a hospital social worker, excluded the mother's attorney from the waiting area outside the examination room, and was advised by a doctor that it was not clear whether the child's bruises were accidental or a result of physical abuse. Not surprisingly, the caseworker received employment reviews indicating he did not always follow proper procedures. Still, the court concluded that "[e]ven if all of the facts alleged . . . were true, [the investigator] did not act in a way that shocks the conscience" (p. 377). Clearly, *Miller* sets a high bar for actionable conduct.

Similarly, in another physical abuse case, county officials acted reasonably when they temporarily removed a 15-year-old daughter based on the fact that her mother pulled her from their car by her hair, wrestled her to the ground, and pushed her face into a gravel driveway, causing minor bruises, cuts and scrapes, and the child arrived at school visibly distressed (*Patterson v. Armstrong County Children and Youth Services,* 2001).

### *CPS Misdeeds Are Sometimes Overlooked When Others Could Correct Them*

Even particularly egregious acts may be insulated from liability where a wronged parent cannot show a connection between the act and the claimed constitutional violation. For instance, one appeals court tossed out a jury verdict for a removed father where he failed to avail himself of opportunities to clarify how long he needed to stay away. In *Terry v. Richardson* (2003), a 3-year-old girl, Jaidah, returned from visits at her father's house withdrawn and afraid of other men. When asked by her mother whether she and her father had any "secrets," Jaidah said yes—at which time her mother, Richelle, contacted Cheryl Richardson, a caseworker (p. 782). Richardson left Jaidah's father, John Terry, a message the next morning informing him that he should not see or contact Jaidah. When Terry called her back, he seemed to understand Richardson's reasoning. Two physicians corroborated the existence of sexual abuse, and for the next month and a half Jaidah continued to implicate her father when questioned about the abuse. During this time, Jaidah missed one scheduled visit with Terry because Jaidah was sick.

Richardson interviewed Terry 15 days into the investigation and again advised him not to contact Jaidah until the investigation was complete. On the 48th day, she called Terry to inform him her investigation was complete and that Jaidah's accusations seemed to be true. Terry denied receiving the message. Richelle then obtained an order prohibiting Terry's visitation with Jaidah. Subsequently, a court found that Jaidah had been abused, but not by Terry. Terry brought suit against Richardson and a jury awarded him $2,062 and Jaidah $7,210.

The United States Court of Appeals for the Seventh Circuit (which covers Illinois, Indiana, and Wisconsin) reversed the verdict, finding no constitutional rights had been infringed (*Terry v. Richardson,* 2003). First, Terry had ample opportunity to ask Richardson about the extent of her authority. Although Terry's attorney spoke with Richardson, he did not ask when Terry could see his daughter. Second, any incursion on Terry's rights was minor—at most, Richardson prevented Terry from seeing Jaidah for 1 day. Finally, while the court noted that "arbitrary abuses of government power are checked by requiring objective justification for steps taken during the investigation" (p. 787), it found such justification here.

Similarly, in *Miller v. City of Philadelphia* (1997), a mother who temporarily lost custody of her three children due to allegations of physical abuse, alleged that a child welfare worker attempted to suborn perjury, induced the examining hospital to falsify records, and misrepresented the physician's medical report to the judge who issued the temporary protection order. Although the trial court initially denied qualified immunity for the caseworker (*Miller v. City of Philadelphia,* 1997), the Third Circuit, after several rounds of appeals, concluded that "even if [the caseworker] did misrepresent the doctor's report to [the prosecutor, the mother] failed to establish a causal connection between the alleged misrepresentation and the Judge's decision to grant a separation order" (*Miller v. City of Philadelphia,* 1999, p. 374). Although she had ample opportunity to do so, the mother chose not to depose the physician or prosecutor, "both of whom would have had direct knowledge of any misstatements or misdeeds" (p. 374) by the caseworker. Moreover, the prosecutor "spoke independently with [the physician] to ascertain his opinion," which "should have served to expose any lies" (p. 374). For this reason, "any subsequent misstatements by [the prosecutor] to the Judge during their telephone hearing would not have been caused by" (p. 374) the caseworker. While no one endorses such questionable practices, it is nonetheless instructive that such actions still did not trigger liability.

Like the actions of caseworkers, court orders also enjoy significant deference. "[O]rders of protection are rarely struck down as 'unreasonable.' Few are appealed, and, when they are, appellate courts tend to rely on the expertise" (Besharov, 2004, n.p.) of the lower court. Protective orders on behalf of sexually abused children have been upheld in numerous cases, even where the order impacts the offending parent's access to a residence he shared with the child (*Campbell v. Campbell,* 1991; *Cooke v. Naylor,* 1990; *Keneker v. Keneker,* 1991).

### *Stepping Over the Line*

Although courts accord caseworkers significant protection, circumstances exist in which caseworkers can and do exceed the wide latitude given them. A caseworker would be advised not to suborn perjury, induce medical providers to falsify records, or misrepresent a medical report to the presiding judge, as alleged in *Miller v. City of Philadelphia* (1997, p. 1066). Reckless disregard for the facts is also not prudent. In *Croft v. Westmoreland County Children and Youth Services* (1997), the court found that a caseworker lacked "objectively reasonable grounds" (p. 1127) when she threatened to remove a child if the father did not exit the home, based only on an anonymous tip passed along a chain of four persons, without any corroboration. The caseworker acknowledged that she renewed the ultimatum even after her interviews with the parties left her with no "opinion one way or the other" (p. 1127) that the father was sexually abusing his son.

Where it is not clear that an objectively reasonable basis existed for acting, courts will also allow litigation to proceed beyond the initial stages—known as summary judgments proceedings. In *Puricelli v. Houston* (2000), a social worker relied upon uncorroborated anonymous reports of abuse in allegedly issuing an ultimatum to a parent to leave his home. By allowing the case against the social worker to proceed to trial, the court permitted a jury to decide whether the social worker had a reasonable basis for issuing the ultimatum, if that is what occurred (p. 8).

In sum, caseworkers have significant latitude to direct alleged offenders to exit the household, rather than immediately proceeding to the usual remedy of removing the victim and other children from their home. This latitude, together with the explicit legal authority granted to them in a number of states, should embolden them to do the obvious—remove the threat from the household rather than the children.

## THE CASE FOR REMOVAL

A strong case can be made for excluding alleged offenders and leaving the children in place. There are compelling reasons for taking this approach.

### *The Consequences for Children of Removal*

By excluding the alleged perpetrator, the home becomes a safer environment not only for the victim, but also for every child in the house (Cross et al., 1999, p. 41; Wilson, 2002). Exclusion offers benefits in addition to safety. The support a child receives from her non-offending mother moderates the long-term effects of the abuse itself (Everson, Hunter, Runyan, Edelsohn, & Coulter, 1989). Exclusion, unlike removal, offers the child the possibility of such support. A child who has endured abuse at the hands of an adult should not then be subjected to the "double victimization" (Bagley & King, 1990, p. 101) of "system-induced trauma" (MacFarlane & Bulkley, 1982, p. 72) that forces him or her to leave familiar surroundings and the comfort of his or her mother and siblings. This trauma can be considerable.

A removed child is often cut off from all contact with his or her non-abusing mother for extended periods of time (Levy, 1989). He or she may "develop feelings of guilt or unworthiness, especially if [he or she] was the one to disclose the abuse" (Ryan et al., 1991, p. 125). While not every removed child is fostered, those who are placed in foster care may experience serious psychological damage (Wald, 1975, pp. 993–994).

Sometimes removal "places a child in a more detrimental situation than he would be in without intervention" (Wald, 1975, pp. 993–994). A child may be sexually victimized in foster care. A 1999 study found that foster care was a significant risk factor for sexual abuse and that foster parents were the perpetrator nearly one-third of the time (Hobbs, Hobbs, & Wynne, 1999). In another study, foster fathers and other foster family members were the perpetrators in over two-thirds of the substantiated cases (Benedict & Zuravin, 1996). Physical abuse may also occur (Gelles & Cornell, 1990).

In many instances, the child's abuse at the hands of a foster parent comes as no surprise to the state. Rosenthal, Motz, Edmonson, and Groze (1991) found that reports of child sexual abuse while in an out-of-home placement—defined to include family foster care, group homes, residential treatment, and institutions—were the most likely to be confirmed and that in 27% of all maltreatment reports, prior allegations against the perpetrator were present. As Gelles (1996) noted, "in some cases, foster parents are actually more dangerous to the child than the biological parents are" (p. 162).

Even where a child is not directly victimized, removal can be a bad idea. Separating the child from his or her mother frustrates the "laborious task of putting lives back together" (Herman & Hirschman, 1981, p. 144). The "essential nucleus" for this healing process is the mother–child relationship (p. 144). Removal also exposes the child to a litany of ills caused by "foster care drift" (Goldstein, 1999, p. 714). The extent of this dislocation cannot be understated. In one study, 13% of sexually abused children placed in foster care experienced six or more moves during their time in foster care (Bolen, 2001, p. 229).

More fundamentally, disrupting the parent's life, rather than the child's, seems preferable where the allegations initially appear to be true. As one court noted in a domestic violence case, "[a] victim of . . . outrageous and life-threatening sort of abuse . . . cannot be held hostage to the potential homelessness of her abuser, who created the intolerable situation in the first instance" (*V.C. v. H.C.*, 1999, p. 453). The equities are especially compelling where the allegations turn out to be substantiated. In that instance, "the father . . . is responsible for the choice to eroticize [his] relationship with [his child]" (Salter, 1988, p. 42) and so should bear the consequences of that choice even when he is not prosecuted. To do otherwise permits offenders to externalize the cost of their behavior on their victims who, ironically, are removed to ensure their safety.

Guam and Hawaii both essentially take this approach. In Guam, the court must first give "due consideration to ordering the removal . . . of the alleged perpetrator from the child's family home" (19 Guam Code Ann. § 13316, 2004) before removing the child. In Guam and Hawaii, the child's family bears the "burden of establishing that it is not in the best interests of the child that the alleged perpetrator be removed from the family's home" (19 Guam Code Ann. § 13316; Haw. Rev. Stat. Ann. § 587-53(f), 1999). Texas errs on the side of the child even more forcefully. There, if the state CPS agency files a petition to exclude the alleged offender, the court has no choice but to exclude the parent if it finds that the child has been sexually abused and "there is substantial risk" he or she will be abused again if the parent is not excluded from the home (Morgan & Gaither, 1999).

While novel in some jurisdictions, excluding an accused parent is certainly no more radical than what we do in private disputes between adults at the time of divorce. Courts routinely direct one spouse to leave the home (which is tantamount to awarding exclusive possession of the marital home to one party) (*Jetter v. Jetter,* 1971). And, of course, we remove children every day without thinking twice about the considerable power being wielded by the state (American Prosecutors Research Institute, 2004).

Importantly, the government acts preemptively before criminal adjudications in other contexts. Bond hearings commonly "place restrictions on . . . place of abode of the person during the period of release" when that person poses an "unreasonable danger to the community" (18 U.S.C. § 3142(c), 2000; S.C. Code Ann. § 17-15-10, 2003). All jurisdictions in the United States take this into consideration (8A Am. Jur. 2d Bail and Recognizance § 34, 1997). Literally thousands of times each day, judges place restrictions on persons presumed innocent. It is true that a bond follows arrest but, as with an allegation of abuse, there has been no hearing on the merits or conviction.

### *Addressing Valid Process Concerns*

There is no doubt that removal of the alleged offender will sometimes raise significant due process concerns. There is some evidence, in fact, that caseworkers have used "voluntary" agreements to leave the home as a means of short-circuiting the normal protections built into the CPS system. Pearson (1998) notes that "authorities sometimes employ coercive tactics . . . as an avoidance of procedural safeguards for the handling of child abuse investigations" (pp. 842–843). This behavior cannot be condoned.

The solution to such overreaching, however, is not to take this remedy out of the state's arsenal. Instead, we should institutionalize and heavily regulate it, as more than a half-dozen states now do. Maine extends the same process protections to parents who are asked to exit as it does when pursuing other equally drastic remedies, like the removal of children from their homes (Me. Rev. Stat. Ann. tit. 22, § 4036(1)(F-1), 1998). These protections include providing legal counsel for the parent, a guardian *ad litem* for the child (Me. Rev. Stat. Ann. tit. 22, § 4005, 1998), notice and opportunity to participate in a hearing (§ 4006), and, where the order was issued on an emergency basis, a preliminary hearing within 21 days (§ 4006).

Texas requires notice, sets a 14-day outer limit for any temporary restraining order, and erects a four-part test that must be satisfied before a temporary restraining order can be issued. Among other things, the state must show that there "is no time, consistent with the physical health or safety of the child, for an adversary hearing" (Morgan & Gaither, 1999). Kentucky courts instruct judges who order alleged perpetrators to "stay out of the family home" (Ky. R. Jefferson Fam. Ct. Rule 6 app., 2003) to do so with great specificity, defining the specific distance the person should stay away. Protective orders in New York must be for a specified time period, not to exceed a year initially, unless certain aggravating circumstances exist (N.Y. Fam. Ct. Act § 842, 2004). These protections balance the state's interests in quick but accurate adjudications with the alleged offender's interests in the least restrictive remedy, and the child's interests in not being cleaved from the security of their family and home. Most important, they reduce significantly legitimate concerns about possible overreaching by CPS caseworkers.

## LIMITATIONS TO EXCLUDING ALLEGED OFFENDERS

Excluding alleged offenders is not without its limitations. Just as a child who is removed from his or her home may experience guilt, so may a child whose parent is ejected, especially when the "family suffers economically" (Ryan et al., 1991, p. 125). In addition, like the decision to remove a child, the decision to exclude an alleged offender is made "against a background of urgency and inadequate information" (Pickett & Maton, 1977, p. 63) and will sometimes turn out to have been unwarranted. The fact that an allegation may later prove unfounded should not, by itself, dissuade us from using this remedy, however. These error costs are no different than those that occur when the state removes a child who is later found not to have been abused.

The real "difficulty with restraining orders is that they are hard to enforce and, in the case of child sexual assault, depend upon the presence of an adult ally for the child to monitor the situation and to report any violation of the restraining order" (Graves & Sgroi, 1982, p. 328). Clearly, it is essential that the non-abusing parent be supportive. In Great Britain, an accused parent may not be excluded from the household during the investigation if another person in the home is not willing to care for the child. The other adult must also consent to the exclusion (Children Act 1989, c. 41 § 38A (3)). For restraining orders to be available in Texas, the court must find that the child "is not in danger of abuse from a parent . . . with whom the child will continue to reside" (Morgan & Gaither, 1999). The remaining parent must "make a reasonable effort to monitor the residence" and agree to report any attempts by the excluded parent to return home. The failure to do these things is a misdemeanor, as is the perpetrator's return to the residence (if the perpetrator has been previously convicted of returning, the return constitutes a felony) (Morgan & Gaither, 1999). Strong empirical evidence demonstrates that most non-offending mothers are capable of performing this critical safety function, and they should be trusted to do so unless screening tools suggest that an individual mother cannot or will not do so.

## CONCLUSION

Nearly everyone recognizes that "[w]e need to develop alternatives to prosecution that can increase children's safety without making them leave their homes" (Cross et al., 1999, p. 43). The easiest, most direct route to this is to take the alleged offender out of the home, not the children. Although the perceived "inability to remove the offender" (Bolen, 2002, p. 58) remains strong, we have come a long way since Florence Rush asked in 1974, "Has anyone thought of the fantastic notion of getting rid of the father?" (p. 71). Over the last quarter century, judges and members of the legislature have done the heavy lifting so that removing alleged offenders is no longer unthinkable. And when practice finally catches up to the law, fewer children will needlessly endure the horror of incest and the trauma of being ripped from the security of their homes.

## REFERENCES


8A Am. Jur. 2d Bail and Recognizance § 34 (1997).

18 U.S.C. § 3142(c) (2000).

19 Guam Code Ann. § 13316 (2004).

Adams-Tucker, C. (1982). Proximate effects of sexual abuse in childhood: A report on 28 children. *American Journal of Psychiatry, 139,* 1252–1256.

Alexander, K. W., Quas, J. A., Goodman, G. S., Ghetti, S., Edelstein, R. S., Redlich, A. D., Cordon, I. M., & Jones, D. P. H. (2005). Traumatic impact predicts long-term memory for documented child sexual abuse. *American Psychological Society, 16*(1), 33–40.

American Prosecutors Research Institute (2004). *Investigation and prosecution of child abuse.* Thousand Oaks, CA: Sage.

Bagley, C., & King, K. (1990). *Child sexual abuse: The search for healing.* New York: Routledge.

Ballard, D. T. et al. (1990). A comparative profile of the incest perpetrator: background, characteristics, abuse history, and use of social skills. In A. L. Horton et al. (Eds.), *The incest perpetrator: A family member no one wants to treat* (pp. 43–64). Newbury Park, CA: Sage.

Barsetti, I., Earls, C. M., Lalumière, M. L., & Bélanger, N. (1998). The differentiation of intrafamilial and extrafamilial heterosexual child molesters. *Journal of Interpersonal Violence, 13,* 275–286.

Benedict, M. I., & Zuravin, S. (1996). The reported health and functioning of children maltreated while in family foster care. *Child Abuse & Neglect, 20,* 561–571.

Besharov, D. J. (2004). Practice Commentary. In N.Y. Fam. Ct. Act § 842 (McKinney 2004).

Bolen, R. M. (2001). *Child sexual abuse: Its scope and our failure.* New York: Kluwer Academic/Plenum.

Bolen, R. M. (2002). Guardian support of sexually abused children: A definition in search of a construct. *Trauma, Violence, & Abuse, 3,* 40–67.

Bolen, R. M. (2003). Nonoffending mothers of sexually abused children: A case of institutionalized sexism? *Violence Against Women, 9,* 1336–1366.

Breckenridge, J., & Baldry, E. (1997). Workers dealing with mother blame in child sexual assault cases. *Journal of Child Sexual Abuse, 6*(1), 65–80.

Campbell v. Campbell, 584 So. 2d 125 (Fla. Dist. Ct. App. 1991).

Children Act 1989, c. 41, § 38A(3) (Eng.).

Conte, J. (1999). The nature of sexual offenses against children. In C.R. Hollins & K. Howells (Eds.), *Clinical approaches to sex offenders and their victims* (p. 11–34). New York: Chichester.

Cooke v. Naylor, 573 A.2d 376 (Me. 1990).

Croft v. Westmoreland County Children and Youth Services, 103 F.3d 1123 (3d Cir. 1997).

Cross, T. P., Martell, D., McDonald, E., & Ahl, M. (1999). The criminal justice system and child placement in child sexual abuse cases. *Child Maltreatment, 4,* 32–44.

De Francis, V. (1969). *Protecting the child victim of sex crimes committed by adults: Final report.* Denver, CO: American Humane Association, Children's Division.

English, C. T. (1995). Stretching the doctrine of absolute quasi-judicial immunity: Wagshal v. Foster. *George Washington Law Review, 63,* 759–794.

Everson, M. D., Hunter, W. M., Runyan, D. K., Edelsohn, G. A., & Coulter, M. L. (1989). Maternal support following disclosure of incest. *American Journal of Orthopsychiatry, 59,* 197–207.

Faller, K. C. (1990). Sexual abuse by paternal caretakers: A comparison of abusers who are biological fathers in intact families, stepfathers and noncustodial fathers. In A.L. Horton et al. (Eds.), *The incest perpetrator: A family member no one wants to treat* (pp. 65–73). Newbury Park, CA: Sage.

Farber, E. D., Showers, J., Johnson, C. F., Joseph, J. A., & Oshins, L. (1984). The sexual abuse of children: A comparison of male and female victims. *Journal of Clinical Child Psychology, 13,* 294–297.

Finkelhor, D. (1986). Abusers: Special topics. In D. Finkelhor & S. Araji (Eds.), *A sourcebook on child sexual abuse* (pp. 119–142). Beverly Hills, CA: Sage.

Firestone, P., Bradford, J. M., McCoy, M., Greenberg, D. M., Larose, M. R., & Curry, S. (1999). Prediction of recidivism in incest offenders. *Journal of Interpersonal Violence, 14,* 511–531.

Fischer, D. G., & McDonald, W.L. (1998). Characteristics of intrafamilial and extrafamilial child sexual abuse. *Child Abuse & Neglect, 22,* 915–929.

Fla. Stat. Ann. § 39.52(1)(b) (West 2003).

Gelles, R. J. (1996). *The book of David: How preserving families can cost children's lives.* New York: Perseus.

Gelles, R. J., & Cornell, C. P. (1990). *Intimate violence in families* (2nd ed.). Newbury Park, CA: Sage.

Goldstein, R. D. (1999). *Child abuse & neglect: Cases and materials.* St. Paul, MN: West Group.

Gottlieb v. Orange County, 871 F. Supp. 625 (S.D.N.Y. 1994).

Gottlieb v. Orange County, 882 F. Supp. 71 (S.D.N.Y. 1995).

Gottlieb v. Orange County, 84 F.3d 511 (2d Cir. 1996).

Graves, P. A., & Sgroi, S. M. (1982). Law enforcement and child sexual abuse. In S.M. Sgroi (Ed.), *Handbook of clinical intervention in child sexual abuse* (pp. 309–334). Lexington, MA: Lexington Books.

Haw. Rev. Stat. Ann. § 586–3(b)(2) (Michie 1999).

Haw. Rev. Stat. Ann. § 587–53(f) (Michie 1999).

Herman, J., & Hirschman, L. (1981). *Father–daughter incest.* Cambridge, MA: Harvard University Press.

Hobbs, G. F., Hobbs, C. J., & Wynne, J. M. (1999). Abuse of children in foster and residential care. *Child Abuse & Neglect, 23,* 1239–1252.

In re Appeal in Pima County Juvenile Dependency Action No. 118537, 912 P.2d 1306 (Ariz. Ct. App. 1994).

In re Burchfield, 555 N.E.2d 325 (Ohio Ct. App. 1988).

In re Cindy B., 471 N.Y.S.2d 193, 194 (Fam. Ct. 1983).

In re Daniel B., 642 A.2d 672 (R.I. 1994).

In re Dorothy I., 209 Cal. Rptr. 5 (Dist. Ct. App. 1984).

In re J.A.H., 502 N.W.2d 120 (S.D. 1993).

In re Lisa D., 146 Cal. Rptr. 178 (Dist. Ct. App. 1978).

In re M.B., 480 N.W. 2d 160 (Neb. 1992).

In re M.F., 770 So. 2d 1189 (Fla. 2000).

In re Rubisela E., 101 Cal. Rptr. 2d 760 (Dist. Ct. App. 2000).

In re S.G., 581 A.2d 771 (D.C. 1990).

In re Starr H., 550 N.Y.S.2d 766 (App. Div. 1989).

Jetter v. Jetter, 323 N.Y.S.2d 305 (N.Y. Sup. Ct. 1971).

Johnson, P. A., Owens, R. G., Dewery, M. E., & Eisenberg, N. E. (1990). Professionals' attributions of censure in father–daughter incest. *Child Abuse & Neglect, 14,* 419–428.

Kalichman, S. C., Craig, M. E., & Follingstad, D. R. (1990). Professionals' adherence to mandatory child abuse reporting laws: Effects of responsibility attribution, confidence ratings, and situational factors. *Child Abuse & Neglect, 14,* 69–77.

Kelly, S. J. (1990). Responsibility and management strategies in child sexual abuse: A comparison of child protective workers, nurses, and police officers. *Child Welfare, 69,* 43–51.

Kendall-Tackett, K. A., Williams, L. M., & Finkelhor, D. (1993). Impact of sexual abuse on children: A review and synthesis of recent empirical studies. *Psychological Bulletin, 113,* 164–180.

Keneker v. Keneker, 579 So. 2d 1083 (La. Ct. App. 1991).

Klein, C. F. & Orloff, L. E. (1993). Providing legal protection for battered women: An analysis of state statutes and case law. *Hofstra Law Review, 21,* 801–1189.

Ky. R. Jefferson Fam. Ct. Rule 6 app. (Banks-Baldwin 2003).

Ky. Rev. Stat. Ann. § 403.725 (Michie 2003 Supp.).

Lane v. Jefferson County Child Welfare Unit, 564 S.W.2d 130 (Tex. Civ. App. 1978).

Larson, C. S., Terman, D. L., Gomby, D. S., Quinn, L. S., & Behrman, R. E. (1994). Sexual abuse of children: Recommendations and analysis. *The Future of Children, 4*(2), 4–30.

Levy, R. J. (1989). Using "scientific" testimony to prove child sexual abuse. *Family Law Quarterly, 23,* 383–409.

MacFarlane, K., & Bulkley, J. (1982). Treating child sexual abuse: An overview of current program models. *Journal of Social Work and Human Sexuality, 1*(1/2), 69–91.

Margolin, L. (1992). Beyond maternal blame: Physical child abuse as a phenomenon of gender. *Journal of Family Issues, 13,* 410–423.

Me. Rev. Stat. Ann. tit. 19A, §§ 4001 to 4007 (1998).

Me. Rev. Stat. Ann. tit. 22, § 4036(1)(F-1) (1998).

Meyer, L., & Romero, J. (1980). *Ten-year follow-up of sex offender recidivism.* Philadelphia: Joseph J. Peters Institute.

Myer, M. H. (1985). A new look at mothers of incest victims. *Journal of Social Work and Human Sexuality, 3,* 47–58.

Mian, M., Wehrspann, W., Klajner-Diamond, H., LeBaron, D., & Winder, C. (1986). Review of 125 children 6 years of age and under who were sexually abused. *Child Abuse & Neglect, 10,* 223–229.

Miller v. City of Philadelphia, 954 F. Supp. 1056 (1997).

Miller v. City of Philadelphia, 174 F.3d 368 (3d Cir. 1999).

Morgan, T. S., & Gaither, H. C. Jr. (1999). Removal of alleged perpetrator only from the home. In *Texas Practice Series: Vol. 29A. Juvenile Law and Practice* (§ 1132). St. Paul, MN: West Group.

N.Y. Fam. Ct. Act § 842 (McKinney 2004).

New Zealand Child, Youth and Family Services, Research and Development Unit. (2004). *Risk estimation system: Reference manual.* Wellington, NZ: Research and Development Unit of the Department of Child, Youth and Family Services.

Patterson v. Armstrong County Children and Youth Services, 141 F. Supp. 2d 512 (W.D. Pa. 2001).

Pearson, K. C. (1998). Cooperate or we'll take your child: The parents' fictional voluntary separation decision and a proposal for change. *Tennessee Law Review, 65,* 835–873.

Pellegrin, A., & Wagner, W. G. (1990). Child sexual abuse: Factors affecting victims' removal from home. *Child Abuse and Neglect, 14,* 53–60.

Phelan, P. (1986). The process of incest: Biologic father and stepfather families. *Child Abuse & Neglect, 10,* 531–539.

Pickett, J., & Maton, A. (1977). Protective Casework: Practice and Problems. In A. White Franklin (Ed.), *The challenge of child abuse* (pp. 56–80). New York: Grune & Stratton.

Puricelli v. Houston, 2000 WL 760522 (E.D. Pa. 2000).

Quinsey, V. L., Lalumière, M. L., Rice, M. E., & Harris, G. T. (1995). Predicting sexual offenses. In J. C. Campbell (Ed.), *Assessing dangerousness: Violence by sexual offenders, batterers, and child abusers* (pp. 114–137). Thousand Oaks, CA: Sage.

Reidy, T. J., & Hochstadt, N. J. (1993). Attribution of blame in incest cases: A comparison of mental health professionals. *Child Abuse & Neglect, 17,* 371–381.

Rosenthal, J. A., Motz, J. K., Edmonson, D. A., & Groze, V. (1991). A descriptive study of abuse and neglect in out-of-home-placement. *Child Abuse & Neglect, 15,* 249–260.

Rush, F. (1974). The sexual abuse of children: A feminist point of view. In N. Connell & C. Wilson (Eds.), *Rape: The first sourcebook for women* (pp. 64–75). New York: New American Library.

Russell, D. E. H. (1986). *The secret trauma: Incest in the lives of girls and women.* New York: Basic Books.

Ryan, P., Warren, B. L., & Weincek, P. (1991). Removal of the perpetrator versus removal of the victim in cases of intrafamilial child sexual abuse. In D. D. Kundsen & J. L. Miller (Eds.), *Abused and battered: Social and legal responses to family violence* (pp. 123–133). New York: A. de Gruyter.

S.C. Code Ann. § 17–15–10 (2003).

Salter, A. C. (1988). *Treating child sex offenders and victims: A practical guide.* Newbury Park, CA: Sage.

Sirles, E. A., & Franke, P. J. (1989). Factors influencing mothers' reactions to intrafamily sexual abuse. *Child Abuse & Neglect, 13,* 131–139.

State ex. rel. Juvenile Department v. Rhoades, 698 P.2d 66 (Or. Ct. App. 1985).

State ex. rel. Juvenile Department v. Smith, 853 P.2d 282 (Or. 1993).

Studer, L. H., Aylwin, A. S., Clelland, S. R., Reddon, J. R., & Frenzel, R. R. (2002). Primary erotic preference in a group of child molesters. *International Journal of Law and Psychiatry, 25,* 173–180.

Studer, L. H., Clelland, S. R., Aylwin, A. S., Reddon, J. R., & Monro, A. (2000). Rethinking risk assessment for incest offenders. *International Journal of Law & Psychiatry, 23,* 15–22.

Sturgeon, V. H., & Taylor, J. (1980). Report of a five-year follow-up study of mentally disordered sex offenders released from Atascadero State Hospital in 1973. *Criminal Justice Journal, 4,* 31–63.

Tenn. Code Ann. § 37-1-152 (2001).

Terry v. Richardson, 346 F.3d 781 (7th Cir. 2003).

V.C. v. H.C., 689 N.Y.S.2d 447 (App. Div. 1999).

W. Va. Code Ann. §§ 48–27–305 & 48–27–204 (Michie 2004).

Wald, M. (1975). State intervention on behalf of "neglected" children: A search for realistic standards. *Stanford Law Review, 27,* 985–1040.

Wickham, R. E., & West, J. (2002). *Therapeutic work with sexually abused children.* London: Sage.

Wilson, R. F. (2002). The cradle of abuse: Evaluating the danger posed by a sexually predatory parent to the victim's siblings. *Emory Law Journal, 51,* 241–307.

Wilson, R. F. (2005). Removing violent parents from the home: A test case for the public health approach. *Virginia Journal of Social Policy & Law, 12*(3), 638–671.

CHAPTER 4

# *Exposure to Pornography as a Cause of Child Sexual Victimization*

DIANA E. H. RUSSELL AND NATALIE J. PURCELL

*Child pornography is the theory, molestation is the practice.*

—(Jenkins, 2001, p. 4)

*We live in a culture which sexualizes children and infantilizes grown women for the gratification of men.*

—(Anderson, 1989, p. 7)

*The increased demand for child pornography directly translates into an increased number of sexual[ly] [sic] abused children.*

—(Crimmins, 1995, p. 2)

*If it wasn't for the Internet I would have never known. I think as the Internet grows, more people will find out their sexual desires just as I did.*

—message posted on a child pornography board by "Dad" (Jenkins, 2001, p. 23)

Researchers almost universally agree that photographing children for child pornography constitutes child sexual victimization. We will argue in this chapter that a causal relationship exists between adult and juvenile males' exposure to child pornography—including computer-generated, written, and oral forms of pornography—and their perpetration of child sexual victimization. Because the theoretical work behind this model comes from the work of Diana Russell over decades, we describe this as "Russell's theory."

According to Russell's theory, there are three causal factors that explain how exposure to child pornography causes some males to commit child sexual abuse. There are many other factors that also contribute to the causation of child sexual victimization. We will not attempt in this chapter to evaluate the relative merits of the different causal factors (a task Russell undertook in *Sexual Exploitation* [1984]). We will merely present evidence that exposure to child pornography is a significant one.

Because child pornography does not negatively affect all viewers to the same degree, some researchers conclude that mere exposure to this material cannot play a causal role in child sexual victimization. This is analogous to the tobacco industry's faulty claim that, since many smokers do not die of lung cancer, smoking does not cause lung cancer. Such reasoning is faulty. When there are multiple causes for a phenomenon, any one of them "may be a sufficient but not necessary condition for the occurrence of the effect or a necessary but not sufficient condition" (Theodorson & Theodorson, 1979, p. 40). In this sense of the term, we argue that exposure to child pornography causes child sexual victimization.

Although women have been known to sexually abuse both male and female children, males form the overwhelming majority of child pornography consumers and perpetrators of child sexual victimization. Therefore, Russell's three-factor causal theory focuses on male perpetrators. (The terms "man," "men," "male," or "males" in this chapter should be understood to include juvenile and adult males.)

## OVERVIEW OF PORNOGRAPHY AND CHILD SEXUAL ABUSE

Many still believe that exposure to pornography is cathartic or provides "a release of wishes, desires or drives such that they do not have to be acted on in reality" (Kelly, Wingfield, & Regan, 1995, p. 23). It is important to critique the catharsis theory before launching into Russell's opposing theory. Similarly, it is important to review existing research on men's propensity to sexually victimize children. This section provides a brief analysis of both topics.

### *Catharsis vs. Intensified Desire*

According to the catharsis theory, the repeated exposure of males to pornography "leads to a steadily decreasing interest" in the material (Bart & Jozsa, 1980, p. 210). This exposure is frequently described as a "safety valve." As applied to child pornography, this theory assumes that repeated viewing of child pornography decreases viewers' desire for sex with children. Hence, according to this theory, viewers of child pornography should be less likely to sexually victimize children.

The very influential but poorly designed experiment of Howard, Reifler, and Liptzin is widely cited as proof of the validity of catharsis theory (Diamond, 1980; Howard, Reifler, & Liptzin, 1991). Howard et al.'s experiment was based on a small sample of 23 white college males and 9 comparable controls. The researchers exposed the subjects and controls to a pornographic movie, then tested both groups for sexual arousal. The subjects were then exposed to adult pornography for 90 minutes a day for 15 days, whereas the controls viewed two nonpornographic movies over the same period. Twenty of the 23 subjects were then shown a third pornographic movie. Howard et al. (1991) found that "all subjects reported being initially stimulated" by the pornography, followed by "a marked decrease in interest in pornography as a result of the exposure" (p. 111).

It is important to note that the "subjects' choice of pornography was severely limited"

(Zillmann, 1989, p. 130). Hence, Howard et al.'s experiment only showed that a tiny sample of males became bored when exposed over time to a limited choice of material. Despite this, many pro-pornography advocates point to Howard et al.'s conclusion that all "legal restrictions to the availability of pornography" should be removed (p. 127). Indeed, this was one of the experiments on which the 1970 Commission on Obscenity and Pornography based its identical conclusion.

Zillmann and Bryant (1986) conducted an experiment based on 160 subjects that demonstrated the invalidity of Howard et al.'s conclusion. They recruited two samples: a student sample that included an equal number of males and females randomly drawn from undergraduate directories at two midwestern universities; and a nonstudent sample of males and females "drawn via random-digit dialing, with proportional sampling within all metropolitan exchanges" (p. 563). Zillmann and Bryant's sample consisted of 20 subjects in each experimental condition.

Zillmann and Bryant gave both their male and female subjects a greater range of pornography to view than the limited materials available to the subjects in Howard et al.'s experiment. These researchers found that the subjects' boredom after repeatedly viewing the same pornographic material motivated them to switch to viewing different and more extreme pornography, such as material involving the infliction of pain, violent pornography, and "uncommon or unusual sexual practices," including bondage, sadomasochism and bestiality (Zillmann & Bryant, 1986, p. 577). Howard et al. had failed to consider this possibility, resulting in their invalid conclusion.

Although masturbation is not addressed in the experiments of Howard et al. and Zillmann and Bryant, this is a major goal of pornography. The ejaculatory pleasure obtained from masturbation intensifies the association between it and the pornography viewed, a theory confirmed by considerable experimental research (Cline, 1974; Osanka & Johann, 1989). Most males consider masturbation a very inferior alternative to sex with the type of individuals they desire. Thus, viewers may desire to act out the sexual acts depicted in pornography. For this reason and others, researchers have concluded that catharsis theory is clearly not substantiated (Sommers & Check, 1987).

Research aside, common sense and rationality unequivocally challenge the catharsis theory. Very few people would likely support a proposal to solve the problem of parents physically beating their children by having them watch movies that show parents battering and torturing their children. Why is it only in the case of misogynistic pornography that so many individuals—including a handful of researchers—believe that exposure dissipates the problem? The plain inconsistency and irrationality of the catharsis theory suffice to dismiss the notion that pornography serves as a "safety valve."

## Males' Propensity to Sexually Victimize Children

In cultures where adult–child sexual contact is taboo, sexual interest in children is typically a critical prerequisite for sexually victimizing children. The studies described below focus on the extent of male desire for sex with children.

### *"Normal" Heterosexual Males as Potential Perpetrators of Child Sexual Victimization*

While some clinicians (Wyre, 1990), law enforcement officers, and the public at large, consider all perpetrators of child sexual abuse to be pedophiles, we and most other researchers do not subscribe to this view. Kurt Freund's classic but still relevant definition of pedophiles described them as individuals with a "sustained erotic preference for children (within the age range up to and including 11 or 12) . . . under the condition that there is a free choice of partner as to sex and other attributes which may co-determine erotic attractiveness" (Freund, 1981, p. 161).

In one experiment, Freund assessed the penile volume changes of "normal" heterosexual males on viewing "colour slides and movies of nude females and males of various ages" (Freund, 1981, p. 162). (The term "normal" as a descriptor of heterosexual males is placed in quotes because there are sound reasons to believe that the sexualities and personalities of heterosexual males are distorted by the patriarchal character of societies. Moreover, there are significant cultural differences regarding what sexual behavior is considered "normal" for heterosexual males.) Freund's results showed that although the "normal" heterosexual males showed a larger penile response to adult females than to children" (Howells, 1981, p. 79), "children have some arousal value even for normal males" (Freund, 1981). In addition, Freund found "that normal heterosexual males respond even to very young girls substantially more than to males of any age group" (Freund, 1981, pp. 161–162).

Kevin Howells (1981), who defined pedophiles as "persons with a dominant and sustained sexual interest in children" (p. 62) maintained that

> There is one classificatory scheme that is pervasive, whether explicitly or implicitly, throughout research and theory in this area. *A distinction is made between offenders whose deviant behaviour is a product of a deviant sexual preference for children, and those whose deviant behaviour is situationally induced and occurs in the context of a normal sexual preference structure.* (p. 76) (emphasis added)

Howells's (1981) situational offender "prefers adult partners" and only becomes involved with a child when there is "some challenge to his sexual adequacy or threat to his sense of competency as a man" (p. 78). Elsewhere, Howells reveals a broader conception of situational offenders as those "whose behaviour is precipitated by unusual life circumstances" (p. 62), or is "situationally induced" (p. 67).

Howells (1981) gives examples of important situational factors that predispose some "normal" males to select a child to serve "as a substitute for an adult woman," such as "marital disruption, loss of sexual partner through the wife's illness or work requirements, the use of alcohol, and multiple life stresses" (p. 67). Situational factors or stressful precipitating events also include "physical, social, sexual, marital, financial and vocational crises to which the offender fails to adapt" (p. 78).

The notion of "normal" males situationally induced to perpetrate sex crimes against children markedly contrasts with the view that all such males are pedophiles. Indeed, Howells (1981) maintains that "*There is good reason to think that such persons [pedophiles] form a minority in the total population of people who become sexually involved with children*" (p. 76) (emphasis added). Other researchers have come to a similar conclusion (Bromberg & Johnson, 2001; Mohr, Turner, & Jerry, 1964; Swanson, 1968).

Psychologists John Briere and Martha Runtz (1989) conducted a study in an attempt to determine the percentage of "pedophiles" in a sample of 193 undergraduate males. These researchers recruited male students in class for a study on "sexual attitudes" (p. 66). The students were assured of complete anonymity and confidentiality. Briere and Runtz failed to describe the percentage of the class who refused to participate in their study, and the possible impact of the refusal rate on their findings. Nor did they mention the grade level or demographic characteristics of the students, calling into question the generalizability of the study. Bearing these limitations in mind, Briere and Runtz reported the following findings in response to the four questions they asked the students about their sexual interest in children:

1. Just over one-fifth (21%) of the male undergraduates "admitted to at least some sexual attraction to some small children" (p. 71).
2. "9% reported fantasies about sex with a child" (p. 71).
3. Over half of the students who reported fantasizing about sex with a child (5% of the total sample) "stated that they had masturbated at least once to such fantasies" (p. 71).
4. Seven percent "indicated [that there was] at least some likelihood of having sex with a child were it possible to do so without detection or punishment" (p. 71).

Significantly, the last figure is substantially lower than the percentage Neil Malamuth obtained in a study using the same or a similar question (Malamuth, personal communication, July 1986). In his study, 10–15% of male students reported some likelihood of sexually abusing a child if they could be sure of getting away with it.

When Briere and Runtz (1989) applied David Finkelhor's (1984) very broad definition of pedophilia requiring only that "the adult has had some sexual contact with a child" *or* "has masturbated to sexual fantasies involving children," they estimated that at least 5% of the university males in their sample were pedophiles (p. 71). When they applied an even broader definition of pedophilia requiring only that the students have at least some sexual attraction to children, the figure for "pedophilia" in Briere and Runtz's sample rose to 21%.

Briere and Runtz (1989) argue that "given the probable social undesirability of such admissions . . . the actual rates of pedophilic interest in this sample were even higher" (p. 71). They maintained that their findings support Vernon Quinsey's conclusion, "based on a review of anthropological and historical data," that adult sexual attraction to children is ubiquitous (Briere & Runtz, 1989, p. 71).

Despite their very broad use of the term pedophilia, Briere and Runtz's (1989) study confirms Freund's (1981) and Howells's (1981) findings that a significant percentage of so-called "normal" heterosexual males have some sexual interest in children. These researchers conclude with good reason that

> The current data offer strong support for the notion that male sexual interest in children is relatively common in our society, even among "normal" (non-incarcerated and nonclinical) males [i.e., non-pedophiles —by the terminology Freund, Howells, and we favor]. (Briere & Runtz, 1989, p. 7)

Also significant is the fact that Briere and Runtz asked about sexual attraction to "small children"—a phrase that suggests prepubescent rather than adolescent children. Had they asked their sample of male students about their sexual attraction to adolescent children at least 5 years younger than themselves, the percentage responding in the affirmative may have been significantly higher. Since we live in a culture that normalizes the eroticization of teenage girls (for example, film star Brooke Shields was described at age 12 as the most beautiful woman in the world), a good case can be made for the claim that only a small percentage of men experience *no* sexual attraction to children. Regarding postpubescent children (adolescents), Dietz and Sears (1987–1988) comment:

> Whether such attraction ought to be regarded as abnormal is a debatable point, for attraction to sexually mature members of the opposite sex of the same species is biologically normal. It is not even clear that our culture, which proscribes sexual *activity* with those below the age of consent, condemns sexual *attraction* to these persons. (p. 28) (emphasis in original)

Philip Jenkins (2001) also emphasizes that "a sexual interest in children is not confined to a tiny segment of hard-core . . . 'pedophiles'" (p. 25). He rejects the notion that there is "a fundamental gulf dividing 'child-lovers' [sic] from 'normal' people" (p. 27).

Referring to the sizable legal market in pseudo-child pornography in which adult women masquerade as young teens on adult sites titled "lolitas" or "child porn," Jenkins (2001, p. 29) infers that "the popularity of such materials indicates a mass popular market for teen sexuality" in the United States (p. 28). Jenkins is struck by pornography merchants' assumption "that a substantial audience would be interested in something that notionally lies so far beyond the pale" (p. 30). From these observations he infers "that those interested in child pornography might not be so far removed from the 'normal' population" (p. 30).

### *Some Causes of Males' Proclivity to Sexually Victimize Children*

Sociologist David Finkelhor (1984) developed a very useful four-factor causal theory to explain the occurrence of child sexual victimization *in cultures where such behavior is illegal or taboo.* According to his model, the following four preconditions must be met in order for child sexual victimization to occur:

> 1. A potential offender needed to have some motivation to abuse a child sexually.
> 2. The potential offender had to overcome internal inhibitions against acting on that motivation.
> 3. The potential offender had to overcome external impediments to committing sexual abuse.
> 4. The potential offender or some other factor had to undermine or overcome a child's possible resistance to the sexual abuse. (Finkelhor, 1984, p. 54)

According to Finkelhor's theory, all four preconditions must be met in order for child sexual victimization to occur. In addition, "the various preconditions come into play in a logical sequence" (Finkelhor, 1984, p.62). (The fourth precondition is problematic because, as Finkelhor himself acknowledges, how the child behaves is irrelevant in circumstances such as when the adult uses force or surprise "to involve the child in sexual activity" [p. 61].)

Whereas Finkelhor's model relates to the causes of child sexual abuse in general, Russell's three-factor theory seeks to demonstrate only that exposure to child pornography is a significant cause of child sexual victimization. Her theory draws heavily on Finkelhor's model, as will become evident shortly.

## PORNOGRAPHY AS A CAUSE OF CHILD SEXUAL VICTIMIZATION

The major objective of this chapter is to challenge the belief that exposure to child pornography is harmless and to demonstrate that exposure to child pornography can cause child sexual victimization in societies where this is proscribed. The diagram of Russell's causal theory schematized in Figure 4.1 should help the reader to follow Russell's theory. This model focuses primarily on female children as victims and on males as perpetrators. There are no equivalent data on females as perpetrators presumably because their proclivity to sexually abuse children is so much less prevalent than that of males.

The list on the top left of Figure 4.1 includes some of the more frequently cited causes of males' proclivity to sexually victimize

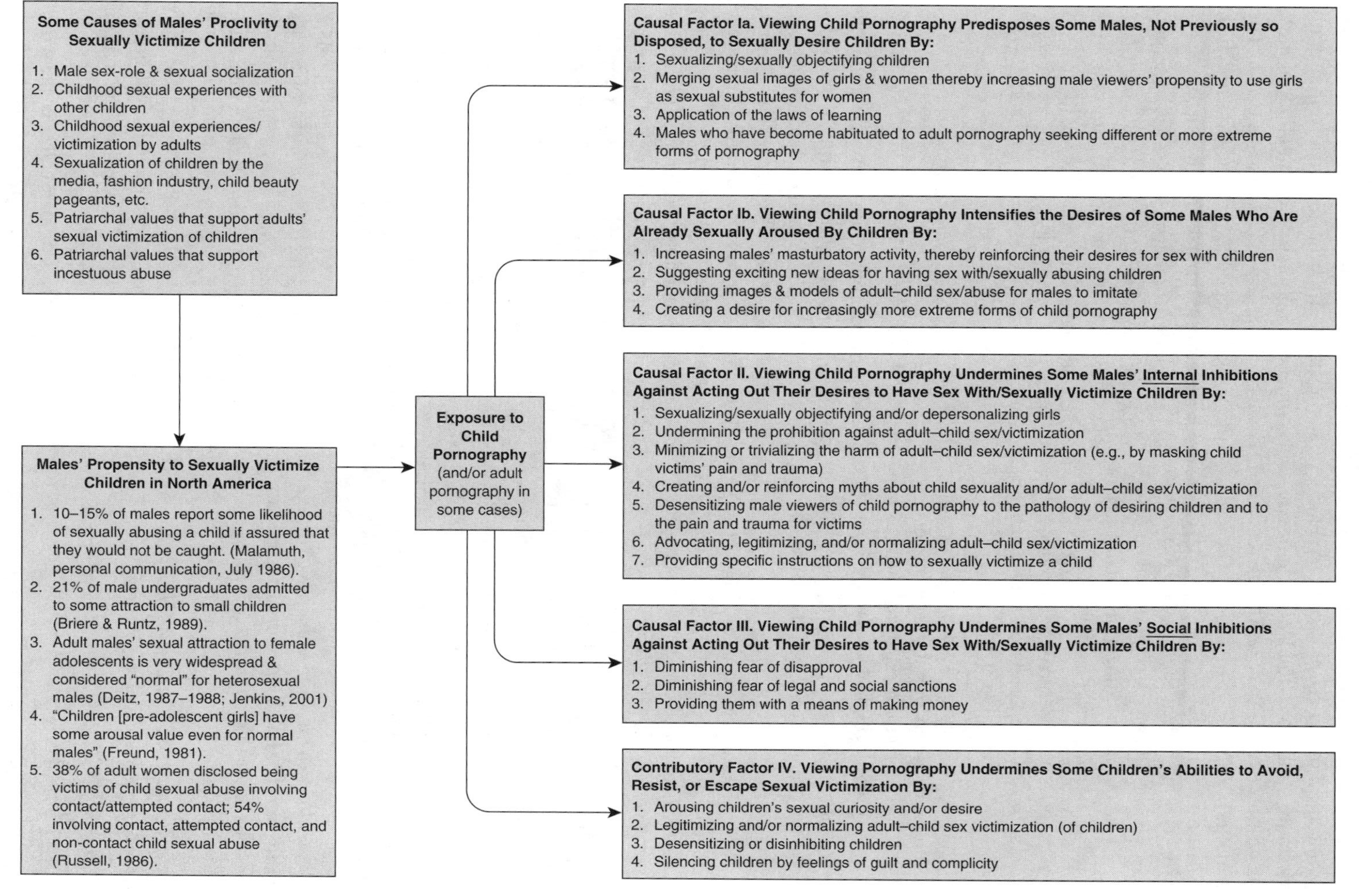


**Figure 4.1** Russell's Causal Model: The Exposure of Males to Child Pornography as a Cause of Child Sexual Victimization

children. The following five quantitative findings of different researchers serve as summary indicators of males' proclivity to sexually victimize children in the United States as of this writing (see the box on the lower left of the figure).

1. 10–15% of males report some likelihood of sexually abusing a child if assured that they would not be caught (N. Malamuth, personal communication, July 1986).
2. 21% of male undergraduates admitted to some sexual attraction to small children (Briere & Runtz, 1989).
3. Adult males' sexual attraction to female adolescents is very prevalent and considered "normal" for heterosexual males (Dietz & Sears, 1987–1988; Jenkins, 2001).
4. "Children [preadolescent girls] have some arousal value even for normal males" (Freund, 1981, p. 137).
5. 38% of adult women disclosed being victims of child sexual abuse involving contact/ attempted contact; 54% involving non-contact (Russell, 1999).

According to Russell's theory, exposure to child pornography causes adult males to perpetrate child sexual victimization when it predisposes them to sexually desire children, or intensifies this desire or undermines internal and external inhibitions against acting out this desire. In addition, children's exposure to pornography can undermine their abilities to avoid, resist, or escape sexual victimization, thereby making them more vulnerable to sexual victimization. The three causal factors do not have to occur in any particular order.

### *Causal Factor Ia: Viewing Child Pornography Predisposes Some Males, Not Previously So Disposed, to Sexually Desire Children*

It is commonly believed that exposure to child pornography cannot create a desire for sexual contact with children in males for whom it did not previously exist. Most people prefer to believe that any man who becomes sexually interested in children must have been predisposed to this interest. The following four points present ways in which exposure to child pornography can cause sexual arousal in some males who were not previously sexually interested in children. These points demonstrate that "normal" heterosexual males can become sexually aroused by depictions of children.

#### *1. By Sexualizing/Sexually Objectifying Children*

Child pornography transforms children into sexual objects designed to appeal to pedophiles and non-pedophilic child molesters. One pornographer declared that "Girls, say between *the a*ges of 8 and 13, are the very salable *objects* . . . young girls without overdevelopment and preferably with little or no pubic hair on their body" (Campagna & Poffenberger, 1988, p. 133) (emphasis added). Similarly, researchers Campagna and Poffenberger maintain that child pornography is "a medium by which the victim is reduced to an *object* or animal state" (p. 138) (emphasis added).

Child pornographers often direct the girls they photograph to get into sexual poses or to engage in masturbation or sexual intercourse like women in adult pornography. These sexualized pictures of girls (often acting as mini-adults) evoke a sexual response in some males who previously had no interest in sex with girls.

O'Connell (2001) notes that "the easy accessibility and transnational distribution of child pornography" sexualizes children for a rapidly growing audience (p. 65). Hence, increasing numbers of males all over the world are developing a sexual interest in children for the first time.

### 2. By Merging Sexual Images of Girls and Women Thereby Increasing Male Viewers' Propensity to Use Girls as Sexual Substitutes for Women

Pseudo-child pornography portrays adult women as if they were young girls—not in the sexual acts they perform, but in the props used and the captions or text accompanying the pictures. The "childification" of women in pseudo-child pornography is accomplished by dressing them in childish clothes, giving them childish hairstyles, having them stand in childlike poses with childlike expressions on their faces, or surrounding them with children's toys. A prevalent form of pornography, childification is also becoming increasingly mainstream (e.g., pop star Britney Spears dressing like a young school girl and dancing seductively in the popular video, "Hit Me Baby One More Time," and the sale of school girl uniforms as lingerie by companies like Emporio Lingerie, Linay Lingerie, and Lollipop Lingerie). Masturbation to pseudo-child pornography can serve as a bridge between adult pornography and child pornography. The transition of a male's arousal to child pornography can be achieved through a step-by-step process of exposure to gradually younger sexualized teenagers and eventually prepubescent girls.

Adultification also merges sexual images of girls and women. This process entails depicting girls as mini-adults with the use of makeup, seductive clothes, sexy adult-like poses, and/or accompanying text (e.g., pictures of 12-year-old Brooke Shields who was named the most beautiful *woman* in the world). Such adultified images are prevalent in advertisements published in the non-pornographic media and in pornography. Like pseudo-child pornography, adultified child images can sexualize girls for some male viewers who never before felt sexual interest in young girls.

Earlier we discussed Freund's (1981) experiment in which he found that a significant percentage of male subjects became sexually aroused by non-sexualized pictures of nude preadolescent girls. For this reason, it seems virtually certain that exposure to child pornography would stimulate even more sexual arousal in "normal" males.

### 3. By Application of the Laws of Learning

While some may believe that only males who are sexually aroused by child pornography would search for it, O'Connell (2001) maintains that "All the evidence is that many people [males] at least browse in this area [of child pornography], if not actively downloading" Web site pictures (p. 7).

A classic experiment by Rachman and Hodgson (1968) demonstrates that male subjects can learn to become sexually aroused by seeing a picture of a woman's boot after repeatedly seeing women's boots in association with sexually arousing slides of nude females. The laws of learning that created the boot fetish can also presumably teach males who previously were not sexually aroused by depictions of adult–child sex, to become aroused after exposure to child pornography.

Masturbation to child pornography during or following exposure to it, reinforces the association between these images and sexual gratification. This constitutes what McGuire, Carlisle, and Young (1965) refer to as "masturbatory conditioning" (p. 185). These researchers hypothesized that "an individual's arousal pattern can be altered by directly changing his masturbatory fantasies" (Abel, Blanchard, & Becker, 1978, p. 192). Abel et al. (1978) have treated violent sexual perpetrators by conditioning them to masturbate and ejaculate to nonviolent consensual portrayals of sex.

Presumably, it is equally possible to change males' non-deviant sexual fantasies and behavior to deviant ones. Hence, when male Internet users with no previous sexual interest in children inadvertently find themselves looking at child pornography, or when curiosity prompts such males to deliberately search out child pornography, they may be surprised to find themselves aroused by sexualized pictures of children. If these male viewers masturbate while viewing sexual pictures of children, this presumably can be the beginning of a growing interest in sex with children. For example, Jenkins (2001) notes that some posts on the Web "*suggest that individuals were 'converted' after discovering the material* [child pornography]" (p. 106) (emphasis added).

Furthermore, *repeated* masturbation to these portrayals may result in increased arousal. The pleasurable experience of orgasm is an exceptionally potent reinforcer. Adult and child pornography are widely used by males as ejaculation material and thus are effective at constructing or reconstructing viewers' patterns of sexual arousal and expression.

#### *4. By Males Who Have Become Habituated to Adult Pornography Seeking Different or More Extreme Forms of Pornography*

It is important to recognize that males who frequently view adult pornography, persons Russell describes as *pornophiles,* can also become interested and sexually aroused by child pornography. (This is the only component of Causal Factor Ia that refers directly to adult pornography.) After invalidating the habituation theory, Zillmann and Bryant (1986) concluded that their findings

> strongly support the view that continued exposure to generally available, nonviolent pornography that exclusively features heterosexual behavior among consenting adults arouses an interest in and creates a taste for pornography that portrays less commonly practiced sexual activities, including those involving the infliction of pain. (p. 574)

It seems reasonable to suppose that some of the males who become bored with ordinary adult pornography would opt to view child pornography since it qualifies as a "less commonly practiced sexual activity." Margaret Healy (2002) supports our conjecture:

> With the emergence of the use of computers to traffic in child pornography, a new and growing segment of producers and consumers is being identified. They are individuals who may not have a sexual preference for children, but who have seen the gamut of adult pornography and who are searching for more bizarre material. (p. 4)

### *Causal Factor Ib: Viewing Child Pornography Intensifies the Desire of Some Males Who Are Already Sexually Aroused by Children*

#### *1. By Increasing Males' Masturbatory Activity Thereby Reinforcing Their Desires for Sex With Children*

When pedophiles and other males who desire sex with children are exposed to child pornography that corresponds to their specific preferences (e.g., the gender and age of the child), their sexual arousal intensifies. For example, John Ferguson, an 18-year-old pedophile, describes his reaction to seeing hardcore child pornography for the first time:

> One of the guys brought in three or four hardcore porno magazines that aroused me so intensely that I could barely control myself. Never in my life had I ever seen or heard of anything like this. Sex . . . oral sex . . . everything . . . close up and in color. I fed on these magazines like a man possessed. Never in my life had I ever been aroused like this. (Ferguson, 1985, p. 285) (ellipses in original)

Although this quote does not mention masturbation, it seems implied. Many males with a sexual interest in children *deliberately* use child pornography to intensify their sexual desire as a prelude to masturbation or the sexual abuse of children. Silbert and Pines (1993) report that a father in their study used to show "his friends pornographic movies to get them sexually aroused before they would rape" his 9-year-old daughter (p. 117–118).

As noted above, the repeated pleasure of sexual arousal and ejaculation typically experienced by males who masturbate to child pornography results in "masturbatory conditioning." Masturbation reinforces the fantasies accompanying the activity, which intensifies the desire for sex with children. For example, Abel, Blanchard, and Becker (1978) described a patient who was a sadistic serial rapist. When he was 9 years old, this man "began having fantasies of injuring women, and by age 12 [he] was masturbating to sadistic or rape fantasies 20 times per month" (p. 195). His rape and sadistic fantasies continued, and he admitted that he raped his first wife (although he did not use this word) and other women when he was 22. Masturbatory conditioning reinforced his sadistic urges and Abel et al. (1978) used masturbatory reconditioning to treat him.

In sum, the more pedophiles and child molesters masturbate to child pornography, the stronger their arousal to this material, and the more it reinforces the association between their fantasies and their desire to have sex with or sexually abuse children.

### *2. By Suggesting Exciting New Ideas for Having Sex With/Sexually Abusing Children*

Jenkins (2001) notes that most pedophiles consider the old child pornography pictures still circulating on the Internet (which he refers to as "oldies") to be boring (p. 84). Consequently, "[a] common theme on the pedo boards is requests for material that is not readily available,"—that is, *novel* kinds of child pornography (p. 84). "The range of requests is bewilderingly perverse," according to Jenkins. "A few themes recur often and arouse real enthusiasm. By far the most common include calls for 'Black loli,' African or African American subjects. . . . Also in demand are incest pictures" (p. 85).

With regard to incestuous abuse, every conceivable relationship is portrayed in pictorial and written forms on the Internet—especially fathers having sex with their daughters. Rare forms of incestuous abuse are greatly overrepresented, including mother–son incest and female-on-female incestuous abuse. Many of the acts demonstrated or described in Internet pornography are portrayed as exciting and unconventional, providing viewers with new ideas for having sex with children. For example, Jenkins (2001) quotes a pedophile who was seeking "hardcore lolita pictures" and requesting pictures in a "Mom & Son Series" (p. 85). A colleague responded, "Yeah! He's right! That would be the best post of the last 2 months! Come on! Everyone with mom&son Pics! PLZ Post!" (p. 85).

### *3. By Providing Images and Models of Adult–Child Sex/ Abuse for Males to Imitate*

Child pornography provides models for males who already have a sexual interest in children. By seeing the different acts perpetrated on children (many of which elicit no negative responses and some of which appear to elicit positive responses or enjoyment), these "newbies" (a term used by many pedophiles) are provided with models that can shape and intensify their desires. Portrayals of child pornography showing only positive consequences for the perpetrators *and* the victims are particularly conducive to imitation. (However, for males who are sadistic, child pornography showing negative consequences for the victim is more likely to intensify sexual arousal and serve as a model to imitate.)

Several examples illustrate the use of pornography as a model for imitation. Catherine Itzin (1996) cites the case of a young girl who was sexually violated between the ages of 4 and 11 by her teenage uncle:

> He'd show me photographs of adults, men and women with whips and leather and children and animals. It would be photographs of oral sex, penetrative sex, both vaginally and anally. Then he would make me act out some of them. (p. 177)

Consider also the young girl who testified in the 1985 Government Commission on Pornography:

> My father had an easel that he put by the bed. He'd pin a picture on the easel and like a teacher he would tell me this is what you're going to learn today. He would then act out the pictures on me. (*Attorney General's Commission on Pornography: Final Report, Vol. 1,* 1986, p. 782)

Tim Tate (1990) provides another example, quoting Len, a pedophile who had molested several hundred young boys during his lifetime:

> Child pornography became important to me because I enjoyed it, fantasized and masturbated to it. It wasn't a safety valve, though. At the time I was looking at the magazine it was OK, I was fine . . . but you're not going to look at a magazine all day. So when I went out in the open I would see another pretty boy and find myself chatting him up. In the end I would put into practice what I had seen in the magazines. (p. 110)

Imitated rape also occurs. The gang rape of a young girl was committed by six adolescent boys "who used a pornographic magazine's pictorial and editorial outlay to recreate a rape in the woods outside of their housing development" (*Attorney General's Commission on Pornography: Final Report, Vol. 1,* 1986, p. 777).

Extrapolating from research on adult pornography, Linz and Imrich (2001) suggest "a profile of what may constitute the most 'risky' set" of pornographic portrayals in films and magazines for motivating "an imitation effect among potential child molesters" (p. 91). Their risky depictions include

i. "Portrayals that show child victims becoming involuntarily sexually aroused or otherwise responding positively to sexual aggression" (p. 91). The potential molesters who are exposed to such portrayals "may come to think that the victim does not suffer and may believe that a larger percentage of children would find forced sex pleasurable" (p. 91).

ii. Portrayals that convey a message "that adult-child sex interaction is 'educational'" (p. 91).

iii. Portrayals that convey the message "that the child was being sexually provocative" (p. 91).

### *4. By Creating a Desire for Increasingly More Extreme Forms of Child Pornography*

Jenkins (2001) maintains that some viewers of child pornography become addicted, with an increasing "hunger for ever more illegal material" (p. 109). Newcomers to child pornography on the Internet may be "amazed and stimulated by the first few soft-core pornographic images" they see (p. 109). However, these images "are all too likely to become routine," motivating the more frequent downloaders to turn "avidly to the harder-core sites" (p. 109).

Tim Tate (1990) interviewed a pedophile who described how child pornography created his desire for increasingly more extreme forms of child pornography:

> I know that my own response to erotica [sic], and that of a number of paedophile acquaintances, is indeed subject to the "law of diminishing kicks." Whereas at one time, when they first became available to me, pictures of [merely] nude boys were a powerful stimulus to masturbation, the response gradually wore off; after this only stronger pictures, showing boys engaged in masturbation or fellatio with other boys, were capable of reproducing a comparably powerful masturbation stimulus to that which I had felt on my first exposure to nudes. . . . Even the response to these stronger pictures diminished slightly with familiarity, but another new stimulus . . . pictures showing anal intercourse with boys . . . revived the response. (p. 177)

Habituation is clearly an intrinsic feature in the escalation described by viewers of child pornography. Some child pornography users acknowledge that "involvement thus becomes a cumulative process" (Jenkins, 2001, p. 109). For example, one pedophile explained, "With this hobby we get bored after a while with the usual and we risk a bit to get new stuff *or get actual experience*. It's a natural progression" (p. 109) (emphasis added). Wyre reports that his "Clients—abusers—have told me of their experience of child pornography which started out as pictures of mutual masturbation and ended with them watching videos of rape, torture and [the] death of a child" (Wyre, as quoted in Tate, 1990, p. 167).

In addition, researchers Max Taylor and Ethel Quayle (2003) interviewed 13 men in Ireland who were convicted of downloading child pornography from the Internet. Quayle and Taylor reported that, "The majority of respondents moved through a variety of pornographies, each time accessing more extreme material. The extremity might manifest in the age of the children in the photographs or to the sexual activities being portrayed" (p. 84). For example, one of these men said,

> it [sic] would go having a look at the teenage sites and then these teenage sites would point you to younger things and it would say like illegal site . . . you'd have a look at the site and the girls are obviously getting younger and it was a steady . . . downward trend. (p. 84)

Rather than child pornography showing child victims with smiling faces, some of these seasoned viewers gravitate to more callous and sadistic images showing children being upset, traumatized, or even killed. For example, a Web site called russianrape.com tries to entice sadistic viewers to "see the poor young girls swallow what they don't want, but have to do . . . see the horror in the eyes of the young girls and see them wild scream [sic] in brutally [sic] rape and pain!" Another Web site called rapedasians.com promises "the very best collection of very young Asian girls brutally raped."

In conclusion, it seems clear that exposure to child pornography often becomes an escalating problem; what may have begun as observation of seemingly nonviolent images of adult–child sexual abuse can lead to sexual interest in increasingly more hardcore and violent images of child sexual victimization.

### *Summary*

Sexual interest in children is the primary motivator for the sexual victimization of children. Factor Ia lists four different ways in which some males who had no prior sexual interest in children can develop this interest as a result of exposure to child pornography. Factor Ib cites four ways in which sexual arousal to children intensifies as a result of exposure to child pornography in some males who already *had* a prior sexual interest in children.

All or most individuals probably *have* had or *will* have desires that are antisocial or illegal at some time in their lives (e.g., the desire to hit someone with whom one is angry).

Clearly, there are many reasons, including internal and external inhibitions, why these desires may not be acted out. The next section focuses on the many ways in which exposure to child pornography undermines some males' internal inhibitions against acting out their desires.

### *Causal Factor II: Viewing Child Pornography Undermines Some Males Internal Inhibitions Against Acting Out Their Desires to Have Sex With/ Sexually Victimize Children*

Each component of Causal Factor II contributes to the undermining of moral beliefs that inhibit some males with a sexual interest in children from acting out their sexual desires.

#### *1. By Sexualizing/Sexually Objectifying and/or Depersonalizing Girls*

It may be remembered that "sexualizing and sexually objectifying children" also constitutes a component of Causal Factor Ia. Exposure to child pornography plays a vital role in both creating a sexual interest in children in some males not previously so disposed and undermining some males' internal inhibitions against acting out their desire to have sex with children. Child pornography portraying girls in sexually provocative poses or happily engaged in sexual acts with other children or with adult men or women can convince those esposed to it that some children want and enjoy sex with adult males. For example, a sexual offender who enjoyed viewing child pornography showing "girls actually having sex," said that the girls "had to look happy . . . I mean I wasn't looking for rape or anything" (Taylor & Quayle, 2003, p. 82).

Just as depersonalizing members of enemy nations in times of war undermines soldiers' internal inhibitions against acting in a violent fashion, so the depersonalization or sexual objectification of girls undermines some males' internal inhibitions against acting out their desire to sexually abuse children. Quayle and Taylor quote two men who were convicted of downloading child pornography from the Internet as saying,

> It wasn't a person at all[;] it was . . . it was just a flat image . . . it was a nothing" (p. 85). "[M]y dad thought exactly the same as me . . . he says, 'well it's only a bloody picture.'" (Taylor & Quayle, 2003, p. 93)

#### *2. By Undermining the Prohibition Against Adult–Child Sex/Victimization*

Although legal ages of consent vary in different countries, adult–child sex *is* proscribed in most countries today.

Despite the prohibition in the United States, there are massive numbers of child pornography Web sites that promote adult–child sexual victimization through photographs, videos, or written stories. For example, an incest Web site titled "Golden Incest Sites!" lists 50 titles (www.incest-gold.com/indes.php, June 6, 2002). The pictures, stories, videos, and other material it makes accessible to interested Internet surfers can serve as highly suggestive models for viewers who may never before have thought of their daughters, sons, nieces, nephews, and other younger relatives in a sexual way. The ubiquity of incest pornography also conveys the popularity of such images, suggesting that large numbers of men must experience such desires.

The prevalence of child pornography sites, their content, and their positive portrayals of adult–child sexual abuse all serve to diminish the deviant nature of incestuous and extra-familial child sexual abuse. This in turn enhances the likelihood that some men's internal inhibitions against acting out incestuous and extrafamilial child sexual victimization will be undermined.

It is also important to note two other ways in which the prohibition against adult–child sex is undermined by child pornography. First, the inclusion of many child pornography cartoons in mainstream men's magazines like *Playboy* and *Penthouse* communicates its social acceptability. Second, the boards on various sites allow visitors to form their own subcultural communities in which such behaviors or desires are not considered deviant and where pedophiles and others interested in child pornography can feel more normal. (Both of these points will be discussed later in greater detail.)

### *3. By Minimizing or Trivializing the Harm of Adult–Child Sex/Victimization (e.g., By Masking Child Victims' Pain and Trauma)*

Masking child victims' pain and trauma is a major way in which the prohibition against child sexual abuse is undermined. A pedophile called Stewart describes how he masked victims' pain when he photographed young girls:

> They couldn't show fear or doubt in the pictures. They had to show happiness or love. . . . To get that look, I'd give them something, from tricycles to stereos. It depended on what they wanted. You have to be able to express [evoke] excitement in the pictures. (Campagna & Poffenberger, 1988, p. 126)

British journalist Davies (1994) describes "a video of a 'girl with her wrists and ankles chained to an iron bar in the ceiling and a grotesque dildo hanging out of her" (cited by Itzin, 1996, p. 185). "The pornographer who was showing the video pointed to the girl's smile as evidence of her consent" (Itzin, 1996, p. 185). The smile also suggests that she enjoys being tortured in this fashion.

Linz and Imrich (2001) note that:

> Potential molesters who watch child sex depictions that supposedly had positive consequences for the victim may come to think that the victim does not suffer and may believe that a larger percentage of children would find forced sex pleasurable. (p. 91)

The evidence cited above confirms that masking the pain and trauma of child pornography victims undermines the internal inhibitions of some males who desire to sexually abuse children.

### *4. By Creating and/or Reinforcing Myths About Child Sexuality and/or Adult–Child Sex/Victimization*

Joseph LoPiccolo (1994) emphasizes that "most sex offenders have a variety of distorted cognitive beliefs that are intimately related to their deviant behavior" (LoPiccolo, personal communication, September 16, 2005. See LoPiccolo, 1994, for examples of these distorted cognitive beliefs). These "flase belief-systems" (Itzin, 1996, p. 170) or myths can be created and reinforced when males view child pornography. For example, child pornography can convince males who sexually desire children "that the feelings and desires they have towards children are not wrong" (Tate, 1990, p. 110).

Following are nine other examples of distorted cognitions or myths commonly held by pedophiles:

1. There's nothing wrong with adult–child sex as long as children consent to it.
2. If children behave seductively toward adults, it means "they're asking for it."

3. Men who love children have sex with them to teach them about sex in a positive, caring, emotional context.

4. Having sex with kids is good sex education for them, to prevent them from having sexual problems as adults.

5. Since children are sexual beings with the capacity to enjoy sexual stimulation, it's fine for an adult to provide them with this enjoyment.

6. Children who don't tell anyone about being molested, can't be upset or bothered about it.

7. If children didn't want to have sex with adults, they would react by crying, fighting, screaming, and resisting.

8. When children initiate sex with adults or allow themselves to be repeatedly molested by adults, it shows that they enjoy having sex with them.

9. Sex between adult males and children is harmless unless force is involved.

Belief in these myths undermines internal inhibitions against acting out the desire to sexually abuse children. For example, Jenkins (2001) notes that many pedophiles justify their sexual behavior with children by claiming that children "consented to the actions," or directly sought sexual contact with their perpetrators (p. 117). These pedophiles consider such experiences to be "consensual. Even if the child is three or five, she was still asking for it" (Jenkins, 2001, p. 117). Jenkins also maintains that "[l]inked to this is the denial of injury, since the sexual activity is seen as rewarding and even educational for the child, rather than selfish or exploitative" (p.117). As Kelly, Wingfield, and Regan (1995) observe, child pornography "enables them [perpetrators] to construct a different version of reality" (p. 34) in which it is possible for them to believe "that both their sexual and non-sexual needs are being met without hurting the child" (Wyre, 1990, pp. 284–285).

The fantasy pedophilic stories on the Internet, the testimonies of pedophiles, the descriptions of child pornography in mainstream men's magazines, and the descriptions of child pornography on the Internet reinforce the myths common believed by pedophiles. Belief in such myths undermines some men's internal inhibitions against victimizing children.

### *5. By Desensitizing Male Viewers to the Pathology of Desiring Children and to the Pain and Trauma for Victims*

Linz and Imrich (2001) maintain that "child pornography can desensitize viewers to the pathology of sexual abuse or exploitation of children, so that it can become acceptable to . . . the viewer" (p. 87). Congress made the same point when they passed the Child Pornography Prevention Act of 1996 banning computer-generated child pornography (Taylor, 2001, p. 51).

Linz and Imrich (2001) suggest that, "One likely source of desensitization to the degrading and abusive aspects of child pornography may be repeated exposure to 'adult' pornography wherein the models, although over the age of 18, are described and depicted as underage" (pseudo-child pornography) (p. 94). Exposure to such material may desensitize viewers to true child pornography.

Many consumers of child pornography become desensitized to the pain and damage that the child victims experience. Desensitization can also result in a preference for increasingly deviant and severely abusive forms of child pornography. Thus, desensitization can undermine internal inhibitions against acting out the desire to sexually victimize children.

### *6. By Advocating, Legitimizing, and/or Normalizing Adult–Child Sex/Victimization*

The legitimatizing and normalizing of adults' sexual victimization of children in child pornography are two of the most frequently cited ways in which this material undermines some viewers' internal inhibitions. As Tate (1990) points out,

> All paedophiles need to reassure themselves that what they are doing or want to do is OK. It [child pornography] validates their feelings, lowers their inhibitions and makes them feel that their behaviour is pretty normal in the context of this pornography—they see other people doing it in the videos or the magazines and it reassures them. (p. 24)

For example, one man testified before Congress, "See, it's okay to do because it's published in magazines" (*Attorney General's Commission on Pornography: Final Report, Vol. 1,* 1986, p. 786). Clearly, child pornography has the power "to reinforce both the paedophile's attraction to children and his self-justification process" (Tate, 1990, p. 110). Pedophiles also "use porn to convince themselves that their behavior is not abnormal, but is shared by others" (Calcetas-Santos, 2001, p. 59). *Playboy, Hustler* magazines all "covertly" normalize adult–child sex and promote sex with children (Mayne, 2000, p. 25). There are many examples—particularly of cartoons in *Hustler*—that quite blatantly legitimize incestuous and extrafamilial child sexual abuse. Many of them trivialize child sexual victimization by repeatedly making jokes about this crime.

### *7. By Providing Specific Instructions on How to Sexually Victimize a Child*

Some males who have never acted on their desire to have sex with a child may be ignorant or anxious about how to proceed with this. Such concerns can inhibit them from perpetrating such an act. Child pornography removes this impediment by providing instructions for the sexual abuse of children. Tyler, a detective sergeant in the San Bernardino, California, Sheriff's Department, testified in hearings on child pornography and pedophilia conducted by Senator Arlen Specter about a child pornography magazine that described "how to have sex with prepubescent children" (*Child Pornography and Pedophilia,* 1984, p. 33). During these hearings, Senator Specter also discussed a book titled *How to Have Sex With Kids* that described "how to meet children, how to entice them, how to develop a relationship with them, and how to have sex with them"(p. 30). Sexually explicit illegal material presumably demonstrates at what ages it is possible for adult males to penetrate young children anally and vaginally. Similarly, Gail Dines, Robert Jensen, and Ann Russo (1998) analyzed a scene in the best-selling pseudo-child pornography video titled *Cherry Poppers Vol. 10* that included "realistic detailed instructions on how to initiate a child into sex" (p. 88). Dines, Jensen, and Russo considered it to be "a manual for how to perpetrate a sexual assault on a child" (p. 88).

In addition, according to law enforcement officials, the *Bulletin* of the North American Man Boy Love Association (NAMBLA), distributed to all NAMBLA members, "has step-by-step 'how to' instructions for locating, seducing, sexually assaulting, and preventing the disclosure of their crime by their child victims" (Linz & Imrich, 2001, p. 92).

According to Tate (1990),

> During the boom days of commercial production a disturbingly large number of magazines showing children undergoing abuse combined with torture came on to the market. Common features were illustrated instructions showing "fathers" clipping padlocks on to the labias of their

> pre-pubescent "daughters," with an encouragement to "keep them all for you." Others, like the American-produced *Child Discipline,* instructed its readers on the best way of deriving sexual pleasure from beating very young boys and girls. (p. 173)

Even more ominously, British professor Harold Thimbleby (1995) reports that he has "found text, film and sound material . . . involving instructions for killing minors."

Presumably, pedophiles and child molesters in general find such instructions useful. Even when explicit instructions on how to sexually victimize a child are not provided in child pornography, this material always provides models that viewers may learn from and attempt to emulate.

*Summary*

Russell's theory specifies seven components for Causal Factor II. Each explains how child pornography can undermine internal inhibitions against acting out sexual desires toward children. The more components that apply, the greater the undermining effect is likely to be. As the next section explains, *social* inhibitions also have to be surmounted before potential molesters are likely to become actual molesters.

### *Causal Factor III: Viewing Child Pornography Undermines Some Males' Social Inhibitions Against Acting Out Their Desires to Have Sex With/Sexually Victimize Children*

Child pornography undermines viewers' social inhibitions against sexually victimizing children. It does so in three distinct ways.

#### *1. By Diminishing Fear of Disapproval*

Potential or actual child molesters who look at or download child pornography on the Internet will quickly become cognizant of the enormous number of child pornography Web sites, videos, and chat rooms. This material makes it abundantly clear that there are many other viewers and collectors of child pornography, as well as many others who act out their sexual attraction to children. As Jenkins (2001) states it, "He [the pedophile viewer] finds that he is not alone in his deviant interests" (p. 106). This revelation "helps support the notion that the boards [where individuals post messages] are safe space that one can visit at will, [and] where like-minded friends can reliably be found," thereby diminishing viewers' fear of universal disapproval for their sexual interest in children (p. 108).

Crimmins (1995) testified at the Senate Judiciary Committee Hearings on Child Pornography on the Internet that, "People who may have never acted on such impulses before, are emboldened when they see that there are so many other individuals who have similar interests" (p. 2). Furthermore, Jenkins (2001) argues that, "The more pedophiles and pornographers are attacked by law enforcement agencies, mass media, and anti-pedos, the greater the sense of community against common enemies" (p. 114). The knowledge that they have a support group of like-minded colleagues contributes to undermining the fear of disapproval for sexually victimizing children.

#### *2. By Diminishing Fear of Legal and Social Sanctions*

Fear of legal sanctions is the most important factor in restraining potential molesters from abusing children. The more effective potential molesters perceive the social sanctions to be, the less likely they are to become perpetrators. Fear of legal sanctions also serves to restrain active child molesters. For example, a pedophile called Duncan said the fear of getting caught "was what stopped me progressing to buggery with the boys" (Tate, 1990, p. 120).

However, child pornography consistently communicates the false message that those who violate children are in no danger of being apprehended or facing other negative consequences. We have not seen any pictorial child pornography that shows a sexual predator being apprehended by the police or ending up in prison. The same applies to written child pornography stories, fantasies, lists of Web sites and videos, as well as child pornography in men's magazines. The outcomes of child sexual abuse are always positive for the perpetrators. Hence, exposure to child pornography gives would-be child molesters a false sense of immunity from legal sanctions, thereby undermining their social inhibitions against acting out their desires.

Users of child pornography who are apprehended are likely to be shamed by the media coverage of their arrest and the charges against them. Such publicity reaches their family members, neighbors, employers, children's school teachers and schoolmates, doctors and dentists, and many others—all of whose disapproval is almost certainly mortifying and devastating for perpetrators. There have been several prominent cases in California in 2004 where pedophiles have been hounded by groups of angry and frightened citizens refusing to have such individuals placed in their neighborhoods. For example, Cary Verse, a four-time convicted child molester, has been "driven by community protests from transient hotels to shelters and from town to town" for 2 years in search of a home in California after his last release from prison (Carey, 2005, p. B5). Even in prison, these perpetrators often have to be isolated to protect them from being attacked by other prisoners who rank them as the most despised of all inmates.

Exposure to large amounts of child pornography undermines viewers' fear of legal sanctions, public shame, and ostracism.

#### *3. By Providing Them With a Means of Making Money*

Exposure to child pornography on the Internet makes it clear to viewers that numerous individuals are making money—sometimes a great deal of it—by providing the material for these Web sites. According to a child pornographer, "the most money is made in child pornography because it's hard to get and willing children are hard to come by" (Campagna & Poffenberger, 1988, p. 133). Hence, child molesters might to infer that they could profit from marketing the photos and videos of children they victimize.

Frequent exposure to child pornography on the Internet promotes the perception that many child pornography producers are "getting away with it" and profiting from it. The desire to benefit financially from the immense economic opportunities available to child pornographers on the Internet could undermine the social inhibitions of some male viewers with a sexual desire for children. The stronger their need or motivation to make money, the more this motivation is likely to overwhelm their social inhibitions.

#### *Summary*

According to Russell's theory, these three causal factors induce some men, who otherwise would not we have sexually abused children, to become child molesters. Contributing Factor IV—the subject of the next section—is not necessary to this causal theory. However, it can be a significant facilitator of child sexual victimization.

### *Contributory Factor IV: Viewing Pornography Undermines Some Children's Abilities to Avoid, Resist, or Escape Sexual Victimization*

Some perpetrators use force to accomplish their acts of child sexual victimization. In these cases, children's abilities to avoid, resist, or escape sexual victimization are irrelevant. There are, however, cases where children's exposure to pornography undermines these abilities and permits sexual abuse to occur where it otherwise would not.

### *1. By Arousing Children's Sexual Curiosity and/or Desire*

Showing pornography to boys and girls is a common seduction strategy of pedophiles who hope thereby to arouse children's sexual curiosity or sexual desire. For example, Katherine Brady (1979) testified as follows before the Senate Subcommittee on Juvenile Justice about her father showing her pornography for the first time:

> As I sat down on the bed, he spread out the pictures of men and naked women in all sorts of sexual positions with each other. Looking at them, I felt a rush spread through my body. . . . I felt intense sexual desire, total revulsion, increasing excitement, abandonment of reason, a sense of sin and guilt, the shame of it all, and a resolve to forget it until next time. (p. 78)

Pedophiles posing as young teenagers in Internet teen chat groups often send pornographic pictures or e-mail messages containing pornographic language to children. These predators use pornographic pictures to arouse the children's curiosity or sexual interest and manipulate them into meeting. These meetings typically culminate in the sexual victimization of the child or children.

Research on adults reveals that many female subjects, in contrast to male subjects, become upset or disturbed when exposed to pornographic pictures (Check, 1995; Check & Maxwell, 1992a, 1992b; Senn, 1993; Stock, 1995). Boys are far more likely than girls to be sexually aroused by pornographic pictures. Consequently, showing pornography tends to be a far more successful "seduction" strategy with boys than with girls. Ann Burgess and Carol Hartman (1987) found in their research on sex rings that "physical sensation and excitement was the dominant pleasure element that kept the boys in the ring" (Burgess & Hartman, 1987, p. 251; Burgess, Hartman, McCausland, & Powers, 1984). It seems reasonable to infer from this finding that the boys' sexual arousal undermines their abilities to escape sex rings.

Thus we conclude that exposure to child or adult pornography can arouse children's sexual curiosity or desire and thereby undermine their abilities to avoid, resist, or escape being sexually abused.

### *2. By Legitimizing and/or Normalizing Child Sexual Victimization for Children*

Many pedophiles and child molesters show pornography to children "in order to persuade them that they would enjoy certain sexual acts" (Kelly, 1992, p. 119). Another motive is "to convince them that what they are being asked to do is alright." Showing them a picture "legitimizes the abuser's requests" (p. 119).

In the following example, an incestuous father's attempts to use pornography to normalize and legitimize having sex with his daughter were unusually persistent.

> The incest started at the age of eight. I did not understand any of it and did not feel that it was right. My dad would try to convince me that it was ok. He would find magazines articles or pictures that would show fathers and daughters or mothers, brothers and sisters having sexual intercourse. (Mostly fathers and daughters.) He would say that if it was published in magazines that it had to be all right because magazines could not publish lies. He would show me these magazines and tell me to look at them or read them and I would turn

> my head and say no. He would leave them with me and tell me to look later. I was afraid not to look or read them because I did not know what he would do. He would ask me later if I had read them and what they said or if I looked real close at the pictures. He would say, "See it's okay to do because it's published in magazines." (*Attorney General's Commission on Pornography: Final Report, Vol. 1,* 1986, p. 786)

Child molesters also send pornography to the children they have targeted for sexual victimization to convince them "that other children are sexually active" (Hughes, 1999, p. 28). Showing children child pornography thus normalizes and legitimatizes adult– child sexual encounters in the minds of some children.

### *3. By Desensitizing or Disinhibiting Children*

A child molester's step-by-step "grooming" of a child serves to gradually desensitize her or him to the culminating act of sexual abuse, which is his goal. He moves from befriending a child, to touching her or him, to introducing her or him to an X-rated video, slowly showing more of it "until the child is able to sit and watch the videos without becoming too uncomfortable" (Whetsell-Mitchell, 1995, p. 201). Juliann Whetsell-Mitchell concludes, "Variations on the grooming ['seduction'] process are many but the end result is desensitizing the child to engaging in sexual acts with the perpetrator, other children, or other adults" (p. 201).

In addition, Calcetas-Santos (2001) notes that "Child pornography can be used by exploiters to lower children's inhibitions in order to seduce or encourage them to freely participate either in prostitution or pornography" (p. 59). Showing adult pornography to children can be "used in the same way [as child pornography] to lower the inhibitions of children" (Tate, 1992, p. 213).

### *4. By Creating Feelings of Guilt and Complicity, Thereby Silencing Children*

When child molesters expose targeted children to pornography, the children often feel guilty and complicit, particularly if they found the material sexually exciting or masturbated to it. According to Scotland Yard, one of the five major ways that pedophiles use pornography is to "ensure the secrecy of any sexual activity with a child who has already been seduced" (Tate, 1990, p. 24). Child molesters can often silence their victims by telling them that their parents would be very upset to learn that they had watched pornography. Even without such warnings, children often fear that their parents will blame and punish them for having looked at this material. Children who are sexually abused following the exposure may feel complicit in the abuse and thus become even more motivated to remain silent. Ultimately, this reduces the likelihood that abused children will disclose the sexual abuse to their parents or others.

## CONCLUSION

More research is urgently needed on child pornography, and especially the causal relationship between exposure to pornography and child sexual victimization. Some research in this area is impossible to conduct for ethical reasons and because of requirements for the protection of human subjects. However, ingenious researchers should be able to design some illuminating experiments that meet ethical standards.

Despite the relative dearth of research, we believe we have provided sufficient evidence to substantiate Russell's theory. This theory explains how exposure to child pornography can create a sexual interest in children in some males who previously had no such interest. When sexual interest in children exists, exposure to child pornography can intensify sexual desires and undermine internal and social inhibitions against acting them out. Thus, exposure to pornography induces some men, who otherwise would not sexually abuse children, to become child molesters.

## REFERENCES


Abel, G., Blanchard, E., & Becker, J. (1978). An integrated treatment program for rapists. In R. Rada (Ed.), *Clinical aspects of the rapist* (pp. 161–214). New York: Grune & Stratton.

Anderson, M. (1989, Summer). *Iconoclast, 7.*

*Attorney General's Commission on Pornography: Final Report, Vol. 1.* (1986). Washington, DC: United States Department of Justice.

Bart, P., & Jozsa, M. (1980). Dirty books, dirty films, and dirty data. In L. Lederer (Ed.), *Take back the night: Women on pornography* (pp. 188–217). New York: William Morrow.

Brady, K. (1979). *Father's Days: A true story of incest.* New York: Seaview Books.

Briere, J., & Runtz, M. (1989). University males' sexual interest in children: Predicting potential indices of "pedophilia" in a nonforensic sample. *Child Abuse and Neglect, 13*(1), 7, 65–75.

Bromberg, D. S., & Johnson, B. T. (2001, July). Sexual interest in children, child sexual abuse, and psychological sequaelae for children. *Psychology in Schools 38*(4), 343–355.

Burgess, A. W., & Hartman, C. R. (1987). Child abuse aspects of child pornography. *Psychiatric Annals, 17*(4), 248–253.

Burgess, A. W., Hartman, C. R., McCausland, M. P., & Powers, P. (1984). Response patterns in children and adolescents exploited through sex rings and pornography. *American Journal of Psychiatry, 141*(5).

Calcetas-Santos, O. (1996, Dec. 9–20). *Rights of the Child: Report of the special rapporteur on the sale of children, child prostitution and child pornography. Addendum: Report on the mission of the special rapporteur to the United States of America on the issues of commercial sexual exploitation of children.* New York: United Nations. Available at http://www.hri.ca/fortherecord1997/documentation/commission/e-cn4–1997–95-add2.htm

Calcetas-Santos, O. (2001). Child pornography on the Internet. In C. Arnaldo (Ed.), *Child abuse on the internet* (pp. 57–60). New York: Berghahn Books.

Campagna, D. S., & Poffenberger, D. L. (1988). *The sexual trafficking in children: An investigation of the child sex trade.* Dover, MA: Auburn House.

Carey, C. A. (2005, January 31). Banishment is not the answer. *San Francisco Chronicle,* B5.

Check, J. (1995). Teenage training: The effects of pornography on adolescent males. In L. Lederer & R. Delgado (Eds.), *The price we pay: The case against racist speech, hate propaganda, and pornography* (pp. 89–91). New York: Hill and Wang.

Check, J., & Maxwell, K. (1992a, June). *Adolescents' rape myth attitudes and acceptance of forced sexual intercourse.* Paper presented at the Canadian Psychological Association Meetings, Quebec.

Check, J., & Maxwell, K. (1992b, June). *Children's consumption of pornography and their attitudes regarding sexual violence.* Paper presented at the Canadian Psychological Association Meetings, Quebec.

*Child pornography and pedophilia* (1984). United States Senate, 98th Congress, second session Sess. 30–37 (1984).

Cline, V. B. (Ed.). (1974). *Where do you draw the line?* Provo, UT: Brigham Young University Press.

Crimmins, B. (1995). Testimony before Congressional Hearing on Child Pornography on the Internet, *Senate Judiciary Committee* (104th Congress ed., pp. 1–15). Washington, DC: Government Printing Office.

Davies, N. (1994, November 26). Dirty business. *Guardian,* pp. 12–17.

Diamond, I. (1980). Pornography and regression: A reconsideration of who and what. In L. Lederer (Ed.), *Take back the night: Women on pornography* (pp. 187–203). New York: William Morrow.

Dietz, P., & Sears, A. (1987–1988). Pornography and obscenity sold in "Adult Bookstores": A survey of 5132 books, magazines, and films in four American cities. *Journal of Law Reform, 21*(1–2), 7–46.

Dines, G., Jensen, R., & Russo, A. (1998). *Pornography: The production and consumption of inequality.* New York: Routledge.

Ferguson, J. (1985). Effect of pornography on women and children (prepared statement). *Subcommittee on Juvenile Justice of the Committee on the Judiciary* (98h Congress, Second Session on Oversight on Pornography, Magazines of a Variety of Courses, Inquiring into the Subject of Their Impact on Child Abuse, Child Molestation, and Problems of Conduct Against Women ed., pp. 281–288). Washington, DC: U.S. Government Printing Office.

Finkelhor, D. (1984). *Child sexual abuse: New theory and research.* New York: The Free Press.

Freund, K. (1981). Assessment of pedophilia. In M. Cook & K. Howells (Eds.), *Adult sexual interest in children* (pp. 137–180). New York: Academic Press.

Healy, M. (2002, February 27). *Child pornography: An international perspective.* Paper presented at the Second World Congress Against Commercial Sexual Exploitation of Children, Yokohama, Japan.

Howard, J., Reifler, C., & Liptzin, M. (1991). *Effects of exposure to pornography.* Washington, DC: Commission on Obscenity and Pornography.

Howells, K. (1981). Adult sexual interest in children: Consideration relevant to theories of aetiology. In M. Cook & K. Howells (Eds.), *Adult sexual interest in children* (pp. 55–94). New York: Academic Press.

Hughes, D. M. (1999). *Pimps and predators on the Internet: Globalizing the sexual exploitation of women and children.* Kingston, RI: The Coalition Against Trafficking in Women.

Itzin, C. (1996). Pornography and the organisation of child sexual abuse. In P. C. Bibby (Ed.), *Organized abuse: The current debate* (pp. 167–196). Hampshire, UK: Aldershot.

Jenkins, P. (2001). *Beyond tolerance: Child pornography on the Internet.* New York: New York University Press.

*Katherine Brady's Testimony to the Senate Subcommittee on Juvenile Justice.* (1984, August 8). 85 CIS S 52115 Testimony No: 1, pp. 28–117.

Kelly, L. (1992). Pornography and child sexual abuse. In C. Itzin (Ed.), *Pornography: Women, violence, and civil liberties* (pp. 113–123). New York: Oxford University Press.

Kelly, L., Wingfield, R., & Regan, L. (1995). *Splintered lives: Sexual exploitation of children in the context of children's rights and child protection.* Ilford, Essex, UK: Barnardos.

Linz, D., & Imrich, D. (2001). Child pornography. In S. O. White (Ed.), *Handbook of youth and justice* (pp. 79–111). New York: Kluwer Academic/Plenum.

LoPiccolo, J. (1994). Acceptance and broad spectrum treatment of paraphilias. In S. C. Hayes, N. Jacobson, V. M. Follette, & M. Dougher (Eds.), *Acceptance and change: Content and context in psychotherapy* (pp. 149–170). Reno, NV: Context Press.

Mayne, A. (2000). Child pornography. In R. Barnes-September, I. Brown-Adam, A. Mayne, D. Kowen, & G. Dyason (Eds.), *Child victims of prostitution in the Western Cape* (p. 25). Cape Town, SA: Institute for Child and Family Development.

McGuire, R.J., Carlisle, J.M., & Young, B.G. (1965). Sexual deviation as a conditioned behavior: A hypothesis. *Behavioral Research and Therapy, 2,* 185–190.

Mohr, J., Turner, R., & Jerry, M. (1964). *Pedophilia and Exhibitionism.* Toronto: University of Toronto Press.

O'Connell, R. (2001). Paedophile networking and the Internet. In C. Arnaldo (Ed.), *Child Abuse on the Internet: Ending the silence* (p. 65). Paris: UNESCO Publishing/Berghahn Books.

Osanka, F. M., & Johann, S. L. (1989). *Sourcebook on pornography.* Lexington, MA: Lexington Books.

Rachman, S., & Hodgson, R. (1968). Experimentally-induced "sexual fetishism": Replication and development. *Psychological Record, 18,* 25–27.

Report of the Commission on Obscenity and Pornography (1970). Washington, DC: U.S. Government Printing Office.

Rush, F. (1980, May 17). *Child pornography.* Paper presented at the Pittsburgh Conference on Pornography: A Feminist Perspective, Pittsburgh, PA.

Russell, D. E. H. (1984). *Sexual exploitation: Rape, child sexual abuse, and workplace harassment.* Beverly Hills, CA: Sage.

Russell, D. E. H. (1999). The *secret trauma: Incest in the lives of girls and women* (Rev. ed.). New York: Basic Books/Perseus.

Russell, D. E. H., & Trocki, K. (1993). Evidence of harm. In D. E. H. Russell (Ed.), *Making violence sexy: Feminist views on pornography* (pp. 194–213). New York: Teachers College Press.

Senn, C. (1993). Women's responses to pornography. In D. E. H. Russell (Ed.), *Making violence sexy: Feminist views on pornography* (pp. 179–193). New York: Teachers College Press.

Silbert, M., & Pines, A. (1993). Pornography and sexual abuse of women. In D. E. H. Russell (Ed.), *Making violence sexy: Feminist views on pornography* (pp. 113–119). New York: Teachers College Press.

Sommers, E., & Check, J. (1987). An empirical investigation of the role of pornography in the verbal and physical abuse of women. *Violence and Victims, 2*(3), 189–209.

Stock, W. (1995). The effects of pornography on women. In L. Lederer & R. Delgado (Eds.), *The price we pay: The case against racist speech, hate propaganda, and pornography* (pp. 80–88). New York: Hill and Wang.

Swanson, D. (1968). Adult sexual abuse of children: The man and circumstances. *Diseases of the Nervous System, 29,* 677–683.

Tate, T. (1990). *Child pornography: An investigation.* London: Methuen.

Tate, T. (1992). The child pornography industry: International trade in child sexual abuse. In C. Itzin (Ed.), *Pornography: Women, violence, and civil liberties* (p. 213). New York: Oxford University Press.

Taylor, M., & Quayle, E. (2003). *Child pornography: An Internet crime.* New York: Brunner-Routledge.

Taylor, S. (2001, March 19). Is it sexual exploitation if victims are virtual? *Newsweek, 137,* 51.

Theodorson, G., & Theodorson, A. (1979). *A modern dictionary of sociology.* New York: Barnes & Noble.

Thimbleby, H. (1995, September 12). *Problems in the global village.* Presented at Discovery and Invention, The British Association Annual Festival of Science (Newcastle). Available: http://www.eff.org/Censorship/Rimm_CMU_Time/thimbleby_global_village_problems_95.paper

Whetsell-Mitchell, J. (1995). *Rape of the innocent: Understanding and preventing child sexual abuse.* Washington, DC: Accelerated Development.

Wyre, R. (1990). Why do men sexually abuse children? In T. Tate (Ed.), *Child pornography: An investigation* (pp. 281–288). London: Methuen.

Zillmann, D. (1989). Effects of prolonged consumption. In D. Zillmann & J. Bryant, (Eds.), *Pornography: Research advances and policy considerations,* pp. 127–157. Hillsdale, NJ: Lawrence Erlbaum.

Zillmann, D., & Bryant, J. (1986). Shifting preferences in pornography consumption. *Communication Research, 12,* 560–578.

CHAPTER 5

# Statutory Rape

## An Empirical Examination of Claims of "Overreaction"

Ross E. Cheit and Laura Braslow

Statutory rape laws have become increasingly controversial as sexual activity among teenagers becomes more common and socially acceptable. These laws, which vary by state, criminalize sexual contact between adults and teenagers above the age at which they are considered children for purposes of child molestation statutes but under the legal age of consent. Originally intended to protect the chastity of girls, these laws are now generally gender-neutral. The current controversy is rooted in a conflict between two radically different perspectives on statutory rape. One view questions the need for such laws, arguing that they are enforced far too strictly, criminalizing what are often cases of "young love" between two teenagers. The other view emphasizes the physical and mental health costs attendant to sexual contact between adults and adolescents, and questions whether adolescents are capable of consenting to sexual activity in such circumstances or whether in fact many of these cases involve complex and often coercive power imbalances. Under this view, law enforcement is too lax.

This chapter subjects these claims to analysis through original trial court research and aggregate statistical analysis of all statutory rape cases filed over 18 years in one state, Rhode Island. We find considerable evidence that arrest and disposition rates are low and sentences are moderate to lenient, indicating little evidence of strict enforcement. In addition, we find that in the majority of cases, defendant characteristics and relationships between complainants and defendants are significantly different from the "young love" picture that one might expect based on the popular image of these cases. These conclusions are subject to various qualifications, and we believe that there is considerable room for further research in this area.

### LEGAL BACKGROUND

Statutory rape laws have been on the books in most states for over 100 years. They were originally intended to protect young girls from older men. In Rhode Island, the first such law was passed in 1889, providing criminal sanctions for "carnal knowledge of a girl under 14" (Rhode Island Public Law 1889, ch. 738, sec. 1). Just 5 years later, the age of consent was raised to 16, where it has remained ever since (Rhode Island General Law 1896, ch. 281, sec. 3). The law was modernized in 1979, when the crime of "seduction" was replaced with "third-degree sexual assault" (Rhode Island General Law 11-37-6). The law applies to anyone over the age of majority, 18, who engages in sexual penetration with someone age 14 or 15. Because young teenagers are under the statutory age of consent, consent per se is not a legal issue in these cases. However, the teenage victims in these cases are generally thought to have been willing participants in the sexual encounter in question. If they did not assent, presumably the case would be charged as rape. However, Rhode Island's rape statute, first-degree sexual assault, requires "force or coercion"—something prosecutors interpret as more than lack of consent. Nonconsensual cases that do not meet the "force or coercion" standard cannot be charged under any sex crimes statute if the victim is over 16. The statutory rape law provides the opportunity for criminal charges in such cases if the adolescent is 14 or 15, as Figure 5.1 illustrates.

Third-degree sexual assault is a felony punishable by up to 5 years in prison. The 1979 reforms increased the scope of the crime, providing protection for boys as well as girls. The new law also significantly reduced the maximum sentence for the crime, from 15 years to 5 years, which at the outset undercuts claims of "sex abuse hysteria" and overzealousness to some extent. The sentencing benchmarks in Rhode Island, written and adopted by the judiciary, specify that the likelihood and severity of a prison sentence depend on the "age difference between perpetrator and victim and the presence or absence of aggravating circumstances" (Sentencing Study Commission, 1997). The "aggravating circumstances" clause is puzzling, since the factors specified in the benchmarks—excessive force for

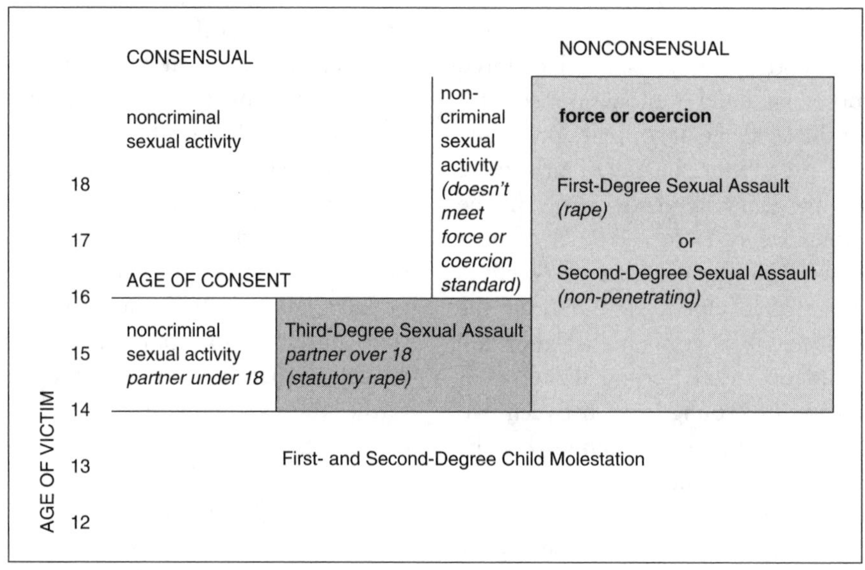


**Figure 5.1** Schematic of Rhode Island Sex Crimes Statutes, Victims Under Age 18

*Note:* The relationship between consensual and nonconsensual cases is unclear, and the positioning of the rectangle representing statutory rape is not meant to represent the actual proportion of these cases in the two categories.

violence, the act having been committed in conjunction with other crimes, moderate to severe mental or physical injury—would all seem to support more severe sexual assault charges in the first place.

Rhode Island's statutory rape law is comparable to many statutes around the country. In 1997, a total of 29 states used 16 as the age of consent, and only 3 states had ages of consent lower than 16 (Elstein & Davis, 1997). Rhode Island's statute does not specify a minimum age difference between victims and offenders, other than the difference between the age of consent, 16, and the age of majority, 18. Thus, the age difference that qualifies for statutory rape in Rhode Island is only 1 day over 2 years, smaller than in some states but generally comparable with the majority. According to the American Bar Association, 16 states have specified minimum age differences of greater than 2 years in their statutes: 6 use three years, 8 use four years, 1 uses five years, and 1 uses six (Elstein & Davis, 1997). Similarly, "aggravated sexual abuse" under the federal criminal code includes sexual contact with a child 13 to 15 by someone at least 4 years older. Thus, 17 jurisdictions required a larger age difference than Rhode Island did in 1997.

## COMPETING NARRATIVES OF STATUTORY RAPE

There are two competing narratives about statutory rape in our society. One is a story of potentially serious public health consequences and undue leniency in law enforcement. That story emphasizes how few cases are ever prosecuted, how leniently they are resolved, and how serious are the potential medical consequences of underage sex. The second narrative centers around the question of teenagers' ability to make their own choices and the validity of their sexual desires. Proponents of this story claim that the psychological and physical health risks associated with teenage sexual activity are minimal, and criticize the criminal justice system for prosecuting consensual relationships and punishing older defendants too harshly.

The public health/undue leniency story reached a peak in popularity at the time of the welfare reforms of 1996. That year the United States Congress called on the states to "aggressively enforce statutory rape laws" in a proclaimed effort to reduce the number of teen pregnancies (Personal Responsibility and Work Opportunity Reconciliation Act of 1996, § 906(a)). In his 1995 State of the State address, then California Governor Pete Wilson said, "And for adult men who impregnate teenage girls . . . [w]e'll give you a year to think about it in county jail" (Gunnison & Lucas, 1996). The American Bar Association issued a report the following year that concluded statutory rape was "a crime that frequently is swept under the rug and remains largely unprosecuted" (Stapleton, 1998, p. 3).

Many medical professionals see neurological and physiological reasons for distinguishing young teens from those over the age of consent. Stuart-Smith (1996, p. 390) notes that "the frontal lobe of the brain, which deals with control of sexual drives as well as abstract reasoning and planning, is not completely [developed] until 14 or 15 years of age." In a report to the federal prosecutor in *United States v. Sacko* (2000), Dr. Carole Jenny, a pediatric child abuse expert, summarized several studies that indicate "the majority of girls younger than 15 years who engage in vaginal intercourse do so involuntarily" (Jenny, 1999, p. 3). If an adolescent is not yet physically mature—a process measured by Tanner Stages, a widely used series of physical benchmarks of development that signal sexual maturity—then sexual intercourse can also cause physical trauma (Tanner, 1962). At age 14, for example, 32.9% of girls have not yet reached

Tanner Stage IV, the physical marker for sexual maturity. Sexually active girls in this age range are also far more susceptible to sexually transmitted diseases (Jenny, 1999). Kaestle, Morisky, and Wiley (2002) found that as the age difference between a young girl and her boyfriend increased, so did the odds of having sexual intercourse. For a 13-year-old in a relationship with a partner 6 years older or more, the odds of sexual intercourse were "more than six times the odds of intercourse with a same age partner" (Kaestle, Morisky, & Wiley, 2002, p. 307). The authors concluded that, in general, "a romantic relationship between a young adolescent female and an older male is risky" because the power and communications dynamics are so skewed (p. 307).

The competing narrative about statutory rape—one that has become dominant in the media and among many academics in recent years—is the story of undue strictness and social constraint of the sexual desires of teenagers. Invoking the phrases "moral panic" and "social hysteria," this narrative claims that the state inappropriately polices teenagers, meting out severe and undeserved prison terms to defendants, almost always men, who are only 3 or 4 years older than their "victims." In the archetypal example of this argument, the sexual relationship of a just-18-year-old boy with his almost-16-year-old girlfriend becomes criminalized by an overbearing, puritanical society.

At age 16, an estimated 98.1% of girls have reached Tanner Stage IV (Jenny, 1999, p. 2). That reality weakens the medical arguments for statutory rape laws applied to 15-year-olds who are close to their 16th birthday. However, the moral panic/social hysteria claim is much broader. Characterizing statutory rape as a "crime of passion"—the title of a recent book chapter on statutory rape by Judith Levine (2002)—Levine and others come down solidly on the side of autonomy and choice, even for the youngest teens. This argument often appears to make no distinction between 15-year-olds and 13-year-olds—even though only 38.1% of girls have reached Tanner Stage IV by age 13 (Jenny, 1999). Indeed, the single case study on which Levine relies involves a 13-year-old girl. That case is described and analyzed in detail below.

### *The Nature of Existing Evidence*

How strong is the evidence for the moral panic/social hysteria position? Far less than meets the eye. For example, Levine's sweeping claims about statutory rape are based largely on a single case, and her characterizations of this case are misleading. She also cites a study of adolescent sexual behavior, playing down the results that contradict her position. The relevant appellate court cases point to leniency among judges, and other studies indicate some degree of leniency among prosecutors. Studies of adolescent sexual behavior, while indicating that there is evidence on both sides, generally suggest that there are significant grounds for concern when young teenagers become sexually involved with older partners. Empirical support for strict enforcement with the goal of decreasing teen pregnancy is quite limited, while a host of other evidence generally contradicts the moral panic argument.

### *Levine's "Dubious" Case Study*

Levine (2002) devotes considerable attention to a highly publicized case involving a man in his twenties who met a 13-year-old on the Internet and fled town with her after the girl's family had obtained a restraining order. Levine claims that the case was "narrated" (Levine, 2002, p. 73) by the police to fit a social text in which the man she calls Dylan was a dangerous predator and the girl she calls Heather was painted as the victim. Levine scoffs at the fact that Dylan was considered armed and dangerous. She also dismisses the reports from two ex-wives (in common law) that Dylan was physically abusive. Levine concludes that the defendant did not deserve punishment for statutory rape; rather it was a complicated case of "young love."

Levine used pseudonyms for both parties in the case, reasoning that they had "returned to private life" since their identities were widely disseminated in 1997. The defendant, however, had not returned to private life; he was serving a lengthy prison sentence. The subjects can be easily identified through simple research. An examination of police reports and court files in the case reveals a host of errors and omissions in Levine's version of the story. First, Levine misstates the defendant's age. Keir Fiore, the defendant, was twenty-two and a half, not twenty-one. While the error is only one and a half years, getting such a critical fact wrong in a case that revolves around age differences raises obvious questions about the accuracy of the rest of the research. Second, Levine omits any mention of the witness-tampering charges to which the defendant pled guilty, the fact that he was sentenced to receive sex-offender treatment (Meersman, Hayward, & Rose, 1997), or the fact that he was in possession of child pornography at the time of his arrest (Sentencing Statement, 1997).

Levine also drastically minimizes the defendant's threatening behavior. His first common-law wife, whom he met when she was 14, says that he verbally and physically abused her and once threatened her with a rifle (Hayward & Meersman, 1997). A few years later, his second common-law wife obtained custody of their newborn child and a restraining order against Fiore, reporting that he threatened her over the telephone, saying, "If you found someone else, you're dead and he's dead," and "I'm gonna get you and I'm gonna get your baby" (Domestic Violence Petition, 1995, p. 1). Levine labeled these facts "disputed" because the defendant, in an undocumented prison interview, apparently said that they were in dispute (Levine, 2002, p. 73). However, the allegations were affirmed by Fiore's statements in court that he was "possessive and jealous" and was "trying to control" Heather (Sentencing Statement, 1997, pp. 2, 4). Levine also minimizes Fiore's threats against another 14-year-old girl a few months before he met Heather. In that case, he tried to lure the girl to a hotel room, where he promised he would pay her for sex. Fiore's final e-mail to the girl read, "You pissed the wrong person off, playing your little game Jew Girl!!!! Watch your back!!!!!!!" (Incident Report, Holliston Police Dept., 1997a, p. 2). Fiore was also charged with trying to lure her 13-year-old friend. A few months later he began his obsessive relationship with Heather (Meersman, Hayward, & Rose, 1997). In short, an examination of the original sources suggests that it was Levine, not the police, who had a predetermined narrative to impose on this case.

### *Rhode Island Appellate Decisions*

The two competing narratives about statutory rape are both present in the limited appellate law concerning sex crimes against children in Rhode Island, the focus of the empirical data in this chapter. There is evidence of leniency in an appellate case from the 1980s. In a case that began with a civil complaint and was subsequently filed as a criminal complaint, the defendant was indicted on first-degree, second-degree, and third-degree sexual assault and kidnapping; he was disposed by plea on third-degree only (*Silveria v. Santos,* 1985).

Two more recent cases provide some support for the overzealous enforcement view. In *State v. Mulchaney* (2000)—one of only two third-degree sexual assault cases to go to trial in Rhode Island since 1995—the defendant was a 23-year-old, described by the court as having engaged "in consensual sexual intercourse with his fifteen-year-old girlfriend when she was a month or so shy of her sixteenth birthday" (p. 1215). He apparently had the approval of the girl's family, leaving it unclear how this became a criminal complaint. But the judge did not mete out a severe penalty. To the contrary, the defendant received a 5-year suspended sentence, even after taking the case to trial and being convicted.

The other relevant case that was taken to the appellate level in Rhode Island is *State v. Yanez* (1998), a child molestation case involving an 18-year-old man convicted of sexual intercourse with a 13-year-old girl. The defendant characterized the relationship as boyfriend and girlfriend and tried, unsuccessfully, to rely on "mistake of age" as a defense. He was convicted of first-degree child molestation and sentenced to 2 years in prison with 18 years suspended. The defendant appealed his conviction to the Rhode Island Supreme Court, alleging that the law should recognize the "mistake of fact" defense. The Court's divided opinion reveals a collision between the competing narratives of statutory rape. The majority strongly condemned the defendant, noting that trial testimony indicated that "this was not an isolated incident and that there were two equally sordid, uncharged encounters" (*State v. Yanez,* p. 761). "[She] is exactly the type of victim whose vulnerability the Legislature had intended to protect," the majority concluded (*State v. Yanez,* p. 770). The sole dissenter, Judge Flanders, strongly disagreed, characterizing the relationship as "dating" and the majority decision as "draconian" and "out of whack with reality" (*State v. Yanez,* pp. 771–772).

In Rhode Island, the newspaper stories about statutory rape cases are virtually all stories of leniency. Several stories describe cases in which defendants pled guilty to third-degree charges in exchange for more serious charges being dropped. One recent headline reads, "Man Given 5 Years' Probation for Having Sex With 14-Year-Old" (Mider, 2004). The story explains that prosecutors agreed to drop five charges of first-degree child molestation in exchange for the plea. In 2001 there was a story about a case in which "two men were convicted of having sex with a 15-year-old girl while she was intoxicated" (Rosenbaum, 2001, p. C1). The story indicates that the state agreed to reduce the charges from first-degree sexual assault; the defendants both received suspended sentences. The stories about cases charged solely as third-degree sexual assault are also stories of leniency. "Man Gets 1-Day Suspended Term for Having Sex With Girl, 14," cries out a 1995 headline about a case involving a 22-year-old defendant ("Man Gets 1-Day Suspended Term," 1995). In one of the few cases involving a female defendant, the headline and subhead are quite similar: "N. Kingstown woman pleads no contest to having sex with a 15-year-old boy; the woman, 24, received a suspended sentence in a plea agreement" (Cassinelli, 1993, p. B8).

### *Studies Concerning Teen Pregnancy*

Beyond individual stories, there are various empirical studies that shed light on the link between statutory rape and teen pregnancy. While many sources agree that there is a problem with older men impregnating young teens, the size of that problem is much smaller than often claimed. In perhaps the most widely cited study on the subject, Landry and Forrest (1995) found that 65% of teen mothers had a partner aged 20 or older. However, the study included a sizable number of 18- and 19-year-old "teenage mothers," so for the oldest teens in that study both partners were above the age of consent and the age difference between them was often only a year or two. Lindberg, Sonenstein, Ku, and Martinez (1997, p. 65) dissected Landry and Forrest's numbers, demonstrating that only 8% of births resulting from teen pregnancy actually involved an unmarried adolescent and a man at least 5 years older. Accordingly, they conclude that even the strictest enforcement of statutory rape laws would accomplish very little since "the number of births resulting from acts covered by such laws is so small" (Lindberg et al., 1997, p. 66). In contrast, a study of 12,317 births to very young adolescents (under age 15) in California from 1993–1995 found that adult fathers, averaging almost 9 years older than the mother, were responsible for 26.7% of the pregnancies (Taylor, Chavez, Adams, Chabra, & Rugmini, 1999). While many sources agree that there is a problem with older men impregnating young teens, cases resulting in birth are only a small portion of the cases involving teenage sex.

### *Studies of Adolescent Sexual Behavior*

Studies of adolescent sexual behavior put the teen pregnancy issue into a larger context. Leitenberg and Saltzman (2000), for example, found that only 12% of those who had first intercourse experiences between 13 and 15 had partners 5 years older or more. In other words, the vast majority of sexual activity among the age group covered by the statutory rape law does not involve older partners. Levine (2002, p. 86) quotes Allie Kilpatrick—author of a retrospective study of 501 women—saying that "the majority of young people who experience some kind of sexual behavior find it pleasurable." That spin, however, came from the interview Levine conducted with Kilpatrick, not from the actual study. As Yarhouse (2004, p. 313) has pointed out, Levine "glosses over the finding that 45% of the children and adolescents [in Kilpatrick's study] found early sexual experiences to be 'abusive' or 'harmful.'" Abma, Driscoll, and Moore (1998) analyzed data from the National Survey of Family Growth specifically to assess age differences and the "wantedness" of first intercourse. They found that one-third of women who had first intercourse at age 14—and 27.3% of those having intercourse first at age 15—later rated the experience in the low range of the "wantedness" scale. The proportion of women who assigned a low wantedness rating "was twice as great among women who had first sex with a man seven or [more] years older" as it was among those with partners closer in age (Abma et al., 1998, p. 15).

Another recent retrospective study analyzed characteristics of the respondent's first sexual partner (Elo, King, & Furstenberg, 1999). The authors report that "the proportion of children born to teen mothers who are fathered by adult men (who are at least 20 years of age) has declined since 1960" (p. 78). Nevertheless, the study provides significant reasons for concern about older men having sexual contact with young teenage girls. Respondents whose first partner was at least 4 years older "were twice as likely to report their first intercourse was not voluntary or was a rape than women whose partners were closer to their own age" (Elo et al., p. 81). Moreover, a large age difference (4 years or more) was "significantly more likely" for women whose first intercourse was before age 15 (p. 81). These data are tempered by the fact that a majority of the youngest women in the sample "initiated intercourse in a steady relationship, and they reported that the intercourse was wanted" (p. 81).

Ultimately, Elo, King, and Furstenberg provide limited support for both of the competing views of statutory rape. On the one hand, they validate concerns about wantedness in sexual interactions involving young teens and older individuals. On the other, they indicate that considerable sexual activity among teens comes in the context of a steady relationship and is viewed entirely as welcome.

### *Studies Involving the Criminal Justice System*

For a crime that received so much national attention as part of the teen pregnancy scare, it is remarkable how little data exists on the prosecution of statutory rape cases. Cheit and Goldschmidt (1997, p. 280) examined all sex crimes against children in Rhode Island from 1985–1993, finding that the incarceration rates for third-degree sexual assault "fluctuate wildly, from 50% in 1986 to zero in 1990." There were so few cases between 1990 and 1993 that it appeared that statutory rape "had largely been decriminalized" (Cheit & Goldschmidt, p. 280). More recently, Walsh and Wolak (2004) examined prosecutorial outcomes in 77 Internet-related sex crimes with adolescent victims and extra-familial adult defendants. They found a surprisingly high incarceration rate of 85%, with 71% of those apparently being sentenced to over 1 year. It remains to be seen whether that pattern of outcomes is restricted to cases involving the Internet, or whether instead there has been an increase in strictness in the legal system since the results observed by Cheit and Goldschmidt in the mid-1990s.

There are also two attitudinal studies that have direct application to statutory rape and the legal system. Miller, Miller, Kenney, and Clark (1998) surveyed district attorneys in Kansas in light of the federal welfare law's admonition to enforce statutory rape laws aggressively. Seventy-three percent of prosecutors agreed (41.8%) or strongly agreed (31.9%) that statutory rape laws should be "aggressively" enforced (Miller et al., p. 179). Less than a quarter of those surveyed, however, thought that aggressive enforcement would reduce teen pregnancy. And only 37% agreed (26.4%) or strongly agreed (11.0%) that the public would support aggressive enforcement. Indeed, the survey reported the reluctance by prosecutors "to prosecute cases in which the parties are close in age" (Miller et al., p. 180). These and other findings led the authors to conclude that prosecutors' "interpretation of appropriate enforcement policy is by definition less aggressive than the limits of Kansas criminal law" (Miller et al. 1998, p. 180). The cases actually prosecuted are likely to involve larger age differences and occur outside "a long-standing, caring relationship" (p. 180). Rather than undue strictness, this study suggests forbearance and an unwillingness to prosecute "young love" cases.

Mock jury research also indicates a public skepticism about blaming others when the "victim" is 13 or older and "willing." Isquith, Levine, and Scheiner (1993) studied the relationship between victim age and the willingness of mock jurors to attribute blame to the victim of sexual abuse. Statutory rape laws tend to cover adolescents in precisely the years that mock jurors believe adolescents are first interested in sex. Mock jurors are significantly more hesitant to convict when the victim is 13 or older, suggesting that juries would be hesitant to enforce the law when a case involves an apparently willing or encouraging adolescent. The authors concluded (Isquith et al., p. 207) that "victim responsibility may be considered in some way by jurors, particularly when the female is as young as 13, and even when consent is not a legal issue." Like the perceptions of Kansas prosecutors, these data suggest limited public support for prosecuting cases where a young teen is said to have "encouraged" sexual contact with someone older.

## AGGREGATE ANALYSIS OF RHODE ISLAND CRIMINAL CASES

This section constitutes the most comprehensive quantitative study to date to investigate the universe of statutory rape claims and case outcomes over time in a single jurisdiction. Our quantitative aggregate analysis is based on two data sources. Data were drawn primarily from a download of the Rhode Island state court internal record-keeping system. This database contains full case information, including disposition and sentencing, for all cases in Rhode Island district and superior courts for January 1985 through December 2002. We also gathered secondary information from a review of all hard-copy case files for the years 1997–2002 ($n = 158$), and a secondary request for police reports in cases involving teenage defendants and defendants over the age of 35 (about 40% of those cases). The overall population consists of all cases with at least one original charge of third-degree sexual assault filed in Rhode Island district or superior court between 1985 and 2002 ($n = 403$). See Appendix A at the end of this chapter for detailed information on sample selection and study methodology.

### *Case Load and Charge Combinations*

Between 1985 and 2002, there were roughly 20 cases per year with at least one third-degree sexual assault charge filed in Rhode Island. The late 1980s were a high point, with 30 cases filed in 1987 and 27 cases filed in 1988. The number fell in the early 1990s, when statutory rape seemed to be almost decriminalized. The number of cases filed reached a low of only 9 in 1990—and, notably, not one of the defendants in these cases was incarcerated for the offense. The number of cases fell below average for the next few years: 15 in 1991, 14 in 1992, and 17 in 1993. The trend reversed in the mid-1990s, with steady increases since 1994. The annual number of cases hovered around the low- to mid-20s until the late 1990s, and increased to a high of 34 cases in 2001. However, this is only a modest increase over the 1985–2002 average of 22.4, and is in keeping with the overall caseload increase in the Rhode Island state court system over this period of time.

Within this sample of 403 cases with at least one charge of third-degree sexual assault, 59% were charged only with third-degree sexual assault ($n = 238$). The remaining 41% ($n = 165$) included other charges, which varied widely over time and lacked any clear pattern. For example, from 1986 to 1987 the ratio of cases involving charges of statutory rape only to those involving charges of statutory rape plus other charges varied from 3:1 to 1:5. From 1997 to 1998 the ratio varied from 5:1 to 1:1. Although the number of cases filed each year is fairly small, as detailed above, the degree of variation from year to year and the lack of consistency during any multi-year period suggests that there is no discernable pattern to these charging practices.

For those cases involving defendants charged with "third only," 58% ($n = 138$) were charged a single count and the remaining 42% ($n = 100$) were charged with multiple counts of third-degree sexual assault. Of the 165 cases involving charges of "third plus," 45% ($n = 74$) had at least one other sexual assault charge, 31.5% ($n = 52$) had at least one charge of child molestation, 24% ($n = 40$) had at least one other sex crime charge, and 45% ($n = 75$) had miscellaneous other charges. In terms of the total sample, 29% of all third-degree cases ($n = 117$) involved charges of third-degree plus sexual assault, child molestation, or other sex crimes. Eighteen percent of cases charged as third-degree were also charged with more serious sexual assault, 13% included charges of child molestation, and 10% had additional sex charges. Based on our case review and general legal practice, we believe that cases with multiple charges represent single, not multiple, victims.

Without reviewing the full case files, it is impossible to characterize the cases involving charges of "third plus." Some or most might resemble the "young love" case, which many proponents of undue strictness claim to be representative of statutory rape charges. But since in a large subset of cases (29%), third-degree charges are brought in combination with more serious sex crimes, it appears that a significant number of these cases differ from that fact pattern, either in terms of the age of the defendant (because repeated sexual contact may have begun before the age of 14), or in whether the sexual contact in question was willing.

### *Distribution of Defendants by Age*

The "social hysteria" view generally portrays statutory rape cases as involving 18- or 19-year-old boys and their 15-year-old girlfriends. The "young love" claim relies on the defendant being no more than about 4 years older than the victim. However, defendants who were 18 or 19 at the time they were charged account for only 20.9% of third-degree sexual assault cases between 1985 and 2002 in Rhode Island. The median age of defendants in these cases is 24, and the average age is 27.9. The universe includes 188 cases (46.6%) where the defendant was 24 or older. Ninety-two of the defendants (22.8%) were 35 or older. However, based on the charge combinations for those defendants, the "young love" narrative seems to have some purchase—young defendants are more likely to be charged with statutory rape only (71%, compared to 59% for the sample as a whole), and are far less likely to be charged with statutory rape plus child molestation (6%, as compared to 13% for the sample as a whole) or more serious sexual assaults (9%, compared to 18% for the entire sample).

The 35-and-older age group is another important subset of the statutory rape universe. Ninety-two defendants (22.8%) in the sample are over the age of 35, and 134 defendants (33.3%) are 30 years of age or older. Thus, offenders who are at least twice as old as their victims comprise a significantly larger percentage of all defendants than teenage defendants who fit the "young love" narrative. How many, if any, of these relationships between adolescents and adults over 35 represent legitimately willing sexual involvements? Charging patterns suggest that the majority appear to be closer to nonconsensual sexual assaults. Older defendants are far less likely to be charged with statutory rape alone (34%, compared to 59% for the sample as a whole), and are twice as likely to be charged with child molestation (25%, compared to 13% for the sample as a whole) and more serious sexual assaults (36%, compared to 18% for the sample as a whole).

### *Dispositions: Dismissed, Guilty Plea, or Trial*

A final resolution was reached in all but 17 of the 403 cases in this study. The remaining 4.4% were pending when this study was completed. Only two of those were active cases, however. In the remainder, the defendant skipped bail and remains at large. Of the 386 cases with final dispositions, 14% were dismissed and 86% were disposed on at least one charge. The 14% dismissal rate is lower than the 16.5% dismissal rate for all three criminal sex offenses against minors in Rhode Island from 1985–1993 (Cheit & Goldschmidt, 1997). On the other hand, it exceeds the dismissal rate in a 2004 national study of Internet-related sex crimes against minors, where only 5% of state charges and 7% of federal charges were dismissed (Walsh & Wallack, 2004). In the period 1997–2002 we found a dismissal rate of 20.6%, suggesting a trend in favor of dismissal.

Almost all of the cases carried forward resulted in guilty pleas or pleas of *nolo contendre*. There were 11 jury trials involving statutory rape charges between 1985 and 2002, and 10 of these resulted in a conviction. Of those, five were charged as third only, and three were charged with third-degree plus either child molestation or more serious sexual assault. The total number of trials represents about 3% of all cases with third-degree charges, significantly lower than the rate that Cheit and Goldschmidt (1997) found for third-degree charges in Rhode Island from 1985–1993 (6%). Indeed, seven of the eleven trials in this study were from the 1980s.

## *Incarceration Rates and Average Sentences*

A fairly modest percentage of those convicted on third-degree charges in Rhode Island during the period 1985 to 2002 were sentenced to prison. Other punishments included probation, suspended sentences, and other options used by judges to satisfy minimum sentencing requirements. Twenty-seven percent of defendants originally charged with third-degree sexual assault received time to serve on one or more charges ($n = 89$), and 23% of defendants were given time to serve on third-degree charges specifically ($n = 69$). In cases where defendants were convicted of third-degree charges only, 20% of defendants ($n = 47$) were sentenced to jail.

For those who received jail sentences in third-degree cases, the length of sentence was moderate. The average sentence on third-degree charges was 25.6 months, with an average of 20.2 months for defendants convicted of statutory rape only. The longest sentence on third-degree charges was 8 years, consisting of two charges with consecutive sentences (an unusual practice in Rhode Island). The second through the tenth longest sentences were the statutory maximum, 5 years. However, most of those cases involve defendants who were convicted on multiple charges. In cases where the defendant was convicted of statutory rape alone, only four defendants received sentences of 5 years or more, and only ten received sentences of 3 years or more. See Appendix B for a discussion of variations in sentence length in third-degree cases disposed on multiple charges.

Using the data available, it is not possible to determine which judge presided over the disposition of a case, but an analysis of sentencing judges indicates that these cases are fairly well distributed between judges. There were 38 judges who sentenced at least one defendant on third-degree charges between 1985 and 2002. That works out to a rough average of nine cases per judge. Fourteen judges sentenced more than 10 cases each. The highest number of cases for any single judge was 23. There were five judges who sentenced between 20 and 23 defendants on these charges. Many judges had only a handful of cases. Seventeen judges had between one and four cases. In short, there are not enough observations to allow meaningful comparisons between judges, although this variable likely has some effect.

Overall incarceration rates and average sentence lengths vary significantly by defendant age. The Rhode Island sentencing benchmarks indicate that sentence severity should depend in large part on the age difference between the parties. That suggests that younger defendants might legitimately avoid incarceration on this charge, while older defendants should not. However, the descriptive statistics paint a slightly more complicated picture. (See Table 5.1.) While the incarceration rate on "third only" for defendants 35 and over (30.6%) is nearly three times the rate for teenage defendants (11.3%), the relationship between age and likelihood of incarceration is not strictly linear. Defendants in the middle two age groups had roughly equivalent incarceration rates, but the rate for the 20–24 group (22.1%) was slightly higher than the rate for the 25–34 group (21.2%).

The relationship between the defendant's age and the likelihood of incarceration was even more complex for those charged with "third plus." There appears to be a shelf of

**Table 5.1** Third Only Versus Third Plus: Incarceration Rates and Average Sentence on Third-Degree Charges by Defendant Age (Rhode Island, 1985-2002)

| | *Incarceration Rate (%)* | | *Average Sentence (in months)* | |
|---|---|---|---|---|
| *Defendant Age* | *3rd Only* | *3rd Plus* | *3rd Only* | *3rd Plus* |
| 18–19 | 11.3 | 20.0 | 8.9 | 3.0 |
| 20–24 | 22.1 | 11.1 | 18.4 | 12.0 |
| 25–34 | 21.2 | 42.9 | 24.7 | 34.7 |
| 35+ | 30.6 | 42.3 | 29.5 | 44.8 |
| ALL | 20.2 | 36.7 | 21.1 | 36.6 |

sorts in these cases—the two youngest groups have very low incarceration rates (only one individual was convicted of third plus and incarcerated from each age group), while the two older groups have equivalent and very high incarceration rates (42–43%). Average sentences increased across the four groups in both categories. These and other descriptive observations are assessed in the next section using multivariate models.

Average sentences were longer for those convicted of "third plus" than those convicted of "third only" for the two oldest groups. Generally, defendants received sentences 30–40% longer if convicted of "third plus" than if convicted of "third only." The younger defendants were an exception—in both the 18–19 group and the 20–24 group, those convicted of third plus served less time than those convicted of third only. However, this finding is extremely weak, due to the fact that there is only one case of incarceration on "third plus" in each of those groups.

Table 5.1 undercuts the narrative of undue strictness. First, the incarceration rates are low to moderate across age groups and across charges of third only *and* third plus. Second, the average sentences, particularly for third only, are also light to moderate. Defendants in the older age groups charged with third plus received sentences that average slightly above the midpoint of what the third-degree statute allows. But even there, the incarceration rate is fairly low. Forty-seven of the 136 defendants convicted in these two age groups received sentences averaging 3 and 4 years. But 27 of the 47 defendants in the two oldest age categories disposed as guilty on "third plus" (15 of whom were also charged with rape or child molestation) were not sentenced to prison on third-degree charges.

## MULTIVARIATE ANALYSIS

Multivariate analysis provides a rigorous way of testing the kinds of observations provided by the descriptive statistics. We used multivariate OLS and logistic regression to assess the impact of five key independent variables on three separate outcome variables: (1) whether third-degree charges were disposed or dismissed, (2) whether the defendant in a case where third-degree charges were disposed received jail time on those charges, and (3) the length of the jail sentence imposed on third-degree charges. Two categories of independent variables were considered—case characteristics and defendant characteristics. Case characteristics include the year the case was filed, the court where the case was prosecuted, and whether the case was charged as "third only." Defendant characteristics include defendant age and prior criminal history. Various interaction and quadratic effects were also assessed, but were not included in the final models.

Detailed descriptions of these variables can be found in Appendix C.

For the disposition model, all cases for which disposition was recorded are included ($n = 386$). To simplify the problem of parsing sentence outcomes for defendants disposed on "third plus," sentencing outcomes are considered only for cases disposed on third-degree sexual assault charges alone ($n = 238$). Two statistical techniques were used for multivariate analyses. On the first two questions (disposition and incarceration), logistic regression was used since the outcome variables are binary. On the third question (length of sentence), OLS regression was used since the outcome variable is continuous. The three models have the same independent variables, although the age variable is formulated slightly differently in the OLS model. Tables 5.2–5.4 below give detailed results of the three models, including coefficients and adjusted $R^2$ values for OLS and coefficients, odds ratios, percentage-point impact (the computed risk difference of 0 or 1 for binary variables or an increase of one unit for continuous variables), percentage correctly predicted, –2 log likelihood, and pseudo-$R^2$ for logistic regression. All three models were highly statistically significant.

### *Model One: Disposition on Statutory Rape Charges*

The only variables that proved statistically significant in this model are Years

**Table 5.2** Disposition on Statutory Rape Charges ($n = 386$)—Logit Regression

| *Variable* | *Coefficient* | *Odds Ratio [Exp(B)]* | *Percentage Point Impact* |
|---|---|---|---|
| Constant | 0.617 | 1.853 | |
| Year | | | |
| 1985–1989 | 0.334 | 1.396 | 5.2 |
| 1990–1993 | 0.373 | 1.452 | 5.6 |
| 1994–1998 | 1.054** | 2.869 | 14.9 |
| 1999–2002 | — | — | — |
| Court | | | |
| Kent County | 0.114 | 1.121 | 1.8 |
| Newport County | — | — | — |
| Providence County | –0.533 | 0.587 | –8.4 |
| Washington County | 0.415 | 1.514 | 6.2 |
| Charged as Third Only | 0.941*** | 2.562 | 15.9 |
| Defendant Age | –0.003 | 0.997 | –0.05 |
| Prior Criminal History | 0.031 | 1.032 | 0.5 |
| Pseudo $R^2$ | 0.084 | 0.084 | |
| % Cases Predicted | 77.2 | 77.2 | |
| –2 Log Likelihood | 380.574 | 380.574 | |

*Significant at $p < 0.10$
**Significant at $p < 0.05$
***Significant at $p < 0.01$
****Significant at $p < 0.001$

1994–1998 and Charged as Third Only. The other three year dummies were not statistically significant, so this is not a particularly strong finding. However, the large and highly significant coefficient for Charged as Third Only is relevant. According to the percentage-point impacts reported in Table 5.2, the probability of conviction on statutory rape charges is almost 16% greater for those charged with statutory rape alone, as compared to those charged with statutory rape in addition to other crimes. Clearly, whether defendants are convicted on statutory rape charges is determined in no small part by the outcome of other charges in the case. At the very least, this suggests that the court system does not assess these charges as distinct from other charges, which is a significant finding. It has important implications for criminal justice studies that do not acknowledge this confounding effect.

There are many possible explanations for this result in cases disposed on multiple charges, but they are impossible to assess statistically as they occur at the level of court practices on individual cases. It is likely that in some cases statutory rape charges are seen as minor included charges where the fact pattern would more appropriately lead to child molestation or sexual assault charges, which could lead to these charges being dropped in plea bargain agreements on more serious charges, or vice versa. Based on descriptive statistics, in some cases it appears that statutory rape charges are dropped and the defendant convicted of a non-sex-related offense. This could be due to an inclination on the part of prosecutors and judges to exercise leniency on this crime, since it is considered fairly minor but, due to sex offender registration laws (commonly known as Megan's Law), it carries heavy penalties unrelated to criminal sentencing. Regardless, again, these are only descriptive theories—no systematic analysis of the root causes of this pattern is possible.

### *Model 2: Incarceration on Statutory Rape Charges*

Two key significant variables in this model are Defendant Age and Prior Criminal History, and both have positive coefficients. This demonstrates that older defendants and those with prior offenses are more likely to be incarcerated when convicted of third-degree only. This finding is consistent with the sentencing benchmarks on defendant age. On the other hand, the model coefficients indicate that criminal history category has an equal to slightly larger impact than does defendant age, which is not appropriate under the sentencing benchmarks on defendant age. According to the percentage-point impacts for Defendant Age and Prior Criminal History reported on Table 5.3, an increase of one criminal history category (on a scale of 1–6) is equivalent to being 13 years older, holding all else constant. Since prior record is not one of the factors mentioned in the Rhode Island sentencing benchmarks, this finding is striking. Finally, the coefficient for 1990–1993 confirms our descriptive finding that Rhode Island courts treated this crime much more lightly during the early 1990s than at other times over the 17-year period studied, particularly in terms of incarceration. However, this variable was significant only at the 10% level. Notably, incarceration rates in the late 1990s were not statistically different from the late 1980s, even though in 1996 the U.S. Congress urged the states to take statutory rape more seriously. There is no evidence for an increase in concern about these cases (in terms of incarceration) in the late 1990s, as has been asserted by supporters of the undue strictness argument.

### *Model 3: Prison Time on Statutory Rape Charges*

Two significant determinants of the length of jail sentences received on statutory rape

**Table 5.3** Incarceration on Statutory Rape Charges ($n = 238$)—Logit Regression

| *Variable* | *Coefficient* | *Odds Ratio [Exp(B)]* | *Percentage Point Impact* |
|---|---|---|---|
| Constant | −3.782**** | 0.023 | |
| Year | | | |
| 1985–1989 | 0.464 | 1.590 | 6.5 |
| 1990–1993 | −2.209* | 0.110 | −17.4 |
| 1994–1998 | 0.126 | 1.134 | 1.6 |
| 1999–2002 | — | — | — |
| Court | | | |
| Kent County | 0.202 | 1.224 | 2.7 |
| Newport County | — | — | — |
| Providence County | 0.449 | 1.567 | 5.6 |
| Washington County | 0.417 | 1.518 | 5.8 |
| Charged as Third Only | −0.261 | 0.770 | −0.04 |
| Defendant Age | 0.041** | 1.042 | 0.5 |
| Prior Criminal History | 0.634**** | 1.886 | 6.5 |
| Pseudo $R^2$ | 0.164 | 0.164 | |
| % Cases Predicted | 83.2 | 83.2 | |
| −2 Log Likelihood | 196.715 | 196.715 | |

*Significant at $p < 0.10$
**Significant at $p < 0.05$
***Significant at $p < 0.01$
****Significant at $p < 0.001$

charges are Charged as Third Only and Defendant Age. The coefficients on defendant age suggest that teenage offenders receive significantly lighter jail sentences on average than defendants in each other age category, in the range of 2–2.5 years less. This finding is affirmed by comparing the two Coefficient columns in Table 5.4 (Model 1 and Model 2). Although original charges do not appear relevant in our incarceration model, as illustrated above, they are significant in terms of sentence length. Defendants charged with "third only" receive roughly 1.5 years shorter sentences on third-degree charges than do defendants charged with "third plus," even if they are disposed on "third only." This suggests that judges are inclined to give longer sentences to those who were originally charged with other (usually more serious) crimes than to defendants charged with statutory rape alone.

## *Multivariate Conclusions*

Each of the three models above provides useful information about what case characteristics and defendant characteristics do and do not impact disposition and sentencing outcomes in statutory rape cases. In general, we conclude that court jurisdiction (by county) has no effect on outcomes, and that case filing year does not have the large and systematic effect suggested by our earlier descriptive analysis. The defendant's age exerts large and significant effects on sentencing apart from the impact of prior criminal history. Prior criminal history has mixed effects—it significantly impacts incarceration,

**Table 5.4** Prison Time on Statutory Rape Charges in Days ($n = 238$)—OLS Regression

| *Variable* | *Coefficient (Model 1)* | *Coefficient (Model 2)* |
|---|---|---|
| Constant | –108.429 | 489.795 |
| Year | | |
| 1985–1989 | 462.727* | 462.727* |
| 1990–1993 | 261.223 | 261.223 |
| 1994–1998 | 147.874 | 147.874 |
| 1999–2002 | — | — |
| Court | | |
| Kent County | 894.825 | 894.825 |
| Newport County | — | — |
| Providence County | 275.747 | 275.747 |
| Washington County | 306.921 | 306.921 |
| Charged as Third Only | –551.200** | –551.200** |
| Defendant Age | | |
| 18–19 | — | –598.224** |
| 20–24 | 607.434** | 9.210 |
| 25–34 | 833.797** | 235.573 |
| 35+ | 598.224** | — |
| Prior Criminal History | 30.972 | 30.972 |
| Adjusted $R^2$ | 0.221 | 0.221 |

*Significant at $p < 0.10$
**Significant at $p < 0.05$
***Significant at $p < 0.01$
****Significant at $p < 0.001$

but not sentence length. The large impact of Charged as Third Only on disposition and sentence length is a highly significant finding and may be a cause of concern for court officials and criminal justice advocates and indicate directions for future research.

## CONTEXTUAL DATA

The electronic court docket contains information about charges, case processing, and disposition, but it contains virtually no contextual information beyond the defendant's date of birth. Neither the story of undue strictness nor the story of undue leniency can be assessed solely on the basis of such information. Contextual information must be obtained in order to characterize the nature of the relationship between the parties and examine important factual questions surrounding consent (or *assent,* since minors are by definition unable legally to consent).

The contextual data for this study were obtained from two sources: court files and police reports. We attempted to examine the court file for every case filed from 1997–2002. Some case files contained significant contextual information, others contained almost nothing, and a small number were simply impossible to access for one reason or another. We sought to supplement the information from court files by requesting police reports from the arresting agency. This was a cumbersome task and it sometimes produced extremely limited information because police departments blacked out far more information than is justified by the state's open records act. We requested reports in every case where the court file was unavailable or contained no information. We also requested police reports for all cases ($n = 47$) covering two specific populations of defendants: the youngest (ages 18 and 19) and oldest (35 and over) defendants, disposed on statutory rape charges only.

## *Overall (1997–2002)*

Based on a case review of the 158 cases filed between 1997 and 2002, we can draw some conclusions about the gender of offenders and victims and, to some extent, characteristics about their relationships. Race data was not available. At least some information was obtained in 157 of the 158 cases. But more detailed factual information was only available in the minority of cases with more intensive research.

Although nominally gender-neutral, statutory rape is still widely conceived of as involving predatory men and young girls. For example, the American Bar Association's 1997 report on statutory rape was titled "*Sexual Relationships Between Adult Males and Young Teen Girls.*" The contextual evidence from Rhode Island largely supports that view. Offenders were overwhelmingly male, and victims were overwhelmingly female. In the 157 cases surveyed, only six offenders were female, or 3.8%. In the 117 cases where victim gender could be identified, only 13 victims were male (11.1%). There were 10 cases with a male victim and a male offender, and 2 cases with a female victim and a female offender. The relatively high proportion of same-sex involvements charged may reflect the process by which otherwise consensual relationships become criminal—namely, if the minor victim's parents disapprove. However, with such a small number of cases there is no way to determine what pattern, if any, differentiates same-sex from opposite-sex statutory rape cases, either in case characteristics or case outcomes. Notably, 39% of the victims in Walsh and Wolak's (2004) study of Internet-related statutory rape cases were male. It remains to be seen whether Internet-related sex crimes have a substantially higher proportion of male victims, or whether the proportion of males is just more accurately reflected in Internet-related crimes.

Some characterization of the nature of the relationship was possible in 88 cases. In 62% of these, the relationship is described in the case files as "dating" (n = 54). This characterization is too broad, however—one of these cases, for example, involved a pimp and an underage prostitute who reported that they were in a "dating" relationship. In 14 cases (16.1%), the relationship was described as friend or acquaintance. In 15 cases (17.2%), the victim and the offender had just met, i.e., had not previously had a relationship of any kind. The remaining five cases involved family members or authority figures—two were family members (an uncle and a cousin), two were school officials (a teacher and a school principal), and one was a priest.

Finally, more extensive contextual information on the relationship between offender and victim was obtained in 56 cases. The information gathered shows little that can be aggregated, because the types of relationships are so varied and complex. In some cases the victim and the offender were apparently in happy committed relationships; in others there was a cycle of domestic abuse. In some cases the victim and the offender had met only that day; in other cases they had known each other for years. Some relationships were reported to the police by the victims' parents, some by the victims themselves, and some were filed in connection to other crimes. All we can conclude, again, is that there is a great degree of variation in the fact patterns that lead to charging on this offense, but that many situations do not fit the "young lovers" pattern.

### *Teenage Defendants*

The 18- and 19-year-old defendants are the ones most likely to fit Levine's description of "young lovers" star-crossed by the criminal justice system. Indeed, given the definition of statutory rape in Rhode Island, a defendant could be just days over 18 years old and the "victim" could be just days under 16. The two parties could attend high school together, suggesting far less of the power imbalance and abuse of trust that characterizes the model of statutory rape as "predatory" adults taking advantage of young teens. There were thirty-three 18- and 19-year-old defendants charged with third-degree sexual assault in Rhode Island between 1997 and 2002. Ten of those cases included other charges, while the remaining twenty-three cases were "third only." Teenage defendants were more likely to be charged on "third only" (71%, compared to 59% for the sample as a whole). Teenage defendants charged with "third plus" were only half as likely to be charged with sexual assault (9%, compared to 18% for the sample as a whole) or child molestation (7%, compared to 13% for the sample as a whole). So this group of young defendants appears, at least at first blush, to involve less serious cases than the overall universe of statutory rape cases, and accordingly may well be appropriate for non-incarceration outcomes. These cases may legitimately raise questions about the possible overzealousness of prosecutors.

The "third plus" cases, however, do not raise these issues. To the contrary, the nature of the offense in these cases appears to be very serious. In seven of these ten third-plus cases, the "other" charges were much more serious sex crimes—either first-degree sexual assault ($n = 4$) and/or child molestation ($n = 3$). These cases suggest something much different than "consensual sex." The former involve charges of force or coercion, the atter involve sexual activity while the victim was 13 years old or younger and could not possibly have assented in any meaningful way.

However serious the third-plus charges, the teenage defendants with these charges were *not* treated harshly by the criminal justice system. All 10 of these cases were disposed on third-degree only, meaning that the other (often more serious) charges were dismissed. Seven of those defendants avoided prison entirely. This is surprising since 5 of the 10 cases involved more serious sexual assault charges as well. Two of the three teenage defendants originally charged with child molestation received prison sentences on third-degree charges. One was sentenced to 3 months (*State v. Mayo,* 2000), the other to 8 months (*State v. Parenteau,* 2001). The other teenage defendant receiving a prison sentence was a 19-year-old male who gave a venereal disease to a 14-year-old girl in what she described as consensual sex. The girl's mother had warned the man away in the past. The other charge in this case, drug possession, was dropped and the defendant pled guilty to third-degree sexual assault only. He received a 4-month sentence (*State v. Natal,* 2001). The defendant had been convicted on four prior charges of breaking and entering, resulting in a surprisingly high prior-record score for a 19-year-old, which may explain his prison sentence.

The 23 teenage defendants charged with "third only" are the most likely to bear out the "young love" vision of statutory rape cases. Not only are these defendants close in age to their victims, but none of them was charged with anything else that would suggest a more coercive fact pattern than statutory rape. Six of these twenty-three cases were dismissed (26%)—a dismissal rate twice as high as the overall dismissal rate among cases with any third-degree charges from 1985 through 2002. Obviously, the dismissed cases do not represent prosecutorial overzealousness. To the contrary, high rates of dismissal raise questions of undue leniency. One of the cases has since been expunged, and no additional information is available. Information on the five others, however, indicates that only one of the cases was described as consensual dating. In two cases, the victim described the defendant as an acquaintance, but no additional information was available. Another case involved two defendants, ages 18 and 19, who assaulted two girls (ages 14 and 15) at a house party (*State v. Kiselica,* 1999). One of the girls was a German foreign exchange student who would be returning home shortly. There is no indication in the public record of why the case was dismissed. An informed guess is the girl who lived in Rhode Island was considered to be a poor witness, or that the facts were deemed undesirable since there were, in all likelihood, drugs and alcohol at the house party. Nevertheless, a case that began with charges of force and coercion ended with a third-degree plea and no time served.

The most likely explanation for the other cases being dismissed is that the "victim" was uncooperative. Even a few of the cases that were carried forward contain clear evidence of reticence by the adolescent "victim." In one dismissed case, a 14-year-old girl was brought to state police barracks to make a statement about having sex with an 18-year-old in a car parked near her house. The responding officer noted that the girl "was reluctant to give the statement and would not elaborate on a lot of the activity that I believe has occurred between the two" (Incident Report, Westerly Police Dept., 2001, p. 2). It is not surprising that this case was dismissed. It seems logical to extrapolate that, if cases are dismissed when the adolescent is reluctant, many of the cases actually carried forward would *not* involve "young lovers,"—at least not young lovers who are still romantically involved at the time of prosecution.

There were 17 cases between 1997 and 2002 in which a teenage defendant was convicted of "third only". This yields an average of three cases per year, in a state with a population of twenty to twenty-five thousand 14- and 15-year-olds during any given year. It is difficult to reconcile these low numbers with the claim that authorities are on the rampage to prosecute such cases. Moreover, it is impossible to reconcile the success of these defendants in avoiding incarceration with the claim that the justice system is hungry to impose long sentences in these situations. All seventeen of these 18- and 19-year-old defendants pled guilty. One was sentenced to home confinement for a year; another was sent to prison on a separate case involving sexual assault charges against a different teenager. The other 15 received suspended sentences or probation. Punishments on these charges, which could have resulted in 5-year prison terms, can only be characterized as minimal. Whether minimal punishment is considered appropriate, however, still turns on the facts of the relationship. If those cases had involved "young lovers" barely more than 2 years apart, then the relative lack of punishment is arguably appropriate. If, on the other hand, those cases were seen as more predatory in nature, then the lack of punishment seems overly lenient.

The available case file review data suggest that at least half of these cases involve much more serious situations than consensual dating. Defendants in only four of the seventeen cases reviewed were described with terms akin to "boyfriend." And in three of those four cases—where there was more than minimal information available—there were allegations of threats and violence beyond the sexual activity. In one case, a pregnant

15-year-old reported that she had been dating the defendant for 1 year. She filed a complaint after the defendant "called and threatened to kill her." The defendant pled *nolo contendre* to "third only" and received a year of home confinement (*State v. Cramer,* 1998). In a similar case, a 15-year-old Hmong girl moved in with an 18-year-old male whom she had been dating for a year and intended to marry. She filed a criminal complaint when he "began assaulting her repeatedly." The man pled *nolo contendre* to third only and received a deferred sentence *(State v. Ly,* 1997). Such threats and violence are the kinds of aggravating factors that under the Rhode Island sentencing benchmarks should result in prison time, but none of these defendants was sentenced to jail.

Six of the remaining cases are specifically described as nonconsensual. In one case, for example, a 14-year-old girl describes her encounter with a 19-year-old acquaintance who took her to a party in a motel room in East Providence (*State v. Domingues,* 2000). Her statement to the police describes "stopping him and saying she didn't want to do anything else" at one point and "asking him to stop" again later. The incident was classified as third-degree sexual assault because, according to the girls' stepmother, "[the victim] didn't feel she could call the assault a rape because she didn't scream or fight off [the defendant]" (Arrest Report, East Providence Police Dept., 1999). The defendant reached a plea agreement and avoided any prison time. In a similar case, a 15-year-old girl was supposed to meet a male acquaintance from school and his friend (*State v. Shloul,* 2001). Only the friend, whom the girl did not previously know, showed up. He drove her to a marina and persistently asked her to have sex. She declined, informing him that she had a boyfriend. He eventually said he would take her home only if she had sex first. She "agreed," but told the police the next day that she "was afraid and almost started to cry" (Police Narrative, Pawtucket Police Dept., 2001, p. 1). The defendant pled guilty to third-degree only and received a suspended sentence.

Four other cases involving acquaintances all resulted in plea agreements without any prison time. In two, consent was questionable given the available information. The remaining cases appear to be consensual. Indeed, several are quite clear in describing the encounter as willing. However, in none of these cases is the defendant actually described as a boyfriend. Rather, all are described as acquaintances—sometimes very recent acquaintances. Were there a social hysteria about adults engaging in sex with promiscuous underage girls, these would be cases ripe for punishment. Many involve parties who met that day. But none of these defendants received any prison time; they all entered into plea agreements.

In sum, the number of teenage defendants charged with third only is so small that it is impossible to conclude that social hysteria or overzealous prosecutors explain these cases. However, few, if any, of the cases brought fit Levine's description of "young lovers" committing nothing more than a "crime of passion." Many involved violence; many others involved more serious sexual assault charges. Yet, even so, this group of defendants was treated with remarkable leniency. Only 11% of the cases with teenage defendants disposed as guilty actually resulted in incarceration. The average sentence was 9 months.

### *The Oldest Defendants*

The other subset of cases that we examined contextually involved defendants 35 and older. Given the enormous age difference between the defendant and the victim, these are the cases where the Rhode Island sentencing benchmarks most clearly call for a prison sentence. Regardless, one would expect the strictest punishments in cases where the defendant was at least 20 years older than the adolescent, since these cases seem most exploitative by definition.

The 5-year contextual sample (1997–2002) includes 14 cases with defendants 35 years old and over who were charged with third degree and disposed on "third only." Again, the police reports and court files in these cases are uneven, but there is sufficient information to ascertain something about the nature of the relationship in 13 of the 14 cases. The relationship between the parties in these cases varied. None are intrafamilial, although one is close. Most of the defendants were acquaintances of some sort: three were the father of a friend, one was the complainant's father's brother-in-law, one was the complainant's pastor, and another was the complainant's judo instructor. Three others were general acquaintances. The parties in two cases met that day—one over the Internet, the other in a telephone chat room. The parties in two other cases were strangers who met at a house party.

All of these defendants pled guilty. Only five, however, were sentenced to prison. Two of those received multi-year sentences, with more severe charges dropped at the time of disposition. A 37-year-old man, charged with second-degree child molestation of his friend's 14-year-old daughter, received a 4-year sentence in a plea agreement on statutory rape charges only (*State v. Fortin*, 2000). A 46-year old man, charged with first-degree sexual assault of a 15-year-old girl, received a 3-year sentence in a plea agreement on third-degree charges (*State v. Cook*, 2001). The other three defendants in this subgroup who received prison time were sentenced to 15 months, 6 months, and 45 days, respectively. The 15-month sentence was given to the 38-year-old pastor of a small church whose victim was a 15-year-old congregant (*State v. Barchiesi*, 1999). Far from being strict, this punishment is surprisingly lenient for a case involving a significant breach of trust and an enormous age difference. No details are available on the case with the 6-month sentence—court clerks were unable to locate the file after repeated requests. But we do know that the defendant had six prior convictions on breaking and entering charges, making him a prime candidate for a prison sentence (*State v. Frisby*, 1998). The final case, which resulted in a 45-day-sentence, involved a 42-year-old defendant. No other details about the case are contained in the "incident narrative" provided by the police (Uniform Report, Providence Police Dept., 1999, p.1). The defendant was convicted in a jury trial, but clerks at superior court and the state archives were unable to locate the transcript after repeated requests.

Nearly two-thirds of the defendants who were 35 or older avoided prison entirely. According to case file review, three of these nine cases were described as non-consensual and two others were borderline. Several others are impossible to assess because the police reports were almost entirely blacked out. In one case, a 36-year-old man lured a 14-year-old boy off the street to play video games in his apartment. He assaulted and threatened the boy, who disclosed the abuse immediately. It appears that the case could have been charged as first- or second-degree sexual assault (Witness Statement, Pawtucket Police Dept., 2002a), but it was resolved on third-degree charges through a plea agreement with no time to serve. The second case involved a 40-year-old man who had sexual contact with a girl who was dating his 18-year-old son. The man apparently had sexual contact with that girl and her friend, both of whom were known to the Department of Children, Youth and Families (Narrative Statement, Warwick Police Dept., 2002, p.1). According to the police report, the abuse began when the complainant was thirteen and a half, so the case could have been charged as first-degree child molestation. The warrant listed that charge, but the Grand Jury indictment was for nine counts of third-degree sexual assault. The case was resolved with no time to serve.

The third case described as non-consensual involved a 45-year-old man who "let" runaways stay at his apartment in exchange for sex. One victim told the police that the defendant had said, "This is what's gonna happen, your [sic] gonna have sex with me and then I'll let you stay here with me" (Witness Statement, Pawtucket Police Dept., 2002b, p. 2). The man was also known to pay teenage girls for sex, to provide them with drugs of various sorts, and, on occasion, to threaten them. Three different girls were implicated in the police report in this case, which came about when one of the girls was suicidal and made threats against the defendant from the hospital. The man pled guilty to third-degree charges and did not serve time.

The files in two other cases contain troubling statements about the issue of consent. One involved a 35-year-old man who exposed himself to two 14-year-old girls in his garage and eventually had sexual contact with one of them. According to the police report, the girl "told him to stop" but he did not. As the police characterized it, "at least initially, vic. was a willing participant" (Incident Report, Westerly Police Dept. 1997, p. 2). The defendant pled *nolo contendre* and received a 4-year suspended sentence and probation. The other case began in a telephone chat room and resembles the popular notion of the Internet predator. A 37-year-old man, who portrayed himself as 27, struck up a conversation with a 14-year-old girl. Enticing her with the promise of a job, the defendant picked her up in his car. He took her to a remote area and sexually assaulted her. The girl reported having objected (Witness Statement, East Providence Police Dept., 2001, p. 1). The man took her home, gave her $40 and told her not to tell anyone. This would seem to be a prime candidate for the maximum sentence under the sentencing benchmarks, since there was a 23-year age gap between the parties and the girl was lured through deception. The case ended with a plea agreement that involved no time to serve.

There were three cases in this subset in which court documents identify the complainant as a "willing participant." One involves a 38-year-old man who was living with his brother-in-law and initiated sexual relations with his 15-year-old daughter. The defendant continued to profess his love for the girl in letters from prison, where he was held before trial. The case was originally charged as "indecent assault on a child." The defendant pled *nolo contendre* to third only and received a deferred sentence (*State v. St. Nelus,* 1998). The second case involved a 36-year-old man who was friends with the father of a 14-year-old girl. The girl described the acts as consensual and affirmed that "at no time did [the defendant] force or coerce her into cooperating" (Officer's Narrative Report, Pawtucket Police Dept., 1999, p. 1). The report also indicates that the defendant told the girl "several times that he could go to jail if anyone found out." Instead, he pled *nolo contendre* to third-degree sexual assault and received 5 years of probation. The third case was the only one in this group where the complainant used the word "boyfriend" to describe the defendant. The complainant, brought in by her parents, was a 15-year-old girl from an affluent suburb. The defendant was her 39-year-old judo teacher. The girl became suicidal when her parents found out about the relationship. The case hardly fits Levine's "crimes of passion" narrative, though. The adult in this case was almost 25 years older than the girl and he was in a position of trust and authority. This defendant would also appear to be a prime candidate for a severe sentence under the sentencing benchmarks. He pled guilty and received a suspended sentence (*State v. White,* 2001).

Without going beyond the public record and interviewing multiple parties, it is impossible to ascertain why the results in these cases were so lenient. All are prime candidates for jail time under the sentencing benchmarks. Perhaps the complainant was not seen as a good witness; perhaps the complainant became less cooperative over time. A victim's advocate in Rhode Island commented recently that cases that begin with a parent bringing his or her child to the police station sometimes unravel when time has passed and the young person's willingness to cooperate wanes. Whatever the reason, the fact that most defendants 35 years old and over avoided prison certainly undercuts the claim of overreaction. Indeed, it provides surprising evidence of leniency.

## CONCLUSIONS

The analysis of statutory rape cases in Rhode Island presented in this chapter has significant implications for researchers, child welfare advocates, and practitioners in the criminal justice system. We found significant evidence to contradict claims of "overreaction" to adult–adolescent sexual contact in the courts—in contrast, our analysis lends substantial support to the view that statutory rape cases are treated with undue leniency. However, it is clear that further studies are needed to contextualize and scrutinize these results.

### *The "Overreaction" Claim Is Not Supported*

Rhode Island's statutory rape caseload has been light, and few cases that have gone forward have resulted in outcomes that could be deemed severe. Very few cases involved anything close to the archetypal portrayal of statutory rape cases as criminalizing "young love." Of the subset of cases in the 6-year contextual sample described as boyfriend–girlfriend or dating, only a handful (less than 10%) resulted in incarceration, and many of those appeared to involve threats or violence. A surprisingly large portion of defendants in statutory rape cases were 35 and older. While the multiple regression analysis shows that age difference is a significant factor in predicting disposition and sentence outcomes, the effect of age is not overwhelmingly strong. In fact, prior record has a marginally larger effect on sentence length than does the age difference between the defendant and victim. While defendant age does help predict case outcomes, dismissal rates were high and sentences were frequently lenient even for the oldest defendants. Although defendants 35 and over were more likely to be incarcerated than defendants in any other age group, the majority of defendants in this age group avoided prison entirely. Defendants in the other age groups were treated even more leniently.

Of course, these conclusions derive entirely from a single U.S. state, and it is unclear how representative the findings are of other jurisdictions. One recent point of comparison is provided by Walsh and Wolak's (2004) study of Internet-related sex crimes with adolescent victims. Based on reports from the National Juvenile Online Victimization (N-JOV) Study, Walsh and Wolak found that teenage defendants constituted 39% of the cases in 2000–2001—a much higher rate than the 21% reported in this study. Moreover, they report an incarceration rate of 85%, with one in five defendants receiving sentences of over 10 years. In the current study, not one of the defendants was sentenced to even 10 years on statutory rape charges. More significantly, the overall incarceration rate for defendants disposed as guilty on third only was only 20.2%, drastically lower than the N-JOV results. Perhaps Rhode Island is significantly more lenient than other jurisdictions. Then again, the N-JOV respondents may disproportionately represent cases with the most severe results.

### *The Argument for "Underreaction" Deserves More Attention*

In a state with approximately 25,000 teenagers who are 14 or 15 years old in any given year, we found an average of 22 statutory rape cases filed per year. Although there are no reliable estimates of the incidence of sexual contact between adults and 14- and 15-year-old adolescents, Leitenberg and Saltzman (2000) specifically examined age differences between partners at first intercourse. They found that 31% of 14- and 15-year-olds were sexually active and that 12% of 13- to 15-year-olds had their first sexual experience with a "much older" partner. Applying those percentages directly to Rhode Island's population of 14- and 15-year-olds suggests that in each year there are roughly 930 first sexual experiences that are apparently in violation of the law. Of course, this rough estimate neglects those who are already sexually active, and including them would undoubtedly raise this number into the thousands. Yet, even using this underestimation, less than 1% of sexual involvements between adults and 14- and 15-years-olds are filed each year as criminal cases.

In addition, in terms of filing and prosecution, we see a trend toward lenience and little evidence of prosecutorial overzealousness. The number of cases has gone up only marginally over time, the increase has not been linear, and it did not go up markedly after Congress's admonition in 1996. But more striking than the analysis of caseloads are our findings regarding lenience in cases that reach the courts. Of the relatively few cases that get filed, most involve claims that appear to justify more serious charges—sometimes for overt rape, other times for threats and violence. Thus, it appears that many cases brought under Rhode Island's statutory rape statute might be more properly charged and disposed as more serious crimes. Statutory rape frequently appears to be a catch-all lesser included charge or substitute for other, more serious sex offenses.

## DIRECTIONS FOR FUTURE RESEARCH

This study's limitations suggest at least four avenues for future research. First, there is a clear need for more state studies. It is difficult to know how to place any state into a national context without more information for comparison. Statutory provisions say little about how a given law is enforced, and enforcement is vital to our understanding and analysis of any criminal statute. The few states that allow for life in prison for statutory rape, for example, might actually have lenient sentencing patterns like those in Rhode Island.

Second, there is a need for studies that more comprehensively examine the permutations of charging patterns and plea agreements. Two years of data under Rhode Island's new data system reveal that a sizable number of cases are charged as third-degree sexual assault and disposed on lesser, non–sex-crimes charges. Those defendants escape the reach of sex offender registration laws, and to date, the scrutiny of criminal justice studies. Further, although dispositions of third-degree charges are intricately linked to other charges in a given case, those additional charges often escape scholarly analysis in studies focused on a single crime.

Third, there is a need to carefully consider conceptualizations of "unwantedness" of sexual activity in reference to contextual data in sex crimes cases. As Abma, Driscoll, and Moore (1998, p.16) noted, "A dichotomy of voluntary versus involuntary is insufficient to capture the meaning" of early sexual experiences. There is a clear need for court-based studies that apply a richer conceptualization of "voluntary" and "involuntary" sexual encounters, especially since those who criticize statutory rape laws often do so in the name of "free will." Complex (and sometimes even contradictory) definitions of consent and wantedness in sex crimes statutes magnify the need for such close analysis.

Fourth, there is a need for studies that consider the early stages of an offense and prosecution. Specifically, these studies should examine not only how cases are disposed and sentenced, but how many incidences become reports and how reports become cases. Numerous studies exist on one side of case filing or the other, but analyses of the full process from incident report to sentencing is rare. The current study, like many criminal justice studies, begins with formal cases and focuses on cases disposed on a particular charge such as statutory rape. There is a clear need to connect the two halves of the criminal justice system in statutory rape cases. This additional insight will allow us to better understand reporting mechanisms and the various ways in which reports fail to become cases, or cases are dismissed or pled out to lesser charges. Such inquiry may uncover an even vaster world of underreaction to statutory rape. Some additional evidence of underreaction, if found, would undoubtedly be considered appropriate, as states like Rhode Island have drawn their statutes narrowly. But deeper research may well uncover more of the type of egregious cases documented in this study, where even enormous age differences; sexual contacts involving violence, force, or coercion; and sexual relationships that began while the victim was still under 14 resulted in no real punishment.

## APPENDICES

### *Appendix A—Methodology*

Data were drawn primarily from a download of the Rhode Island state court Banner database, the court's internal record-keeping system. The Banner database contains full case information, including disposition and sentencing, for all cases in Rhode Island district and superior courts for January 1985 through December 2002. Due to space limitations, methodological details cannot be included in this text. However, the complete methodological appendix is available online at http://www.brown.edu/PublicPolicy/webdocs

### *Appendix B—Note on Sentence Length in Third-Plus Cases*

The longer sentences on third-degree charges for defendants convicted of third degree plus other charges reflects the fact that although sentences are recorded for each charge separately, the sentences are almost always interrelated. For example, in a case where a defendant is convicted of third degree plus a more serious charge, the defendant might be more likely to receive concurrent "time to serve" on the lesser charge of third degree than he or she would be to receive time to serve if convicted of third degree alone, even if the two charges are factually unrelated (for example, statutory rape and a drug charge). This also translates to sentence length—if a defendant is sentenced to 5 years or more on a more serious charge, he or she will often be sentenced to 5 years to serve concurrently on the third-degree charge, again, even if the two charges are factually unrelated. This could be viewed as simply an idiosyncrasy in the Rhode Island sentencing system, but it does make it difficult to parse the patterns of disposition and sentencing on lesser included offenses when defendants are disposed on multiple charges.

## *Appendix C—Coding of Key Variables for Multivariate Analysis*

### *Case Characteristics*

**Case Filing Year**—Based on the assessment of variation through time observed using descriptive statistics (and outlined above), 4-year dummies were created: 1985–1989, 1990–1993, 1994–1998, and 1999–2002. The 1999–2002 dummy was not included in the models.

**Court**—Court dummies for the four counties in Rhode Island were included. The county dummies include district and superior court cases in the relevant county. These variables are Kent, Newport, Providence, and Washington. The Newport County dummy was not included in the models.

**Charged as Third Only**—A binary dummy variable for whether the defendant was originally charged with statutory rape only, as opposed to statutory rape in addition to other charges, was included.

### *Defendant Characteristics*

**Defendant Age**—The age of the defendant was included in each model. In the logit regressions, a continuous variable of age was used. In the OLS regression, age dummies were used. These dummies were coded (based on descriptive stats) as 18–19, 20–24, 25–34, and 35+.

**Prior Severity Category**—Defendants were assigned a prior criminal history score based on federal sentencing criminal history guidelines. Values range from 1 to 6.

### *Other Tested Variables*

A quadratic of defendant age term, an interaction term of prior category and defendant age, and an interaction term of prior category and case filing year were assessed, but none of the three was statistically significant in any model.

## REFERENCES

Abma, J., Driscoll, A., & Moore, K. (1998). Young women's degree of control over first intercourse: An exploratory analysis. *Family Planning Perspectives, 30*(1), 12–18.

Arrest Report. (1999, October 18). Incident No. 99-4879-OF. East Providence [R.I.] Police Dept.

Cassinelli, R. (1993, February 23). N. Kingstown woman pleads no contest to having sex with a 15-year-old boy. *Providence Journal,* p. B8.

Cheit, R. E., & Goldschmidt, E. B. (1997). Child molesters in the criminal justice system: A comprehensive case-flow analysis of the Rhode Island docket (1985–1993). *New England Journal on Criminal and Civil Confinement, 23*(2), 267–299.

Domestic Violence Petition. (1995, March 6). Docket No. 95-DV-111. Manchester District Court, New Hampshire.

Elo, I. T., King, R. B., & Furstenberg, Jr., F. F. (1999). Adolescent females: Their sexual partners and the fathers of their children. *Journal of Marriage and the Family, 61*(1), 74–84.

Elstein, S. G., & Davis, N. S. (1997). *Sexual relationships between adult males and young teen girls: Exploring the legal and social responses.* Chicago: American Bar Association, Center on Children and the Law.

Gunnison, R. B., & Lucas G. (1996, January 9). Wilson seeks school vouchers with a new twist. *San Francisco Chronicle,* p. A1.

Hayward, M., & Meersman, N. (1997, April 18). Fiore has a dark, abusive history. *The Union Leader* (Manchester, NH), p. A1.

Incident Report. (1997a, January 20). Incident No. I9700226. Holliston [N.H.] Police Dept.

Incident Report. (1997, November 25). Incident No. I9715265. Westerly [R.I.] Police Dept.

Incident Report. (2001, September 4). Incident No. I0111040. Westerly [R.I.] Police Dept.

Isquith, P. K., Levine, M., & Scheiner, J. (1993). Blaming the child: Attribution of responsibility to victims of child sexual abuse. In G. S. Goodman & B. L. Bottoms (Eds.), *Child victims, child witnesses: Understanding and improving testimony* (pp. 203–228). New York: The Guilford Press.

Jenny, C. (1999, September 28). Correspondence re *U.S. v. Sacko* to James H. Leavey, Assistant U.S. Attorney, District of Rhode Island.

Kaestle, C. E., Morisky, D. E., & Wiley, D. J. (2002). Sexual intercourse and the age difference between adolescent females and their romantic partners. *Perspectives on Sexual and Reproductive Health, 34*(6), 304–309.

Landry, D. J., & Forrest, J. D. (1995). How old are U.S. fathers? *Family Planning Perspectives, 27*(4), 159–161, 165.

Leitenberg, H., & Saltzman, H. (2000). A statewide survey of age at first intercourse for adolescent females and age of their male partners: Relation to other risk behaviors and statutory rape implications. *Archives of Sexual Behavior*, *29*(3), 203–215.

Levine, J. (2002). *Harmful to minors: The perils of protecting children from sex.* Minneapolis: University of Minnesota Press.

Lindberg, L. D., Sonenstein, F. L., Ku, L., & Martinez, G. (1997). Age differences between minors who give birth and their adult partners. *Family Planning Perspectives, 29*(2), 61–66.

Man gets 1-day suspended term for having sex with girl, 14. (1995, February 15). *Providence Journal,* p. B4.

Meersman, N., Hayward, M., & Rose, D. (1997, April 18). Internet "Romeo" arrested. *The Union Leader* (Manchester, NH), p. A1.

Mider, Z. (2004). Man given 5 years' probation for having sex with 14-year-old. *Providence Journal,* D6.

Miller, H. L., Miller, C. E., Kenney, L., & Clark, J. W. (1998). Issues in statutory rape law enforcement: The views of district attorneys in Kansas. *Family Planning Perspective, 30*(4), 177–182.

Narrative Statement. (2002, June 18). Incident No. 02–4002-OF. Warwick [R.I.] Police Dept.

Officer's Narrative Report. (1999, September 21). Report No. 99–6796-OF/99–3133-AR. Pawtucket [R.I.] Police Dept.

The Personal Responsibility and Work Opportunity Reconciliation Act of 1996, P.L. 104–354, § 906(a) (1996).

Police Narrative. (2001, May 1). Incident No. 01–923-AR. Pawtucket [R.I.] Police Dept.

Rhode Island P.L. 1889, ch. 738.

Rhode Island G.L. 1896, ch. 281.

Rhode Island G.L. 11-37-6.

Rosenbaum, S. I. (2001, March 1). Judges pares his sentences for molester. *Providence Journal,* p. C1.

Sentencing Statement, Keir Fiore. (1997, October 20). U.S. v. Fiore, C.R. 97–66–01-JD. U.S. District Court, District of New Hampshire.

Sentencing Study Commission. (1997, March). *Rhode Island Sentencing Benchmarks*. Rhode Island Bar Journal, XLV, 27–31.

Silveira v. Santos, 490 A.2d 969; 1985 R.I. Lexis 477 (R.I. Supreme Court 1985).

Stapleton, M. A. System should get tougher on statutory rape. *Chicago Daily Law Bulletin* (January 7, 1998): p. 3.

State v. Barchiesi, Providence [R.I.] Superior Court, No. P2-1999-2560A (1999).

State v. Boyle, Providence [R.I.] Superior Court, No. P2-2002-1599A (2002).

State v. Brown, Kent County [R.I.] Superior Court, No. K1-2002-0644A (2002).

State v. Bruno, Providence [R.I.] Superior Court, No. P2-2001-2593A (2001).

State v. Cook, Woonsocket [R.I.] Superior Court, No. W1-2001-0292A (2001).

State v. Cramer, Kent County [R.I.] Superior Court, No. K2-1998-0521A (1998).

State v. Crook, Providence [R.I.] Superior Court, No. P2-1999-3458A (1999).

State v. Domingues, Providence [R.I.] Superior Court, No. P2-2000-0448A (2000).

State v. Edwards, Woonsocket [R.I.] Superior Court, No. W2-1998-0134A (1998).

State v. Fortin, Kent County [R.I.] Superior Court, No. K2-2000-0342A (2000).

State v. Frisby, Providence [R.I.] Superior Court, No. P2-1998-1364A (1998).

State v. Garnes, Providence [R.I.] Superior Court, No. P2–2003-0945A (2003).

State v. Kiselica, Providence [R.I.] District Court, No. 66-1999-11642 (1999).

State v. Ly, Providence [R.I.] Superior Court, No. P1-1997-2242A (1997).

State v. Mayo, Woonsocket [R.I.] Superior Court, No. W1-2000-0420A (2000).

State v. Mulchaney, 762 A.2d 1214; 2000 R.I. Lexis 237 (R.I. Supreme Court 2000).

State v. Natal, Providence [R.I.] Superior Court, No. P2-2001-4118A (2001).

State v. Parenteau, Woonsocket [R.I.] Superior Court, No. W2-2001-0215A (2001).

State v. Parmenter, Providence [R.I.] Superior Court, No. P2-1999-3632A (1999).

State v. Shloul, Providence [R.I.] Superior Court, No. P2-2001-1415A (2001).

State v. St. Nelus, Providence [R.I.] Superior Court, No. P2-1998-3394A (1998).

State v. White, Providence [R.I.] Superior Court, No. P2-2001–0332A (2001).

State v. Yanez, 716 A.2d 759; 1998 R.I. Lexis 273 (R.I. Supreme Court 1998).

Stuart-Smith, S. (1996). Teenage sex: Cognitive immaturity increases the risks. *British Medical Journal, 312*(7028), 390–391.

Tanner J. M. (1962). *Growth at adolescence.* Oxford, UK: Blackwell Scientific.

Taylor, D. J., Chavez, G. F., Adams, E. J., Chabra, A., & Rugmini, S. S. (1999). Demographic characteristics in adult paternity for first births to adolescents under 15 years of age. *Journal of Adolescent Health, 24*(4), 251–258.

Uniform Report, Providence [R.I.] Police Dept., 1999. CCR No. 99-030228 (August 23).

United States v. Sacko, 103 F. Supp. 2d 85; 2000 U.S. Dist. Lexis 9110 (R. I. District Court 2000).

Walsh, W. A., & Wolak, J. (2004). *Nonforcible Internet-related sex crimes with adolescent victims.* Durham: University of New Hampshire, Crimes Against Children Research Center.

Witness Statement. (2001, January 29). Incident No. 01-128-OF. East Providence [R.I.] Police Dept.

Witness Statement. (2002a, April 25). Incident No. 02-2999-OF. Pawtucket [R.I.] Police Dept.

Witness Statement. (2002b, November 24). Incident No. 02–3164-AR. Pawtucket [R.I.] Police Dept.

Yarhouse, M. A. (2004). Book review. *Archives of Sexual Behavior, 33*(3), 312–313.

CHAPTER 6

# *Mitigating the Impact of Publicity on Child Crime Victims and Witnesses*

CHARLES PUTNAM AND DAVID FINKELHOR

Children and adolescents become crime victims at shockingly high rates. They are twice as likely to suffer violent crimes as adults (Hashima & Finkelhor, 1999; Klaus & Rennison, 2002). This disproportion has remained consistent even as overall crime rates have dropped. Children and adolescents are the victims of 75% of the sex offenses that come to police attention (Finkelhor & Ormrod, 2000).

When the perpetrator of a crime against a child is another child, both the victim and the offender are generally shielded from public scrutiny (*Globe Newspaper Co. v. Superior Court,* 1982; Laubenstein, 1995; McLatchey, 1991). As a society, we generally believe that shielding young offenders from public attention promotes their rehabilitation and healthy development. Because criminal proceedings against adult offenders are generally public, when the perpetrator is an adult, which occurs in about half of all reported violent offenses against children, both the victim and the offender are thrown into the public arena. For news organizations, reporting the identity of the victim and the witness increases the story's human interest value. This creates a paradox for children in the justice system: for offenders, proceedings remain confidential in most states, while victims harmed by adults often have no such confidentiality.

Victims' identities are almost always revealed in news stories regarding abductions ("Elizabeth's Journey," 2003; "Kidnapped Pair Safe," 2002) and homicides ("Slain Girl Used Internet to Seek Sex, Police Say," 2002). Although greater privacy is afforded for sex crimes, in some states information about rape victims is public, which some news organizations publicize. Disclosing a rape victim's identity and graphic details of her rape is the subject of ongoing controversy, including when the victim is an adult (Elliott, 1989; Finkelhor, 2003; Gartner, 1991; Hackney, 2003; Magowan, 2003; Roeper, 2002).

While publicizing victims' names may not be the norm for all crimes committed against children, it occurs quite often. The disclosure of victims' identities and the details of the crimes raises legal and ethical issues. From the legal standpoint, how should the law resolve the conflict between children's privacy interests and freedom of the press? From the standpoint of ethics, how can society balance the media's power to promote sympathy and justice for child victims against the danger that it may increase the victim's anxiety and shame and impede the individual's healing? These issues raise the question of whether the legal system could do a better job of protecting young crime victims and witnesses from the potentially adverse impact of becoming the object of media and public scrutiny. Such questions arise in sensational cases but also with routine crimes reported in the local newspaper, where a victim's schoolmates, friends, or neighbors may see it.

Concerns about confidentiality extend to young witnesses as well. Children who witness criminal acts are sometimes required to reveal embarrassing or unflattering personal information in direct testimony or cross-examination. Young witnesses may also be concerned about retaliation or the attention a notorious criminal case may draw. Thus, the confidentiality accorded to juvenile offenders might also benefit juvenile witnesses as well as victims if it were available.

The practice of identifying child victims or witnesses in criminal cases raises many important questions of public and legal policy. How should the law balance the interests of individual crime victims and witnesses against the public's need or desire to know the details of crimes? Should the protections vary depending on the stage of the proceedings? Which crimes raise the specter of public stigma for child victims and witnesses such that they should be protected from public scrutiny? Should victims, young witnesses, and their parents choose whether the children should be identified publicly or should the law presume or forbid that choice? Should the burden be on victims in the first instance to prove that their privacy should be protected, or should the law presume that those interests will be protected and place the burden on parties seeking disclosure of victim and witness identities?

Part I of this chapter describes the effects of publicity on young persons. Part II traces how we shield young offenders, but not young victims or witnesses, from intense scrutiny. Part III outlines various statutory approaches to protecting the privacy interests of child victims and witnesses. Part IV explores whether other potential responses for protecting young witnesses and crime victims such as personal injury lawsuits, systems of applied ethics for journalists, or informal measures would likely be more helpful than statutes in protecting victims' privacy interests and rejects these mechanisms as impractical. Ultimately we conclude that greater and more uniform laws to protect the identities of child victims and witnesses from publicity are warranted.

## IMPACT OF VICTIMIZATION AND PUBLICITY

Crime victimization of a child is a major trauma that poses considerable peril for the child's subsequent development, including increased risks of depression, substance abuse, post-traumatic stress disorder, conduct disorder, delinquency, and additional child and adulthood victimization (Boney-McCoy & Finkelhor, 1995a, 1995b, 1996; Kendall-Tackett, Williams, & Finkelhor, 1993; Kilpatrick, Saunders, & Smith, 2002). Little research has isolated the specific contribution that publicity makes to these problematic outcomes. Nonetheless, many specific theoretical and empirical findings point strongly to their probable negative contribution.

Most models of the serious negative impact of childhood sex offenses posit a major role for stigma or shame in the etiology of subsequent problems (Andrews, 1995; Finkelhor & Browne, 1985). Indeed, victims with greater levels of shame and negative self-perceptions related to the offense tend to be more negatively affected (Mannarino & Cohen, 1996). Victims who recant disclosures made to the authorities or fail to disclose the more embarrassing elements of the episodes often do so because of shame and the realization that a larger audience than the victim originally anticipated will know.

The experience of testifying in criminal cases also provokes anxiety in children (Goodman et al., 1992). Children who experience more intensive cross-examination or are involved in cases that drag on over a longer period of time have higher levels of anxiety and depression than children who lack these experiences. Prosecutors and courts have adopted reforms to minimize these anxieties (Myers, 1994), especially children's concern that their testimony will result in public exposure of embarrassing information.

Reputational issues are very important and sensitive for school children. Negative life events, family circumstances, and sex-related biographical details frequently are the basis for bullying and exclusionary behavior (Ross, 1996). Reputations among school children, once established, are difficult to alter (Jacobs-Sandstrom & Coie, 1999). In addition, young victims and witnesses are more likely than other children to experience subsequent victimization because they are seen as legitimate victims or easy targets.

Thus, publicity may compromise the recovery of juvenile crime victims in several ways. First, the anticipation that people will learn about an embarrassing victimization may increase the victim's anxiety, embarrassment, and shame. This concern depends not just on the number of people who will potentially know, but also on whether specific individuals, such as classmates, relatives, or church members, will likely learn the details. Second, publicity may extend the recovery time for child victims because more individuals may potentially remind children about their victimization. Recovery from crime victimization is more rapid when children are able to put the experiences behind them and escape the victim role (Runyan, Everson, Edelsohn, Hunter, & Coulter, 1988). Third, publicity about victimization may in some cases cause children to be targeted for hazing, exclusion, or even additional victimization.

While all crime victims may suffer from publicity, several aspects of childhood elevate the costs of exposure for child victims. First, children are less able to directly represent their experience to journalists or to analyze and correct misrepresentations in portrayals of their experience. Second, school-age children cannot easily insulate themselves from a large and frequently harsh community of peers, short of leaving school entirely. Third, early formative sexual experiences laced with shame and humiliation have consequences that are sometimes difficult to reverse, so that anything that heightens the shame poses a serious risk.

Not all effects of publicity are necessarily negative. Publicity may marshal outpourings of support and protection, and it may allow victims the opportunity to shed stigmas and unrealistic expectations of rejection. Obviously, reactions will differ greatly according to circumstances and individuals. Nonetheless, social scientific findings and anecdotal experience both suggest that publicity is a burden on many child crime victims.

## PRIVACY AND AN EVOLVING LEGAL LANDSCAPE

Before we explore whether legislatures might do a better job of protecting victims' privacy rights, we should analyze the sources and limits of crime victims' legal rights to privacy. States' efforts to protect the privacy of child victims have clashed with the news media's First Amendment protections. It is thus essential to understand the controlling legal doctrines before proposing alternative rules or practices to protect child victims' privacy rights in criminal litigation.

In this section we briefly review the origins of notions about privacy, inventory the various contexts in which the United States Constitution has been held to establish a right to "privacy," and analyze cases in which the First Amendment limits states' ability to enact legislation to protect the privacy rights of crime victims.

## Constitutional Privacy

The word "privacy" has several meanings. In what is perhaps the oldest and most common use, it means the state or condition of being withdrawn from the society of others, or from public interest; seclusion, especially in one's home (Hall, 1990; Oxford English Dictionary, 2003). Beginning in the 19th century, however, the word came to be associated with the notion of rights. In this context, "privacy" means the state or condition of being alone, undisturbed, or free from public attention, as a matter of choice or right; and includes freedom from interference or intrusion (Oxford English Dictionary, 2003). It might thus be argued that although the idea of being withdrawn from society is deeply rooted, the idea that it is a human right protected by law is of more recent origin (Hall, 1990; Perrot, 1990).

The seminal discussion of "the right to privacy" in American law appeared in 1890 in a law review article of that name by Samuel Warren and Louis Brandeis (1890). Since then, it has been the subject of extensive scholarly debate (Kalven Jr., 1966; Zimmerman, 1983). Warren and Brandeis theorized that the right to privacy originated in the common law, meaning the body of cases decided by courts, not in the Constitution or legislation. They equated this right with common-law legal rights that traditionally require a balancing of interests, rather than creating absolute protections. Describing privacy as a desirable and protected mental and emotional state, Warren and Brandeis argued that the "next step" that the law should take in protecting the "right to be let alone," would be to establish better protections from the intrusions of photographers and newspaper reporters (p. 195).

For the first 80 years after the article's publication, tort law remained the focus for privacy. Beginning in the 1960s, legislatures enacted laws to protect a variety of privacy interests, especially in information held by government agencies (Stevens, 2003). Although some scholars believe the privacy tort is in decline (Kalven Jr., 1966; Zimmerman, 1983), statutes regulating access to and disclosure of information that the government possesses about individuals continue to increase.

## Classifying Privacy

### *Freedom from public intrusion into personal matters*

The "right" to be free from public intrusion into private matters has poorly defined constitutional underpinnings and has largely been left to state regulation (*Whalen v. Roe,* 1977).

Information gathered about individuals and held by government agencies, however, stands on slightly different footing. Federal legislation extensively regulates both government and private access to information in a variety of contexts (The Family Educational Rights and Privacy Act of 1974; The Privacy Act of 1974; Stevens, 2003; Warren & Brandeis, 1890). Although these regulatory schemes are both detailed and extensive, they generally govern the collection, access, and dissemination of data by subject matter. The breadth of federal and state legislation in this area suggests two things: first, respect for privacy has taken deep root; and second, statutory rights expressing this respect are likely to give way when they conflict with specific rights granted by the Constitution. As we shall see below, this has been especially true when statutory privacy rights conflict with the media's First Amendment's rights to publish truthful information.

## *FLORIDA STAR V. B.J.F.*: FIRST AMENDMENT V. PRIVACY

A child victim's or witness's interest in preventing the publication of his or her name and identifying characteristics arises from the interest in avoiding intrusion into personal matters. This branch of privacy law is not derived from the Constitution, but from state and federal statutes that have been enacted during the last 30 years. Many state laws that restrict the news media's ability to report public facts have been found unconstitutional, as *Florida Star v. B.J.F* (1989) illustrates.

In *Florida Star,* a woman reported to the Duval County Sheriff's Department ("Department") that she had been robbed and sexually assaulted. The Department prepared an incident report and placed it in its press relations room, an area open to the public. A reporter from the *Florida Star* prepared a story that included the victim's full name, which the paper published. The publication of B.J.F.'s full name violated both a Florida statute that made it unlawful to "print, publish, or broadcast . . . in any instrument of mass communication" (p. 524) the name of a sexual assault victim, and the paper's own internal policies. B.J.F. sued the Department and the *Florida Star* for negligent violation of the state statute. The Department settled, while the *Florida Star* defended itself, arguing that the statute violated the First Amendment.

B.J.F. testified at trial that she learned about the article from fellow workers and acquaintances. Her mother received several phone calls from an individual who threatened to rape B.J.F. again. These events caused B.J.F. to move from her home, change her phone number, seek police protection, and get psychotherapy. The jury awarded B.J.F. $75,000 in compensatory damages and $25,000 in punitive damages, and the *Florida Star* appealed. The newspaper lost in Florida's appellate courts and then appealed to the United States Supreme Court, which reversed.

Writing for the court, Justice Marshall first distinguished the earlier case of *Cox Broadcasting Corp v. Cohen* (1975), which struck down a state statute prohibiting the dissemination of a rape victim's name. Here, the newspaper publicized information gleaned from a police report, not a trial or court record. Justice Marshall characterized both press freedom and privacy rights as "plainly rooted in the traditions and significant concerns of our society" (p. 535), and did not "rule out the possibility that, in a proper case imposing civil sanctions for publication of the name of a rape victim might be so overwhelmingly necessary to advance" (p. 537) state interests as to survive First Amendment scrutiny. He located the privacy interest in "the protections which various statutes and common-law doctrines accord to personal privacy" (p. 530) (*Cox Broadcasting Corp v. Cohen,* 1975; Kalven Jr., 1966; *Oklahoma Publishing Co. v. Oklahoma County District Court,* 1977; *Smith v. Daily Mail Publishing Co.*, 1979) and held that the statute was unconstitutional. For Justice Marshall, the fact that the *Florida Star* obtained B.J.F.'s name lawfully, through a news release provided by the government, was a fact of paramount importance.

## IMPLICATIONS FOR LEGISLATION DESIGNED TO PROTECT PRIVACY

The line of cases ending with *B.J.F.* establishes this rule: when a state statute that seeks to preserve a crime victim's privacy conflicts with the First Amendment, the statute must pass exacting constitutional scrutiny. Such a statute must be narrowly tailored to serve a state interest of the highest order (*Florida Star v. B.J.F.*, 1989; Marcus & McMahon, 1991). The difficulty for state legislatures and those seeking to better protect crime victims' privacy interests is that the *B.J.F.* court effectively determined that those interests are not of the highest order, where a news-gathering organization has lawfully acquired information about a crime victim and publishes it.

## *Protective Statutes*

The federal government and numerous states have adopted a variety of measures designed to protect the privacy of victims and witnesses. A review of these statutes and cases analyzing their constitutionality allows us to draw some preliminary conclusions as to which protections are likely to be effective in protecting children and withstand constitutional muster.

Three state interests underpin state victim confidentiality statutes:

- promoting the well-being of crime victims by preventing stigmatization, even inadvertent stigmatization, by press, peers, or community;
- encouraging crime victims to report crimes committed against them, thereby both aiding the process of psychological healing and preventing additional crimes against them; and
- enabling crime victims better to endure the rigors of the investigative and litigation process.

All of these interests are stronger when the object of the protection is a child. The law has traditionally viewed children as meriting greater protection than adults, and allowed states greater freedom to enact protections for children (*Ginsberg v. New York,* 1968; *Maryland v. Craig,* 1990; *Prince v. Massachusetts,* 1944). While this interest in protecting children will not overcome a First Amendment violation, it might support limiting the access of the press to court proceedings and documents involving child crime victims.

## *Federal Law: 18 U.S.C. § 3509*

18 U.S.C. § 3509 establishes significant protections for children who are either witnesses or victims of a broad category of crimes. The statute provides that child victims may testify under some circumstances by closed-circuit television or videotaped deposition (18 U.S.C. § 3509 (b)(1) & (2)) and requires that challenges to the competency of child witnesses be supported by an offer of proof. The latter does not require a hearing unless the court finds compelling reasons for one, and any competency hearing that is conducted must occur outside the jury's presence (18 U.S.C. § 3509 (c)).

Most importantly, the statute prevents information about child victims and witnesses from falling into the public domain (18 U.S.C. § 3509 (a)(2)). It imposes a duty to safeguard information on the entire trial work group, which encompasses everyone involved with the trial, including investigators, prosecutors, defense counsel, and court personnel (18 U.S.C. § 3509 (d)(1)(B)). The entire work group must keep all documents containing the child's name or any other information concerning a child in a secure place, and may disclose them only to persons who have reason to know the information they contain (18 U.S.C. § 3509 (d)(1)(A)). Court papers referring to child witnesses and victims are filed under seal, and counsel must prepare redacted copies for filing in the public record of the proceedings (18 U.S.C. § 3509 (d)(2)). Finally, the trial judge may exclude members of the public and the press from the court room who do not have a direct interest in the case if the trial judge finds that requiring the child to testify in open court would cause substantial psychological harm to the child or would result in the child's inability to effectively communicate (18 U.S.C. § 3509 (e)).

The statute's constitutionality has been challenged only at the district court level (*United States v. Broussard,* 1991). In that case a newspaper challenged the seal requirement that resulted in redactions to otherwise public documents. The district court found the requirement was narrowly tailored to serve the compelling interest of protecting the identity of children and avoiding unwanted pretrial exposure. It interfered neither with the defendant's Sixth Amendment right to public trial nor the press's First Amendment right of access to criminal proceedings and documents (*United States v. Broussard,* 1991; *United States v. Carrier,* 1993; *United States v. Farley,* 1993; *United States v. Rouse,* 1997).

Although the federal statute imposes additional procedures and related expenses on law enforcement officials, prosecutors, defense counsel, and court officials, it provides excellent protection for child victims and witnesses. Unfortunately, it only applies in federal courts and no state has adopted this comprehensive model.

### Overview of State Statutes

Many states have attempted to protect sex-crime victims' privacy by enacting legislation that allows public officials to withhold information about the victim from the press and public, including Alaska, Arizona, California, Florida, Indiana, Massachusetts, Michigan, Montana, Nebraska, Ohio, Texas, Virginia, Washington, and Wyoming, among others (Alaska Statute § 12.61.140, 2003; Ariz. Rev. Stat. Ann. § 13-4434, 2003; Calif. Gov't Code § 54961, 1995; Fla. Stat. Ann. § 92.56, 2002; Ind. Code Ann. § 35-37-4-12, 1995; Mass. Ann. Laws ch. 265 § 24C, 2003; Mich. Comp. Laws § 780.758, 2003; Montana Code Ann. § 44-5-311, 2002; Neb. Rev. Stat. § 81-1842. 1995; Nev. Rev. Stat. Ann. § 200.3772–200.3774, 2003; Ohio Rev. Code Ann. § 2930.07, 1995; Tex. Code Crim. P. Ann. art. 57.02, 2002; Utah Code Ann. § 77-38-6, 2003; Va. Code Ann. § 19.2-11.2, 1995; Wash. Rev. Code § 42.17.310, 2003; Wyo. Stat. Ann. § 14-3-106, 2003).

State legislators have pursued a number of strategies to protect crime victims from the potential stigma of publicity, including prohibiting the publication of victim identity, requiring the redaction names or use of pseudonyms in police reports and court filings, allowing victims to request redaction or the use of pseudonyms in official documents, protecting victims from the normal requirement that witnesses identify themselves on the public record at trial, exempting police reports and court filings relating to certain crimes from public records requirements, and allowing trials to be closed to the public in some circumstances.

These laws vary in scope. Although state legislators have created a variety of protections, no state statute is as comprehensive as the federal statute. Some protect the identities of sex-crime victims during all stages of the investigation, pretrial, and trial proceedings (Fla. Stat. Ann. § 92.56, 2002; Mass. Ann. Laws ch. 265 § 24C, 2003; Nev. Rev. Stat. Ann. § 200.3772–200.3774, 2003; Tex. Code Crim Code art. 57.02, 2002). Some apply only to certain public documents or only until the victim testifies at trial (Alaska Statute § 12.61.140, 2003; Calif. Gov't Code § 54961, 1995; Ind. Code Ann. § 35-37-4-12, 1995; Mich. Comp. Laws § 780.758, 2003; Mont. Code Ann. § 44-5-311, 2002; Neb. Rev. Stat. § 81-1842, 1995; Ohio Rev. Code Ann. § 2930.07, 1995, Utah Code Ann. § 77-38-6, 2003; Va. Code Ann. § 19.2-11.2, 1995; Wash. Rev. Code § 42.17.310, 2003; Wyo. Stat. Ann. § 14-3-106, 2003). In four states, the law protects the identities of only *child* sex-crime victims (Iowa Code § 910A.13, 1995; Maine Rev. Stat. Ann. tit. 30-A § 288, 2003; N.J. Rev. Stat. § 2A:82-46, 2004; N.D. Cent. Code § 12.1-35-03, 2003; R.I. Gen. Laws § 11-37-8.5, 1995). A few states protect child witnesses as well as victims.

### *Prohibitions on Publication*

South Carolina's statute, similar to the statute in *B.J.F.*, criminalizes publication of a rape victim's name. The statute makes it a misdemeanor to publish the name (but not the image or other identifying information) of victims of criminal sexual conduct (S.C. Code Ann. § 16-3-652-656, 2002). The statute exempts from criminal liability names published by order of a court. It does not establish a private cause of action for invasion of privacy, meaning the victim cannot sue the publisher (*Dorman v. Aikman Communications Inc.*, 1990). A Georgia statute also prohibits the publication of victim identities (Ga. Code Ann., § 16-6-23, 2004). Although state courts have not yet declared these statutes unconstitutional, the *B.J.F.* and *Cox Broadcasting* decisions cast significant doubt on the validity of such statutes, at least as they apply to the publication of truthful information lawfully acquired from public documents or court records.

### *Voluntary Protections*

Some states permit victims or prosecutors to make the victim's identity confidential or to initiate proceedings to do so. After *B.J.F.*, Florida enacted a statute permitting crime victims to obtain court orders restricting the use of their names and other identifying information. It protects the victims of sexual offenses, child abuse, and other crimes directed toward children (Fla. Stat. Ann. 92.56(1), 2002). Crime victims must show three things in order to protect their names and identities:

- The victim must establish that nothing has occurred to disqualify him or her from receiving the court's protection; the victim's identity is not already known in the community; the victim has not called public attention to the offense; and the victim's identity has not already become a "reasonable subject" of public concern (Fla. Stat. Ann. § 92.56 (1) (a)–(c), 2002).
- The victim must establish that disclosure of his or her identity would be offensive to a reasonable person (Fla. Stat. Ann. § 92.56 (1)(d), 2002).
- The victim must show harm from disclosure, such as likelihood of retaliation, severe emotional harm, or interference with trial testimony (Fla. Stat. Ann. § 92.56 (1)(e), 2002).

Once a protective order is granted, the defendant in the case is entitled to access to identifying information, but may not disclose the information to persons not connected with his or her defense (Fla. Stat. Ann. § 92.56 (2), 2002). The statute authorizes the parties to use pseudonyms in court filings to protect the victim's identity (Fla. Stat. Ann. § 92.56 (3), 2002). In addition, it imposes a duty on law enforcement personnel, court staff, counsel, and litigants to maintain the confidentiality of victims' identification.

Rather than criminalizing the publication of a victim's name or identifying information, the statute treats disclosure or publication of such information as a contempt of court. In this regard, it is significantly different from its predecessor in *B.J.F.* and the South Carolina and Georgia statutes, which impose criminal sanctions for the publication of names and identifying information.

The revised Florida statute acts preemptively to prevent the identity of a qualifying victim from reaching the public domain. The Florida statute should pass constitutional muster. It requires a case-by-case showing of need, a demonstration that disclosure would be offensive to a reasonable person, and a particularized showing of harm.

The Florida statute nevertheless suffers from at least three drawbacks. First, it requires crime victims to take the initiative and move for the court's protection. Second, it requires victims to shoulder significant evidentiary burdens in order to invoke the court's protection (Anderson, 2002). Third, by requiring victims to prove that their identity has not already been disclosed, it creates the real possibility that they cannot carry that burden if a charging document or other court filing inadvertently includes their name. It may even create some incentive for the media to discover and disclose a victim's identity before the victim has a chance to apply for a protective order. The Florida procedure is thus of limited practical usefulness.

Other states impose fewer burdens on crime victims seeking to preserve the confidentiality of their identity. Texas gives victims of sexual crimes the right to be referred to by pseudonym in all public files and records concerning the offense, including police summary reports, press releases, and records of judicial proceedings. Victims who elect to use this procedure complete a "pseudonym form" developed and distributed by the Sexual Assault Prevention and Crisis Services Program of the Texas Department of Health, which records their name, address, telephone number, and pseudonym (*Greeno v. State,* 2001; *Stevens v. State,* 1995; Tex. Code Crim. Proc. art. 57.02, 2002.

Completed pseudonym forms are confidential. After victims complete the form, the investigating law enforcement agency may not disclose the victim's name, address, or telephone number in the offense's investigation or prosecution (Tex. Code Crim. Proc. art. 57.02, 2002), and must take steps to protect the form's confidentiality. The form may be disclosed to defendants and their attorneys but not to anyone else without a court order. Prosecutors must designate the victims by their chosen pseudonyms in all legal proceedings (Tex. Code Crim. Proc. art. 57.02, 2002). This protection extends to victims of a wide variety of sexual crimes, including indecency with a child, sexual assault, aggravated sexual assault, compelling prostitution, and sexual performance by a child. While the statute does not expressly address child victims, it also does not exclude them from the procedure. A public servant's wrongful disclosure of a victim's identifying information is a misdemeanor (Tex. Code Crim. Proc. art. 57.02, 2002).

The Texas statute provides two routes for disclosure of identifying information about victims. A court may order the disclosure if it finds that the information is "essential" in the trial or the victim's identity is disputed (Tex. Code Crim. Proc. Art. 57.02 (g), 2002). Victims or their parents or guardians may consent to disclosure. The Texas statute has been twice challenged on non-constitutional grounds and has withstood those challenges both times (*Greeno v. State,* 2001; *Stevens v. State,* 1995). One lower court has noted that it is an error to identify a child crime victim by name at trial where the victim had followed the statutory procedure for using a pseudonym, meaning that this practice is barred by the statute (*Stevens v. State,* 1995). Although the Texas statute has not yet been challenged on constitutional grounds, it appears likely to withstand constitutional scrutiny because it requires the use of a pseudonym after steps have been taken to prevent victims' names from falling into the public domain (*KPNX Broadcasting Co. v. Arizona Superior Court,* 1982; *Nixon v. Warner Communications, Inc.,* 1978a).

The concept of allowing crime victims to control public access to their identities is appealing on the surface. The choice protects those who want their identity to remain private while allowing those who want to come forward to do so. For some victims it is beneficial to confront possible stigma head-on, and coming forward helps educate the public about the impact of crime.

Three policy arguments against such an approach, however, should be considered. First, the relatively infrequent utilization of the Texas procedure suggests that without a mandate, the justice system may be fairly passive. At a minimum, more resources should be invested in informing the law enforcement and victim services communities about the procedure. Second, where a crime occurred recently, victims or their parents may be in a poor psychological condition to rationally consider their privacy needs, and may later regret a decision to disclose their identity because it cannot be revoked. Finally, putting the burden on victims to invoke privacy protections clearly runs the risk that ill-informed victims who would otherwise invoke the protections will be publicly identified, a policy that seems inequitable to crime victims, especially to children.

### *Mandatory Redaction or Use of Pseudonym*

Some states have required that the names of crime victims be treated as confidential under some circumstances unless a court or the victim releases the identity. New Jersey is one such state. It enacted a statute to protect the privacy of child victims of aggravated sexual assault, sexual assault, aggravated criminal sexual conduct endangering the welfare of a child, and abuse and neglect actions. The statute requires the use of initials or a pseudonym in all court filings and provides that police reports, to the extent to which they would ordinarily be public, are confidential and unavailable to the public (N.J. Stat. Ann. § 2A:82-46, 2004).

Unlike statutes that require victims to invoke confidentiality protections, the New Jersey law prevents information from falling into the public record, where the First Amendment protects the news media from regulation or sanction. In this respect the statute works like laws requiring that court records relating to juvenile *offenders* be confidential (N.J. Stat. Ann. § 2A:82-46, 2004). Such statutes probably should withstand constitutional challenge.

Although no reported cases test the constitutionality of the New Jersey statute, we believe it should be found constitutional. Rather than punishing the publication of victim information after it enters the public domain, the New Jersey statute, like other confidentiality statutes, protects the information from making its way into the public domain in the first place. Similar laws have withstood constitutional challenge (*Nixon v. Warner Communications, Inc.,* 1978a).

This is the right result. The First Amendment generally does not grant the press a right to information about criminal proceedings superior to that of the general public (*Nixon v. Warner Communications, Inc.,* 1978b). Because protective statutes keep details of victims' identity out of the public record in the first instance, they do not restrict the news media's right to copy and publish information open to the public.

These statutes offer a number of benefits. Crime victims are not required to shoulder the burden of triggering confidentiality protections. These statutes do not depend upon victims being notified of the availability of such protections. Uniform procedures requiring that identifying information in certain categories of offenses be withheld from the public are less burdensome than the dual record-keeping procedures under a Texas-style opt-in statute.

Although we favor a mandatory approach, it also has its drawbacks. First, it requires investigators, prosecutors, defense counsel, and court officials to maintain one set of records containing victims' identifying information for their own use and a second set without that information for public disclosure. The approach thus imposes significant costs and administrative burdens. Second, it can be difficult to design an effective enforcement mechanism, given that the targets of enforcement action (police, prosecutors, defense counsel, and court administrators) generally derive no personal benefit from violating the statutes. Finally, for reasons that will be discussed further below, such statutes may not deal effectively with protecting victim privacy after the criminal verdict.

### *Public Access to Investigative and Court Records*

Another approach to protecting the privacy of victims and witnesses is to exempt certain identifying information in public records from disclosure. A number of states take this approach (e.g., Alaska Stat. § 12.61.110, 2003; Mass. Ann. Laws ch. 265, § 24C, 2003; N.D. Cent. Code, § 12.1-35-03, 2003; N.J. Stat. § 2A:82-46, 2004; R.I. Gen. Laws § 11-37-8.5, 2002; Wash. Revised Code § 10.97.130, 2003). In Massachusetts, identifying information about victims of sexual crimes in law enforcement and court records is not subject to disclosure under the Massachusetts public records law (Mass. Ann. Laws ch. 265, § 24C, 2003).

Changes to public records laws offer the same advantages that mandatory protections provide. They offer the additional advantage that if structured correctly, they can continue to shield identifying information about child victims and witnesses from disclosure after a criminal case has been adjudicated. Moreover, from a functional standpoint, law enforcement agencies and courts generally deal with requests for disclosure in the analytical context of public records laws. Their chief disadvantages are (a) that they are not always applicable to court records, and (b) they often put the burden to establish that records are exempt from disclosure on the party opposing disclosure (*Ames v. City of Fircrest,* 1993).

Shielding information from public disclosure brings two important values into conflict: protecting the privacy interests of crime victims and preserving transparent governmental function. While there is a right to inspect and copy public records and documents, including judicial records (*Nixon v. Warner Communications, Inc.,* 1978a), that right is not absolute. It is subject to the court's supervisory power over its own records and files and the trial judge's discretion.

### *Protections at Trial*

Protection for young crime victims and witnesses during criminal trials takes two forms: protections against being required to divulge identifying information during trial testimony, and procedures to close the courtroom to the public and news media during the child's testimony.

Several states provide that victims may not be compelled to provide identifying information during court testimony under some circumstances. By themselves such statutes probably do not go far enough. But when coupled with statutes requiring or allowing redaction, they provide important protection.

In contrast, closure of trial proceedings burdens the court system and the public in ways that the use of pseudonyms in court filings or allowing children not to provide detailed identifying information in trial testimony do not. Only Massachusetts and the federal statute expressly provide that criminal trials may be closed to protect child crime victims (Mass. Ann. Laws ch. 278, § 16A, 2003; 18 USC § 3509 (e), 2004; Alaska Stat. § 12.61.150, 2003). In Massachusetts, a trial judge must exclude the public and the press from the trial proceedings of a variety of cases in which a child is the victim of a sexual crime (Mass. Ann. Laws ch. 278, § 16A, 2003). In 1982, the *Boston Globe's* parent company requested access to the trial of a defendant charged with sexual crimes against three girls (*Globe Newspaper Co. v. Superior Court,* 1982), and the district court denied it. The United States Supreme Court struck the statute down on First Amendment grounds.

Writing for the court, Justice Brennan observed that the right of access to criminal trials has constitutional stature, but is not absolute. Orders to close criminal trials, however, must be supported by a compelling government interest and be narrowly tailored to serve that interest. Justice Brennan identified two interests in the Massachusetts statute: protecting minor victims of sex crimes from further harm, and encouraging such victims to come forward and testify fully and credibly.

While safeguarding the physical and psychological well-being of young crime victims is a compelling state interest, the Court concluded that this did not justify mandatory closure of all criminal trials. Rather, it requires a more narrowly tailored approach, including a case-by-case analysis to decide whether closure is necessary to protect the victim. Factors that the trial court must consider include the victim's age and psychological maturity, the nature of the crime, the interests of parents and relatives, and the victim's preference.

After the Supreme Court's decision, the Massachusetts legislature neither repealed nor amended the statute. Massachusetts courts have interpreted the statute to require the findings and narrowly tailored protections mandated by the United States Supreme Court. Courts outside Massachusetts also use a case-by-case analysis to decide whether closure is necessary to protect the victim (*Commonwealth v. Martin,* 1994). In highly newsworthy cases, where public and press interests are at their highest, a judge may be reluctant to close a trial.

The federal statute largely tracks the *Boston Globe* requirements. Thus, carefully drawn statutes allowing judges to close hearings to the public are constitutional.

### *Protections for Witnesses*

A few states give crime witnesses a general right to keep their identities confidential in police reports and court documents (see Alaska Stat. § 12.61.130, 2003; N.D. Cent. Code, § 12.1-35-03, 2003; Rev. Code Wash. (ARCW) § 7.69A.050, 2003; Wash. Rev. Code. § 42.17.310, 2003) or trial proceedings (see Utah Code Ann. § 77-38-6, 2003). Such statutes should be found constitutional to the same extent as statutes protecting crime victims. They offer the benefit of protecting children collaterally involved in crimes performed by adults or other children, who may become subjects of publicity themselves.

Such statutes suffer from a number of practical drawbacks. First, stigmatizing publicity appears to affect crime witnesses less often than victims, and imposing this burden on law enforcement, prosecutors, defenders, and court administrators may be unnecessary. Second, it is not always clear who will become a witness at trial, especially during the investigation or pretrial phase. Finally, public records of a criminal case, especially investigative records that often become public when the adjudicative phase ends, often include the names of dozens of persons categorized as "witnesses," both laypersons and professionals; requiring nondisclosure of their names could be difficult and consume public resources better spent elsewhere.

### *Enforcement*

States have chosen a variety of enforcement mechanisms for statutes protecting the privacy of victims and witnesses. Some make disclosure a crime (see, N.J. Stat. § 2A:82-46 (b), 2004), others punish disclosure as contempt of court (see, R.I. Gen. Laws § 11-37-8.5 (c), 2002), others establish a fine (Mass. Ann. Laws ch. 265, § 24C, 2003), others treat disclosure as a professional conduct violation (see Alaska Stat. § 12.61.125, 2003), and others are silent on enforcement (see, N.D. Cent. Code, § 12.1-35-03, 2003; Tex. Code Crim. Proc. art. 57.02, 2002).

Statutes shielding the identity of a crime victim face several practical barriers to enforcement. Absent new direction from the United States Supreme Court, there would be significant constitutional barriers to punishing representatives of the news media for publishing truthful information obtained by a wrongful disclosure (*Bartnicki v. Vopper*, 2001; Halstuk, 2003; Leone, 1993). Thus, the likely targets of enforcement would be law enforcement personnel, prosecutors, defense attorneys, court employees, and other public employees. It might be unwise as a policy to impose criminal sanctions for negligent or reckless disclosure of confidential information against persons who do not personally benefit from the disclosure (see Nev. Rev. Stat. § 200.3772 (7), 2003). Proving willful disclosure by public employees might be difficult, and legislators are probably justified in assuming that such disclosures will be rare. It thus may be beneficial for such statutes to establish a variety of enforcement measures, including contempt remedies, fines, and referrals to licensing agencies in such statutes, and to allow courts and prosecutors to select the most appropriate remedy.

## Scope

States use a wide variety of strategies in determining the scope of privacy protections extended to crime victims. Some states limit protections to minors or to a small class of offenses (Nev. Rev. Stat. § 200.3772 (1), 2003; R.I. Gen. Laws § 11-37-8.5, 2002; Wyo. Stat. § 14-3-106, 2003); others appear to grant the protections to all crimes (Alaska Stat. § 12.61.130 & Alaska Stat. § 12.61.125, 2003; Ariz. Rev. Stat. § 13-4434, 2003; N.D. Cent. Code, § 12.1-35-03 (2), 2003; Utah Code Ann. § 77-38-6 (1), 2003); and others tailor the protections to the offense involved (see, Conn. Gen. Stat. § 1-210 (b)(3)(F), 2003; Fla. Stat. § 92.56, 2002; Maine Rev. Stat. 30-A M.R.S. § 288, 2003; Mass. Ann. Laws ch. 265, § 24C, 2003; Mich. Comp. Laws § 780.758 (2), 2003; Mont. Code Ann., § 44-5-311, 2002; N.J. Stat. Ann. § 2A:82-46, 2004).

Obviously the scope of protections offered to crime victims is a matter of legislative policy. Protections that are too narrow may not promote victims' privacy interest and encourage cooperation with law enforcement efforts, while extending the protections too broadly may impose costly administrative burdens.

## Elements of a Model Statute

Although many states have enacted statutes to protect the identities of crime victims or witnesses, few establish a comprehensive approach to such protections at the investigative, trial, and posttrial phases of the case. It may be that effective models for protecting the privacy of crime victims have simply not received sufficient dissemination. Child and victim advocates could draw upon such models in their efforts to protect children and adults more effectively.

Although a detailed legislative proposal is beyond the scope of this chapter, several objectives for such a proposal emerge from the foregoing analysis. These include the following:

- Establish a right for child victims and witnesses of enumerated crimes to be identified by pseudonym in police reports, charging documents, and court filings, thus preventing public disclosure of identifying information, rather than seeking to punish publication after it arrives in the public domain.
- Make the protections mandatory. This avoids imposing the burden and expense of requiring special findings or detailed showings of harm on victims, while allowing victims to choose to disclose their identities.
- Designate a list or class of crimes for which victim and witness information will be protected. Although sexual assault is

too narrow a category, because children can feel deep shame about being victims of bullying, physical assaults, and offenses by caretakers, including too many crimes, especially for adult victims, may increase administrative burdens and costs and compromise the fundamentally public nature of criminal proceedings. It may even be desirable to establish separate lists of "eligible" crimes for adults and children.

- Establish procedures for defense counsel to obtain the identities of victims and witnesses, subject to the requirement not to disclose or re-disclose the information.
- Do not limit the privacy protections to adult females; include both children and sexual crimes against men and boys within the scope of the protective statute.
- Even if the protections are mandatory, exempt from prosecution victims who purposely or inadvertently put their identifying information in the public domain.
- Establish an exception allowing courts to order prosecutors to disclose identifying information when a victim's identity is disputed or when disclosure is otherwise necessary to protect a defendant's constitutional rights.
- Ensure that law enforcement personnel, prosecutors (and their staff), defense counsel (and their staff), and court administrative personnel are all subject to the statute to avoid allowing some actors with knowledge of the victim's identity to place identifying information in the public domain. Provide protections for negligent disclosure of identifying information by law enforcement officials, prosecutors, and court officials, even when common law or statutory privileges would arguably be a defense to prosecution.
- Amend public records laws so that the portions of investigative, prosecution, and court records that identify child victims and witnesses remain confidential after the disposition of the case.
- If protections of the statute are to be extended to witnesses, do so only for child witnesses who have requested, individually or through their parent or guardian, that their identity remain confidential.
- Adopt a variety of enforcement measures for knowing violations, ranging from contempt, referral to licensing bodies, and criminal sanctions, to encourage compliance without unduly penalizing negligent acts by law enforcement, administrative officials, or attorneys.
- Although the scope of protection is at the heart of legislative policymaking here, statutes that make confidential identifying information for (a) child victims and witnesses in all crimes, and (b) all victims of sexual crimes seem generally to strike the best balance between promoting crime victims' privacy interests and protecting the transparency of the criminal justice process.

### *Summary*

The federal government and several states have chosen to fashion laws to protect crime victims' privacy. Those statutes have been subjected to vigorous constitutional challenges. When considered in light of controlling constitutional principles, however, statutes requiring or allowing victims to be identified by pseudonyms in police reports, charging documents, and court filings appear to be constitutional. They thus serve as useful models for other states to draw upon in their efforts to serve the needs of child and adult crime victims. In particular, the federal statute offers the most thorough protections in terms of its scope, its protections for victims and witnesses, and its consideration of the need in some cases to close evidentiary hearings.

## OTHER RESPONSES TO PROTECTING VICTIMS' PRIVACY INTERESTS

There are no guarantees that protective legislation will either be enacted or survive constitutional challenges. We thus turn to an analysis of whether informal measures would provide better assurances that victims' privacy interests can be protected in the criminal process.

### *Informal Measures to Protect Victims*

Although it appears impractical to protect victims' privacy through expanded rights under personal injury law, it is important for victims and victim advocates to understand a few practical considerations that may limit intrusion on victims' privacy interests.

#### *Avoid relying on oral or vague promises*

Reporters and news producers request interviews with crime victims with some frequency. They often promise to provide "favorable" treatment to victims in the resulting stories and to use their broader understanding of the crime's "context" gleaned from the interview to "inform" their coverage of the case. The unexpressed promise in these instances is that unfavorable facts will be minimized and balanced with favorable facts. In addition, reporters or victims may wish to classify some comments or subjects as being "off the record."

Although there may be cases where victims or victim advocates have prior personal experience with a reporter and may reasonably rely on such representations, there are at least two reasons why reporters are unlikely to protect crime victims from intrusive publicity. First, such promises are likely to be found to be legally unenforceable because oral promises are hard to prove and written promises are rare. Second, reporters' and producers' promises usually are too vague to be enforced even when they can be proven.

#### *Protect the victim's physical space*

The First Amendment protects nearly everything that the news media obtains from public documents and public places. It does not, however, give representatives of the news media a license to trespass into private property or into nonpublic areas on public property. Whenever possible, prosecutors and court officials should cooperate in providing crime victims with nonpublic places to sit while waiting to testify or to learn of a jury's verdict. In addition, reporters, photographers, and producers should not be allowed to invade victims' homes and yards. Police officers generally are willing to assist in removing reporters and producers from victims' front lawns. Victims are not required to consent to the entry of reporters or producers into their homes or other nonpublic places.

#### *Choose when to make statements*

Reporters and producers sometimes imply that a victim is morally or legally obligated to provide them with an interview or statement merely because the victim has provided a statement to the police or testified in court. This is not true. Reporters are entitled to publish and broadcast information obtained from public statements and public documents, but they cannot compel a person to provide additional statements. Indeed, the most compelling and effective victim accounts often emerge after the criminal case has been fully litigated and both the reporter and the victim understand how any potentially unfavorable aspects of a victim's life or experience relate to the case.

### *Special Considerations for Children and Adolescents*

Finally, it is worth noting that special care must be taken in explaining these considerations to the parents and guardians of children who are the victims of crime. It appears that it is not infrequent for parents to effectively waive their child's privacy through hasty, angry, or unsophisticated judgments about what statements to disclose to the news media. Children and adolescents may be unable to cope effectively with the additional burdens of publicity, even if they initially express a willingness to enter the public spotlight. Three questions may help guide parents and guardians in this situation: (1) What facts would I want disclosed if I were the crime victim? (2) What press disclosures will help this child heal the most quickly? (3) What help is available to this child to cope with the effects of publicity?

### *Practical Considerations for Officials*

Although we favor the adoption of protective statutes modeled after 18 USC § 3509, we believe that there are informal steps that law enforcement officers, victim advocates, prosecutors, and court administrators can consider in the meantime to protect the privacy of child victims and witnesses. Such measures include the following:

- Asking victims, witnesses, and their families during investigations if they are anxious about publicity and documenting their concerns and any factual basis for them with some care. For instance, care must be taken to document the concerns in a way that does not lead to the child being unfairly impeached as unbelievable or otherwise emotionally unstable if that is not the case;
- Developing, where appropriate, procedures for creating and maintaining police investigatory reports and records so as to protect the identities of child victims and witnesses from public disclosure;
- Advising victims and witnesses as part of their debriefing about how they may choose to avoid publicity, and providing informational brochures to them outlining their rights vis-à-vis the press;
- Refusing to disclose identities of victims and witnesses to reporters if disclosure is not legally required, and advising reporters of the wishes of victims and their families regarding their identities and related publicity;
- Requiring a demonstrated factual basis for any challenge to the competency of a child victim or witness to testify, and holding closed hearings on competency;
- Where state criminal procedure allows it, voluntarily using pseudonyms instead of actual names of child victims and witnesses in charging and other documents filed in court, subject to defendants' rights to adequate notice and discovery;
- Considering issues of trial publicity at pretrial structuring conferences in appropriate cases, which will inform the court of the needs of child victims and witnesses and may result in protective orders regarding the procedures for identifying and safeguarding information about child victims and witnesses; and
- Requesting closed evidentiary hearings when it can be established that publicity is likely to harm a child victim or witness.

These ad hoc measures cannot protect the privacy of child victims and witnesses as easily as statutory protections, because they require a greater expenditure of resources in the form of specialized motions and orders on a case-by-case basis to make them effective. Nevertheless, they may improve the chances that publicity will not adversely affect a child victim or witness, especially where the child is particularly vulnerable.

## CONCLUSION

Efforts to protect crime victims, especially children, from the adverse impact of publicity have been hampered by perceived constitutional limitations. However, protective legislation can be designed (a) to protect the identities of child crime victims in police reports and court filings from public disclosure and (b) to allow courts to close hearings where potential harm to a child can be demonstrated. Such legislation appears likely to withstand constitutional challenge. Even in those jurisdictions that have yet to enact legislation to shield children from publicity, families and child advocates can take a number of preventive measures to minimize the harm from publicity to children who have been victimized or have witnessed a crime.

## REFERENCES


18 USC § 3509 (2004).

Alaska Statute § 12.61.125, 12.61.130, 12.61.140 (2003).

Ames v. City of Fircrest, 71 Wn. App. 284 (1993).

Anderson, C. (2002). A prevention view on the compliant child victim. *APSAC Advisor (Special Issue): The compliant child victim, 14*(2), 16–18.

Andrews, B. (1995). Bodily shame as a mediator between abusive experiences and depression. *Journal of Abnormal Psychology, 104*(2), 277–285.

Ariz. Rev. Stat. Ann. § 13–4434 (2003).

Bartnicki v. Vopper, 532 U.S. 514, 533–534 (2001).

Boney-McCoy, S., & Finkelhor, D. (1995a). Prior victimization: A risk factor for child sexual abuse and for PTSD-related symptomatology among sexually abused youth. *Child Abuse & Neglect, 19*(12), 1401–1421.

Boney-McCoy, S., & Finkelhor, D. (1995b). The psychosocial impact of violent victimization on a national youth sample. *Journal of Consulting and Clinical Psychology, 63*(5), 726–736.

Boney-McCoy, S., & Finkelhor, D. (1996). Is youth victimization related to trauma symptoms and depression after controlling for prior symptoms and family relationships? A longitudinal, prospective study. *Journal of Consulting and Clinical Psychology, 64*(6), 1406–1416.

Calif. Gov't Code § 54961 (1995).

Commonwealth v. Martin, 417 Mass 629 (1994).

Conn. Gen. Stat. § 1–210 (b)(3)(F) (2003).

Cox Broadcasting Corp v. Cohen, 420 U.S. 469 (1975).

Dorman v. Aikman Communications Inc., 303 S.C. 63 (1990).

Elizabeth's journey. (March 14, 2003). *USA Today,* p. 1A.

Elliott, D. S. (1989). Anonymity for rape victims . . . should the rules change? *FineLine: The Newsletter on Journalism Ethics, 1*(3), 1–2.

The Family Educational Rights and Privacy Act of 1974 20 U.S.C. § 1232g (1974).

Finkelhor, D. (June 18, 2003). Child victims suffer doubly under public's scrutiny. *USA Today,* p. 13A.

Finkelhor, D., & Browne, A. (1985). The traumatic impact of child sexual abuse: A conceptualization. *American Journal of Orthopsychiatry, 55*(4), 530–541.

Finkelhor, D., & Ormrod, R. (2000). Characteristics of crimes against juveniles (*Juvenile Justice Bulletin No. NCJ 179034*). Washington, DC: Office of Juvenile Justice and Delinquency Prevention.

Fla. Pub. L. ch. 207 § 3 (1995).

Fla. Stat. Ann. § 92.56 (2002).

Florida Star v. B.J.F., 491 U.S. 524 (1989).

Gartner, M. (1991, July/Aug). *Naming the victim. Columbia Journalism Review.*

Ga. Code Ann., § 16-6-23 (2004).

Ginsberg v. New York, 390 U.S. 629, 640 (1968).

Globe Newspaper Co. v. Superior Court, 457 U.S. 596 (1982) (Burger, C.J., dissenting).

Goodman, G. S., Taub, E. P., Jones, D. P., England, P., Port, L. K., Rudy, L., et al. (1992). Testifying in criminal court: Emotional effects on child sexual assault victims. *Monographs of the Society for Research in Child Development, Vol 57*(5) (229), v. 142.

Greeno v. State, 46 S.W.3d 409, 412–414 (Tex. Ct. App., 2001).

Hackney, S. (2003). Covering crime and its victims. *Covering Crime and Justice, A Guide for Journalists.* Available at http://www.justicejournalism.org/crimeguide/index.html

Hall, C. (1990). The sweet delights of home. In M. Perrot (Ed.), A. Goldhammer (Trans.), *A history of private life* (pp. 47–93). Cambridge: Belnap Press.

Halstuk, M. (2003). Analyzing the implications of Bartnicki for the balance between press access and personal privacy. *Community Law Conspectus, 11,* 71, 84–92.

Hashima, P., & Finkelhor, D. (1999). Violent victimization of youth versus adults in the National Crime Victimization Survey. *Journal of Interpersonal Violence, 14*(8), 799–820.

Ind. Code Ann. § 35–37–4-12 (1995).

Iowa Code § 910A.13 (1995).

Jacobs-Sandstrom, M., & Coie, J. D. (1999). A developmental perspective on peer rejection: Mechanisms of stability and change. *Child Development, 70*(4), 955–966.

Kalven Jr., H. (1966). Privacy in tort law—where were Warren and Brandeis wrong? *Law and Contemporary Problems, 31*(326–327).

Kendall-Tackett, K. A., Williams, L. M., & Finkelhor, D. (1993). Impact of sexual abuse on children: A review and synthesis of recent empirical studies. *Psychological Bulletin, 113,* 164–180.

Kidnapped pair safe. (2002, August 1). *The San Francisco Chronicle,* p. A1.

Kilpatrick, D. G., Saunders, B. E., & Smith, D. W. (2002). *Youth victimization: Prevalence and implications* (Research in Brief No. NCJ194972). Washington, DC: US Department of Justice/National Institute of Justice.

Klaus, P., & Rennison, C. M. (2002). *Age patterns in violent victimization, 1976–2000* (Crime Data Brief No. NCJ190104). Washington, DC: Bureau of Justice Statistics.

KPNX Broadcasting Co. v. Arizona Superior Court, 459 U.S. 1302 (1982).

Laubenstein, K. M. (1995). Comment: Media access to juvenile justice: Should freedom of the press be limited to promote rehabilitation of youthful offenders? *Temple Law Review, 68,* 1897–1901.

Leone, S. (1993). Protecting rape victims' identities: Balance between the right to privacy and the First Amendment. *New England Law Review, 27,* 883–901.

Magowan, M. (2003). *The shame of rape.* Retrieved July 7, 2003, from http://www.salon.com/mwt/feature/2002/08/09/stigma/

Maine Rev. Stat. Ann. titles 30-A § 288 (2003).

Mannarino, A. P., & Cohen, J. A. (1996). Abuse-related attributions and perceptions, general attributions, and locus of control in sexually abused girls. *Journal of Interpersonal Violence, 11*(2), 162–180.

Marcus, P., & McMahon, T. (1991). Limiting disclosure of rape victims' identities. *Southern California Law Review, 64,* 1019.

Maryland v. Craig, 497 U.S. 836, 852–857 (1990).

Mass. Ann. Laws ch. 265 § 24C (2003).

McLatchey, S. F. (1991). Media access to juvenile records: In search of a solution. *Georgia State University Law Review, 16,* 337–340.

Mich. Comp. Laws § 780.758 (2003).

Mont. Code Ann. § 44-5-311 (2002).

Myers, J. E. B. (1994). Adjudication of child sexual abuse cases. *The Future of Children, 4*(2), 84–101.

Neb. Rev. Stat. § 81-1842 (1995).

Nev. Rev. Stat. Ann. § 200.3772–200.3774 (2003).

N.H. Rev. Stat. Ann. 169-B:32 (2004).

N.J. Stat. Ann. § 2A:82-46 (2004).

Nixon v. Warner Communications, Inc., 435 U.S. 589, 597 (1978a).

Nixon v. Warner Communications, Inc., 435 U.S. 609 (1978b).

N.D. Cent. Code § 12.1–35–03 (2003).

Oklahoma Publishing Co. v. Oklahoma County District Court, 430 U.S. 308 (1977).

Ohio Rev. Code Ann. § 2930.07 (1995).

Oxford English Dictionary. (2003). Available at http://dictionary.oed.com/cgi/entry/00188918

Perrot, M. (1990). *A history of private life.* Cambridge: Harvard University Press.

Prince v. Massachusetts, 321 U.S. 158, 165 (1944).

The Privacy Act of 1974, 5 U.S.C. § 552a (2004).

R.I. Gen. Laws § 11–37.8.5 (2002).

Roeper, R. (August 5, 2002). Case shows absurdity of media's rape ID policy. *Chicago Sun-Times,* p. 11.

Ross, D. M. (1996). *Childhood bullying and teasing: What school personnel, other professionals, and parents can do.* Alexandria, VA: American Counseling Association.

Runyan, D. K., Everson, M. D., Edelsohn, G. A., Hunter, W. M., & Coulter, M. L. (1988). Impact of legal intervention on sexually abused children. *Journal of Pediatrics, 113,* 647–653.

Slain girl used internet to seek sex, police say. (May 22, 2002). *The New York Times,* p. 5.

Smith v. Daily Mail Publishing Co., 443 U.S. 97 (1979).

S.C. Code Ann. § 16-3-652–656 (2002).

Stevens, G. (2003). *Privacy: Total information awareness programs and related information access, collection, and protection laws.* Washington, DC: Congressional Research Service.

Stevens v. State, 891 S.W.2d 649 (Tex. Crim. App. 1995).

Tex. Code Crim. Proc. art. 57.02 (2002).

United States v. Broussard, 767 Federal Supplement 1545 (1991).

United States v. Carrier, 9 Federal Reporter 3d 867 (10th Cir. 1993).

United States v. Farley, 992 Federal Reporter 2d 1122 (10th Cir. 1993).

United States v. Rouse, 111 Federal Reporter 3d 561 (8th Cir. 1997).

Utah Code Ann. § 77-38-6 (2003).

Va. Code Ann. § 19.2-11.2 (1995).

Warren, S., & Brandeis, L. (1890). The right to privacy. *Harvard Law Review, 4,* 193–195.

Wash. Rev. Code § 42.17.310 (2003).

Wash. Rev. Code § 10.97.130 (2003).

Whalen v. Roe, 429 U.S. 589, 607–608 (1977) (Stewart, J. concurring).

Wyo. Stat. Ann. § 14-3-106 (2003).

Zimmerman, D. (1983). Requiem for a heavyweight: A farewell to Warren and Brandeis's privacy tort. *Cornell Law Review, 68,* 291.

# Part II

## CHILDREN AS CONSUMERS OF VIOLENCE

CHAPTER 7

# *The Violent Shadows of Children's Culture*

JOHN CECH

> *Childhood is a difficult time. . . . The realities of childhood put to shame the half-true notions in some children's books. These offer a gilded world unshadowed by the least suggestion of conflict or pain, a world manufactured by those who cannot—or don't care to—remember the truth of their own childhood. Their expurgated vision has no relation to the way real children live.*
>
> —Maurice Sendak, Caldecott Medal Acceptance Speech (1963)

Violence is an inescapable fact in the lives of children, whether it occurs in the real world around them, or in the works of the imagination that a culture produces for them. Every day we are reminded of the violence that many children are subjected to in their families, neighborhoods, and schools. Globally, children's haunted faces look at us from the pages of newspapers, magazines, and our television screens as the victims of war, famine, disease, and natural disaster. We see young people marched before the television cameras who are the perpetrators of violent acts against adults and other children. We read the accounts of children's accidents with firearms, and we read the studies of the violence that has been deliberately committed by young people with firearms or other weapons in their communities. And sadly we wonder if anything will ever change the tragic course of this history.

## ANCIENT BEGINNINGS: THE VIOLENT LITERATURE OF THE NURSERY

Certainly the literature and other aspects of the cultures that we have created for children reflect this history of violence in children's lives. In fact, one of the earliest works for children in the oral tradition of most cultures, the lullaby, derives its name in Western culture and its premise universally, as a protective response to the violent threat to a child's well-being. "Lullaby," comes from semitic sources that refer to a "lillu demon," the mythological Lillith, Adam's first wife in the ancient Midrashim, who stole the souls of children while they were sleeping (Gaster, 1980). In the ancient Middle East, amulets were hung over the cradles of infants to ward off any harm that might come to them, and a charm was sung for them—a tradition that continues into the present though we may not be aware of its origins (Gaster, 1980). Some traditional lullabies also express the violence that takes place in the life of the caregiver and the child for whom she is singing—the threats of a drunken husband or, no less threatening, the presence of starvation and illness. Sometimes these cradle songs are filled with the inward singing of the caregiver who laments her own and her child's plights, expressing her anguish over the difficult circumstances of her existence, as in the Spanish cradle song that begins,

> All labours are for us poor women
>
> Who wait at night for our husbands to come.
>
> Some return drunk, others return merry,
>
> Others say, "lads, let us kill the women."
>
> They ask for their supper,
>
> But we have nothing to give them
>
> —*(Daiken 1959, p. 14).*

Even a familiar song like "Rock-a-Bye Baby" suggests the perilous turn that life can suddenly and ominously take: "and down will come baby, cradle and all."

Nursery rhymes—those often mysterious doggerel verses that, despite their literary shortcomings, begin the process of tuning our young ears to the rhythms of our world and its cultures—are also vessels for some extraordinarily violent images. In *Mother Goose's Melodies* (1833), a popular printed collection of oral rhymes, we encounter alcoholism, madness, pyromania, prostitution, murder, child abuse, and mayhem of almost every variety. All verses are told to rollicking rhythms, easily memorized and passed along for centuries, as in the following ditty:

> Snail, Snail,
>
> Come out of your hole,
>
> Or else I'll beat you black as coal,
>
> Snail, snail
>
> Put out your head,
>
> Or else I'll beat you till you're dead.

The long history of horrific content to be found in nursery rhymes led critics as early as 1641 to criticize them as being "unfit for childish ears" (Baring-Gould & Baring-Gould, 1962, p. 20). During the early part of the 20th century, a group of concerned citizens in England organized themselves into The Society for Nursery Rhyme Reform. One scholar of this movement wrote that "The average collection of 200 traditional nursery rhymes contains approximately 100 rhymes which personify all that is glorious and ideal for the child. Unfortunately, the remaining 100 harbour unsavory elements" (Baring-Gould & Baring-Gould, p. 20). Among those elements are

8 allusions to murder

2 cases of choking to death

1 case of death by devouring

1 case of cutting a human in half

1 case of decapitation

1 case of death by squeezing

1 case of death by shriveling

Catalogues of human woes were, of course, part of the raw material of these poems; many were adult songs, sung in taverns, while traveling or working, celebrating or soldiering. Much as we might wish to keep these rhymes from toddlers today, they were once shared by a common audience that did not object to their contents or make distinctions between an audience of adults and one that included children. Indeed, a mistake that is commonly made about children's literature from previous centuries is the assumption that the Mother Goose figure was exclusively surrounded by children when, in fact, her audience was multigenerational and her subject matter was adamantly populist and non-discriminatory. In the world of Mother Goose, everyone and everything is rolled together in the same rough and ready, rollicking mix.

The same is true for the stories passed across generations through the oral tradition, which include among its myriad forms myths, legends, fables, folktales, puppet and other theater, pageants, jokes, anecdotes, and songs. This literature was meant to be heard across generations, and usually across classes. Often societies have constructed elaborate story cycles that were part of ritualized performances intended for specific times of the year. While the stories in these traditions frequently contain violent episodes, children are usually not deliberately excluded from the public events during which these materials were presented. To the contrary, the cultural attitudes that children were supposed to be absorbing were contained in these stories. The epic and violent deeds of the young Sumerian king, Gilgamesh, for example, which comprise the oldest story that exists in the West, were carved, the poem tells us, upon the walls of the ancient city of Uruk so the entire population could read about his exploits (Sandars, 1972, p. 117). Myths are often bloody, but because their narratives relay the essential beliefs of a people, they are also considered essential for children to experience because, through them, children are exposed to the core values of their culture.

Art has been similarly directed toward an intergenerational audience since its beginnings. For instance, the paintings that appeared in paleolithic caves did not, as far as we know, spare the children of the tribe from representations of hunting, and the lethal accidents and injuries that sometimes befell the hunters. Nor did the bas reliefs of Egypt, the mosaics of Mycenae, the frescoes of Rome, or public sculptures of the Renaissance try to expunge violence from their subject matter, despite the fact that children would also be part of their audience. Certainly, one cannot adequately represent a number of the crucial stories of the Old or New Testaments of the Bible in visual or verbal forms without some reference to the physical violence that is enacted in many of the central episodes of these ancient texts and works of art. In his recent film, "The Passion of the Christ," Mel Gibson unsparingly (and controversially) recreated the violence that would have been inflicted on Christ, and during the movie's theatrical release in the United States, whole congregations, including children, attended screenings together.

Although we may find this alarming, we should remember that children have historically witnessed a wide variety of public spectacles, from self-flagellation, executions, and violent games to puppet plays, like the Balinese Dalang and the Punch and Judy shows, both of which contain violent material and were performed in public spaces. Relatively little thought has been given to censoring these events or the arts from a child's environment until the 20th century. Two horrific World Wars, the threat of global annihilation, and the advent of movements for nonviolence and peaceful resolution of conflict have linked with the arguments of modern psychologists and parenting experts about the need for adults to minimize potentially traumatic experiences for their children, even the kind found in the arts and literature.

## CHILDREN'S FOLKLORE: THE ROUGH AND TUMBLE PLAYGROUND

As children grow older, the folklore of games, songs, rhymes, stories, rituals, and beliefs that they create and perpetuate solely among themselves, is just as challenging and often downright shocking to adult ears. The English scholar Douglas Newton called children "the greatest of savage tribes, and the only one which shows no sign of dying out" (Opie & Opie, 1959, p. 2). Two scholars of children's folklore, Iona and Peter Opie, in their classic study, *The Lore and Language of Schoolchildren* (1959), collected thousands of rhymes that included a group they called "jeers and other torments." These include a wide range of verbal taunts, such as this warning to a tattle tale:

> Tell tale tit,
> Your tongue shall be slit,
> And all the little dickey birds
> Will have a little bit. (p. 190)

Other "torments" include forms of ritualized physical violence that English children have inflicted on one another for centuries, passing this tradition on from generation to generation. One of these "tortures," depicted by Pieter Brueghel the Elder in his renowned 16th-century painting, *Kinderspiele,* was called "Running the Gauntlet." The Opies recorded this ritual as still being practiced in 20th-century England. It was meant to teach bullies a lesson, as the Opies' young informant explained:

> When boys are not agreeable and are bullies they are put through the mill. This is a kind of torture, and about twenty boys or less, as the case may be, put their hands flat on the wall, with arms outstretched to form a tunnel. The bully has to go through the mill four times. The first time he has rain, this is a good slap from each boy. The second time he gets lightning, this is a rabbit-punch. The third time he gets thunder, this is a prod with the knee. Fourth time he gets hailstones, this is a very hard punch in the back. I can assure you the bully will behave after this. (p. 200)

In their illuminating study of U.S. children's folklore, *One Potato, Two Potato: The Secret Education of American Children* (1976), Mary and Herbert Knapp include folklore that is particular to the cultural dynamics of the United States. One of their many fascinating discussions concerns the centuries-old practice of verbal taunting in the African American oral tradition, "doing the dozens." Antagonists hurl insults at each other to demonstrate their verbal prowess, including the well-known kinds of ever-escalating exchanges that begin with "Yo' mama. . . ." The Knapps argue that the verbal violence that is often displayed in these shouting matches on the streets and playgrounds, in school yards and hallways, provide ways that children construct their social hierarchies and establish the range and dynamics of individual power. The loudest, most fluid, most imaginative insulter gains prestige among his or her peers. Cruel as these "cuts" can be, they also serve as a sublimated substitute for actual, physical conflict.

## THE PAINFUL LESSONS OF THE CAUTIONARY TALE

Along with these rhymes and their often cruel content, violence has also entered into

[...] the earliest in literature, but Aesop could not have dreamed of the exquisite torments that would be meted out to American children along with their alphabets. In one of the most famous tales from England, "The Prodigal Daughter" (ca. 1737), a girl makes a pact with the Devil in order to increase her allowance. The only catch is that she must agree to kill her mother and father (copying the murder of Hamlet's father) by pouring poison into their ears while they sleep. Only angelic divine intercession prevents the parenticide, and the now repentant girl, risen literally from her coffin that is about to be interred, takes it upon herself to warn other children not to follow a similar road to perdition.

Eighteenth- and nineteenth-century children's literature on both sides of the Atlantic carried on this didactic tradition in secular, though no less bloody terms. By the late 18th century, the Zeitgeist with regard to children was moving in a new direction. In its first edition, *The New England Primer* presented children as innately flawed creatures: "In Adam's fall, we sinned all" (*The New England Primer,* 1727). But a century later, in one of the many revised editions of the *Primer,* the verse had morphed into "Adam and Eve, Their God did grieve" (*Beauties of the New-England Primer,* ca. 1825, p. 1). This change of just a few words indicated a dramatic shift in the doctrine that governed thinking about the core, moral condition of both adults and children. It represented, in essence, a paradigmatic shift vis-à-vis children, brought about by a number of factors, including the mellowing of theological opinion from the Calvinist view of the fallen child and the influence of rationalists like John Locke, who argued that the child was a "tabula rasa," and thus adults should be very careful what was written on that clean slate. In addition, the idealistic philosophies about childhood expressed by writers like Rousseau and the artistic intuitions of the Romantic movement like those of William Blake, whose poetry likens the child's primal nature to a state of innocence, and William Wordsworth, for whom the child came into this world "trailing clouds of glory" also contributed to this shift. Quite simply, the child was no longer being summarily dismissed as a brutish creature.

Despite this distinctly progressive turn, the child was still seen in many quarters as being in need of constant and often harsh instruction, lest something terrible befall him or her. Even a quick dash could be deadly, as one story, "The Dangers of the Streets" (ca. 1820), lets its young readers know:

> [George] was thoughtless and giddy, would run across streets when carriages were driving up a full speed, and often very narrowly escaped being run over. . . .
>
> But see the dreadful consequences of his giddiness and folly! His foot slipped; he fell

> under the loaded wagon; the wheel passed over one of his legs, and shattered it in a most shocking manner.
>
> Thus mangled and racked with pain, he shrieked most piteously and repented his folly when too late. (Arnold, 1969, p. 20)

In these new, secular cautionary tales, children who do not listen are not, in Jonathan Edwards's well-known phrase, young "sinners in the hands of an angry God," ready to fall into Hell (1741). Rather, they accidentally tumble from rooftops or are crushed beneath wagon wheels. In other such tales, children are injured by fireworks, unsafe railings, floorboards, and ferocious animals. The 19th century would produce a number of authors who would satirize these horrific stories, including Lewis Carroll in *Alice in Wonderland.* In his story, Carroll, who was himself a member of the clergy as well as a mathematician, poked fun at such moralistic tracts as those to be found in Isaac Watts's *Divine Songs* (1971): The "little busy bee" of Watts's poem, for example, becomes, with some tweaking from Carroll, a "little crocodile."

Others in this tradition include the German doctor, Heinrich Hoffmann, who created *Struwwelpeter* (1845), a series of stories about children who do not listen to their parents and suffer extremely gruesome, over-the-top consequences: Harriet, who loves to play with matches, burns herself up—leaving only her little shoes. Conrad is deaf to the warnings of his mother about sucking his thumbs, and, while she is out, the Scissors Man appears and cuts them off. The artist Wilhelm Busch, one of the inventors of the comic book, wrote a series of adventures of two bad boys, Max and Moritz (1865), who play tricks on people, some quite violent (like loading the pipe of the church organist, Master Lämpel, with gunpowder). The boys' final trick lands them in the miller's hopper, where they are ground up into pellets, and eaten by the miller's ducks, much to the merriment of the villagers, who are delighted to be rid of the two rapscallions. By the end of the 19th century, Hilaire Belloc wrote the hilarious "Jim," first published in *Cautionary Tales for Children* (1908). This story tells of a little boy who slips out of his nurse's hands while at the zoo, and is eaten by a lion, leaving only his head. The poem ends,

> When Nurse informed his Parents, they
> Were more Concerned than I can say:—
> His Mother, as she dried her eyes,
> Said, "Well—it give me no surprise,
> He would not do as he was told!"
> His Father, who was self-controlled,
> Bade all the children round attend
> To James's miserable end,
> And always keep ahold of Nurse
> For fear of finding something worse.

One might think that these satires of cautionary tales would have hastened the demise of this genre of children's literature, but these kinds of didactic tales resurfaced again in an even stronger form in the schoolrooms of the United States from the late 1940s through the 1970s. In a genre collectively called "mental hygiene" movies, one film, *Live and Learn* (1951), warned about everyday carelessness—playing in the street, jumping from rooftops, lighting fires with gasoline, running with scissors. Each of the brief episodes in this short film ends up with a child in the emergency room, swathed in bandages, with the weary voice-over repeating "if only he had listened. . . ." For older children, the violence was ratcheted up, as in *Age 13* (1955), an exploration of a "confused" boy's downward spiral into juvenile delinquency, or *The Last Prom* (1972), about an alcohol-precipitated car wreck. Dozens of films from the 1950s through the 1970s gave their grim warnings about substance abuse (see Ken Smith's book, *Mental Hygiene: Classroom Films 1945–1970*).

Fairy tales and other traditional folk stories have been among the most controversial of any genres in the children's literature canon since Sara Trimmer first attacked the tales in her magazine, *The Guardian of Education,* in the early 1800s. Many of these stories, which were originally part of oral, pre-literate traditions, were unsparing in their graphic violence, even as they morphed over the centuries from oral to written forms. "Little Red Riding Hood," first in print in Charles Perrault's *Histoires ou contes du temps passé* (Stories or tales of times past) (1697), initially ended with the wolf devouring both the grandmother and her granddaughter. No passing huntsman arrives to rescue the victims, and the tale becomes a fable, complete with the moral,

> Little girls, this seems to say,
> Never stop upon your way.
> Never trust a stranger-friend;
> No one knows how it will end.
> As you're pretty, so be wise;
> Wolves may lurk in every guise
> Handsome they may be, and kind,
> Gay or charming—never mind!
> Now, as then, 'tis simple truth–
> Sweetest tongue has sharpest tooth!
>
> —(*Perrault's Fairy Tales,* p. 29)

In a 1939 retelling of this tale in *Fables for Our Times,* James Thurber armed his little girl with an automatic pistol. His heroine is not to be fooled because "even in a nightcap a wolf does not look any more like your grandmother than the Metro-Goldwyn lion looks like Calvin Coolidge" (p. 5). Other retellings make use of the familiar ending in which the hunter saves the grandmother and her daughter by killing the wolf who has eaten them. In a controversial version of the tale published with illustrations by the late Trina Schart Hyman in 1986, the grandmother and the huntsman have a celebratory glass of wine after their ordeal.

The Brothers Grimm first published their famous *Household Stories* in 1812, to preserve important aspects of oral Germanic culture they feared were dying. The Grimms chose to edit out much of the sexual and political content of these well-known stories but maintained the violence. They left in the chilling wedding reception party that ends "Snow-White," in which the wicked stepmother is meted out justice in horrifyingly understated terms: "And when she saw her she knew her for Snow-White and could not stir from the place for anger and terror. For they had ready red-hot iron shoes, in which she had to dance until she fell down dead" (Grimm & Grimm, 1886, p. 221). Though fairy tales have been contested literary works in children's culture for years, the concern has usually been about the sexist, authoritarian, or classist elements of the tales and not their violent content. In his now famous defense of fairy tales, *The Uses of Enchantment* (1976), noted child psychiatrist Bruno Bettelheim urged parents to retell to their children the traditional stories in their original forms, without censoring the violence. He argued that the tales' violence, especially the endings, should not be taken literally. These tales were metaphors that worked through universal questions young people have about growing up and coming into their own as distinct, valuable human beings. The symbolic nature of the final, violent acts in the tales, Bettelheim stressed, often served an important psychological function for both the teller and listener: that of restoring a sense of justness and order to the imaginary world the child has entered and vicariously lived through in the stories. Since Bettelheim's widely publicized defense of the tales, the subject of violence has hardly come up for discussion. Instead, general challenges to Bettelheim and his advocacy of the tales in their original forms have been over his seeming acceptance of the gender and class stereotypes that some have argued the tales in their original forms tend to perpetuate. More recently, the magical, supernatural elements of the tales have become a subject of concern for some adults who find these facets of the stories to be in conflict with their religious beliefs. Still, one must wonder if Bettelheim is right about offering these traditional, often violent tales to young children, despite the "just" and "happy" endings of these stories, since a young child may well be unable to process the violent content of this material.

If we look at the history of children's literature prior to this century, when the violence contained in a story for children is seen as serving to teach a lesson—whether moral, ethical, psychological, or even political—violence has usually been permitted. One of the earliest books published in English, *Aesop's Fables* (1484), originally was meant for adults. It soon became a favorite of teachers, full of instructive tales frequently underscored by a violent punch line. Gullible animals always pay a mortal price to the clever foxes, hawks, and lions that prey upon them. The boy who cries wolf when there isn't any danger, is not able to summon help when there is. When the trees of the forest agree to give the woodsman enough timber to make the handle for his axe, they fail to realize until too late that he will chop them all down.

A stomach for violence among the rough edges of pre-literate societies can hardly explain the presence of violence in a good number of more "refined" children's classics, from the 19th century to the present. Violence is part of the fabric of the action-packed stories of Sir Walter Scott and James Fennimore Cooper, just as it is in Dickens and Dumas, all of whom were read widely by boys and young men. The violence was even more pronounced and less justified by narrative brilliance when it invariably appeared in the inexpensive action literature of its time, the dime novels and "penny dreadfuls" that filled the popular imagination with tales of derring-do in exotic locales where young men dreamed of finding fame and fortune. Closer to home, Twain's *The Adventures of Tom Sawyer* and *The Adventures of Huckleberry Finn* have, at their heart, violent episodes that threaten the physical safety of their young heroes. In the case of Huck Finn, it shakes his sense of psychological invulnerability to the core. Huck is so powerfully affected by his dangerous journey down the Mississippi, the brutality of his alcoholic father, several horrendous mob scenes, and the sens less death of a young friend, that he refuses to go back up the river to civilization. "I been there before," he says in the book's closing lines.

## OVER THE RAINBOW AND RIGHT NEXT DOOR: FICTIONAL VIOLENCE

As we move into the 21st century, we also see the presence of violence in the works of Rudyard Kipling, Howard Pyle, and Jack London, where violence is essential to the character-building in the novels' young men. Even L. Frank Baum, who wished in *The Wizard of Oz* (1900) to write "a modernized fairy tale, in which the wonderment and joy are retained and the heartaches and nightmares are left out," could not quite manage to expel violence from his imagined world of Oz (p. 4).

If we leap forward to the present—over Tolkien's battle-scarred landscape in *The Lord of the Rings* series and C. S. Lewis's *The Chronicles of Narnia* (a place which is redeemed through the sacrifice of its King, Aslan) and Ursula Le Guin's *Earthsea Trilogy* (in which a young wizard contends with the dark forces of his world)—we find a contemporary landscape of children's books that is anything but violence-free, especially in the longer narratives meant for older children and adolescents. The wildly popular Harry Potter books, to pick just one example from the contemporary mix, are fueled by violent episodes and threats—from the abuse Harry receives from his human foster family, to the extremely dangerous sport he plays at the school for young wizards, to the life-or-death struggles that he engages in with evil characters who keep turning up. Interestingly enough, the controversy that these books have stirred does not concern possible violent physical harm in the story line, but rather the magic that is practiced throughout the series by the adults and young people.

It is one thing for there to be violence in fantasy literature where it could, presumably, be viewed as a part of the general nostalgia associated with fantasies that are set in other times, or galaxies "far, far away," and another for the violence to be set in the present, "real" world. Thus, to the literalist's way of thinking, there would be little danger of a teenager imitating the sword and sorcery violence of a work of high fantasy: it would be a physical impossibility. But since the 1960s, the fiction produced for teenagers and young adults has insisted on depicting the realities of life for young people. One of the key works to try to truthfully portray the experiences of adolescents was S. E. Hinton's first novel, *The Outsiders* (1967). This was a sympathetic tale, told from a point of view inside a gang of teenage boys from the wrong side of the tracks, who are continually forced to protect themselves against another gang. The period's other breakthrough work was Robert Cormier's *The Chocolate War* (1974), which regularly appears on banned books lists. However, the extreme nature of its violence is not the source of controversy: instead, it is the book's language and the hero's thoughts about sex. "They murdered him," begins the first chapter, set at a high school football practice. This tone continues to the end when the hero is taken away in an ambulance, beaten senseless by the school bully, while a teacher nonchalantly comments, "Boys will be boys."

These books were part of a long-standing discussion about violence that began in the United States in the late 1940s with a concern about the rise of juvenile crime and gangs. "Juvenile delinquency" became a common topic explored in Hollywood films like *The Wild One* (1953) and *Rebel Without a Cause* (1955). Both of these movies made their respective young heroes, Marlon Brando and James Dean, instant stars. This growing separation between generations continued throughout the 1950s with the Beats, Elvis, and the youth movement of the 1960s. A generic stance was taken in these works against all forms of authority—parents, teachers, politicians, institutions—and the perceived hypocrisy and lack of sympathy in their treatment of the aspirations and yearnings of young people. The Vietnam War in the late 1960s became the ultimate symbol of these generational conflicts.

All was not quiet in picture books for younger children at this time either. Dr. Seuss suggested the unconscious rebelliousness in young people was about to break loose in *The Cat in the Hat* (1957). Seuss continued for three decades in books like *The Lorax* (1971) and *The Butter Battle Book* (1984) to satirize the destructive folly of "leaders" ravaging the environment and threatening to unleash another world war.

Maurice Sendak broke onto the scene with his award-winning *Where the Wild Things Are* (1962), about a little boy who tames the threatening creatures of his own imagination by "staring into all their yellow eyes without blinking once." Sendak created a map of the emotional and visionary terrain of childhood, where he dealt with subjects considered taboo for the writers of books for younger children—explosive anger, frustration, intense sibling rivalry, existential angst, and death.

Other writers and illustrators from the 1960s to the present—William Steig, Louise Fitzhugh, Tomi Ungerer, Eve Merriam, and Raymond Briggs, to name just a few—have worked with volatile, often violent material as an intrinsic part of their books and their vision. More recently we have seen picture books include larger, violent issues affecting our society, as artist David Diaz and author Eve Bunting did with their treatment of the Los Angeles race riots, *Smokey Night* (1994).

## THE NEW UNMEDIATED REALITIES

If we add to these established literary forms the newer digital genres of video games and the Internet; the reenergized comics industry; and electronic media like television, movies, and popular music, we find that our children have returned to a new, immediately accessible Mother Goose world in which anything and everything is produced and available, almost instantly, for an audience that crosses generations and societal strata. Despite widespread parental concerns over the Internet and cable television, and some ability to filter obscene or violent images, there isn't any comprehensive, socially agreed-upon structure of protection for children other than the problematic one of constant parental vigilance. At some point, most parents or concerned adults experience shock and stupefaction over children's access to media that Ian Wojcik-Andrews describes in the introduction to his book, *Children's Films: History, Ideology, Pedagogy, Theory* (2000, p. 1). He writes:

> My own understanding of children's films grew out of various personal experiences. One day my then eight- and five-year-old boys Eric and Ryan came home from school declaring they had outgrown *Barney, Sesame Street, Lamb Chop, Reading Rainbow, The Land Before Time, Ferngully, Fantasia, Home Alone* and *Home Alone 2: Lost in New York,* and were now old enough to watch instead cartoons such as *The Power Rangers, The Centurions, Captain Planet, Dragon Ball Z, Swat Cat, Beavis and Butthead,* and *South Park,* and films such as *Free Willy, Batman, Batman Forever, The Mask, Ace Ventura: Pet Detective, Terminator 2: Judgment Day,* and *Starship Troopers.* For Eric and Ryan, appropriate viewing no longer meant children's shows such as *Sesame Street,* but films for older viewers such as *Scream.*

The reasons for this breakdown in the separation between adult and children's media have been extensively and continuously debated by Neil Postman (*The End of Childhood,* 1982) and many others. With regard to violence, exposure is pervasive in our culture from early childhood through adulthood. Regulation in a democratic, market-driven society seems impossible. The language and images of violence have taken over what one thinks of as our most reasoned, cautious levels of discussion and debate.

Currently, the visual and verbal vocabularies of war have come to occupy a prominent place in our contemporary environment, an environment that is clearly within the listening range of children. During the 2004 U.S. presidential election, both candidates spoke forcefully, repeatedly, explicitly about tracking down the terrorist enemies of America and killing them. The candidates themselves suited up, like action figures, ready to rumble in battle flight gear for the press, or in one case, carrying a shotgun over his arm. In this context, the ban on automatic assault rifles was allowed to expire without significant public debate. This potentially dangerous, sanctioned expansion of powerful weapons into everyday life was essentially ignored.

On every level, the unspoken message is that one best be well-armed. The enemy is at the gates. And young people, some in their teens, will be sent, as always, to fight in places around the world where enemies wait in ambush. Not only is the acquisition of real weapons a given in our culture, but virtual weapons and virtual violence are seen as providing a useful dimension of preparedness. The reflexes of our soldiers are being honed for combat through the "first-person shooter" video games that once shocked parent groups and led to age-appropriate ratings of the games. What purpose could these games possibly have, except to train young people to use weapons? Those concerns and questions seem absurdly rhetorical now. The inviolate sheltering of our children from violence has suddenly evaporated.

We are seeing a proliferation of toys, video games, animated films, anime, and movies unconcerned with the need to protect our young from the disquieting and potentially tragic effects of violence in their lives. Almost anything can be obtained via the Internet, including a new video game in which the player attempts to mimic the shots that claimed the life of the late President Kennedy from the vantage point of his alleged assassin, Lee Harvey Oswald (*JFK Reloaded,* 2004). Almost anything can be heard in contemporary music, including Eminem's (2004) video, "Mosh," in which the vice president suffers a heart attack before an angry mob of protesters. Virtually anything can be seen on television during the hours reserved for family viewing. According to the Parents Television Council, "the third most watched program on TV for children under fourteen" in 2004 was *Fear Factor,* which airs during family viewing time and includes having the contestants engage in gross and dangerous stunts, "everything from eating animal genitals to freeing themselves from a submerged body bag" (Sizemore, 2004). In fact, we now celebrate violent arch villains, like Uncle Olaf in Lemony Snicket's *Series of Unfortunate Events,* or the "teenage criminal mastermind," Artemis Fowl, in the series of novels by Eoin Colfer.

## AN ARCHETYPAL HOPE: SHADOW WORK

Something is happening in our culture and another paradigm has shifted. In the 21st century, unlike the last, preemptive violence is once again redemptive and ultimately good. We have seen released in our culture, among children and adults, what the psychologist Carl Jung calls the shadow—that part of our individual and collective psyches that contains all that we do not wish to acknowledge about ourselves. In the United States, there is a new prevailing mythos, floated on certain national media, that refuses to see this country as anything but ultimately correct, profoundly exceptional, perfect in all its imperfections—indeed, chosen by God to fulfill its new destiny. What has been pushed aside by this particular Zeitgeist is any real sense of moral and ethical responsibility for our actions, the notion of playing by rules, of cooperation, of understanding other perspectives.

The novelist Ursula Le Guin (1980) offers an insightful summary of Jung's concept of the archetypal shadow when she writes,

> The shadow is on the other side of our psyche, the dark brother of the conscious mind. It is Cain, Caliban, Frankenstein's monster, Mr. Hyde. It is Virgil who guided Dante through hell, Gilgamesh's friend Enkidu, Frodo's enemy Gollum. It is the Doppelgänger. It is Mowgli's Grey Brother; the werewolf; the wolf, the bear, the tiger of a thousand folktales; it is the serpent, Lucifer. The shadow stands on the threshold between the conscious and the unconscious mind, and we meet it in our dreams as sister, brother, friend, beast, monster,

> enemy, guide. It is all that we do not want to, cannot, admit into our conscious self, all the qualities and tendencies within us which have been repressed, denied, or not used. . . . Unadmitted to consciousness, the shadow is projected outward onto others. There's nothing wrong with me—it's *them.* I'm not a monster, other people are monsters. All foreigners are evil. All communists are evil. All capitalists are evil. It was the cat that made me kick him, Mummy. . . . If the individual wants to live in the real world, he must withdraw his projections; he must admit that the hateful, the evil exists within himself. This isn't easy. It is very hard not to be able to blame anybody else. But it may be worth it. Jung says, "If he only learns to deal with his own shadow he has done something real for the world. He has succeeded in shouldering at least an infinitesimal part of the gigantic, unsolved social problems of our day." (p. 64)

This shouldering of the burden of the shadow is addressed in Le Guin's *Earthsea Trilogy,* where the main character, Ged, charts his development into a wise adult from an enormously talented, enormously proud, enormously foolish teenager. This important journey of self-discovery serves as an example for both young people and adults about our personal confrontations with our own shadows. We can understand, on an abstract level, how our literature and art provide a kind of "container" for the violent darkness within us as individuals and our society as a whole.

The expression of the violent "other" in myths and stories, video games and movies, poetry and picture books, is one way we can make some sense of it, attempt to frame it and possibly gain some control over it. Children are constantly doing this in their own attempts to master the bogeymen and other "Wild Things" that inhabit their world. Like the rest of life, alas, some parts of children's cultural experience will remain eternally violent, unruly, and unremittingly resistant to any forms of adult restraint. But, when we challenge children and adolescents over this material and seek to guide them through its emotional labyrinths, we also need to examine for ourselves our adult justifications and acceptance of violence in our homes, communities, country, and world. After all, we still have our own adult bogeymen to meet, daily.

## REFERENCES

Arnold, A. (1969). *Pictures and stories from forgotten children's books of the past.* New York: Dover.

Baring-Gould, W. S., & Baring-Gould, C. (Eds). (1962). *The annotated Mother Goose.* New York: Clarkson N. Potter.

Baum, L. F. (1900). *The wizard of Oz.* New York: Rand McNally.

*Beauties of the New-England Primer.* (n.d. ca. 1825). New York: Samuel Wood.

Bettleheim, B. (1976). *The uses of enchantment: The meaning and importance of fairy tales.* New York: Knopf.

Daiken, L. (1959). *The lullaby book.* London: Edmund Ward.

Edwards, J. (1741). *Sinners in the hands of an angry God.* New Haven, CT: Yale University, Jonathan Edwards Center. Retrieved from www.edwards.yale.edu/major-works/sinners-in-the-hands-of-an-angry-god/

Eminem. (2004). *Mosh* [music video]. Available: http://www.gnn.tv/videos/video.php?id=27

Gaster, T. H. (1980). *The holy and the profane: Evolution of Jewish folkways.* New York: William Morrow.

Grimm, J., & Grimm, W. (1886). *Household stories from the collections of the Brothers Grimm* (L. Crane, Trans.). New York: Macmillan.

Knapp, M., & Knapp, H. (1976). *One potato, two potato: The secret education of American children.* New York: Norton.

Le Guin, U. K. (1980). *The language of the night: Essays on fantasy and science fiction.* New York: Perigee.

*JFK reloaded.* (2004). Retrieved from www.jfkreloaded.net

*Mother Goose's melodies.* (1970. Facsimile of 1833 edition). New York: Dover.

*New-England Primer.* (1727). Boston: S. Kneeland & T. Green.

Opie, I., & Opie, P. (1959). *The lore and language of schoolchildren.* Oxford: Clarendon.

Perrault, C. (1697). *Histoires ou contes du temps passé.* Translated into English as *Histories, or tales of past times.* (1729). York, UK: J. Kendrew, Colliergate.

*Perrault's fairy tales: Stories or tales from times past, with morals.* (1969). (A. E. Johnson, Trans.; originally published as *Old-Time Stories Told by Master Charles Perrault.* New York: Dodd Mead, 1921; Verse morals translated by S. R. Littlewood, London: Herbert & Daniel, 1912; Illustrations by Gustave Doré, first published in *Les Contes de Perrault, dessins par Gustave Doré.* Paris: J. Hetzel, 1867) New York: Dover.

Sandars, N. K. (Trans.). (1972). *The epic of Gilgamesh.* London: Penguin.

Sizemore, F. (2004, February 28). *Fear factor.* Parents Television Council Publications. www.parentstv.org/ptc/publications/bw/2004/0228worst.asp

Smith, K. (1999). *Mental hygiene: Classroom films 1945–1970.* New York: Blast Books.

Thurber, J. (1939). *Fables for our time.* New York: Harper & Row.

Watts, I. (1971). *Divine songs attempted in easy language for the use of children: Facsimile reproductions of the first edition of 1715 and an illustrated edition of ca. 1840.* London: Oxford University Press.

Wojcik-Andrews, I. (2000). *Children's films: History, ideology, pedagogy, theory.* New York: Garland.

CHAPTER 8

# *A Preliminary Demography of Television Violence*

NANCY SIGNORIELLI

Television is the central and most pervasive mass medium in American culture. It plays a distinctive and historically unprecedented role as our nation's, and increasingly the world's, most common, constant, and vivid learning environment. Americans spend much of their time watching television. In the average home the television set is turned on for about 7 hours each day and the average person watches more than 3 hours a day (Nielsen, 2000). Few people escape exposure to television's vivid and recurrent patterns of images, information, and values. Moreover, today's delivery systems, including broadcast television, cable, satellite, video tapes, and DVDs, provide numerous venues for viewing.

Television is first and foremost a storyteller—telling most of the stories to most of the people, most of the time. It is the wholesale distributor of images and the mainstream of our popular culture. Today, the children of the world are born into homes in which, for the first time in human history, centralized commercial institutions rather than parents, churches, or schools tell most of the stories. Television shows and tells us about life—people, places, power, striving, what people do and how they do it. It tells us who is good and who is bad, who wins and who loses, what works and what does not, and what it means to be a man or a woman or a member of a particular racial group. As such, television has become a socialization agent. It gives us messages about violence, its prevalence, who gets hurt or killed, and who is likely to do the hurting or killing. These images of perpetrators and victims are particularly compelling because they provide viewers with a calculus of life's chances—the likelihood that a particular person, or group of people, might hurt or kill someone, or more importantly, the likelihood of getting hurt or killed. Consequently, our understanding of televised images about the demography of violence can help us to understand better the media's important role in people's lives. This chapter focuses specifically on these messages, using the results from an analysis conducted specifically for this discussion as well as information and data from the most important and relevant studies of television violence to date—the Cultural Indicators project (see Gerbner,

Gross, Morgan, Signorielli, & Shanahan, 2002) and the National Television Violence Study (1998).

## THEORETICAL PERSPECTIVE

Numerous theories explain why the study of television violence is important and how it may affect viewers, especially children. Desensitization (see Potter, 1999) and social learning-cognitive theory (Bandura, 2002), for example, examine the immediate and typically harmful effects of viewing violence. *Desensitization* posits that watching violence leads to insensitivity and callousness. *Social learning-cognitive theory* predicts that viewing violence provides viewers with potential scripts or models of violent behaviors or reactions to them and may teach viewers to behave aggressively. *Cultivation theory,* on the other hand, looks at viewing violence from a cumulative, long-term perspective (Gerbner et al., 2002). It posits that television violence illustrates and provides lessons about power, which in turn contribute to viewers' perceptions of the world as a mean and scary place and their own chances of being a victim or perpetrator of violence.

These theoretical perspectives also explain the importance of understanding the demography of violence. According to social learning-cognitive theory, images of those who do the hurting or killing may enable viewers to develop scripts about their own likelihood of becoming involved in violence. If, for example, you find that people like you are typically the perpetrators or victims of violence, then you may have a different set of scripts than someone for whom these images rarely apply. Similarly, according to cultivation theory, viewers whose demography is similar to or resonates with the primary demography of being hurt or killed on television or other media, may feel their own personal or societal vulnerability is affected (Morgan, 1983). This could then translate to exhibiting behaviors of a more protective nature (such as buying a watchdog or gun for protection) or perceiving the world as dangerous (Gerbner, Gross, Morgan, & Signorielli, 1980).

Children, in particular, are likely to be affected by messages of violence. These messages may be particularly salient if those depicted in the violent images are children or adolescents. Children typically like to watch programs whose main characters are youngsters and find these programs more appealing (Harwood, 1997). Moreover, characters who are similar to children in age and sex are their favorites (Hoffner, 1996). From a social learning-cognitive theoretical perspective, children may focus on television characters who are "like" them to guide their behavior or help them form scripts of acceptable behaviors and possible outcomes, particularly those of an aggressive nature (Bandura, 2002). In addition, recent studies have found that the lessons learned from viewing violence may be related to the characters who are involved in violence (Wilson, Colvin, & Smith, 2002). The sex, race, and age of characters involved in violence could provide powerful messages about power and vulnerability.

There are relatively few studies focusing on how children and adolescents are portrayed on television. The existing studies tell us that this age group has been consistently underrepresented and devalued during prime time (Greenberg, 1980; Signorielli, 1987). Signorielli (1987) found that while children under 10 made up about 15% of the U.S. population, they made up less than 2% of the characters in prime-time programs. This study of prime-time programs broadcast between 1969 and 1985 found that children and adolescents were much more likely to be victimized than older characters. The only group that was equally likely to hurt others and be hurt themselves was young girls

(9 years of age and younger). Overall, however, boys under 10 years of age were more likely than girls to be battered on prime time—they were more likely to get hurt than to hurt other characters. Young boys were also the most underrepresented and the most racially mixed group. While young girls were also underrepresented, the analysis found that as girls move into adolescence, particularly later adolescence, they become more numerous on prime time but more vulnerable in terms of their likelihood of getting hurt. Signorielli (1987) concluded that the overall image of children and adolescence on television was one of unimportance and devaluation. Similarly, Peck (1982) noted, "(t)he young are either played for laughs, kept subordinate to adult roles, or cast as victims—three states they are anxious to avoid in their own lives" (p. 63).

## VIOLENCE ON TELEVISION

Most of our knowledge about television violence comes from studies conducted during the past 35 years as part of the Cultural Indicators project (CI), the longest-running, consistent, and stable research project on television violence; and the research conducted in the mid-1990s in the National Television Violence Study (NTVS). Through the early 1990s, CI measured the amount of physical violence on television by monitoring intact weeks of prime-time network broadcast television programming (Gerbner et al., 2002), periodically publishing the results as a Violence Profile, the last in 1994 (Gerbner, Morgan, & Signorielli, 1994). This perspective has continued into the 21st century in the work of Signorielli (2003b). The CI studies examined 37 separate samples of prime-time network broadcast programs with a total of 2,836 programs and 10,294 leading characters. The NTVS (1998) also examined physical violence using a different sampling procedure. This study focused on three yearly samples (1994–1995, 1995–1996, and 1996–1997) made up of composite weeks of programming across 23 channels operating between 6:00 A.M. and 11:00 P.M. each day ($N = 8,200$). This sample included programs on broadcast channels (commercial networks, independent stations, and public television) and cable channels (basic and premium offerings) seen between October and June of each year sampled. The samples included all genres except game shows, religious programs, "infomercials" or home shopping channels, sports, instructional programs, and news. NTVS thus provides a more expansive examination of television violence because it sampled a larger universe of television programming. Taken together, however, both research programs provide a unique and detailed understanding of television violence.

## DEFINITIONS AND MEASURES

CI and NTVS both define violence in terms of physical force. CI defines violence as "the overt expression of physical force (with or without a weapon, against self or other) compelling action against one's will on pain of being hurt or killed, or actually hurting or killing" (Signorielli, Gross, & Morgan, 1982, p. 163). This focus includes all plausible and credible violence, including humorous violence. Although some have argued that humorous violence is not problematic (Blank, 1977; Coffin & Tuchman, 1972–1973), in actuality, humorous or comic violence may increase the risk of learning aggressive behaviors because it is not perceived as "bad" or problematic violence and the public often sees cartoon violence as harmless (Baron, 1978; Berkowitz, 1970; Potter, 1999). "Accidental" violence and violent "acts of nature" are also included because such actions are purposeful, claim victims, and demonstrate power. Writers add such scenes to programs in order to propel the story and perhaps to eliminate or incapacitate certain characters. NTVS defines violence as "any overt depiction of a credible threat of physical force or the actual use of such force intended to physically harm an animate being or group of beings" (Wilson et al., 2002, p. 41). NTVS focuses on physical violence, rather than psychological or emotional violence, and includes "depictions of the harmful consequences of unseen violence" (Wilson et al., 2002, p. 41).

These two research programs examine who is involved in violence differently. CI focuses on all characters whose roles are central to the story line or action. The data from this study can thus be analyzed to examine prevalence of violence among all the characters as well as those involved in violence. Several measures are used to examine how characters are involved in violence. Two distinct variables measure involvement—being a perpetrator of violence or being a victim of violence. An overall measure of involvement in violence is calculated from the intersection of these two variables and labels a character as either a perpetrator or a victim of violence. A fourth measure looks at the overlap of these two variables to isolate those characters who are both perpetrators and victims. Several variables also measure the context of the character's involvement in violence. All of the variables used in the CI studies met standards of reliability as set out by Krippendorff (1980) and discussed in more detail in Signorielli (2003b).

NTVS (1998), in contrast, focuses only on characters who were actually involved in violence, specifically, the characters who took part in interactions consisting of perpetrators (P) who use unique violent actions (A) to aggress against a target (T), known as PAT interactions. Consequently the NTVS discusses characterizations only in terms of violent interactions. The CI studies present a broader picture by looking at a character's involvement in violence from the perspective of the entire group of leading and supporting characters, not just those involved in violence. The CI studies thus tell us about the overall likelihood of involvement in violence of specific demographic subgroups of characters.

## WHO'S INVOLVED

Physical violence is extremely prevalent on television. The CI project found that violence appears in about 60% of all network prime-time broadcast programs at the rate of 5 incidents per program (Signorielli, 2003b). More recent samples of network prime-time programs broadcast between the fall of 2000 and the fall of 2003 (Signorielli, 2003b, 2005) show that violence appears most in crime programs, dramas, and reality shows, and least in situation comedies and news magazine shows. While violence was a little more likely to occur in programs broadcast between 9 P.M. and 11 P.M. (67% were violent) than those broadcast between 7 P.M. and 9 P.M. (54% were violent), the rate of violent actions per program was higher in the early-evening programs (5.3 acts per program) compared to later programs (4.3 per program). Moreover, about a third of the leading and supporting characters in late-evening programs were involved in violence, compared to a little more than a quarter of the leading and supporting characters in the early-evening programs. Similarly, NTVS found that violence appears in roughly 60% of all the programs in their entire sample (6 A.M. to midnight) as well as those programs seen during prime time (Smith, Nathanson, & Wilson, 2002).

The early CI studies found a demographic power structure, with women and minorities more likely to be hurt than to hurt others. "Violence Profile No. 11" (Gerbner, Gross, Morgan, & Signorielli, 1980), for example, found that between 1969 and 1979, 60% of the male major characters compared to 40% of the female major characters were involved in violence (either hurting others or being hurt themselves). Whites were slightly more likely than minorities to be involved in violence; more than half of the minority men, compared to 60% of the White men, either hurt others or were hurt themselves. This was true for less than one-quarter of the minority women, compared to 40% of the White women. During the 1970s these patterns favored victimization for women and minorities—characters were more likely to be hurt or killed themselves than to hurt or kill other characters.

During the 1980s, male characters were slightly less likely to be involved in violence than in the 1970s (Gerbner, Morgan, & Signorielli, 1994). More than half of the male characters (56%) in the 1980s, compared to 60% in the 1970s, either hurt others or were hurt themselves. The percentage of women involved in violence, on the other hand, increased slightly during the 1980s. In the 1970s, 40% of the women were involved in violence while 44% were involved during the 1980s. Once again, characters were somewhat more likely to be victimized than to hurt others.

Ongoing research by the author in the Cultural Indicators perspective conducted specifically for this chapter and other projects (see Signorielli, 2003b, 2005) shows that by the end and turn of the century, patterns of committing violence and being victimized on prime time changed. Analyses of week-long samples of prime-time programs broadcast between 1993 and 2003 show that, overall, fewer major and leading characters were involved in violence—only one-third were involved in violence either by hurting or killing others or being hurt or killed themselves. In the 1960s and 1970s and into the 1980s about half of the leading characters were typically involved in some type of violence. Thus, during the last 40 years, the percentages of leading characters involved in violence decreased.

Although fewer characters are involved in violence overall, demographic differences mark their involvement in violence. Between the fall of 2000 and the fall of 2003, those characters involved in violence, as perpetrators or victims, were more likely to be male (68%) than female (32%), reflecting the continued overrepresentation of men on television (Signorielli & Bacue, 1999). But, as this data set of programming has an overall 60%–40% male–female split, it is clear that involvement in violence is much more an activity of male than female characters. Perpetrators of violence are 69% male compared to 31% female, while 66% of the males compared to 34% of the females are victims of violence. Similarly, looking at the entire sample of characters, those involved in violence as either perpetrators or victims are more likely to be White characters (77%) than minority characters (23%), a split that reflects the overall racial makeup in prime-time broadcast programs (Signorielli, Horry, & Carlton, 2004). Moreover, the distributions are similar for just the perpetrators and just the victims of violence. The distributions by involvement also are similar when comparing characters by both race and sex. These figures again reflect prime time's overall White–minority distribution of 80% to 20%.

There are considerable differences when the data about the involvement in violence are examined and isolated in terms of just men, just women, just Whites, and just minorities. This analysis provides information about how many men, women, Whites, or minorities are involved in violence and gives a somewhat different picture of how characters are involved in violence during prime time. The data from the fall of 2000 to the fall of 2003 show that one-third of the men compared to one-quarter of the women are involved in violence as either perpetrators or victims of violence. Interestingly 15% of the men compared to 10% of the women are categorized as both perpetrators and victims of violence (Signorielli, 2005). If we look at how many men and women are only perpetrators or only victims of violence on prime time, we find that one-quarter of the men compared to less than one-fifth of the women fall in these two groups.

In these samples, we find that proportionally more of the minorities (33%) than the Whites (29%) are involved in violence. Minorities are a little more likely than Whites to be perpetrators or victims of violence (1 in 4 minorities compared to 1 in 5 Whites), and minorities are more likely than Whites to be both perpetrators and victims (17% of the minorities compared to 11% of the Whites). Adding sex to the equation, both minority men and women are slightly more likely to be involved in violence than White men and women.

Another way the CI studies have examined involvement in violence is by comparing the ratio of who does the hurting or killing to who gets hurt or killed. Interestingly, during the 1990s and early part of the 21st century, these ratios changed (Signorielli, 1990). In the 1970s and early 1980s, for every 10 male characters who hurt or killed other characters, 11 men were victimized. From 2000 to 2003, male characters were about equally likely to hurt or kill than be hurt or killed. For women, the differences vary. In the 1970s, 16 women were victimized for every 10 women who hurt or killed others. However, the odds have now changed. In the most recent samples of programs broadcast in prime time, women are also equally likely to hurt or kill as be hurt or killed (Signorielli, 2005).

There are few differences by race. While, as noted above, Whites are less likely than minorities to be involved in violence, both groups are equally likely to hurt or kill as be hurt or killed. However, when we add sex to the mix, there are some differences. Both White men and minority men are slightly more likely to do the hurting than be hurt (for every 10 White or minority males who are hurt, 11 hurt others). On the other hand, White women are slightly more likely than minority women to hurt others (for every 10 White woman who are hurt, 11 do the hurting), while minority women are more likely to be hurt than hurt others (for every 10 minority women who hurt others, 11 are hurt).

While NTVS (1998) did not generate a profile of all characters on television, it examined the demographic makeup of perpetrators and targets of violence. Most of the perpetrators (close to three-quarters) were men while only 1 in 10 was a woman. Few perpetrators were categorized as heroes and most were White. More than 4 out of 10 perpetrators (43%) were "bad" while more than a quarter (28%) were "good" and 1 in 10 was both "good and bad." Similarly, about three-quarters of the targets were men while only 1 in 10 was a woman. Three-quarters of both the perpetrators and targets of violence were White. Potter, Vaughan, Warren, Howley, Land, and Hagemeyer (1995) also found that men were more likely than women to perpetuate aggressive acts, particularly those of a serious nature. They note, however, that these higher rates of aggression are due to the overrepresentation of men on television, and this explains the unrealistic nature of TV portrayals of violence. Potter and colleagues (1995) also found that the television world typically presents an unrealistic picture of serious aggression in regard to the race of those who commit the acts as well as those who are victimized. In short, television overrepresents both White perpetrators and White victims of aggression.

## AGE-RELATED DIFFERENCES

Looking first at those characters in prime time who are perpetrators or victims of violence in the early 21st century, there are interesting age differences. An analysis of the data set used by the author in previous publications (see Signorielli, 2003b, 2005) conducted specifically for this discussion found that, overall, middle-aged characters are most likely to be involved in violence (53%), followed by young adults (40%), children and adolescents (6%), and almost none of the elderly (less than 1%). The same age-related distributions exist for White and minority characters. There are some differences, however, for women—47% of both the young adults and middle-aged women, 6% of the girls and adolescent girls, but no elderly women are involved in violence. Again, the figures are quite stable when looking only at perpetrators and only at victims of violence. Likewise, the NTVS found that about 75% of both White and minority characters in the PATs were adults, about 10% were children or teens, and only 1% were classified as elderly.

This special analysis also isolated interesting differences when looking at characters in four specific age groups: children and teens, young adults, middle-aged adults, and the elderly. The data show that minority and White boys, adolescents, and young men are the groups most likely to be involved in violence on prime time. Old or elderly characters, on the other hand, particularly old women, and young or adolescent girls are the least likely to be involved in violence. Except for minority girls, children and adolescents are more likely to be victims than to commit violence. For every 10 young boys who hurt others, 17 are hurt, and an identical ratio appears for young girls. On the other hand, young adult men and women as well as middle-aged women are equally likely to hurt others and be hurt themselves. Middle-aged men, however, are more likely to hurt others than be hurt themselves—for every 10 who are hurt, 12 hurt others. Overall, elderly women were not involved in violence in any of these samples, while 15 elderly men were victimized for every 10 who hurt others.

Adding race to the picture shows some interesting differences. Among White male characters, children, adolescents, and young adults are somewhat more likely to be involved in violence than middle-aged men—about 40% of the younger male characters compared to 30% of the middle-aged men and only 9% of the elderly men. There are larger differences for minority males—60% of the children and adolescents, 40% of the young adults, 33% of the middle-aged men, and 25% of the elderly men are involved in violence. Except for the middle-aged minority men, the ratios of involvement for minorities favor victimization over being a perpetrator of violence. For every 10 minority boys who hurt, 14 are hurt; while young minority men are equally likely to hurt as be hurt themselves. Elderly minority men are only victims of violence—none of this group hurt other characters. For middle-aged minority men, however, 14 hurt others for every 10 who are hurt.

Minority females have an interesting constellation. Minority girls are more likely to hurt others than be hurt on prime time—for every 10 minority girls who are hurt, 15 do the hurting. Young minority women are more likely to be victimized—for every 10 who hurt others, 14 are hurt. Middle-aged minority women, on the other hand, are equally likely to hurt or be hurt, while none of the elderly minority women were involved in violence.

Wilson, Colvin, and Smith (2002), in an analysis of the NTVS data set, found that while younger perpetrators of violence do not appear very frequently, when they do appear they are presented as attractive and may not be punished as often as adult perpetrators. Moreover, the type of violence in which they are involved typically produces fewer negative consequences for the target and may be found in a humorous context, most often in cartoon programming. Youthful perpetrators are important, however, because during a typical day's viewing, a child will probably encounter two incidences of violence committed by a youthful perpetrator. Most violence, however, is perpetrated by adults who are more likely to be punished and typically cause more harm to their targets of violence.

## INVOLVEMENT IN KILLING

Overall, less than 10% of the leading and supporting characters in prime-time broadcast programs are involved in killing. More than 70% of this small number of characters are men. These figures show that both men and minorities are somewhat overrepresented when compared to their overall proportions in programming. While 1 in 5 characters is a minority, more than one-quarter of those involved in killing are minorities. Similarly while 6 out of 10 characters are men, they represent 7 out of 10 of those involved in killing. Killing is also most likely to involve adults and young adults. Children and the elderly are not involved in killing very often.

In terms of proportions, almost 1 in 10 men are involved in killing, compared to 1 in 20 women. The comparison by race shows that proportionally more minorities than Whites are involved in killing—7% of the White characters compared to 10% of minority characters. These differences also exist when looking at sex and race—for the White characters, 8% of the men compared to 5% of the women are involved in killing. For minorities, 11% of the men and 8% of the women are so involved. Thus, both minority men and minority women are more likely to be involved in killing than White men and White women. About 8% of both young adults and middle-aged characters are involved in killing, while about 4% of both children and the elderly are involved in killing.

Adding race to the mix shows some interesting differences. The involvement in killing for White characters of different ages does not change from the figures for the entire sample of characters. However, minorities in all age groups, except the young adults, are more likely to be involved in killing. Minorities involved in killing include 7% of the children and adolescents, 7% of the young adults, 11% of the middle-aged adults, and 17% of the elderly. Comparing rates by sex, boys are more likely to be involved in killing than girls (5% compared to 2%), young men are more likely than young women (11% compared to 4%), and middle-aged men are more likely than middle-aged women (9% compared to 7%). Moreover, there are no elderly women involved in killing, only elderly men.

The ratio of being a killer to being killed favors killers. Overall, there are 21 killers for every 10 characters who are killed, ratios that are similar for both men and women. Whites are more likely to be killers than minority characters. For every 24 White killers, 10 Whites are killed, while for every 16 minority killers, 10 minorities are killed. The intersection of sex and race shows that White males are the most likely to be killers (25 killers for every 10 killed), followed by minority women (22 killers for every 10 killed), White women (21 killers for every 10 killed), and minority men (14 killers for every 10 killed).

This analysis found that these patterns remain when characters are broken down by age. There are roughly 20 killers for every 10 young boys and young men who are killed, and 25 adult male killers for every adult man who is killed. Elderly men are equally likely to kill as be killed. Young girls (children or adolescents) are only likely to be killed rather than be killers (no young girls kill other characters). Young women, on the other hand, are more likely to kill than be killed, with 46 young female killers for every

10 young women who are killed. Similarly, there are 22 adult woman killers for every 10 women who are killed. As noted above, no elderly characters are killers or victims. While the ratios for the White characters are similar to these figures, the ratios for minorities differ somewhat. Both minority boys and girls are cast only as being killed (there are no minority killers). Among young adult characters, there are 16 young minority men who kill for every 10 who are killed, compared to female young adults, who are only victims. Adult minority women are much more likely to kill than be killed, while there are 18 killers for every 10 middle-aged minority men who are killed. Elderly minority men are only killed, while elderly minority women are neither likely to kill or be killed.

## CONSEQUENCES OF VIOLENCE

On television, violence often occurs in a vacuum. Consequences for characters involved in violence, whether presented as rewards or punishments, are rarely shown. In an analysis of programs from the 1990s and the early 2000s, Signorielli (2003b) found that, overall, there are no consequences for violent behavior for more than 50% of the men, about 33% of the women, and about 60% of the White and minority characters. No consequences are shown for 56% of the White men and minority men, while 69% of the White women compared to 60% of the minority women commit violence without consequences.

Interestingly, violence has consequences most often for the very young (52%) and the very old (47%). In addition, characters, whether men or women, Whites or minorities, rarely exhibit any remorse for their violent behavior—only about 15% of any of these groups showed remorse. The only groups that show slightly more remorse are children (about a quarter) and the elderly (about a quarter). Finally, while about half of the violence exhibited by characters is presented as justified, there are some interesting differences by sex and race. Specifically, about 50% of the White men, compared to 60% of the minority men, commit violence that is seen as justified. The patterns are reversed for women: about 60% of White women, compared to about 50% of minority women, commit justified acts. Last, only one-third of the children commit violence presented as justified (Signorielli, 2003b).

The NTVS defined the consequences of violence primarily in terms of depicted harm and pain. This research found no negative consequences of violence in 3 out of 10 programs and that half of the programs only showed short-term negative consequences. In regard to the portrayal of harm to the targets, one-third of the violence interactions presented unrealistically low levels of harm, with more than half showing the victim in no obvious pain. Almost three-quarters of the violent interactions portrayed violence that went unpunished. Overall, both the CI studies and the NTVS found that television presents very few consequences of violence.

## MENTAL ILLNESS AND VIOLENCE

There is one group on television for whom involvement in violence paints a very different picture. Characters judged to be mentally ill are considerably more likely to be involved in violence than "normal" characters. While the surgeon general posits that roughly 20% of the U.S. population may exhibit some degree of mental illness (U. S. Department of Health and Human Services, 1999), such illnesses appear very infrequently on television—in about 15% of the prime-time programs and less than 5% of the characters in leading roles. Nevertheless, when it is a story element, violence often is part of the picture (Signorielli, 2003a).

There is a decided relationship between the appearance of mental illness and elements of violence in programs. Overall, slightly more than 6 out of 10 programs contain elements of violence; among programs with mental illness themes, however, 8 out of 10 focus on violence. While 45% of all programs have themes of law enforcement, 70% of the programs with mental illness include themes relating to law enforcement. Similarly, while 40% of all programs have themes relating to crime, 66% of the programs with mental illness have a crime theme.

In the two most recent samples, fall of 2002 and 2003, there are very few mentally ill characters in leading or supporting roles—less than 2% of the characters. They are more likely to be men than women. Consistent with earlier analyses (Signorielli, 1989), mentally ill characters are much more likely to be involved in violence than characters who are not mentally ill: 56% commit violence and 25% hurt other characters while more than 30% kill. Mentally ill characters are also somewhat more likely than non–mentally ill characters to be hurt or killed. Similarly, Diefenbach (1997) found that mentally ill characters are much more likely to be involved in violent crimes, and are portrayed as considerably more violent than non-mentally ill characters. Moreover, television characters who are mentally ill are much more violent than actual people living in the United States who are mentally ill. This finding more than likely reflects the tendency of writers to build their stories on stereotypes that those with mental illnesses are more likely to be violent than "normal" people.

## CONCLUSION

Although Potter et al.'s (1995) research as well as the NTVS and CI reports differ somewhat in how they isolate characters' involvement in violence, the patterns are similar. Overall, we find that more men than women, more Whites than minorities, and more middle-aged adult characters than younger or older characters are involved in violence. The role of women in violence, particularly in prime-time programming, has undergone important changes. In the 1970s through the mid-1980s, a time when network programming was "the only game in town" and the "big three" (ABC, CBS, and NBC) typically garnered 95% of the viewing audience most nights, the presence of women in a program generally signaled less violence. Today, the presence of women in a program does little to reduce the level of violence. Women are now as likely to be involved in violence and to kill as men. Consequently, in this venue, women have achieved greater parity with men, but at what price?

Moreover, the patterns of being hurt or hurting others in the portrayal of children and adolescents on television have changed very little since the 1980s. As seen in earlier analyses (Signorielli, 1987), youngsters are still more likely to be victimized and consequently remain a devalued group on prime-time network broadcast programs.

The patterns of violence and victimization continue to demonstrate power. Cultivation theory posits that these depictions serve to intimidate rather than incite and to paralyze rather than trigger action (Gerbner, 2002). Those who watch more television tend to overestimate their chances of being involved in violence, believe that their neighborhoods are unsafe, and believe that crime is a very serious problem and is rising, despite data to the contrary (Gerbner, Gross, Morgan, & Signorielli, 1984). Moreover, Morgan (1983) found that viewers who watch more programs in which their demographic counterparts are consistently seen as powerless victims of violence rather than as the powerful characters who commit violence, tended to overestimate their likelihood of being involved in violence, particularly as a victim. Morgan does not imply that a one-to-one mapping, or that identification with all demographically similar characters, occurs. Rather, "the cultivation of a heightened sense of danger and risk is strongly enhanced among viewers who see characters 'like themselves' on the bottom of the symbolic power hierarchy" (p. 156).

Similarly, the NTVS (1998) posits that some of the most hazardous violence on television is that seen by children under 7. Specifically, in 16% of the programs with violence, children see attractive characters who "use violence in a morally defensible way to solve problems" (p. 136). This violence is sanitized of consequences—the violence is not criticized or punished, and the character typically does not regret his or her involvement. In addition, Wilson, Colvin, and Smith (2002) note that the depiction of younger characters as perpetrators of violence poses particular risks for younger viewers because such characters are attractive, are cast as good characters, often serve as role models, do not cause much damage, present violence in a humorous way, and are found in programs and on channels that specifically cater to younger viewers. Importantly, many of the programs in which this violence is found are cartoons for the youngest viewers; this, in turn, tends to exacerbate the potential problems because the youngest viewers may not be able to differentiate between fantasy and reality and may learn that aggression is an effective and useful way to solve problems rather than seeing violence as a technique that typically causes more trouble.

The changes in the demography of television violence, as noted above, are particularly troubling. New research should determine how these new patterns of committing violence and being victimized in the 21st century relate to viewers' perceptions of their likelihood of being involved in violence. In particular, it is important to ascertain whether those whose demographic counterparts are more likely to be involved in violence continue to overestimate their own risks of becoming embroiled in violence. Research should also examine if today's reality-based prime-time television contributes to the cultivation of real-world fear. In short, we need to determine if viewers, particularly children, have come to perceive the world as an even meaner and scarier place because no one is immune from violence.

## REFERENCES

Bandura, A. (2002). Social cognitive theory of mass communication. In J. Bryant & D. Zillmann (Eds.), *Media effects: Advances in theory and research* (2nd ed., pp. 121–154). Hillsdale, NJ: Lawrence Erlbaum.

Baron, R. A. (1978). The influence of hostile and non hostile humor upon physical aggression. *Personality and Social Psychology Bulletin, 4,* 77–80.

Berkowitz, L. (1970). Aggressive humor as a stimulus to aggressive responses. *Journal of Personality and Social Psychology, 16,* 710–717.

Blank, D. M. (1977). The Gerbner violence profile. *Journal of Broadcasting, 21,* 273–279.

Center for Communication and Social Policy. (Ed.). (1998). *The National Television Violence Study (NTVS), Vol 3.* Thousand Oaks, CA: Sage.

Coffin, T. E., & Tuchman, S. (1972–1973). Rating television programs for violence: A comparison of five surveys. *Journal of Broadcasting, 17*(1), 3–20.

Diefenbach, D. L. (1997). The portrayal of mental illness on prime time television. *Journal of Community Psychology, 25*(3), 289–302.

Gerbner, G. (2002). Mass media and dissent. In M. Morgan (Ed.), *Against the mainstream: The selected works of George Gerbner* (pp. 479–481). New York: Peter Lang.

Gerbner, G., Gross, L., Morgan, M., & Signorielli, N. (1980). The "mainstreaming" of America: Violence profile No. 11. *Journal of Communication, 30*(3), 10–29.

Gerbner, G., Gross, L., Morgan, M., & Signorielli, N. (1984). Political correlates of television viewing. *Public Opinion Quarterly, 48*(1), 283–300.

Gerbner, G., Gross, L., Morgan, M., Signorielli, N., & Shanahan, J. (2002). Growing up with television: Cultivation processes. In. J. Bryant & D. Zillmann (Eds.), *Media effects: Advances in theory and research* (2nd ed., pp. 43–68). Hillsdale, NJ: Lawrence Erlbaum.

Gerbner, G., Morgan, M., & Signorielli, N. (1994). *Television violence profile No. 14: The turning point.* Philadelphia: The Annenberg School for Communication.

Greenberg, B. (1980). *Life on television: Content analyses of U. S. TV drama.* Norwood, NJ: Ablex.

Harwood, J. (1997). Viewing age: Lifespan identity and television viewing choices. *Journal of Broadcasting & Electronic Media, 41,* 203–213.

Hoffner, C. (1996). Children's wishful identification and parasocial interaction with favorite television characters. *Journal of Broadcasting & Electronic Media, 40,* 389–402.

Krippendorff, K. (1980). *Content Analysis.* Newbury Park, CA; Sage.

Morgan, M. (1983). Symbolic victimization and real world fear. *Human Communication Research, 9*(2), 146–157.

Nielsen, A. C. (2000). *Report on television.* New York: A. C. Nielsen.

Peck, R. (1982). Teenage stereotypes. In M. Schwarz (Ed.), *TV and teens: Experts look at the issues* (pp. 62–65). Reading, MA: Addison-Wesley.

Potter, W. J. (1999). *On media violence.* Thousand Oaks, CA: Sage.

Potter, W. J., Vaughan, M. W., Warren, R., Howley, K., Land, A., & Hagemeyer, J. C. (1995). How real is the portrayal of aggression in television entertainment programming? *Journal of Broadcasting & Electronic Media, 39*(4), 496–516.

Signorielli, N. (1987). Children and adolescents on television: A consistent pattern of devaluation. *Journal of Early Adolescence, 7*(3), 255–268.

Signorielli, N. (1989). The stigma of mental illness on television. *Journal of Broadcasting and Electronic Media, 33*(3), 325–331.

Signorielli, N. (1990). Television's mean and dangerous world: A continuation of the cultural indicators perspective. In N. Signorielli and M. Morgan (Eds.), *Cultivation analysis: New directions in media effects research* (pp. 85–106). Newbury Park, CA: Sage.

Signorielli, N. (2003a). *Mental illness on TV: A stigmatized presentation.* Paper presented at the annual conference of the National Communication Association, Miami, FL.

Signorielli, N. (2003b). Prime-time violence 1993–2001: Has the picture really changed? *Journal of Broadcasting & Electronic Media, 47*(1), 36–57.

Signorielli, N. (2005). *Violence in the media: A reference handbook.* Santa Barbara, CA: ABC-CLIO.

Signorielli, N., & Bacue, A. (1999). Recognition and respect: A content analysis of prime-time television characters across three decades. *Sex Roles, 40*(7/8), 527–544.

Signorielli, N., Gross, L., & Morgan, M. (1982). Violence in television programs: Ten years later. In D. Pearl, L. Bouthilet, & J. Lazar (Eds.), *Television and social behavior: Ten years of scientific progress and implications for the eighties* (pp. 158–173). Rockville, MD: National Institute of Mental Health.

Signorielli, N., Horry, A., & Carlton, K. (2004, November). *Minorities on prime time: Is there parity?* Paper presented at the annual conference of the National Communication Association, Chicago, IL.

Smith, S. L., Nathanson, A. I., & Wilson, B. J. (2002). Prime-time television: Assessing violence during the most popular viewing hours. *Journal of Communication, 52*(1), 84–111.

U. S. Department of Health and Human Services. (1999). *Mental Health: A Report of the Surgeon General.* Rockville, MD: U.S. Department of Health and Human Services, Substance Abuse and Mental Health Services Administration, Center for Mental Health Services, National Institutes of Health, National Institute of Mental Health.

Wilson, B. J., Colvin, C. M., & Smith, S. (2002). Engaging in violence on American television: A comparison of child, teen, and adult perpetrators. *Journal of Communication, 52*(1), 36–60.

CHAPTER 9

# *Protecting Children's Welfare in an Anxiety-Provoking Media Environment*

JOANNE CANTOR

> *Our anxiety does not empty tomorrow of its sorrow but only empties today of its strength.*
>
> —Charles H. Spurgeon (1834–1892)

In 2000, an intriguing research report suggested that we are living in an age of anxiety. Twenge (2000) conducted a meta-analysis of all the studies produced between 1952 and 1993 in which standard measures of self-reported anxiety were included. The results showed a dramatic, linear increase in anxiety over the years. In fact, the level of anxiety coinciding with the 50th percentile in the early 1990s would have represented the 84th percentile in the 1950s. Although Twenge concluded that the change is most consistent with evolving social forces such as increasing crime rates and decreases in family stability, she also argued that media coverage of unsettling events has led people to *perceive* a higher level of threat than actually exists. Perhaps not coincidentally over the same years, the amount of time spent watching television in American homes also increased dramatically, from 4.5 hours per day in 1950 to more than 7 hours per day in the 1990s (Bushman & Huesmann, 2001). Research shows that a substantial proportion of what television offers involves violence and other frightening images (Cantor, 1998; Center for Communication and Social Policy, 1998). Although it is difficult to isolate the impact of the media over the course of a half century in which so much social change took place, there is a growing body of literature demonstrating that media exposure contributes to viewers' anxieties in significant ways—particularly among children.

This chapter summarizes research on the impact of media on children's fears and anxieties. It describes developmental differences in the media stimuli that frighten children as well as in the coping strategies that are effective for children of different ages. It concludes by describing a series of different approaches that have been taken to attempt to protect children from media-induced harm.

## RESEARCH ON THE MEDIA'S EFFECTS ON CHILDREN'S FEARS AND ANXIETIES

Although the relationship between exposure to media violence and antisocial behavior has been a central focus of public debates for decades, researchers have also studied the impact of media on children's emotions. Blumer (1933) reported that 93% of the children he interviewed had been frightened or horrified by a motion picture. Other researchers in the 1930s and 1940s also noted the prevalence of children's fright reactions to movies and radio crime dramas (Eisenberg, 1936; Preston, 1941). Early television researchers (Himmelweit, Oppenheim, & Vince, 1958; Schramm, Lyle, & Parker, 1961) explored the frequency with which this new medium induced fright reactions as well. These studies reported that enduring anxieties, sleep disturbances, and nightmares were common consequences of exposure to mass media.

Research interest in the media's impact on fears reawakened in the 1980s after such frightening films as *Jaws, The Exorcist,* and *Poltergeist* became extremely successful, and the press reported ruined beach vacations, extreme emotional reactions, and sleepless nights associated with these movies. Brian R. Johnson (1980) asked a random sample of adults whether they had ever seen a motion picture that disturbed them "a great deal." Forty percent said they had had such an experience, with 3 days as the median length of the disturbance. Respondents also reported on the type, intensity, and duration of symptoms such as nervousness, depression, fear of specific things, and recurring thoughts and images. Based on these reports, Johnson judged that 48% of these respondents experienced what he termed a "significant stress reaction" for at least 2 days as the result of watching a movie. Johnson argued,

> It is one thing to walk away from a frightening or disturbing event with mild residue of the images and quite another thing to ruminate about it, feel anxious or depressed for days, and/or to avoid anything that might create the same unpleasant experience. (p. 786)

Correlational studies have shown that watching television is related to the occurrence of both anxiety and sleep disturbances. A survey of elementary and middle school children reported that the more television a child watched, the more likely he or she was to report the symptoms of anxiety, depression, and posttraumatic stress (Singer, Slovak, Frierson, & York, 1998). A survey of parents of elementary school children reported that more hours of television viewing (especially at bedtime) were associated with higher rates of nightmares, difficulties with falling asleep, and the inability to sleep through the night (Owens, Maxim, McGuinn, Nobile, Msall, & Alario, 1999). Nine percent of the children studied experienced television-induced nightmares at least once a week.

Although simple correlational studies cannot rule out the alternative explanation that anxious children or those with sleep problems seek out greater levels of television viewing, a recent longitudinal survey supports the interpretation that viewing precedes and promotes these problems. Jeffrey G. Johnson and colleagues (Johnson, Cohen, Kasen, First, & Brook, 2004) conducted a prospective panel survey that measured children's television viewing and sleep problems at ages 14, 16, and 22 years. They reported that adolescents who watched more than 3 hours of television at age 14 were significantly more likely than lighter viewers to experience sleep problems at ages 16 and 22, even after controlling for previous sleep problems and other factors such as psychiatric disorders, parental education, income, and neglect. In contrast, early sleep problems were not independently related to later television viewing. Moreover, respondents who reduced their amount of television viewing between the ages of 14 and 16 were significantly less likely to experience sleep disturbances at ages 16 and 22. These findings suggest that heavy viewing leads to difficulty falling asleep and to frequent nighttime awakenings, and that the correlation between viewing and sleep problems is not simply due to sleepless youth turning to television for relief.

Experiments are better suited than correlational studies to determine cause and effect. The problem with experiments, however, is that it is unethical to show frightening television programs and movies to children for the purpose of demonstrating that they produce intense anxieties and sleep disturbances. Experimental research on frightening media employs only small excerpts from frightening programs to test theories regarding age differences or differences in features of presentations (Cantor, 2002). Even though many children are exposed to horrifying media images on their own, the long-term negative effects of these images cannot be studied using experimental procedures.

One way that research has circumvented this ethical obstacle is to study the long-term effects of media exposure through retrospective reports. Adults' detailed memories of having been frightened by a television show or movie provide vivid evidence of the severity and duration of fear induced by the media. In two independently conducted studies (Harrison & Cantor, 1999; Hoekstra, Harris, & Helmick, 1999) involving samples of undergraduates from three universities, the presence of vivid memories of enduring media-induced fear was nearly universal. All of the participants in one study (Hoekstra et al., 1999) reported such an incident. In the other study (Harrison & Cantor, 1999), 90% reported an intense fear reaction to something in the media, in spite of the fact that they could have avoided writing a paper and filling out a three-page questionnaire by simply saying they had never had such an experience.

Both studies revealed a variety of intense reactions. In Hoekstra et al.'s (1999) study, 61% of the participants reported a generalized fear or free-floating anxiety after viewing; 46% reported what they called "wild imagination" ("monsters under the bed" or "someone sneaking up on you"); 29% reported a specific fear (e.g., sharks, power tools, spiders); and more than 20% reported a variety of sleep disturbances, including fear of sleeping alone, nightmares, insomnia, or needing to sleep with the lights on. Of the students reporting fright reactions in Harrison and Cantor's (1999) study, 52% reported disturbances in eating or sleeping, 22% reported mental preoccupation with the disturbing material, and 35% reported subsequently avoiding or dreading the situation depicted in the program or movie. Moreover, one third of those who reported fright said that the fear effects had lasted more than a year. Indeed, more than one fourth of the respondents said that the emotional impact of the program or movie was still with them at the time of reporting, on average 6 years after exposure. Eighty-three percent had viewed the frightening program with someone else. Most reported watching because someone else wanted to watch (44%) or because they stumbled onto it accidentally (12%).

A recent content analysis of more than 500 papers written by students about their fright reactions demonstrates how frequently irrational media-induced fears continue well into adulthood (Cantor, 2004a). The two most commonly cited frightening media offerings in this study were the movies *Jaws* and *Poltergeist*. Of the 29 students who wrote about *Poltergeist,* 72% reported that it had interfered with their ability to sleep, and 76% reported that it had affected their waking behavior, typically making them extremely uncomfortable in the presence of real-world objects similar to threatening objects in the movie (e.g., clowns, trees, televisions). Although all 29 saw the movie before the age of 12, 31% reported lingering effects in adulthood. Of the 23 students who wrote about *Jaws,* only 39% reported sleep problems, but 83% reported an influence on their waking life. Most effects involved activities in or near water. In fact, 65% indicated the movie made them anxious while swimming. For most, this anxiety occurred not only in the ocean, but in lakes and pools, and other venues without sharks. For 43%, these effects were continuing at the time the papers were written. These findings are consistent with research on the neurophysiology of fear, which shows that intensely traumatic events produce nonconscious memories, including bodily reactions, that are virtually "indelible" (LeDoux, 1996, p. 252; see also Cantor, 2004a).

The research demonstrates, therefore, that television and movies contribute to children's feelings of anxiety. In some cases, a single exposure to an extremely frightening offering can produce powerful effects that linger and interfere with normal activities. These findings suggest that it is advisable to observe caution in exposing children to mass media and to avoid specific programs and movies that are likely to be intensely frightening. Research demonstrates, however, that what will frighten a child is not always easy to anticipate.

## PREDICTING WHAT WILL BE FRIGHTENING

It is not difficult to explain why a movie showing bloody shark attacks or a documentary about terrorist attacks would produce fear. However, age differences in cognitive development account for the fact that many children experience intense fear in response to programs and movies that most adults would not consider scary. Cantor and colleagues (see Cantor, 2002, for a review) have conducted a series of studies to explore developmental differences in what frightens children.

### *The Role of Appearance*

The importance of appearance to instilling fright in a child declines as children get older. Preschool children (up to the age of 7 or 8) are more likely to be frightened by something that looks scary but is actually harmless, than by something that looks attractive but is actually harmful. By the end of elementary school, appearance carries much less weight in causing fear, relative to the behavior, destructive potential, or intent of characters or objects. For example, in a survey conducted in 1981 (Cantor & Sparks, 1984), parents were asked to name the programs and movies that had frightened their children the most. Parents of preschool children most often mentioned those with grotesque-looking characters, such as the television series *The Incredible Hulk* and the movie *The Wizard of Oz;* parents of older elementary school children more often named programs and movies involving threats that did not have a strong visual component.

Another study looked at children's reactions to *The Incredible Hulk* (Sparks & Cantor, 1986) more directly. When children were shown a shortened episode of this program, preschool children reported the most fear after the attractive, mild-mannered hero transformed into the monstrous-looking Hulk in order to save a man who was trapped in a fire. Older elementary school children reported the least fear at this time because they understood that the monster was really the benevolent hero in another form, and that he was using his superhuman power to rescue the man. Preschool children's unexpectedly intense reactions to this program seem to have been partially due to their over-response to the visual image of the Hulk character and their inability to look beyond his appearance and appreciate his benevolent behavior.

A third study (Hoffner & Cantor, 1985) tested the effect of appearance in a more controlled fashion. A program was created in four versions so that a major character was either attractive and grandmotherly looking or ugly and grotesque, and in her attractive or ugly form she was shown behaving in either a kind or cruel manner. Children in three age groups (3–5, 6–7, and 9–10 years) saw one of these versions and were asked to indicate how nice or mean the woman was and to predict what she would do next. Preschool children were more influenced than older children by the character's looks and less influenced by her kind or cruel behavior. As the age of the child increased, the character's looks became less relevant and her behavior carried increasing weight. These studies help explain why many children are frightened by characters like E.T., the extraterrestrial, who are intended to be kind, benevolent heroes but whose grotesque appearance makes them disturbing (Cantor, 1998).

### *Fantasy vs. Reality*

A second developmental difference in what frightens children is that preschool children are just as likely to be frightened by a fantasy offering (depicting something that could not possibly occur in the real world) as by something that is realistic. This is not surprising since the ability to distinguish fantasy from reality develops only gradually during the first 8 years. Young children, in fact, are often more frightened by fantastic depictions than real ones because fantastic depictions are usually more visually grotesque. In contrast, by the age of 8 or 9, children are much more likely to be frightened by something that is realistic than by something fantastic. In Cantor and Sparks's (1984) survey of what had frightened children, the parents' tendency to name fantasy offerings decreased as the child's age increased, while the tendency to identify realistic fictional offerings increased. Similarly, Cantor and Nathanson (1996) reported that children's fear responses to fantasy depictions declined throughout the elementary school years, but their fear responses to the news increased. Because of young children's inability to distinguish between fantasy and reality, they often surprise their parents by worrying about preposterous outcomes after viewing children's programs or movies. For example, after seeing *Pinocchio,* children often report worrying that their nose will grow if they lie, and after seeing *The Wizard of Oz* they often cannot sleep from fear that the Wicked Witch of the West or the flying monkeys will capture them (Cantor, 1998).

### *Abstract Concepts*

A third generalization is that as children mature, they become frightened by media depictions involving increasingly abstract concepts. Data supporting this generalization come from a survey of children's responses to the television movie *The Day After,* which depicted the devastation of a Kansas community by a nuclear attack (Cantor, Wilson, & Hoffner, 1986). The visual depictions of injury in the movie were quite mild compared to the enormity of the consequences implied by the plot. In a random telephone survey of parents conducted the night after the broadcast of this movie, children under 12 were reportedly much less disturbed by the film than were teenagers, and parents were the most disturbed. The very youngest children were the least frightened. The findings seem to be due to the fact that the emotional response comes from contemplating the potential annihilation of the earth as we know it—a concept that is beyond the grasp of the young child.

Studies of children's reactions to major news events reveal that younger and older children tend to react to different components of media coverage, as a function of their level of abstraction. A survey evaluating children's reactions to televised coverage of the 1991 Persian Gulf War (Cantor, Mares, & Oliver, 1993) reported that although children in the first, fourth, seventh, and eleventh grades had similarly intense emotional reactions, younger children were most affected by the visual aspects of the coverage and the direct, concrete consequences of combat (e.g., the missiles exploding), whereas older children responded more to the more abstract, conceptual aspects of the coverage (e.g., the possibility of the conflict spreading). The same trend has recently been observed in children's responses to the war in Iraq (Smith & Moyer-Guse, in press).

## HELPING CHILDREN COPE WITH THEIR MEDIA-INDUCED FEARS

Even the most careful parents will not be able to completely shield their children from terrifying content in the media. Because of the frequent need of parents to help their children cope with their media-induced fears and anxieties, Cantor and associates (see Cantor, 1998, for review) have explored the types of strategies that are most effective for children of different ages. In general, nonverbal strategies, those that involve actions rather than words and ideas, work best for young children (up to the age of 7 or 8). Verbal strategies work best for older children and adults.

### *Nonverbal Strategies*

The process of visual desensitization, or gradual exposure to threatening images in a nonthreatening context, is one nonverbal strategy that is effective for both preschool and older elementary school children (e.g., Wilson & Cantor, 1987). In several experiments, prior exposure to filmed footage of snakes, still photographs of worms, rubber replicas of spiders, and live lizards reduced children's fear in response to movie scenes featuring similar creatures. In addition, fear of the Incredible Hulk was reduced by exposure to footage of the actor having his makeup applied so that he gradually took on the menacing appearance of the character (Cantor, Sparks, & Hoffner, 1988).

A nonverbal strategy that has been shown to have both more appeal and greater effectiveness for younger than for older children is covering one's eyes during frightening scenes. In one experiment (Wilson, 1989), for example, when covering the eyes was suggested as an option, younger children used this strategy more often than older children. Moreover, the suggestion of this option reduced the fear of younger children, but actually increased the fear of older children. Wilson noted that the older children recognized the limited effectiveness of covering their eyes (while still being able to hear the program) and may have felt *less* in control, and therefore more vulnerable, when this strategy was suggested to them.

Other nonverbal strategies involve physical activities, such as clinging to an attachment object or having something to eat or drink. Younger children report using these strategies more often, and the children themselves think these physical techniques work better for younger than older children (Wilson, Hoffner, & Cantor, 1987).

### *Verbal Coping Strategies*

In contrast to nonverbal strategies, verbal techniques provide information that casts the threat in a different light. These strategies involve relatively complex cognitive operations, and research consistently finds such strategies to be more effective for older than for younger children. When dealing with fantasy depictions, for example, the most typical cognitive strategy seems to be to provide an explanation focusing on the unreality of the situation. In one experiment (Cantor & Wilson, 1984), older elementary school children who were told to remember that what they were seeing in *The Wizard of Oz* was not real, showed less fear than their classmates who received no instructions. The same instructions did not help preschoolers, however, who, in addition to being unable to perform complex cognitive operations, do not have a full grasp of the implications of the fantasy–reality distinction.

For media depictions involving realistic threats, the most prevalent verbal strategy is to provide an explanation that minimizes the perceived severity of the depicted danger. This type of strategy is not only more reassuring for older than for younger children, in certain situations it enhances fear rather than reduces anxiety for younger children. In an experiment involving the snake-pit scene from *Raiders of the Lost Ark* (Wilson & Cantor, 1987), prior reassuring information about snakes (e.g., stating that most snakes are not poisonous) reduced the fear of older elementary school children (approaching significance). However, kindergarten and first-grade children seem to have only partially understood the information, responding to the word "poisonous" more intensely than to the word "not." For them, the supposedly reassuring information increased feelings of fear.

Research exploring ways to improve the effectiveness of verbal strategies for young children shows that asking children to repeat unequivocal but limited reassuring information is effective in reducing their fears. For example, young children who repeated the phrase "tarantulas cannot kill people" while viewing a movie involving a tarantula showed reduced fear levels (Wilson, 1987). Moreover, when children are frightened by something they have seen in the media, it is an especially good time to teach them safety guidelines and techniques to prevent similar events from happening to them (Cantor & Omdahl, 1999).

### *Expressive Communication as a Coping Strategy*

Research on coping with emotional distress produced by situations other than media exposure suggests that certain ways of communicating about frightening media may also be useful. Cognitive therapy, one of the most widely studied psychological interventions for anxiety disorders, is based on the notion that individuals may gain control over their emotions by talking over disturbing situations with a caring listener. Cognitive therapies are effective in treating some anxiety disorders (Deacon & Abramowitz, 2004).

A good deal of research has been conducted on the therapeutic value of writing about one's past frightening experiences. In his book *Opening Up: The Healing Power of Expressing Emotions,* Pennebaker (1997) provides evidence of the physical as well as the psychological benefits of writing about traumatic events. These benefits include fewer medical visits and improved immune function as well as reports of psychological well-being (Lepore & Smyth, 2002). Although young children are often unable to talk about their feelings and are not equipped to write about them, many art therapists have reported that children can reduce their anxieties by drawing pictures of what frightens them in conjunction with interaction with a therapist or caregiver (Horovitz, 1983; Roje, 1995).

In an effort to help young children and their parents cope with frightening images on television and in the movies, Cantor (2004b) recently published a children's story. *Teddy's TV Troubles* is an illustrated picture book about a little bear who has been frightened by something on TV. After recognizing that words do not work, he and his mother go through a series of calming activities that help him cope with his feelings. These include drawing a picture of what scared him and making it look less scary, repeating reassuring phrases to his favorite stuffed animal, and going to bed happy and secure. The book is intended to promote the type of parent–child interaction that helps young children cope with their fearful feelings.

## RECENT APPROACHES TO PROTECTING CHILDREN FROM HARM

Because it is increasingly clear that children's mental health is at stake if they have unlimited exposure to the media, a variety of approaches to protecting children have emerged. These approaches range from practices within individual homes and schools to activities involving federal agencies, Congress, state legislatures, and the courts. This section reviews some recent developments.

The first line of defense has been to foster greater parental involvement. Major public health organizations, such as the American Academy of Pediatrics (www.aap.org) and the American Psychological Association (www.apa.org), urge parents to monitor their children's viewing and restrict both the amount of time and the content of the electronic media to which they are exposed. Other organizations, such as the Alliance for a Media Literate America (www.amlainfo.org) and the Center for Media Literacy (www.medialit.org), promote school curricula involving "critical viewing skills" that may help children protect themselves from harmful effects (e.g., Brown, 2001; Potter, 1998). Some organizations, such as the Center for Successful Parenting (www.sosparents.org) and Common Sense Media (www.commonsensemedia.org), are dedicated specifically to educating the public about the harmful effects of the media and to lobbying the media industries to engage in more child-friendly practices. In addition, many books give guidance to parents on their children's media exposure (e.g., Cantor, 1998; Steyer, 2002; Walsh, 1994). All of these sources urge parents to keep abreast of the content of media so that they can make wise choices for their children.

### *Rating Systems*

Although the ideal situation might be for parents to preview every program or movie before their child sees it, this option is not possible with live television, and is impracticable for most other media. One potential solution to this problem has been the development of rating systems for media. Dale Kunkel and Lara Zwarun discuss this in detail in this volume. The media industries have introduced rating systems in efforts to ward off censorship or other government intervention (Bushman & Cantor, 2003). Media ratings in the United States are confusing, however, because every mass media delivery mode has a different rating system, with a distinct rating systems for movies (The Motion Picture Association of America [MPAA] Ratings), television (The TV Parental Guidelines), and music (Parental Advisories), and two different ratings systems for video games (The Electronic Software Rating Board [ESRB] Ratings, The Parental Advisory System). (See Table 9.1 for various features of these rating systems.) Some rating systems give age recommendations; others give information about content; some provide both age and content information; and some simply post an advisory. Although many parents report using the rating systems, many also find them confusing. Moreover, awareness of the *television* rating system has declined over the years

**Table 9.1** A Guide to the Most Commonly Used Industry-Developed Rating Systems in the United States**

| *Medium/Name* | *Evaluative Ratings (Recommendations & Warnings)* | *Content Indicators* | *Assignment (Who Decides?)* |
|---|---|---|---|
| **Movies**/Motion Picture Association of America (MPAA) Ratings | **G:** General Audiences<br>**PG:** Parental Guidance Suggested<br>**PG-13:** Parents Strongly Cautioned<br>**R:** Restricted<br>**NC-17:** No One 17 and Under Admitted | None; reasons for ratings of recent films available at www.mpaa.org; reasons also available in some large newspaper ads and some television ads | Assigned by paid, anonymous panel of parents; rating may be appealed to Industry Panel |
| **TV**/TV Parental Guidelines (V-chip ratings) | **TV-Y:** [All Children]*<br>**TV-Y7:** [Directed to Older Children]<br>**TV-G:** [General Audience]<br>**TV-PG:** [Parental Guidance Suggested]<br>**TV-14:** [Parents Strongly Cautioned]<br>**TV-MA:** [Mature Audiences Only] | **FV:** [Fantasy Violence]<br>**V:** [Violence]*<br>**S:** [Sex]<br>**L:** [Coarse Language]<br>**D:** [Sexual Dialog or Innuendo] | Self-assigned by producer or distributor; designed to be applied to all programming except news and sports |
| **Music** Advisories | "Parental Advisory: Explicit Content" | None | Self-assigned by producer or distributor |
| **Video Games**/Electronic Software Ratings Board (ESRB) Ratings | **EC:** Early Childhood: Ages 3+<br>**E:** Everyone: Ages 6+<br>**E:10+:** Everyone Ages 10+<br>**T:** Teen: Ages 13+<br>**M:** Mature: Ages 17+<br>**AO:** Adults Only | Variety of phrases, e.g., "cartoon violence," "fantasy violence," "intense violence," "sexual violence," "comic mischief," "strong language," "mature sexual themes" | Assigned by Rating Board based on submitted tape and questionnaire |
| **Arcade Games**/Parental Advisory System | None | Animated Violence, Life-like Violence, Sexual Content, Language (three levels of each—green: "suitable for everyone"; yellow: "mild"; red: "strong") | Self-assigned by producer or distributor |

*Material in brackets is not usually given with the ratings.

**Adapted from www.joannecantor.com

and understanding of the meaning of the ratings is very low (Bushman & Cantor, 2003; Rideout, 2004). A 2004 study (Rideout, 2004) showed that while parents have more concerns about the effects of television than other media, they consider the television ratings less useful than other media ratings.

Because of many parents' dissatisfaction with the existing media ratings, independently developed rating systems, such as the PSV Ratings (PSVRatings.com) have been introduced, and several Web sites have been designed (e.g., Moviereports.org, Screenit.com, Commonsensemedia.org) to provide parents with more detailed information about media content.

In light of the difficulty that parents have found in mastering the various rating systems, several bills have been introduced in the U.S. Congress to mandate the development of a universal rating system for all media. For example, The Twenty-First Century Media Responsibility Act of 2001 would have amended the Federal Cigarette Labeling and Advertising Act to state that "it is the policy of Congress to provide for the establishment, use, and enforcement of a consistent and comprehensive system for labeling violent content in audio and visual media products, including the appropriateness of such products for minors." The bill, like many others of its type, was never passed, in large part because the media industries have consistently lobbied against this type of legislation.

### *Blocking Technologies for Television*

Blocking technologies like the V-chip have been developed as a way to give parents more control over their children's TV exposure without needing to always be in the room where their children are watching television. The V-chip was mandated by the Telecommunications Act of 1996 and was designed to allow programs to be blocked on the basis of their ratings. However, only 15% of parents have used the V-chip and many parents whose TVs are equipped with the device do not know it (Rideout, 2004). As currently configured, the V-chip is extremely difficult for parents to learn to use (Jordan & Woodard, 2003). Its effectiveness depends on the accuracy and appropriateness of programs' ratings, which many critics argue are not fairly and consistently applied (e.g., Federman, 2002; Rideout, 2004). Although the V-chip was originally designed to work only with the TV Parental Guidelines and the MPAA Ratings, a recent Federal Communications Commission Report and Order (2004) mandates that the device become more flexible in the conversion to digital television, enabling it to work with modifications to the TV Parental Guidelines and with other rating systems.

### *Third-Party Editing and Filtering of Movies*

Because many families are seeking a way to view films while avoiding scenes of intense violence, nudity, and profanity, several companies have emerged that sell or rent movies whose more controversial content has been edited or "sanitized." Companies such as CleanFlicks (www.cleanflicks.com) and CleanFilms (www.cleanfilms.com) offer such fare over the Internet and in stores. These companies are in a legal struggle with the Directors Guild of America and major movie studios over whether their practice violates copyright laws (Aho, 2004; Hilden, 2002).

Another method to sanitize recorded movies has been developed by a company called ClearPlay (www.ClearPlay.com), which creates specialized filters through which an unedited DVD can be played. The ClearPlay system allows the customer to choose to filter out varying levels of sex, violence, and profanity, and as a function of the customer's choices, the device automatically mutes or skips images, dialogue, or scenes without altering the disk itself. This company was also challenged by the Directors Guild. However, ClearPlay maintains that it is different from the companies that edit and re-sell copyrighted properties, arguing that its customers are analogous to those who use their remote control to skip unwanted parts of a movie. Members of Congress weighed in on this controversy. In a hearing on the issue (*Derivative Rights, Moral Rights, and Movie Filtering Technology,* 2004), the rights and needs of families to protect their children from media violence were discussed in relation to the copyright and First Amendment rights of movie makers. Following that hearing, a bill was introduced into Congress that would exempt from copyright infringement the use of technologies that skip or mute limited portions of movies in the course of private home viewing (Family Movie Act of 2004). Language from this bill was later introduced into The Family Entertainment and Copyright Act of 2005, which was passed by Congress and became law in April of 2005.

### *Discouraging the Marketing of Media Violence to Children*

At the request of President Clinton and Congress, the Federal Trade Commission (FTC) in September of 2000 issued a report on the marketing of violent entertainment products to children. This report concluded that the media industries were conducting "aggressive and persistent marketing of violent movies, music, and electronic games to children" in a manner inconsistent with the industries' own ratings of the products (FTC, 2000, p. i). They further reported that advertisements for violent media products often failed to contain rating information and that it was relatively easy for teenagers to gain access to R-rated movies, parental advisory-labeled music, and M-rated videogames in the absence of parental accompaniment. The Commission urged improvements on all these fronts, but limited its recommendations to industry self-regulation. Since the 2000 report, the FTC has issued four follow-up reports, the most recent occurring in July of 2004. Each report notes progress in certain domains and points out areas where improvement is still needed. The FTC has created mechanisms for consumer complaints about media violence, and called for continuing follow-up reports on the industries' marketing practices.

### *Restricting Children's Access to Violent Video Games*

In the wake of several highly publicized school shootings by students who were heavy users of video games, there have been several attempts to pass legislation restricting children's access to such games. In a recent attempt, a bill introduced into Congress (Protect Children From Video Game Sex and Violence Act of 2003) sought to prohibit the sale to minors of adult-rated video games that contain content deemed harmful to minors, including graphic violence, sexual violence, or strong sexual content. This bill was referred to the House Judiciary Committee's Subcommittee on Crime, Terrorism, and Homeland Security, but did not receive further action. In July of 2005, Senator Hillary Rodham Clinton announced that she would introduce another bill restricting children's access to violent video games by implementing financial penalties for retailers who fail to enforce the games' rating system (Clinton, 2005).

Several localities have passed ordinances restricting the access of minors to adult-rated violent video games. The city of

Indianapolis enacted an ordinance in 2000 that would require video arcade operators to label video games that contain graphic violence or strong sexual content and to prohibit minors from playing them without their parents' consent ("Peterson Signs Violent Video Game Ordinance," 2000). A more narrowly tailored ordinance was passed in Washington State in 2003, which prohibited the sale or rental to a minor of video games depicting violence against law enforcement officers (Prohibiting Sale of Violent Computer and Video Games to Minors, 2003). Both laws were challenged by the video game industry and both were declared unconstitutional by the courts (Carnell, 2002; "Judge Strikes Down Washington Video Game Law," 2004). Similar ordinances are being discussed in a variety of locales, including Illinois and New York City (see Citizens for Responsible Media, www.medialegislation.org, for an overview of past and pending legislation). It remains to be seen whether any of these will survive court challenges.

### *Other Approaches Involving Governmental Bodies*

Occasionally, the courts become involved in the issue of media violence on a more individual level. For example, one increasingly common area of dispute in divorce and joint custody cases relates to situations in which one parent wishes to control his or her children's access to media violence and the other does not. Another example is the desire of some professionals who work with juveniles involved with violent crimes to restrict their access to violent media. The Center for Successful Parenting (www.sosparents.org) has led a campaign to educate family court judges on the issue of media violence. They have developed model child custody orders and model child probation orders that provide guidance for outlining restrictions to children's access to violent media in such situations.

At the urging of Congress, the Federal Communications Commission (FCC) sent out a Notice of Inquiry in the summer of 2004 on the presentation of violence on television and its impact on children, soliciting comments from researchers, media producers, and the general public on this issue. The FCC sought information about current trends in the amount and type of violence on television and its effects on children. They also asked for data regarding the use and effectiveness of the TV Parental Guidelines and the V-chip, and sought opinions regarding whether further public policy measures to help protect children were appropriate, and whether constitutional barriers exist to the enactment of such measures.

### *Conclusion*

Proposed solutions and heated debates will continue as the media remain a dominant force in children's lives, and as controversial content becomes even more accessible to children. Our society continues to grapple with the problem of balancing the government's interest in protecting children's welfare and parents' interest in protecting their children, on one hand, with artists' rights to free expression and the entertainment industries' desires to maximize their profits, on the other. No matter how specific policy issues are resolved, children's mental health will benefit if parents and other caregivers are well informed about the content and effects of the media that children consume and about effective ways of reducing the unhealthy effects.

## REFERENCES

Aho, B. (2004, May 20). Prepared statement. In *Derivative rights, moral rights, and movie filtering technology: Hearing before the Subcommittee on Courts, the Internet, and Intellectual Property, Committee on the Judiciary, House of Representatives,* 108th Cong, Serial No. 93. Available: http://commdocs.house.gov/committees/judiciary/hju93773.000/hju93773_0f.htm

Blumer, H. (1933). *Movies and conduct.* New York: Macmillan.

Brown, J. A. (2001). Media literacy and critical television viewing in education. In D. G. Singer & J. L. Singer (Eds.), *Handbook of children and the media* (pp. 681–697). Thousand Oaks, CA: Sage.

Bushman, B. J., & Cantor, J. (2003). Media ratings for violence and sex: Implications for policy makers and parents. *American Psychologist, 58,* 130–141.

Bushman, B. J., & Huesmann, L. R. (2001). Effects of televised violence on aggression. In D. G. Singer & J. L. Singer (Eds.), *Handbook of children and the media* (pp. 223–254). Thousand Oaks, CA: Sage.

Cantor, J. (1998). *"Mommy, I'm scared": How TV and movies frighten children and what we can do to protect them.* San Diego, CA: Harcourt.

Cantor, J. (2002). Fright reactions to mass media. In J. Bryant & D. Zillmann (Eds.), *Media effects: Advances in theory and research* (2d ed., pp. 287–306). Mahwah, NJ: Lawrence Erlbaum.

Cantor, J. (2004a). "I'll never have a clown in my house": Why movie horror lives on. *Poetics Today: International Journal for Theory and Analysis of Literature and Communication, 25,* 283–304.

Cantor, J. (2004b). *Teddy's TV troubles.* Madison, WI: Goblin Fern Press.

Cantor, J., Mares, M. L., & Oliver, M. B. (1993). Parents' and children's emotional reactions to televised coverage of the Gulf War. In B. Greenberg & W. Gantz (Eds.), *Desert storm and the mass media* (pp. 325–340). Cresskill, NJ: Hampton Press.

Cantor, J., & Nathanson, A. (1996). Children's fright reactions to television news. *Journal of Communication, 46* (4), 139–152.

Cantor, J., & Omdahl, B. (1999). Children's acceptance of safety guidelines after exposure to televised dramas depicting accidents. *Western Journal of Communication, 63,* 1–15.

Cantor, J., & Sparks, G. G. (1984). Children's fear responses to mass media: Testing some Piagetian predictions. *Journal of Communication, 34,* (2), 90–103.

Cantor, J., Sparks, G. G., & Hoffner, C. (1988). Calming children's television fears: Mr. Rogers vs. the Incredible Hulk. *Journal of Broadcasting & Electronic Media, 32,* 271–188.

Cantor, J., & Wilson, B. J. (1984). Modifying fear responses to mass media in preschool and elementary school children. *Journal of Broadcasting, 28,* 431–443.

Cantor, J., & Wilson, B. J. (1988). Helping children cope with frightening media presentations. *Current Psychology: Research & Reviews, 7,* 58–75.

Cantor, J., Wilson, B. J., & Hoffner, C. (1986). Emotional responses to a televised nuclear holocaust film. *Communication Research, 13,* 257–277.

Carnell, B. (2002). Indianapolis to pay heavy price for video game ban. Available: http://www.libertysearch.com/articles/2002/000004.html

Center for Communication and Social Policy (1998). *National television violence study, Vol. 3.* Thousand Oaks, CA: Sage.

Citizens for Responsible Media. (2004). Media violence laws and legislation. www.medialegislation.org

Clinton, H. R. (2005, July 14). *Senator Clinton announces legislation to keep inappropriate video games out of the hands of children.* Senator Clinton's Web page: Statements and Releases. Available: http://clinton.senate.gov/news/statements/details.cfm?id=240603&&

Deacon, B. J., & Abramowitz, J. S. (2004). Cognitive and behavioral treatments for anxiety disorders. A review of meta-analytic findings. *Journal of Clinical Psychology, 60,* 429–441.

*Derivative rights, moral rights, and movie filtering technology: Hearing before the Subcommittee on Courts, the Internet, and Intellectual Property, Committee on the Judiciary, House of Representatives,* 108th Cong., Serial No. 93 (2004, May 20). Available: http://commdocs.house.gov/committees/judiciary/hju93773.000/hju93773_0f.htm

Eisenberg, A. L. (1936). *Children and radio programs: A study of more than three thousand children in the New York metropolitan area.* New York: Columbia University Press.

Family Entertainment and Copyright Act of 2005. P.L. 109-9 (2005).

Family Movie Act of 2004, H.R. 4586, 108th Cong. (2004).

Federal Communications Commission Notice of Inquiry (2004). *In the matter of violent television programming and its impact on children.* MB Docket No. 04–261.

Federal Communications Commission Report and Order (2004). *In the matter of second periodic review of the commission's rules and policies affecting the conversion to digital television.* MB Docket No. 03–15, RM 9832.

Federal Trade Commission (FTC). (2000). *Marketing violence to children: A review of self-regulation and industry practices in the motion picture, music recording, and electronic game industries.* Washington, DC: Author.

Federal Trade Commission (FTC). (2004). *Marketing violence to children: A fourth follow-up review of industry practices in the motion picture, music recording, and electronic game industries.* Washington, DC: Author.

Federman, J. (2002). *Rating sex and violence in the media: Media ratings and proposals for reform.* Menlo Park, CA: Kaiser Family Foundation.

Harrison, K., & Cantor, J. (1999). Tales from the screen: Enduring fright reactions to scary media. *Media Psychology, 1*(2), 97–116.

Hilden, J. (2002). The CleanFlicks case: Is it illegal to rent out a copyrighted video after editing it to omit "objectionable" content? *FindLaw's Writ, Legal Commentary.* http://writ.news.findlaw.com/hilden/20020903.html

Himelweit, H. T., Oppenheim, A. N., & Vince, P. (1958). *Television and the child.* London: Oxford University Press.

Hoekstra, S. J., Harris, R. J., & Helmick, A. L. (1999). Autobiographical memories about the experience of seeing frightening movies in childhood. *Media Psychology, 1*(2), 117–140.

Hoffner, C., & Cantor, J. (1985). Developmental differences in responses to a television character's appearance and behavior. *Developmental Psychology, 21,* 1065–1074.

Horovitz, E. G., (1983). Preschool aged children: When art therapy becomes the modality of choice. *Arts in Psychotherapy, 10,* 23–32.

Johnson, B. R. (1980). General occurrence of stressful reactions to commercial motion pictures and elements in films subjectively identified as stressors. *Psychological Reports, 47,* 775–786.

Johnson, J. G., Cohen, P., Kasen, S., First, M. B., & Brook, J. S. (2004). Association between television viewing and sleep problems during adolescence and early adulthood. *Archives of Pediatrics and Adolescent Medicine, 158,* 562–568.

Jordan, A., & Woodard, E. H. (2003). *Parents' use of the V-chip to supervise children's television use.* Paper presented at the Children and Television Media Policy Roundtable Discussion, Annenberg Public Policy Center, University of Pennsylvania. http://www.annenbergpublicpolicycenter.org/05_media_developing_child/childrensprogramming/2003_Parentsuseofvchip.pdf

Judge strikes down Washington video game law (2004). *Tech Law Advisor.* http://techlawadvisor.com/2004/07/judge-strikes-wa-video-game-sales-law.html

LeDoux, J. (1996). *The emotional brain: The mysterious underpinnings of emotional life.* New York: Simon & Schuster.

Lepore, S. J., & Smyth, J. M. (2002). *The writing cure: How expressive writing promotes health and emotional well-being.* Washington, DC: American Psychological Association Books.

Owens, J., Maxim, R., McGuinn, M., Nobile, C., Msall, M., & Alario, A. (1999). Television-viewing habits and sleep disturbance in school children. *Pediatrics, 104*(3), 552, e 27. http://pediatrics.aappublications.org/cgi/content/ full/104/3/e27

Pennebaker, J. W. (1997). *Opening up: The healing power of expressing emotions.* New York: Guilford Press.

Peterson signs violent video game ordinance into law (2000). City of Indianapolis Web Site. http://www.indygov.org/eGov/Mayor/PR/2000/7/20000717a.htm

Preston, M. I. (1941). Children's reactions to movie horrors and radio crime. *Journal of Pediatrics, 19,* 147–168.

Prohibiting Sale of Violent Computer and Video Games to Minors (2003). Washington State Legislature, H.B. 1009.

Protect Children From Video Game Sex and Violence Act of 2003, H.R. 669, 108th Cong. (2003).

Rideout, V. (2004). *Parents, media, and public policy: A Kaiser Family Foundation survey.* Menlo Park, CA: The Henry J. Kaiser Family Foundation.

Roje, J. (1995). LA '94 earthquake in the eyes of children: Art therapy with elementary school children who were victims of disaster. *Art Therapy, 12,* 237–243.

Schramm, W., Lyle, J., & Parker, E. P. (1961). *Television in the lives of our children.* Stanford, CA: Stanford University Press.

Singer, M. I., Slovak, K., Frierson, T., & York, P. (1998). Viewing preferences, symptoms of psychological trauma, and violent behaviors among children who watch television. *Journal of the American Academy of Child and Adolescent Psychiatry, 37*(10), 1041–1048.

Smith, S. L., & Moyer-Guse, E. (in press). Children's fear responses to the war in Iraq. *Media Psychology.*

Sparks, G. G., & Cantor, J. (1986). Developmental differences in fright responses to a television program depicting a character transformation. *Journal of Broadcasting and Electronic Media, 30,* 309–323.

Steyer, J. P. (2002). *The other parent: The inside story of the media's effect on our children.* New York: Atria Books.

Twenge, J. M. (2000). The age of anxiety? Birth cohort change in anxiety and neuroticism, 1952–1993. *Journal of Personality and Social Psychology, 79,* 1007–1021.

Twenty-First Century Media Responsibility Act of 2001, H.R. 1916. 107th Cong. (2001).

Walsh, D. (1994). *Selling out America's children: How America puts profits before values—and what parents can do*. Minneapolis: Fairview Press.

Wilson, B. J. (1987). Reducing children's emotional reactions to mass media through rehearsed explanation and exposure to a replica of a fear object. *Human Communication Research, 14,* 3–26.

Wilson, B. J. (1989). The effects of two control strategies on children's emotional reactions to a frightening movie scene. *Journal of Broadcasting & Electronic Media, 33,* 397–418.

Wilson, B. J., & Cantor, J. (1987). Reducing children's fear reactions to mass media: Effects of visual exposure and verbal explanation. In M. McLaughlin (Ed.), *Communication Yearbook 10,* (pp. 553–573). Beverly Hills, CA: Sage.

Wilson, B. J., Hoffner, C., & Cantor, J. (1987). Children's perceptions of the effectiveness of techniques to reduce fear from mass media. *Journal of Applied Developmental Psychology, 8,* 39–52.

CHAPTER 10

# *The Impact of Violent Music on Youth*

BARBARA J. WILSON AND NICOLE MARTINS

In 1999 in Littleton, Colorado, parents of the Columbine shooting victims linked gothic punk rocker Marilyn Manson to the killings at Columbine High School. They argued that Manson's (1996) *AntiChrist Superstar* album, along with other forms of violent media, inspired Dylan Klebold and Eric Harris to walk into their school heavily armed and shoot their classmates ("Forget God," 1999). In 2004, in *Confession Part II,* Rapper Joe Budden sang about the beating of a pregnant woman who is unwilling to abort her baby: "Pray that she abort that, if she's talkin' 'bout keepin' it / One hit to the stomach, she's leakin' it" ("Island/Def Jam Rap Song," 2004). The song was pulled from radio stations all across the United States after pregnancy crisis centers claimed the song advocated violence against women. In the same year another rapper, Jay-Z, produced a music video that featured a dramatization of the singer being shot and killed. Controversy over the video resulted in MTV restricting its airtime and including a disclaimer stating that the network does not promote gun violence (Rotter, 2004).

These are just a few examples of popular music that have come under public scrutiny in recent years because of violent content. But they are not isolated cases. Gangsta rap, which emerged as a genre of hip-hop in the late 1980s, is known for its raw and explicit lyrics detailing the street violence, drugs, and sexual experiences of urban gangs. For example, in his 2003 song "What Up Gangsta," controversial rapper 50 Cent chants the following:

> They say I walk around like got an "S" on my chest
>
> Naw, that's a semi-auto, and a vest on my chest
>
> I try not to say nothing, the DA might want to play in court
>
> But I'll hunt or duck a nigga down like it's sport
>
> Front on me, I'll cut ya, gun-butt ya or bump ya
>
> You getting money? I can't get none with ya then fuck ya

The album featuring this song, *Get Rich or Die Tryin'*, sold 872,000 copies in its first week, and went on to become the number-one selling CD in 2003 in the United States ("50 Cent Tops Album Charts," 2004).

Indeed, rap is the fastest-growing music genre in the United States (Recording Industry Association of America, 2003a). The success of this genre is due primarily to youth listeners. In one nationally representative study of U.S. teens, 53% of 12- to 18-year-olds reported that they had listened to rap music on the previous day (Roberts & Foehr, 2004). The popularity of such music raises alarms for many parents and critics. One well-known sports commentator for the British Broadcasting Corporation recently called gangsta rap "a deadly virus" that is "killing some of our children" (Denny & Suchet, 2004). According to one study, nearly 50% of mothers with children in junior high school believe that violent rap music contributes "a great deal" to school violence (Kandakai, Price, Telljohann, & Wilson, 1999).

This chapter explores the impact of violent music on youth. We begin by describing the music listening habits of children and adolescents, looking at total time spent with music compared to other media, preferences for different genres, and motivations for listening. We also examine how these patterns differ according to age, sex, and race and ethnicity. We then explore the content of music that youth find most appealing. In the third section, we examine young people's comprehension of music lyrics and videos. This section will be framed in terms of cognitive development and the requisite skills for processing musical lyrics and videos. The chapter then turns to the effects of violent music on children and adolescents. Most research to date has assessed the impact of exposure to violent music on aggressive attitudes and behaviors, but some studies have looked at other outcomes such as depression, risk taking, and even racial stereotyping. The chapter concludes with a discussion of various policy-making efforts launched over the years to deal with violent music.

## MUSIC HABITS AND PREFERENCES

Children in the United States are immersed in music. The typical child in this country lives in a home with three radios, three cassette players, and two CD players (Roberts & Foehr, 2004). Moreover, a full 53% of children under age 8 and 92% of 8- to 18-year-olds have a music medium of some kind in their bedroom (Roberts & Foehr, 2004). Higher levels of household income and parent education increase the chances that a younger child will have a CD player or radio, but possession of music equipment is so high among preteens and teens that it does not vary with income or education. Personal CD players, MP3 players, and iPods are becoming standard gadgets for adolescents.

As might be expected with all this equipment, young people devote a great deal of time to listening to music (see Roberts & Christenson, 2000). Children under 6 years of age spend an average of an hour a day listening to some type of music (Rideout, Vandewater, & Wartella, 2003). Exposure to audio media nearly doubles between the preteen and teen years, so that by age 15 the average adolescent spends 2½ hours a day listening to music (Roberts & Foehr, 2004). During the teenage years, young people also begin showing a preference for listening to music over watching television (Roberts & Foehr, 2004). In fact, in one study, teens were asked to select which of various media they would take if they were stranded on a desert island (Roberts & Henriksen, 1990, as cited in Christenson & Roberts, 1998). Junior and senior high students selected music media (radio/recordings) as their first choice substantially more often than they did any other medium, including television. Based on data like these, many scholars have argued that music is *the* most important medium for adolescents (Christenson & Roberts, 1998).

In addition to age, gender predicts use of audio media. Girls and boys in early elementary school, do not differ in their music listening, but toward the end of grade school, gender-based differences emerge. In a nationally representative sample of over 3,000 U.S. youth, Roberts and Foehr (2004) found that girls between the ages of 8 and 14, the "tween" years, spend more time listening to music than boys of the same age do. Although previous studies found that this sex difference continues through high school (e.g., Lyle & Hoffman, 1972), recent research suggests it may disappear by late adolescence (Roberts & Foehr, 2004).

The large-scale study by Roberts and Foehr (2004) revealed no substantial differences in time spent with music by race and ethnicity, although earlier studies employing less representative samples found greater music listening by African American youth (Brown, Childers, Bauman, & Koch, 1990) and by Hispanic youth (Lyle & Hoffman, 1972). Based on their findings, Roberts and Foehr (2004) concluded that, "one of the more striking characteristics of audio media is how very democratic they seem to be, at least in terms of how much they appeal to young people from all backgrounds" (p. 90).

Young people not only listen to music, but they can also "watch" it on television with the advent of MTV and other music video channels. The vast majority of preadolescents and adolescents watch music videos at least occasionally (Christenson, 1992b). Yet most studies indicate that listening to music is a far more frequent activity for youth than is watching music videos on television (see Christenson & Roberts, 1998). In the national study by Roberts and Foehr (2004), for example, 96% of 15- to 18-year-olds had listened to some kind of music on the previous day, whereas only 9% of these same teens had watched a music video on television on that same day.

## CONTENT PREFERENCES

Sorting music into genres is challenging because the industry is constantly changing. Not only do we have rock, hip-hop, jazz, Christian, country western, new age, and rhythm and blues, but we also have a proliferation of subgenres for many of these categories. For instance, Latin music can be divided into salsa, flamenco, samba, tango, mariachi, Latin pop, tejano, Caribbean, and Andean folk music, to name a few. Despite the ever-changing music scene, young people show strong preferences for certain types of music and these preferences vary considerably across individuals. Music styles are powerful social markers for youth (Christenson & Roberts, 1998), as evidenced by terms such as "punker" and "metalheads." Musical genres are also important because they differ widely in terms of violent content, as we will explore in a subsequent section.

Children under the age of 8 mostly listen to music created specifically for child audiences (Roberts & Foehr, 2004), such as Jim Gill, Raffi, and Disney tunes. Nevertheless, even very young children can be exposed to music that is violent, presumably because they are in the room with an older sibling or parent. In the Roberts and Foehr (2004) national survey, 7% of children between the ages of 2 and 7 had listened to rap music on the previous day; only 1% had heard hard rock or heavy metal.

By third or fourth grade, children clearly migrate toward popular music (Christenson, 1994). Two genres dominate the preferences of preteens and teens: rap/hip-hop and rock. In the national study by Roberts and Foehr (2004), 52% of the seventh through twelfth graders had listened to rap/hip-hop on the previous day, and 42% had listened to alternative or "modern" rock. The third most popular genre was heavy metal/hard rock, with 19%.

There are some sex differences in musical tastes. Boys are more likely to listen to heavy metal and "harder" forms of rock than girls are; girls are more likely to listen to soft rock, country western, and top 40 (Christenson & Peterson, 1988). However, musical tastes generally vary more strongly by race and ethnicity than by sex. African American youth tend to listen predominately to rap/hip-hop, but also like rhythm and blues/soul, and to a lesser extent, gospel music (Christenson & Roberts, 1998), all of which are linked to Black performers and Black culture. In one study, a full 84% of African American teens had listened to rap/hip-hop on the previous day (Roberts & Foehr, 2004). Hispanic youth also select rap/hip-hop as their favorite, but they listen to alternative rock, rhythm and blues, Latin, and heavy metal as well (Roberts & Foehr, 2004). Caucasian teens spread their listening over a wider range of genres. The two most popular are alternative rock and rap/hip-hop (Roberts & Foehr, 2004). Caucasian youth also report listening to heavy metal, country western, classic rock, and punk in greater numbers than do African American and Hispanic teens. Two generalizations can be drawn here. First, the only genre that is popular with all racial/ethnic groups is rap/hip-hop. Second, African American youth listen primarily to what has been labeled "Black" music in the industry; Caucasian youth listen to both "Black" and "White" music; and Hispanic youth listen to "Black," "White," and "Latin" music (Roberts & Foehr, 2004).

## *Uses and Gratifications*

Preadolescence and adolescence are developmental periods often characterized as challenging and sometimes even turbulent (Roth & Brooks-Gunn, 2000). As early as age 9 or 10, youth are beginning to experience physical and hormonal changes (Archibald, Graber, & Brooks-Gunn, 2003), an increased interest in sexuality (Crockett, Raffaelli, & Moilanen, 2003), questions about their identity (Kroger, 2003), and a growing independence from parents (Zimmer-Gembeck & Collins, 2003; see also the Prologue in this volume dealing with developmental differences). During this time, music is a form of communication that plays a central role in the lives of young people (Lull, 1992). Particular songs and even genres of music are often a source of comfort and a way to connect to the peer group, which takes on increasing importance during this time (Berndt, 1996).

When asked why they listen to music, young people list several reasons. Among the most prominent is to manage their moods (Christenson, 1994). In one study of junior high and college students (Gantz, Gartenberg, Pearson, & Schiller, 1978), high proportions of youth said they frequently listen to music to relieve tension or troubles (83%), to get into a certain mood (79%), and to relieve loneliness (67%). Interestingly, males are more likely to use music to get energized or "pumped up," whereas females are more likely to report using music when they feel lonely or troubled (Larson, Kubey, & Colletti, 1989). Such findings correspond with the different genres that boys and girl prefer. In one study, almost half of heavy metal fans, which are mostly male, reported that they were most likely to listen to the music when they are feeling angry (Arnett, 1991a).

A second gratification sought from music is to relax or relieve boredom. In the Gantz et al. study (1978), a full 91% of young people reported that music helps them pass the time while engaging in other activities such as homework, driving, and even trying to sleep. A third use of music is to establish and maintain social identities (Lull, 1992). Music helps young people make friends, connect to social groups, and even socialize at gatherings. In one study, over half of the teens reported that musical knowledge was an important factor in judging the status of their classmates (Brown & O'Leary, 1971); only school performance and clothing were ranked higher.

Finally, children and teens listen to music for informational purposes. Rock music introduces preteens and teens to explicit themes involving violence and sex that are often not contained on television or in popular films (Lull, 1985). Although young people seldom acknowledge the socialization function of music (Christenson & Roberts, 1998), there is ample evidence that such learning occurs. High schoolers in one study were asked to compare music against other possible sources of guidance on moral and social issues, including church, parents, and friends (Rouner, 1990). A full 25% of the teens ranked music in the top three sources for obtaining information about social interaction, and 16% ranked it in the top three for moral guidance. In another study, 66% of 11- to 15-year-olds indicated that music has "some" or "a lot" of influence on how they deal with problems in their lives, and nearly 50% reported that a particular song had influenced the way they thought about an important topic (Leming, 1987).

Part of the way in which young people learn from music is by listening to the lyrics. There is actually some debate about whether children pay much attention to the words in songs. Certainly the melody and the performers are key aspects of what makes a song popular. But words matter, too. Boyle and colleagues asked nearly 400 students in 5th, 7th, 9th, and 11th grades and in college what their reasons were for liking favorite songs (Boyle, Hosterman, & Ramsey, 1981). The lyrics of the song were ranked as the fourth most important reason, after melody, mood, and rhythm. The singer or group, the danceability of a song, and whether friends liked it were three other features that followed lyrics in order of importance. Christenson (1994) found that first through sixth graders also rated lyrics as less important than aspects of the sound and the mood a song encouraged, but the significance of lyrics increased with age. Still, certain genres of music are defined by the very nature of the messages they convey. Heavy metal fans report that they like such music because the lyrics resonate with the way they see the world (Arnett, 1991a), and avid rap listeners cite the lyrics as the most important feature of the music for them, more important than the rhythm or the danceability of a song (Kuwahara, 1992). In other words, the lyrics that are most explicit and oppositional may get the most attention from young people.

## AMOUNT OF VIOLENCE IN MUSIC AND MUSIC VIDEOS

Although many would agree that music has become more explicitly violent in nature, few studies have systematically analyzed the content of songs. In fact, only one published study could be found that assesses song lyrics for violence. Armstrong (2001) analyzed the content of 490 gangsta rap songs produced between 1987 and 1993. He found that 22% of the songs contained violent and misogynistic (i.e., expressing hatred of women) lyrics. Of those songs with violence, assault was the most frequently occurring criminal offense (50%), followed by murder (31%), rape (11%), and rape and murder combined (8%). Unfortunately, the study did not assess the frequency of violence within particular songs. Also, the sample represents an early period in the genre's development when lyrics were tamer than they have since become, according to Armstrong. As evidence of this trend, Armstrong analyzed a single top-selling rap album released in 2000, *Marshall Mathers LP* by Eminem, and found that 11 of the album's 14 songs (78%) contained violent lyrics. Thus, the figure of 22% is likely to considerably underestimate the amount of violence in gangsta rap today.

One possible reason that lyrics have received so little research attention is because of the advent of music videos. Since MTV's inception in 1981, critics have charged that violent and sexually explicit videos can have negative effects on adolescent viewers (Duff, 1995). Now, with as many as four music networks offering a constant stream of videos, social scientists have turned away from lyrics to focus more on the visual images that accompany popular music. In one early study, Baxter and colleagues analyzed a random sample of 62 videos that aired on MTV in 1984 (Baxter, DeRiemer, Landini, Leslie, & Singletary, 1985). They found that 53% contained violence. Most of the antisocial behavior consisted of physical aggression against another person. Weapons were seldom used. In a similar study around that same time, Sherman and Dominick (1986) analyzed 166 music videos featured on three different channels, including MTV. The researchers only coded "concept" videos or those that told a dramatized story rather than just showing a group performing. They found that 57% of the concept videos featured violence, a figure very close to that found by Baxter et al. (1985). On average, the videos contained nearly three separate acts of violence. Most of the violence was perpetrated by White male characters between the ages of 18 and 34. Like in the Baxter et al. study, hand-to-hand combat was the most common form of aggression. Only 3% of the violent videos portrayed death of the victim.

More recent content analyses suggest that violence may be a bit less prevalent than the above research suggests. Tapper, Thorson, and Black (1994) analyzed 161 videos that aired on four music channels in 1992. Fifteen percent contained violence. Rich, Woods, Goodman, Emans, and DuRant (1998) also found that 15% of the 518 videos they analyzed from 1994 contained violence. In the most comprehensive analysis to date, Smith and Boyson (2002) analyzed a sample of 1,962 videos drawn randomly to create a composite week of music video programming across three channels. They also found that 15% of the videos featured violence. At first glance, it appears that the amount of violence in music videos has declined since the 1980s. However, several of the earlier studies looked only at concept videos (e.g., Sherman & Dominick, 1986), which inflates the percentages because performance videos typically are nonviolent. Moreover, earlier studies did not assess the range of channels that have been examined more recently. Rich et al. (1998), for example, included the Country Music Television network and Tapper et al. (1994) included the Nashville Network in their samples. When a broader range of networks is examined, the study encompasses more genres, some of which are less violent.

Despite the fact that only about 15% of music videos features physical aggression, the variation by genre is substantial. Rap music videos are consistently more likely to feature violence than other types of videos are (DuRant et al., 1997; Tapper et al., 1994). Smith and Boyson (2002) found that nearly 30% of rap videos contained violence compared to only 12% of rock videos and 9% of rhythm and blues videos. The second-most violent genre is heavy metal (Tapper et al., 1994). Smith and Boyson (2002) found that a full 27% of heavy metal videos contained violence. Music channels also vary in violent content. MTV consistently features more violence than other music channels do (DuRant et al., 1997; Smith & Boyson, 2002). Black Entertainment Television (BET) is also more violent than channels such as VH-1 (Smith & Boyson, 2002). These patterns are primarily due to genre differences in programming. MTV features rap, heavy metal, and alternative rock in almost equal proportions, whereas BET concentrates on rap and soul/rhythm and blues (Tapper et al., 1994). In general, the more a television network carries rap and heavy metal, the more violent are its videos.

What is the nature of the violence featured in music videos, particularly rap videos? As part of their content analysis, Smith and Boyson (2002) assessed a number of contextual factors such as whether the violence is rewarded or punished, who the perpetrator is, and what the motive for violence is, all of which affect the likelihood that a viewer will learn aggressive behaviors from violent content (see Wilson et al., 1997). Smith and Boyson (2002) found that the majority of perpetrators and victims in rap videos are Black males. In contrast, the majority of characters involved in violence in rock videos are White males. The violence in rap videos is also more likely to be presented as justified than in other videos, is more likely to involved repeated acts of aggression against the same target, and is less likely to be punished. Unfortunately, the researchers could not assess the contextual features in heavy metal videos, the second-most violent genre, because too few were contained in their sample.

To summarize, we know much more about the violent content in music videos than in songs themselves. In the mid-1990s, roughly one in five rap songs contained violent lyrics (Armstrong, 2001). Some speculate that rap music is becoming more violent, but we have no clear data to substantiate that. Future research should assess the nature of lyrics more systematically, with particular attention to rap and heavy metal music. With regard to music videos, about one in six contain some violence. Most of this physical aggression is found in rap and heavy metal videos, two highly popular genres among youth. Nevertheless, content analyses of music videos have concentrated on the visual images and have yet to simultaneously analyze the lyrics for violence. In most cases the visuals reinforce the lyrics. But sometimes the lyrics contain additional information. Guns, for example, are displayed in only 17% of violent rap videos (Smith & Boyson, 2002), but guns are *talked about* in nearly 50% of rap videos (Jones, 1997). Presumably, the combination of violent words and violent images sends a powerful message regarding antisocial behavior.

## YOUNG PEOPLE'S COMPREHENSION OF MUSIC LYRICS

The impact of violent music on children depends to a great extent on what sense young listeners make of the content. We have already noted that the words of a song may not be the most important factor in determining what becomes popular, but youth do pay attention to lyrics. Moreover, young people who are attracted to songs that are controversial or oppositional seem to pay closer attention to the lyrics than do fans of more conventional music (Wass et al., 1989). But how well do young listeners truly understand the meaning of popular songs, especially those that are violent?

One of the challenges in comprehending music is that the lyrics often contain oblique references to risqué or illicit topics. Innuendos about violence and sex are common, as is the use of metaphors to express ideas. For example, Insane Clown Posse, a heavy metal/rap band known for its violent lyrics and carnival-like live shows featuring fires and chainsaws, released a song in 2004 titled "Bowling Balls." Parts of the lyrics are as follows:

> We take a quick ride, homicide, then I confide in you
>
> And I can love you and technically even though you're dead
>
> You'll always be around cause I'm keeping your head
>
> I keep heads on shelves everywhere in my cellar. . . .
>
> Your head would mean so much to me
>
> Sometimes I put 'em in my bowling bag and bring 'em to work
>
> Play with their hair under my desk, with my bare feet

The song's title sounds innocent enough but in fact refers to a murderer collecting the heads of his victims.

Understanding lyrics such as these is likely to be a challenge for youth. In one early study, Rosenbaum and Prinsky (1987) asked a sample of 266 12- to 18-year-olds to name their three favorite songs and then to describe the songs in a few sentences. Students were unable to explain 37% of the songs listed as their favorites. Many teens reported that they had no idea what their selected song meant but that they liked the rhythm or melody. Although no precise percentages were given, the researchers found that teens frequently misinterpreted the songs they liked. A number of them thought, for example, that the song "Stairway to Heaven" by Led Zeppelin, which focuses on a young woman's quest for meaning in life, was about going to heaven on a stairway. The researchers pointed out that students, often unable to grasp complex metaphors, provided very literal descriptions of the songs.

Leming (1987) played three "Top 40" songs to a sample of 11- through 15-year-olds and asked them to describe in their own words what the songs meant. Roughly 25% of the youth reported that they had no idea what each of the songs meant, even though nearly all had heard the music before and knew the artists. Misinterpretations were also common. For example, 36% of the youth thought Olivia Newton-John's song "Physical" was a plea for physical exercise. Only one third of the sample correctly interpreted the song as advocating sexual relations. Likewise, only 26% of the youth understood that "I Want a New Drug" by Huey Lewis and the News was a song advocating drug use. A higher proportion of teens understood Madonna's "Material Girl" (67%), but comprehension was still far from universal.

In one of the few studies to assess age differences in comprehension, Greenfield and colleagues (1987) presented two popular rock songs, Bruce Springsteen's "Born in the USA" and Madonna's "Like a Virgin," to a sample of fourth, eighth, and twelfth graders, and college students. Participants received a copy of the lyrics as they listened to the songs and then were asked a series of questions about the lyrics' meaning. Strong differences in understanding among different age levels were observed for both songs. Only 20% of the fourth graders understood the term "hometown jam" in the Springsteen song, whereas 60% of the eighth graders and nearly all of the twelfth graders and college students understood it. None of the fourth graders comprehended that Springsteen was singing about his despair and disillusionment over living in this country, compared to 30% of the eighth graders, 40% of the twelfth graders, and 50% of the college students.

Although participants showed a slightly better understanding of Madonna's song, age differences still existed. Only 10% of the fourth graders correctly understood Madonna's feelings in the song, whereas 50% of the eighth graders, 60% of the twelfth graders, and 80% of the college students did. Overall, younger children were more literal and concrete in their interpretations of the songs, whereas high school and college students were more abstract and metaphorical.

Age differences have also been found in the comprehension of music videos. Christenson (1992b) exposed 54 fourth- through sixth graders to Billy Ocean's music video "Get Outta My Dreams, Get Into My Car" and then asked the children to describe what the story was about. The video features Billy Ocean pulling into a carwash and asking the female attendant to get into his car. The couple then goes through the carwash and later to a drive-in movie. Roughly half of the children knew the video was about a romantic relationship, but the remaining half did not. Next the children were presented with three forced-choice alternatives about the meaning of the song: an abstract one that focused on the budding relationship between the characters ("a guy who likes a girl and wants to know her better") and two that were more concrete ("a guy who wants to take a girl for a ride in his car," "a guy who is getting his car washed"). Sixth graders were more likely to pick the abstract, more correct interpretation of the song (88%) than were fourth graders (51%).

We can expect children's comprehension of music to improve with development, in part because of the preponderance of symbolism and figurative language in popular songs. Other media-related research supports this idea. In one study, second, fourth, and sixth graders were exposed to print ads that featured either a literal or a metaphorical message about the same product (Pawlowski, Badzinski, & Mitchell, 1998). Sixth graders were better able to interpret the metaphors than were the younger two age groups. In another study, children between the ages of 12 and 16 were exposed to a series of television clips that contained sexual innuendos about intercourse, rape, and prostitution (Silverman-Watkins & Sprafkin, 1983). Children over the age of 13 generally understood the televised innuendos better than did the 12-year-olds.

As it turns out, the age differences in comprehension of the media are quite consistent with research on children's understanding of symbolic language such as metaphors (Wilson, 2001). In general, children aged 6 and under have difficulty interpreting even common metaphors (Johnson & Pascual-Leone, 1989). By age 7 or 8, children can understand those metaphors that bare strong physical resemblance to their referents. Not until 11 or 12 can children reliably interpret most types of metaphors. These patterns are congruent with broad shifts in cognitive development in which children move from concrete thought processes closely tied to how things appear (Flavell, Miller, & Miller, 2002) to more abstract and flexible thinking during the adolescent years (Byrnes, 2003).

Age is not the only factor that can affect comprehension. Being a committed fan seems to encourage a differential response to music (Kuwahara, 1992), as suggested above. In one study, Wass et al. (1989) surveyed 694 middle and high school students about their music preferences and favorite songs. Nearly 20% of the students qualified as heavy metal fans and most were White males. The researchers found that 41% of the heavy metal fans knew all the lyrics to their favorite songs as compared to only 25% of students who liked other types of music. Unfortunately, the researchers did not test actual lyric comprehension, but it stands to reason that those who pay more attention to the words will show increased comprehension of them. Fans will have more experience with a genre's themes and conventions, and this experience should result in the development of "scripts" or routinized mental expectations for the sequence of actions that constitute a typical story or event (Schank & Abelson, 1977). According to script theory, songs that are scripted should be easier to understand and memorize than songs that are novel or unfamiliar (Desmond, 1987).

To test this idea indirectly, Hansen and Hansen (1991) conducted an experiment in which undergraduates were either given a written copy of the lyrics (low cognitive load) or not (high cognitive load) while they listened to four heavy metal songs. Providing the lyrics was designed to reduce the mental effort or load required to make sense of the songs. The researchers reasoned that their low cognitive load condition is parallel to an avid fan's experience in that repeated exposure to a song should also reduce the mental resources needed to process its meaning. Across three experiments, those in the low cognitive load condition showed better recall, song comprehension, and extraction of detailed content than did those in the high cognitive load condition. However, even when the lyrics were provided, most participants showed far from perfect comprehension of the songs.

Several conclusions can be drawn from this research. First, comprehension of music is particularly challenging because of the symbolic language and complex metaphors involved. Second, comprehension varies greatly with age; the more obscure the lyrics are, the more likely that a child under the age of 11 or 12 will not understand their meaning. Some have argued that this lack of comprehension might in fact protect younger children from possible harmful effects of explicit or violent songs (Greenfield et al., 1987).

Third, fans of musical genres are more likely to pay attention to and understand song lyrics than are casual listeners. With regard to violence, we should be most concerned, then, about fans of rap and heavy metal music. Notably, these are the very genres that place a strong emphasis on the words as central to the music. Finally, it is not at all clear that a "correct" or absolute understanding even exists with regard to music, given the multiple meanings inherent in this artistic form (Hansen & Hansen, 1991). Furthermore, we do not have any evidence to suggest that a fuller understanding leads to more learning or imitation. It may be enough to simply understand the themes of violence in order to learn from such content. We now turn to the research on effects.

## EFFECTS OF VIOLENT MUSIC ON AGGRESSIVE ATTITUDES AND BEHAVIORS

Most research on the impact of violent music has focused on whether such content encourages aggressive attitudes and behaviors in listeners. There are literally hundreds of studies showing that exposure to violent television programming increases aggression (see Bushman & Anderson, 2001). By contrast, there are far fewer studies of the effects of violent music and music videos. However, several prominent theories suggest that music would have the same effects as television programs do. Social learning theory posits that children can learn new behaviors by observing others in their social environment (Bandura, 1977, 1994). According to this theory, children are more likely to imitate models that are rewarded than those that are punished. Children are also more likely to imitate a model that is perceived as attractive or similar to the self (Bandura, 1986). Therefore, highly popular singers and bands can serve as potent role models for young people. When Arnett (1991a) asked a group of high school students to list people they admired, 60% of heavy metal fans named a favorite musician. Indeed, a casual observer can find numerous examples of preteen and teen fans trying to emulate the gothic style of punk rocker Marilyn Manson or the pop style of Britney Spears.

Social learning theory is a useful framework for understanding how children can learn new attitudes and behaviors from role models in the media. Once such behaviors are acquired, cognitive priming theory explains how the media can prompt their enactment in certain situations. According to priming theory (Berkowitz, 1990; Jo & Berkowitz, 1994), violent stimuli in the media can activate aggressive thoughts, feelings, and even motor tendencies stored in a person's memory. For a short time after exposure, then, a person is in a "primed" state and several conditions can encourage these thoughts and feelings to unfold into aggressive behavior. One such condition is the person's own emotional state. Individuals who are angry or hostile are more likely to be primed to act aggressively by the media because they are in a state of readiness to respond (Berkowitz, 1990). Another condition that encourages priming is justified violence. If media violence is portrayed as morally proper, it can help to temporarily reduce a person's inhibitions against behaving in an antisocial way (Jo & Berkowitz, 1994). Finally, reminders in the immediate environment of violence that a person has just witnessed can trigger aggressive behavior (Jo & Berkowitz, 1994).

Both social learning and priming explain the short-term effects of exposure to media violence. Huesmann (1998) has developed an information-processing model that helps to account for the long-term effects of media violence. The model focuses on the learning and reinforcement of scripts, or mental routines stored in memory. A script typically includes information about what events are likely to happen, how a person should respond, and what the likely outcome of these responses will be. According to Huesmann, a child who has been exposed to a great deal of violence, either in real life or through the media, is likely to develop scripts that encourage aggression as a way of dealing with problems. Consistent and repeated exposure to violent messages helps to reinforce these scripts and make them easy to retrieve in memory. In other words, a preteen or teen who listens to a great deal of gangsta rap should have a stable and enduring set of cognitive scripts that accentuate aggression, particularly aggression against women, as an appropriate response to social situations. How well does the research on violent music support these theories? We turn now to the evidence.

### *Correlational Studies*

Several studies have found a relationship between preference for violent music and aggressive behavior. In one study, Rubin et al. (2001) surveyed 243 college students about their listening habits, emotions, aggressive attitudes, and attitudes toward women. Rap and heavy metal listeners exhibited significantly more aggressive attitudes than did fans of classic rock, rhythm and blues, country, and alternative rock. Heavy metal listeners also expressed more negative attitudes toward women and rap listeners exhibited significantly more distrust of other people than did listeners of the other genres.

Took and Weiss (1994) found that adolescents who like rap and heavy metal music were more likely to have been suspended or expelled from school for behavior problems and to have arrest records. Other studies have found that heavy metal fans in particular are more likely than other teens to engage in delinquent behaviors (Arnett, 1991b; Martin, Clarke, & Pearce, 1993) and to experience conflict in family relationships (Christenson & van Nouhuys, 1995, as reported in Christenson & Roberts, 1998). The findings are consonant with social learning, priming, and Huesmann's model in that exposure to the most violent music is associated with increased aggression. The data, however, are correlational and therefore impossible to untangle in terms of causality. Do violent lyrics cause adolescent aggression or do troubled, violent youth seek out such content? The only way to resolve this issue is to use more controlled studies.

## *Experiments Assessing Violent Lyrics*

Several experiments have assessed the impact of listening to violent music. One important caveat here is that the vast majority of these laboratory studies have used college-aged students rather than children and teens. In such cases, the best we can do is extrapolate from what is known about older teens and young adults to what is likely to occur with younger listeners.

Wannamaker and Reznikoff (1989) assessed feelings of hostility after exposure to a single heavy metal song that had either aggressive lyrics and aggressive music (i.e., "hard, driving beat") or just aggressive music but nonaggressive lyrics. Compared to a group who heard a completely nonaggressive song, no differences in hostility were found in the two heavy metal conditions, although the researchers acknowledged that the vast majority of participants did not understand the theme in either of the two heavy metal songs used.

In another experiment, male college students listened to four rap songs that were either misogynous (sexually violent) or neutral (no sex or violence) in nature (Barongan & Hall, 1995). Participants then viewed a violent, a sexually violent, or a neutral vignette from the movie *I Spit on Your Grave* and chose one of the vignettes for a female confederate to watch. Males who had heard the misogynous rap music were significantly more likely to select the violent vignette for the female confederate than were males who had heard the neutral rap. The researchers argued that selecting a violent movie clip to show another person is a proxy for aggressive behavior, although others have questioned the validity of such a measure (Anderson, Carnagey, & Eubanks, 2003).

In the most extensive research to date, Anderson and colleagues reported five experiments on the impact of violent lyrics on aggression (Anderson et al., 2003). In the first experiment, college students listened to a violent song or a nonviolent song, both performed by the same band, and then rated their feelings on a standard hostility scale (e.g., "I feel furious," "I feel like yelling at somebody"). Results revealed that the violent song produced higher levels of hostility than did the nonviolent song. Experiment 2 was identical except that it assessed aggressive cognitions rather than feelings. After listening, participants were presented with a series of ambiguous words and asked to rate how similar they were to other words. As predicted, the violent song led participants to interpret ambiguous words such as "rock" and "stick" in an aggressive way. The researchers argued that the violent song made aggressive thoughts more accessible, as priming theory suggests.

In Experiment 3, the researchers added a no-song control condition and increased the number of songs tested in the violent and nonviolent conditions. Again, participants who heard a violent song reported a higher level of hostility, but only when measured immediately after exposure, suggesting that the impact of music on aggressive feelings may be fleeting. In addition, those who heard a violent song reacted more quickly when reading aggressive words than did those in the nonviolent and control conditions. In Experiment 4, participants listened to a violent humorous song, a nonviolent humorous song, or no song. As predicted, the violent humorous group showed the same level of hostility as the control group did, supporting the idea that humor can cancel out the impact of violent lyrics. Nevertheless, those who listened to the violent humorous song were still more likely than those who heard the nonviolent song to create aggressive words out of word fragments (e.g., make "h_t" into "hit" rather than "hat").

Experiment 5 tested song violence and humor independently in a 2 (violent vs.

nonviolent lyrics) X 2 (humorous vs. nonhumorous lyrics) design. Irrespective of humor, those who heard the violent song had higher hostility scores and produced more aggressive word completions afterward than did those who heard a nonviolent song. To summarize, songs with violent lyrics increased feelings of hostility in four of the five experiments, and this effect occurred across the range of humorous and nonhumorous songs. In addition, violent songs led to more aggressive cognitions in four of the experiments.

Two studies have assessed whether violent songs enhance aggression against women in particular. St. Lawrence and Joyner (1991) exposed 75 male undergraduates to 17 minutes of sexually violent heavy metal rock, Christian heavy metal rock, or classical music and then measured attitudes toward women, acceptance of violence against women, and self-reported arousal. Males in both heavy metal song conditions were significantly more likely to endorse sex-role stereotypes than were males who had listened to classical music. Furthermore, both the sexually violent and the Christian heavy metal music increased acceptance of interpersonal violence against women and of rape myths (e.g., "Women who get raped hitchhiking get what they deserve"), although the increase was statistically significant only for the Christian heavy metal listeners.

Wester, Crown, Quatman, and Heesacker (1997) looked at gangsta rap and its impact on attitudes toward women. Male participants with little exposure to gangsta rap were randomly assigned to one of four conditions: listened to five gangsta rap songs (music only), listened to the same songs while reading the lyrics (music plus lyrics), read the lyrics but did not hear the songs (lyrics only), or neither heard the songs nor read the lyrics (control). Men exposed to the gangsta lyrics, regardless of whether music accompanied them, expressed more adversarial views about sexual relations with women than did those who were not exposed to the lyrics. Music alone, the researchers concluded, might not suffice to affect naïve listeners who have no prior scripts in memory for such content. Instead, consistent with social learning, more explicit exposure to a song's words may be necessary to foster the creation of new scripts.

### *Experiments Assessing Violent Music Videos*

Several scholars have argued that music videos are likely to have more impact than songs alone (Strasburger & Hendren, 1995). Adding a visual portrayal of violence to reinforce violent words certainly enhances the number of aggressive cues in the message. Consistent with this idea, college students evaluate music videos more favorably and rate them to be more "potent" than audio-only versions of the same music (Rubin et al., 1986). One of the main reasons young people like music videos is because the visual portrayals help in interpreting the song's meaning (Sun & Lull, 1986). Thus, a video may make complex or ambiguous lyrics more accessible and meaningful, especially to a younger child.

In one of the earliest experiments on music videos, Greeson and Williams (1986) had seventh and tenth graders watch either a randomly compiled group of videos from MTV or a pre-selected group of high-impact videos containing sex, violence, and anti-establishment overtones. The high-impact videos increased tenth graders' self-reported acceptance of the use of interpersonal violence. The same videos unexpectedly tended to decrease seventh graders' acceptance of violence, although this difference was not statistically significant. Unfortunately, because the high-impact videos contained numerous themes and because some low-impact videos actually contained violence, this study does not provide a clean test of the effects of violent music videos.

In a more tightly controlled experiment, Hansen and Hansen (1990) had 56 undergraduates watch three rock videos portraying antisocial behavior (e.g., destroying a home during a wild party) or three neutral rock videos containing no antisocial acts. Afterward, participants watched a videotape of a confederate who was ostensibly on a job interview and who made either an obscene hand gesture toward the experimenter or no such gesture during the interview. Overall, those who had seen the neutral videos rated the confederate as less likeable, more threatening, and more irrational when he made the gesture than when he did not. In contrast, those who had seen the antisocial videos rated the confederate the same regardless of the obscene gesture, suggesting an increased tolerance for antisocial behavior.

Johnson, Jackson, and Gatto (1995) conducted an experiment on the impact of rap music videos in particular. African American males between the ages of 11 and 16 were exposed to eight violent rap videos, eight nonviolent rap videos, or no music videos. Next, the teens read two vignettes ostensibly as part of another study, one of which involved a jealous man who assaulted his girlfriend as well as another man who vied for her attention. Participants were then asked about their attitudes regarding the use of violence in the vignette and about the likelihood that they themselves would respond similarly. Teens in the violent video group expressed greater acceptance of the use of violence against the man than did teens in the nonviolent and control groups. Compared to the control group, participants in the violent video group also reported a greater acceptance of the use of violence against the girlfriend and a greater likelihood of personally engaging in similar violence. In a subsequent study, Johnson and colleagues found that even nonviolent rap videos could increase African American adolescents' acceptance of teen dating violence, but only among girls and not among boys who were already high in acceptance (Johnson, Adams, Ashburn, & Reed, 1995). The researchers argued that nonviolent videos still contain images of women as sexually subordinate, which could lead to increased tolerance for violence against females.

In a study conducted outside the laboratory, researchers assessed the level of violence in a maximum-security forensic hospital before and after the removal of MTV (Waite, Hillbrand, & Foster, 1992). The study was prompted by clinical staff observations that MTV was continuously on in at least one of two television rooms and that patients often experienced behavioral problems after prolonged exposure to such content. The hospital staff measured verbal and physical aggression of 222 patients over a 55-week period, 33 weeks before and 22 weeks after MTV was banned from the viewing options. Following MTV's removal, aggression dropped from an average of 44 incidents per week to 28 incidents per week, with significant decreases in verbal as well as physical aggression. Although the study lacks a true control group, it is the only evidence we are aware of that links exposure to violent music with changes in aggressive behavior observed in a naturalistic environment.

To summarize, a modest amount of evidence links exposure to violent music with aggression. Even brief periods of listening to or watching violent material can increase aggression. Certain violent music, particularly that which is misogynistic in nature, can also increase aggression toward women. Most research has focused on rap and heavy metal music, the two most violent genres. All of the studies have looked at short-term effects only, predominantly with college students.

Future research can take several directions. First, we simply need more studies. Compared to the database on violent television programming, the literature on violent music is scant and unsystematic. Second, researchers need to pay more attention to the music and the aggression measures they select so that stronger conclusions can be drawn across studies. If violent rap music is tested, for example, the experimenter needs to specify whether the lyrics are explicit or vague, whether the songs employed also contain sexual content, and what type of violence the song endorses. As mentioned previously, justified violence, rewarded violence, and attractive perpetrators all enhance the impact of *television* violence on aggression, warranting their assessment in music as well. Third, more studies should assess actual aggressive behavior as an outcome variable rather than self-reports of hostile feelings and attitudes. Fourth, we need to study younger age groups, especially preteen and teens, who spend a great deal of time with music and are still developing scripts for social problem solving and for dating relationships. We also need to focus specifically on teens that are ardent fans of violent music. Finally, we need to conduct longitudinal research to ascertain the long-term impact of exposure to violent music. Tracking youth over time will help determine whether rebellious teens are simply attracted to violent music or whether such music actually contributes to aggression.

## OTHER ANTISOCIAL EFFECTS OF VIOLENT MUSIC

Although the vast majority of studies have concentrated on the impact of violent music on aggression, there may be other negative outcomes of listening to violent songs. We review three here: increased depression, risk taking, and racial stereotyping.

### *Violent Music and Depression/Suicide*

Several studies have explored whether violent music is linked to mental health problems in youth. In an experiment, Ballard and Coates (1995) had college students listen to one of six songs that varied by genre (rap vs. heavy metal) and by content (homicidal, suicidal, or nonviolent). Rap music generally made students feel angrier than heavy metal did, but none of the songs increased depression or suicidal thoughts. This is not surprising given that changes in mental health are not likely to occur after short-term exposure to a single song.

Correlational studies suggest more of a link. One survey of 247 Australian teens found that a preference for rock/heavy metal music was positively correlated with suicidal thoughts, acts of deliberate self-harm, and depression, particularly among females (Martin, Clarke, & Pearce, 1993). For example, 62% of female teens who liked rock/heavy metal reported that they had deliberately tried to harm themselves within the last 6 months, compared to only 14% of females who preferred pop music. Unfortunately, the study combined those who listened to rock with those who listened to heavy metal, so it is difficult to isolate the effect of *violent* music.

Scheel and Westefeld (1999) surveyed 121 U.S. high schoolers and found that 40% liked or strongly liked heavy metal music. They also found a positive correlation between heavy metal fanship and suicidal ideation or thinking about killing oneself. The relationship was especially prominent among females: 74% of female heavy metal fans reported that they had occasionally or seriously thought about killing themselves, whereas only 35% of nonfans did. Heavy metal listening was also associated with significantly lower scores on the Reasons for Living Inventory (RFL), which taps reasons to live and reasons not to commit suicide. In contrast, being a rap or rock fan was associated with higher scores on the RFL. Like most teens in the study, heavy metal fans reported that listening to their favorite music put them in a positive rather than negative mood (only

9% said the music made them feel angrier). This self-reported mood elevation has led some scholars to argue that the pessimistic lyrics of heavy metal may actually be therapeutic for teens coping with stress (Arnett, 1991a). Disentangling whether heavy metal music attracts or creates troubled youth is an important challenge for future research.

### *Violent Music and Reckless Behavior*

Several studies have found a link between violent music and risk taking. Arnett (1991b) surveyed tenth and twelfth graders about a variety of reckless activities they might have engaged in over the past year. For males, liking heavy metal music was positively associated with drunken driving and with marijuana use. These relationships held even after controlling for individual differences in sensation seeking and in satisfaction with family relationships. For females, liking heavy metal was positively associated with having sex without contraception, marijuana use, and shoplifting.

Looking at a sample of teens treated for problems at clinics and psychiatric units, Took and Weiss (1994) found that those who liked heavy metal and rap music were more likely to have used illegal drugs and alcohol and to have engaged in sexual activity than were those who did not like such music. Many of these teens had a history of problems dating back to elementary school, leading the researchers to speculate that troubled teens may gravitate to violent music rather than that violent music causes such turmoil.

To resolve the directionality issue, two longitudinal studies have been conducted. Robinson, Chen, and Killen (1998) surveyed 1,533 ninth graders at a baseline point and again 18 months later about their alcohol use. Results showed that after controlling for age, sex, ethnicity, and other media use, music video viewing was significantly associated with the onset of drinking. In fact, each increase of 1 hour per day of music video exposure was associated with a 31% increased risk of starting to drink during the next 18 months. Unfortunately, the study did not assess the types of videos viewed so it is impossible to know whether violence, or some other content feature such as drinking portrayals, contributed to this effect. The study also did not control for parental influence.

Wingood, DiClemente, and Bernhardt (2003) surveyed 522 African American girls between the ages of 14 and 18 at two points in time concerning their exposure to rap music videos and their sexual activity, drug use, and aggressive behavior. After controlling for parental monitoring as well as teen employment, age, involvement in extracurricular activities, and participation in religious events, early exposure to rap music videos was found to be a significant predictor of subsequent risk-taking behaviors 12 months after exposure. In particular, those who reported greater exposure to rap at baseline were twice as likely to have had multiple sex partners, more than 1.5 times as likely to have contracted a new sexually transmitted disease, and more than 1.5 times as likely to have used drugs and alcohol by the follow-up.

Longitudinal studies begin to address whether at-risk teens are merely attracted to violent music or whether such music contributes to teen recklessness. In the end, it may be a cyclical process whereby violent music and risky behavior are mutually reinforcing over time. At a minimum, we can conclude that a strong preference for violent music is one of many factors that can signal adolescent turbulence.

### *Violent Music and Racial Stereotyping*

Fictional television shows and even television news often portray Blacks as violent and as engaged in disproportionate amounts of criminal behavior (Dixon & Linz, 2000; Oliver, 1994). Rap music has also been criticized for stereotyping (Morano, 2004).

Only two published studies exist, to our knowledge, on the impact of rap music on racial stereotyping. In one experiment (Johnson, Trawalter, & Dovido, 2000), 180 Caucasian and African American undergraduates were randomly assigned to listen to 4 minutes of violent rap music, 4 minutes of nonviolent rap, or no music. Students then participated in an ostensibly unrelated study in which they read three stories, one about a young man who threatened his fiancée with violence, one about a job applicant interested in a management position that required "demonstrated intelligence," and one about an ROTC graduate seeking a position in a helicopter training school that required "excellent spatial skills." Participants were either told that the man in each story was Black or that he was White. When the target in the story was Black, participants exposed to the violent rap were significantly more likely to make negative attributions about the Black man's violent personality than were those exposed to either nonviolent rap or no rap. When the target was White, rap music had no impact on attributions about the violence. This stereotyping effect occurred regardless of the participants' race. Similarly, compared to the nonviolent rap and the no-music conditions, exposure to violent rap music led participants to rate the Black man as less qualified for a job requiring intelligence. Yet violent rap music had no impact on judgments regarding the Black ROTC applicant, consistent with the idea that spatial skills are not part of people's stereotypes about race.

In another experiment, Rudman and Lee (2002) exposed mostly Caucasian undergraduates to either six violent and misogynistic rap songs or six pop/rap songs with no violent or sexist content. Students who listened to the violent and misogynistic rap rated a Black target that behaved ambiguously as more violent, more sexist, and less intelligent than controls did. Violent rap music did not affect judgments when the ambiguous target was White. These findings are consistent with research indicating that other types of violent media content can also prime racial stereotypes (see Greenberg, Mastro, & Brand, 2002).

## POLICY IMPLICATIONS AND CONCLUSIONS REGARDING VIOLENT MUSIC

In the last two decades, violent music has provoked spirited debate between members of the music industry, parents, and policy makers. As early as 1985, the wives of several members of the United States Congress formed the Parents Music Resource Center (PMRC). Spearheaded by Tipper Gore, the PMRC's mission was to educate parents about the "alarming trends" in popular music, particularly the increasingly violent and sexual lyrics as well as the graphic album covers (PMRC, 2004). As a way to combat this issue, the PMRC asked the Recording Industry Association of America (RIAA) to provide parental advisory labels on recordings that contained explicit content. Contemporaneously, the U.S. Senate Commerce, Technology, and Transportation Committee, responding to pressure from the PMRC, began an investigation into the content of rock music. Several famous rock musicians were called to testify before the committee, including Frank Zappa who called Tipper Gore a "cultural terrorist." Before the hearing ended, the RIAA agreed to label explicit audio recordings. Today, the labels are applied by individual record companies and artists, and are in the form of a black and white logo with the words "parental advisory, explicit content" placed on the packaging. As of 2000, one third of the 100 top-selling

CDs contained a parental advisory label (FTC, 2000).

Some retail chains like Wal-Mart have refused to stock any music containing such advisories ("Wal-Mart Cleans Up," 1997). Record companies have responded by altering certain songs and creating "clean" copies to meet retailing standards. Notably, these edited versions often outsell the original releases (FTC, 2000). Despite the efforts by the RIAA and some retail chains to help parents, the advisory labels may make little difference as more and more music becomes available on the Internet. In one recent poll, 70% of preteens and teens (ages 12–18) reported that they are more likely to download music off the Web than go to a record store (Holland, 2002).

The effectiveness of the labels may also be hampered by the parents themselves. Although 75% of parents report being concerned about the music their children listen to (Woodard, 2000), many do not seem to use the advisory labels. In one national survey, 84% of parents reported that they had used the MPAA film rating system to make media choices for their children, but only 50% had used the parental advisory labels on music (Kaiser Family Foundation, 2001).

Another problem with advisory labels is that they may actually attract young consumers to the very content that parents want their children to avoid. Bushman and Cantor (2003) tested this "forbidden fruit" idea in a meta-analysis of 18 studies conducted on the impact of ratings and advisories on attraction to different types of media content. They found that ratings and advisories generally increased rather than decreased attraction to media, particularly among males. But the effects varied with age. Ratings served as a repellent for children under age 8, but as an enticement for older children and adolescents.

Other approaches for dealing with violent music are more direct. Some schools have forbidden young people to dress in any style that represents punk or heavy metal music (Garza, 2004), and some communities have devised workshops for parents to "depunk" or "demetal" their children (Rosenbaum & Prinsky, 1991). The American Academy of Pediatrics (1996) issued a statement that, "It is in children's best interest to listen to lyrics that are not violent, sexist, drug-oriented, or antisocial," (p.1219) and it recommends that pediatricians encourage parents to monitor the music that their children listen to and purchase. And in one national poll, over 70% of parents supported the outright prohibition of the sale of gangsta rap music to children under the age of 18 (Joint Center for Political and Economic Studies, 1997).

The music industry and avid fans have charged that any efforts at music censorship are a violation of the First Amendment (RIAA, 2003b). Yet governmental pressure continues. In 2000, the Federal Trade Commission issued a report stating that the marketing of explicit-labeled music to children under 17 is pervasive. The report encourages the music industry and independent retailers to require parental permission before selling labeled music to minors. At the same time, rap music is becoming increasingly popular and, some argue, more explicit. In addition, heavy metal music attracts a smaller but just as avid group of fans who are mostly young White males.

The research to date indicates that exposure to violent music can lead to short-term increases in aggressive attitudes and cognitions, and that some forms of rap music can prime racial stereotypes. We need far more evidence about the long-term effects of violent lyrics on aggressive behavior, risk taking, depression, and even desensitization to violence. As with all forms of violent media, we should be most concerned about those young people who are frustrated, isolated from social support, surrounded by aggressive cues in their environment, and strongly attracted to musicians who glorify violence in their songs.

## REFERENCES


50 Cent. (2003). What up gangsta. On *Get rich or die tryin'* [CD]. Santa Monica, CA: Interscope Records.

50 Cent tops album charts. (2004, January 2). *Associated Press.* Retrieved September 3, 2004, from Lexis Nexis database.

American Academy of Pediatrics. (1996). Impact of music lyrics and music videos on children and youth. *Pediatrics, 98*(6), 1219–1221.

Anderson, C. A., Carnagey, N. L., & Eubanks, J. (2003). Exposure to violent media: The effects of songs with violent lyrics on aggressive thoughts and feelings. *Journal of Personality and Social Psychology, 84,* 960–971.

Archibald, A. B., Graber, J. A., & Brooks-Gunn, J. (2003). Pubertal processes and physiological growth in adolescence. In G. R. Adams & M. D. Berzonsky (Eds.), *Blackwell handbook of adolescence* (pp. 24–48). Malden, MA: Blackwell.

Armstrong, E. G. (2001). Gangsta misogyny: A content analysis of the portrayals of violence against women in rap music, 1987–1993. *Journal of Criminal Justice and Popular Culture, 8*(2), 96–126.

Arnett, J. (1991a). Adolescence and heavy metal music: From the mouths of metalheads. *Youth and Society, 23*(1), 76–98.

Arnett, J. (1991b). Heavy metal music and reckless behavior among adolescents. *Journal of Youth and Adolescence, 20,* 573–592.

Ballard, M. E., & Coates, S. (1995). The immediate effects of homicidal, suicidal, and nonviolent heavy metal and rap songs on the moods of college students. *Youth & Society, 27*(2), 148–168.

Bandura, A. (1977). *Social learning theory.* Englewood Cliffs, NJ: Prentice Hall.

Bandura, A. (1986). *Social foundations of thought and action: A social cognitive theory.* Englewood Cliffs, NJ: Prentice Hall.

Bandura, A. (1994). Social cognitive theory of mass communication. In J. Bryant & D. Zillmann (Eds.), *Media effects: Advances in theory and research* (pp. 61–90). Hillsdale, NJ: Lawrence Erlbaum.

Barongan, C., & Hall, G. C. N. (1995). The influence of misogynous rap music on sexual aggression against women. *Psychology of Women Quarterly, 19,* 195–207.

Baxter, R. L., DeRiemer, C., Landini, A., Leslie, L., & Singletary, M. W. (1985). A content analysis of music videos. *Journal of Broadcasting and Electronic Media, 29,* 333–340.

Berkowitz, L. (1990). On the formation and regulation of anger and aggression: A cognitive neoassociationistic analysis. *American Psychologist, 45,* 494–503.

Berndt, T. J. (1996). Transitions in friendship and friends' influence. In J. A. Graber, J. Brooks-Gunn, & A. C. Peterson (Eds.), *Transitions through adolescence: Interpersonal domains and context* (pp.57–85). Mahwah, NJ: Lawrence Erlbaum.

Boyle, J. D., Hosterman, G., L., & Ramsey, D. S. (1981). Factors influencing pop music preferences of young people. *Journal of Research in Music Education, 29*(1), 47–55.

Brown, J. D., Childers, K. W., Bauman, K. E., & Koch, G. G. (1990). The influence of new media and family structure on young adolescents' television and radio use. *Communication Research, 17,* 65–82.

Brown, R. L., & O'Leary, M. (Eds.). (1971). *Pop music in an English secondary school.* London: Sage.

Budden, J. *Confessions, part II* [single] (2004). New York: The Island Def Jam Music Group.

Bushman, B. J., & Anderson, C. A. (2001). Media violence and the American public: Scientific fact versus media misinformation. *American Psychological Association, 56,* 477–489.

Bushman, B. J., & Cantor, J. (2003). Media ratings for violence and sex: Implications for policymakers and parents. *American Psychological Association, 58*(2), 130–141.

Byrnes, J. P. (Ed.). (2003). Cognitive development during adolescence In G. R. Adams & M. D. Berzonsky (Eds.), *Blackwell handbook of adolescence* (pp. 227–246). Malden, MA: Blackwell.

Christenson, P. G. (1992a). Advisory labels and adolescent music preferences. *Journal of Communication, 42*(1), 106–113.

Christenson, P. G. (1992b). Preadolescent perceptions and interpretations of music videos. *Popular Music and Society, 16,* 63–73.

Christenson, P. G. (1994). Childhood patterns of music use and preferences. *Communication Reports, 7*(2), 136–144.

Christenson, P. G., & Peterson, J. (1988). Genre and gender in the structure of music preferences. *Communication Research, 15,* 282–301.

Christenson, P. G., & Roberts, D. F. (1998). *It's not only rock and roll: Popular music in the lives of adolescents.* Creskill, NJ: Hampton Press.

Christenson, P. G., & Roberts, D. F. (2001). Popular music in childhood and adolescence. In D. G. Singer & J. L. Singer (Eds.), *Handbook of children and media* (pp. 395–413). Thousand Oaks, CA: Sage.

Christenson, P. G., & van Nouhuys, B. (1995, May). *From the fringe to the center: A comparison of heavy metal and rap fandom.* Paper presented at the annual meeting of the International Communication Association, Albuquerque, NM.

Crokett, L. J., Raffaelli, M., & Moilanen, K. L. (2003). Adolescent sexuality: Behavior and meaning. In G. R. Adams & M. D. Berzonsky (Eds.), *Blackwell handbook of adolescence* (pp. 371–392). Malden, MA: Blackwell.

Denny, J., & Suchet, R. (2004). *Gangsta rap culture "is a deadly virus."* Retrieved February 9, 2004, from http://www.telegraph.couk/news/main

Desmond, R. J. (1987). Adolescents and music lyrics: Implications of a cognitive perspective. *Communication Quarterly, 35*(3), 276–284.

Dixon,T. L., & Linz, D. (2000). Overrepresentation and underrepresentation of African Americans and Latinos as lawbreakers on television news. *Journal of Communication, 50*(2), 131–154.

Duff, Marilyn. (1995). MTV continues as purveyor of smut, violence to kids. *Human Events, 51*(25), 11–13. Retrieved September 30, 2004, from Lexis Nexis database.

DuRant, R. H., Rich, M., Emans, S. J., Rome, E. S., Allred, E., & Woods, E. R. (1997). Violence and weapon carrying in music videos: A content analysis. *Archives of Pediatrics & Adolescent Medicine, 151*(5), 443–448.

Eminem. *Marshall Mathers LP.* (2000) [CD]. Santa Monica, CA: Interscope Records.

Federal Trade Commission (FTC). (2000). *Marketing violent entertainment to children: A review of self-regulation and industry practices in the motion picture, music recording & electronic game industries.* Washington, DC: Author.

Flavell, J. H., Miller, P. H., & Miller, S. A. (2002). *Cognitive development* (4th ed.). Upper Saddle River, NJ: Prentice Hall.

Forget God, get Littleton. (1999). *Human Events, 55*(16), 1–2.

Gantz, W., Gartenberg, H. M., Pearson, M. L., & Schiller, S. O. (1978). Gratifications and expectations associated with music among adolescents. *Popular Music and Society, 6*(1), 81–89.

Garza, E. (2004). PSJA students protest ban on solid black attire, deny relation to gangs, Satanism. *The Monitor*. Retrieved September 4, 2004, from http://www.themonitor.com

Greenberg, B. S., Mastro, D., & Brand, J. E. (2002). Minorities in the mass media: television into the 21st century. In J. Bryant & D. Zillmann (Eds.), *Media effects: Advances in theory and research* (2nd ed., pp. 333–351). Hillsdale, NJ: Lawrence Erlbaum.

Greenfield, P. M., Bruzzone, L., Koyamatsu, K., Satuloff, W., Nixon, K., Brodie, M., & Kingsdale, D. (1987). What is rock music doing to the minds of our youth? A first experimental look at the effects of rock videos. *Journal of Early Adolescence, 7*, 315–329.

Greeson, L. E., & Williams, R. A. (1986). Social implications of music videos for youth: Analysis of the content and effects of MTV. *Youth & Society, 18*(2), 177–189.

Hansen, C. H., & Hansen, R. D. (1990). Rock music videos and antisocial behavior. *Basic and Applied Social Psychology, 11*(4), 357–369.

Hansen, C. H., & Hansen, R. D. (1991). Schematic information processing of heavy metal lyrics. *Communication Research, 18*, 373–411.

Holland, B. (2002, October 12). Industry claims piracy by teens undercuts labeling. *Billboard, 114*, p.8. Retrieved September 30, 2004, from Lexis Nexis database.

Huesmann, L. R. (1998). The role of social information processing and cognitive schema in the acquisition and maintenance of habitual aggressive behavior. In R. G. Green & E. Donnerstein (Eds.), *Human aggression: Theories, research, and implications for social policy* (pp. 73–103). San Diego, CA: Academic Press.

Insane Clown Posse. (2004). Bowling balls. On *Hells pit* [CD]. Royal Oaks, MI: Psychopathic.

Island/Def Jam rap song advocates violence. (June, 2004). *U.S. Newswire*. Retrieved September 3, 2004, from Lexis Nexis database.

Jo, E., & Berkowitz, L. (1994). A priming effect analysis of media influences: An update. In J. Bryant & D. Zillmann (Eds.), *Media effects: Advances in theory and research* (pp. 43–60). Hillsdale, NJ: Lawrence Erlbaum.

Johnson, J. D., Adams, G. R., Ashburn, L., & Reed, W. (1995). Differential gender effects of exposure to rap music on African American adolescents' acceptance of teen dating violence. *Sex Roles, 33*(7/8), 597–605.

Johnson, J. D., Jackson, A. L., & Gatto, L. (1995). Violent attitudes and deferred academic aspirations: Deleterious effects of exposure to rap music. *Basic and Applied Social Psychology, 16*(1 & 2), 27–41.

Johnson, J., & Pascual-Leone, J. (1989). Developmental levels of processing in metaphor interpretation. *Journal of Experimental Child Psychology 48*, 1–31.

Johnson, J. D., Trawalter, S., & Dovidio, J. F. (2000). Converging interracial consequences of exposure to violent rap music on stereotypical attributions of blacks. *Journal of Experimental Social Psychology, 36*, 233–251.

Joint Center for Political and Economic Studies. (1997). *1997 National Opinion Poll: Children's Issues*. (1997). Washington, DC: Author.

Jones, K. (1997). Are rap videos more violent? Style differences and the prevalence of sex and violence in the age of MTV. *Howard Journal of Communications, 8,* 343–356.

Kaiser Family Foundation. (2001). *Parents and the V-chip 2001: How parents feel about TV, the TV ratings system, and the V-chip.* Menlo Park, CA: Author.

Kandakai, T. L., Price, J. H., Telljohann, S. K., & Wilson, C. A. (1999). Mothers' perceptions of factors influencing violence in schools. *Journal of School Health, 69*(5), 189–195.

Kroger, J. (2003). Identity development during adolescence. In G. R. Adams & M. D. Berzonsky (Eds.), *Blackwell handbook of adolescence* (pp. 205–226). Malden, MA: Blackwell.

Kuwahara, Y. (1992). Power to the people y'all: Rap music, resistance and Black college students. *Humanity and Society, 16,* 54–73.

Larson, R., Kubey, R., & Colletti, J. (1989). Changing channels: Early adolescent media choices and shifting investments in family and friends. *Journal of Youth and Adolescence, 18,* 583–599.

Leming, J. S. (1987). Rock music and the socialization of moral values in early adolescence. *Youth and Society, 18*(4), 363–383.

Lull, J. (1985). On the communicative properties of music. *Communication Research, 12*(3), 363–372.

Lull, J. (1992). Popular music and communication: An introduction. In J. Lull (Ed.), *Popular music and communication* (2nd ed., pp.1–32). Newbury Park, CA: Sage.

Lyle, J., & Hoffman, H. R. (1972). *Children's use of television and other media.* Washington, DC: U.S. Government Printing Office.

Manson, M. (1996). *AntiChrist Superstar* [CD]. Santa Monica, CA: Interscope Records.

Martin, G., Clarke, P., & Pearce, C. (1993). Adolescent suicide: Music preference as an indicator of vulnerability. *Journal of the American Academy of Child Adolescent Psychology, 32*(3), 530–535.

Morano, M. (2004). Bill Cosby to blacks: Stop blaming "the white man." Retrieved July 2, 2004, from http://www.cnsnew.com

Oliver, M. B. (1994). Portrayals of crime, race, and aggression in "reality based" police shows: A content analysis. *Journal of Broadcasting and Electronic Media, 38,* 179–192.

Parent Music Resource Center (PMRC). (2004). Available: http://www.wikipedia.org

Pawlowski, D. R., Badzinski, D. M., & Mitchell, N. (1998). Effects of metaphors on children's comprehension of and perception of print advertisements. *Journal of Advertising, 27*(2), 83–98.

Recording Industry Association of America (RIAA). (2003a). *2003 Consumer Profile.* Washington, DC: Author. Retrieved September 3, 2004, from http://www.riaa.com

Recording Industry Association of America (RIAA). (2003b). *What the RIAA is doing for freedom of speech.* Washington, DC: Author. Retrieved September 30, 2004, from http://www.riaa.com

Rich, M., Woods, E. R., Goodman, E., Emans, S. J., & DuRant, R. H. (1998). Aggressors or victims: Gender and race in music video violence. *Pediatrics, 101*(4), 669–674.

Rideout, V. J., Vandewater, E. A., & Wartella, E. A. (2003). *Zero to six: Electronic media in the lives of infants, toddlers and preschoolers. A Kaiser Family Foundation Report.* Menlo Park, CA: The Kaiser Family Foundation.

Roberts, D. F. & Christenson, P. G. (2000). Popular Music in Childhood and Adolescence. In D. G. Singer & F. L. Singer (Eds.), *Handbook of Children and the Media,* (pp. 395–414). Thousand Oaks, CA: Sage.

Roberts, D. F., & Foehr, U. G. (2004). *Kids and media in America.* New York: Cambridge University Press.

Roberts, D. F., & Henriksen, L. (1990, June). *Music listening vs. television viewing among older adolescents.* Paper presented at the annual meeting of the International Communication Association, Dublin, Ireland.

Robinson, T. N., Chen, H. L., & Killen, J. D. (1998). Television and music video exposure and risk of adolescent alcohol use. *Pediatrics, 102*(5), 54.

Rosenbaum, J. L., & Prinsky, L. E. (1987). Sex, violence and rock 'n' roll: Youths' perceptions of popular music. *Popular Music and Society, 11,* 78–89.

Rosenbaum, J. L., & Prinsky, L. E. (1991). The presumption of influence: Recent responses to popular music subcultures. *Crime & Delinquency, 37*(4), 528–535.

Roth, J., & Brooks-Gunn, J. (2000). What do adolescents need for healthy development? Implications for youth policy. *Social Policy Report, 14,* 3–19.

Rotter, J. (2004). Jay-Z wants to kill himself. *New York Times,* p. 13. Retrieved September 3, 2004, from Lexis Nexis database.

Rouner, D. (1990). Rock music use as a socializing function. *Popular Music and Society, 14*(1), 97–107.

Rubin, A. M., West, D. V., & Mitchell, W. S. (2001). Differences in aggression, attitudes toward women, and distrust as reflected in popular music preferences. *Psychology of Women Quarterly, 3,* 25–42.

Rubin, B., Rubin, A. M., Perse, E. M., Armstrong, C., McHugh, M., & Faix, N. (1986). Media use and meaning of music video. *Journalism Quarterly,* 63, 353–359.

Rudman, L. A., & Lee, M. R. (2002). Implicit and explicit consequences of exposure to violent and misogynous rap music. *Group Processes & Intergroup Relations, 5*(2), 133–150.

Schank, R. C., & Abelson, R. (1977). *Scripts, plans, goals, and understanding.* Hillsdale, NJ: Lawrence Erlbaum.

Scheel, K. R., & Westefeld, J. S. (1999). Heavy metal music and adolescent suicidality: An empirical investigation. *Adolescence, 34*(134), 253–273.

Sherman, B. L., & Dominick, J. R. (1986). Violence and sex in music videos: TV and rock 'n' roll. *Journal of Communication, 36*(1), 79–93.

Silverman-Watkins, L. T., & Sprafkin, J. N. (1983). Adolescents' comprehension of televised sexual innuendos. *Journal of Applied Developmental Psychology, 4,* 359–369.

Smith, S. L., & Boyson, A. R. (2002). Violence in music videos: Examining the prevalence and context of physical aggression. *Journal of Communication, 52*(1), 61–83.

Strasburger, V. C., & Hendren, R. O. (1995). Rock music and rock music videos. *Pediatric Annals, 24,* 97–103.

Sun, S. W., & Lull, J. (1986). The adolescent audience for music videos and why they watch. *Journal of Communication, 36*(1), 115–125.

St. Lawrence, J. S. & Joyner, D. J. (1991). The effects of sexually violent rock music on males' acceptance of violence against women. *Psychology of Women Quarterly, 15,* 49–63.

Tapper, J., Thorson, E., & Black, D. (1994). Variations in music videos as a function of their musical genre. *Journal of Broadcasting and Electronic Media, 38*(1), 103–114.

Took, K. J., & Weiss, D. S. (1994). The relationship between heavy metal and rap music and adolescent turmoil: Real or artifact? *Adolescence, 29*(115), 613–623.

Waite, B. M., Hillbrand, M., & Foster, H. G. (1992). Reduction of aggressive behavior after removal of music television. *Hospital and Community Psychiatry, 43,* 173–175.

Wal-Mart cleans up musicians' acts. (1997, January). *Consumers' Research Magazine, 80,* p. 40. Retrieved September 30, 2004, from Lexis Nexis database.

Wannamaker, C.E., & Reznikoff, M. (1989). The effects of aggressive and nonaggressive rock songs on projective and structured tests. *The Journal of Psychology, 123,* 561–570.

Wass, H., Raup, J. L., Cerullo, K., Martel, L. G., Minngione, L. A., & Sperring, A. M. (1989). Adolescents' interest in and views of destructive themes in rock music. *Omega Journal of Death and Dying, 19*(3), 177–186.

Wester, S. R., Crown, C. L., Quatman, G. L., & Heesacker, M. (1997). The influence of sexually violent rap music on attitudes of men with little prior exposure. *Psychology of Women Quarterly, 21,* 497–508.

Wilson, B. J., Kunkel, D., Potter, W. J., Donnerstein, E., Smith, S. L., Blumenthal, E., & Gray, T. E. (1997). Violence in television programming overall: University of California, Santa Barbara study. *National television violence study, Vol. 1* (pp. 3–268). Thousand Oaks, CA: Sage.

Wilson, S. L. A. (2001). "A metaphor is pinning air to the wall": A literature review of the child's use of metaphor. *Childhood Education, 77*(2), 96–99.

Wingood, G. M., DiClemente, R. J., & Bernhardt, J. M. (2003). A prospective study of exposure to rap music videos and African American female adolescents' health. *American Journal of Public Health, 93*(3), 437–439.

Woodard, E. H. (2000). *Media in the home 2000: The fifth annual survey of parents and children.* Philadelphia: Annenberg Public Policy Center.

Zimmer-Gembeck, M. J., & Collins, A. W. (2003). Autonomy development during adolescence. In G. R. Adams & M. D. Berzonsky (Eds.), *Blackwell handbook of adolescence* (pp. 175–204). Malden, MA: Blackwell.

CHAPTER 11

# *How Real Is the Problem of TV Violence?*

## *Research and Policy Perspectives*

DALE KUNKEL AND LARA ZWARUN

Concern on the part of the public and policy makers about the harmful influence of media violence on children dates back to the 1950s and 1960s (Murray, 1996; Potter & Warren, 1996). The legitimacy of that concern is corroborated by extensive scientific research that has accumulated since that time. Indeed, in reviewing the totality of empirical evidence regarding the impact of media violence, the conclusion that exposure to violent portrayals poses a risk of harmful effects on children has been reached by the U.S. Surgeon General (Surgeon General's Scientific Advisory Committee, 1972), the National Institute of Mental Health (Pearl, Bouthilet, & Lazar, 1982), the National Academy of Sciences (Reiss & Roth, 1993), the American Medical Association (1996), the American Psychological Association (1993), the American Academy of Pediatrics (Cook, 2000), and a host of other scientific and public health agencies and organizations.

It is well established by a compelling body of scientific evidence that television violence is harmful to children. These harmful effects include (1) children's learning of aggressive attitudes and behaviors; (2) desensitization, or an increased callousness toward victims of violence; and (3) increased or exaggerated fear of being victimized by violence (Wilson et al., 1997). While exposure to media violence is not necessarily the most potent factor contributing to real-world violence and aggression in the United States today, it is certainly the most pervasive. The average American child spends roughly 20 hours per week watching television (Roberts & Foehr, 2004), and the cumulative exposure to violent images over time can shape young minds in unhealthy ways.

While brief conclusions such as these may be helpful and important in understanding the problem of television violence, they also risk masking or oversimplifying complex issues and relationships. Despite the compelling evidence of harmful effects, not all children are adversely affected and not all portrayals of violence pose a risk of harm. In this chapter, we seek to explicate this and other complexities of the research findings on media violence. More specifically, we will (1) review and summarize the evidence regarding the risk of harmful effects from children's viewing of televised violence; (2) examine the nature of violence depicted on television, linking our analysis directly to the known risk factors; and (3) consider the implications of the findings about media violence for public policy makers, reviewing previous efforts and analyzing future prospects for resolving the concerns.

## THE EVOLUTION OF RESEARCH ON MEDIA VIOLENCE EFFECTS

Although concern about television violence first surfaced in the 1950s and received some attention in the 1960s, it was not until the 1970s that researchers began to study the topic in depth. At that time, the U.S. Surgeon General was commissioned by Congress to examine the issue and to draw conclusions upon which policy makers could act.

The Surgeon General's final report on the topic (Surgeon General's Scientific Advisory Committee, 1972) was complicated and filled with caveats, reflecting its status as both a political and scientific document (Cater & Strickland, 1975). Indeed, the process by which the study was conducted afforded the television industry extraordinary influence and control, such that leading academic scholars who had published evidence of harmful effects were "blackballed" from participation on its advisory board, while researchers employed by the industry were allowed onto the committee (Cater & Strickland, 1975; Liebert & Sprafkin, 1988). The American Association for the Advancement of Science (AAAS) voiced a public complaint at this blatant politicization of science (Boffey & Walsh, 1970).

In the end, critics of the television industry found within the Surgeon General's report strong confirmation of the harmful effects of children's exposure to televised violence, while television industry officials argued that the conclusions were too equivocal to be definitive (Kunkel, 2003). Certainly the report triggered more controversy than it resolved, with subsequent debates pursued concurrently in the popular press and the policy arena as well as in the scientific community (Bok, 1998).

By the 1980s, much more empirical research and scientific analysis had been accomplished, and a strong consensus began to emerge in the academic community that exposure to television violence was harmful for children. The effects were not understood to be direct and powerful such that every child who watched would be adversely affected; rather, exposure to violent media was viewed as a risk factor in contributing to the likelihood that children would behave aggressively. This viewpoint is well summarized in an overview of the evidence published by the National Institute of Mental Health (Pearl, Bouthilet, & Lazar, 1982):

> The consensus among most of the research community is that violence on television does lead to aggressive behavior by children and teenagers. . . . Not all children become aggressive, of course, but the correlations between [viewing] violence and aggression are positive. In magnitude, television violence is as strongly correlated with aggressive behavior as any other behavioral variable that has been measured. (p. 6)

In the 1990s, the public health community began to play a more active and prominent role in the debate about media violence. Physicians regarded violence as an "epidemic" (American Medical Association, 1996), and approached the topic as they would any other epidemiological analysis in which causes and cures are examined. Research articles on the topic of media violence started to surface at least as often in medical and public health journals as in the social science literature, their traditional home. The most visible action by the public health community was the Joint Statement on the Impact of Entertainment Violence on Children (Joint Statement, 2000) issued at a Congressional briefing by the American Academy of Pediatrics, the American Psychological Association, the American Medical Association, and the American Academy of Child and Adolescent Psychiatry. This document declared that research points "overwhelmingly to a causal connection between media violence and aggressive behavior" (p. 1), putting the credibility of these organizations behind a push for policy makers to do something to address the problem.

The frequency of new studies of television violence effects has diminished in the past decade, largely as a function of the strong consensus about the conclusion that viewing violence is harmful to children. Yet even in this context, several significant new empirical findings from longitudinal studies have emerged in recent years. One of these, a panel study that followed 6- and 10-year-old subjects over a 15-year period into adulthood, found that childhood exposure to media violence predicted adult aggressive behavior (Huesmann, Moise-Titus, Podolski, & Eron, 2003). Another similar project, published in the AAAS journal *Science* (arguably the nation's most respected scientific venue), demonstrated that the level of violence viewed at an average age of 14 is significantly related to assaults and fights resulting in injury at an average age of 22 (Johnson, Cohen, Smalles, Kasen, & Brook, 2002). In both of these studies, the influence of exposure to media violence remained significant even when controlling statistically for a wide range of other factors known to be associated with aggression, such as childhood neglect, family income, parental education, and neighborhood violence.

It is abundantly clear that exposure to television violence poses a risk of harmful effects for children. That conclusion is strongly affirmed by both the social scientific and public health communities, based upon consistent research evidence produced over the past 40 years.

## Summary of Key Findings About Media Violence Effects

Over the years, studies of the impact of media violence have encompassed the full range of research methodologies, including experiments, surveys, field research, and longitudinal studies, among others. It is the convergence of findings across the totality of empirical evidence that yields the key conclusions offered here.

### *Children learn aggressive attitudes and behaviors from viewing televised violence*

Employing both social learning theory and its more recent derivative, social cognitive theory, Albert Bandura (1977, 1978, 2002) has established that observational learning is a critical component of human social behavior. Learning that occurs by observing others is particularly important for young children, who are early in the process of developing an understanding of normative behavioral patterns. While Bandura was one of the first to demonstrate that children may learn and imitate aggressive acts observed in the media (Bandura, Ross, & Ross, 1961, 1963a, 1963b), he has been followed by many other experimenters who have produced comparable results (Comstock & Paik, 1991; Potter, 1999).

Complementing these laboratory studies, an impressive collection of field research has documented a strong association between children's viewing of televised violence and subsequent aggressive behavior (Huesmann & Eron, 1986; Huesmann, Eron, Lefkowitz, & Walder, 1984). Exposure to television portrayals where problems are resolved by violence may contribute to scripts that children learn and then apply in their own world under trying circumstances. Berkowitz (1984) and his colleagues (Berkowitz & Rogers, 1986; Jo & Berkowitz, 1994) refer to this as "media priming."

Literally hundreds of experimental and longitudinal studies support the conclusion that viewing televised violence leads to increases in subsequent aggression, and that such aggression can become part of a lasting behavioral pattern. As Huesmann (1986) notes,

> Aggressive habits seem to be learned early in life, and once established, are resistant to change and predictive of serious adult antisocial behavior. If a child's observation of media violence promotes the learning of aggressive habits, it can have harmful lifelong consequences. Consistent with this theory, early television habits are in fact correlated with adult criminality. (pp. 129–130)

Clearly, children's exposure to media violence, particularly at young ages, can lead to serious adverse consequences. Some who are affected directly may suffer by committing their own acts of aggression; while others may be impacted indirectly as they become the victims of violent actions committed against them. The evidence is overwhelming that viewing televised violence contributes significantly to increases in real-world violence and aggression. An occasional critic has challenged this conclusion (Fowles, 1999; Freedman, 1984), but their arguments or objections have never been sustained (Friedrich-Cofer & Huston, 1986; Huesmann & Taylor, 2003).

### *Heavy viewing of televised violence desensitizes children to violence and its victims in the real world*

Over the years, research has examined the relationship between exposure to media violence and feelings of concern, empathy, or sympathy that viewers may have regarding victims of actual violence. Numerous studies indicate that heavier viewers of media violence demonstrate less physiological reactivity to violent film clips compared to lighter viewers; that general physiological arousal decreases as viewers watch more violent media; and that children as well as adults are susceptible to this effect (Cline, Croft, & Courrier, 1973; Drabman & Thomas, 1974; Thomas, Horton, Lippincott, & Drabman, 1977).

While desensitization effects from exposure to typical action-adventure program portrayals of violence have been well documented, there is also evidence that viewing more explicit or graphic depictions of violence enhances the effect (Linz, Donnerstein, & Penrod, 1984, 1988; Mullin & Linz, 1995).

### *Viewing of media violence increases children's fear of being victimized by others*

George Gerbner and his colleagues (Gerbner & Gross, 1976; Gerbner, Gross, Morgan, & Signorielli, 1986) have repeatedly demonstrated the cultivation effect, by which viewers exposed to heavy doses of television violence come to believe that the world is a violent and scary place. This effect leads to an exaggerated fear of crime or victimization that persists over time, in both children and adults (Wilson et al., 1997). While most of this evidence is correlational, there are also experimental studies that demonstrate the same effect (e.g., Bryant, Carveth, & Brown, 1981).

In addition, more transitory reactions such as extreme emotional fright and sleep disturbances may result from children's exposure to graphic violence or intense scenes of danger, particularly associated with concrete threats such as from monsters (Cantor, 1994; Cantor & Wilson, 1988; Wilson & Smith, 1998).

These three effects—increases in children's aggressive attitudes and behaviors, desensitization to real-world victims of violence, and heightened fear of victimization—represent the most significant impacts of children's exposure to media violence. They occur largely as the product of a slow, cumulative process of watching countless acts of violence across years of viewing. Particularly because this influence process is so gradual, it is important to consider the broad patterns regarding how violence is presented on television over time. Fortunately, as we discuss below, there is an abundance of content-analysis evidence about the depiction of violence on television from which to draw.

## *Patterns of Violence on Television*

Studies of the nature and extent of televised violence have been conducted since the 1960s and remain common today (Comstock & Sharrer, 1999; Gunter, Harrison, & Wykes, 2003; Potter, 1999). Most tend to employ somewhat different definitions of violence for purposes of the tallies employed, and hence they yield somewhat different findings. For example, if one study defines violence to include comic or slapstick actions, its count of violence will likely yield a higher figure than would a comparable study that excluded such actions in its definition. Despite these differences, virtually every study of the topic finds that violent behavior is widespread across the television landscape, with violence typically observed in the majority of programs examined.

Gerbner defined violence as "the overt expression of physical force (with or without a weapon) against self or other, compelling action against one's will on pain of being hurt or killed, or actually hurting or killing" (Gerbner, Gross, Morgan, & Signorielli, 1980). Using this definition, Gerbner and his colleagues reported findings of approximately 5 to 6 violent acts per hour of television over many years in the 1970s and 1980s. Other scholars have used broader definitions of violence, including actions that cause psychological or emotional harm rather than solely physical damage, and have reported averages ranging from 18 to 38 violent acts per hour (Greenberg, Edison, Korzenny, Fernandez-Collado, & Atkin, 1980; Potter et al., 1995; Williams, Zabrak, & Joy, 1982). Still other researchers count differently, measuring the number of scenes with violence, rather than the number of violent acts. For example, Lichter and Amundson (1994) reported that an average of 10.7 scenes per hour of prime-time programming in 1992 contained violence. Note that a scene could contain 1, 5, 10, or any number of violent actions and it would still be coded identically as simply "contains violence" under this approach.

It is apparent that the strategy for measuring violence on television plays an important role in shaping the results. Most studies employ a highly reductionistic approach in framing their central findings, by which we mean that their summary statistics count all acts of violence as equivalent to one another in adding the totals. This common tactic poses a significant validity problem if one is trying to draw implications for effects in the three critical areas we have presented above—learning aggressive attitudes and behaviors, becoming desensitized, and developing an exaggerated fear of violent attack. That is because there is strong evidence that not all portrayals of violence pose the same degree of risk for contributing to each of these various outcomes, as we explicate below.

### *The Importance of Context*

In the debate about television violence, a frequent oversimplification—and a critical focus here—is to assume that all violence is essentially the same in terms of its implications for effects. Such an assumption is implicit in any analysis that aggregates all observations of violent behavior. Upon closer examination, however, such an assumption is clearly unwarranted, though it is easy to understand why this perspective has become so widespread over time. From the 1960s to the 1980s, the most visible researcher who studied media violence was George Gerbner, and his violence index tracked the overall levels of violent behavior from year to year, indicating whether violence on television was "up or down" (Rowland, 1983). The news media embraced this angle and reported the annual findings dutifully (Hoffner, 1998). Policy makers typically gave these reports careful scrutiny (Cooper, 1996; Murray, 1996). Given that Gerbner and his colleagues were interested primarily in predicting television's influence on beliefs and perceptions about social reality, such a tactic may well have been reasonable. It is not, however, a prudent approach for examining the impact of television violence on subsequent aggressive behavior.

There are many ways in which to depict violence on television. For example, the violence may occur on-screen and be shown graphically or it may occur offscreen but be clearly implied. Violent acts may be shown close-up or at a distance. There are differences in the types of characters who commit violence and their reasons for doing so. And there are differences in the outcomes of violence—some depictions focus on the pain and suffering of victims, whereas others avoid showing the negative consequences of physical aggression. Simply put, not all portrayals of violence are the same. Their context can vary on many important dimensions. These differences matter because there is substantial evidence that such differences in the message characteristics hold important implications for the impact of particular violent scenes on viewers (Kunkel et al., 1995; Wilson et al., 1997).

In the mid-1990s, a large-scale project called the National Television Violence Study (NTVS) reviewed all existing effects of research that had previously examined the influence of various contextual features, and devised a content-analysis framework that measured attributes known to either increase or diminish the likelihood of one of the three basic types of harmful influence (Wilson et al., 1997). For example, violence that is rewarded or shown without punishment is known to increase the likelihood of subsequent viewer aggression, whereas violence that is punished tends to diminish the risk of such effects. Similarly, violent actions that are more realistic increase the probability of subsequent aggression, whereas portrayals that are less realistic reduce that prospect. A summary table of the key contextual features associated with violence on television, and their relationship to the three basic types of harmful effects, is presented in Table 11.1.

Employing this analytical framework, the NTVS project examined approximately 10,000 television programs across all times of day on the most frequently viewed channels over a 3-year period, from 1994 to 1997. Its definition of violence was similar to Gerbner's and focused on physical harm:

> Violence is defined as any overt depiction of a credible threat of physical force or the actual use of such force intended to physically harm an animate being or group of beings. Violence also includes certain depictions of physically harmful consequences against an animate being or group that occur as a result of unseen violent means. (Wilson et al., 1997, p. 53)

Based upon this project, which is certainly among the largest scientific studies of

**Table 11.1** How Contextual Features Affect the Risks Associated With TV Violence

| | *Harmful Effects of TV Violence* | | |
|---|---|---|---|
| | *Learning Aggression* | *Fear* | *Desensitization* |
| CONTEXTUAL FEATURES | | | |
| Attractive Perpetrator | ▲ | | |
| Attractive Victim | | ▲ | |
| Justified Violence | ▲ | | |
| Unjustified Violence | ▼ | ▲ | |
| Conventional Weapons | ▲ | | |
| Extensive/Graphic Violence | ▲ | ▲ | ▲ |
| Realistic Violence | ▲ | ▲ | |
| Rewards | ▲ | ▲ | |
| Punishments | ▼ | ▼ | |
| Pain/Harm Cues | ▼ | | |
| Humor | ▲ | | ▲ |



*Note:* Predicted effects are based on a comprehensive review of social science research on the different contextual features of violence. Blank spaces indicate that there is no relationship or adequate research to make a prediction.

▲ = likely to increase the outcome

▼ = likely to decrease the outcome

television violence, the following three key conclusions were drawn.

### *Violence is widespread across the television landscape*

When viewers turn on a television set and pick a channel at random, the odds are better than 50–50 that the program they encounter will contain violent material. More specifically, 60% of all shows sampled across the entire 3-year project contained some form of violence. An average of 6,000 violent interactions were observed in a single week of programming across the 23 channels studied each year, including both broadcast and cable networks. More than half of the violent shows (53%) contained lethal acts, and 1 in 4 of the programs with violence (25%) depicted the use of a gun (Smith et al., 1998).

### *Most violence on television is presented in a manner that increases its risk of harmful effects on child viewers*

Most violence on television follows a highly formulaic pattern that is both sanitized and glamorized. A sanitized depiction of violence means that the portrayal fails to show realistic harm to victims, both from a short- and long-term perspective. Immediate pain and suffering by victims of violence is included in less than half (46%) of all scenes of violence. More than a third of violent interactions (36%) depict unrealistically mild harm to victims, grossly understating the severity of injury that would occur from such actions in the real world. Most depictions sanitize violence by making it appear to be much less painful and less harmful than it really is.

A glamorized depiction refers to violence that is performed by attractive role models who are often justified for acting aggressively and who suffer no remorse, criticism, or penalty for their violent behavior. More than a third of all violence (35%) is committed by attractive characters, and more than two-thirds of the violence they engage in (73%) occurs without any signs of punishment. All of these patterns are important because violence that is sanitized or glamorized increases the risk of harmful effects on child viewers.

*There is remarkable stability in the presentation of violence on television*

A summary of findings comparing the 1994–1995, 1995–1996, and 1996–1997 television seasons (see Table 11.2) illustrates the tremendous degree of consistency that is found in both the nature and extent of violence on television. On each of the critical contextual attributes associated with the presentation of violence, the frequency statistics varied no more than a few percentages from year to year over the 3 years studied and across roughly 10,000 programs. That consistency demonstrates that the portrayal of violence is highly stable and formulaic—and unfortunately, this formula of presenting violence as glamorized and sanitized is one that enhances the risk of harmful effects for the child audience.

The NTVS study establishes clearly that the level of violence on television poses substantial cause for concern. It demonstrates that violence is a central aspect of television programming that enjoys remarkable consistency and stability over time. The emergence of these data in the 1990s, coupled with the growing consensus from both the social scientific and public health communities about the harmful effects of media violence, created an impetus for policy makers to consider the issue more closely. In the next section, we examine the history of how policy makers have sought to address the problem of television violence.

## MEDIA VIOLENCE AND PUBLIC POLICY

Public concern about violent content in motion pictures (Jowett, Jarvie, & Fuller, 1996) and comic books (Wertham, 1954) long preceded the advent of television. Thus, it is not entirely surprising that policy makers seemed eager to engage with the issue of television violence, even while the medium was still in its infancy. Congressional hearings on the topic were conducted beginning in the mid-1950s, before a single study of the effects of televised violence had yet been completed (Cooper, 1996; Kunkel & Wilcox, 2001).

In the early years of television, all programming viewed in the United States was delivered by broadcast stations; cable television did not emerge as a viable consumer option until the 1980s (LeDuc, 1987). Interestingly, the regulatory framework applied to broadcast television is more stringent than that applied to other electronic media such as cable television. That is because broadcasters transmit their signals over the publicly owned airwaves.

To use the public airwaves, broadcasters must be licensed by the government, and by accepting a license they agree to serve the "public interest, convenience, and necessity." The power both to license broadcasters and to establish the public-interest policies they must follow was granted by Congress to the Federal Communications Commission (FCC) in the Communications Act of 1934. This power has been used at times to place

**Table 11.2** Overall Industry Averages: Three-Year Comparisons

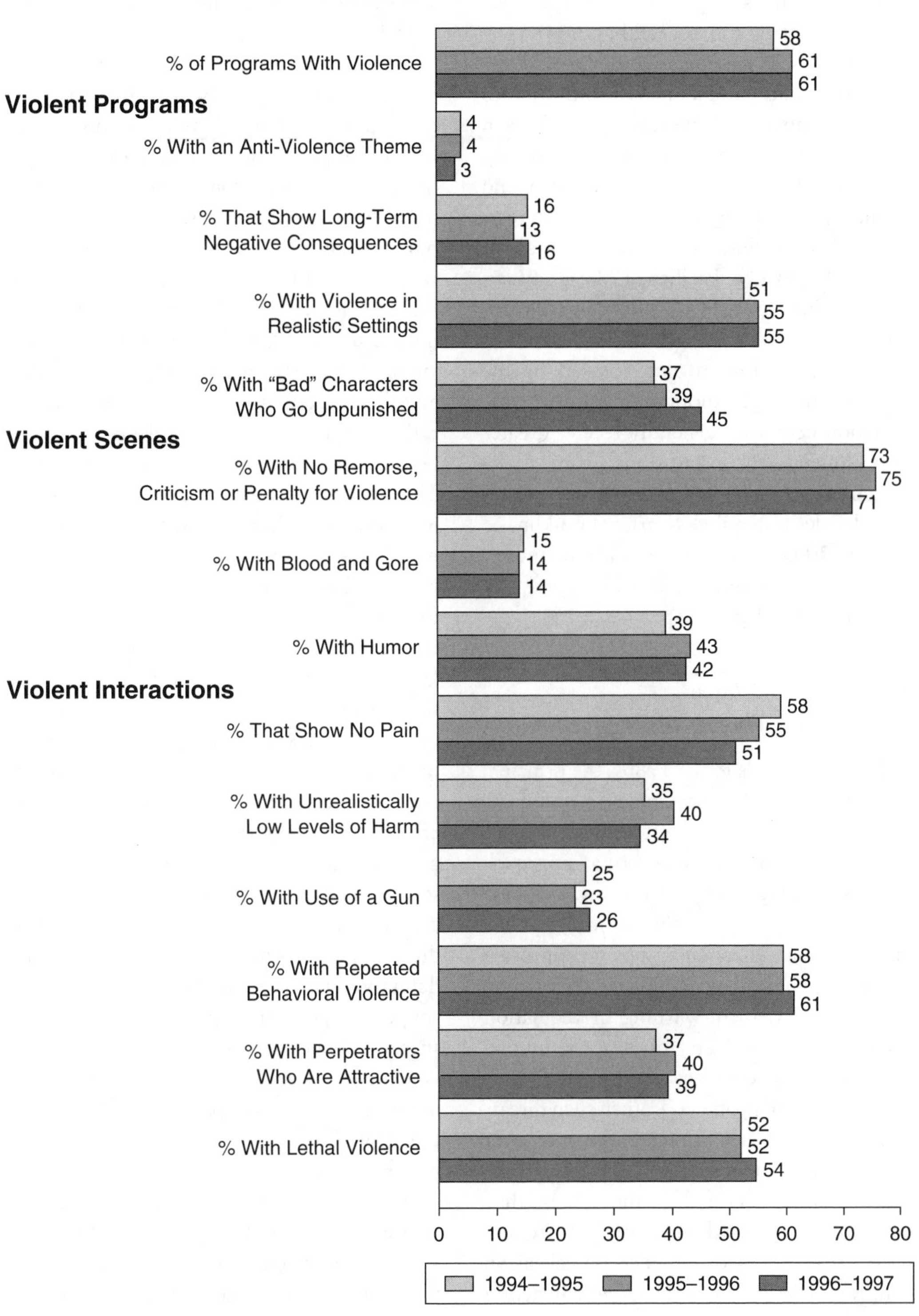

content-specific regulations on the broadcast industry, such as in the area of indecency restrictions (Hilliard & Keith, 2003). The Supreme Court has consistently upheld the constitutionality of the FCC's authority to regulate content on broadcast channels even in the face of the First Amendment, so long as the regulations are narrowly drawn and further compelling government interests (Action for Children's Television et al. v. FCC, 1995; FCC v. Pacifica, 1978; Red Lion Broadcasting Co. v. FCC, 1969). In contrast, other media that do not use the public airwaves and thus are not licensed by the government (e.g., motion pictures, cable television networks) generally receive greater First Amendment protections from direct content regulation, which in theory makes them harder to regulate (Carter, Franklin, & Wright, 2003). Thus, governmental interest in violence on broadcast television is uniquely justified from a legal perspective.

### *The 1950s to 1980s: Diminishing Threats of Regulation*

From the 1950s to the 1980s, the principal tactic employed by the Congress and FCC to address concern about televised violence was known as the "raised eyebrow" approach (Cole & Oettinger, 1978; Krasnow, Longley, & Terry, 1982). With this strategy, policy makers assume threatening postures in hearings and public statements, voicing their strong concern and vaguely warning of regulation if the television industry does not voluntarily address the concern, or euphemistically speaking, "clean up its act." When such threats about television violence were sustained over time and viewed as serious by industry officials, as often occurred in the 1970s, they indeed have resulted in significant reductions in the levels of violence on television (Murray, 1980). But because violent action is an important staple for attracting large audiences to television (Bartholow, Dill, Anderson, & Lindsay, 2003; Hamilton, 1998), such reductions tend to diminish quickly once the intensity of the regulatory threat seems to abate.

The "raised eyebrow" tactic was well tailored to fit the equivocal status of the research evidence that was still accumulating during this period. Policy makers never had to have an "air-tight" case to use their bully pulpit, since no specific regulatory action was ever formally proposed. During this time, the television industry used its political muscle to focus the debate about television violence squarely on the question of whether any harms could actually be established, rather than on whether violence ought to be regulated (Baumgartner & Jones, 1993). This strategy effectively defined the debate in a way that inherently weakened its opponents' position. For example, the ABC network published its own report (American Broadcasting Companies, 1983) in response to the National Institute of Mental Health (1982) review of research that had drawn the first strong causal conclusions about harmful effects. Acknowledging that "the body of literature on television and violence continues to expand" (p. 1), the ABC report criticized the NIMH's emphasis on convergence of the evidence, stating that "in social science, convergence—the analysis of many different studies which point in the same direction—is sometimes used when no definitive evidence can be found to clearly support a position" (p. 6). In the face of such challenges, and in the absence of overwhelming research evidence, the broadcast industry successfully parried all the raised eyebrow threats and concerns from policy makers for several decades.

The policy debate about televised violence quieted for a time by the late 1980s. From a regulatory perspective, this was a period that emphasized deregulation throughout the government (Derthick & Quirk, 1985), and in particular at the FCC (Fowler & Brenner,

1982). In this context, threats of regulation lacked much of their punch as compared to the past. Moreover, after decades of ritual warnings without any formal sanctions ever being adopted, the industry seemed to have grasped the hollow nature of the threats and appeared less concerned than ever. Starting in the early 1990s, however, the efforts of a single U.S senator, Paul Simon of Illinois, reinvigorated the debate.

### *The 1990s: Finally Some Firm Policy Action*

Convinced by his own reading of the evidence that violent portrayals were harmful to children, yet uncomfortable with the prospect of any governmental censorship of program content, Senator Paul Simon sought an alternative path to resolve the issue. He sponsored legislation enacted by Congress in 1990 that encouraged the television industry to adopt industrywide guidelines regarding its treatment of violence (MacCarthy, 1995). Technically speaking, the legislation merely exempted the networks from federal antitrust law that might preclude them from reaching industrywide agreements affecting their business. In other words, no formal action by the industry was required by Senator Simon's legislation; rather, it simply provided a clear opportunity for a socially responsible initiative. In speeches and public appearances, Senator Simon implored television officials to both reduce the amount of violence on television, and to avoid glamorized and sanitized violence, which research has shown to increase the risk of harmful effects.

Perhaps braced by too many years of successfully dodging policy makers' concerns, the television industry turned a blind eye to Senator Simon's legislation and proposal. This time, however, the industry faced a much different political context, which ultimately led to a much different policy outcome. Public concern about the issue of violence in society was at an all-time high, fueled in part by sensationalistic media coverage of school shootings and other violent attacks by youth (Chyi & McCombs, 2004; Pew Research Center for People and the Press, 1999). At the same time, the growing body of research evidence about the harmful effects of television violence had generated an unprecedented consensus from the scientific and public health communities indicting the media as a causal factor in real-world violence and aggression. Similarly, public opinion about television violence reflected more impressive levels of concern. Surveys at the time reported that strong majorities agreed that television violence is harmful to children and that there is too much violence on television (Duston, 1993; Guttman, 1994; Times Mirror Center for People and the Press, 1993).

In the eyes of policy makers and the public, the industry appeared callous to the growing concern about televised violence. Its long-standing tactic of contesting the research evidence was no longer tenable, and its failure to respond more forcefully to Senator Simon's initiatives left it more vulnerable than ever before to some sort of government regulation. In this context, policy makers were poised to act. The focus of debate had clearly shifted from *whether* television violence should be regulated to *how* such regulation might be best accomplished. The challenge, as legal scholar Kevin Saunders (1996) put it, "lies in finding a way to work with and within the First Amendment" (p. 58).

If the government were to adopt any limits on the depiction of violence on television, such restrictions would face numerous hurdles in order to be considered constitutional. According to legal precedent, the research evidence must establish a "compelling governmental interest" in reducing children's exposure to such content; the policy must effectively accomplish the goal of significantly reducing children's exposure to violence known to be harmful; and the policy must be the "least restrictive means" of accomplishing the goal, avoiding restraints on the rights of adults to see violent media content if they wish (Edwards & Berman, 1995; Prettyman & Hook, 1987). These challenges have no doubt contributed to policy makers' long-standing reluctance to formally regulate television violence. Indeed, legislators have long searched for "First Amendment–friendly" solutions such as industry self-regulation, but had not yet succeeded in finding any that seem promising.

### *The V-Chip: A New Technology Offers a New Policy Solution*

A technological development in the early 1990s offered the prospect of an innovative solution that had the potential to skirt most of the First Amendment concerns. That development was the V-chip, an electronic device that could serve as a filter to block programming that posed any risk of harmful effects on children. If television programming could be categorized with ratings that identified violent content, then parents could implement the electronic blocking technology to shield their children from exposure to inappropriate content. By shifting the policy intervention from a sender-based to a receiver-based restriction, the government was removed "from the constitutionally disfavored position of having to decide what its citizens are allowed to see and hear" (Samoriski, Huffman, & Trauth, 1997, p. 146).

Legislation to adopt the V-Chip had been pending in Congress when President Clinton emphatically praised the device in his 1996 State of the Union address. Congress responded to this exhortation by including a section on the V-chip in the Telecommunications Act of 1996, which was passed shortly following the president's speech. The law requires that all televisions sold in the United States include a V-chip device that will facilitate program-blocking capabilities, and establishes uniform technical standards for its use. In order to avoid First Amendment controversies, the legislation does not formally require the television industry to devise a rating system by which its programming must be clearly identified. Of course, without such a rating system the V-chip would be worthless, but the industry quickly acquiesced and agreed to implement a ratings framework (Spitzer, 1998). Under the law, the FCC must review the industry's system for rating programs and deem it acceptable in order to link it to the electronic blocking capability. This review was accomplished in 1997. Even if it was not approved, however, no sanctions could be applied. Thus, the ratings system is considered "voluntary" from a legal perspective.

As currently implemented, there are two key dimensions to the V-chip ratings: age-based advisory categories, and content-based descriptors (Federman, 2002). The age-based advisory categories fall into two groups: shows directed to adults and shows for children. Adult programming includes four rating categories: TV-G (suitable for all ages); TV-PG (parental guidance may be necessary); TV-14 (unsuitable for children under 14); and TV-MA (specifically designed for adults). Children's programs may be rated in either of two rating categories: TV-Y (appropriate for all children) or TV-Y7 (designed for children aged 7 and above).

In addition, the V-chip rating system also includes content descriptors to help clarify why a program received the age-based rating it was assigned. In adopting the V-chip legislation, Congress called upon the television industry to rate its programs not just for violence, but also for sex and other material that parents might find objectionable for their children. Thus, programs for adults may include the content descriptors V for violence, S for sexual behavior, D for sexual dialogue, or L for adult language. A "V" rating indicates moderate violence when attached to a TV-PG program, intense violence when attached to a TV-14 program, and graphic violence when attached to a TV-MA program. V ratings are not applied to TV-G programs. In addition, an FV rating may be attached to children's programs designated TV-Y7 to identify intense or combative fantasy violence.

By the end of 1997, V-chip ratings were being applied to most programs on television. A small billboard in the upper corner of the screen displays the rating during the first 15 seconds of each show. By 2000, the V-chip device was included in all new television sets sold in the United States with 13-inch or larger screens. At that point, use of the V-chip's electronic blocking capability became feasible for those families who had obtained a television set featuring this new technology.

### *Evaluating the V-Chip*

In the early years of the V-chip's availability, studies showed that the electronic blocking capability was used by only modest numbers of parents (Foehr, Rideout, & Miller, 2001; Stanger & Gridina 1999). This is hardly surprising due to the limited diffusion of the technology, which essentially required the purchase of a new television set. In contrast, more than half of parents typically reported that they had used information about a program's V-chip rating (as opposed to the electronic blocking capability) to help them decide whether or not their child should view a particular program (Foehr et al., 2001; Kaiser Family Foundation, 2001; Krcmar, Pulaski, & Curtis, 2001).

Several years later, additional data indicate that use of ratings information by parents has remained stable over time at about 50%, while use of the V-chip's blocking technology has increased significantly (Kaiser Family Foundation, 2004). Of parents who have a V-chip–equipped television set and know it, 42% report using the electronic blocking capability; and of that group, nearly two-thirds (61%) say they found it "very useful." In sum, it appears that the utility of the V-chip for parents is increasing over time, although substantial numbers remain unaware or uninterested.

The nature of the program content being blocked is also a critically important factor to consider in evaluating the impact of the V-chip. Content-analysis research indicates that many shows containing substantial amounts of potentially harmful violence do not receive a V rating (Kunkel et al., 2002). Perhaps more importantly, the V-chip rating system is not devised to rate programs according to their risk of harmful effects on children, but rather relies upon vague and subjective standards to differentiate "moderate," intense," and "graphic" portrayals of violence. Furthermore, the rating judgments are obtained not by child development or media effects experts, but rather by television industry officials who are responsible for rating their own programming. To date, no network has publicly revealed any policies, rules, or criteria that are used for classifying its programs.

Given this context, it is not surprising that parents often disagree with rating judgments. One study found that 39% of parents say that most shows on television are not rated accurately (Kaiser Family Foundation, 2004), while another that asked parents to apply their own ratings to videotaped programs revealed that most judge programs more restrictively than did the television industry (Walsh & Gentile, 2001). A further complication is that many parents are confused by the rating system, potentially limiting its utility (Bushman & Cantor, 2003). For example, many parents believe that the rating FV stands for family values rather than fantasy violence, while others mistakenly assume TV-Y7 identifies programming that is safe for children 7 and under, rather than the opposite (Kaiser Family Foundation, 2004). Clearly, the V-chip cannot be effective in addressing the issue of televised violence unless the ratings are applied accurately and consistently, and parents understand the meaning of the various categories.

Notwithstanding the challenges of comprehending the V-chip ratings, parents are also faced with mastering unique media rating systems for such different platforms as motion pictures, videogames, and Internet sites, among others. According to a national survey, a strong majority of parents (78%) support the creation of a single, universal rating system rather than the mix of media ratings currently used; and a similar proportion (70%) would prefer that an independent group of parents, educators, and child development experts oversee the ratings (Common Sense Media, 2003). This prospect has received support from academic scholars (Walsh & Gentile, 2001) and has begun to draw the attention of public policy makers.

An important lesson gained from research could certainly be applied to development of a universal media ratings system: emphasize descriptive information about the content rather than age-based advisory categories. Parents clearly prefer descriptive ratings (e.g., five levels to describe the intensity of violence) over judgments about the age of children for which the material is appropriate (Bushman & Cantor, 2003). Furthermore, age-based ratings pose the risk of a "forbidden fruit" effect by which children's interest is increased once they learn they are too young to be allowed access to the content; whereas this effect is not observed with the use of content-descriptive ratings that merely indicate levels or types of violence (Bushman & Cantor, 2003; Cantor, 1998).

It remains to be seen whether the V-chip policy will play an important role in resolving the concern about television violence. Many issues persist about the proper design and functioning of the system. But even under optimal conditions, the V-chip system can only protect youth in families where the parents play an active role in supervising their children's media use. It would seem that latchkey children and youngsters who live in at-risk households with less attentive parents have much greater need for protection from media violence; while ironically, the V-chip is most likely to be used for children in the lower-risk families. The greatest asset of the V-chip is that it allows individual choice for each family. The greatest limitation is that it does nothing to protect society against increased violence and aggression that results from violence viewing by children whose families ignore the V-chip.

### *Other TV Violence Policy Alternatives*

Despite the existence of the V-chip, there still seems to be interest in considering other policy alternatives for combating television violence. A recent national poll reported that 63% of parents favor new regulations to limit sex and violence during the early evening hours, when children are most likely to be watching television (Kaiser Family Foundation, 2004). The industry implemented its own self-regulatory policy in the 1970s known as the "Family Hour," with broadcast networks voluntarily committing to air family-friendly material (i.e., no sex or violence) in the first hour of prime time. Adoption of the Family Hour policy was prompted by strong pressure from the FCC, and because of this the courts ultimately judged that the industry's action was not voluntary, and therefore overturned it on First Amendment grounds (Cowan, 1979). It is unlikely that such a policy could legally be implemented by the government, although a related proposal has received substantial attention in recent years.

Beginning in 1993, Senator Ernest Hollings of South Carolina (now retired) introduced legislation in every session of Congress that would regulate television violence in essentially the same manner as broadcast indecency (Kunkel, 2003). Under the FCC's indecency policy, stations may air indecent material late at night, but cannot do so between the hours of 6:00 A.M. and 10:00 P.M. when children are likely to be in the audience. This approach is termed a "safe harbor" policy, though ironically the safe harbor refers to the hours late at night when the broadcast of sensitive material is permitted. This safe harbor period makes the policy legally safe or compliant with the First Amendment by helping the government to meet the "least restrictive means" test applied in the courts, as opposed to the more restrictive alternative of banning such material entirely.

Senator Hollings argued that the social science evidence documenting the risk of harmful effects from children's viewing of televised violence constitutes a "compelling governmental interest," which therefore legitimizes intrusions on otherwise protected speech. His proposal is controversial for several reasons: It attracts strong opposition from free-speech advocates, who are troubled by its strong degree of government censorship. It faces a difficult practical challenge of identifying the violence that would be subject to the policy, while allowing adults access to important political information such as news depictions of violence. And finally, to be effective, the policy would have to be applied to cable as well as broadcast television, which would pose even greater challenges to the law's constitutionality. It is well established that non-broadcast media such as cable qualify for greater First Amendment protection than do broadcast media (Carter, Franklin, & Wright, 2003).

Finally, another policy option that has long been discussed involves the prospect of tort liability, whereby the media would be held accountable for damages when exposure to their products contributes to real-world violence and aggression. This tactic faces particular difficulty given the nature of the process by which media violence influences the audience. It is rarely the case that a direct and powerful response occurs after viewing a single program. Rather, the effects of media violence are typically slow, gradual, and cumulative, in much the same way that cigarette smoking contributes to adverse physical health outcomes. This makes causality more difficult to demonstrate, though not any less real (Gentile & Sesma, 2003).

In the case of *Zamora v. Columbia Broadcasting System et al.* (1979), a 15-year-old plaintiff sued three major television networks, claiming that his cumulative exposure to televised violence since the age of 5 led him to murder an elderly neighbor. The case failed on legal grounds having to do with the lack of evidence about the degree of causality and the foreseeability of the outcome by the broadcasters, among other factors (Prettyman & Hook, 1987).

Another case that involved more direct imitative violence (*Olivia N. vs. National Broadcasting Company*, 1981) also met the same outcome. In this case, 9-year-old Olivia N. was attacked and raped by a group of youths using a plumber's helper handle 4 days following the broadcast of the movie "Born Innocent," in which an identical event was depicted. Again the court said that the plaintiffs had failed to establish that the criminal conduct had been facilitated or made particularly tempting by the broadcast (Prettyman & Hook, 1987).

The duty for media industries to guard against negligent or criminal actions by others after viewing their products increases if the harmful outcome is foreseeable. This factor is particularly relevant for a program such as "Jackass," a Music Television Network (MTV) show that features a host who performs dangerous stunts for comic effect.

Although MTV claims that the show targets 18- to 24-year-olds, one-third of its audience is 17 or younger, and several incidents have occurred in which younger viewers harmed themselves or others in efforts to imitate such actions. For example, a 13-year-old poured gasoline on his arms and legs and lit himself on fire in an attempt to mimic a human barbeque stunt presented on the show (Minow & Minow, 2003). At the outset of each episode, "Jackass" delivers a warning to viewers not to imitate the stunts shown on the program, but the disclaimer was initially conveyed in a humorous, mocking tone that seemed to trivialize its importance. A network spokesperson observed in the press that it is "incredibly upsetting" when young people hurt themselves, but that MTV is not responsible ("MTV Shuns Responsibility," 2001). Following the copycat incidents, the warnings were changed to a much more serious format.

The use of legal torts to hold the media industries accountable when their violent products contribute to physical harm in the real world remains theoretically possible, but rather impotent in practice given existing legal precedent. It is worth noting that most of the key legal decisions were accomplished at a point in time historically when the scientific evidence regarding media violence effects was much less developed than is the case today. Although the hurdles remain high for demonstrating legal culpability, many view this avenue as one of the most promising for exerting an impact on the industry's depictions of violence, should a legal breakthrough in this area occur.

## CONCLUSION

In this chapter, we have demonstrated the clarity of the evidence that media violence is a significant factor contributing to real-world violence and aggression. Various observers have estimated the strength of the correlation between exposure to media violence and subsequent aggression at between +.11 (Hogben, 1998) and +.31 (Comstock & Scharrer, 2003), which on average would be greater than the strength of the relationship between homework and academic achievement or between calcium intake and bone mass (Bushman & Anderson, 2001). As the science has grown in this realm, we have come to understand that not all violence poses the same degree of risk of harmful effects. Indeed, it is theoretically possible that media violence could be presented in a manner that appears so ineffective or repugnant that exposure to such depictions could actually have beneficial outcomes, reducing the likelihood that viewers would subsequently behave aggressively. Unfortunately, content-analysis research establishes clearly that such portrayals are extraordinarily uncommon, and that the most frequent patterns associated with the violence shown on television serve to increase the risk of harmful effects, particularly for child viewers.

It is this scenario that leads policy makers to invest significant efforts to address the issue of media violence. Resolving the issue is no simple matter, as important First Amendment protections must be balanced against the risks of harm from viewing violent material. Policy makers have focused their efforts over the years on broadcast television, which affords the easiest avenue for any direct regulation of content, but this medium is diminishing in importance in an era of increasing media competition and technological innovation. The V-chip stands as the most noteworthy policy to date to address the concerns about media violence. It seems unlikely it will be the last such effort at policy making in this area. The importance of the issue warrants continued careful scrutiny from all interested parties, including parents, policy makers, media practitioners, and health care providers.

## REFERENCES


Action for Children's Television et al. v. Federal Communications Commission, 58F.3d 654 (D.C. Circuit, 1995).

American Broadcasting Companies. (1983). *A research perspective on television violence.* New York: ABC Social Research Unit.

American Medical Association. (1996). *Physician's guide to media violence.* Chicago: Author.

American Psychological Association. (1993). *Violence and youth: Psychology's response.* Washington, DC: Author.

Bandura, A. (1977). *Social learning theory.* Englewood Cliffs, NJ: Prentice Hall.

Bandura, A. (1978). Social learning theory of aggression. *Journal of Communication, 28*(3), 12–29.

Bandura, A. (2002). Social cognitive theory of mass communication. In J. Bryant & D. Zillmann (Eds.), *Media effects: Advances in theory and research* (pp. 121–154). Mahwah, NJ: Lawrence Erlbaum.

Bandura, A., Ross, D., & Ross, S. (1961). Transmission of aggression through imitation of aggressive models. *Journal of Abnormal and Social Psychology, 63,* 575–582.

Bandura, A., Ross, D., & Ross, S. (1963a). Imitation of film-mediated aggressive models. *Journal of Abnormal and Social Psychology, 66,* 3–11.

Bandura, A., Ross, D., & Ross, S. (1963b). Vicarious reinforcement and imitative learning. *Journal of Abnormal and Social Psychology, 67,* 601–607.

Bartholow, B. D., Dill, K. E., Anderson, K. B., & Lindsay, J. J. (2003). Proliferation of media violence and its economic underpinnings. In D. Gentile (Ed.), *Media violence and children: A complete guide for parents and professionals* (pp. 1–18). Westport, CT: Praeger.

Baumgartner, F. R., & Jones, B. D. (1993). *Agendas and instability in American politics.* Chicago: University of Chicago Press.

Berkowitz, L. (1984). Some effects of thoughts on anti- and pro-social influences of media events: A cognitive-neoassociation analysis. *Psychological Bulletin, 95,* 410–427.

Berkowitz, L., & Rogers, K. H. (1986). A priming effect analysis of media influences. In J. Bryant & D. Zillmann (Eds.), *Perspectives on media effects* (pp. 57–82). Hillsdale, NJ: Lawrence Erlbaum.

Boffey, P., & Walsh, J. (1970). Study of TV violence: Seven top researchers blackballed from panel. *Science, 168* (3934), 949–952.

Bok, S. (1998). *Mayhem: Violence as public entertainment.* Reading, MA: Addison-Wesley.

Bryant, J., Carveth, R. A., & Brown, D. (1981). Television viewing and anxiety: An experimental examination. *Journal of Communication, 31* (1), 106–119.

Bushman, B., & Anderson, C. (2001). Media violence and the American public: Scientific facts versus media misinformation. *American Psychologist, 56,* 477–489.

Bushman, B., & Cantor, J. (2003). Media ratings for violence and sex: Implications for policymakers and parents. *American Psychologist, 58,* 130–141.

Cantor, J. (1994). Fright reactions to mass media. In J. Bryant & D. Zillmann (Eds.), *Responding to the screen* (pp. 213–245). Hillsdale, NJ: Lawrence Erlbaum.

Cantor, J. (1998). Ratings for program content: The role of research findings. *Annals of the American Academy of Political and Social Science, 557,* 54–69.

Cantor, J., & Wilson, B. J. (1988). Helping children cope with frightening media presentations. *Current Psychology: Research and Reviews, 7,* 58–75.

Carter, T. B., Franklin, M. A., & Wright, J. B. (2003). *The First Amendment and the fifth estate: Regulation of electronic mass media.* New York: Foundation Press.

Cater, D., & Strickland, S. (1975). *TV violence and the child: The evolution and fate of the Surgeon General's Report.* New York: Russell Sage Foundation.

Chyi, H. I., & McCombs, M. (2004). Media salience and the process of framing: Coverage of the Columbine school shootings. *Journalism & Mass Communication Quarterly, 81,* 22–35.

Cline, V. B., Croft, R. G., & Courrier, S. (1973). Desensitization of children to television violence. *Journal of Personality and Social Psychology, 27,* 360–365.

Cole, B., & Oettinger, M. (1978). *Reluctant regulators: The FCC and the broadcast audience.* Reading, MA: Addison-Wesley.

Common Sense Media. (2003). The 2003 Common Sense Media poll of American parents. Retrieved January 31, 2005, from http://www.commonsensemedia.org/resources/polls.php#p0112

Communications Act of 1934, 47 U.S.C. 151 et seq. (1934).

Comstock, G., & Paik, H. (1991). *Television and the American child.* New York: Academic Press.

Comstock, G., & Sharrer, E. (1999). *Television: What's on, who's watching, and what it means.* New York: Academic Press.

Comstock, G., & Scharrer, E. (2003). Meta-analyzing the controversy over television violence and aggression. In D. Gentile (Ed.), *Media violence and children* (pp. 205–226). Westport, CT: Praeger.

Cook, D. E. (2000, September 13). *Testimony of the American Academy of Pediatrics on media violence before the U.S. Senate Commerce Committee.* Retrieved January 31, 2005, from http://www.aap.org/advocacy/releases/medvioltest.htm

Cooper, C. A. (1996). *Violence on television: Congressional inquiry, public criticism, and industry response: A policy analysis.* Lanham, MD: University Press of America.

Cowan, G. (1979). *See no evil: The backstage battle over sex and violence on television.* New York: Simon & Schuster.

Derthick, M., & Quirk, P. J. (1985). *The politics of deregulation.* Washington, DC: The Brookings Institution.

Drabman, R. S., & Thomas, M. H. (1974). Does media violence increase children's tolerance of real-life aggression? *Developmental Psychology, 10,* 418–421.

Duston, D. (1993, March 24). Majority of Americans are "personally bothered" by TV violence. *Washington Post,* p. C1.

Edwards, H., & Berman, M. (1995). Regulating violence on television. *Northwestern University Law Review, 89,* 1487–1566.

Federal Communications Commission v. Pacifica Foundation, 438 U.S. 726 (Supreme Court, 1978).

Federman, J. (2002). *Rating sex and violence in the media: Media ratings and proposals for reform.* Menlo Park, CA: Author. Retrieved January 31, 2005, from http://www.kff.org/entmedia/3278-index.cfm

Foehr, U., Rideout, V., & Miller, C. (2001). Parents and the TV rating system: A national study. In B. Greenberg (Ed.), *The alphabet soup of television program ratings* (pp. 195–215). Cresskill, NJ: Hampton Press.

Fowler, M., & Brenner, D. (1982). A marketplace approach to broadcast regulation. *Texas Law Review, 60,* 205–257.

Fowles, J. (1999). *The case for television violence.* Thousand Oaks, CA: Sage.

Freedman, J. L. (1984). Effect of television violence on aggressiveness. *Psychological Bulletin, 96,* 227–246.

Friedrich-Cofer, L., & Huston, A. C. (1986). Television violence and aggression: The debate continues. *Psychological Bulletin, 100,* 364–371.

Gentile, D., & Sesma, A. (2003). Developmental approaches to understanding media effects on individuals. In D. Gentile (Ed.), *Media violence and children: A complete guide for parents and professionals* (pp. 19–37). Westport, CT: Praeger.

Gerbner, G., & Gross, L. (1976). Living with television: The violence profile. *Journal of Communication, 26*(2), 172–199.

Gerbner, G., Gross, L., Morgan, M., & Signorielli, N. (1980). The "mainstreaming" of America: Violence profile No. 11. *Journal of Communication, 30*(3), 10–29.

Gerbner, G., Gross, L., Morgan, M., & Signorielli, N. (1986). Living with television: The dynamics of the cultivation process. In J. Bryant & D. Zillmann (Eds.), *Perspectives on media effects* (pp. 17–40). Hillsdale, NJ: Lawrence Erlbaum.

Greenberg, B. S., Edison, K., Korzenny, F., Fernandez-Collado, C., & Atkin, C. (1980). Antisocial and prosocial behaviors on television. In B. S. Greenberg (Ed.), *Life on television: Content analysis of U.S. TV drama* (pp. 99–128). Norwood, NJ: Ablex.

Gunter, B., Harrison, J., & Wykes, M. (2003). *Violence on television: Distribution, form, context, and themes.* Mahwah, NJ: Lawrence Erlbaum.

Guttman, M. (1994, May 9). Violence in entertainment: A kinder, gentler Hollywood. *U.S. News & World Report,* pp. 39–46.

Hamilton, J. T. (1998). *Channeling violence: The economic market for violent television programming.* Princeton, NJ: Princeton University Press.

Hilliard, R. L., & Keith, M. C. (2003*). Dirty discourse: Sex and indecency in American radio.* Ames: Iowa State Press.

Hoffner, C. (1998). Framing of the television violence issue in newspaper coverage. In J. T. Hamilton (Ed.), *Television violence and public policy* (pp. 313–333). Ann Arbor: University of Michigan Press.

Hogben, M. (1998). Factors moderating the effect of television aggression on viewer behavior. *Communication Research, 25,* 220–247.

Huesmann, L. R. (1986). Psychological processes promoting the relation between exposure to media violence and aggressive behavior by the viewer. *Journal of Social Issues, 42*(3) 125–140.

Huesmann, L. R., & Eron, E. (Eds.). (1986). *Television and the aggressive child: A cross-national comparison.* Hillsdale, NJ: Lawrence Erlbaum.

Huesmann, L. R., Eron, L., Lefkowitz, M. M., & Walder, L. O. (1984). The stability of aggression over time and generations. *Developmental Psychology, 20,* 1120–1134.

Huesmann, L., Moise-Titus, J., Podolski, C., & Eron, L. (2003). Longitudinal relations between children's exposure to TV violence and their aggressive and violent behavior in young adulthood: 1977–1992. *Developmental Psychology, 39,* 201–221.

Huesmann, L. R., & Taylor, L. D. (2003). The case against the case against media violence. In D. Gentile (Ed.), *Media violence and children: A complete guide for parents and professionals* (pp. 107–130). Westport, CT: Praeger.

Jo, E., & Berkowitz, L. (1994). A priming effect analysis of media influences: An update. In J. Bryant & D. Zillmann (Eds.), *Perspectives on media effects* (pp. 43–60). Hillsdale, NJ: Lawrence Erlbaum.

Johnson, J., Cohen, P., Smalles, E., Kasen, S., & Brook, J. (2002). Television viewing and aggressive behavior during adolescence and adulthood. *Science, 295,* 2468–2471.

Joint Statement on the Impact of Entertainment Violence on Children. (2000, July 26). Congressional Public Health Summit, Washington, DC. Retrieved January 31, 2005, from http://www.aap.org/advocacy/releases/jstmtevc.htm

Jowett, G. S., Jarvie, I. C., & Fuller, K. H. (1996). *Children and the movies: Media influence and the Payne Fund controversy.* Cambridge, MA: Cambridge University Press.

Kaiser Family Foundation. (2001). *Parents and the V-chip, 2001.* Menlo Park, CA; Author. Retrieved January 31, 2005, from http://www.kff.org/entmedia/3158-index.cfm

Kaiser Family Foundation. (2004). *Parents, media, and public policy: A Kaiser Family Foundation survey.* Menlo Park, CA: Author. Retrieved January 31, 2005, from http://www.kff.org/entmedia/entmedia092304pkg.cfm

Krasnow, E., Longley, L., & Terry, H. (1982). *The politics of broadcast regulation,* 3rd ed. New York: St. Martin's Press.

Krcmar, M., Pulaski, M., & Curtis, S. (2001). *Parents' use and understanding of the television rating system: A national survey.* Paper presented at the annual conference of the National Communication Association, Atlanta, GA.

Kunkel, D. (2003). The road to the V-chip: Television violence and public policy. In D. Gentile (Ed.), *Media violence and children: A complete guide for parents and professionals* (pp. 227–245). Westport, CT: Praeger.

Kunkel, D., Farinola, W., Cope, K., Donnerstein, E., Biely, E., Zwarun, L., et al. (2001). Assessing the validity of V-chip rating judgments: The labeling of high-risk programs. In B. Greenberg (Ed.), *The alphabet soup of television program ratings* (pp. 51–68). Cresskill, NJ: Hampton Press.

Kunkel, D., Farinola, W., Cope-Farrar, K., Donnerstein, E., Biely, E., & Zwarun, L. (2002). Deciphering the V-Chip: An examination of the television industry's program rating judgments. *Journal of Communication, 52*(1), 112–138.

Kunkel, D., & Wilcox, B. (2001). Children and media policy. In D. Singer & J. Singer (Eds.), *Handbook of children and the media* (pp. 589–604). Thousand Oaks, CA: Sage.

Kunkel, D., Wilson, B., Donnerstein, E., Linz, D., Smith, S., Gray, T., et al. (1995). Measuring television violence: The importance of context. *Journal of Broadcasting and Electronic Media, 39,* 284–291.

LeDuc, D. R. (1987). *Beyond broadcasting: Patterns in policy and law.* New York: Longman.

Lichter, S. R., & Amundson, D. (1994). *A day of TV violence 1992 vs. 1994.* Washington, DC: Center for Media and Public Affairs.

Liebert, R., & Sprafkin, J. (1988). *The early window: Effects of television on children and youth* (3rd ed.). New York: Pergamon.

Linz, D., Donnerstein, E., & Penrod, S. (1984). The effects of multiple exposures to filmed violence against women. *Journal of Communication, 34*(3), 130–147.

Linz, D., Donnerstein, E., & Penrod, S. (1988). Effects of long-term exposure to violent and sexually degrading depictions of women. *Journal of Personality and Social Psychology, 55,* 758–768.

MacCarthy, M. (1995). Broadcast self-regulation: The NAB Codes, Family Viewing Hour, and television violence. *Cardozo Arts & Entertainment Law Journal, 13,* 667–696.

Minow, N., & Minow, N. (2003). The role of government in a free society. In D. Ravitch & J. Viteritti (Eds.), *Kid stuff: Marketing sex and violence to America's children* (pp. 240–257). Baltimore: Johns Hopkins University Press.

MTV shuns responsibility for stunts. (2001, April 21). *USA Today,* p. D1.

Mullin, C. R., & Linz, D. (1995). Desensitization and resensitization to violence against women: Effects of exposure to sexually violent films on judgments of domestic violence victims. *Journal of Personality and Social Psychology, 69,* 449–459.

Murray, J. (1980). *Television and youth: 25 years of research and controversy.* Boys Town, NE: Boys Town Center for the Study of Youth Development.

Murray, J. (1996). Media violence and youth. In J. Osofsky (Ed.), *Children, youth, and violence: Searching for solutions* (pp. 72–96). New York: Guilford Press.

National Institute of Mental Health. (1982). *Television and behavior: Ten years of scientific progress and implications for the eighties, Volume 1:* Summary report. Rockville, MD: Author.

Olivia N. v. National Broadcasting Company, 126 Cal.App.3d 488 (California Court of Appeals, First District, 1981).

Paik, H., & Comstock, G. (1994). The effects of television violence on anti-social behavior: A meta-analysis. *Communication Research, 21,* 516–546.

Pearl, D., Bouthilet, E., & Lazar, J. (Eds.). (1982). *Television and behavior: Ten years of scientific progress and implications for the eighties, Volume 2.* Rockville, MD: National Institute of Mental Health.

Pew Research Center for People and the Press. (1999, December 28*). Columbine shooting biggest news draw of 1999.* Retrieved January 31, 2005, from http://people-press.org/reports/display.php3?ReportID=48

Potter, W. J. (1999). *On media violence.* Thousand Oaks, CA: Sage.

Potter, W. J., Vaughan, M., Warren, R., Howley, K., Land, A., & Hagemeyer, J. (1995). How real is the portrayal of aggression in television entertainment? *Journal of Broadcasting & Electronic Media, 39,* 496–516.

Potter, W. J., & Warren, R. (1996). Considering policies to protect children from media violence. *Journal of Communication, 46*(4), 116–138.

Prettyman, E. B., & Hook, L. A. (1987). The control of media-related imitative violence. *Federal Communications Law Journal, 38,* 317–382.

Red Lion Broadcasting Co., Inc. et al. v. Federal Communications Commission et al., 395 U.S. 367 (Supreme Court, 1969).

Reiss, A., & Roth, J. (Eds.). (1993*). Understanding and preventing violence.* Washington, DC: National Academy Press.

Roberts, D., & Foehr, U. (2004). *Kids and media in America.* Cambridge, MA: Cambridge University Press.

Rowland, W. D. (1983). *The politics of TV violence: Policy uses of communication research.* Beverly Hills, CA: Sage.

Samoriski, J. H., Huffman, J. L., & Trauth, D. M. (1997). The V-chip and cyber cops: Technology vs. regulation. *Communication Law and Policy, 2,* 143–164.

Saunders, K. W. (1996). *Violence as obscenity: Limiting the media's First Amendment protection.* Durham, NC: Duke University Press.

Smith, S., Wilson, B., Kunkel, D., Linz, D., Potter, W. J., Colvin, C., et al. (1998). Violence in television programming overall: University of California, Santa

Barbara study. In Center for Communication and Social Policy (Ed.), *National Television Violence Study, Volume 3* (pp. 5–220). Thousand Oaks, CA: Sage.

Spitzer, M. L. (1998). A first glance at the Constitutionality of the V-chip rating system. In J. T. Hamilton (Ed.). *Television violence and public policy* (pp. 335–383). Ann Arbor: University of Michigan Press.

Stanger, J., & Gridina, N. (1999). *Media in the home, 1999: The fourth annual survey of parents and children.* Philadelphia: University of Pennsylvania, Annenberg Public Policy Center.

Surgeon General's Scientific Advisory Committee on Television and Social Behavior. (1972). *Television and growing up: The impact of televised violence. Report to the Surgeon General, U.S. Public Health Service.* Washington, DC: U.S. Government Printing Office.

Thomas, M. H., Horton, R. W., Lippincott, E. C., & Drabman, R. S. (1977). Desensitization to portrayals of real-life aggression as a function of exposure to television violence. *Journal of Personality and Social Psychology, 35,* 450–458.

Times Mirror Center for People and the Press. (1993). *TV violence: More objectionable in entertainment than in newscasts.* Washington, DC: Author.

Walsh, D., & Gentile, D. (2001). A validity test of movie, television, and video game ratings. *Pediatrics, 107,* 1302–1308.

Wertham, F. (1954). *Seduction of the innocent.* New York: Rinehart.

Williams, T. M., Zabrak, M. L., & Joy, L. A. (1982). The portrayal of aggression on North American television. *Journal of Applied Social Psychology, 12,* 360–380.

Wilson, B., Kunkel, D., Linz, D., Potter, W. J., Donnerstein, E., Smith, S., et al. (1997). Violence in television programming overall: University of California Santa Barbara study. In *National Television Violence Study, Volume 1* (pp. 3– 158). Thousand Oaks, CA: Sage.

Wilson, B. J., & Smith, S. L. (1998). Children's responses to emotional portrayals on television. In P. Anderson & L Guerero (Eds.), *Handbook of communication and emotion: Research, theory, applications, and contexts* (pp. 533–569). New York: Academic Press.

Zamora v. Columbia Broadcasting System et al., 480 F.Supp. 199 (S.D. Fla., 1979).

CHAPTER 12

# *Violent Video Games: Effects on Youth and Public Policy Implications*

DOUGLAS A. GENTILE AND CRAIG A. ANDERSON

Years of research documents how witnessing violence and aggression leads to a range of negative outcomes for children. These outcomes result both from witnessing real violence (Osofsky, 1995) as well as from viewing media violence (Anderson et al., 2003; Gentile, 2003). Ironically, the same parents who take great pains to keep children from witnessing violence in the home and neighborhood often do little to keep them from viewing large quantities of violence on television, in movies, and in video games.

The apparent lack of parental concern about media violence is particularly perplexing given the clear research on the negative effects of such violence and the strong critique of such violence by pediatricians. The most recent comprehensive review of the literature on media violence effects—coauthored by eight leading media violence researchers—documents the "unequivocal evidence that media violence increases the likelihood of aggressive and violent behavior in both immediate and long-term contexts" (Anderson et al., 2003, p. 81). In a 2004 survey of pediatricians, over 98% believe that the media affect childhood aggression (Gentile et al., 2004). Somehow, this message has failed to be delivered successfully to the average American parent.

Although there is a large and impressive body of research on the effects of violent television and film on aggressive behavior, there is less research on the effects of violent video games on aggressive behavior. The research that does exist, however, suggests an equally strong connection to negative effects on children. The importance of this research to parents is as critical as the work on television and film. This chapter will review the available research on video games, including the history of violence in video games and the research on the effects of playing violent video games. The chapter will also discuss the political and public policy implications of this research.

## THE HISTORY OF VIOLENCE IN VIDEO GAMES

The first commercial video game, *Pong,* was released in 1972. It was like a game of table tennis (or *ping pong*), in which players had to hit a "ball" with "paddles." As the commercial possibilities became known, game developers began to push the creative and technological envelopes in order to gain greater profits and market share. The developers not only worked to create better technological capacities and graphics abilities, but also experimented with content to see what the market would bear, including violent content.

We, like many other researchers, define *aggression* as behavior (verbal or physical) that (a) is intended to harm another individual; (b) is expected by the perpetrator to have some chance of actually harming that individual; and (c) is believed by the perpetrator to be something that the target individual wishes to avoid. In recent years, there has been a convergence of opinion among psychological scholars that physical aggression should be conceived as existing along a severity continuum ranging from mild (e.g., a weak slap) to severe (e.g., shooting), and that violence (or violent behavior) refers to physical aggression toward the severe end of this continuum (e.g., Anderson et al., 2003; Anderson & Huesmann, 2003). In other words, *violence* is simply physical aggression at the high end of a severity dimension. These definitions can be applied both to the violence shown in video games as well as to the types of aggressive behaviors that playing such games might influence.

The first violent commercial video game to receive much attention was *Death Race,* a driving simulator. Released in 1976, the game's working title had been *Pedestrian.* The goal was to run down stick-figure pedestrians, called "gremlins," who would then scream and turn into gravestones. The violent content of this game spurred a public outcry, causing some communities to ban it. The controversy actually increased sales of the game about tenfold (Kent, 2001). This market outcome was not lost on game developers. Although many game developers created standards for their games, including "No excessive blood and violence" and "No sex" (Kent, 2001, p. 465), it gradually became clear that games sold better if they contained more violence, at least in part because of the free publicity generated by outcries against the violence. In the late 1980s and early 1990s, one-on-one fighting games such as *Double Dragon* and *Mortal Kombat* pushed the boundaries of violence and became all-time best sellers. The economic benefits of more explicit violence became apparent when Nintendo and Sega both created versions of *Mortal Kombat* for their competing systems. Nintendo had toned down the blood and gore in their version, and the Sega Genesis version outsold Nintendo's version three to one (Kent, 2001). (The games mentioned in this chapter are described in Appendix A.)

During the 1980s and early 1990s, the violence in video games was still fairly stylized, in large part because of technological constraints. In 1992, a major step forward in realism was taken by the game *Wolfenstein 3D,* the first major "first-person shooter" game. In this kind of game, one "sees" the video game world through the eyes of the character one controls, rather than seeing it from afar, as in almost all previous fighting games. The player moves around, exploring a three-dimensional environment, and can shoot at various game characters. The effect is to put the player *in the game,* fighting, killing, and being killed. This additional realism was followed by other realistic touches. Video game historian Steven Kent (2001) has noted that, "part of *Wolfenstein*'s popularity sprang from its shock value. In previous games, when players shot enemies, the injured targets fell and disappeared. In

*Wolfenstein 3D,* enemies fell and bled on the floor" (p. 458). This caused a revolution in the way violent games were designed. In 1993, *Doom,* the next major first-person shooter game was released. It included more blood and gore and also allowed players to hunt and kill each other.

Partially in response to these advances in video game violence, Senators Joseph Lieberman (D-CT) and Herbert Kohl (D-WI) initiated Congressional hearings to examine the marketing of violent games. The hearings examined whether games with what seemed to be the equivalent of the content in R-rated movies (e.g., violence and sexuality) were being sold to children (Kent, 2001). The hearings included testimony from media effects researchers, child advocates, and video game industry executives. Although there was far less research on the effects of violent video games then than now, the combined pressure caused the video game industry to create its own trade organization (the Interactive Digital Software Association, now renamed the Entertainment Software Association), as well as an organization to create and provide ratings for video games (the Entertainment Software Ratings Board [ESRB]). Thus, the hearings resulted in the video game industry agreeing to implement a voluntary ratings system. Senator Lieberman had hoped that this would cause the video game industry to reduce the violent content of their games, by making them pay attention to the potential effects of the games (Kent, 1997). However, the adoption of ratings did not have this effect, and by 1997 Senator Lieberman admitted that, "The rating system has not stopped game producers from putting out some very violent games" (Kent, 1997). In fact, it had the same effect that the movie ratings system had had on films—now that there were ratings, producers felt able to make even more violent games because they did not need to be designed for general audiences. Thus, when *Mortal Kombat 2* was released, the Nintendo version had just as much gore as the Sega version, and this time the Nintendo version sold better than Sega's (Kent, 2001).

The technological advances in computing and graphics power have continued to increase at a geometric rate during the past decade, allowing the graphics and gameplay to become more violent and more realistic. For example, the first-person shooter game *Soldier of Fortune* (SOF) was created in collaboration with an ex-army colonel, and it featured 26 different "killing zones" in the body. The characters in the game respond realistically to different shots depending on where in the body they are shot, with what weapons, and from what distance. Shooting a character in the arm at close range with a shotgun rips the arm from the socket leaving exposed bone and sinew while blood rushes from the wound. In 2004, the violent game *Doom* got an update, and in the words of one reviewer, "the illusion the game creates is so realistic. . . . There is a crispness to details, a weight and solidity to objects and figures, a lifelike sheen to surfaces in Doom 3 that is unlike anything we've seen before" (Grossman, 2004, p. 83).

As the violence in video games has increased, the concern about the potential effects of playing these games has also increased. One benefit of this concern has been a corresponding increase in empirical research on the effects of video games on players.

## RESEARCH ON THE EFFECTS OF VIDEO GAMES

Researchers require that theories be created, tested, and revised based on the results of the tests. The revisions are further tested and revised, ultimately resulting in a theory that has solid theoretical and empirical bases. Several theories have received empirical support and explain why playing violent video games might increase aggressive behaviors. These theories range from specific theories of learning (e.g., Gentile & Gentile, under review) to broad psychological theories of aggression (e.g., the General Aggression Model; see Anderson & Bushman, 2002; Anderson, Gentile, & Buckley, in press; Anderson & Huesmann, 2003).

There are several types of research designs that social scientists can use, and each type allows different sorts of conclusions to be drawn. No single study can ever be called "conclusive," a point that the video game industry has continued to exploit semantically: Recently, in response to California Bill 1793, which would require that stores make signs and brochures to explain the video game ratings to customers, the president of the Interactive Entertainment Merchants' Association stated, "To-date there has been no conclusive research to prove a causal linkage between playing videogames and asocial behavior" (Halpin, 2004). To accept this statement, one must misunderstand how behavioral science is conducted. Because no one study can ever be wholly conclusive, researchers create and test theories, conducting several studies, each of which has different strengths. It is the total picture of combined studies that answers the question of a causal link.

The three major types of studies—experimental, correlational, and longitudinal—have different strengths and weaknesses. Experimental studies randomly assign participants to different groups—for example, to play either a violent or nonviolent video game. All other factors are carefully controlled, so that the two groups should differ only on the type of game played. After playing, the experimenter might measure aggressive thoughts or aggressive behaviors for both groups. If the groups differ in their responses, causality *can be inferred,* because the game played was the only apparent way in which the groups differed (because participants are randomly assigned to different groups, any individual differences should be equally distributed between the groups). The ability to determine causality is the great strength of experimental studies. Their major weakness in this context is that it is usually impossible to use strong "real-world" measures of aggressive behavior. It would be unethical to actually allow study participants to hit each other, for example, so more ethical measures must be used. The researcher must then prove that the laboratory measures of aggression predict real-world types of aggression.

Correlational studies allow researchers to get beyond this limitation of experimental studies. In a correlational study, for example, researchers might survey children about the video games they play, and about several real-world types of aggressive behavior, such as how many physical fights they get into. The major weakness of correlational studies is that *causality cannot be proven* by them, at least, not in a single correlational study. It might be that playing violent games causes aggressive behavior, or that aggressive children play violent games, or some third variable that causes both (such as being male, which predicts both aggressive behavior and interest in violent video games). Correlational studies are strong where experimental studies are weak and vice versa. Therefore, if both types of studies show similar results, we can start to be reasonably comfortable that we have discovered a real effect.

A third type of study, longitudinal studies, can document changes over a longer period of time. In a longitudinal study, for example, one might measure children's video game play and aggressive behavior at two points in time. In this way, one can test whether children who play violent games at the beginning of the study *change* to become more aggressive by the end of the study. The major limitation of longitudinal studies is that they are difficult and expensive to conduct.

Before scientists are willing to believe that playing violent video games predicts aggressive behavior, they would want to see studies of each type performed, and determine whether the results of the different studies converged. A strong case for a real effect arises if the same results are found no matter what way one studies it. Furthermore, behavioral scientists would want to see that the studies had controlled for several other variables that might be related to both video game play and aggression, such as sex, personality trait hostility, parental education level, parental monitoring of media, and so forth. Although more research is needed, all of these types of studies have been conducted with similar results: playing violent video games can indeed cause increases in aggressive thoughts, feelings, and behaviors.

These same methods have also been used to document potentially *positive* effects of certain types of video games. Video games have been successful at imparting the attitudes, skills, and behaviors that they were designed to teach (Lieberman, 1997, 2001). For instance, they can teach children healthy skills for the self-care of asthma and diabetes (Lieberman, 1997, 2001). In a study of college students, playing a golf video game improved students' actual control of force when putting, even though the video game gave no physical feedback on students' actual putting movement or force (Fery & Ponserre, 2001). Correlational studies with adults show that experience with video games is related to better surgical skills (e.g., Rosser et al., 2004; Tsai & Heinrichs, 1994). Research also suggests that people can learn iconic, spatial, and visual attention skills from video games (De Lisi & Wolford, 2002; Dorval & Pepin, 1986; Green & Bavelier, 2003; Greenfield, deWinstanley, Kilpatrick, & Kaye, 1994; Griffith, Volschin, Gibb, & Bailey, 1983; Okagaki & Frensch, 1994). Finally, research on educational software has shown that educational video games can have very significant effects on improving student achievement (Murphy, Penuel, Means, Korbak, & Whaley, 2001). In sum, video games are great teachers, but what they teach very much depends on the content (Buckley & Anderson, in press; Gentile & Gentile, in press). Therefore, we do not consider video games "bad"; rather, we consider them to be powerful teaching tools, and this compels us to study whether violent video games may be powerful teachers of aggressive thoughts, feelings, and behaviors. It is ironic, though not surprising, that even though the studies documenting positive effects as a set are considerably weaker than the studies documenting negative effects of violent games, people seem to want to believe that video games can have positive effects but not that they can have negative effects.

### *Experimental Studies*

Over a dozen experimental studies have been conducted on the short-term effects of playing violent video games (e.g., Ballard & Weist, 1996; Calvert & Tan, 1994; Chambers & Ascione, 1987; Deselms & Altman, 2003). The best experimental studies share at least four common characteristics: sample size of 200 or more; violent and nonviolent games equated on potentially confounding dimensions (e.g., difficulty); violent and nonviolent games that are truly violent and nonviolent (respectively); and a clear and valid measure of aggression or aggression-related variables assessed for the game-playing participant. Though these characteristics might seem obvious, a number of experimental studies (published and unpublished) do not have all four. Many have small samples. Some present no evidence that the violent and nonviolent games are equated on difficulty or other potentially confounding dimensions. A few (mostly unpublished) have used games that include violence in the nonviolent condition, or games with relatively little violence in the violent condition. Still others have used self-reports of past aggression as the dependent variable of aggressive behavior, which is problematic since playing a violent video game for 20 minutes in an experiment would not logically increase aggression committed prior to starting the experiment.

Although the first published experimental study of violent video games appeared in 1985 (Graybill, Kirsch, & Esselman), the first that contained all four of these high-quality characteristics appeared in 2000 (Anderson & Dill, Study 2). In this study, college students were randomly assigned to play either a violent or nonviolent game. The games were matched on several important dimensions, including arousal and frustration levels. Participants played their assigned game and completed measures of aggressive cognition (a word-speed reading task) and of aggressive behavior (a standard competitive game involving the setting of punishment levels for one's opponent). The results were that playing a violent video game increased both aggressive cognition and aggressive behavior.

This pattern of results has also been documented with children and adolescents playing age-appropriate (based on the video game ratings) violent video games (Anderson, Gentile, & Buckley, in press; Study 1). E-rated video games (those labeled as appropriate for "Everyone") with violent content increased aggressive behavior in the laboratory, whereas matched nonviolent E-rated games did not. This experimental effect occurred with males and females, with children and older adolescents/young adults, with high and low media violence-exposure individuals, and with high and low media violence-preference individuals. Perhaps surprisingly, among the older adolescents the E-rated violent games produced an increase in aggression at least as large as the T-rated video games (those labeled as appropriate for "Teens"). Although both types included violent content, the E-rated violent games were rated by players as *less* violent than the T-rated games. Combined, these findings contradict two basic assumptions made by parents, the video game industry, and various public policy groups: (1) that E-rated games (even those with violent content) are safe for all ages; and (2) that T-rated violent games have a significantly bigger immediate negative impact on players than E-rated violent games.

### Correlational Studies

Several correlational studies have been conducted on the long-term correlates of playing violent video games, including the relation to real-world physical aggression (e.g., Anderson & Dill, 2000; Dominick, 1984; Gentile, Lynch, Linder, & Walsh, 2004; Krahé & Möller, 2004; Wiegman & Van Schie, 1998). The best correlational studies also share several characteristics: adequate sample size (at least 200); a reliable measure of exposure to violent video games; and a reliable measure of aggression or of an aggression-related variable (e.g., aggressive cognitions). The first published correlational study with all three characteristics appeared in 2000 (Anderson & Dill, Study 1), but the first studies with these methodological characteristics to focus on children did not appear until 2004. Krahé and Möller (2004) found a significant correlation between video game violence exposure and acceptance of physical aggression norms in a sample of eighth graders in Germany ($r = .30$, $p < .01$). Gentile et al. (2004) reported significant correlations between video game violence exposure and: trait hostility ($r = .21$, $p < .001$), arguments with teachers ($r = .20$, $p < .001$), and physical fights ($r = .32$, $p < .001$). The effect on physical fights of violent video games remained significant even after statistically controlling for sex, trait hostility, and overall amount of video game play. Anderson et al. (2004) replicated many of these findings with a college student sample, and also provided correlational evidence that aggressive cognitions at least partially mediate the effects of repeated exposure to violent video games on aggressive and violent behavior. In other words, it is not as simple as people just copying what they have seen. Instead, playing violent video games may first increase aggressive and hostile thoughts, and these thoughts in turn increase the odds of behaving aggressively.

In a series of studies with children and adolescents, Anderson et al. (2004, under review) found that video game violence exposure was related to a wide array of aggression (e.g., verbal aggression, moderate physical aggression, violent behaviors). For example, among high school students, the correlation with violent behavior was $r = .35$, and with moderate physical aggression was $r = .46$ (Study 2). Violent video game exposure was also significantly related to a host of aggression-related variables such as trait anger and hostility, attitudes toward violence, and hostile attribution bias. Importantly, video game violence was a significant risk factor for aggression and violence even when other important risk factors were statistically controlled.

### *Longitudinal Studies*

As this chapter goes to press, to our knowledge, only two longitudinal studies of violent video games have been conducted. In the first study, 807 Japanese fifth and sixth graders were surveyed twice during a school year (Ihori, Sakamoto, Kobayashi, & Kimura, 2003). They found that the amount of video game play at Time 1 was significantly (but weakly, $r = .08$) related to later physical aggression, but aggression at Time 1 was not related to later video game play. There are at least two potential problems with this study. First, it relies only on self-report. More importantly, however, the authors only measured the *amount* of video game play, and not whether the children were playing violent games, a point addressed in more detail later.

In the second longitudinal study, both concerns were addressed. In this study, 430 third, fourth, and fifth graders; their teachers; and their peers were surveyed at two points in the school year (Anderson, Gentile, & Buckley, in press; Study 3). The results showed that students who played more violent video games began to see the world more in terms of aggression (i.e., they had an increase in hostile attribution bias). Research has shown that children who exhibit this cognitive bias (to assume that negative things happen due to hostile intent rather than by accident) are far more likely to react aggressively (Bensley & Eenwyk, 2001; Crick, 1995, 1996; Crick & Dodge, 1994). Indeed, children who had high exposure to violent video games changed over the school year to become more verbally aggressive, more physically aggressive, and less prosocial (as rated by their peers and teachers; raw Pearson correlations ranged between .24 and .40). It appears that not only does repeated exposure to violent video games increase aggressive behavior, but it also decreases empathic helpful behavior. This may be especially noteworthy because increased aggressive behaviors and decreased prosocial behaviors also predicted peer rejection (Anderson et al., in press).

This last finding has particularly important implications because it addresses one of the most common criticisms of the media violence literature. It is often claimed that the correlation between media violence exposure and aggression is due to the fact that aggressive children like to consume media violence, and not because media violence increases children's aggressive thoughts and behaviors. This is a reasonable criticism of correlational research, but it does not explain the findings from experimental research in which both aggressive and nonaggressive children become more aggressive after playing a violent video game. In our view, it does not matter what starts the ball rolling—whether aggressive children watch more violence, or whether watching violence makes children more aggressive. What is clear is that regardless of the *initial cause,* playing violent video games still makes children *more* aggressive. It is certainly plausible that this sets a child on a very bad negative trajectory as the effect snowballs. As children become more aggressive and less prosocial, other children are more likely to reject them from the main peer group. These aggressive children then form a non-mainstream clique with other socially rejected and aggressive children, who then reinforce each other's aggressive attitudes and violent media habits. Ultimately, aggressive children are significantly more likely to have negative outcomes, such as lower academic performance and lower self-esteem (Geen, 2001; National Research Council, 1993), which may perpetuate a cycle of increasingly worse outcomes. Because only one longitudinal study with a measure of *violent* video game exposure has been conducted to date, these conclusions must be considered tentative.

### *Meta-Analytic Procedures*

There is a statistical technique called meta-analysis that is basically a composite of all of the studies, published and unpublished, in a particular area. This statistical technique allows for general conclusions of all the studies done without relying on any single research method or sample population. One recent meta-analysis specifically examined the effects of violent video games effects (Anderson, 2003). The results showed that across all of the studies conducted, video game violence exposure is positively associated with aggressive behavior ($r$ = .21), aggressive affect ($r$ = .16), and aggressive cognition ($r$ = .18), and negatively associated with helping or prosocial behavior ($r$ = –.19).

### *Early Research Compared to Recent Research*

Because video games have changed to include more violence over time, one might predict that early studies looking at the effects of the games might be less consistent in their findings than in later studies. That is, one might expect the difference between the violent and nonviolent games in 1985 to have been a much smaller difference than exists today, and therefore should have a correspondingly smaller and harder-to-detect effect. In fact, this is exactly the pattern researchers have found. In experimental studies where the difference in amount of violent content can be quantified, studies with larger differences between the violent and nonviolent games show larger effects on aggressive behavior (Gentile & Anderson, 2003). In correlational studies, where it is much harder to quantify differences between games, an analysis of the year the studies were conducted shows an increase in effects over the years. Much smaller effect sizes occurred in the 1980s than in the late 1990s and early 2000s (Gentile & Anderson, 2003).

### *Amount of Play vs. Content of Play*

By now, the scientific evidence of potentially harmful effects from violent video games is becoming clearer—playing violent video games appears to increase aggressive thoughts, feelings, and behaviors, both short-term and long-term. It is important, however, to note a critical distinction implicit throughout this chapter—that there may be important differences in the potential effects based on *amount* of game play compared to those based on the *content* of the games played. Many studies (particularly those using data from the 1980s) treated amount of game play as a correlate and found mixed results. More recent studies that carefully separate amount of play from the content of play have shown that amount seems to be negatively related to school performance, but it is only weakly associated with aggressive and antisocial behaviors, most likely because only some of the games played have violent content. Conversely, playing games with violent content is positively related to aggressive variables, but is at most only marginally related to school performance (e.g., Anderson & Dill, 2000; Anderson et al., in press; Gentile et al., 2004). This finding again makes it clear that the question, "Are video games good or bad?" is a false dichotomy. Playing a moderate amount of nonviolent games seems to be benign; and if one plays games with educational content (even relatively infrequently), the effect is likely to be positive, at least on knowledge in that educational domain. But if one plays games with violent content, the effects seem to be negative. These findings appear to result from the simple fact that children learn whatever content their video games teach.

### *The Question of Youth "Vulnerability"*

Many people have assumed that children might be especially "vulnerable" to the effects of violent video games. There are several plausible reasons why this might be true. First, children have less real-life experience to which they can compare portrayals of violence in video games, and therefore may learn more from them. Second, children (especially young children under 8) do not have the same understanding of the fantasy–reality distinction that adults do, and therefore may accept media violence portrayals as more "real." Each of these reasons is theoretically justifiable. Unfortunately, little research supports the idea that children aged 7 or above are more vulnerable to the effects of playing violent video games than adults (Anderson et al., in press). Adults who play violent video games also show both short-term and long-term effects on aggressive thoughts, feelings, and behaviors (Anderson & Bushman, 2001).

## MEDIA VIOLENCE AS A RISK FACTOR FOR AGGRESSION

Violent video games came under intense scrutiny in the public eye in the late 1990s as a result of tragic school shootings in which the shooters had a history of playing violent video games (e.g., West Paducah, KY [December, 1997]; Jonesboro, AR [March, 1998]; Springfield, OR [May, 1998]; Littleton, CO [April, 1999]; Santee, CA [March, 2001]; Wellsboro, PA [June, 2003] and Red Lion, PA [April, 2003]). The news media have linked violent video games to other violent crimes, including a violent crime spree in Oakland, CA (January, 2003); five homicides in Long Prairie and Minneapolis, MN (May, 2003); beating deaths in Medina, OH (November, 2002); and Wyoming, Michigan (November, 2002); and the Washington, D.C., "Beltway" sniper shootings (Fall, 2002). As early as 2000, the U.S. Federal Bureau of Investigation reported that one of the warning signs characteristic of school shooters was that the high-risk student "spends inordinate amounts of time playing video games with violent themes, and seems more interested in the violent images than in the game itself" (O'Toole, 2000, p. 20).

Although these highly publicized tragedies have drawn attention to the potential effects of playing violent video games, these are actually *not* good examples of the effects. In each of these cases, the shooters had several risk factors for aggressive behavior. Research has shown that there are very many risk factors for aggression, such as poverty, a history of having been abused, psychological disorders, gang membership, drug use, media violence, and inflated self-esteem (U.S. Department of Health and Human Services, 2001). We argue that in order for a "normal" child to become seriously violent, he or she would need to have several of these risk factors present (Gentile & Sesma, 2003). No single risk factor is typically strong enough to cause such an extreme behavior as a school shooting. That said, however, there is one important difference between media violence and most of the other risk factors for aggression—it is the one that is *easily controlled.* Even the parent in a family living in poverty (and many families living in poverty have video game systems) can say, "No, you can't play that game. Play this one instead."

If one adopts the view that media violence exposure is a risk factor for aggression, it provides a much clearer understanding of the research. For example, the lack of evidence for youth vulnerability suggests that violent video game exposure is a risk factor for everyone who plays, regardless of age, sex, or other factors. However, this does not mean that most people who play violent video games will later become violent. It *does* mean that their risk is elevated. If there are additional risk factors, the risk is further elevated. With enough risk factors, it becomes extremely likely that an individual will behave with inappropriate aggression at some point. This is similar to predicting heart disease: Smoking elevates the risk of having a heart attack. Smoking is not the sole "cause" of the heart attack, but it does increase the risk—it is a causal factor. If one also does not exercise, the risk is further increased. With each additional risk factor, such as family history of heart disease, or poor diet, the risk increases until it becomes statistically very predictable whether one is likely to have a heart attack. This approach to understanding violent video games can be empirically tested.

In the longitudinal study of third-to-fifth graders, several risk factors for aggressive behavior were measured, including sex, hostile attribution bias, prior aggression, and video game violence exposure. As predicted by a risk factor approach, the group with the least predicted risk of physical fights at Time 2 are (1) girls who have (2) a low hostile attribution bias, (3) have not been involved in fights previously, and (4) who do not play violent video games. The group with the greatest predicted risk of physical fights are (1) boys who have (2) a high hostile attribution bias, (3) have been involved in fights previously, and (4) who play a lot of violent video games. As is shown in Figure 12.1, this is exactly the pattern that was found (Anderson et al., in press). This pattern is identical to that found in a study of adolescents where violent video game play and trait hostility were both measured (Gentile et al., 2004). In that study, both hostility and violent game play were related to physical fights, but the combination was greater than either alone.

The utility of a risk factor approach is further evidenced by considering the opposite side—protective factors. Theoretically, active parental involvement in children's media habits should serve as a protective factor for later aggressive habits (Austin, 1993, Dorr & Rabin, 1995; Lin & Atkin, 1989), a prediction that has received some confirmation. Although boys are more likely than girls to be involved in physical fights, if their parents are more involved in their media habits, their risk of fighting is decreased. In addition, although girls are less likely overall to get into physical fights, if their parents are involved in their media habits, their risk for fighting is diminished by almost half (Anderson et al., in press). Putting the risk and protective factors together, the group with the least predicted risk of physical fights would be (1) girls who have (2) a low hostile attribution bias, (3) have not been involved in fights previously, (4) who do not play violent video games, and (5) who have parents who are highly involved in their media habits. Children with the greatest predicted risk of

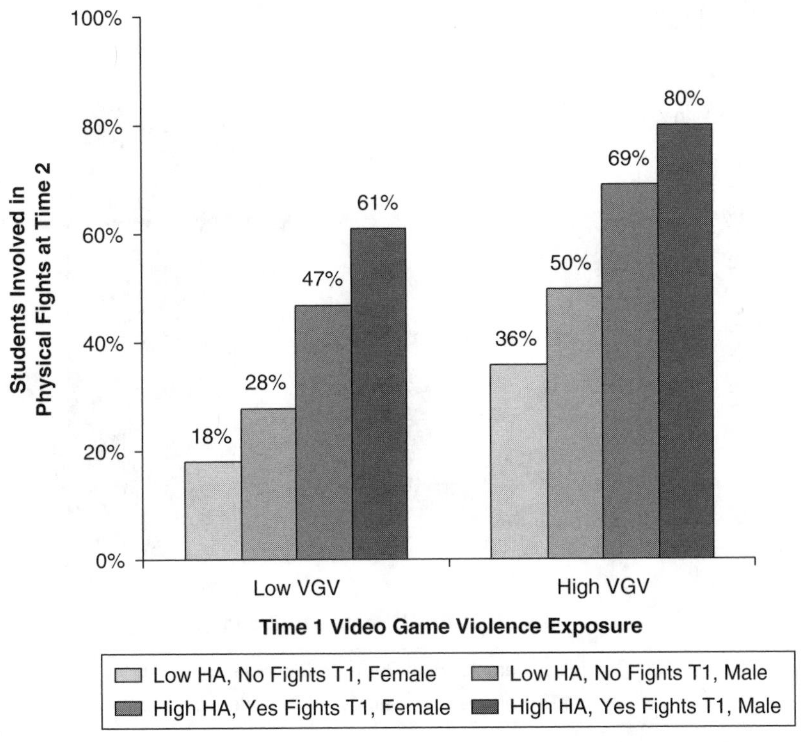


**Figure 12.1** Predicted Likelihood of Physical Fights at Time 2 as a Function of Hostile Attribution Bias, (HA) Involvement in Physical Fights at Time 1, Sex, and Video Game Violence Exposure (VGV)

*Source:* Anderson, C. A., Gentile, D. A., & Buckley, K. E. (in press). Reprinted by permission.

physical fights would be (1) boys who have (2) a high hostile attribution bias, (3) have been involved in fights previously, (4) who play a lot of violent video games, and (5) whose parents are not involved in their media habits. This is exactly the pattern that is found in Figure 12.2. The highest risk group is over five times more likely than the lowest risk group to become involved in physical fights by Time 2, 16% compared to 84%.

## IMPLICATIONS FOR PUBLIC POLICY

Adopting a risk factor approach may be particularly beneficial when attempting to determine public policies regarding children's exposure to media violence. This is similar to the risks associated with smoking, and resembles how scientists studying criminology attempt to understand the predictors of criminal behaviors. Scientific evidence is an important factor in the adoption of good public policies, but it is usually divorced from what the "appropriate" policies could or should be. Only one-third of smokers ever get lung cancer, but that does not mean that smoking is "good" for the other two-thirds. Smoking is a risk factor for all smokers, regardless of whether they ever actually get cancer. Public policy regarding smoking has tended to have a two-tiered approach. For adults, most modern societies provide information about the risks associated with smoking, but allow adults the freedom to accept those risks. For children, most societies support parents' efforts to keep their children from beginning to smoke, which includes

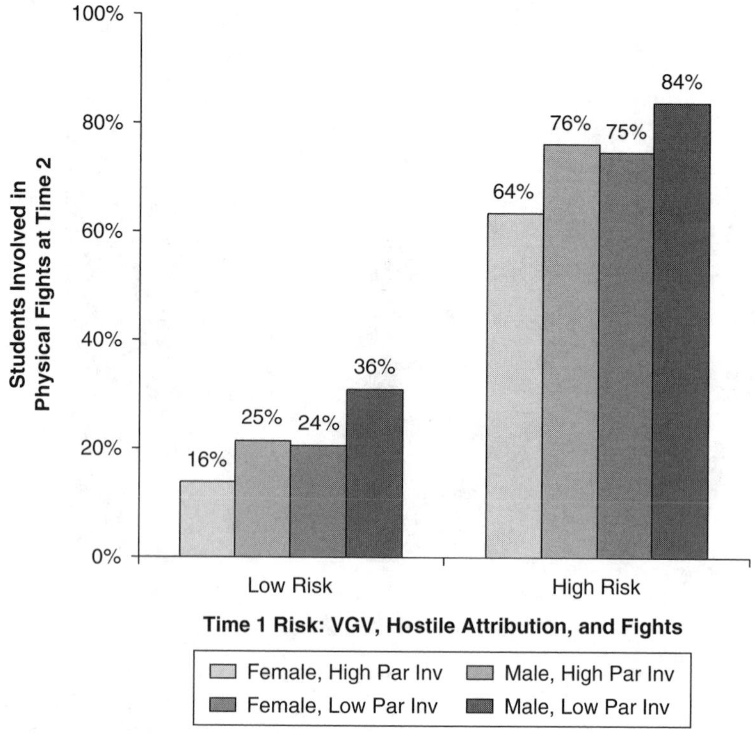


**Figure 12.2** Predicted Likelihood of Physical Fights at Time 2 as a Function of Hostile Attribution Bias, Physical Fights at Time 1, Sex, Video Game Violence Exposure (VGV), and Parental Involvement

*Source:* Anderson, C. A., Gentile, D. A., & Buckley, K. E. (in press). Reprinted by permission.

making the purchase of tobacco products by minors illegal. This two-tiered approach was not determined by scientific research, which suggests that smoking is likely harmful for all who smoke, regardless of age. Instead, the research evidence was one part of the information used in conjunction with several other nonscientific considerations deemed relevant to public policy decisions.

Although we agree that the research on both general media violence and specific video game violence is sufficiently definitive and clear to contribute to public policy debates, we also believe that it is important to focus on the scientific merits of various possible policies. Scientific evidence does not and cannot automatically translate into effective public policy. There are at least four very different and important sources of information underlying the formulation of effective public policy, as Figure 12.3 illustrates, science facts, legal issues, personal values, and political realities. Good scientific facts can and should influence public policy in at least two major ways. First, well-developed science can identify societal problems that might require some sort of public policy intervention. Second, it can identify policies that are likely to work (e.g., Head Start programs) as well as those unlikely to work (e.g., midnight basketball). In both cases, science contributes by providing key answers to factual questions.

## *The Three Pillars of Responsibility*

As the evidence of negative effects of violent games becomes more compelling, parents, educators, and policy makers are increasingly

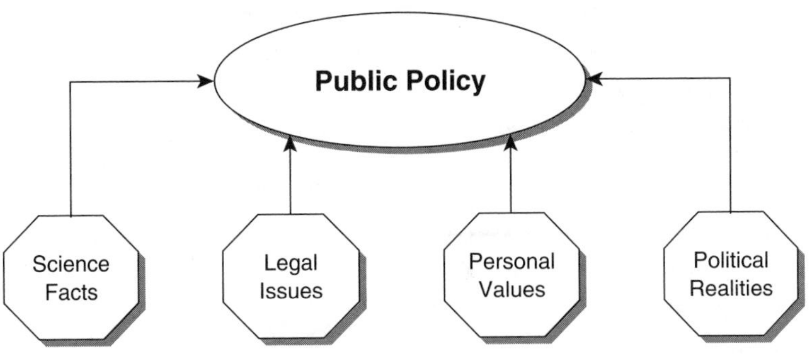


**Figure 12.3** Relation of Scientific Information to Public Policy

concerned about what to do. From our perspective, there are at least three pillars of responsibility—the video game industry, the rental and retail industry, and parents.

The video game industry has at least three responsibilities. First, it must clearly and accurately label the content of games, so that parents know what they are getting before buying. Recently, the authors of a study of "Teen"-rated games pointed out that there is a "significant amount of content in T-rated video games that might surprise adolescent players and their parents" (Hanninger & Thompson, 2004, p. 856). Both the ratings and the content descriptors being provided by the current system are suspect and need improvement (Gentile, Humphrey, & Walsh, 2005). The second responsibility of the video game industry is to market their products appropriately. Advertisements for mature-rated ("M"-rated) games have been seen in *Sports Illustrated for Kids* and other magazines with high proportions of youth readers (Federal Trade Commission, 2000, 2001, 2004). Indeed, the Federal Trade Commission (FTC) has documented numerous ways in which game manufacturers have explicitly marketed their M-rated games to children (although this practice has declined in response to actions taken by the Entertainment Software Association). It is inappropriate and unethical for the video game industry to label some games as "not for kids" while vigorously marketing those same games to children. The video game industry's third responsibility is to help educate parents about why ratings matter. The industry has provided what amounts to, at best, a mixed message to parents. On the one hand, they tout how good their rating system is (e.g., Entertainment Software Association, 2004), while on the other hand they claim (in television, newspaper, and magazine reports and interviews; in courtroom briefs; in conference addresses) that no research shows that violent games can lead to negative outcomes. For example, Doug Lowenstein, president of the ESA, stated in a May 12, 2000, interview on CNN, "There is absolutely no evidence, none, that playing a violent video game leads to aggressive behavior." Beyond not being truthful, this approach only serves to confuse the public about why they should learn about and use ratings.

The rental and retail industries have two responsibilities. First, they must create policies under which children under 17 (18 would seem a more appropriate age cutoff) may not buy or rent mature-rated games without parental permission. Many stores, including large chains and superstores, have dragged their heels in instituting such policies. Second, retailers must enforce these policies. In one "sting operation" conducted by the National Institute on Media and the Family, children as young as 7 were able in half of all attempts to purchase M-rated games (Walsh, Gentile, Gieske, Walsh, & Chasco, 2003). Similar sting operations conducted by the FTC found that teenagers are able to purchase M-rated games 69% to 85% of the time (FTC, 2000, 2001, 2004). Parents should be able to expect that stores will not allow children access to M-rated games in much the same way that they expect movie theaters to deny children entry to R-rated movies when parents drop them off at the theatre, or that bars and liquor stores will not allow underage people to purchase alcohol products.

The third pillar of responsibility is parents. Parents have three principal responsibilities. First, they need to educate themselves about the video game ratings (there are three main ones—"E" for everyone, "T" for teen, "M" for mature) and the content descriptors associated with the games. Second, they need to learn why it is important to pay attention to the ratings and descriptors. Here is where the research is so useful. In short, both *amount* and *content* matter. Parents who put limits on the amount and content of games that children play have children who get better grades and have fewer aggressive outcomes (e.g., Anderson et al., under review; Gentile et al., 2004). Finally, parents need to act on their knowledge. Just as playing violent games is a risk factor for negative outcomes for children, active parental involvement in children's video game habits appears to act as a protective factor (although the specific mechanisms for this have not yet been identified).

## Public Policy Options

What public policy options exist to help encourage and support the responsibilities identified above? Several options are available, including supporting education, voluntary industry ratings, mandatory industry ratings, governmental ratings, mandatory independent ratings, legal access restrictions, and restrictions on production. Each will be described briefly below, although we recognize that these do not exhaust the list of possible options.

### *Education*

One obvious solution is to provide much better public education about the deleterious effects of exposing children and youth to media violence. The main idea is that if people truly understood the consequences, they would cut consumption of violent media. Although 95% of parents claim to be concerned that children are exposed to too much inappropriate content in entertainment media, only half of parents (52%) say they have *ever* used the video game ratings (Rideout, 2004). Even this may be a generous statistic. In a study of adolescents, only 31% said that their parents understand the ratings, and fewer than one in five (19%) say that their parents have ever used the ratings to keep them from getting a game (Gentile et al., 2004). There have been few publicly funded efforts to educate parents about media ratings and the need to use them. Numerous parent and child advocacy groups have attempted to provide such education, and the video game industry has made attempts to provide information about the ratings without explaining why it is important to use them. The high rate of media violence consumption demonstrates that such small, underfunded, piecemeal efforts have largely failed to influence the general population.

### *Voluntary ratings by the industries*

This has been the dominant approach in the United States for many years. Although nominally "voluntary," the ratings systems for television, films, music, and video games were in each case created only after Congress threatened the industries with government regulation. This approach has failed for several reasons. First, existing rating systems are flawed in numerous ways (Gentile et al., 2005). They are based on invalid assumptions about what is safe versus harmful for individuals of various ages; the rating criteria are frequently misapplied; the rating criteria have become more lenient over time (e.g., Thompson & Yokota, 2004); and age-based systems often encourage underage consumption. For example, in content analyses of E-rated games (purportedly fine for "Everyone"), intentional violence against game characters was rewarded or required for advancement in 60% of the games, and more importantly, there was no content descriptor to alert parents to the violent content for almost half of them, 44% (Thompson & Haninger, 2001). In a content analysis of T-rated games ("Teen"), nearly half, 48%, of the games included content that was not described on the box (Haninger & Thompson, 2004). Second, the entertainment industries frequently fail to follow their own guidelines, thereby allowing, and in many cases actively encouraging, underage consumption. For example, in a validity study of video game ratings, parents felt that under half of T-rated games, 43%, were completely appropriate for teenagers (Walsh & Gentile, 2001). Third, as shown above, parents frequently fail to understand the different rating systems (i.e., TV, video game, movie, music, etc.), how to use them, or the serious consequences of allowing one's children to be repeatedly exposed to media violence.

### *Mandatory ratings by the industries*

Governments could require the industries to provide and enforce their own ratings systems. This has never been done in the United States or anywhere else as far as we know. The 1996 Telecommunications Act required that television ratings be created, but it did not specify how or by whom. We suspect that there would be many unsolvable problems with a government-mandated, industry-controlled system. For example, conflicts between the competing interests of the government (to act in the best interests of children) and the industry (to maximize sales and profits) would be likely, with resulting First Amendment dilemmas.

### *Governmental ratings of an advisory nature*

Governments could create their own ratings system and agency, and require that all entertainment media products be rated by the government agency prior to distribution and sale. Many countries have such systems in place (e.g., Australia, the United Kingdom). However, we know of no studies of their effectiveness in reducing children's exposure to harmful materials.

### *Mandatory universal ratings provided or validated by an independent third party*

Currently, there are different ratings for television shows, movies, home video games, video games in arcades, music, Internet sites, and so forth. Because multiple ratings systems are confusing and often contradictory for parents, governments could enact legislation requiring that the entertainment industries create one universal rating system so that parents need not learn the full "alphabet soup" of different ratings systems. Furthermore, legislation could mandate that the ratings be administered independently of each medium. Currently, U.S. TV ratings are assigned by the TV networks, movie ratings are created by the Motion Picture Association of America, video game ratings are assigned by the Entertainment Software Rating Board, and so on. Legislation might also mandate that an independent ratings review board be created to conduct research on the validity of the ratings and to maintain standards. Many industry representatives have argued that a universal ratings system is not possible, and that ratings systems must be different because the various media are different (e.g., Baldwin, 2001; Lowenstein, 2001; Rosen, 2001). These claims seem very difficult to support. First, organizations like the National Institute on

Media and the Family have already created universal ratings systems and applied them successfully across media types (e.g., Walsh, Gentile, & van Brederode, 2002). Second, although TV, movies, music, and video games certainly are different in important ways, the concerns that parents have about violence, offensive language, and sexual content are similar across all types of media. There has been a great deal of research on how to create better and more effective ratings systems (Gentile et al., 2005). It appears to us that such a system could be created and that there are several good options for creating or selecting a third-party organization to oversee the system.

### *Legal-access restrictions*

Governments could (and sometimes do) restrict access to certain types of material. Government-enforced, age-based ratings and restrictions are fairly common (e.g., the United Kingdom, Australia, Canada, Germany), but are almost entirely absent in the United States. Nonetheless, this approach seems feasible in the United States for two reasons. First, the media industries concede that some media products are not appropriate for children (and give them R [movie], TV-MA [TV], or M [video games] ratings). Second, legal precedent in the United States has established that the government has an entirely appropriate role in specific instances in limiting the influences and activities to which children are exposed. For example, state and local authorities routinely restrict minors' access to tobacco, guns, pornography, and gambling. In fact, the U.S. Supreme Court, in *Ginsberg v. New York* (1968) upheld restrictions on minors' access to pornography where it was "rational for the legislature to find that the minors' exposure to [such] material *might be harmful*" (emphasis added). The media violence research conducted to date has clearly met this test, demonstrating that exposing children and youth to violent media *is* harmful (although legislatures have yet to concur with the consensus among scientific and public health organizations). It is important to note that this is not the only legal precedent under which regulating access could be legally defensible while still being sensitive to First Amendment concerns (see Saunders, 2003, for an excellent review).

At all levels of government, bills have been introduced to restrict youth access to M-rated games (e.g., Congressional House Resolution 669, see Protect Children Act of 2003; Washington House Bill 1009; Florida House Bill 663; St. Louis County Ordinance 20193; Indianapolis City Council Violent Video Games Ordinance; for more examples, go to http://www.medialegislation.org). Most have been overturned after legal challenges by the video game industry. We find it ironic that the video game industry has fought every legislative attempt to restrict the sale of M-rated games to minors as this suggests that the industry is unwilling to stand behind its own ratings. The result is that over half of fourth- through twelfth-grade boys report buying M-rated games, with almost one in four admitting that they purchased M-rated games without parental knowledge (Walsh et al., 2003).

### *Governmental restrictions on production*

Many governments (including the U.S.) have made the production of certain types of materials illegal. For example, making sexually explicit films using minors is illegal in the United States. "Snuff" films, in which people are filmed being killed, are also illegal. In a sense, such productions are illegal because the activities involved in the making of such materials are themselves illegal (sex with a minor, murder). However, further restrictions on production of entertainment materials involving otherwise legal behaviors are likely to encounter the greatest problems, given the high value most people (ourselves included) place on freedom of expression.

## CONCLUSION

There has been too little serious public policy debate concerning how best to reduce exposure of children and youth to media violence. Many of the debates that have occurred in Congress, the popular press, and conferences have often focused on *whether* there is sufficient scientific evidence of harmful effects to support public policy actions. Some debates have conflated other public policy issues with the basic scientific question of whether there are significant harmful effects. Some U.S. First Amendment proponents who are vociferous critics of media violence research do not seem to understand that the scientific question (Are there harmful effects?) is different from the legal question (Are proposed policies legal under the U.S. Constitution?).

As the medical, public health, and psychological scientific communities have repeatedly stated, the scientific debate about *whether* there are harmful effects of media violence is over. We believe that it is time to move on to the more difficult public policy questions concerning whether modern societies should take action to reduce the high rates of exposure of children and youth to media violence, and if so, what public policies would likely be the most effective.

## APPENDIX

**Table 12.1** Descriptions of Video Games Mentioned

| *Name* | *Year of Release* | *Description* |
|---|---|---|
| Death Race | 1976 | Driving simulator in which the goal is to run down as many stick-figure people as possible |
| Double Dragon | 1987 | Hand-to-hand fighting game, in which two martial arts masters must defeat the Black Warriors gang to rescue a captive woman |
| Mortal Kombat | 1992 | Hand-to-hand fighting game in which one advances by inflicting fatal damage to a series of opponents. Included blood and gore |
| Mortal Kombat II | 1993 | Hand-to-hand fighting game in which one advances by inflicting fatal damage to a series of opponents. Included blood and gore |
| Castle Wolfenstein 3D | 1992 | The first "First-Person Shooter," in which one advances by exploring a maze-like fortress while killing Nazi soldiers |
| Doom | 1993 | A First-Person Shooter game in which one advances by exploring a maze-like environment while killing monsters |
| Soldier of Fortune | 1999 | A First-Person Shooter game in which one advances by exploring an urban setting while killing terrorists and rescuing hostages. This game boasted a new level of realistic violence |
| Doom III | 2004 | A First-Person Shooter game in which one advances by exploring a maze-like environment while killing graphically realistic monsters |

For more details, see www.klov.com

## REFERENCES


Anderson, C. A. (2003). Video games and aggressive behavior. In D. Ravitch and J. P. Viteritti (Eds.), *Kid stuff: Marketing sex and violence to America's children* (pp. 143–167). Baltimore: Johns Hopkins University Press.

Anderson, C. A. (2004). An update on the effects of violent video games. *Journal of Adolescence, 27,* 133–122.

Anderson, C.A., Berkowitz, L., Donnerstein, E., Huesmann, R. L., Johnson, J., Linz, D., Malamuth, N., & Wartella, E. (2003). The influence of media violence on youth. *Psychological Science in the Public Interest, 4,* 81–110.

Anderson, C. A., & Bushman, B. J. (2001). Effects of violent video games on aggressive behavior, aggressive cognition, aggressive affect, physiological arousal, and prosocial behavior: A meta-analytic review of the scientific literature. *Psychological Science, 12,* 353–359.

Anderson, C. A., & Bushman, B. J. (2002). Human aggression. *Annual Review of Psychology, 53,* 27–51.

Anderson, C. A., Carnagey, N. L., Flanagan, M., Benjamin, A. J., Eubanks, J., & Valentine, J. C. (2004). Violent video games: Specific effects of violent content on aggressive thoughts and behavior. *Advances in Experimental Social Psychology, 36,* 199–249.

Anderson, C. A., & Dill, K. E. (2000). Video games and aggressive thoughts, feelings, and behavior in the laboratory and in life. *Journal of Personality & Social Psychology, 78,* 772–791.

Anderson, C. A., Gentile, D. A., & Buckley, K. E. (in press). *Violent video game effects on children and adolescents.* New York: Oxford University Press.

Anderson, C. A., & Huesmann, L. R. (2003). Human aggression: A social-cognitive view. In M.A. Hogg & J. Cooper (Eds.), *Handbook of Social Psychology* (pp. 296–323). London: Sage.

Austin, E. W. (1993). Exploring the effects of active parental mediation of television content. *Journal of Broadcasting & Electronic Media, 37,* 147–158.

Baldwin, W. (2001). Testimony submitted to the Committee on Governmental Affairs, United States Senate. Retrieved July 25, 2001, from http://www.senate.gov/~gov_affairs/072501_baldwin.htm

Ballard, M. E., & Weist, J. R. (1996). Mortal Kombat: The effects of violent video game play on males' hostility and cardiovascular responding. *Journal of Applied Social Psychology, 26,* 717–730.

Bensley, L., & Eenwyk, J. (2001). Video games and real-life aggression: Review of the literature. *Journal of Adolescent Health, 29,* 244–257.

Buckley, K. E., & Anderson, C. A. (in press). A theoretical model of the effects and consequences of playing video games. Chapter to appear in P. Vorderer & J. Bryant (Eds.), *Playing video games—Motives, responses, and consequences.* Mahwah, NJ: Lawrence Erlbaum.

Calvert, S. L., & Tan, S. (1994). Impact of virtual reality on young adults' physiological arousal and aggressive thoughts: Interaction versus observation. *Journal of Applied Developmental Psychology, 15,* 125–139.

Chambers, J. H., & Ascione, F. R. (1987). The effects of prosocial and aggressive video games on children's donating and helping. *Journal of Genetic Psychology, 148,* 499–505.

Crick, N. R. (1995). Relational aggression: The role of intent attributions, feelings of distress, and provocation type. *Development and Psychopathology, 7,* 313–322.

Crick, N. R. (1996). The role of overt aggression, relational aggression, and prosocial behavior in children's future social adjustment. *Child Development, 67,* 2317–2327.

Crick, N., & Dodge, K. (1994). A review and reformulation of social information-processing mechanisms in children's social adjustment. *Psychological Bulletin, 115,* 74–101.

De Lisi, R. & Wolford, J. L. (2002). Improving children's mental rotation accuracy with computer game playing. *Journal of Genetic Psychology, 163,* 272–282.

Deselms, J. L., & Altman, J. D. (2003). Immediate and prolonged effects of videogame violence. *Journal of Applied Social Psychology, 33,* 1553–1563.

Dominick, J. R. (1984). Videogames, television violence, and aggression in teenagers. *Journal of Communication, 34,* 136–147.

Dorr, A., & Rabin, B. E. (1995). Parents, children, and television. In M. Bornstein (Ed.), *Handbook of parenting: Vol. 4* (pp. 323–351). Mahwah, NJ: Lawrence Erlbaum.

Dorval, M., & Pepin, M. (1986). Effect of playing a video game on a measure of spatial visualization. *Perception and Motor Skills, 62,* 159–162.

Entertainment Software Association (2004). *Games, parents and ratings.* Available: http://www.theesa.com/pressroom.html

Federal Trade Commission (FTC). (2000). *Marketing violent entertainment to children: A review of self-regulation and industry practices in the motion picture, music recording, and electronic game industries.* Retrieved December 22, 2003, from http://www.ftc.gov/reports/violence/vioreport.pdf

Federal Trade Commission (FTC). (2001). *Marketing violent entertainment to children: A one-year follow-up review of industry practices in the motion picture, music recording, and electronic game industries.* Available http://www.ftc.gov/os/2001/12/violencereport1.pdf

Federal Trade Commission (FTC). (2004). *Marketing violent entertainment to children: A fourth follow-up review of industry practices in the motion picture, music recording, and electronic game industries.* Available: http://www.ftc.gov/os/2004/07/040708kidsviolencerpt.pdf

Fery, Y., & Ponserre, S. (2001). Enhancing the control of force in putting by video game training. *Ergonomics, 44,* 1025–1037.

Geen, R. G. (2001). *Human aggression* (2nd ed). Philadelphia: Open University Press.

Gentile, D. A. (Ed.). (2003). Media violence and children. In I. Sigel (Series Ed.), *Advances in applied developmental psychology.* Westport, CT: Praeger.

Gentile, D. A., & Anderson, C. A. (2003). Violent video games: The newest media violence hazard. In D. A. Gentile (Ed.), *Media violence and children* (pp. 131–152). Westport, CT: Praeger.

Gentile, D. A., & Gentile, J. R. (under review). Violent video games as exemplary teachers.

Gentile, D. A., Humphrey, J., & Walsh, D. A. (2005). Media ratings for movies, music, video games, & television: A review of the research and recommendations for improvements. *Adolescent Medicine Clinics, 16,* 427–446.

Gentile, D. A., Lynch, P. L., Linder, J. R., & Walsh, D. A. (2004). The effects of violent video game habits on adolescent hostility, aggressive behaviors, and school performance. *Journal of Adolescence, 27,* 5–22.

Gentile, D. A., Oberg, C., Sherwood, N. E., Story, M., Walsh, D. A., & Hogan, M. (2004). Well-child exams in the video age: Pediatricians and the AAP guidelines for children's media use. *Pediatrics, 114,* 1235–1241.

Gentile, D. A., & Sesma, A. (2003). Developmental approaches to understanding media effects on individuals. In D. A. Gentile (Ed.), *Media violence and children* (pp. 19–37). Westport, CT: Praeger.

Ginsburg v. New York, 390 U.S. 629 (1968).

Graybill, D., Kirsch, J. R., & Esselman, E. D. (1985). Effects of playing violent versus nonviolent video games on the aggressive ideation of aggressive and nonaggressive children. *Child Study Journal, 15,* 199–205.

Green, C. S., & Bavelier, D. (2003, May 29). Action video game modifies visual selective attention. *Nature, 423,* 534–537.

Greenfield, P. M., deWinstanley, P., Kilpatrick, H., & Kaye, D. (1994). Action video games and informal education: Effects on strategies for dividing visual attention. *Journal of Applied Developmental Psychology, 15,* 105–123.

Griffith, J. L., Volschin, P., Gibb, G. D., & Bailey, J. R. (1983). Differences in eye-hand motor coordination of video-game users and non-users. *Perception and Motor Skills, 57,* 155–158.

Grossman, L. (2004, August 9). The age of doom. *Time,* 82–84.

Halpin, H. (2004, September 24). *IEMA criticizes Governor Schwarzenegger* [Press Release]. Available: http://www.gameindustry.com/ih/item.asp?id=330

Haninger, K., & Thompson, K. M. (2004). Content and ratings of teen-rated video games. *Journal of the American Medical Association, 291,* 856–865.

Ihori, N., Sakamoto, A., Kobayashi, K., & Kimura, F. (2003, August). Does video game use grow children's aggressiveness? Results from a panel study. In K. Arai (Ed.), *Social contributions and responsibilities of simulation and gaming: Proceedings of the 34th Annual Conference of the International Simulation and Gaming Association.* Tokyo, Japan: Japan Association of Simulation and Gaming.

Indianapolis City Council Violent Video Games Ordinance. (2000, March). Introduced by Mayor Peterson.

Kent, S. (1997, November 25). The good of the games. Retrieved from http://zdnet.com.com/2100–11_2–505968.html

Kent, S. (2001). *The ultimate history of video games.* Roseville, CA: Prima.

Krahé, B., & Möller, I. (2004). Playing violent electronic games, hostile attributional style, and aggression-related norms in German adolescents. *Journal of Adolescence, 27,* 53–69.

Lieberman, D. A. (1997). Interactive video games for health promotion: Effects on knowledge, self-efficacy, social support, and health. In R. L. Street, W. R. Gold, & T. Manning (Eds.), *Health promotion and interactive technology: Theoretical applications and future directions* (pp. 103–120). Mahwah, NJ: Lawrence Erlbaum.

Lieberman, D. A. (2001). Management of chronic pediatric diseases with interactive health games: Theory and research findings. *Journal of Ambulatory Care Management, 24,* 26–38.

Lin, C. A., & Atkin, D. J. (1989). Parental mediation and rulemaking for adolescent use of television and VCRs. *Journal of Broadcasting & Electronic Media, 33,* 53–67.

Lowenstein, D. (2001). Testimony submitted to the Committee on Governmental Affairs, United States Senate. Retrieved July 25, 2001, from http://www.senate.gov/~gov_affairs/072501_lowenstein.htm

Murphy, R., Penuel, W., Means, B., Korbak, C., & Whaley, A. (2001). *E-DESK: A review of recent evidence on the effectiveness of discrete educational software.* Menlo Park, CA: SRI International. Retrieved May 19, 2004, from http://ctl.sri.com/publications/downloads/Task3_FinalReport3.pdf

National Research Council (1993). *Understanding and preventing violence.* Washington, DC: National Academy Press.

Okagaki, L., & Frensch, P. A. (1994). Effects of interactive entertainment technologies on development. *Journal of Applied Developmental Psychology, 15,* 33–58.

Osofsky, J. D. (1995). The effects of exposure to violence on young children. *American Psychologist, 50,* 782–788.

O'Toole, M.E. (2000). *The school shooter: A threat assessment perspective.* U.S. Department of Justice, Federal Bureau of Investigation.

Protect Children From Video Game Sex and Violence Act of 2003 (introduced by Rep. Baca, CA). H.R. 669 108th Cong. (2003).

Rideout, V. (2004). *Parents, media and public policy: A Kaiser Family Foundation survey.* Menlo Park, CA: Kaiser Family Foundation.

Rosen, H. (2001). Testimony submitted to the Committee on Governmental Affairs, United States Senate. Retrieved July 25, 2001, from http://www.senate.gov/~gov_affairs/072501_rosen.htm

Rosser, J. C. Jr., Lynch, P. J., Haskamp, L. A., Yalif, A., Gentile, D. A., & Giammaria, L. (2004, January). *Are video game players better at laparoscopic surgery?* Paper presented at the Medicine Meets Virtual Reality Conference, Newport Beach, CA.

Saunders, K. W. (2003). Regulating youth access to violent video games: Three responses to First Amendment concerns. *Michigan State DCL Law Review, 2003(3),* 51–114.

St. Louis County, MO, Ordinance Number 20193. (2000, September). *Accessibility to children of video games with violent content.*

Telecommunications Act of 1996, P. L. No. 104–104, 110 Stat. 56 (1996).

Thompson, K. M., & Haninger, K. (2001). Violence in E-rated video games. *Journal of the American Medical Association, 286,* 591–598.

Thompson, K. M., & Yokota, F. (2004, July 12). Violence, sex, and profanity in films: Correlation of movie ratings with content. *Medscape General Medicine.* Available: http://www.medscape.com/viewarticle/480900

Tsai, C. L., & Heinrichs, W. L. (1994). Acquisition of eye-hand coordination skills for videoendoscopic surgery. *Journal of the American Association of Gynecological Laparoscopy, 1*(4, part 2), S37.

U.S. Department of Health and Human Services. (2001). *Youth violence: A report of the Surgeon General.* Rockville, MD: U.S. Department of Health and Human Services, Centers for Disease Control and Prevention, National Center for Injury Prevention and Control; Substance Abuse and Mental Health Services Administration, Center for Mental Health Services; and National Institutes of Health, National Institute of Mental Health.

Walsh, D. A., & Gentile, D. A. (2001). A validity test of movie, television, and videogame ratings. *Pediatrics, 107,* 1302–1308.

Walsh, D. A., Gentile, D. A., Gieske, J., Walsh, M., & Chasco, E. (2003). *The eighth annual MediaWise video game report card.* Minneapolis, MN: National Institute on Media and the Family.

Walsh, D. A., Gentile, D. A., & van Brederode, T. M. (2002). Parents rate the ratings: A test of the validity of the American movie, television, and video game ratings. *Minerva Pediatrica, 54,* 1–11.

Washington State H.B. 1009, Chapter 365, Laws of 2003 (ESHB 1009).

Wiegman, O., & van Schie, E. G. M. (1998). Video game playing and its relations with aggressive and prosocial behavior. *British Journal of Social Psychology, 37,* 367–378.

Yuji, H. (1996). Computer games and information-processing skills. *Perception and Motor Skills, 83,* 643–647.

CHAPTER 13

# *Positive Features of Video Games*

LAURIE N. TAYLOR

The ongoing debate over violence in the media has focused recently on the danger that violent and mature-themed video games pose to children. There are valid concerns that children should not have access through video games to material like graphic depictions of sex and violence that are denied to them in other visual media such as film and television. However, the problems surrounding rating, regulating, and even banning violent video games are not easily solved. This chapter seeks to analyze the themes and concepts that underlie these games, and argues that, for many children, certain video games can be both positive and necessary.

The debate over video games and violence is based largely on the question of whether there is a negative impact on the children who play them. Many studies analyzing the effects of watching and engaging in violent acts while playing video games have yielded inconclusive or contradictory results (Anderson & Bushman, 2001; "A Calm View of Video Violence," 2003; Sherry, 2001). Empirical evidence is not the only issue in this debate. As noted in one meta-analysis of studies on violence and gaming,

> Conspicuously absent from the video game research are other designs used in the study of television violence such as longitudinal designs and field experiments. These types of research designs are more complex and expensive to undertake, so their absence may merely reflect the fact that video game research has only recently begun. However, these designs often provide the greatest ecological validity and allow researchers to make stronger predictions of social significance. (Sherry, 2001, p. 426)

Even those studies that conclusively show a negative impact (Anderson et al., 2003; Anderson & Bushman, 2001) fail to address the manner in which the violent acts in video games are contextually presented within the video games themselves and for the children that play these games. In some games, violence occurs within the game stories of survival and friendship and the violence is in self-defense (in Appendix, see *Resident Evil*, *Final Fantasy VII*, and *The Legend of Zelda*). Other games use violence as a means for conflict with guns easily exchanged for water hoses or vacuums (in Appendix, see *Super Mario Sunshine* and *Luigi's Mansion*). Violence is also defined differently in different studies:

> There is the most basic problem of how the term violence is defined by the various social scientists investigating it. Depending on how the term is explicated, a video game like Ms. Pac Man that does not depict any human or human-like figures and that does not entail the use of point-and-shoot artificial guns may be defined as violent. (Calvert, 2002, p. 25)

Further, even those researchers who have found a positive correlation between video games and arousal, or the propensity for violence, nevertheless suggest video games could be used beneficially: "[W]e wonder whether exciting video games can be created to teach and reinforce nonviolent solutions to social conflicts" (Anderson & Bushman, 2001, p. 359).

This chapter will canvass the benefits of video games, including the learning of cultural and community rules, problem and puzzle solving, strategic and critical thinking skills, alternative spatial exploration when other spaces prove unsafe, and other benefits more directly accessible through video games. Ultimately, this chapter argues that certain video games can present both positives and negatives for children, and offers suggestions about how best to balance these so that access by the children who can benefit from violent video games remains unimpeded.

## VIDEO GAME POSITIVES: THEMES AND CONCEPTS

Video games most often focus on one centralized narrative. This can be a quest narrative with the lone hero or band of heroes accomplishing multiple quests for fame, to save kingdoms, or to save themselves. This is perhaps the most common video game theme, with the next most common being games of skill (sports and racing games), or elaborate puzzle games (like blocks, matching, *Tetris,* and riddle-solving games). Using these basic themes, individual video games offer various permutations in terms of game style, explicit game narrative, and the mechanics of game play. Within these, games offer similar concepts as those found in fairy tales and other stories for children (Murray, 1998).

Elementary-age school children are often required to read books like Wilson Rawls' *Where the Red Fern Grows* or Fred Gipson's *Old Yeller* for the purpose of learning about death. Other common assignments attempt to teach children about other cultures. Video games similar to the *Final Fantasy* series do both. In *Final Fantasy VIII,* the game presents a group of orphans working together, struggling to grow into adulthood, and to make the world a better place after an apocalypse destroyed much of the world, removed their parents, and stole their memories. The game was made in Japan and the themes and concepts of the game—the idea of spirits within each part of the Earth and the apocalypse—draw on the Shinto religion and the nuclear bombings of World War II (in Appendix, see *Final Fantasy VIII*). These and other cultural aspects are threaded within a story that presents a group of children working together to help themselves and others around them. The game narrative deals with the loss of the children's parents and their ability to cope and survive while working with other children.

Similarly, other games like the violent *Resident Evil* series present narratives in which brothers and sisters work together to protect themselves from monsters and to survive in unbearable situations. This common element offers comfort by showing that the child playing is not alone and that she can succeed despite her conditions. These tales of survival in the face of adversity are often couched within violent games, like the violent bloody zombie-fighting in *Resident Evil,* mentioned above, and the tournament fights in *Street Fighter.* They also provide inspiration and comfort as narratives in other media have done for so many years (in Appendix, see *Resident Evil* and *Street Fighter*). Other games offer the option of story- or non–story-based play, like *Tony Hawk's Pro Skater,* where players can play by roaming around, and potentially falling and showing blood from falling (with the appearance of blood changing the age rating), or players can compete in simulated tournaments to become professional skaters. In each of these games, the narrative acts as a factor in the representation of violence in the game.

In addition to providing stories that both educate and comfort, certain video games also present children with heroes. While many children have access to heroes in the form of everyday people (parents, teachers, scout leaders, and coaches), other children do not. Heroes can prove extremely influential and important for children, which is part of the reason for the ongoing popularity of such comic books as *Spider-Man* and *X-Men*. Video games can present heroes that are age appropriate. Some heroes in video games come straight out of comic books, like those in *Spider-Man* (2004) and *X-Men* (2002), while others exist within more complicated worlds like those in which Jade, from *Beyond Good and Evil* (2002), exists. Jones (2001) suggests that children need both the heroes and the make-believe violence found in video games to be better able to cope and grow in their own, real lives. While violence in these games may be particularly problematic for young players, for older or more mature children and teenagers, the importance and influence of heroes may temper the effects of violence. Working with video games as cathartic or coping mechanisms, therapists have also found them to be useful in treating children's anxieties (Bertolini & Nissim, 2002). Whether or not the violence itself is useful, the heroes are, and those heroes need to be able to grow with children in order to retain their usefulness.

Video games are generally designed to present some sort of conflict through which players apply their skills, whether those are problem-solving skills or deft eye-hand coordination, to accomplish certain goals. Video games most often rely on simple scenarios of violence to implement these goals. Violence in these games exists as part of the context in which the game narrative occurs and can easily be replaced by nonviolent contexts in order to decrease overt violence in the games. In fact, games like *Super Mario Sunshine* (2002), the most recent in the Super Mario Brothers' line of games, have already replaced violence as the context for game play. In previous *Super Mario* games, two brothers would fight evil mushrooms and turtles to save innocent people from the villain Bowser. In *Super Mario Sunshine,* Mario fights graffiti with a water hose to clean a tropical island. In this and the earlier Mario games, the violence against mushrooms acts as only a means for conflict and can easily be supplanted with nonviolent concepts like cleaning graffiti.

In games that seek to be seen as explicitly nonviolent, the symbolic nature of the conflict is easily shown through the exchange of weapons for vacuums, stop watches, grappling hooks, or other items. In *The Legend of Zelda* games, the character of Link fights monsters with a sword; however, in *Pikmin* (2001), Captain Olimar avoids bugs to reassemble his spaceship with the help of the Pikmin plant creatures. Both games have heroes and monsters, and both have a means by which to fight, but the means by which the conflict is portrayed is altered. In the game *Luigi's Mansion,* it does not matter if Luigi hits an evil Boo Brother monster-ghost, or if he has to make contact by sucking the Boo Brother into the vacuum. Either way, Luigi confronts and removes the Boo Brother as a threat (even when Luigi hits the Boo Brother, there is no indication whatsoever that the Boo Brother is dead). Because video games have so frequently used violence as a lazy shorthand for game design, video games can often be changed from violent to nonviolent with the simple exchange of basic style and images.

For other games that are expressly violent, like the mature-rated *Resident Evil* series in which the player kills gruesome monsters, the violence is in self-defense and the player only kills zombies to prevent the zombies from killing the player. The whole point of the game is for the player to escape from the evil zombies. Other games like *Halo* (2001) and *Metal Gear Solid* (1998) are violent because the player must fight and kill evil characters in order to save the world. Bolter and Grusin (1999) have argued that this type of violence is prosocial because it attempts to protect the innocent and maintain society at large: "Ideologically, the player is asked to defend or reestablish the status quo, so that even though the violence of games appears to be antisocial, the ultimate message is not" (p. 93). Just as the negatives of video games cannot be weighed without an examination of their positives, the violence in video games cannot be treated independently from the stories in which that violence takes place.

Like Bolter and Grusin's argument that video game narratives use violence to reaffirm social norms, Dee (2003) argues that

> A game like Max Payne or Enter the Matrix or Grand Theft Auto may depend heavily upon simulated violence, but the object of the game is to make the story tell itself. Piling up or losing points (or dollars or blood) is relevant to the gaming experience only in that it allows you to keep the story going, to find out, if you want, what happens at the end. . . . Plot is the reward. (pp. 52–53)

Dee's remarks demonstrate how violence is used as a shorthand by which video games are designed; in addition, Dee's remarks show the importance of the story to the video game players. Most video game players play for the stories, just as children often read books and watch movies and television for their stories.

## CHARACTERISTICS OF CHILDREN'S VIDEO GAME PLAY

In order to provide meaningful guidance to lawmakers and others who regulate video games, studies of violence and video games need to address the entirety of video game play for children. As many researchers have shown, play in general for elementary school age children is a dynamic activity in which rules change and evolve rapidly (Beck & Wade, 2004; Caillois, 2001; Gee, 2003; Hughes, 1983). Because of this rapid change of rules during play, any children's game cannot easily be classed as violent or nonviolent. As applied to video games, one can see examples of this principle. Players often play normally violent games in nonviolent ways, for instance by playing tag, or by making movies within the games (this is known as "machinima"—machine animation), rather than playing within the explicitly violent narratives also provided in the games (Consalvo, 2003; Johnson, 2002). This sort of play occurs frequently because children most often play video games with other children, even if the games are made for single players (Valkenburg, 2004). Players may also play normally nonviolent games, like racing games, in violent ways by purposely trying to crash their cars into other cars instead of trying to win the races. However, many games prevent players from doing this. In racing games, such as *Crazy Taxi* (2001), players are prevented from hitting bystanders when driving cars.

Caillois (2001) devoted an entire book to exploring the changing methods of play within games. Hughes also studied how children play games, noting that the published rules of any game are often idealized and "that the 'real' rules of the game differ markedly from those commonly reported by players (and by researchers)" (1983, p. 189). By playing outside of the official rules, children can and do play violent games in nonviolent ways (Sutton-Smith, 1997). Gee (2003) also notes that well-designed video games encourage just this type of atypical play, stating, "Good games—and the games get better in this respect all the time—are crafted in ways that encourage and facilitate active and critical learning and thinking" (p. 46). By encouraging critical thinking, the best-designed video games also encourage players to attempt to change the game rules and the game systems for additional types of play. By imposing a unidimensional standard of "violent or not violent" to characterize games, researchers overlook the fact that children often do not play games by the rules. Further, the very definition of violence proves difficult when some games position players to fight with guns and others have characters fighting by taking photographs or squirting water hoses (in Appendix, see *Super Mario Sunshine*). Given the benefits of games in terms of encouraging generalized play and critical thinking, one option for regulation could be a sliding rating scale based on both the positives and negatives in the games. A sliding scale could weigh the game positives along with the game negatives to ensure that games are not simply classed as violent and therefore negative when positives may exist alongside the violence in the game.

Many games inherently include the ability to change the game play. Games like *Doom* (1993) and *Quake* (1996), which are notoriously violent, allow children to build their own play arenas, which can be and often are used to play virtual versions of hide-and-seek and tag (Johnson, 2002). While these types of play are not the first prescribed by the games, they are possible avenues of play that players can explore, even within the most violent video games available (Salen & Zimmerman, 2004, pp. 464–465). Players often collaboratively create social game rules when playing these games:

> In computer games, the rules as enforced by the game software are black-and-white: a manoeuvre is either possible or it is not; a shot either hits a defined target area or it misses. . . . Because the rules enforced by the game software itself are so clearly defined, the player is ostensibly freed from making any moral choices in the game—anything that is possible is permissible. One phenomenon observed in multiplayer gaming is the development of social rules and restraints, however, in which certain actions are considered to be unsporting or forms of cheating even though they are well within the possibilities of the game. (Morris, 2002, p. 94)

Other nonviolent or less violent games present similar options for varied play, and all of these are positive play aspects that video games provide. While offering nonviolent methods of play does not negate the violence in the games, it does show that the dynamic field of children's play cannot be fully captured by a regulation based simply on violence or nonviolence of games as a sort of closed media.

## CHANGING RULES

Just as children playing four square play by their own rules, they can play all games by modifying the existing rules for the game: "Games aren't much 'fun' when rules, rather than relationships, dominate the activity, when there is no attention to 'flow,' 'fairness,' 'respect,' and 'nice'" (Hughes, 1983, p. 197). For video games, this means that children both play the game in ways that differ from the expressed game rules, and play the game in social settings that likewise have rules. In these cases, video games provide a wealth of benefits by teaching social and community rules and standards for fairness, politeness, and decency. Video games also create shared social situations that engender helping attitudes and friendly play (Beck & Wade, 2004). Children often play video games together, and one of the common unwritten laws of video game play is that the playing child will pass the game controller on to the next child when the playing child loses during the game. While taking turns playing games, both violent and nonviolent, does not teach a child to be nonviolent, it does teach other social norms, like fairness and cooperation. This can occur during a fighting game like *Street Fighter* (1997), where two children play by fighting against each other in the game, and then when one is knocked out, another child plays against the winner. This is also the case in single-player games like the role-playing game *The Legend of Zelda*. This game—like so many video games—has only one player, so game play must be shared between many children. While the fighting may well have some negative impact on the behavior of the players, the act of sharing and navigating the spoken and unspoken norms of children's play that occurs may have other positive, socializing effects.

In cases where one child is significantly more skilled than the other children playing, the players normally impose different game rules (PBS, 2003; Burn & Carr, 2003). In addition to taking turns, the extremely skilled player might be given a maximum number of games or a time limit to make sure that all of the players receive equal play time. Other player-imposed rules are regularly used to ensure fair play that are not intrinsically present in the games (Morris, 2002). These rules make game play a social activity where the game serves as the focus of play. In addition to these social rules, most team-based games—including the incredibly violent *Doom* series—allow players to build new rooms for new challenges. Clearly, a game cannot be fair if one player already knows the puzzles and game world layout, so the game allows players to modify the game levels and worlds. In doing so, the games allow the players to build and play in collaborative spaces. These games even have chat features for player communication, providing a collaborative, communicative, and nonviolent side to these violent games (Morris, 2002). Thus, while the game itself allows violent, unfriendly play, the game is not always played in this manner. Competitive video games, from sports-inspired football or NBA games, to fighting games like *Mortal Kombat II* (1996), present friendly competition. Some of the games viewed as most intrinsically violent, like *Quake* and *Doom*, are even referred to as sports games by their players because they play them as they do sports games—with the goal to play fairly and to win, but to have a pleasant time doing so.

Hughes (1983) noted that children applied the same sort of "nice" rules, called Rooie Rules, for street games that children now use for playing video games:

> How are Rooie Rules "nice"? First, even though they are not explicitly mentioned and most of the players could not list all of them, Rooie Rules are understood to prohibit all kinds of what the kids call "rough stuff." . . . Second, Rooie Rules are "nice" because they prohibit "'rough stuff'" in a "nice" way. . . . Fairness, it seems, is an important component of "nice." (p. 192)

Fairness is a point that children seek in all aspects of video game play, including requiring the video game itself to be fair (Herdlick, 2002; Rothstein, 2002). This also means that children have different rules for different gaming situations. Video game arcades, for instance, are normally played by "arcade style" rules. Because arcade games require money for play, arcade style rules allow for play that would be considered unfair in a home video game situation—for instance, repeatedly using only one unblockable attack in a fighting game (Herdlick, 2002; Myers, 2004;). Thus, while the games themselves have varying degrees of violence, this violence is enclosed within a space of child-determined play.

In addition to teaching social rules and other unwritten rules of play, video games also teach internal rules that dictate how players can win the games themselves. Video games teach strategy, such as how to conserve resources for long winters and how to create and build resources before trying to expand. Some of these strategies are implemented within war scenarios in games like *Warcraft II* (1996) and *Lords of the Realm II* (1996). Other games like *SIMCITY* (2000), *The SIMS* (2000), and *The Oregon Trail* (2004) use the simulations themselves as the basis for the games. Certain games also lend themselves more easily to social, rather than predetermined, rules. In exploring the history of card games, Parlett (1990) notes that card games are rarely played by their official rules; instead, they are most often played by "house" rules, or rules agreed upon by the players. Parlett also notes that card games teach patience because of their structures and the manner of their play. These structures and play are then replicated in video games of card games and in video games that include card games as smaller, nonviolent subgames as with the card subgames in *Knights of the Old Republic* (2003).

Not only do children create their own rules for fairness and game play, but they also play in a manner different from the way that adults perceive their play. Schwartzman (1983) and Sherry (2001) have noted that researchers generally study adult-structured play, which is play that is extremely structured and follows preset rules, but largely neglect child-structured play, which is play that is open for change and is not dictated by preset rules. Studying games as adult-centered neglects that video game play is often collaborative, with multiple players helping each other through the game by sharing game secrets and "supermoves," and providing discussion and ideas about better ways to play and to win (Beck & Wade, 2004; Singer, 1994). Within this collaborative environment, video games teach children that different people have different skills that can all be equally useful in solving problems. Studies most often assess players in laboratory environments so that the study can collect exact data for a number of players in the same situation. While this research provides extremely valuable insights, research is also needed on video game play in a "normal" setting, which for the majority of players is playing together in groups within a family or home environment (Valkenburg, 2004). Studies of game play in these "normal" settings should assess the effects of violence and the reduction of violence when video games are played cooperatively:

> What is needed in media research is, first, a contextual view of the experiences of representative members of the audience, and, second, a critical approach that does not break the continuities of earlier research. (Alloway, 1993, p. 68)

Child-structured play incorporates all of the unwritten rules that children create for play and games. Studying children's play in an artificial environment disrupts the social rules for play such that children may rely on different social rules (Linzmayer, 1983), or they may be unsure of which social-gaming rules to use.

A complement to these unwritten rules are other codes of conduct for game play that have become "semi-official" in online multiplayer games. *Everquest* bars players from cheating in the game even when performing acts that are permissible by the game rules like "ninja looting" and "stealing kills" (Sony, 2004). Players often hold the video game to the same standards of fairness that they use for play with other children, so when video games seem to cheat, children view the game as cheating (Myers, 2004). Reeves and Nass (1996) have shown that people of all ages treat computers as other people, and consequently, cheating by the computer or video game is perceived as equal to cheating by another real player. As Huizinga (1950) has noted, cheaters and spoil-sports can both be detrimental to a game or to play in general because cheating breaks the magic circle of the fictional realm of play. Because video games are machines and repeat their actions, their "cheating behaviors" are repeated, making it appear all the more unfair.

Video games can seem to "cheat" because of technological limitations like "slow-down" and "clipping" (*Game Developer*, 2004). Slow-down occurs when there are too many elements moving at one time and the video game machine cannot process all of them properly. When slow-down occurs, one or more game elements literally slow down. Sometimes, this means that the game enemies move more slowly; other times it means that the player moves more slowly. During slow-down, the game itself can miscalculate time and movement. Thus a player can perform a move or a jump successfully, and still fail because of the game rather than an error on the player's part.

Clipping, in which video games "clip" visual elements, can cause the same sort of unfair gaming situations. Clipping causes video game images to be lost or disappear temporarily. By losing images, players can lose or be injured because the game failed to display an enemy or other obstacle. Because the games "cheat" in this manner, players must learn to control their frustration with video games, even in violent games where players must be aggressive in terms of their movement inside the game, but be quiet and calm outside the game in the act of playing (Luedtke et al., 2003).

Like other types of play and learning, many positives are available in video games; however, players can always choose not to use or accept the positives. For instance, in playing a game like *Crazy Taxi,* which is currently rated "T" for teenager players, the player cannot harm pedestrians while driving the taxi. The goal of the game is for the player to drive passengers from one place to another as quickly as possible without damaging the car, and without scaring the passenger. If the passenger is scared, he or she will leave the car and the player will not be paid. In this game, the player must learn to navigate the road systems effectively and safely in order to win. The player can simply drive around and scare passengers and attempt to hit pedestrians (which is explicitly impossible because of the game design). Playing in this manner would cause the player to lose, but it is still a possible method of play. Similarly, in the more violent *Resident Evil* (1996) game series, players must leave equipment—including guns, lighters, typewriter ribbon, and other items—for another character to use because the two characters share items in order to stay alive in the game. The player must facilitate this sharing in order to win the game, but the player can always avoid this sharing and lose the game. While players can play in ways that subvert the positives offered by video games, the themes and concepts present in the games may still reinforce positive play.

Direct positives of video games include children learning technological standards from video game play because video games are designed with those standards in mind. Further, as Reeves and Nass (1996) have shown, video games teach children normal behavior in response to technology, which includes treating the video games as "rude" when they break unwritten rules, or treating the video games as unhelpful when they present poor advice.

Many video games allow players to "mod" or modify the games, enabling players to learn computer programming from video games. By modifying existing games, players can connect to gaming communities, explore additional methods of play for a single game, and possibly learn job skills. Kushner's (2003) examination of the *Doom* game programmers shows how video games allowed underprivileged youths to succeed by programming games. Pelletier (2004) also argues that many game developers today learn game design through their love of games:

> As we know from the biographies of its leading luminaries, the games industry emerged from the bedrooms of 12 year olds programming games on rustic computers less powerful than contemporary digital alarm clocks. (para. 1)

Games often include internal editors that help players learn to alter and manipulate the games. While it is uncommon for most players to completely design video games, most children do learn some basics about technology while also learning to be more comfortable with technology (Sutton-Smith, 1986, p. 65). As the *Doom* designers illustrate, video games can present an avenue for success that would otherwise be closed to some children.

Video games as possible teachers of technology are especially important for girls and children from lower socioeconomic groups who have fewer opportunities to play and work with technology. Graner Ray (2004) stresses the need to teach girls technology and argues that video games offer one way to do so. Currently, the greater experience that boys have with technology offers later educational and career advantages. Video game play offers girls and boys the chance to experience and learn about technology in a useful and productive manner, while also *un*learning fears of technology, a pivotal point for later education. Video games teach technology and a degree of comfort with technology to many children, including girls, who have limited access to computers in their schools or homes (Beck & Wade, 2004).

## VIDEO GAMES PROVIDE A SAFE SPACE FOR PLAY

Video games offer a complement to the shrinking play spaces available to children. The changing landscape and spaces of childhood often demand new types of play for children, play that both enriches their lives and protects them from unsafe areas. Many researchers have noted that video games have the ability to present virtual spaces that can supplement real spaces. Poole (2000) states that

> Children have always made up their own "exploration games," playing, for instance, in a deserted house and imbuing it with magical qualities. Now the technological prosthesis afforded by a videogame such as Tomb Raider or Zelda 64 allows such activity to be far more complex and cognitively challenging, so that the gamer really can, in Walter Benjamin's phrase, "calmly and adventurously go traveling." (p. 164)

Similarly, researchers (Jenkins, 1998; Rivkin, 1995) have indicated that the changing landscape of childhood has moved children inside apartments instead of offering them backyards, forests, and other spaces to explore. One prevalent and potentially dangerous situation is due to the changing landscapes of neighborhood environments. While unsupervised play is dangerous, many previous generations of children felt safe playing without adult supervision in neighborhood parks and neighborhood streets with older children or with a few neighboring adults watching. With the changing urban and suburban landscapes, the majority of parents and children are no longer comfortable with this sort of unsupervised outdoor play (Jenkins, 1998; Rivkin, 1995). As children play and live in more dominantly indoor environments (Rivkin, 1995), their options for play and activity change. With the streets seen as less safe, children spend increasing amounts of time inside their homes, often alone or only with other children. As a result, video games afford, virtually, the benefits of exploration that children were offered directly in previous years.

Video games are a medium predicated on the creation and exploration of virtual spaces. They can provide free play spaces and places of wonder for children. Most games rely on conflict as the primary focal point for game play, so that the spatial exploration is punctuated with fights. Many games are designed with linear violent plots that are easily constructed (Luban & Meziane, 2001). Many games also include free-play options that extend the game's enjoyable play time and its value in terms of cost. These free-play segments are generally constructed for multiple players, or for additional play time (Salen & Zimmerman, 2004). Video games remain expensive toys for individual children. Because most games are played in the shared space of a living room connected to a television set, the free-play portions of the games are generally played and replayed frequently, especially by children who use the free-play areas as virtual play spaces (Jenkins, 1998).

Researchers (Gee, 2003; Hughes, 1983; Squire, 2002) have shown the positives associated with games and play. Analysis of earlier outdoor games is relevant to video games because, as many children are forced inside their homes for safety, video games offer the same sort of play as found in earlier street games. For indoor play, video games are the most recent entry in the history of toys that allow and encourage social play. Toys, like other forms of play, can increase or decrease sociability:

> Children who have siblings or peers in the neighborhood will, of course, be more likely to convert toy play into some form of social play. . . . Toys decrease the sociability of play. We hasten to add, however, that new toys also, in time, make a contribution to new forms of social play. (Sutton-Smith, 1986, p. 38)

Sutton-Smith (1986) notes that toys are often used to keep children occupied when parents cannot otherwise entertain or watch them. Sutton-Smith also states that, "Today, although children will still nearly always prefer playing with other children than on their own, for the greater part of their time, they are confined to playing alone" (p. 26). Video games provide a toy that children can easily share with other children in order to create a safe space for social play. For singular play, video games also allow children a space of autonomy:

> Games are typically played by a relatively powerless segment of society—younger teenagers. Nonetheless, these players find meaning in the games that lets them resist, for a rather short time, forms of social control, allowing them to form their own cultural identity. (Dominick, 2002, pp. 52–53)

When combined with game narratives and themes that include children struggling to survive and succeed, video games offer children fictionalized versions of their own experiences. In doing so, games allow children to have a sense of authority and autonomy that can build self-esteem. Certain video games offer children hours of cooperative play with siblings and friends, opportunities that are difficult to find in other indoor games, or at least for an equivalent time duration. "Video games—like many other games—are inherently social" (Gee, 2003, p. 7) because they are played within the direct social realm of play with multiple players and because they exist within a culture of play even when being played by a single player. For some children, video games may be a net positive because they provide safer opportunities for play and encourage norms of sharing and cooperation. Legislative responses need to take into account both those children for whom video games are a positive overall and those for whom they create a negative balance.

## REGULATION: BENEFITS AND DISADVANTAGES

In discussions of video game violence, video games are most often depicted as laced with violence that is seamlessly transmitted to children playing the game. However, this linear vision breaks down when the entire context of video game play—a social and active experience—is considered. Video games often have violent content, but that content is only one part of the overall play.

Describing video games as violent simplifies the problems and benefits of video games. The positives of video games and the need for those positives are omitted. Further, the division into either violent or nonviolent video games assumes that an exterior standard of violence can be applied to video games. In much the same way that children's stories often contain violence—the threat of murder from Snow White's Queen and the death of Bambi's mother, to name just two examples—video games most often present violence contextualized within the game narratives, as well as within the structure of play, as when Claire Redfield fights and kills zombies in *Resident Evil* to protect herself and her brother Chris.

Despite all the positives that video games present, video games disturbingly offer many extremely violent images. There are also an increasing number of sexually explicit games. The benefits that video games offer should be considered before any policies that regulate video game play and usage are enacted:

> The reality, despite media attention on games like Doom, may also be that the vast majority of video games are nonviolent, indicating that federal, state and local regulations restricting video games may represent, at best, legislative overkill and, at worst, politicians pandering to public opinion. (Calvert, 2002, p. 23)

For any sort of video game regulation, video games do currently offer a rating system that can serve as a guide, but this is a guide that needs further industry input and clarification. The current video game rating system is much like the movie industry rating system, but the video game system is only loosely enforced at this time. Video games are currently rated by the Entertainment Software Rating Board (ESRB), which categorizes games based on age appropriateness. Their ratings appear in Table 13.1.

If the ESRB system is used as a reference for legislating violent games, the categories effectively divide children, defined as those under 18, into four groups: those 3 and older, 6 and older, 13 and older, and those who are 17. These are somewhat useful categories because they parallel the rating system for films. However, legislation based on these categories is insufficient because the rating system lacks complexity. In fact, the current rating system is based on evaluators watching videos and then evaluating the games based on those videos instead of having the evaluators actually play the games (*Official U.S. Playstation,* 2004). Even within the rating system, the game ratings themselves are inadequate because many games have been rated for older ages based on depictions of blood and the use of profanity. This may seem logical, but a skateboarding game like *Tony Hawk* (1999) is rated "T" for Teen because of blood, comic mischief, mild lyrics, and suggestive themes. The blood is not from players fighting or beating up enemies; instead, the blood is shown when the player's character falls from

**Table 13.1** Entertainment Software Rating Board (ESRB) Rating System for Games

| | |
|---|---|
| EARLY CHILDHOOD (EC) | Titles rated EC have content that may be suitable for ages 3 and older. Contains no material that parents would find inappropriate. |
| EVERYONE (E) | Titles rated E have content that may be suitable for persons ages 6 and older. Titles in this category may contain minimal violence, some comic mischief, or mild language. |
| TEEN (T) | Titles rated T have content that may be suitable for persons ages 13 and older. May contain violent content, mild or strong language, or suggestive themes. |
| MATURE (M) | Titles rated M have content that may be suitable for persons ages 17 and older. Titles in this category may contain mature sexual themes, more intense violence, or strong language. |
| ADULTS ONLY (AO) | Titles rated AO have content suitable only for adults. Titles in this category may include graphic depictions of sex or violence. Adult Only products are not intended for persons under the age of 18. |
| RATING PENDING (RP) | Titles listed as RP have been submitted to the ESRB and are awaiting final rating. |

*Source:* ESRB, 2004.

failing to properly perform a skateboarding trick and is injured. The *Tony Hawk* games, which have repeatedly won game of the year and player's choice awards, offer countless hours and weeks of indoor play within a fun, interesting, and intelligent frame. The games also offer the heroic figure of the champion skater and loving father, *Tony Hawk*. Players can also choose to play as different characters, including female characters and characters from many different races.

Given the inherent problems in the game rating system, and the benefits offered by video games, legislative controls should not be enacted until additional data can be gathered as to the exact benefits and detriments of violent video games based on the actual experience and situation of game play. Once these studies are completed, legislative controls should only be enacted after taking into account the benefits of video game play, and only after creating a rating system that can both weigh the positives and negatives of video games in their entirety and as they are actually played.

## CONCLUSION

Children and adults play video games because they are enjoyable and rewarding (Gee, 2003). For many children, the same rewards offered by video game play are also offered in school, neighborhood play, family relationships, extracurricular activities, and other media. When a child's situation is more limited, video games may provide benefits that are not provided elsewhere. As one researcher notes,

> The potential uses of video games extends far beyond the playing of games. They could be excellent teaching devices. In playing a game, you have to learn an amazing variety of skills and knowledge. . . . You read books and study the game thoroughly, doing active problem solving and working with other people. (Gee, 2003, p. 44)

Video games can be productive teaching tools; moreover, they can provide educational and social value to children who do not otherwise have access to similar resources. This value cannot be dismissed in the debates over video games and violence. In fact, one of the more positive avenues for change and improvement exists within the game industry. As more game designers realize that their games are not suitable for all players, an increasing number are trying new possibilities for game design that either exclude violence or include violence only for educational purposes. Some of these games include violence and death in order to teach history, and others include violence to teach about disease—for instance, a player acts as a white blood cell and fights against diseases like cancer. This has therapeutic value for sick children who can feel as though they can do something to fight their ailments (Ball, 2004; Johnson, 2004). In more mainstream design, game companies like Nintendo are re-releasing classic friendly and nonviolent games while also creating innovative, nonviolent new games (see Appendix, *Super Mario Sunshine* and *Luigi's Mansion*).

Other avenues in game design include the Serious Games Initiative, the Games for Health Initiative, and the rising numbers of organized female game developers in companies like Her Interactive—all of which aim to create more inclusive and innovative games that further focus on collaboration; self-esteem; and other nonviolent, positive goals (Ray, 2004; Squire, 2002). By actually working with the industry, discussions of violence and video games could shift to include some of the more problematic issues in video games for children, like gender issues and the lack of racial diversity. Many games present women as sexualized objects instead of realistic depictions of women. Working with the industry could also help parents, teachers, and others to explore the positives that video games present. As Dewey (1963) remarked on the nature of education and learning,

> Perhaps the greatest of all pedagogical fallacies is the notion that a person learns only what he is studying at the time. Collateral learning in the way of formation of enduring attitudes . . . may be and often is more important than the spelling lesson or lesson in geography or history. . . . For these attitudes are fundamentally what count in the future. (p. 48)

Collateral learning in video games includes critical thinking, exploratory play, and many other positives that researchers are currently building on to create even more positive effects. Many researchers like Sawyer and Squire of the Serious Games Initiative are already exploring how video games can be better designed for use in improved education, physical fitness, self-esteem, and other areas. Squire (2002) in particular has studied how video games in their current form can be used to teach critical thinking, strategy, and history.

## APPENDIX

Bioware. (2003). *Knights of the Old Republic.* (XBox). San Rafael, CA: LucasArts.

*Knights of the Old Republic* is a role-playing game within the Star Wars world. Players play as Jedi Knights and develop skills while completing quests to make the universe safer. The game includes many sub-games, like card games.

Blizzard. (1996). *Warcraft II.* (PC). Irvine, CA: Author.

*Warcraft* is a real-time strategy game where players manage resources to gain territory and build colonies to control land. It is one of the founding games of the real-time strategy genre, and it relies on resource management for game play. It can be played as a single- or multiplayer game. As a multiplayer game, it is often played through networked computers and online.

Bungie Software. (2001). *Halo: Combat Evolved.* (XBox). Redmond, WA: Microsoft.

*Halo* is one of the most popular first-person shooter (FPS) games to be released in the past few years. It is generally played by two to four players on the XBox or larger groups for computerized play. Players often play by chasing each other, sometimes shooting and sometimes playing tag. *Halo* has an enormous player community and the community often experiments with different types of play. For instance, players have performed theatrical plays by each performing a role and recording that performance.

Capcom. (1996). *Resident Evil.* (Playstation). Sunnyvale, CA: Author.

The *Resident Evil* series is extremely popular. Each game focuses on several characters as they fight zombies while trying to survive. The games fixate on sibling relationships—brothers and sisters working together—and on cooperation in general to succeed in the games.

Capcom. (1997). *Street Fighter Collection.* (Playstation). Sunnyvale, CA: Author.

The *Street Fighter* games are typical fighter games in that they are played by either one player competing with the computer or by two players competing together. In single-player mode, the story for each fighter-character is told.

Digital Eclipse. (2004). *Spider-Man.* (Game Boy Advance). Santa Monica, CA: Activision.

*Spider-Man* puts the player in the role of the title character, fighting villains and solving mysteries to save New York City. This is a basic action game in that the play is based mainly around fighting villains and accomplishing difficult movement maneuvers.

Hitmaker. (2001). *Crazy Taxi.* (PS2). Glen Cove, NY: Acclaim.

*Crazy Taxi* places the player as a taxi driver who must drive fares from one location to the next as quickly and safely as possible. Extra points and money are awarded for speed and safety; however, the player can lose a fare simply by making the passenger uncomfortable with unsafe driving. The game includes multiple sub-games for learning city spaces, performing driving tricks, and so on.

id Software. (1993). *Doom.* (PC). Santa Monica, CA: Activision.

id Software. (1996). *Quake.* (PC). Santa Monica, CA: Activision.

*Doom* and *Quake* are classic FPS games (first-person shooter) and are most often played in multiplayer games. Like *Halo* and other FPS games, tournaments are regularly held at gaming arcades and players can win endorsements as cyberathletes for their skill in these games. *Doom* and *Quake* allow players to modify the game system so that they can build their own characters and their own game levels, which has led to many gaming communities that devote themselves to certain "mods," including large all-female gaming communities.

Impressions Games. (1996). *Lords of the Realm II.* Bellevue, WA: Sierra.

*Lords of the Realm* is a real-time strategy (RTS) game like *Warcraft,* but *Lords* is set in a more realistic medieval time period as compared to the more fantastic *Warcraft.* Like all RTS games, *Lords* focuses on resource management and growth, including such variables as keeping the peasant population content.

KCEJ. (1998). *Metal Gear Solid.* (PS). Los Angeles: Konami.

*Metal Gear Solid* is a stealth game where the player plays as a spy who sneaks into evil rogue military bases (normally not aligned with a country) and gathers data. Fighting is included in these games, but the player is more likely to lose with more fighting; the goal is stealth and conflict avoidance.

Learning Company. (2004). *The Oregon Trail,* 5th ed. (PC). Novato, CA: Broderbund.

*The Oregon Trail* has been around and in use in schools for years to teach students about the trail and about pioneer life. The game also teaches information about more general related topics, like what types of plants are edible, diseases that come from malnutrition, resource management, and so on.

Maxis (EA). (2000). *SIMCITY 3000 Unlimited.* (PC). Redwood City, CA: Author.

The *SIMCITY* games offer city management simulations where players must build their cities while managing resources to encourage population growth and to prevent the townspeople from being angry or unsafe. The game includes intensive resource management, planning, and strategy.

Neversoft. (1999). *Tony Hawk's Pro Skater.* (Playstation). Santa Monica, CA: Activision.

*Tony Hawk's Pro Skater* was lauded for its innovative game design where players can play missions to become competitive skateboarders, or can play to just roam around and skate in virtual skate parks.

Nintendo. (1985). *Super Mario Brothers.* (NES). Redmond, WA: Nintendo of America.

*Super Mario Brothers* is played through the character of either Mario or Luigi as they fight evil mushrooms, other plants, turtles, and fish, to save Princess Mushroom and the Mushroom Kingdom from the evil turtle Bowser. The game is mainly jumping and running. It can be won without ever attacking another character; in fact, the player cannot defeat many of the enemies and must run. The two brother characters are one of the early examples of a multiplayer environment where only one player plays the game at any given time.

Nintendo. (1987). *The Legend of Zelda.* (NES). Redmond, WA: Nintendo of America.

*The Legend of Zelda* focuses on the character of Link as he fights to save the land of Hyrule and Princess Zelda. The elfen-esque Link is helped by various wise people and by fairies in the fantasy setting while gaining new items and skills to travel to new areas.

Nintendo. (2001). *Luigi's Mansion.* (Nintendo GameCube). Redmond, WA: Nintendo of America.

*Luigi's Mansion* is played through Luigi and his friends as Luigi cleans out a house that he has won. The house is filled with ghosts and Luigi has to vacuum them up in order to clean. The game has many puzzles, including those that are visual and musical, as in one instance where the puzzle's solution requires the player to correctly play a piece of music.

Nintendo. (2001). *Pikmin.* (GameCube). Redmond, WA: Nintendo of America.

Pikmin focuses on the character of Captain Olimar, who crash lands on an alien planet and who must then work with plant creatures that he names Pikmin to repair his ship. There are several types of Pikmin—blue, red, and yellow—and they all have separate skills. Players learn to work with, and to manage, the Pikmin.

Nintendo. (2002). *Super Mario Sunshine.* (GameCube). Redmond, WA: Nintendo of America.

*Super Mario Sunshine* focuses on Mario on vacation. When Mario arrives at the tropical island, he learns that someone impersonating him has been polluting and putting graffiti on the island. Mario, in order to protect his good name, cleans the island and uncovers the secret of the missing "shines," which help protect the island and which are missing.

Probe. (1996). *Mortal Kombat II.* (Sega Saturn). Chicago: Midway.

Like *Street Fighter,* this is a fighting game that is most often played by multiple players. *Mortal Kombat* became infamous by including blood codes so that the game could display blood, and by including super-death moves where the knock-out blow was graphically illustrated.

Rockstar North. (2001). *Grand Theft Auto 3 (GTA3).* (PC, PS2). New York: Rockstar Games.

*Grand Theft Auto 3* is at the heart of the current worries over video games and violence because it presents a completely amoral world where the player plays as a criminal. The game is very violent, offers no positive moral reinforcement, and is extremely ironic in that it presents a world in which all choices are wrong. The police, pedestrians, and all members of the town are corrupt versions of normal people. Even the radio reinforces this point by mocking music, talk radio programming, and society with advertisements that highlight the absurdity of driving to a gym as well as the absurdity of single people driving oversized sport utility vehicles. It has internal racing games, taxi games, firefighting games, and more. The game's popularity was due in part to the completely mature content, a huge departure from other games in 2001, and in part to its incredibly rich game world that includes multiple spoof radio stations, complete with comedic commercials.

Square Enix. (1999). *Final Fantasy VIII.* Los Angeles: Square.

The *Final Fantasy* series is a role-playing game with a group of heroes, each with specific skills, that solve puzzles and fight monsters to save the world. The heroes are all young adults, and they are all orphans, who fight to protect each other, their only loved ones. The game has internal racing and card games.

Ubisoft. (2002). *Beyond Good and Evil.* (GameCube). San Francisco: Author.

*Beyond Good and Evil* focuses on Jade, who investigates an alien invasion, winning points by taking photographs and notes. Jade also works with team members to fight the aliens. Internal card games are included.

## REFERENCES

Alloway, L. (1993). *Violent America: The movies 1946–1964.* Greenwich, CT: Museum of Modern Art.

Anderson, C. A., Berkowitz, L., Donnerstein, E., Huesmann, L. R., Johnson, J. D., Linz, D., et al. (2003). The influence of media violence on youth. *Psychological Science in the Public Interest,* 4(3), 81–110.

Anderson, C. A., & Bushman, B. J. (2001). Effects of violent video games on aggressive behavior, aggressive cognition, aggressive affect, physiological arousal, and prosocial behavior: A meta-analytic review of the scientific literature. *Psychological Science, 12*(5), 353–359.

Ball, J. (2004, June 28). Boy inspires cancer video game. *BBC News*. Retrieved October 6, 2004, from http://news.bbc.co.uk/2/hi/technology/3839091.stm

Beck, J. C., & Wade, M. (2004). *Got game: How the gamer generation is reshaping business forever*. Boston: Harvard Business School Press.

Bertolini, R., & Nissim, S. (2002). Video games and children's imagination. *Journal of Child Psychotherapy, 28*(3), 305–325.

Bolter, J. D., & Grusin, R. (1999). *Remediation: Understanding new media*. Cambridge, MA: MIT Press.

Burn, A., & Carr, D. (2003). Signs from a strange planet: Role play and social: performance in Anarchy Online. *COSIGN Conference Proceedings* (pp. 14–21). University of Teesside, Middlesbrough, UK: School of Computing.

Caillois, R. (2001). *Man, play and games* (M. Barash, Trans.). Urbana, IL: University of Chicago Press.

A calm view of video violence [Editorial]. (2003, July 24). *Nature, 424*, 355.

Calvert, C. (2002). Violence, video games, and a voice of reason: Judge Posner to the defense of kids' culture and the First Amendment. *The San Diego Law Review, 39*(1), 1–30.

Capizzano, J., Tout, K., & Adams, G. (2000). *Child care patterns of school-age children with employed mothers*. Urbana Institute. Retrieved December 12, 2003, from http://www.urban.org/url.cfm?ID=310283

Consalvo, M. (2003). Zelda 64 and video game fans: A walkthrough of games, intertextuality, and narrative. *Television and New Media, 4*(3), 321–334.

Dee, J. (2003, December 21). Playing mogul. *The New York Times Magazine*, pp. 36–41, 52–53, 66–68.

Dewey, J. (1963). Experience and education. *The Kappa Delta Pi Lectures*. London: Collier Books.

Dominick, J. R. (2002). *The dynamics of mass communication: Media in the digital age* (7th ed.). New York: McGraw-Hill.

Entertainment Software Rating Board. *ESRB game ratings–Game ratings and descriptor guide*. Entertainment Software Rating Board Web site. Retrieved October 1, 2004, from http://www.esrb.org/esrbratings_guide.asp

Game Developer. (2004). *Dictionary*. Game Developer Network. Retrieved December 12, 2004, from http://www.gamedev.net/dict/search.asp

Gee, J. P. (2003). *What video games have to teach us about learning and literacy*. New York: Palgrave Macmillan.

Herdlick, C. (2002). *The projected playscape: Enabling new play scenarios with computer vision and non-structured rule sets*. Unpublished master's thesis, Parsons School of Design, New York.

Hughes, L. A. (1983). Beyond the rules of the game: Why are rooie rules nice? In F. E. Manning (Ed.), *World of play: Proceedings of the 7th Annual Meeting of the Association of the Anthropological Study of Play* (pp. 188–199). West Point, NY: Leisure Press.

Huizinga, J. (1950). *Homo ludens: A study of the play element in culture*. Boston: Beacon Press.

Jenkins, H. (1998). "Complete freedom of movement:" Video games as gendered play spaces. In J. Cassell & H. Jenkins (Eds.), *From Barbie to Mortal Kombat: Gender and computer games* (pp. 262–297). Cambridge, MA: MIT Press.

Johnson, L. (2004, Dec. 9). Video games better than tranquilizers at keeping children calm before surgery, study finds. *San Francisco Chronicle.* Retrieved December 10, 2004, from http://sfgate.com/cgi-bin/article.cgi?f=/news/a/2004/12/09/nationa11316EST0597.DTL

Johnson, S. (2002, May 24). Review of Wreckless: The Yakuza missions. NetJak Old School. Retrieved October 1, 2004, from http://www.netjak.com/review.php/40

Jones, G. (2001). *Killing monsters: Why children need fantasy, super heroes, and make-believe violence.* New York: Basic Books.

Kushner, D. (2003). *Masters of Doom: How two guys created an empire and transformed pop culture.* New York: Random House.

Linzmayer, O. (1983). The ultimate coin-op arcade machine. *Creative Computing Video & Arcade Games, 1*(1), 26.

Luban, P., & Meziane, J. (2001). *Turning a linear story into a game: The missing link between fiction and interactive entertainment.* Gamasutra. Retrieved December 12, 2004, from http://www.gamasutra.com/features/20010615/luban_01.shtml

Luedtke, J., Harwood, C., Matlock, A., Fernando, M., Keene, C., Oracheski, R., et al. (2003, Feb. 24). *Editors' roundtable.* Gaming World X. Retrieved October 6, 2004, from http://www.gamingworldx.com/features/EditorsRoundtable22403.shtml

Morris, S. (2002). First-person shooters—A game apparatus. In G. King & T. Krzywinska (Eds.), *Screenplay: Cinema/videogames/interfaces* (pp. 81–97). London: Wallflower Press.

Murray, J. (1998). *Hamlet on the holodeck: The future of narrative in cyberspace.* Cambridge: MIT Press.

Myers, D. (2004). The anti-poetic: Interactivity, immersion, and other semiotic functions of digital play. *COSIGN Conference Proceedings.* Split, Croatia: University of Split.

OK to Play? E-M? (2004, August). *Official U.S. Playstation Magazine, 83,* 66.

Parlett, D. (1990). *Oxford guide to card games.* Oxford: Oxford University Press.

PBS. (2003). *PBS parents guide to children and media: Video games, grade schoolers.* PBS Web site. Retrieved Oct. 9, 2004, from http://www.pbs.org/parents/issuesadvice/childrenandmedia/videogames-grade.html

Pelletier, C. (July 2004). *What scope is there for game researchers, developers and players to collaborate in making games?* IGDA Ivory Tower. Retrieved July 1, 2004, from http://www.igda.org/columns/ivorytower/

Poole, S. (2000). New York: Arcade.

Ray, S. G. (2004). *Gender inclusive game design: Expanding the market.* Hingham, MA: Charles River Media.

Reeves, B., & Nass, C. (1996). *The media equation: How people treat computers, television and new media like real people and places.* New York: Cambridge University Press.

Rivkin, M. S. (1995). *The great outdoors: Restoring children's right to play outside.* Washington, DC: National Association for the Education of Young Children.

Rothstein, E. (2002, April 6). Realism may be taking the fun out of games. *New York Times,* p. B7.

Salen, K., & Zimmerman, E. (2004). *Rules of play: Game design fundamentals.* Cambridge, MA: MIT Press.

Schwartzman, H. B. (1983). Child-Structured play. In F. E. Manning (Ed.), *World of play: Proceedings of the 7th Annual Meeting of the Association of the Anthropological Study of Play* (pp. 200–214). West Point, NY: Leisure Press.

Sherry, J. L. (2001). The effects of violent video games on aggression: A meta-analysis. *Human Communication Research, 27*(3), 409–431.

Singer, J. (1994). The scientific foundations of play therapy. In J. Hellendoorn, R. van der Kooij, & B. Sutton-Smith (Eds.), *Play and intervention* (pp. 27–38). Albany: State University of New York Press.

Sony Computer Entertainment America. (2004). *Everquest rules of conduct.* Everquest Live Online. Retrieved Oct. 7, 2004, from http://eqlive.station.sony.com/support/customer_service/cs_rules_of_conduct.jsp

Squire, K. (2002). Cultural framing of computer/video games. *Game Studies: The International Journal of Computer Game Research, 2*(1). Retrieved July 1, 2004, from http://www.gamestudies.org/0102/squire/

Sutton-Smith, B. (1986). *Toys as culture.* New York: Gardner Press.

Sutton-Smith, B. (1997). *The ambiguity of play.* Cambridge, MA: Harvard University Press.

Valkenburg, M. (2004). *Children's responses to the screen: A media psychological approach.* Mahwah, NJ: Lawrence Erlbaum.

CHAPTER 14

# *Children, Adolescents, and the Culture of Online Hate*

BRENDESHA TYNES

As hate groups have proliferated in the United States over the last decade, there has been a corresponding increase in the number of online environments where their adherents congregate. Scholars have argued that a "virtual culture" of racism is now forming as a result (Back, 2002; Zickmund, 1997). While most members of such groups are adults, the widespread adoption of computer technology by children and teens has made it easier for hate groups to reach out to young people. Recent surveys suggest that some 97% of children and adolescents in the United States have Internet access (Center for the Digital Future, 2004). Nearly three-quarters of these youth use the Internet as an information source in doing their schoolwork (Lenhart, Simon, & Graziano, 2001). While parents may be pleased that their children are finding help with mathematics, science, or social studies, evidence is mounting that some are studying a new online subject: hate.

Hate groups and racist individuals carefully construct their online sales pitches to appeal to youth, using multimedia and other persuasive tactics (McDonald, 1999). In some research, children are portrayed as passive victims who might stumble upon online hate while doing homework or surfing the Internet (Perry, 2000). But the exposure of children to online hate sites run by adults is only part of the problem. Children are also becoming perpetrators. Recent news articles and studies have shown that children and adolescents are increasingly involved in online hate speech (Gerstenfeld, Grant, & Chiang, 2003; Greenfield, 2000; McKelvey, 2001; Tynes, Reynolds, & Greenfield, 2004). Acting both alone and in conjunction with peers or family members, children as young as 11—and perhaps younger—are active agents in the creation of hate materials and the use of deprecating speech online. Encouraged by the interactivity and anonymity of cyberspace, children and adolescents from around the world can lead their own personal hate movements, all in the privacy of their homes.

The potential impact on children is worrisome at several levels. First, hate speech can directly hurt youngsters who are members of the target groups when they encounter this material online. Second, by making their messages attractive to children and adolescents, hate groups are able to recruit, teach, and maintain alliances with youth, swelling the ranks of potential supporters and members. And finally, there is the possibility that hate speech online may directly incite or otherwise enable youth to commit violent acts offline. Perhaps the best-known example is the Columbine school massacre of 1999, where the young killers used the Internet to learn how to make pipe bombs, to plan their strategy (using an online video game), and to post online threats to their classmates (Biegel, 1999; Greenfield & Juvonen, 1999). One of the perpetrators, Eric Harris, also used the Internet to communicate with others who shared his admiration for Hitler's philosophy.

This chapter begins by describing the global environment of online hate and the computer tools used to disseminate hate materials, especially to children and adolescents. Discourse strategies used by both adults and children to recruit, socialize with, and persuade others within the online hate movement and derogate targets outside are analyzed. Next, the chapter briefly discusses why some children rather than others participate in online hate and the risk factors for involvement. The final sections look at the potential impact of these discourses on young people and suggest policy implications.

## METHODOLOGY

The analysis in this chapter draws on literature from various disciplines dealing with racist and anti-Semitic online hate. A search was conducted of major online social science databases, including PsycINFO, JSTOR, ISI Web of Science, Linguistics and Language Behavior Abstracts, Sociological Abstracts, and Communication Abstracts. Keywords used in the search were "online hate and racism," "Internet and racism," "Internet and anti-Semitism," and "children, Internet and racism." A search of major composition journals was also conducted using the same keywords. Articles resulting from each of these searches were gathered and their reference lists were used to find other studies. This chapter includes both examples drawn from the studies reviewed and examples retrieved directly from online sites.

Because the literature has focused primarily on adults, selected Web sites, discussion boards, and chat rooms geared toward youth were also monitored and used to provide examples of hate speech, both targeting young people and carried out by them. Three discussion boards were chosen: the racism board of the online version of a widely distributed teen magazine, and two extremist discussion boards linked to the Resistance Youth and Panzerfaust Web sites. Also examined was Stormfront.org for Kids, the youth section of the extremist Stormfront Web site. Mainstream teen-monitored chat rooms on a popular paid service were followed as well. Monitored chat rooms have a trained adult host that intermittently monitors the room and electronically "evicts" participants who violate chat rules, while unmonitored chat rooms have no monitors and no such rules. These sites provide a window into the range of spaces where online hate is present, including monitored forums, as well as those directed to extremists and the general public.

Each example of hate speech is transcribed here just as it was written by the perpetrator. The language is extreme and includes racially degrading terms. In presenting these examples, no attempt has been made to omit or modify offensive words, as mitigating the language could "convey unwittingly that the material is less extreme, both politically and morally, than it actually is" (Billig, 2001, p. 272). Misspellings and other errors in the originals have been retained as well.

## THE GLOBAL ENVIRONMENT OF ONLINE HATE

Online hate, also known as cyber racism (Back, 2002), includes hate speech and so-called persuasive rhetoric. There is no generally agreed-upon definition of hate speech, but many scholars refer to Matsuda (1993), who defines it as "speech that has a message of racial inferiority; is directed against a member of an historically oppressed group; and is persecutory, hateful, and degrading" (Boeckmann & Turpin-Petrosino, 2002, p. 209). Online hate speech may appear in the form of text, music, online radio broadcasts, or visual images that directly or indirectly exhort users to act against target groups (Thiesmeyer, 1999). While most hate speech is protected under the First Amendment, speech may rise to the level of hate crime when it creates clear danger of imminent lawless action and when it constitutes "fighting words" or defamation (Leets, 2001).

Online hate speech simultaneously targets two different audiences: on one hand, potential members and adherents of hate groups; and on the other hand, the targets of the hatred, usually minorities. While the Internet is used to promote all types of bigotry, this chapter focuses on racism and anti-Semitism disseminated by White racialists. The term White racialist refers broadly to groups or individuals who subscribe to ideologies of White racial superiority. The literature uses various terms to describe this population, including far-right extremists, White nationalists, White supremacists, and White racists. When discussing a specific author's research, this chapter uses the term chosen by the researcher. Racism and anti-Semitism underlie most of the hate crimes White racialist groups commit offline; accordingly, the focus here is on parallel online phenomena.

A number of sociologists and criminologists have conducted content and social network analyses in an attempt to document the nature and extent of online hate (Donelan, 2004; Gerstenfeld, Grant, & Chiang, 2003; Mann, Sutton, & Tuffin, 2003). Their findings indicate that the online hate movement is promoted by a loose global network of racist organizations that use Web sites, along with discussion boards, chat rooms, and other interactive media, to create an online presence. This network appears to be growing, both offline and on. The Southern Poverty Law Center (2004a, 2004b) reported a resurgence in hate group activity in 2003, with several racist groups more than doubling their number of chapters from the year before. The organization's *Intelligence Report* (2004b) listed 497 hate Web sites based in the United States alone that year, a 12% increase over 2002. While it is impossible to get a definitive count of the sites that exist, some estimates are well into the thousands.

A handful of prominent hate groups have played key roles in setting the ideological tone for the movement (Anti-Defamation League 2001a; Gerstenfeld et al., 2003; Southern Poverty Law Center 2004a, 2004b). They include the Ku Klux Klan; Skinheads; and neo-Nazi groups such as Aryan Nations, Christian Identity, and Holocaust Denial. The Ku Klux Klan is one of the oldest hate organizations, founded in 1865 by veterans of the Confederate Army. The organization has died out and reemerged a number of times but its ideology of White superiority over other races has remained constant. The organization now has a number of different factions throughout the United States. Skinheads, with roots in Britain, and neo-Nazi groups share a belief in Hitler's anti-Semitic, racist philosophy. Skinheads, however, often have a younger membership and advocate violence more vehemently than most groups (Gerstenfeld et al., 2003). Christian Identity groups believe that Anglo Saxons are the true Jews of the Bible, that the Jews of today are descendants of Satan, and that all other minorities are inferior "mud people" (Anti-Defamation League, 2001a).

There are hundreds of different branches and chapters of these organizations and similar ones in the United States, with corresponding Web sites (Southern Poverty Law Center, 2004b). Membership in the groups is fluid, with people moving in and out and often maintaining affiliations with several groups simultaneously (Perry, 2000). These complex linkages are also present online. Gerstenfeld, Grant, and Chiang's (2003) content analysis of 157 online hate sites showed that more than 80% of the sites had external links to other hate sites. No one group dominates the cyber world of hate. In a social network analysis of 80 White supremacist organizations with a presence on the Internet, Burris, Smith, and Strahm (2000) found that the online movement is decentralized, with multiple centers of influence.

There is little evident division between groups along doctrinal lines. Though they may differ in their practices and national visibility, the groups share a common goal that might be broadly described as ridding the world of "cultural pollution" (Perry, 1999). This pollution is defined differently by different groups, but it is most often equated with racial, ethnic, and religious minorities, with most groups espousing an anti-Semitic and White supremacist platform (Perry, 2000). Burris et al. (2000) confirm that strong links have been forged between organizations and suggest that ideologies are merging, with many groups undergoing "Nazification" or adopting neo-Nazi ideologies. Other researchers have argued that Christian Identity beliefs are increasingly shared among groups (Sharpe, 2000). In many cases, boundaries between groups are no longer sharply defined.

Recently, hate group activities offline have become increasingly mainstream. Louis Beam's essay *Leaderless Resistance* (1992) encourages White racialists to infiltrate mainstream institutions. Beam also suggests in this essay that White racialist groups become more decentralized, and that members wear less conspicuous dress so that they will not be easily identifiable. This melding into the fabric of society occurs even more seamlessly on the Internet.

While organized hate groups and their adherents may account for a significant proportion of those involved in online hate, a person does not have to be affiliated with any group to espouse hateful ideologies and commit racist acts online. One only needs access to the electronic tools often used to spread hate.

### *Tools of Online Hate*

Web sites, e-mail, chat rooms, multiuser domains (MUDs), discussion boards, music, video games, audiotapes and videotapes, games, and literature are some of the most common tools used to disseminate online hate (Donelan, 2004; Gerstenfeld et al., 2003; McDonald, 1999; Schafer, 2002). Most of these are widely known; however, chat rooms, MUDs, and discussion boards may be less familiar to some readers and therefore require some explanation.

Chat rooms directly link the senders and recipients of text messages. Participants engage in what is called synchronous communication, in which comments of all participants may be viewed in real time. This differentiates chat rooms from e-mail exchanges, where messages can languish for hours or days before being read. Users may enter a goal-oriented chat room, where the discussion centers around one topic, or an open-topic chat room, where the discussion is freewheeling. In either case, they partake in the online equivalent of a dinner party conversation with one or hundreds of friends—or strangers—at once. The language produced forms a multidimensional text that juxtaposes dissimilar lines of conversation.

These various dialogues float toward the top of the screen and then off at a speed that depends on the number of people in the chat room and how fast they type.

Multiuser domains are similar to chat rooms, but they often allow users to create graphic representations or "avatars" of themselves. Participants communicate with one another through a virtual body graphically represented on the screen, which may take the form of a human or, in some cases, an animal or monster.

Discussion boards are a type of conferencing system used to discuss a wide range of topics in an asynchronous format. Like e-mail messages, discussion board messages may be read and responded to in a matter of seconds, hours, or months. An important distinction between e-mail and discussion boards, however, is that e-mail is a "push" medium—messages can be sent to people who have not solicited them. In contrast, discussion boards is a "pull" medium—people must select groups and messages they want to read and actively request them (Smith & Kollock, 1999). The participant who engages in discussion boards has sought out others who are interested in the same issues (e.g., a teen health bulletin board; see Suzuki & Calzo, 2004). Unlike many chat rooms that are open-topic, most discussion boards are created to discuss specific subject areas. Posted messages and their responses are clearly demarcated by topic in what is known as a thread.

Chat rooms and discussion boards are key tools in the dissemination of online hate. They are often linked to Web sites. Schafer's (2002) content analysis of 132 extremist Web sites found that 18.2% of the sample offered either a discussion board or chatroom to the site's visitors. These tools allow for interactivity in ways that other materials may not and help to facilitate the formation of a global "community." While some of these online spaces are created specifically for hate group members and have strict guidelines for entry and participation, the bulk of online forums where hate speech takes place are open to the general public. One of the earliest types of discussion boards, Usenet newsgroups, still serves as a space for the recruitment of new members, dissemination of racist materials, and bullying of target groups (Mann, Sutton, & Tuffin, 2003). In addition to maintaining these targeted online spaces, White racialists have developed a strategy of infiltrating mainstream chat rooms and discussion boards (Whine, 1999).

## HOW HATE SITES TARGET CHILDREN

Hate groups use a number of strategies to reach out to young people online. First, they create Web pages that are specifically geared to children and teens. Of the 157 extremist sites examined by Gerstenfeld et al. (2003), 7% had children's pages. On these pages, ideas may be worded in ways that are easily understood by a younger audience. They may even feature messages by youth, directed to other youth. For example, on Stormfront.org for Kids, the children's section of the Stormfront Web site, the creator of the page, 15-year-old Derek Black, introduces himself:

> Hello, welcome to my site, I can see by the fact that you have visited my page that you are interested in the subject of race. I will start by introducing myself, my name is Derek. I am fifteen years old and I am the webmaster of kids.stormfront.org. I used to be in public school, it is a shame how many White minds are wasted in that system. I am now in home school. I am no longer attacked by gangs of non-whites and I spend most of my day learning, instead of tutoring the slowest kids in my class. In addition to my schoolwork, I am also learning pride in myself, my family and my people. (www.kids.stormfront.org)

Web pages may also be organized in such a way as to appear legitimate to a younger audience. Site creators often invite children and adolescents to use the information to complete homework assignments. Further along on the Stormfront.org for Kids site, Derek asks, "Need to do a school report of M.L.King? Visit this website for all your needs: www.martinlutherking.org." The viewer is then redirected to the site and can click on a number of links, including one that reads, "The truth about Martin Luther King." Those who go there encounter a myriad of disparaging articles, speeches, and "facts" about this historical figure. Since children and adolescents are generally less able than adults to differentiate between truth and fiction online, hate messages masquerading as facts may be interpreted as truth.

In addition to creating sections of Web sites geared toward youth, hate groups use multimedia, including video games, regular games, and music, to appeal to young audiences (Gerstenfeld et al., 2003). For example, sites may allow viewers to order the video game *Ethnic Cleansing.* A promotion for the game reads,

> The Race War has begun. Your skin is your uniform in this battle for the survival of your kind. The White Race depends on you to secure its existence. Your peoples enemies surround you in a sea of decay and filth that they have brought to your once clean and White nation. Not one of their numbers shall be spared. (Gerstenfeld et al., 2003, p. 39)

White power and "Oi" music, a sub-genre of punk rock created by working-class British youth in the 1980s, often convey a similar message. For example, a song called "Aryan Rage" calls on all White men to get off the fence because "it's time to kick some ass, pulverize the niggers, trash the fuckin fags. Grab yourself a club and beat down a lousy Jew" ("William Pierce," 2000). One researcher suggests that listening to Oi music is the single greatest predictor of racist beliefs and violent behavior in hate group members (Hamm, 1999).

Children may also access entire works of racist literature through Web sites. One of the most commonly encountered is *The Turner Diaries: A Novel,* written by William Pierce under the pseudonym Andrew Macdonald (1980). Considered the bible for many White racialists, this fictional account features a race war, the overthrow of the U.S. government, and the establishment of an Aryan world (Leets, 2002). A copy of the book was found in Timothy McVeigh's car after the Oklahoma City bombing, and it is widely believed that he drew inspiration from its message. Downloaded from the Web, the novel may effectively provide blueprints for violence for young people, who need not be members of an organized hate group to retrieve this information, but need only a computer with Internet access.

Another way that hate groups ensnare children is by giving Web sites ambiguous titles, so that they are easily mistaken for more innocuous sites. Children can unknowingly stumble upon these sites while searching for information online. A high school student researching weather systems, for example, might access www.stormfront.org (Perry, 2000). In search engines like Google, all sites resulting from online searches appear one after the other and often for several pages. Hate sites compete with credible sources of information for the browser's attention. As hate sites continue to proliferate, it will likely become increasingly difficult to distinguish them from other more reputable cites.

White racialists also use a number of "foot-in-the-door" techniques to get the attention of young browsers. McDonald's (1999) content analysis of 30 racist/White nationalist sites revealed five such techniques, including warnings, disclaimers, objectives/ purposes, social approaches, and more sophisticated counterargument strategies. Twenty percent of the sample warned of the offensive content on the site, using language such as "Warning! This site contains white nationalist views. If you do not have an open mind, do not enter." Such announcements serve a dual purpose: warning casual browsers, but also enticing them to read further. Thirty-seven percent of McDonald's sample attracted attention by stating the group's objectives, standards, values, credo, or manifesto. Many others used a "social approach," adding jokes, quotes, prayers, symbols, photos, or cartoons to appeal to viewers' emotions. The most prevalent strategies in the sample, however, were the objective approach and counterargument strategies. Sites using an "objective" approach stated their views neutrally, free of overtly derisory comments, in an effort to appear rational. Those using the counterargument strategy attempted to change potential constituents' views about White nationalism and racism by explicitly countering mainstream conceptions of their group, often using poems, sayings, or historical facts as "moderating symbols."

## DISCOURSE STRATEGIES AND MECHANISMS FOR EXPRESSING ONLINE HATE

The computer technologies used to teach hate are in themselves neutral. Their negative power comes from discourse whose overarching goal is to establish the racial supremacy, superiority, separation, and preservation of an in-group and the racial "otherness" of one or more out-groups (Back, 2002; Back, Keith, & Solomos, 1998). This is accomplished with a repertoire of discourse strategies that fall into two broad categories: hate speech and persuasive rhetoric.

Hate speech includes verbal harassment and intimidation; displaying of racist symbols such as swastikas; expressive action, such as cross-burning; conveying an intention to discriminate or incitement to discriminate; fighting words, threats, and incitement to violence; and epithets or group libel (Goldschmid, 2001). The most common forms occurring online include threats, epithets, and an additional form gleaned from Internet research—*cybertyping,* or online stereotyping. Persuasive rhetoric includes such tactics as moral appeals, historical revisionism, and humor. All these forms of discourse may be found in any of the previously described online modes of communication. However, overtly racist hate speech is more likely to be encountered in music, videos, discussion boards, and chat rooms, while persuasive rhetoric is more likely to be seen on Web pages. As will become clear, the same strategies are used to communicate with both adults and youth.

### *Hate Speech*

The presence of hate speech on the Internet is a burgeoning topic of study, engaging scholars in fields as diverse as law, communications, and psychology. Legal scholars have been by far the greatest contributors, with much of their work focused on which types of speech are liable and which enjoy constitutional protection, and the legal establishment of harm. The less extensive contributions from the social sciences focus primarily on White racialists and their use of hate speech online (Sharpe, 2000; Whine, 1999; Zickmund, 1997), or measuring the harm hate speech inflicts (Lee & Leets, 2002).

Sharpe's (2000) qualitative analysis of the Christian Identity movement's print and Internet materials details how hate speech is used to establish the beliefs, doctrines, and practices of this group. Blacks are referred to as "talking apes" or "talking beasts." Anti-Semitism, however, is the most powerful theme in the Christian Identity doctrine. The

Kingdom Identity Ministries Doctrinal Statement of Beliefs proclaims the following: "We believe in an existing being known as the Devil or Satan and called the Serpent (Gen. 3:1; Rev. 12:9), who has the literal seed or posterity in the earth (Gen. 3:15) commonly called Jews today (Rev. 2:9, 3:9; Isa. 65;15). . . . The ultimate end of this evil race whose hands bear the blood of our Savior (Matt. 27:25) and all the righteous slain upon the earth (Matt. 23:35), is Divine judgment (Matt. 13:38–42, 15:13; Zech. 14:21)" (quoted in Sharpe, 2000, p. 611; also see the Kingdom Identity Ministries Web site). Adherents to this doctrine cite these principles as divine justification for acts of violence against Jews and people of color. Those who commit these acts, specifically murder, are considered heroes of the faith, honored for their deeds (Blazak, 2001; Sharpe, 2000).

In much of the White racialist discourse online, notably the Usenet discussion board alt.politics.white-power, minorities are portrayed as a cultural disease or social contaminant. These sites typically depict African Americans as savages and subhuman destroyers of cities, the "counter-image" of civilized, productive society (Zickmund, 1997, p. 193). Jews, on the other hand, often are purported to be conspiring to take over the world.

These themes that are so prevalent on adult hate sites are increasingly surfacing in youth chat rooms and discussion boards. In the excerpt below from the Panzerfaust discussion board for teens, a youth expresses his disdain for "wiggers" (combination of the words white and nigger) who may date interracially and listen to hip-hop music. Using the screen name Onewiggerhater88, he explicitly calls Black people racially inferior in his rant, using epithets such as "smelly," "buck nigger," and "monkeys." He claims that hip-hop music has changed the dating patterns of White females and predicts that if the pattern persists, the racially superior White man will be "bred out of existence."

> Was I absent from school the day the teacher told everyone its okay to go and fuck a smelly nigger? That shit is the worst thing a girl can do, its the lowest life thing in the world, worse than bestiality, which is really what it is: an extreme form of bestiality. All because of this lame, illiterate, non-musical, hip hop shit. How is a buck nigger talking fast about his automatic weapons and his "hennessey" and weed such a powerful phenomenon that it changes the breeding habits of an entire race of females, and makes them breed with the racially inferior? . . . The nigger of course, is trying to genetically better himself, no matter how it justifies it. Also, how come if they hate whitey so much, they will only fuck white women? Charles Darwin would be as perplexed as I am. . . . I am so sick of all this shit. Know this, it will only get worse. This shit has been building up since 1986, when those sell outs Aerosmith made that fucking video with RunDmc of "Walk This Way . . . the NIGGERS [WILL] CONTINUE TO BREED THE WHITE MAN OUT OF EXISTENCE WITH THEIR FUCKING HIP HOP RAP SHIT, they will only grow in number. These monkeys are incapable of advancing to a higher level of expression. Rap is here to stay. When I look at white kids, in the FIRST GRADE wearing this hip hop "gear," I see where it is going. It is getting stronger and stronger and reaching deeper and deeper. The gene pool is moving towards this shit. The wiggers are getting younger and younger. This did not happen with any other cultural trend, like disco, or new wave, or flower power. I fear that this shit will only continue to grow, WHILE WE GET BRED OUT OF EXISTENCE. (www.panzerfaust.com/forum)

This teen's message parallels those espoused in adult discussion boards. Like adult White racialists, he asserts that the out-group is innately inferior. However, his message is tailored toward his peer group. Hip-hop music is a global phenomenon, with over 75% of its album sales to White suburban youth (Reese, 1998). Onewiggerhater88 links its popularity to the disintegration of society and argues that the White people who sympathize with Blacks and adopt cultural styles that might be considered Black are getting younger and younger. He is, in a sense, calling youth to arms, warning that Black cultural practices and race-mixing have the potential to strip White youth of their White identities.

His message can be categorized as *flaming*—hostile, aggressive online language characterized by profanity, obscenity, and insults. Flaming is often seen on discussion boards and is a central mechanism through which hate speech is spread. White racialists may flame among themselves or go into mainstream discussion boards and start flame wars. Other aggressive tactics developed to harass out-groups include the "mail bomb," an e-mail sent to one or many targets who have demonstrated liberal sentiments or ideologies that counter those of the perpetrator (Back, Keith, & Solomos, 1998). Nineteen-year-old Richard Machado, a student at the University of California at Irvine, sent the equivalent of a mail bomb to 59 Asian students on campus in 1996. The message was titled "FUck You Asian Shit" and read:

> As you can see in the name, I hate Asians, including you. If it weren't for asias at UCI, it would be a much more popular campus. You are responsible for ALL the crimes that occur on campus. YOU are why I want you and your stupid ass comrades to get the fuck out of UCI. IF you don't I will hunt you down and kill your stupid asses. Do you hear me? I personally will make it my life carreer to find and kill everyone one of you personally. OK?????? That's how determined I am.

The message was signed, "Get the fuck out, MOther FUcker (Asian Hater)" (Computing Cases.org, n.d.).

Glaser, Dixit, and Green's (2002) semi-structured interviews of 38 seemingly adult participants (no demographic data were obtained) in White racist Internet chat rooms highlight possible motivations behind racist acts such as these. Interviewees were asked questions related to interracial marriage, minority in-migration, and job competition. Respondents felt most threatened by interracial marriage; Blacks moving into White neighborhoods came second. Questions about in-migration incited strong emotions as participants described the actions they would take if minorities moved in nearby. One respondent said he would "run the niggers and all non-whites oit of my city . . . kill some nigger ass." Another said he would "spraypaint 'niggers beware' on the door before they even move in" (Glaser et al., 2002, p. 185).

Such comments are not exclusive to online spaces that are geared toward extremists. Studies of chat rooms for general use by children and teens document aggressive language in these spaces as well (Bremer & Rauch, 1998; Tynes et al., 2004). However, studies do show significant differences between monitored and unmonitored teen chat rooms, with more negative race-related language in the unmonitored forums (Tynes et al., 2004). This suggests that without social controls, latent negative attitudes are more likely to surface among youth.

This becomes evident in monitored chat rooms when monitors leave the room, as negative race-related language and hate speech increase dramatically in their absence. For example, in the transcript below from a monitored teen chat room on May 25, 2003, the monitor (HostTeens) is out of the room until midway through the conversation. This transcript was included in the quantitative analysis in a previous study (Tynes et. al., 2004), but has not previously been published. Black Cord is mistaken for a Black person and is threatened for using the word "cracker" (line 106). In the transcript, only those lines that pertain to this conversation are shown.

| | |
|---|---|
| 106. Black Cord: | yo snappy cracker |
| 109. Star: | you start in on crackers and i'll break ur face |
| 113. Black Cord: | home fry on the french fri |
| 117. Black Cord: | im hip |
| 119. Black Cord: | im cool |
| 121. Black Cord: | im a dude |
| 124. Star: | cord u wanna get beat to death |
| 131. Black Cord: | u gotta find me first |
| 134. Star: | ur black in a white mans world my friend |
| 136. Black Cord: | whos gonna beat my ass |
| 140. Black Cord: | whos gonna beat my ass |
| 141. Zora: | I am |
| 143. HostTeens: | * © * © * |
| 144. HostTeens: | @}——>——§ Hey Everyone! §——<——{@ |
| 145. HostTeens: | * © * © * |
| 146. Star: | me and my white cracker ass and shoe |
| 148. HostTeens: | hmmmm |
| 149. Black Cord: | o no |
| 150. NUT: | NO ITS A BLACK MANS WORLD |
| 151. Zora: | no not really |
| 152. Black Cord: | wait |
| 160. HostTeens: | actually it's a purple alien's world :-D |
| 166. Star: | ok host that was a lil gay there |
| 172. Zora: | yo who said its a white mans world who said black mans world all I know is God that made black and white said it was his world |
| 177. HostTeens: | Star, Maybe . . . except it won't start a race war :-) |
| 178. Honey: | Amen Zora! |
| 179. Black Cord: | i'm not blak |
| 182. Black Cord: | i like pearl jam |
| | [ . . . ] |
| 236. Star: | race wars rock |

—(from a paid monitored chat service)

Offended that the term "cracker" is apparently being used by a person of color, Star replies "yo you start in on crackers and I'll break ur face" (line 109). Rather than responding to Star's comments, Black Cord continues to antagonistically joke that he's "hip" (line 117) and "cool" (line 119). Star then threatens to beat Black Cord to death (line 124).

The message of out-group inferiority reverberates here as it does in adult online spaces. In an effort to affirm his superiority over Black Cord, Star says that Black Cord is Black in a White man's world. Note that prior to the host reentering the room, the hate messages include overt threats of physical violence. When the host reenters (lines 143–145) and attempts, although weakly, to quell the intensity of the conflict by saying it's a "purple alien's world," the conversation becomes slightly less vitriolic. When Black Cord says he is not Black, the "race war" peters out and Star makes the final statement that "race wars rock" (line 236).

Placing ethnic or racial identifiers in screen names is a common practice in teen chat, but one that can actually invite conflict (Tynes et al., 2004). By including the word "Black" in his screen name, Black Cord made himself a target of racial attack. Such attacks can take place not only in chat rooms, but also on discussion boards and in instant messages (private online messages sent back and forth between two or more individuals in real time).

Another mainstream forum where hate speech can sometimes be found is the racism message board from an online version of a popular teen magazine. This is an open forum where teens go to discuss their attitudes about racism, get advice about interracial dating, and make connections with people from other cultural groups. While much of the communication is positive, it is often interlaced with negative stereotypes. For example, Dirtbiker2002 posted a message that read,

> black people always cause mischeif and steal, they are very rotten how they have their stupid acents i mean come on man "axe" its ask. however i admit there is one black boy in my school and he is ok. (online magazine)

Dirtbiker2002 invokes images of Blacks as thieves and uneducated people, even while acknowledging that an individual he knows personally does not fit the norm described. Nakamura (2002) coined the term *cybertypes* to describe the distinctive images of race and racism that are propagated and disseminated through the Internet. Although cybertyping often occurs through the interaction in multiuser domains, it takes place in other forums as well. The appearance of such language on this message board, a space where many teens claim to have moved past the racism of their parents, suggests the resilience and power of racial stereotypes on the Internet (Burkhalter, 1999).

## *Persuasive Rhetoric*

A second type of discourse used in online hate is indirect hate speech, also called persuasive rhetoric (Thiesmeyer, 1999). These techniques of persuasion are geared mainly, though not exclusively, toward potential hate group recruits, and are also used to further indoctrinate less fervent hate group members. Being tailored to these specific audiences, persuasive rhetoric is often more subtle and less explicitly offensive than the hate speech presented in the previous section. In his study of rhetoric on neo-Nazi Web sites, Thiesmeyer (1999) lists seven strategies of persuasion, including (1) pedantism or preaching; (2) urgency; (3) historicism, fake tradition, and folk etymology; (4) delegitimization of other discourses; (5) use of virtual community to create the illusion of "real community"; (6) production of different materials for those who are already a part of the movement and for those who must be convinced; and (7) factualization, or phrasing of a perception as though it were an established fact (p. 120).

According to Lee and Leets (2002), storytelling is one of the most powerful tools for persuasion found in online environments. These scholars differentiate between so-called high narratives, which have well-developed stories with plots and characters, and low narratives, which have less-developed narrative content. "Explicit messages" within these narratives are aligned with the speaker's intentions and convey only one meaning, while "implicit messages" may be inconsistent with speaker's intentions and convey multiple meanings. Lee and Leets asked adolescent respondents ages 13 to 17 to rate the persuasiveness of stories from hate group Web sites. The stories focused on five topics: interracial dating, being born White, immigration, joining a White supremacist group, and *The Turner Diaries*. The authors found that neutral, or uncommitted, youths found implicit messages more persuasive than explicit ones. Those youths already predisposed to accept the ideas found explicit messages more persuasive than implicit ones.

High-narrative, implicit messages had more effect in the short term, but low-narrative, explicit messages had more lasting effects that persisted or even increased over time. Though this may seem counterintuitive, it has important implications for the potential ability of online hate to effect lasting changes in attitudes and beliefs.

In addition to these various forms of persuasive rhetoric, several others deserve special mention: appeals to morality or tradition, paradoxical language, historical revisionism, and comedic racism.

### *Moral appeal*

Virtually all adult hate sites make reference to fairness, justice, and morality. Groups often seek to legitimize their activity on the grounds that they are "God's chosen people" and have been denied justice (Duffy, 2003). A Web site visitor is solicited as a potential hero who can bring justice to his or her race and restore the world to its "proper" order after joining the hate group. Similar appeals are made on children's sites. A site for the Ku Klux Klan's "Youth Corp" explains that

> kids are in the KKK because they want to learn about their heritage and they want to help make the world a better place. Men join because they want to protect their families and their Christian friends and neighbors from being destroyed in the future. We are all working together because we love Jesus and we want to help our people and the world. (www.kkk.bz/just_for_kids.htm)

### *Paradoxical language*

In George Orwell's book *1984,* the characters speak a language called Newspeak, in which the true meanings of words and phrases are veiled through the use of paradoxical language. Truths are distorted into half-truths and in some cases, the polar opposite of truth, as in the slogan "Freedom Is Slavery." Similar language is common on hate Web sites. In one study, as many as 21.7% of racist sites claimed to be nonracist, with some even going so far as to claim that minority groups are the real racists (Gerstenfeld et al., 2003). The KKK, for example, vehemently denies that it is a hate group. Its youth site offers a list of "bad things" people say about the KKK, such as that they burn crosses, to which the Web site responds, "This couldn't be further from the truth." Cross burning is a celebrated religious ceremony, the site claims, and not an act of terror. In fact, it argues that Klansmen "love the cross and would never desecrate it." The KKK is thus portrayed as a group of love rather than a hate group.

### *Historical revisionism*

Another key strategy used to deprecate racially oppressed groups is historical revisionism. This form of discourse is used to reconstruct an event or, in some cases, deny that it has occurred in order to further racist agendas. Extremist groups often promote revisionist rhetoric about the Holocaust in order to promote anti-Semitism. This typically includes claims that Jews were not killed in gas chambers on any significant scale, that the number of Jews murdered was substantially lower than reported, and that the Holocaust is a myth invented during the war in order to finance the state of Israel (Levin, 2001, 2002).

While the literature has documented the existence of Holocaust revisionism on the Internet (Tador-Shimony, 1995), we know very little about the role children and adolescents may play in advancing these ideologies. The example below is drawn from the Resistance Youth message board. On it, more senior members of the message board (as indicated underneath their screen names) tutor junior members in hate ideology. In a thread titled "Holahoax in English class,"

Pinsafety, a junior member, poses a question to the group:

> [W]e are studying about the biggest lie ever and i need good questions and comments to ask/say to make this left wing commie wench look stupid. I have allready gotten 2 other kids to say it never happened but the mo[r]e movies and crap she shows the more the kids are like poor jews. I need something to say that will unpanzifiy these people and make her look uncretitable.

A senior member named Wolfwoman then posts an extended reply that includes more than 10 questions for Pinsafety to ask his teacher, among them,

> The NAzi's wanted to kill all the Jews? Then why would they, during a war, with limited fuel supply, gather up all the Jews, ship them in railroads hundreds of miles, to camps they built specifially to house them, to shave and clothe them, to tattoo them for identification, only to kill them?
>
> How could Anne Frank have written her diary, which was mostly in ball point pen, when she died in 1945 of Typhus and the ball point pen wasnt invented till like 1949–50???
>
> IF 6 million were killed, then that is 3000 people a day. Is that really possible??
>
> How come it is illegal in some countries, like Canada and most Euopean countries to even ask questions about the numbers of Jews who died in the Holocaust? What about freedom of speech? What are they afraid of ? If these revionists are full of crap then why not just let them spout thier crap and prove them wrong in trial? (www.resistance.com/forum/viewforum.php?f=1)

Through this exchange, we may speculate, Pinsafety is further persuaded that his preconceived beliefs are true. Because of the instructive nature of Wolfwoman's questions, Pinsafety is not only learning how to argue against the existence of the Holocaust, but also gaining strategies for instructing others in his class. This suggests that transmission of cultural knowledge is taking place, with anti-Semitic and racist hate learned online subsequently taught offline. Other researchers have found that violence committed offline mimics the discourse of online hate (Thiesmeyer, 1999).

### *Comedic racism*

Another means of teaching hate is through parody and humor. Ronkin and Karn (1999) examined text-based parodies of Ebonics (African American English) on the Internet. They found that beliefs about the inferiority of this language, and by extension its speakers, are expressed through mocking discourse. Billig (2001) has explored the seemingly innocuous practice of telling jokes and found that it is common on Web sites, in chat rooms, and on discussion boards. His study of the sites Nigger Jokes KKK, Nigger Jokes, and Nigger Joke Central suggests that joking provides a way to breach the constraints of political correctness, since jokes may not be condemned as readily as outright racist statements. He argues that taboos against race have replaced the Victorian taboos against sex and that joking permits their infringement (Billig, 1999). Racist attitudes and stereotypes are easily disguised as "just jokes," ostensibly not to be taken seriously as indicators of racist beliefs.

Comedic racism is popular in online spaces for youth. The following jokes appeared on the Resistance Youth Web site, reportedly posted by teens participating in the discussion board:

> you hear they were improvong transportation in harlem? yea they planted more trees.

> what don't you want to call a black person that starts with n and ends with r? Neighbor.

> whats the difference between a pizza and a jew (pizza doesnt scream in the oven)
>
> How many Jews does it take to change a Light Bulb? 1, but he'll swear blind it was 6 million!!! (www.resistance.com/forum/view forum.php?f=1)

## YOUTH AND ONLINE HATE: WHY AND WHO?

Aside from slight differences in the themes and tools, the discourses of hate practiced by children, adolescents, and adults are very similar. The differences, as might be expected, reflect the melding of youth culture with the culture of online hate. For example, adolescents and young adults are more likely than older adults to listen to and create White power music, which is heavily distributed online. They are also more likely to perceive racial differences through the lens of youth culture. For example, as in the Panzerfaust message cited above, some teens are concerned that hip-hop culture will influence young White people to form alliances with Blacks and that it would ultimately lead to the extinction of the White race.

Why do children come to adopt or express such extreme beliefs? Part of the answer may lie in the effectiveness of the Internet as a medium for reaching and persuading computer-savvy youth. Messages online often achieve a level of legitimacy based solely on the fact that they appear on the Internet. Indeed, the information found online is often taken for literal truth (Perry, 2000). Children are not usually taught to be critical of the text that they read online and may be unable to filter out that which may be untrue. In addition, hate groups and racist individuals package their online messages in a visually persuasive manner. The engaging, interactive nature of the medium, along with its perceived credibility, may desensitize young people and make them particularly vulnerable to hate messages (Duffy, 2003).

Some researchers have used symbolic convergence theory to explain how a young person might become indoctrinated into online hate. This theory posits that groups create and exchange fantasies about themselves and others, thereby co-constructing a shared reality. In-group members tell stories and perform rituals with other group members that ultimately lead to a shared understanding of the group and of the behaviors of typical group members (Bormann, Cragan, & Shields, 1994; Duffy, 2003). These stories create a rhetorical vision of key events in history as well as of the future. If this vision speaks to an individual's current state of mind, that person may adopt it as a credible interpretation of reality (Duffy, 2003).

Because many of the physical cues present in face-to-face interaction are absent online, participants in interactive online environments often have to recreate their physical bodies in their text. Social identity theorists would argue that the mere act of having to construct online bodies, to categorize both the self and others, leads to much of the out-group derogation that occurs in online contexts. Individuals strive to maintain a positive social identity for their own group, and the in-group must be positively differentiated from out-groups (Tajfel & Turner, 1979). Categorization is a normal process that facilitates information processing, but it may not always be based on real similarities or differences and may ultimately lead to ethnocentrism (Devine, 1995).

Anonymity is another factor that may lead to increased expressions of online hate. The facelessness of the Internet is disinhibiting—and often causes people to write things they would not consider saying in face-to-face settings. Alonzo and Aiken's (2002) study of flaming explains this behavior with "uses and gratifications theory"—the idea that people use certain media to satisfy certain needs (p. 3). These researchers argue that flaming may fill cognitive and affective needs by providing an outlet for stimulation, tension reduction, expression, and assertion. People can fulfill these needs at little risk to themselves because of the anonymity of many cyberspace applications.

Although the computer as a medium may encourage the uninhibited expression of hate, the computer itself clearly does not "make" children and adolescents—or anyone else—commit racist acts. Multiple factors contribute to antisocial online behaviors. Research on children in offline environments has consistently shown that young people are far from color-blind. Indeed, even toddlers may exhibit indicators of racial bias (Doyle & Aboud, 1995; Katz, 2003). The origins of this bias are multiple and may include children's cognitive abilities, their peer group, their social environment, and their parents' behaviors and values (Katz, 2003). As children grow into adolescents, research shows that many of the same predictors determine their racial attitudes (Fishbein, 2002). While the Internet is a powerful tool, there are many social and psychological factors that may influence children's and adolescents' attitudes about their own and other ethnic groups, as well as their decisions about whether to act on these beliefs.

### *Risk Factors for Involvement*

Who engages in online hate? One might expect the most common profile to be that of a Southern, White, adult male. Some of the most prominent leaders of hate movements fit this description, including David Duke, former national director of the Knights of the KKK; William Pierce, author of *The Turner Diaries;* and Donald Black, creator of Stormfront.org, one of the first racist Web sites. With the proliferation of online hate and the widespread adoption of computer technology by young people, however, the face of hate is changing (Perry, 2000).

Youths of all regional, educational, and socioeconomic backgrounds are susceptible to engaging in hate group activity (Turpin-Petrosino, 2002). Those involved are found in every part of the country, although there may be higher concentrations along the East Coast (Southern Poverty Law Center, 2004b). There is evidence, however, that youth in areas experiencing economic distress may be more open to accepting hate messages (Blazak, 2001). In fact, a key strategy for offline recruiting is to visit schools in towns that have recently experienced an economic downturn, such as a factory closing (Southern Poverty Law Center, n.d.).

In addition, certain characteristics appear to place some children at greater risk. A study of youth involved in White extremist organizations found that 62.2% of the sample came from single-parent homes (McCurrie, 1998). Alienation from school and family is one predictor of whether young people will access violent media content, including hate Web sites (Slater, 2003). Similarly, youths who experience psychological distress as a result of factors such as blocked goal attainment and a lack of established social norms are particularly vulnerable (Blazak, 1995). Anger and frustration in these individuals can ultimately lead to group delinquency (Slater, 2003).

A number of other personal characteristics may contribute to making individuals of any age more likely to engage in online hate. Higher levels of disinhibition (or sensation-seeking behavior) are positively correlated with verbal attacks online. Aggression (Slater, 2003) and anxiety have also been implicated in these practices. In some instances, people who have experienced social deprivation—or economic, racial, or gender-based threats—may be drawn to hate-group ideology and activities (Blazak, 2001; Turpin-Petrosino, 2002). Others may perceive "genetic" threats in the form of interracial dating as a key reason to advocate racist violence (Glaser, Dixit, & Green, 2002).

### *Impact: From Speech to Action*

It is nearly impossible to establish with any certainty the precise impacts of online hate speech involving youth. But research suggests that effects may be occurring on at least three levels.

First, out-group members, typically minorities, may be directly harmed by witnessing online hate directed toward their group or toward them as individuals. Leets and colleagues have researched hate speech and the harm it inflicts both on- and offline (Lee & Leets, 2002; Leets, 2001, 2002; Leets & Giles, 1997). They found that members of different racial and ethnic groups may have different perceptions of and reactions to the language on hate sites. Participants in one study generally considered hate Web sites to be harmful, but people of color perceived more social harm than Whites (Leets, 2001). This may be attributable to the fact that messages were not directed toward Whites. When a person witnesses his or her own social or ethnic group being attacked, there are likely to be, at the very least, short-term emotional effects; these may include mood swings, guilt, anger, loneliness, and fear. For example, a Latina participant in an unmonitored chat group, confronted with death threats against her ethnic group and stereotypes of Mexicans as "dumb," commented, "I have heart probs [problems]. . . and I don't want to end up in the hospital because of these muther fucker" (transcript collected May 2, 2003, Tynes et al., 2004). Long-term attitudes and behavior may also be influenced, with victims developing more defensive or vigilant attitudes and behaviors (Leets, 2002). The effects of victimization may linger for months or even years (Bard & Sangrey; 1986; see also Leets, 2002).

One of the earliest studies of computer messages and their influence on young people's violent behavior suggested that being able to voice hatred through the medium of technology might actually be beneficial (Hamm, 1993, 1999). Online hate was seen as a substitute for action, allowing "the unfettered enjoyment of racial desires and fantasies . . . to be expressed through psychological catharsis, thereby quelling the impulse toward physical aggression" (Hamm, 1999, p. 9). Even if this were true for online spaces that are restricted to people who adhere to racist ideology, the message of hate is now spreading into mainstream online groups where the targets of these racial attacks are more likely to be present (Beckles, 1997). The psychological and emotional pain inflicted by this deprecating speech can often be as devastating as physical pain and material loss (Leets & Giles, 1997). Online hate, rather than being seen as an alternative to physical violence, may be viewed *as* violence, albeit in written form.

At a second level of impact, Internet hate strengthens the work of organized right-wing extremists. It does so by providing anonymous access to propaganda that guides criminal activity, by helping members to effectively coordinate their activities, and by creating venues for generating both legal and illegal income (Wolf, 2004). Children may be drawn into the network of hate groups by online materials. Resistance Records, a leading online distributor of White power music, sells most of its products to teens and young adults. This music may serve as the main point of entry into the online and offline hate movement for these young people (Blazak, 2001).

Finally, online hate may be a precursor to violent crime offline. Though a causal link between Internet hate and physical violence has not been proven empirically, scholars have argued that hate messages on the Internet incite hatred and promote harmful action against racial, ethnic, and religious minorities (Biegel, 1999). The Columbine case and countless hate crimes in recent years demonstrate that the Internet is, at the very least, an important educational and recruitment tool for perpetrators (Greenfield & Juvonen, 1999).

A key element in this incitement to violence is the dehumanization of target groups, making action against them seem justifiable. Minorities are dehumanized through "invalidation myths"—statements alleging that they are innately inferior (Kallen, 1998, p. 6). Kallen conceptualizes this dehumanization as a three-stage process: an invalidation myth is put forth, a theory of vilification is developed, and a course of action is planned that includes incitement to hatred and harm. These hateful messages accumulate and contribute to an atmosphere in which power structures are created and maintained, and in which violence against target groups appears socially sanctioned. Repeated often enough, these messages can eventually lead to physical harm (Calvert, 1997).

## POLICY IMPLICATIONS

Parents, Internet service providers (ISPs), the courts, and the federal government have all taken steps to protect children from hate on the Internet, but these strategies face significant obstacles. Some parents use filtering software programs including NetNanny, CyberPatrol, and Filter Logix to block access to inappropriate material. While some filters work via artificial intelligence, instantaneously scanning sites for offensive content, others work by using URL and keyword lists for filtering. Both types of filters work crudely at best: they may block access to important sites while allowing access to illicit ones (Mossberg, 2004). And because they screen only for text, graphic images of violent acts can be freely accessed. Filtering software programs created by ISPs are more effective, but still not perfect solutions. Additional attempts to protect minors from online hate include installing monitors in chat rooms. But this also has limitations, since it can be effective only when the monitor is actually present and decisively enforces chat rules.

While other developed countries such as Canada and Germany have established regulations against hateful content on the Internet, the United States has not done so, because regulation is quickly challenged as a violation of free speech. To the extent that First Amendment doctrine fails to recognize hate speech as a category of speech that justifies an exception from First Amendment protection, regulation is extremely difficult. Attempts to subject Internet communication to stricter regulation than what is applied to public communication in more traditional arenas, such as the broadcast media or the public square, have been struck down (Partners Against Hate, n.d.).

Legal prosecution of online hate speech is also problematic. Most of the blatant statements of hatred and prejudice described in this chapter enjoy constitutional protection under the First Amendment (Leets, 2001). However, there are several types of speech that do not, including speech that threatens specific individuals. Any online communication that expresses an intention or threat to commit an unlawful act against a specific person is punishable by law (Anti-Defamation League, 2001b). The precedent for this was set with the 1998 case of *United States v. Machado,* which followed the arrest of the college student who sent e-mail threats to Asians. After serving a 1-year jail term, Machado was fined $1,000 and sentenced to a year of probation (Deirmenjian, 2000). Other speech that is not protected includes persistent harassment aimed at specific persons. However, to be prosecutable, the harassment cannot be an isolated instance, but must be an established trend (Anti Defamation League, 2000). In addition, statements must be traceable to specific individuals or organizations. With the proliferation of new ways to send anonymous messages through cyberspace, this can prove very difficult.

Recently, legislation has been passed to protect children from many of the negative aspects of the Internet. The Dot Kids Implementation and Efficiency Act of 2002 mandated the establishment of a secondary-level Internet domain name within the "us" domain for children 13 and under (Saunders, 2003). The new domain is "kids.us" and only material appropriate for children is allowed to be posted. Links outside the domain are prohibited along with multiuser interactive services unless they show compliance with goals of the statute (Saunders, 2003). While this act would protect children from inappropriate material, it does not protect children from other children. It is likely that even those multiuser services that comply with the statutes would have difficulties monitoring every child at all times.

Stemming the spread of online hate and reducing the involvement of children and adolescents will require more than new laws or a new domain, though these can be part of the answer. The entire community must work collaboratively toward this goal. A first step is to get a better grasp on what really goes on in cyberspace, and how young people are involved as targets and perpetrators. Just as the government now monitors hate crimes offline, a task force should be established to monitor hate online, with special attention to sites frequented by youth.

Second, steps should be taken to determine what constitutes an online hate crime and to take these crimes seriously with appropriate enforcement (Deirmenjian, 2000). Criminal activity on the Internet is often regarded as beyond the bounds of detection and enforcement because of its "virtual" status (Williams, 2000, p. 95). For this reason, law enforcement agencies should receive special training to enable them to recognize and handle these types of cases (Deirmenjian, 2000).

Even with such measures, however, the nature of cyberspace makes it unlikely that effective controls can be imposed on the content of all, or even much, online communication. In the end, the best hope of limiting the damage to young people and the larger society from hate speech may lie in establishing a counterdiscourse of tolerance. Speaking to a United Nations seminar on the Internet and racial discrimination, the Global Internet Liberty Campaign (1997) asserted that "when encountering racist or hateful speech, the best remedy to be applied is generally more speech, not enforced silence." More spaces both online and offline should be created where children of different backgrounds can learn together about other cultures and openly discuss their racial and ethnic similarities and differences. It has been argued that these integrated discussions can reduce prejudice (Burnette, 1997; Kang, 2000). Ultimately, such open communication may benefit both young people and society at large by helping to promote a culture of online tolerance that stands in clear opposition to the culture of online hate.

## REFERENCES

Alonzo, M., & Aiken, M. (2002). Flaming in electronic communication. *Decision Support Systems, 36*(3), 205–213.

Anti-Defamation League (2000). *Combating extremism in cyberspace: The legal issues affecting Internet hate speech.* Retrieved September 8, 2004, from http://www.adl.org/main_about_adl.asp

Anti-Defamation League. (2001a). *Hate on the World Wide Web: A brief guide to cyberspace bigotry.* Retrieved September 8, 2004, from www.adl.org/special_reports/hate_on_www/print.asp

Anti-Defamation League. (2001b). *Responding to extremist speech online; 10 frequently asked questions.* Retrieved September 8, 2004, from www.adl.org/issue_combating_hate/10faq_print.asp

Back, L. (2002). Aryans reading Adorno: Cyber-culture and twenty-first century racism. *Ethnic and Racial Studies, 25*(4), 628–651.

Back, L., Keith, M., & Solomos, J. (1998). Racism on the Internet: Mapping Neo-Fascist subcultures in cyberspace. In J. Kaplan and T. Bjorgo (Eds.), *Nation and Race,* pp. 73–101. York, PA: The Maple Press Company.

Bard, M., & Sangrey, D. (1986). *The Crime Victim's Book* (2nd ed.). New York: Brunner/Mazel.

Beam, L. (1992). *Leaderless resistance.* Retrieved October 26, 2004, from http://www.louisbeam.com/sedition.htm

Beckles, C. (1997). Black struggles in cyberspace: Cyber-segregation and Cyber-Nazis. *The Western Journal of Black Studies, 21*(1), 12–19.

Biegel, S. (1999). *Online threats in the aftermath of the events at Littleton, Colorado.* UCLA Online Institute for Cyberspace Law and Policy. Retrieved August 25, 2004, from http://www.gseis.ucla.edu/iclp/threats.htm

Billig, M. (1999). *Freudian repression: Conversation creating the unconscious.* Cambridge, MA: Cambridge University Press.

Billig, M. (2001). Humour and hatred: The racist jokes of the Ku Klux Klan. *Discourse and Society, 12*(3), 267–289.

Blazak, R. (1995). *The suburbanization of hate: An ethnographic study of the skinhead subculture.* Unpublished doctoral dissertation, Emory University, Atlanta, GA.

Blazak, R. (2001). White boys to terrorist men: Target recruitment of Nazi skinheads. *American Behavioral Scientist, 44*(6), 982–1000.

Boeckmann, R. J., & Turpin-Petrosino, C. (2002). Understanding the harm of hate crime. *Journal of Social Issues, 58*(2), 207–225.

Bormann, E. G., Cragan, J. F., & Shields, D.C. (1994). In defense of symbolic convergence theory. *Communication Theory, 4*(4), 259–94.

Bremer, J., & Rauch, P. K. (1998). Children and computers: Risks and benefits. *Journal of the American Academy of Child & Adolescent Psychiatry, 37*(5), 559–60.

Burnette, E. (1997). Talking openly about race thwarts racism in children. *APA Monitor, 28*(6), 33.

Burkhalter, B. (1999). Reading race online: Discovering racial identity in Usenet discussions. In P. Kollock & M. A. Smith (Eds.), *Communities in cyberspace.* New York: Routledge.

Burris, V., Smith, E., & Strahm, A. (2000). White supremacist networks on the Internet. *Sociological Focus, 33*(2), 215–35.

Calvert, C. (1997). Hate speech and its harms: A communication theory perspective. *Journal of Communication, 47*(1), 4–19.

Center for the Digital Future. (2004). *Ten years, ten trends: The Digital Future Report.* Retrieved October 13, 2004, from www.digitalcenter.org/downloads/DigitalFutureReport-Year4–2004.pdf

Computing Cases.org. (n.d.). *Machado case history.* Retrieved October 14, 2004, from http://www.computingcases.org/case_materials/machado/case_history/case_history.html

Deirmenjian, J. M. (2000). Hate crimes on the Internet. *Journal of Forensic Science, 45*(5), 1020–2.

Devine, P. G. (1995). Prejudice and out-group perception. In A. Tesser (Ed.), *Advanced social psychology*, pp. 467–524. New York : McGraw-Hill.

Donelan, B. (2004). Extremist groups of the Midwest: A content analysis of Internet websites. *Great Plains Sociologist, 16*(1), 1–27.

Doyle, A., & Aboud, F. (1995). A longitudinal study of white children's racial prejudice as a social cognitive development. *Merrill-Palmer Quarterly, 41*, 213–23.

Duffy, M.E. (2003). Web of hate: A fantasy theme analysis of the rhetorical vision of hate groups online. *Journal of Communication Theory, 27*(3), 291–312.

Fishbein, H. D. (2002). *Peer prejudice and discrimination: The origins of prejudice* (2nd ed.). Mahwah, NJ: Lawrence Erlbaum.

Gerstenfeld, P. B., Grant, D. R., & Chiang, C. (2003). Hate online: A content analysis of extremist Internet sites. *Analyses of Social Issues and Public Policy, 3*(1), 29–44.

Glaser, J., Dixit, J., & Green, D. P. (2002). Studying hate crime with the Internet: What makes racists advocate racial violence? *Journal of Social Issues, 58*(1), 177–193.

Global Internet Liberty Campaign. (1997, November 10). *GILC resolution on hate speech: Statement to the United Nations Seminar on the role of Internet with regard to the provisions of the International Convention on the Elimination of All Forms of Racial Discrimination.* Geneva. Available: http://www.gilc.nl/speech/un/gilc-hate-speech.html

Goldschmid, R. (2001). *Promoting equality in the Information Age.* Vancouver, B.C., Canada: Canadian Jewish Congress.

Greenfield, P. M. (2000, December 13). *Developmental considerations for determining appropriate internet use guidelines for children and adolescents.* Paper presented at the Workshop on Non-Technical Strategies to Protect Youth From Inappropriate Material on the Internet, Washington, DC.

Greenfield, P. M., & Juvonen, J. (1999, July/August). A developmental look at Columbine, public interest. *APA Monitor.*

Hamm, M. S. (1993). *American Skinheads: The criminology and control of hate crime.* Westport, CT: Praeger.

Hamm, M. S. (1999, November/December). Cyberhate: Computers, violence, and the racist right. *Congress Monthly*, pp. 8–11.

Kallen, E. (1998). Hate on the net: A question of rights/A question of power. *Electronic Journal of Sociology.* Retrieved September 23, 2004, from www.sociology.org/content/v01003.002/kallen.html

Kang, J. (2000). Cyberrace. *Harvard Law Review, 113*, 1130–1208.

Katz, P. A. (2003). Racists or tolerant multi-culturalists? How do they begin? *American Psychologist, 58*(11), 897–909.

Lee, E., & Leets, L. (2002). Persuasive storytelling by hate groups online. *American Behavioral Scientist, 45*(6), 927–957.

Leets, L. (2001). Responses to Internet hate sites: Is speech too free in cyberspace? *Communication Law and Policy, 6*(2), 287–317.

Leets, L. (2002). Experiencing hate speech: Perceptions and responses to Anti-Semitism and Antigay speech. *Journal of Social Issues, 58*(2), 341–361.

Leets, L., & Giles, H. (1997). Words as weapons—When do they wound? Investigations of harmful speech. *Human Communications Research, 24*(2), 260–302.

Lenhart, A., Simon, M., & Graziano, M. (2001). *The Internet and education: Findings of the Pew Internet & American Life Project.* Washington, DC: Pew Internet and American Life Project.

Levin, B. (2001). History as a weapon: How extremists deny the Holocaust in North America. *American Behavioral Scientist, 44*(6), 1001–1031.

Levin, B. (2002). Cyberhate: A legal and historical analysis of extremists' use of computer networks in America. *American Behavioral Scientist, 45*(6), 958–988.

Mann, D., Sutton, M., & Tuffin, R. (2003). The evolution of hate: Social dynamics in white racist newsgroups. *Internet Journal of Criminology.* www.flashmouse publishing.com

Matsuda, M. J. (1993). Public response to racist speech: Considering the victim's story. In M. J. Matsuda, C. R. Lawrence, R. Delgado, & K. W. Crenshaw (Eds.), *Words that wound: Critical race theory, assaultive speech, and the First Amendment.* Boulder, CO: Westview Press.

McCurrie, T.F. (1998). White racist extremist gang members: A behavioral profile. *Journal of Gang Research, 5*(2), 51–60.

Macdonald, A. [William Pierce]. (1980). *The Turner Diaries* (2nd ed.). Washington, DC: National Alliance.

McDonald, M. (1999). Cyberhate: Extending persuasive techniques of low credibility sources to the World Wide Web. In D. W. Schumann & E. Thorson (Eds.), *Advertising and the world wide web.* Mahweh, NJ: Lawrence Erlbaum.

McKelvey, T. (2001, July 16). Father and son team on hate site. *USA Today Online.* Web document, accessed August 9, 2004. Available online: http://www.usato day.com/life/2001–07–16-kid-hate-sites.htm

Mossberg, W. S. (2004, August 18). More software aims to make Web safer for kids. *The Wall Street Journal Online.* Retrieved September 8, 2004, from http://online.wsj.com/article_print/0,SB109277830006294021,00.html

Nakamura, L. (2002). *Cybertypes: Race, ethnicity, and identity on the Internet.* New York: Routledge.

Partners Against Hate (n.d.). Hate crime definitions and trends. Retrieved February 28, 2005, from http://www.partnersagainsthate.org/about_hate_crimes/faq .html#13

Perry, B. (1999). Defenders of the faith: Hate groups and ideologies of power. *Patterns of Prejudice, 32*(3), 32–54.

Perry, B. (2000). "Button-down terror": The metamorphosis of the hate movement. *Sociological Focus, 33*(2), 113–131.

Reese, R. (1998). From the fringe: The Hip Hop culture and ethnic relations. Retrieved February 14, 2005, from http://www.csupomona.edu/~rrreese/ HIPHOP.HTML

Ronkin, M., & Karn, H. E. (1999). Mock Ebonics: Linguistic racism in parodies of Ebonics on the Internet. *Journal of Sociolinguistics, 3*(3), 360–380.

Saunders, K. W. (2003). *Saving our children from the First Amendment.* New York: New York University Press.

Schafer, J. A. (2002). Spinning the web of hate: Web-based hate propagation by extremist organizations. *Journal of Criminal Justice and Popular Culture,* 9(2), 69–88.

Sharpe, T. T. (2000). The Identity Christian Movement: Ideology of domestic terrorism. *Journal of Black Studies, 30*(4), 604–623.

Slater, M. D. (2003). Alienation, aggression, and sensation seeking as predictors of adolescent use of violent film, computer, and website content. *Journal of Communication, 53*(1), 105–121.

Smith, M. A., & Kollock, P. (1999). *Communities in cyberspace.* New York: Routledge.

Southern Poverty Law Center (2004a). *Hate groups, militias on rise as extremists stage comeback.* Retrieved September 15, 2004, from www.splcenter.org/center/splcreport/article.jsp?aid=71&printable=1

Southern Poverty Law Center (2004b). *The Southern Poverty Law Center's Intelligence Report,* 113.

Southern Poverty Law Center (n.d.). *Youth and hate: A sociologist who has investigated and worked with white supremacist youth discusses the roots of racism.* Retrieved September 15, 2004, from www.splcenter.org/intel/intelreport/article.jsp?aid=307&printable=1

Suzuki, L. K., & Calzo, J. P. (2004). The search for peer advice in cyberspace: An examination of online teen health bulletin boards. *Journal of Applied Developmental Psychology, 25,* 685–698.

Tador-Shimony, T. (1995). Antisemitism on the information superhighway: A case study of a UseNet discussion group (ACTA No. 6). *Analysis of Current Trends in Antisemitism.* Vidal Sassoon International Center for the Study of Antisemitism (SICSA), Jerusalem. Retrieved October 12, 2004, from http://sicsa.huji.ac.il/6tali.htm

Tajfel, H., & Turner, J. (1979). An integrative theory of intergroup conflict. In W. G. Austin & S. Worchel (Eds.), *The social psychology of intergroup relations* (pp. 33–47). Monterey, CA: Brooks/Cole.

Thiesmeyer, L. (1999). Racism on the Web: Its rhetoric and marketing. *Ethics and Information Technology, 1,* 117–125.

Turpin-Petrosino, C. (2002). Hateful sirens . . . who hears their song? An examination of student attitudes toward hate groups and affiliation potential. *Journal of Social Issues, 58*(2), 281–301.

Tynes, B., Reynolds, L., & Greenfield, P. M. (2004). Adolescence, race and ethnicity on the Internet: A comparison of discourse in monitored and unmonitored chat rooms. *Journal of Applied Developmental Psychology, 25*(6) 667–684.

Whine, M. (1999, August 30). The use of the Internet by far right extremists. In B. Loader & D. Thomas (Eds.), *Cybercrime: Law, security, and privacy in the Information Age.* New York: Routledge. Available online: www.ict.org.il/articles/articledet.cfm?articleid=413

William Pierce: The Internet's leading peddler of racial hate. (2000, Spring). *Journal of Blacks in Higher Education, 27,* 11.

Williams, M. (2000). Virtually criminal: Discourse, deviance, and anxiety within virtual communities. *International Review of Law Computers & Technology, 14*(1), 95–104.

Wolf, C. (2004, June 16). *Needed: Diagnostic tools to gauge the full effect of online anti-Semitism and hate.* Paper presented at OSCE Meeting on the Relationship Between Racist, Xenophobic and Anti-Semitic Propaganda on the Internet and Hate Crimes, Paris. Retrieved September 5, 2004, from http://www.adl.org/osce/osce_wolf.pdf

Zickmund, S. (1997). Approaching the radical other: The discursive culture of cyber hate. In S. G. Jones (Ed.) *Virtual culture.* Thousand Oaks, CA: Sage.

## WEB SITE REFERENCES

Kingdom Identity Ministries: http://www.kingidentity.com/index.html
Knights of the Ku Klux Klan Youth Corp: www.kkk.bz/just_for_kids.htm
Panzerfaust White Nationalist Discussion Forum: www.panzerfaust.com/forum
Resistance Youth message board: www.resistance.com/forum/viewforum.php?f=1
Stormfront.org for Kids: http://kids.stormfront.org

# CHAPTER 15

# *Constitutional Obstacles to Regulating Violence in the Media*

CATHERINE J. ROSS

At the start of the 21st century, roughly 80% of Americans believe that too much violence is displayed in the media (Bok, 1997). Many parents, social scientists, and educators wish that the government would intervene to protect children from violent images. They worry that graphic media violence has a "deleterious influence on the young" and contributes to violence in the real world. Parents have long been warned to protect their children from violence found in cheap novels and popular music, in comics, movies and television, and, most recently, in computer materials and video games (Broadcast Decency Enforcement Act, 2004; Ross, 1997, 2000).

When harm to children is invoked, the average citizen, legislator, and even judge is too often tempted to disregard the strictures of the Constitution which pose formidable obstacles to any government effort to restrict violent speech (Ross, 2000, as cited in *ACLU v. Reno,* 2000, p. 181). The Speech Clause of the First Amendment provides in pertinent part, "Congress shall make no law . . . abridging the freedom of speech, or the press" (U.S. Const., Amend. 1). This chapter separates speech containing violent imagery from other forms of speech that become controversial when made available to children, and considers whether such "violent speech" can be subjected to government regulation that will survive constitutional scrutiny.

The first section of this chapter briefly reviews the limits the Speech Clause places on the government's power to regulate speech. The second section demonstrates that violent speech may not be regulated based on its content (i.e., "violence") because it does not fit the limited legal categories constituting "unprotected" speech, such as obscenity. The third section examines the government's burden to demonstrate that violent speech harms children before it can regulate such speech, and concludes that current social science evidence does not meet the constitutional standard. The fourth section discusses the inherent difficulties in defining violent speech in a way that satisfies the demands of the First Amendment. The fifth section argues that private efforts by parents and industry provide the best, and probably the only constitutional, response to the problem of media violence.

## AN INTRODUCTION TO FREEDOM OF SPEECH

The Speech Clause occupies a privileged place among the guarantees of the Bill of Rights. It is the key to an open marketplace of ideas that, in turn, is critical to a functioning democracy. The marketplace of ideas, through which "good" speech will presumably overcome "bad" speech, is a prerequisite for an informed citizenry that is seen as essential to democracy (Dienes, Levine, & Lind, 1999).

Freedom of speech, like other civil liberties, is not absolute. It may, for example, be subject to "reasonable time, place, and manner regulations," (*Police Dep't of the City of Chicago v. Mosley,* 1972, p. 98), but never on the basis of its content or viewpoint. As the Supreme Court has explained, "above all else, the First Amendment means that government has no power to restrict expression because of its message, its ideas, its subject matter or its content" (*Mosley,* p. 95). Because the Speech Clause is designed to prevent any suppression of speech that is motivated by the state's disapproval of the ideas expressed, the essence of censorship, "[c]ontent-based regulations are presumptively invalid" (*R.A.V. v. City of St. Paul,* 1992, p. 382). The Supreme Court has emphasized that, "if there is a bedrock principle underlying the First Amendment it is that the government may not prohibit the expression of an idea simply because society finds the idea itself offensive or disagreeable" (*Texas v. Johnson,* 1989, p. 414). The source of the government's regulation—legislative or regulatory, at the federal, state, or local level—is irrelevant to the analysis. All are governed by the First Amendment.

Any government effort to restrict speech containing violence or violent imagery would, on its face, be aimed at the content of the speech, and therefore would be presumptively invalid. "Violent speech" defies clear definition, as discussed in Part IV below. It includes pictures and conduct as well as words about violence or depicting violence. The lack of agreement about what sorts of violence to worry about has led to dissatisfaction with industry ratings systems. For example, when one mother screened a family-rated film, *Fiddler on the Roof,* her son ran screaming from the room as the Cossacks tormented the Jews, yelling "what kind of parents would show a scary movie like this to a little kid?" (Salamon, 2005). The same 8-year-old had happily watched films rated "parents strongly cautioned" and "not appropriate for those under age 17" such as *The Matrix* and the *Lord of the Rings,* both of which clearly involved fantasy worlds rather than history.

When a government regulation affecting speech is challenged in court, the regulation is subjected to "strict scrutiny," as opposed to the deferential "rational basis" or mere "legitimacy" standard governing most reviews of government actions. Under strict scrutiny, a regulation based on the content of speech (such as any regulation of "violent speech") will be found unconstitutional unless the government can demonstrate: (i) a compelling government interest that justifies regulation and (ii) that the regulation is "narrowly tailored" to achieve the state's goal without limiting more speech than is absolutely necessary (*Sable Communications, Inc. v. FCC,* 1989). The impact of these principles on potential government regulations designed to limit the exposure of minors to violent speech is considered in the following sections.

## IS VIOLENT SPEECH CONSTITUTIONALLY PROTECTED SPEECH?

The easiest way to justify regulation of violence in any form of media, and avoid the rigors of strict scrutiny, would be to argue that it is not "speech" protected by the First Amendment. If "violent speech" were shown not to be "speech" within the protection of the First Amendment, government regulation would only be subject to deferential "rational basis" review. Efforts to claim that violent speech is not protected speech are, however, unlikely to succeed.

Most scholars agree that the Supreme Court has already rejected the notion that violent speech is unprotected speech. More than a half century ago, the Supreme Court overturned a New York City statute criminalizing the publication and distribution of "publications devoted principally to criminal news and stories of bloodshed, lust or crime" (*Winters v. New York,* 1948, p. 667). The Court rejected the notion that the Speech Clause only covered "the exposition of ideas" (p. 667). The Court explained that line-drawing between "ideas" and other forms of communication was impossible:

> The line between informing and entertaining is too elusive for the protection of that basic right. Everyone is familiar with instances of propaganda through fiction. What is one man's amusement, teaches another's doctrine. Though we can see nothing of any possible value in these [crime] magazines, they are as much entitled to the protection of free speech as the best of literature. (p. 667)

Some lower federal courts initially viewed video games as simply not speech. In the 1980s, a handful of federal lower courts accepted the argument that violence in one particular form of media—video games—did not comprise speech (Phillips, 2004). Judges held that games like "Pacman" lacked content, were not communicative, and therefore were not speech (*American Best Family Showplace Corp. v. City of New York,* 1982). Since that time, however, federal appellate courts have found that modern, sophisticated video games have story lines, and therefore are communicative and fall within the legal definition of speech (*American Amusement Machine Ass'n v. Kendrick,* 2000; *Interactive Digital Software Ass'n v. St. Louis County,* 2003). The rare lower court judge who has denied First Amendment protection to video games on any grounds has been reversed in the appellate courts (*American Amusement Machine Ass'n v. Kendrick,* 2000; *Interactive Digital Software Ass'n v. St. Louis Country,* 2002). Violence in every other form of media—from print to music, cable television, and movies—has uniformly been treated as speech protected by the First Amendment. Thus, any regulation of such speech based on its violent content would be subject to strict scrutiny regardless of the form in which it appears.

One might argue that violent speech could be subsumed into categories that the Supreme Court views as "unprotected" speech. The Court has carved out narrow categories of speech that are subject to government regulation because they are "of such slight social value that any benefit that may be derived from them is clearly outweighed by the social interest in order and morality" (*Chaplinsky v. New Hampshire,* 1942, p. 572). The categories of such "low-value" speech are (i) defamation (*New York Times v. Sullivan,* 1964); (ii) "fighting words" (*Chaplinsky v. New Hampshire,* 1942) and incitement (*Brandenberg v. Ohio,* 1969); and (iii) obscenity (*Miller v. California,* 1973). If one of those categories could be stretched to encompass violent speech, the government could regulate the imagery. The government, however, would have to regulate the entire category. The government may proscribe an entire category of so-called low-value speech based on its content, but may not pick and choose within the category based on the speaker's viewpoint. For example, libel of government officials could not be banned while allowing other forms of libel.

Under this analysis, the threshold question is whether speech containing violent content fits within the rubric of one of the narrow categories of speech subject to content-based regulation.

## DEFAMATION

The treatment of defamation as unprotected speech adapts the common law of libel to a constitutional standard. The common law provided an individual with the opportunity to sue a speaker for damages when the speaker had made or published false statements that damaged the individual's reputation. At the risk of oversimplification, the constitutional adaptations made by the Supreme Court protect vigorous debate about public figures (Kalven, 1989), while otherwise permitting a cause of action for defamation to proceed. Defamation clearly does not overlap with violence, even if it involves a false accusation that an individual acted in a violent manner.

### *Fighting Words and Incitement*

The concept of "fighting words" at first glance appears to offer a much more likely possibility that it might incorporate some forms of violent speech. But "fighting words" that may be constitutionally subject to criminal penalties has an extremely narrow scope. It applies only when the speaker says something that would provoke most people to fight (*Chaplinsky v. New Hampshire,* 1942; Kalven, 1989). The government's interest in such cases is to prevent immediate physical and social disorder. Violent speech contained in various forms of media entertainment cannot be squeezed into the rubric of "fighting words" because the imagery is normally too far removed from any action to which it might arguably contribute.

"Incitement to violence" is also very narrow. It requires specific incitement to engage in "imminent unlawful activity" (*Brandenburg v. Ohio,* 1969). Under this doctrine, the speaker must intend to incite listeners to immediate action (*Hess v. Indiana,* 1973; Li, 2003). Finding promise in this approach, some individuals have brought tort actions against the producers of violent movies, video games, and rock music. Each of the cases was brought by parents whose children had died, either as suicides or as the victims of what the plaintiffs considered to be imitation of violence portrayed in various forms of entertainment. These crimes included several notorious school shootings, allegedly inspired by films or video games. None of these suits has succeeded. Indeed, according to Montz (2002), no claim survived the earliest stages of a lawsuit, defendants' motions for dismissal or summary judgment, at either the trial court or appellate level. Courts have rejected these tort claims on their face after applying tort law or the doctrine of "imminent unlawful activity" enunciated in *Brandenberg.* Among other things, courts have held that such violence is not reasonably foreseeable, and that, absent any intent to incite violence, the producers owe no duty to the victims under tort law. More important for this discussion, the speech at issue is protected by the First Amendment unless it satisfies the high demands of the incitement exception, including intent and immediacy.

### *Obscenity*

Another category of unprotected speech that might seem to subsume some forms of violent speech is "obscenity." The Supreme Court has struggled since it first considered the problem of obscenity in 1957 to define and apply a standard distinguishing hardcore "obscene" speech, which is outside the protection of the First Amendment, from merely indecent speech, which is protected from government regulation (*Miller v. California,* 1973; *Roth v. United States,* 1957). The confusion over what constitutes obscenity is so great that one member of the Court metaphorically threw up his hands, saying "I know it when I see it" (*Jacobellis v. Ohio,* 1964, p. 197).

The current test for obscenity, crafted by the Supreme Court in *Miller* v. *California* (1973) has three parts, each of which must be satisfied before a work is deemed obscene:

(a) whether "the average person, applying contemporary community standards," would find that the work, taken as a whole, appeals to the prurient interest;

(b) whether the work depicts or describes, in a patently offensive way, sexual conduct specifically defined by the applicable state law; and

(c) whether the work, taken as a whole, lacks serious literary, artistic, political, or scientific value (p. 24).

Perhaps the most difficult problem in applying *Miller v. California* is who defines which works have "serious literary, artistic, political or scientific value." This phrase and other variables have made the test for legal obscenity difficult to administer. The Court's efforts to define obscenity in order to distinguish protected from unprotected speech have generated much criticism (*Paris Adult Theatre I v. Slaton,* 1973).

It is important to appreciate the constitutional protection accorded even to highly sexualized speech that does not meet the test for obscenity. As the Supreme Court stated in *United States v. Playboy Entertainment Group, Inc.* (2000), "we shall assume that many adults themselves would find the material highly offensive" (p. 811). But if it is not obscene, "adults have a constitutional right to view it" (p. 812). It has long been a foundational principle of Speech Clause doctrine that adults may not be reduced "to reading only what is fit for children," (*Butler v. Michigan,* 1957, p. 383) or, to put it more dramatically, the "level of discourse reaching a mailbox simply cannot be limited to that which would be suitable for a sandbox" (*Bolger v. Youngs Drug Products Corp.,* 1983, p.74).

Minors also have rights under the Speech Clause, both to speak and to receive speech (*Tinker v. Des Moines Ind. Schl. Dist.,* 1969; Ross, 1999). The rights of minors are not, in this instance as in many others, coextensive with those of adults. Under the legal concept of "variable obscenity," the state may place special burdens on speech deemed obscene for minors, even if it is not obscene for adults (*Ginsberg v. New York,* 1968). Contemporary legislation designed to limit minors' access to speech that is protected for adults is generally modeled after the *Miller* test, with additional words such as "appeals to the prurient interest *of minors*" (*Ginsberg,* p. 633, emphasis added). Variable obscenity statutes will generally survive constitutional scrutiny only if the speech remains available to adults, and if the statute allows parents to make the material available to their children if they choose to do so (*Ginsberg v. New York,* 1968; *Reno v. ACLU,* 1997; *Sable Communications, Inc. v. FCC,* 1989).

Obscenity doctrine has had a tortured history even when properly applied to depictions of sex as required by the express language of *Miller,* which states that the regulated work must depict or describe "sexual conduct" in a "patently offensive way" (p. 15). Ignoring the Court's holding that obscene speech is limited to certain speech involving sex, many advocates of limiting violent speech to protect children have pinned their hopes on the obscenity model. They seek to expand the concept of obscenity to encompass excessive or egregious media depictions of violence. Kevin Saunders (1996, 2003), the leading proponent of this approach, argues that both sexual materials and graphic violence were historically treated as "obscene," and that graphic violence should be merged into modern obscenity law to protect children. People frequently refer to extreme violence in real life—such as decapitations—as "obscene." In conversation, "'obscene' is often just a synonym for repulsive, with no sexual overtones at all" (*American Amusement Machine Ass'n v. Kendrick,* 2000, p. 575).

This real-world usage does not apply in the world of legal analysis. The Supreme Court draws a clear line between obscene speech under the *Miller* test and speech involving even the most graphic violent imagery. Courts have rejected every claim that violent imagery should be incorporated into the definition of obscene speech as applied to children (*American Amusement Machine Ass'n v. Kendrick,* 2000; *Bookfriends v. Taft,* 2002; *Eclipse Enterprises v. Gulotta,* 1997; *Video Software Dealers Ass'n v. Maleng,* 2004).

For example, a federal court enjoined enforcement of a broad Ohio criminal statute that labeled as "obscene" the dissemination to minors of material "harmful to juveniles" in all forms of media. In addition to the displays or depictions of sexual activity or bodily elimination deemed obscene to minors, commonly reached by variable obscenity statutes, the Ohio law banned depictions of "extreme or bizarre violence," and representations "in lurid detail of the violent physical torture, dismemberment, destruction or death of a human being" (p. 936). Even more troubling, Ohio sought to ban glorification of criminal activity in a manner tending to corrupt juveniles. The court squarely rejected Ohio's argument that it merely codified the *Roth* obscenity test as modified for juveniles by *Ginsberg* and updated by *Miller.* The court relied on the Supreme Court's statement in *Erznoznik v. City of Jacksonville* (1975) that "an expression 'must be, in some significant way, erotic'" in order for the state to limit distribution to juveniles (*Bookfriends v. Taft,* 2002, p. 941).

Similarly, in overturning a narrower Indianapolis statute limiting minors' access to arcade video games depicting graphic violence, Judge Richard Posner, writing for the United States Court of Appeals for the Seventh Circuit, declined the City's invitation to "squeeze the provision on violence into a familiar legal pigeonhole, that of obscenity, which is normally concerned with sex. . . . Violence and obscenity are distinct categories of objectionable depiction" (*American Amusement Machine Ass'n v. Kendrick,* 2000, p. 574). He distinguished the effort to ban violent speech as quasi-obscene when made available to minors from efforts to protect children from harm. The concerns animating the two approaches were quite different, he concluded. Obscene speech is not banned because it is harmful, but because it is offensive: "disgusting, embarrassing, degrading, disturbing, outrageous and insulting." But, Judge Posner noted, obscenity "is not believed to inflict temporal (as distinct from spiritual) harm" (*American Amusement Machine Ass'n v. Kendrick,* 2000, p. 575).

These decisions make clear that violent imagery cannot be shoehorned into obscene or otherwise unprotected speech that can be regulated based on its content.

## THE STATE'S BURDEN TO DEMONSTRATE THAT VIOLENT SPEECH HARMS CHILDREN

This section examines the fate of other limitations on speech that were justified on the basis of preventing speech that is "harmful to minors" from reaching them. It then sets forth the standards that the government must meet in order to establish a compelling interest in regulating speech to protect children. Finally, it asks whether the government is likely to meet that burden based on the available evidence about the effect of violent speech on minors, and concludes that it will not.

### *The Fate of the "Harmful to Minors" Argument in the Supreme Court*

The Supreme Court has expressly stated that the "salutary purpose of protecting children" does not insulate government action from constitutional scrutiny" (*Interstate Circuit v. City of Dallas,* 1968, p. 689). Over the last two decades, the Supreme Court has overturned most of the federal statutes it reviewed that were intended to shield children from speech that Congress regarded as indecent but not obscene (hereinafter, "controversial" speech) (Ross, 2000). The statutes the Supreme Court struck down were not narrowly tailored to protect the rights of adults as required to survive scrutiny under the Speech Clause. The laws struck down included federal efforts to shelter children from commercial telephone sex messages (*Sable Communications, Inc. v. FCC,* 1989); limit indecency on leased and public access cable television channels (*Denver Area Educ. Telecom Consortium, Inc. v. FCC,* 1996); and control transmissions from subscription adult cable channels so that they did not inadvertently reach children whose parents did not subscribe (*United States v. Playboy Entertainment Group, Inc.,* 2000). The Supreme Court has also overturned or sent back to lower courts for further consideration several Congressional efforts to regulate indecent speech on the Internet (*ACLU v. Reno,* 2000; *Ashcroft v. ACLU,* 2002, 2004; *Reno v. ACLU,* 1997).

In addition to *Ginsberg,* discussed above, there are only two other cases in which the Supreme Court has upheld federal regulation of indecency designed to protect children. The first, decided more than 25 years ago, is widely regarded as the apex of the Court's expansion of the concept of indecency and the government's ability to regulate it in a specific form of media. In *FCC v. Pacifica Foundation* (1978), the Court upheld Federal Communications Commission sanctions imposed on a radio station for programming that used foul language during the afternoon. The Court distinguished radio from other forms of communication, keeping up a long tradition of court rulings discussing speech rights in the context of the form of communication at issue (such as print, radio, broadcast television, cable, Internet). Regulations governing when certain material may be broadcast on radio, known as "safe harbors," remain in effect today. But when the FCC overreaches by, for example, banning all indecent broadcasts, regardless of the time of day, lower courts have overturned the agency's regulations and decisions (*Action for Children's Television v. FCC,* 1991).

The only other instance in which the Supreme Court has upheld regulations of speech designed to protect minors involved a federal statute that required public libraries to install filtering software to block images constituting obscenity or child pornography on all computers, and to install software filtering all materials "harmful to minors" on all computers available to them, as a condition of receiving federal funding (Children's Internet Protection Act, 2000). Once again, Congress was concerned about exposing children to sexual, rather than violent, speech. The plurality opinion by Chief Justice Rehnquist (an opinion expressing the reasoning of the winning side but signed by less than half of the Justices) turned on the distinction between government regulation of private speech and the right of the government to define the limits of the programs it chooses to finance. The two concurring opinions by Justices Breyer and Kennedy (at least one of which was needed to make up a majority) emphasize that the material intercepted by the filters remained available to adult users on request (*United States v. American Library Ass'n,* 2003). In instances where children's access to violent speech is not underwritten by the government, this case does not provide a useful precedent for limiting children's access.

In all of these cases, regardless of the outcome, the Supreme Court, like most lower courts, has failed to evaluate whether the targeted speech actually harmed children.

Thus, the courts have generally accepted the government's argument that protecting children from indecent or sexually explicit speech constitutes a compelling government interest that justifies regulations on speech. With few exceptions, the courts have rubber-stamped the government's compelling interest argument and focused almost exclusively on whether the regulation was narrowly crafted to achieve the government's goal, as required under the Speech Clause (Ross, 2000). None of the cases discussed in this section involved violent imagery.

### *Standards for Establishing That the Government Has a Compelling Interest in Regulating Violent Speech*

It is not sufficient for the government merely to assert an abstract or generalized interest in children's development to establish that it has a compelling interest in limiting speech (Ross, 2000). *Turner Broadcasting System v. FCC* (1994) articulates an exacting test: "[W]hen the [g]overnment defends a regulation on speech as a means to . . . prevent anticipated harms, it must do more than simply 'posit the existence of the disease sought to be cured. . . . It must demonstrate that the recited harms are real, not merely conjectural, and that the regulation will in fact alleviate these harms in a direct and material way" (*Turner Broadcasting System v. FCC*, Kennedy opinion, p. 664). If *Turner* is taken seriously, as it should be, courts must carefully review the government's claim of a compelling interest in regulating controversial speech to protect the young. In order to meet its burden, the government must demonstrate that (i) children's social, moral, or emotional development is at stake; (ii) the speech is the direct cause of the risk; and (iii) restricting the speech will in fact reduce the risk of harm. Significantly, a court must determine whether the government has demonstrated and defined its compelling interest in regulating any given form of speech before it asks hether the regulation is narrowly tailored to achieve the government interest without imposing an undue burden on speech (Ross, 2000).

Applying this standard to the social science literature concerning the impact of sexual speech on children, I have previously concluded that "it is nearly impossible to find an iota of evidence that controversial speech about sex harms children" (Ross, 2000, p. 504). Concededly, the case for regulating violent imagery might be stronger. Substantial social science research supports the allegation that violent speech may lead some children to violent actions or attitudes, but such evidence is not uncontroverted (Ross, 2000, p. 505; Ross, 2000, as cited in *American Amusement Machine Ass'n v. Kendrick*, 2000).

### *Can the Government Establish That Violent Speech Harms Children?*

Some observers argue that it is not necessary for the government to provide "scientifically certain criteria" in support of regulations affecting speech, based on the language upholding variable obscenity standards (*American Amusement Machine Ass'n v. Kendrick*, 2000; *Ginsberg v. New York*, 1968, p. 643). But in *Ginsberg*, the Supreme Court treated the indecent speech at issue as obscene when provided to minors and therefore outside the protection of the Speech Clause. Consequently, the Court did not apply strict scrutiny to the statute before it, using instead the lower standard of rational basis. The Court held that it was "rational" for the state to conclude that the speech it sought to regulate was "harmful to children." More is demanded when the state seeks to regulate violent speech, however, because violent speech is protected speech. Therefore any efforts to regulate it, even those reaching only minors, are subject to strict scrutiny. Strict scrutiny always begins with an analysis of whether the government has a compelling interest in regulating the speech it seeks to limit.

Two important and legally relevant questions about whether limiting violent speech would reduce societal violence are (i) whether some identifiable "subset" of violent speech in particular media causes "antisocial behavior of a sort that the state has a compelling interest in eliminating or reducing," and (ii) how much "societal violence the regulation would curb" (Edwards & Berman, 1995, pp. 1546, 1549). In 1995, Edwards and Berman concluded that despite all of the congressional hearings on television violence since the early 1950s, and despite the extensive research that has examined the "violence hypothesis" that viewing televised violence causes aggression, "there is scant data on the magnitude of the effect of television violence" (p. 1549). A decade later, a federal court in Washington State concluded after expert testimony that "no causal connection between playing violent video games and real-life violence has been established" (*Video Software Dealers Ass'n v. Maleng,* 2004, p. 1188). A federal appeals court also expressly rejected Missouri's argument that violent video games harmed children. The court observed that while the state's interest in protecting the "psychological well-being of minors" sounded "compelling in the abstract," the government had not met its burden to "demonstrate that the recited harms are real, not merely conjectural, and that the regulation will in fact alleviate these harms in a direct and material way" (*Interactive Digital Software Ass'n v. St. Louis Co.,* 2003, p. 958, *quoting Turner Broad. Sys. Inc. v. FCC,* 1994, p. 664). Although social scientists such as Bushman and Anderson (2001) argue that society should be concerned even if violent media make only 1% of the population more aggressive, such a small effect would be insufficient to overcome constitutional values protecting speech.

Edwards and Berman (1995) argue that even "acceptance of the violence hypothesis does not establish that television violence is harmful to children viewers" (p. 1552). They point out that antisocial behavior in itself does not establish pathology, and assert that a different research question must be posed to determine whether televised violence harms children in some manner that does not gain expression in aggressive behavior. The authors found "little direct support" in the social science and medical literature for the hypothesis that watching violent television threatens the health of young viewers (p. 1552).

A more recent review of the social science literature from a legal viewpoint echoed Edwards and Berman's (1995) conclusion that the studies establish neither causation nor harm. Heins (2001, 2004) argues that the studies oversimplify the effect of viewing controversial material and ignore the social cognition perspective. In other words, different viewers (at different ages) respond differently to different types of expression.

This chapter does not undertake a new review of the literature. The inquiry here is limited to pointing out the nature and specificity of the evidence necessary to establish a compelling interest in state regulation of media violence. The confusion between correlation and causation continues to infect the literature on the links between violent entertainment and subsequent aggression. The authors of a leading study concede that even longitudinal studies provide weak evidence of causation, and that the effects found are modest (Huesmann, Moise-Titus, Podolski, & Eron, 2003).

As Judge Posner has explained, the state cannot rest its case on "what everyone knows" about the harm violence in media causes to children. Common sense, he observed, may be just another name for "prejudice." He rejected the government's argument that two social science studies supported a link between playing violent video games and aggressive behavior. "The studies," the court held, "do not find that video games have ever caused anyone to commit a violent act, as opposed to feeling aggressive, or have caused the average level of violence to increase anywhere." In light of the flood of violent material available to children, Judge Posner concluded that as a matter of common sense, the claim of harm from video games alone was "implausible, at best wildly speculative" (*American Amusement Machine Ass'n v. Kendrick,* 2000, pp. 578–579).

The impact of television violence has been the subject of more scientific inquiry than violence in other media. An impressive array of experts has proclaimed that television violence endangers our children and our society. In 2000, six major public health organizations, including the Academy of Pediatrics, the American Psychological Association, and the American Medical Association, issued a joint statement on televised violence. They concluded the following:

> Well over 1,000 studies—including reports from the Surgeon General's office, the National Institute of Mental Health, and numerous studies conducted by leading figures within our medical and public health organizations— . . . point overwhelmingly to a causal connection between media violence and aggressive behavior in some children. The conclusion of the public health community, based on over 30 years of research, is that viewing entertainment violence can lead to increases in aggressive attitudes, values and behavior, particularly in children. Its effects are measurable and long lasting. Moreover, prolonged viewing of media violence can lead to emotional desensitization toward violence in real life. (quoted in Broadcast Decency Enforcement Act, 2004, pp. 7–8)

The 2004 report on television violence from a committee of the United States Senate pointed to this statement as establishing a consensus among behavioral scientists (Broadcast Decency Enforcement Act, 2004, p. 8). But as Freedman (2002, p. 13) has pointed out, there are only about 200 studies, not "thousands"; Freedman argues that those 200 studies do not live up to their claims. The respected British medical journal, *The Lancet,* has taken a similar position, stating, "it is inaccurate to imply that the published work strongly indicates a causal link between virtual and actual violence" (Heins, 2004, p. 244). These challenges to the significance of the research linking media violence to aggression have in turn provoked ongoing controversy.

Environmental factors may be at least as important as exposure to violence in the media as a causal factor for aggressive behavior. The same Senate committee quoted above observed that the risks of exposure to television violence were "especially acute for residents of inner city neighborhoods. One witness testified that "[v]iolence is the No. 1 cause of death in the African-American community. . . . The environment is permeated with violence. It is unsafe for children to walk to and from school" (Broadcast Decency Enforcement Act, 2004, p. 17). Each day in the United States, eight children are killed by firearms, on average three of them African American and one a Latino (Children's Defense Fund, 2004). Many other children, not themselves the victims of violence, witness violence around them and experience the fear that accompanies it. Research confirms that children exposed to high levels of neighborhood violence are more prone to think and behave aggressively than children who live in safer neighborhoods (Guerra, Huesmann, & Spindler, 2003).

Johnson and colleagues (Johnson, Cohen, Smailes, Kasen, & Brook, 2002) considered the common hypothesis that some or all of the correlation between watching violent material on television and aggression later in life could reflect the initial preferences of aggressive young people who desire violent entertainment. They identified a "bi-directional" relationship between television violence and aggressive behavior. The authors concluded that growing up in an unsafe neighborhood, in poverty, and having parents who had not graduated from high school—all acknowledged as childhood risk factors—were significantly associated with heavy television viewing, which, in turn, was associated with subsequent aggressive behavior.

The standard of proof that allows reasonable people to be concerned about the impact of media violence is much lower than the causal link required before the state restricts protected speech. To provide legally convincing evidence that viewing media violence or playing violent video games actually harms children, studies would need to distinguish more carefully among factors such as the level of exposure to violent entertainment, and violence and poverty in the community, than they generally have done to date. According to Huesmann et al. (2003), most scholars who study aggression "agree that severe aggressive and violent behavior seldom occurs unless there is a convergence of multiple predisposing and precipitating factors such as neurophysiological abnormalities, poor child rearing, socioeconomic deprivation, poor peer relations, attitudes and beliefs supporting aggression, drug and alcohol abuse, frustration, provocation and other factors" (p. 201). This complexity suggests that it would be hard to establish more than a simple positive correlation between watching violence on television and long-term aggression. Studies other than those that examine the impact of media violence offer variables that should be integrated into ongoing research. One study suggests that children who are the direct victims of violence (including domestic violence) demonstrate the highest level of behavioral problems, followed by children who have personally witnessed violence, and then by those "who were exposed through other people's report" or news coverage (Purugganan, Stein, Silver, & Benenson, 2003).

Any enterprising youngster can easily find violence in newspapers, television news, and on Internet news pages. Even parents who are careful about what their children are exposed to in the media may find that headlines about violent realities that will be covered in the next scheduled news report interrupt programming for children. These exposures may not be comfortable, and parents may go to great lengths to avoid them, but they are constitutionally protected.

News coverage routinely contains abundant and graphic violence, but violent speech in the news cannot be regulated in any way consistent with the First Amendment (*Miami Herald v. Tornillo*, 1974). Suicide bombings in the Middle East and elsewhere, decapitations of hostages, the torture of Iraqi prisoners of war in Abu Ghraib prison, ethnic slaughter in Africa, Scott Peterson's murder of his wife and the fetus she was carrying, as well as myriad local assaults, homicides, and incidents of child abuse, are all shown without a thought of legal censorship.

The contrast to countries that lack our strong legal protection for speech is striking. Venezuela, for example, recently adopted a law prohibiting scenes of violence and sex from being broadcast during the daylight hours, ostensibly in order to shield children from harm. Opponents of the law charge that its real purpose is to block news coverage of violent protests and government crackdowns on demonstrators (Forero, 2004).

Although the Federal Communications Commission (FCC) has occasionally denied that the newsworthiness of a broadcast would necessarily protect the program from federal regulation, scholars disagree (Ross, 2000). An effort to control newscasts such as the one in place in Venezuela is unimaginable and certainly would not be legal in the United States. Moreover, the sliding scale of protection for indecent speech in the United States, from complete protection for news, to lesser protection for cable television, with broadcast television and radio subjected to higher levels of FCC regulation (Ross, 2000), suggests that it would be difficult to devise regulations addressing the problem of violent speech that would reach all depictions of violence regardless of their source. This broader context makes it much harder for the government to demonstrate that any proposed regulation of violent speech applied to any single method of communication would directly and effectively reduce "harm to children."

When freedom of speech is implicated, the Constitution requires that legislatures proceed cautiously and that courts exercise vigilant oversight. Scientific studies purporting to demonstrate the state's compelling interest in regulating violent speech to protect children must be carefully crafted to identify the precise harm caused by the speech, and to show that restrictions on speech would directly and materially alleviate the harm. The studies to date do not appear to have met that standard.

## DEFINING VIOLENT SPEECH

The intertwined problems of how to define violent speech and who would define it pose yet another obstacle to regulation. One reason that the multitude of studies linking violent entertainment to aggression fail to identify a precise harm is that many or most of the studies fail to define what they count as media violence. The studies that do offer definitions do not use the same definition. As a result, even if the findings regarding causation were more compelling, the studies would not identify a precise harm (such as a heightened level of aggression or insecurity) or be able to show how restrictions on speech would directly alleviate the harm.

The problem of definition is central to the dilemma facing lawmakers who wish to regulate violent speech. Laws carrying criminal penalties must be crafted precisely in order to provide notice to people who might unwittingly violate them, such as television producers and broadcasters, or video game manufacturers. The failure to provide such notice is a fatal flaw in a criminal statute affecting speech (*Reno v. ACLU,* 1997). Equally important, in First Amendment parlance, it leads to "chill," a process in which speakers censor their own protected speech out of fear of prosecution.

The Broadcast Decency Enforcement Act of 2004 was one of a handful of congressional efforts to address media violence. The portion of the proposed legislation devoted to violent speech was adopted in the Senate, but not in the House of Representatives, and the legislation languished at the end of the congressional term (Broadcast Decency Enforcement Act, 2004; Steinberg, 2004). The Senate bill envisioned channeling violent programming to "safe harbor" hours when children were not "reasonably likely to comprise a substantial portion of the audience" (p. 21), but only if further FCC study confirmed the legislators' suspicion that the current industry-administered rating system and blocking technology, the violence- or V-chip, did not sufficiently protect children. Although the bill has not become law, the proposal is worth examining because it exemplifies the difficulties inherent in attempts to regulate violent speech.

The proposed legislation instructed the FCC to define the term "violent video programming" within 9 months as a prerequisite to further study and, if justified, to ultimate regulation (Broadcast Decency Enforcement Act, 2004, § 715 (b) (3)). The Senate committee report appreciated that defining the speech it intended to reach was not an easy task: "While it may be difficult to craft a definition of violent video programming, that is not overbroad, that is not vague, and that is consistent with the research of harm caused to children, these are exactly the tasks that the FCC was created to perform" (Broadcast Decency Enforcement Act, 2004, p. 19). The committee noted that state efforts to restrict the display to minors for sale or rental of any material containing "excess violence," have been overturned where the state defined the term inadequately (*Davis-Kidd Booksellers, Inc. v. McWherter,* 1993). The committee nonetheless concluded that although the "case demonstrates the difficulty of defining violent programming, it does not stand for the proposition that such term is incapable of being defined" (Broadcast Decency Enforcement Act, 2004, p. 20).

This flies in the face of the FCC's conclusion in 1972 that it could not prohibit broadcast violence because the subject matter would prove impossible to define. The Commission asked how it would treat the children's classic *Peter Pan,* in which the crocodile bites off the captain's hand, and ultimately eats him (Wise, 1996, pp. 34–35). The passage of time has not made violence any easier to define. As one congressman wondered in 1999, does violence mean "a movie like '*Home Alone*' . . . a movie like '*Ben Hur*' . . . [or] a movie like '*[Saving] Private Ryan*?'" (Mitchell & Bruni, 1999).

Five years later, numerous ABC affiliate stations refused to broadcast the unedited Academy Award–winning *Saving Private Ryan,* because they feared being sanctioned under the FCC's broadening expansion of standards governing indecency. The soldiers apparently swore like sailors. Station owners requested, but did not receive, an advance waiver from the FCC, which told them to use "their own good faith judgment" (de Moraes, 2004, p. C-7).

In this classic example of chilled speech, the station owners were intimidated by the FCC's perceived crackdown after notorious incidents in which rock star Janet Jackson bared her breast during the Super Bowl, and singer Bono used the f-word when being honored at a ceremony broadcast on network television. ABC inserted 11 parental advisories during *Saving Private Ryan,* but that did not reassure its mutinous affiliates. ABC's affiliates emphasized that their concern about the film lay in the FCC's reaction to profanity, *not* the violent matter contained in prolonged and realistic battle scenes, since the FCC does not regulate violence. The Parents Television Council, a watchdog group, agreed with ABC that in context, "the content is not meant to shock, nor is it gratuitous" (de Moraes, 2004, p. C-7).

Context is hard to capture in legislation, and perceptions may differ. Even if legislators could agree on a specific definition of violent speech, presumably some sort of protection would need to be accorded to speech containing violent images that (to paraphrase the *Miller* obscenity standard), "taken as a whole," demonstrate serious literary, artistic, political, or scientific value. Under First Amendment doctrine, even when the government has established a compelling interest in regulating speech, the regulation must be narrowly crafted so that it reaches no more speech than is absolutely necessary. While this chapter does not detail how a regulation designed to limit children's exposure to violent speech might be narrowly tailored in order to pass muster, any proposed government regulation would need to define speech in a way that assures that "legitimate speech is not chilled or punished" (*Ashcroft v. ACLU,* 2004, p. 2791).

Shakespeare's *Romeo & Juliet,* for example, contains sex and violence. In fact, the violence is more graphic than the sex, resulting in the suicide of both teenagers. Hunters shoot Bambi's mother early in the classic children's film, and Babar's mother is similarly disposed of in the first volume of the book series.

Consideration of whether violence is "gratuitous" in context also requires differentiation among minors of varying ages and levels of maturity. Legislation designed to restrict the access of children to violent speech to date has lacked such subtlety.

As noted above, children have First Amendment rights. Judge Posner, presuming that the statute before him did not intend to limit the access of young people to such classic works of literature as *The Odyssey, War and Peace,* or Edgar Allen Poe's writing, explained,

> [v]iolence has always been and remains a central interest of humankind and a recurrent, even obsessive theme of culture high and low. It engages the interest of children from an early age, as anyone familiar with the classic tales collected by Grimm, Andersen, and Perrault is aware. To shield children right up to the age of 18 from exposure to violent descriptions and images would not only be quixotic, but deforming: it would leave them unequipped to cope with the world as we know it. (*American Amusement Machine Ass'n v. Kendrick,* 2000, p. 577)

Judge Posner pointed out that since young people may vote at age 18, "it is obvious that they must be allowed to form their political views on the basis of uncensored speech *before* they turn eighteen, so that their minds are not a blank when they first exercise the franchise" (*American Amusement Machine Ass'n v. Kendrick,* 2000, p. 577). Likewise, since 18-year-olds may also enlist in the armed forces without parental permission, it might prove useful for them to have already seen *Saving Private Ryan,* or read *War and Peace,* so that they would understand the risks of military service before signing up.

Whose values will we, as a society, trust to draw the lines between permissible and impermissible violence in the context of art? There is no objective, ascertainable standard with which to measure value. As Justice Scalia has stated with reference to the third prong of the *Miller* test for obscenity, asking jurors to make reasonable judgments about such matters is "quite impossible . . . there being many accomplished people who have found literature in Dada, and art in the replications of a soup can." Such decisions, he observed, if not always impossible, are "at least impossible in the cases that matter" (*Pope v. Illinois,* 1987, pp. 504–505 [Scalia, J., *concurring*]).

## PARENTAL RIGHTS AND RESPONSIBILITIES

Reasonable parents differ. When the state seeks to regulate speech that reaches children, it often argues that in trying to protect children directly, it also seeks to empower parents by helping them to enforce the rules they impose on their children. But this argument is misleading because parents do not all exercise discretion over their children in identical ways. Parental values and judgments may vary considerably, and are affected by parents' knowledge of their individual children.

For heuristic purposes, three categories of families reflect the complex relationship among government actors, mainstream mores, and each family's values. First, in an "idealized normative family," the parents share the values of government actors and also share an identical understanding of how to best transmit those values to the next generation. Second, in the "imperfect normative family," the parents share the general preferences of the government actors but fail, through lack of information, fatigue, or overextension, to protect their children from speech they view as potentially harmful. Third, the "nonconformist family" does not share the values and choices of the dominant culture as interpreted by lawmakers. The nonconformist family comes in countless varieties, at both ends of the spectrum of tolerance for controversial speech in all of its forms, including violent speech (Ross, 2000).

When the government seeks to make any kind of controversial speech more difficult for minors to obtain in the name of helping parents, it tacitly discounts the ability of parents in all categories of families to raise their children as they see fit. If 90% of parents do not use the V-chip to limit their children's television viewing, only a fraction of parents know the meaning of all of the content-rating categories, and the majority of children have television sets in their own bedrooms (Broadcast Decency Enforcement Act, 2004), these facts reflect parental choices.

Another message, based on the presumed prevalence of imperfect normative families, is that responsible parenting is virtually impossible even for the most well-intentioned parents. This line of argument suggests that the transmission of values ought to be delegated, at least in part, to the state even outside of school hours. But government regulation based on this premise would trample minority views.

When the state divides speech that reaches children into favored and disfavored categories, it sends a message that nonconformist parenting is irresponsible at best. If the parenting is irresponsible enough to rise to the level of abuse or neglect, laws are already in place allowing government intervention. When government favors one set of values over others, the government risks marginalizing at least some types of nonconformist families. The government's endorsement of one position sends a message to neighbors and schoolmates that the nonconformist family is a bad family. Parents, however, have a constitutional right, recognized by the Supreme Court, to make decisions affecting how their children are raised (*Troxel v. Granville,* 2000), as long as they do not cross the line to neglect or abuse. The government may regulate children's access to substances such as tobacco and alcohol, which pose demonstrated risks to health and do not involve speech or any other protected right, but may not regulate children's exposure to ideas made available in their homes.

The argument that the state may not regulate the violent speech available to children does not in any way constrain parental efforts to limit the violent imagery to which their own children are exposed. On the contrary, it may strengthen the argument that parents should set some limits on what their children see, limits that convey their own judgments about the specific material and the specific child.

Judge Harry T. Edwards of the Court of Appeals for the D.C. Circuit has authored several thoughtful separate opinions in cases that raise issues about the government's ability to limit speech in order to protect children (*Action for Children's Television v. FCC,* 1995; *Alliance for Community Media v. FCC,* 1995). Edwards & Berman (1995) concluded that television violence is protected speech not subject to government regulation. Judge Edwards has eloquently captured the distinction between decisions made by the government and those made by parents and the limits imposed on government regulation by the Constitution:

> As a constitutional scholar, long-time law teacher, and fervent advocate of the First Amendment, I am not surprised by the conclusions I have reached. But, as a father and step-father of four children, the husband of a trial judge in Washington, D.C. who works with the perpetrators and victims of juvenile violence every day, and an Afro-American who has watched the younger generation of his race slaughtered by the blight of violence and drugs in the inner-cities of America, I am disappointed that more regulation is not possible. . . . It is no answer for a parent like me to know that

> I can (and will) regulate the behavior of my children, because I know that there are so many other children in society who do not have the benefit of the nurturing home that I provide. If I could play God, I would give content to the notion of "gratuitous" violence, and then I would ban it from the earth. I am not God, however, so I do not know how to reach gratuitous violence without doing violence to our Constitution (Edwards & Berman, 1995, p. 1566)

Certainly individual parents will make different choices about what kind of speech threatens to harm their children, and how much help they want or need in making or enforcing their child-rearing decisions. If the state makes distribution of violent material to minors a crime, it does violence to parental discretion as well as to the Constitution. When the governor of Illinois proposed legislation in 2004 to bar the distribution to minors of video games containing violence, an informal sampling of parental opinion revealed that some parents did not welcome the help. As one mother of three teenagers put it, "I don't feel that the state Legislature can do a good job of dictating to parents on how to raise our children. [Under the proposed legislation] we're putting our responsibility as a parent now onto a retailer. That is not going to work" (National Public Radio, 2004).

Sensitive ratings and filters can assist parents who *do* want help in making judgments about content. To the extent that producers and retailers voluntarily adopt such systems and parents can choose whether or not to use them, they pose no constitutional problem (*Delgado v. American Multi-Cinema,* 1999). The Constitution does not appear to pose any obstacles to government actions designed to facilitate the technical availability of filtering systems, such as imposing technical regulations that insure the compatibility of filtering mechanisms with transmission, or requiring manufacturers to install V-chips in television sets as Congress did in the mid-1990s (Telecommunications Act of 1996). In addition, while Congress may not require that parents use filters on televisions or computers, it may encourage the use of filtering mechanisms. Voluntary parental use of filters or lock devices helps those parents who wish to restrict their children's access to violent speech, and who seek help in doing so, without either imposing the government's views on parents who have different opinions or subjecting protected speech to penalties (*Ashcroft v. ACLU,* 2004).

Current flaws in the ratings systems for television and video games fuel the momentum for governmental action. According to recent Senate findings, nearly 80% of violent television programming remains unrated for violence, rendering V-chips programmed for violence useless. Age-based ratings for both television and video games may also fail to identify violent content (Broadcast Decency Enforcement Act, 2004, § 202; National Public Radio, 2004). Similarly, filters for computers may be both under-inclusive (failing to block all objectionable speech) and over-inclusive (blocking valuable and harmless speech).

In order to accomplish their intended goal, ratings and filters should provide parents with as much information as possible so they can understand the basis for industry classifications. Development of a variety of rating systems attuned to different sensibilities offers a rich arena for child advocates concerned about violent speech.

Families might also benefit from information regarding the scientific research in this area, written in nonscientific and accessible language, that can help parents form their own opinions. One recent study found that "the violent films and TV programs that probably have the most deleterious effects on children are not always the ones that adults and critics believe are the most violent." The authors concluded that children were most likely to be influenced by depictions of violence when they identified with the perpetrator, perceived the story as "telling about life like it is," and saw the perpetrator as being "rewarded for the violence." Parents, they argued, "need to be educated about these facts" (Huesmann et al., 2003, p. 218). If ratings reflected more nuanced thinking and contained more information, parents who wish to shelter their children from violent material as well as those who wish to share and discuss some types of violent material with their children would both be empowered. Media literacy education that teaches children how to think critically about what they see and hear offers another constructive and constitutional response to societal and parental concerns (Heins, 2004).

## CONCLUSION

As a society, we cannot begin to approach the problem of violent speech in a thoughtful way until we can define the speech that is too violent, and do so in a way that takes into account its context, including its social value and the listener's age. Even if the proponents of regulation could solve the dilemma of how to define violent speech with precision, which seems unlikely, any effort to regulate violent speech must meet the demands of the First Amendment. Thus, the state must justify any proposed regulation of violent speech by establishing that it causes a specific harm to minors and that regulation will decrease that harm. The current evidence supports neither proposition. If the state could meet all of these demands, it would also have to succeed in crafting a narrowly tailored regulation that inhibits no more speech than necessary to achieve the precisely defined goal. The inherent difficulty is that this final task underscores, and is entwined with, the seemingly intractable initial problem of how to define violent speech.

While this chapter does not demonstrate that no constitutionally sound approach could ever exist in response to popular concerns about violent speech, it does conclude that difficult obstacles confront any government effort to shelter children from violence in the media. Violent speech is protected under the First Amendment. Ever since video games have been recognized as speech, no city or state has succeeded in crafting a regulation of violent speech in any medium that has survived judicial review. The prospects for any regulation that will comport with the Speech Clause seem dim at best. And this is just as well. The rights of parents to exercise discretion in raising their children, the rights of older minors to be exposed to speech of all kinds, as well as the rights of speakers are at stake. The best public response to violent speech remains information and education, not censorship.

## REFERENCES

ACLU v. Ashcroft, 322 F. 3d 240 (3rd Cir. 2003), *aff'd and remanded sub nom* Ashcroft v. ACLU, 124 S. Ct. 2783 (2004).

ACLU v. Reno, 217 F. 3d 162 (3rd Cir, 2000), *vacated and remanded sub nom* Ashcroft v. ACLU, 535 U.S. 564 (2002).

Action for Children's Television v. FCC, 932 F.2d 1504 (D.C. Cir. 1991).

Action for Children's Television v. FCC, 59 F.3d 1249 (D.C. Cir. 1995), *cert. denied,* 516 U.S. 1072 (1996).

Alliance for Community Media v. FCC, 56 F. 3d 105 (D.C. 1995), *rev'd sub nom* Turner Broadcasting System v. FCC, 512 U.S. 622 (1994).

American Amusement Machine Ass'n v. Kendrick, 115 F. Supp.2d 943 (S.D. Indiana, 2000) *rev'd*, 244 F.3d 572 (7th Cir. 2001) (Posner, J.), *cert. denied*, 534 U.S. 994 (2001).

American Best Family Showplace Corp. v. City of New York, 536 F. Supp. 170 (E.D.N.Y. 1982).

Ashcroft v. ACLU, 535 U.S. 564 (2002).

Ashcroft v. ACLU, 1542 U.S. 656 (2004).

Bok, S. (1997). Censorship and media violence. *Michigan Law Review, 95*, 2160–2161.

Bolger v. Youngs Drug Products Corp., 463 U.S. 60, 74 (1983).

Bookfriends v. Taft, 223 F. Supp.2d 932 (S.D. Ohio, 2002).

Brandenburg v. Ohio, 395 U.S. 444, 447–48 (1969).

Broadcast Decency Enforcement Act (2004). 108th Cong. 2d Sess. S. 2056 (April 5, 2004). Report of the Committee on Commerce, Science, and Transportation on S. 2056, Report 108–253.

Bushman, B. J., & Anderson, C. A. (2001). Media violence and the American public: Scientific facts versus media misinformation. *American Psychologist, 56*, 477–489.

Butler v. Michigan, 352 U.S. 380, 383 (1957).

Chaplinsky v. New Hampshire, 315 U.S. 568 (1942).

Children's Defense Fund. (2004). *Each day in America, August 2004*. Retrieved December 8, 2004, from www.children'sdefensefund.org/data/eachday.asp

Children's Internet Protection Act. (2000). P. L. No. 106–554, tit. XVII, 114 Stat, 2763A-335.

Davis-Kidd Booksellers, Inc. v. McWherter, 866 S.W. 2d (Tenn. 1993).

Delgado v. American Multi-Cinema, 85 Cal Rptr. 2d 838 (1999).

de Moraes, L. (2004, November 11) "Saving Private Ryan": A new casualty of the indecency war. *The Washington Post*, C-1, C-7.

Denver Area Educ. Telecom Consortium, Inc. v. FCC, 518 U.S. 727 (1996).

Dienes, C. T., Levine, L., & Lind, R. C. (1999). *Newsgathering and the law* (2nd ed.). Charlottesville, VA: Lexis Law.

Eclipse Enterprises v. Gulotta, 134 F.3d 63 (2d Cir. 1997).

Edwards, H. T, & Berman, M. N. (1995). Regulating violence on television. *Northwestern University Law Review, 89*, 1487–1566.

Erznoznik v. City of Jacksonville, 422 U.S. 205 (1975).

FCC v. Pacifica Fdn., 438 U.S. 726 (1978).

Forero, J. (2004, December 9). Venezuela chief signs press law some see as aimed at his critics. *New York Times*, p. A-5.

Freedman, J. L. (2002). *Media violence and its effect on aggression: Assessing the scientific evidence*. Toronto: University of Toronto Press.

Ginsberg v. New York, 390 U.S. 629 (1968).

Guerra, N., Huesmann, L. R., & Spindler, A. (2003). Community violence exposure, social cognition, and aggression among urban elementary school children. *Child Development, 74*(5), 1561–1576.

Heins, M. (2001). *Not in front of the children: "Indecency," censorship, and the innocence of youth*. New York: Hill & Wang.

Heins, M. (2004). On protecting children—from censorship: A reply to Amitai Etzioni. *Chicago-Kent Law Review, 79*, 229–255.

Hess v. Indiana, 414 U.S. 105 (1973).

Huesmann, L. R., Moise-Titus, J., Podolski, C., & Eron, L. D. (2003). Longitudinal relations between children's exposure to TV violence and their aggressive and violent behavior in young adulthood: 1977–1992, *Development Psychology,* 39, 201–221.

Interactive Digital Software Ass'n v. St. Louis County, 200 F. Supp.2d 1126 (E.D. Mo. 2002), *rev'd* 329 F. 3d 954 (8th Cir. 2003).

Interstate Circuit v. City of Dallas, 390 U.S. 676 (1968).

Jacobellis v. Ohio, 378 U.S. 184 (1964) (Stewart, J., *concurring*).

Johnson, J. G., Cohen, P., Smailes, E. M., Kasen, S., & Brook, J. S. (2002). Television viewing and aggressive behavior during adolescence and adulthood. *Science, 295,* 2468–2471.

Kalven, H., Jr. (1989). *A worthy tradition: Freedom of speech in America* (J. Kalven, Ed.). New York: Harper & Row.

Krattenmaker, T. G., & Powe, L. A., Jr. (1995). Converging first amendment principles for converging communications media. *Yale Law Journal,* 104, 1719.

Li, W. (2003). Unbaking the adolescent cake: The constitutional implications of imposing tort liability on publishers of violent video games. *Arizona Law Review, 45,* 467–483.

Miami Herald v. Tornillo, 418 U.S. 241 (1974).

Miller v. California, 413 U.S. 15 (1973).

Mitchell, A., & Bruni, F. (1999, June 17). House undertakes days-long battle on youth violence. *New York Times,* A-1, A-26.

Montz, V. T. (2002). Recent incitement claims against publishers and filmmakers: Restraints on first amendment rights or proper limits on violent speech? *Virginia Sports and Entertainment Law Journal, 1,* 171–210.

National Public Radio. (2004, December 16). *Analysis: Illinois Governor Rod Blagojevich wants to make selling or renting violent or sexual video games to minors a crime* [radio broadcast]. Chicago: Author.

New York Times v. Sullivan, 376 N.Y. 254 (1964).

Paris Adult Theater I v. Slaton, 413 U.S. 49, 70–114 (Douglas, J., *dissenting;* Brennan, J., *dissenting*) (1973).

Phillips, N. (2004). Interactive Digital Software Ass'n v. St. Louis County: The first amendment and minors' access to violent video games. *Berkeley Technology Law Journal, 19,* 585–592.

Police Dep't of the City of Chicago v. Mosley, 408 U.S. 92 (1972).

Pope v. Illinois, 481 U.S. 497 (Scalia, J., *concurring*) (1987).

Purugganan, O. H., Stein, R. E., Silver, E. J., & Benenson, B. S. (2003). Exposure to violence and psychosocial adjustment among urban school-aged children, *J. Dev. Behav. Pediatrics,* 24, 424–30.

R.A.V. v. City of St. Paul, 505 U.S. 377, 382 (1992).

Reno v. ACLU, 521 U.S. 844 (1997).

Ross, C. J. (1997). Comments, Association of American Law Schools, section on Mass Communications Law, 1997 Annual Conference Panel: Sex, violence, children, and the media: Legal, historical, and empirical perspectives. 5 *CommLaw Conspectus 41,* 349–351.

Ross, C. J. (1999). An emerging right for mature minors to receive information. *University of Pennsylvania Journal of Constitutional Law, 2,* 223–275.

Ross, C. J. (2000). Anything goes: Examining the state's interest in protecting children from controversial speech. *Vanderbilt Law Review, 53,* 427–524.

Roth v. United States, 354 U.S. 476 (1957).

Sable Communications, Inc. v. FCC, 492 U.S. 115 (1989).

Salamon, J. (2005, Jan. 7). The rating says PG, but is that guidance enough? *New York Times,* E-1.

Saunders, K. W. (2003) *Saving our children from the first amendment.* New York: New York University Press.

Saunders, K. W. (1996). *Violence as obscenity: Limiting the media's first amendment protection.* Durham, NC, and London: Duke University Press.

Steinberg, J. (2004, June 7). Move to stiffen decency rules is losing steam in Washington. *New York Times,* C-1.

Telecommunications Act of 1996 (1996). P. L. No. 104–104, 110 Stat. 56.

Texas v. Johnson, 491 U.S. 397 (1989).

Tinker v. Des Moines Independent Community School Dist., 393 U.S. 503 (1969).

Troxel v. Granville, 530 U.S. 57 (2000).

Turner Broadcasting System v. FCC, 512 U.S. 622 (1994).

United States v. American Library Ass'n, 539 U.S. 194 (2003).

United States Constitution, Amendment 1.

United States v. Playboy Entertainment Group, Inc., 529 U.S. 803, 812 (2000).

Video Software Dealers Ass'n v. Maleng, 325 F. Supp.2d 1180 (W.D. Washington, 2004).

Winters v. New York, 333 U.S. 506 (1948).

Wise, E. (1996). A historical perspective on the protection of children from broadcast indecency. *Villanova Sports & Entertainment Law Journal, 3,* 15–43.

# Part III

# CHILDREN AS PERPETRATORS OF VIOLENCE

CHAPTER 16

# Peer Victimization

## The Nature and Prevalence of Bullying Among Children and Youth

SUSAN P. LIMBER

Although bullying is an age-old phenomenon, it has only recently been recognized as a serious and pervasive problem among children and youth in the United States. Research regarding peer bullying in Scandinavia has been active for more than three decades, and wide-scale public attention to the problem was aroused there in the early 1980s, after the suicides of several young victims of bullying were brought to light (Olweus, 1993a). In the United States, such wide-scale interest in bullying was not triggered until the spring of 1999, when media accounts of the tragic shootings at Columbine High School identified the perpetrators as victims of bullying by classmates. Research on the nature and extent of bullying among children and youth ballooned after Columbine as we rushed (belatedly) to better understand and prevent the phenomenon.

Bullying is most commonly defined as repeated, aggressive behavior, in which there is an imbalance of power or strength between the parties (Nansel, Overpeck, Pilla, Ruan, Simmons-Morton, et al., 2001; Olweus, 993a). Bullying behaviors may be direct (e.g., hitting, kicking, taunting, malicious teasing, name-calling) or indirect (e.g., rumor-spreading, social exclusion, friendship manipulation, cyber-bullying) (Olweus, 1993a; Rigby, 1996).

Research in recent years confirms that bullying is a complex phenomenon with no single cause. Rather, bullying among children and youth is best understood as the result of a dynamic interaction between an individual and his or her social ecology—his or her family, peer group, school, and broader community (Espelage & Swearer, 2004; Olweus, Limber, & Mihalic, 1999). This chapter summarizes current research on the nature and prevalence of bullying among children and youth, and identifies aspects of a child's social ecology that may increase or decrease the risk of bullying.

### PREVALENCE OF BULLYING

The earliest systematic studies assessing the prevalence of bullying were conducted by Olweus (1993a) with 150,000 Norwegian and Swedish children aged 8 to 15. Using anonymous, self-report measures, Olweus found that 15% of children and youth reported being involved in bully-victim problems 2 to 3 times per month or more often. Nine percent reported having been bullied by their peers, 7% had bullied others, and approximately 2% had both bullied others and been bullied with this frequency.

Surveys of children and youth in the United States typically have found higher rates of bullying than those in Scandinavia (Melton Limber, Cunningham, Osgood, Chambers, et al., 1998; Nansel et al., 2001). In a nationally representative sample of more than 15,000 students in Grades 6 through 10, Nansel and colleagues (2001) found that 17% of children and youth reported having been bullied "sometimes" or more often during the school term and 19% had bullied others "sometimes" or more frequently. Of five specific types of bullying that were examined by the authors (being "belittled about religion or race"; being "belittled about looks or speech;" being "hit, slapped, or pushed;" being "subjects of rumors;" or being "subjects of sexual comments or gestures"), being belittled about one's looks or speech was most common. Most recently, Finkelhor and colleagues (2005) conducted telephone interviews with children and parents to assess a wide range of victimization among children and youth aged 2 to 17. In this nationally representative sample, the researchers observed that 22% of children and youth had been physically bullied in the last year (resulting in a national estimate of 13.7 million children and youth), and 25% had been teased or emotionally bullied within the past year (an estimated 15.7 million children and youth nationally).

## DEMOGRAPHIC INFLUENCES ON BULLY VICTIMIZATION

The prevalence of bullying among children and youth is correlated with a variety of demographic characteristics, including age, gender, race, and ethnicity. Despite popular mythology, it is not more prevalent in urban as opposed to rural or suburban settings.

### *Age and Developmental Stage*

Somewhat different developmental trends have been observed depending upon whether the focus is on victims or perpetrators. Although few studies have systematically examined bullying across broad age groups of children, researchers who have focused on victimization experiences have found the highest rates of bully victimization among elementary-aged children, somewhat lower rates among middle school students, and lower rates still among high school students (Finkelhor et al., 2005; Limber, 2002; Nansel et al., 2001; Olweus, 1991). Finkelhor and colleagues (2005) compared victimization experiences of children aged 2 to 5, 6 to 12, and 13 to 17, and observed that children aged 6 to 12 experienced the highest rates of physical bullying. They also experienced the highest rates of teasing or emotional bullying. Preschool-aged children experienced the second-highest rates of physical bullying, and children and youth aged 13 to 17 experienced the least amount of physical bullying. There were no significant differences in rates of teasing or emotional bullying among children in the 2- to 5-year-old group compared to the 13- to 17-year-old group.

Nansel et al. (2001) found that rates of occasional ("sometimes") or weekly bully victimization decreased steadily among sixth through tenth graders in the United States. Although 24% of children in Grade 6 reported being bullied "sometimes" or more often, only 9.4% of students in tenth grade reported being bullied with this frequency. Similarly, in his study of more than 150,000 Norwegian and Swedish students age 8 to 15, Olweus (1991) observed steadily decreasing rates of victimization from children aged

8 through 15. Rates of bully victimization were twice as high for 8-year-old boys (17.5%) compared with 12-year-old boys (8.4%), and nearly three times as high for 8-year-old girls (16%) compared with 12-year-old girls (5.5%). By age 15, rates of bully victimization had decreased to 6.4% among boys and 3% among girls.

Children and youth typically report being bullied either by same-aged peers or by older children and youth (Olweus, 1993b). This finding may explain why somewhat different age trends are found when focusing on rates of bullying others versus rates of bully victimization. Most researchers have found peaks of self-reported bullying during early to mid-adolescence (Eisenberg & Aalsma, 2005; Espelage & Swearer, 2003; Nansel et al., 2001; Olweus, 1991). Olweus (1991) found the highest rates of self-reported bullying among 14- and 15-year-olds. Similarly, Nansel et al. (2001) noted in their sample that the highest rates of self-reported bullying were among eighth graders. Because of the heightened prevalence of bullying among elementary and middle school children, most bullying prevention and intervention efforts have appropriately focused at these grade levels. Although some researchers have noted a decrease in physical bullying and an increase in verbal bullying with age (Craig, 1998; Rivers & Smith, 1994), more research is needed to examine age trends in various types of bullying experienced by children at different ages.

### *Gender Differences*

Although both girls and boys are frequently engaged in bullying problems, researchers have debated the relative frequency with which they engage in and experience bullying. Studies relying on self-report measures typically have found that boys are more likely than girls to bully (Duncan, 1999; Haynie, Nansel, Eitel, Crump, Saylor, et al., 2001; Nansel et al., 2001; Olweus, 1993a; Seals & Young, 2003). Findings are less consistent when examining gender differences in peer victimization. Some studies (Boulton & Underwood, 1992; Haynie et al., 2001; Nansel et al., 2001; Olweus, 1993a; Perry, Kusel, & Perry, 1988; Rigby & Slee, 1991; Ronning, Handergaard, & Sourander, 2004; Whitney & Smith, 1993) have found that boys report higher rates of victimization than girls. Other studies, however, have found either no gender differences or only marginal differences (Boulton & Smith, 1994; Charach, Pepler, & Ziegler, 1995; Duncan, 1999; Hoover, Oliver, & Hazler, 1992; Melton et al., 1998). What is clear is that girls are bullied by both boys and girls, while boys are most often bullied by other boys (Limber, 2002; Melton et al., 1998; Olweus, 1993a).

Perhaps more important than the relative frequency with which boys and girls are bullied is the different *types* of bullying that they engage in and experience. Boys are more likely than girls to experience physical bullying by their peers (Finkelhor et al., 2005; Harris, Petrie, & Willoughby, 2002; Nansel et al., 2001; Ronning et al., 2004). The picture is somewhat less clear when examining gender differences for other forms of bullying. Ronning and colleagues (2004) found that boys in grades 6 and 10 were more likely than girls to be verbally bullied, but they found no such gender differences in Grades 7 to 9. Finkelhor and colleagues (2005) found no gender differences in rates with which boys and girls aged 2 to 17 had been teased or emotionally bullied. However, Nansel and colleagues (2001) found that girls were more likely than boys to be bullied through rumor-spreading or being the subjects of sexual comments or gestures. Olweus (cited in Limber, 2002) studied the nature of same-gender bullying (e.g., bullying of girls by girls) and found that girls are more likely than boys to be bullied through social exclusion.

There are inconsistent findings of gender differences in children's use of indirect or relational forms of bullying (Crick & Grotpeter, 1995; Espelage, Holt, & Henkel, 2003; Espelage & Swearer, 2003; Rys & Bear, 1997). For example, although Crick & Grotpeter (1995) found that third- through sixth-grade girls were much more likely than their male peers to be rated as relationally aggressive (i.e., behaviors intended to "damage another child's friendships or feelings of inclusion by the peer group" [p. 711]), others have failed to replicate these findings (Espelage et al., 2003; Rys & Bear, 1997).

### *Racial and Ethnic Differences*

Although relatively few large-scale studies have systematically examined race and ethnic factors in bullying, several researchers have observed significant differences in rates of peer victimization among children and youth from different racial and ethnic groups (Graham & Juvonen, 2002; Hanish & Guerra, 2000; Nansel et al., 2001). For example, in their nationally-representative survey of more than 15,000 U.S. students in Grades 6 to 10, Nansel and colleagues (2001) found that Black youth reported being bullied less frequently than White or Hispanic children, and Hispanic youth reported slightly higher involvement in moderate and frequent bullying of others compared with White or Black students. A different pattern emerged in Graham and Juvonen's (2002) study of students from a multiethnic middle school. Black students were more likely than Latino and multiethnic students to be named by their peers as aggressive, and less likely to be nominated as victims of peer victimization. Additional research is needed to further explore how numerical majority/minority status within schools and communities, status hierarchy (e.g., economic and social mobility of different racial and ethnic groups), and cultural views of or experiences with aggression influence rates of bullying among peers (Graham & Juvonen, 2002).

### *Bullying in Urban, Suburban, and Rural Communities*

Although bullying has often been viewed as a problem primarily of urban schools, there is no evidence to support this claim (Nansel et al., 2001; Seals & Young, 2003). To the contrary, bullying has been documented in widely diverse communities. In their nationally representative study of sixth through tenth graders in the United States, Nansel and colleagues (2001) found no significant differences in rates of bully victimization among youth from urban, suburban, town, and rural areas. They observed only very small differences in students' reports of bullying others. By self-report, suburban youth were 2 to 3% less likely to report participating in bullying with moderate frequency (i.e., "sometimes" or more often), and rural youth were 3 to 5% more likely to ever bully their peers.

## BEHAVIORAL CHARACTERISTICS OF CHILDREN INVOLVED IN BULLYING

In order to understand how to best intervene to prevent and address bullying among children and youth, it is useful to understand the behavioral characteristics of children who bully and those who are bullied. Although researchers have documented some common behavioral patterns, it is also important to note that (a) not all children fit these patterns, and (b) these patterns may not be static.

### *Children Who Bully*

Researchers have identified a number of general characteristics of children who bully their peers regularly. These children tend to have impulsive, dominant personalities; have difficulty conforming to rules; and view violence in a positive light (Limber, 2002; Olweus, 1993a; Olweus et al., 1999). These children engage in both proactive aggression (i.e., goal-directed, deliberate aggression) and reactive aggression (defensive responses to provocation) (Camodeca & Goossens, 2005). Contrary to the common myth that children who bully are "loners," these children are not socially isolated (Cairnes, Cairnes, Neckerman, Gest, & Gariepy, 1988; Nansel et al., 2001; Olweus, 1978; Juvonen, Graham, & Schuster, 2003). For example, Nansel and colleagues (2001) noted that among the sixth to tenth graders in their study, children who bullied their peers had an easier time making friends than other children.

In their study of sixth-grade students from low–socioeconomic status urban communities, Juvonen and colleagues (2003) observed that children who bully were less depressed, socially anxious, and lonely than their peers (according to self-report measures of psychological distress). Their classmates rated them as having high social status, and teachers confirmed that children who bully were the most popular of all students. Recent research by Sutton and colleagues (Sutton, Smith, & Swettenham, 1999a, 1999b) reveals that children who bully (and particularly those who are "ringleaders") have high scores on tests of social cognition. As Sutton and colleagues (1999b) note, "In contrast to the popular stereotype and research tradition of the 'oafish' bully lacking in social skills and understanding, the bully may be a cold, manipulative expert in social situations, organizing gangs and using subtle, indirect methods" (p. 435).

Children who bully are more likely than their peers to be engaged in a variety of antisocial, violent, or troubling behaviors (Haynie et al., 2001). They are more likely to be involved in vandalism (Olweus, 1993a), fighting (Nansel, Overpeck, Haynie, Ruan, & Scheidt, 2003; Olweus, 1993a), theft (Olweus, 1993a), and weapon-carrying (Nansel et al., 2003), and are more likely than non-bullying peers to consume alcohol (Nansel et al., 2001; Olweus, 1993a) and smoke (Nansel et al., 2001). They may exhibit poorer school adjustment in terms of academic achievement, assessments of school climate (Nansel et al., 2001), and school dropout rate (Byrne, 1994). In a study of fifth to seventh graders in rural southern communities, and colleagues (Cunningham, Henggeler, Limber, Melton, & Nation, 2000) observed that rates of self-reported bullying were related to students' reasons for gun ownership. Those students who owned guns in order to gain respect or frighten others (high-risk gun owners) reported higher rates of bullying others than did their peers who owned guns for reasons of protection or sport (low-risk gun owners) or those who did not own guns at all.

Bullying also may be an indicator that boys are at risk for engaging in later troublesome and criminal behavior (Limber, 2002; Loeber & Dishion, 1983; Olweus, 1993a; Pellegrini, 2001, 2002). Preliminary findings from a longitudinal study by Pellegrini (2001) suggest that male perpetrators of sexual harassment at the end of middle school had been identified as bullies in elementary school and at the beginning of middle school. In a longitudinal study conducted by Olweus (1993a) in Norway, 60% of boys identified as bullies in middle school had at least one criminal conviction by age 24, and 35 to 40% had three or more convictions. To date, no such longitudinal studies have focused on girls who bully their peers.

### *Children Who Are Bullied*

Children who are bullied by their peers are commonly characterized as being either "passive victims" or "bully-victims" (also referred to as "aggressive victims" or "provocative victims") (Limber, 2002; Olweus, 1993a). Care should be taken to ensure that these terms are not used pejoratively or to blame children for being bullied. Although estimates vary somewhat from study to study, passive victims comprise a larger proportion of victimized children than do bully-victims (Limber, 2002; Nansel et al., 2001; Olweus, 2001). For example, Nansel and colleagues (2001) observed that 11% of their nationally representative sample were passive victims of bullying, whereas only 6% were characterized as bully-victims. Passive victims of bullying have been described in the literature as being distanced from and submissive to their peers. In a study by Juvonen and colleagues (2003), teachers rated victims of bullying as being unpopular, and their peers rated them as having very low social status. Frequently, victims of bullying are socially isolated from their peers (Nansel et al., 2001; Olweus, 1993a) and report feeling lonely (Hawker & Boulton, 2000; Juvonen, Graham, & Schuster, 2003; Kochenderfer & Ladd, 1996; Nansel et al., 2001).

Victims of bullying are also more likely than their non-bullied peers to report feeling anxious (Craig, 1998; Fekkes, Pijpers, & Verloove-Vanhorick, 2004; Hawker & Boulton, 2000; Hodges & Perry, 1996; Juvonen et al., 2003; Olweus, 1978). Anxiety among bullied children may be viewed both as a precursor to and a consequence of bully victimization (Olweus, 2001; Swearer, Grills, Haye, & Cary, 2004). For example, anxious behaviors may signal to others that a child is an easy target for victimization. On the other hand, anxious symptoms may develop among bullied children as a result of their experience, as they react to their threatening environment with hypervigilance (Roth, Coles, & Heimberg, 2002; Swearer et al., 2004).

Depression is another internalizing behavior that is more common among bullied versus non-bullied children (Craig, 1998; Hawker & Boulton, 2000; Hodges & Perry, 1996; Juvonen et al., 2003; Kumpulainen, Rasanen, & Puura, 2001; Olweus, 1978; Rigby & Slee, 1993; Seals & Young, 2003; Slee, 1995; van der Wal, de Wit, & Hirasing, 2003). In a study of 2,700 Dutch children aged 9 to 12, Fekkes and colleagues (2004) observed that bullied children were four times as likely as their non-bullied peers to report feeling unhappy. They also were three times as likely to show moderate signs of depression, and eight times as likely to exhibit strong indications of depression. Several studies also have linked bully victimization with suicidal ideation (van der Wal, et al., 2003; Rigby, 1996; Roland, 2002). For example, Rigby (1996) observed that children who are frequently bullied (e.g., at least once a week) were twice as likely as their peers to wish they were dead or to admit to having recurring thoughts of suicide. Van der Wal and colleagues (2003) found that the associations between bully victimization and depression and suicidal ideation are stronger for indirect (e.g., "They pretend they don't see me") than direct (e.g., "They hit me") forms of bullying.

Bullied children are more likely than their peers to suffer from low self-esteem (Eagan & Perry, 1998; Hawker & Boulton, 2000; Hodges & Perry, 1996; Olweus, 1978; Rigby & Slee, 1993). Although children's self-esteem may be lowered as a consequence of being bullied, Eagan and Perry (1998) observed that low self-regard, especially when assessed in terms of children's self-perceptions of low social competence within their peer group, also contributes to peer victimization. The authors speculate that there are likely a number of explanations for this finding. A child's confidence in his or her standing within the peer group may protect him or her from being victimized. Thus, although most children are occasionally tested by threats from their peers, those with high self-regard refuse to tolerate these attacks and defend themselves more assertively than others. Children who have low self-perceived peer social competence also may exhibit behaviors that "signal" to their peers that they may be "easy targets" for bullying (Eagan & Perry, 1998; Limber, 2002).

Research also reveals common health effects of bullying. In a recent study of 2,766 Dutch elementary school children aged 9 to 12, Fekkes and colleagues (2004) compared self-reports of psychosomatic complaints among bullied children, children who bullied, and children not directly involved in bullying incidents. The researchers observed a consistent association between bully victimization and all measured health symptoms. For example, compared with children who were not involved in bullying, bullied children were approximately three times as likely to experience headaches, feel listless, and wet their beds. They were about twice as likely to experience problems sleeping, have abdominal pain, feel tense, be tired, and have a poor appetite.

Finally, there is some indication that bullying may affect not only the health but also the academic work of bullied children. Bullied children are more likely than their peers to report wanting to avoid attending school (Kochenderfer & Ladd, 1996) and have higher absenteeism rates (Rigby, 1996; Smith, Talamelli, Cowie, Naylor, & Chauhan, 2004). In a cross-sectional study of students in Grades 7 to 12, Eisenberg, Neumark-Sztainer, and Perry (2003) found that those students who were most frequently bullied by peers were more likely than others to report disliking school. They also received the lowest grades. Although these findings do not necessarily imply a causal relationship between bullying and academic achievement, the authors speculate that "young people mistreated by peers may not want to be in school and may thereby miss out on the benefits of school connectedness as well as educational advancement" (Eisenberg et al., 2003, p. 315).

### *Children at particular risk for being bullied*

As noted above, children who are anxious and who have low self-esteem are at increased risk of being bullied by their peers. In addition, research suggests that bully victimization is higher among boys who are physically weaker than their peers (Olweus, 1993b), and among children and adolescents who are gay, lesbian, or bisexual (Eisenberg & Aalsma, 2005; Garofalo, Wolf, Kessel, Palfrey, & DuRant, 1998). There also is a small but growing literature on the bullying of children with disabilities and special needs in mainstream settings (Martlew & Hodson, 1991; Mishna, 2003; Nabuzoka & Smith, 1993; Thompson, Whitney, & Smith, 1993). Children with chronic diseases or special health care needs may be at increased risk of being bullied or harassed by their peers. Researchers have observed higher rates of victimization among children with medical conditions that affect their appearance (e.g., cerebral palsy, muscular dystrophy, spina bifida) (Dawkins, 1996), children with hemiplagia (paralysis on one side of the body) (Yude, Goodman, & McConachie, 1998), and children with diabetes (Storch , Lewin, & Silverstein, 2004a; Storch, Lewin, Silverstein, Heidgerken, Strawser, et al., 2004b).

There also is some indication that overweight and obese school children are more likely than their normal-weight peers to be bullied (Janssen, Craig, Boyce, & Pickett (2004). In a representative study involving more than 5,700 Canadian children aged 11 to 16, researchers found a direct and significant relationship between Body Mass Index (BMI) and victimization among all ages of girls studied, and among the youngest group of boys (aged 11–12). Specifically, overweight and obese girls and boys were more likely than normal-weight peers to experience verbal victimization (be teased or made fun of) and relational bullying (e.g., be socially excluded). Moreover, overweight or obese girls were more likely than their peers to be physically bullied.

*Lasting effects of bullying*

Compared to the extensive research that has been conducted on the immediate effects of peer victimization, there has been a dearth of research on its possible long-term effects (Roth et al., 2002). In a retrospective study of young adults, Olweus (1993b) found that former victims of bullying were more likely than their non-bullied peers to be depressed and have low self-esteem, even though they were no longer experiencing bullying. Similarly, Roth and colleagues (2002) found a relationship between teasing during childhood and depression and trait anxiety in young adulthood. They speculate that, "Children who are repeatedly teased may develop beliefs that the world is a dangerous place and that they have little control over outcomes in their lives" (p. 161). These are characteristic thinking patterns of individuals suffering from anxiety and depression. In a study assessing possible long-term effects of childhood bullying on lesbian, gay, and bisexual, and transgendered adults, Rivers (2001) noted that lesbian, gay, and bisexual individuals who were former victims of bullying were more likely than comparison groups (e.g., lesbians, gays and bisexuals who had *not* been bullied, or heterosexuals who had been bullied) to be prone to depression but not anxiety.

## *Aggressive Victims of Bullying (Bully-Victims)*

As noted previously, some children are bullied with regularity but also bully other children. Referred to as aggressive victims, bully-victims, or provocative victims, these children may tend to be hyperactive (Kumpulainen & Rasanen, 2000), restless, and have difficulty concentrating (Olweus, 1993a, 2001). They may be more clumsy and immature than other peers their age, and they may have difficulty reading the social cues of their peers. These children tend to be quick-tempered and may try to fight back when they feel that they have been insulted or attacked. Not only are they bullied by their peers, but they also may try to bully weaker children (Olweus, 1993a, 2001).

Research suggests that there is particular reason to be concerned about aggressive victims of bullying, as they may display some of the social and emotional problems of victimized children and the behavioral problems of children who bully (Haynie et al., 2001; Limber, 2002; Nansel et al., 2001). For example, Nansel and colleagues (2001) observed that bully-victims in Grades 6 to 10 were more likely to report poor relationships with classmates and be lonely. They also were at higher risk of smoking, fighting, and lower academic achievement. Similarly, Haynie and colleagues (2001) found that bully-victims rated more poorly than other children (victims, bullies, or children not involved in bullying) across a wide spectrum of variables, including problem behaviors, behavioral misconduct, self-control, deviant peer influences, social competence, school adjustment and bonding, and depressive symptoms.

In a recent study involving 1,985 mostly Latino and Black sixth graders, Juvonen and colleagues (2003) assessed self-reports of psychological distress, peer ratings, and teacher ratings of students who were categorized based on peer nominations as "bullies," "bully-victims," "borderline," or "uninvolved." The bully-victims were the most troubled group of the four. They were identified by their peers as the children who were most avoided. Teachers rated bully-victims as being low in popularity, high in conduct problems, and high in school disengagement.

Kim and colleagues (2005) studied suicidal and self-injurious behaviors among a sample of 1,700 seventh- and eighth-grade students in Korea. Compared with bullies, victims, and students not involved in bullying, those students who were identified as bully-victims were most likely to report suicidal or self-injurious behavior ("I deliberately try to hurt or kill myself") and suicidal ideation ("I think about killing myself") (Kim et al., 2005, p. 358).

Finally, authors of at least two recent retrospective studies of violent acts at school (Anderson, Kaufman, Somon, Barrios, Paulozzi, et al., 2001; Fein, Vossekuil, Pollack, Borum, Modzeliski, et al., 2002) have observed that many of the violent youth in their studies had also been bullied. Anderson et al. (2001) speculated that these children "may represent the 'provocative' or 'aggressive' victims described in recent studies on bullying behavior, who often retaliate in an aggressive manner in response to being bullied" (p. 2702). The literature clearly identifies this group of children to be at very high risk of a range of troublesome behaviors, which suggests that educators and practitioners should pay particular attention to them in prevention and intervention efforts.

## FAMILY INFLUENCES ON BULLYING

Not only do certain characteristics of individual children place them at risk of being involved in bullying, but there also are family characteristics that may increase a child's likelihood of bullying or of being bullied (Duncan, 2004; Espelage, Bosworth, & Simon, 2000; Olweus, 1993a; Olweus et al., 1999).

### *Family Characteristics of Children Who Bully*

Common characteristics of parents of children who bully include a lack of warmth and involvement, a lack of supervision, and inconsistent but corporal discipline (Duncan, 2004; Olweus, 1993a; Olweus et al., 1999). Children who bully report high negative affect within their families (Rigby, 1993), poor relationships with their parents (Rigby, 1993), and little emotional support (Rigby, 1994). Children who bully their peers are also more likely than other children to be engaged in or exposed to violence within the home. They are, for example, more likely to bully their siblings (Duncan, 1999). In a study involving middle school students in the United States, Duncan (1999) found that 57% of children who bullied their peers and 77% of children who were bully-victims also bullied their siblings, whereas only 38% of bullied children and 32% of children not involved in peer bullying indicated that they bullied their siblings. Children who bully also are nearly twice as likely to have been exposed to domestic violence (Baldry, 2003). Research by Shields and Cicchetti (2001) also reveals that children who were maltreated by a parent are more likely to bully their peers.

### *Family Characteristics of Children Who Are Bullied*

Several researchers have examined familial characteristics of bullied children (Duncan, 2004; Fosse & Holen, 2002; Ladd & Ladd, 1998; Olweus, 1993a; Rigby, 1993, 1994). Although care must be taken not to blame bullied children or their families for abuse that their peers inflict, recognition of familial risk factors may be helpful in prevention and intervention efforts. Somewhat different familial characteristics emerge for bullied boys and girls. Male victims of bullying tend to have close relationships with their mothers (Olweus, 1994; Duncan, 2004). Mothers of bullied boys have been described as being overprotective (Hodges & Perry, 1996; Olweus, 1993a), intense, and overly involved in their sons' lives (Bowers, Smith, & Binney, 1994). Bullied girls, on the other hand, are more likely to report having negative attitudes toward their mothers (Duncan, 2004; Rigby, 1993), poor family functioning and communication, and low family affect (Rigby, 1994). Mothers of bullied girls have been described in the research literature as being "emotionally abus[ive], hostile, and rejecting of their daughters" (Duncan, 2004, p. 235). Both boys and girls who have been maltreated by parents are more likely to be bullied by their peers (Shields & Cicchetti, 2001). Moreover, boys and girls exposed to domestic violence are more likely to be bullied than those who are not exposed to violence between their parents (Baldry, 2003). Finally, children who are bullied by their peers may be slightly more likely than non-involved children to also be bullied by their siblings. Duncan (1999) found that 36% of victims of peer abuse were also bullied by their siblings, compared with 24% of children who were not involved in peer bullying.

### *Family Characteristics of Aggressive Victims*

Very little research has focused on the family characteristics of bully-victims. Bowers and colleagues (1994) observed that bully-victims report troubled parent–child relationships, low parental warmth, abusive and inconsistent monitoring and discipline, and neglect. Duncan (1999) found that sibling bullying was most common among children who were characterized as bully-victims at school. As Duncan notes, "the majority of bully/victims reported that they were at the receiving *and* the giving end of bullying with their siblings" (p. 882).

## THE PEER CONTEXT AND BULLYING

Although adults may tend to view bullying as an aggressive exchange between two individuals (a child who bullies and his or her victim), it is more accurately understood as a group phenomenon (Hanish, Kochenderfer-Ladd, Fabes, Martin, & Denning, 2004; Olweus et al., 1999; Pellegrini, 2002; Salmiavelli, Lagerspetz, Björkqvist, Österman, & Kaukianen, 1996) in which children may play a variety of roles as aggressors, victims, observers, and defenders. Olweus et al. (1999) identified at least six distinct roles that children may play in acute bullying situations: bullies (who initiate the bullying), followers (who may take an active part in the bullying but do not initiate it), supporters (who support the bullying but do not take an active role), passive supporters (who like the bullying but do not show open support), disengaged onlookers, possible defenders (who dislike the bullying but do not take action to help), defenders (who try to help the child being bullied), and victims. In a study of sixth graders in Finland, Salmiavelli and colleagues (1996) observed that the vast majority of students (87%) assumed participant roles in bullying situations as reinforcers, assistants, defenders of the victim, or outsiders. Unfortunately, the important roles of these various bystanders has tended to be somewhat overlooked by researchers and educators (Hazler, 1996).

### *Students' Attitudes Toward and Responses to Bullying*

Bullying appears to thrive in school environments in which there are positive (or at least accepting) attitudes on the part of peers and adults toward aggressive behavior. Therefore, it is important to understand how children view bullying. Most studies have found that children have generally negative views toward bullying and positive or sympathetic responses toward victims of bullying (Baldry, 2004; Rigby & Slee, 1993). For example, Unnever and Cornell (2003) found that 80% of the students in their middle school sample reported feeling sorry for victims of bullying. Sympathy, however, did not translate into action. Most students, 64%, also noted that other students actually try to prevent bullying only "once in a while" or "almost never." Hazler (1996) notes that bystanders frequently comprise a "silent majority" who may remain on the sidelines because they may be uncertain about how to respond to bullying, are afraid that they might make the situation worse for the victim, or are fearful of becoming targets themselves (p. 19).

Not only do children often fail to take action to stop or prevent bullying, but a disturbing minority of children display attitudes that are supportive of bullying or blaming of the victims of bullying (Baldry, 2004; Unnever & Cornell, 2003). When asked, "When you see a student your age being bullied at school, what do you think or feel?," 20% of the students surveyed by Unnerver and Cornell admitted either that the bullying did not bother them much or that the victim deserved the bullying. These attitudes may contribute to a culture supportive of bullying at schools and within communities. Prevention and intervention efforts must, therefore, target bystanders as potential agents for change, as deLara argues in this volume.

### *Risk and Protective Factors Associated With Peer Relations*

Not only do peers play a role in influencing a school culture that is generally supportive of or opposed to bullying, but they may also make it more or less likely that individual children are bullied or bully others. Research has confirmed that the number and quality of friends is important in protecting children from possible bullying by peers (Pellegrini, 2002; Pellegrini & Long, 2004). If children affiliate with large numbers of peers, it is less likely that they will be bullied, as bullies may risk disapproval and possible retaliation from the target's friends (Pellegrini, 2002). Moreover, it appears that affiliation with particular types of peers (those who are rated as popular and strong) may be particularly helpful in preventing bullying (Pelligrini & Long, 2004). Finally, there also are peer-related risk factors associated with bullying behavior among children and youth. Children who bully are more likely to associate with other aggressive or bullying children (Olweus, 1993a).

## CHARACTERISTICS OF SCHOOLS THAT INFLUENCE BULLYING

Not only are bullying rates influenced by characteristics associated with individual children, family units, and peer groups, but they also may be affected by characteristics of the child's school. One particular variable of interest is the transition from elementary to middle school. Drawing upon data from studies of bullying in five countries, Pellegrini (2002) observed that bullying rates tend to decline across the primary school years, increase with the transition to secondary school, and then resume their decline. He notes that this pattern changes, however, if students remain in the same schools during this age period, in which case rates of bullying decline steadily through elementary, middle, and high school. Pellegrini notes that there are a number of characteristics of middle and junior high schools that may be responsible for this increase in bullying, including their size and impersonal nature, a relative lack of supervision, increased focus on competition and social comparisons among peers, teacher attitudes, and a loss of a sense of community.

Studying students in Norway, Olweus (1993a) did not observe that rates of bullying were explained by competition among students or school size. However, it is not certain that the negative findings related to school size would translate to U.S. schools, which typically are significantly larger and structured differently than corresponding schools in Norway. The structure of U.S. middle and junior high schools is also such that they tend to lack the sense of community, familiarity, and closeness that more commonly characterize elementary school settings (and corresponding schools) in Norway (Limber, 2004). When children transition from elementary school, they typically trade the closeness of a single classroom setting (in which they have a primary teacher and interact regularly with 20–30 peers) for the comparative anonymity of a middle school setting in which they frequently change classrooms, may have five or more teachers, and interact with different cohorts of peers. Whereas the closeness and familiarity of the elementary setting may foster cooperation and minimize aggression among students (Pellegrini, 2002), its absence may contribute to increased bullying. Several bullying prevention efforts in the United States (e.g., Olweus et al., 1999) have encouraged school staff to hold regular classroom meetings in an effort to increase familiarity and cohesion among students. Additional research in the United States is needed to better understand how the structure of middle school settings affects children's sense of closeness and familiarity, and in turn, rates of bullying.

Not only may middle school settings lack the close sense of community that characterizes elementary schools, but they also may have less direct supervision from adults. Olweus (1993a) and others (Boulton, 1994; Pellegrini & Bartini, 2000; Smith & Sharp, 1994) have documented that rates of bullying are significantly affected by the quality and amount of adult supervision of students, particularly during break times. Boulton (1994) found, for example, that the training of playground supervisors reduced rates of various forms of bullying by 40–50%. The U.S. Department of Education (1998) and the Health Resources and Services Administration (Maternal and Child Health Bureau, 2005) also have emphasized the role of adult supervision in reducing bullying in schools.

In a two-and-one-half-year longitudinal study with more than 500 youth from 250 schools in the United States, Kasen and colleagues (Kasen, Berenson, Cohen, & Johnson, 2004) examined a number of aspects of school climate that may affect rates of bullying in school: (a) conflict (i.e., the extent to which teachers are ineffective in maintaining control and students discount authority); (b) learning focus (i.e., the extent to which schools are well-organized to make learning a priority); (c) social facilitation ("which reflects an open and informal atmosphere where personal concerns may be voiced and social ties encouraged" [p. 196]); and (d) autonomy (in which students are encouraged to have a voice in school politics and decisions). Kasen and colleagues (2004) found that adolescents who attended schools high in conflict and social facilitation issues increased their bullying behaviors during the course of the study. Conversely, schools that were high in learning focus and in granting autonomy appeared to have a positive influence on youth; researchers saw a decrease in bullying-related behaviors among youth who attended schools with these characteristics.

The attitudes and behaviors of teachers and other staff members with regard to bullying also may significantly affect rates of bullying within a school (Limber, 2002; Olweus, 1993a; Pellegrini, 2002). The majority of studies find that most teachers have generally negative attitudes about bullying, are sympathetic toward children who are bullied, and feel a responsibility to prevent bullying (Boulton, 1997). For example, in a study of nearly 800 elementary through high school teachers, Holt and Keyes (2004) noted that 97% agreed that adults in the school "usually stop hurtful comments from students toward other students" (p. 127).

However, teachers fairly consistently perceive less bullying at school than do students (Holt & Keyes, 2004). They also are less likely to accurately identify children as bullies or victims in middle school as opposed to elementary school (Leff, Kupersmidt, Patterson, & Power, 1999). There may be several reasons why teachers are not as aware of bullying as students are. A small minority may discount its seriousness or view bullying as a rite of passage. Others may hold somewhat limited definitions of what constitutes bullying (Holt & Keyes, 2004). For example, Boulton (1997) observed that although 96% of teachers considered hitting, pushing, and kicking to be forms of bullying, one quarter of teachers did not consider name-calling, rumor-spreading, or intimidation (by staring) to be bullying. Approximately half did not view social exclusion as a form of bullying. Pellegrini (2002) also noted that teachers may be especially likely to ignore or fail to detect indirect forms of bullying.

Teachers also may perceive less bullying at school because it often goes unreported by students (Holt & Keyes, 2004; Limber, 2002; O'Moore, 2000; Pellegrini, 2002). For example, studies in England revealed that less than one quarter of those students who had been bullied with some frequency reported the incidents to teachers or other staff at school (Boulton & Underwood, 1992; Whitney & Smith, 1993). Many students likely fail to report bullying because they fear retaliation. Others may not feel that their concerns will be taken seriously by adults or be dealt with effectively. In their survey of middle school youth, for example, Unnever and Cornell (2003) found that 42% of the students believed that their teachers had done fairly little, little, or nothing to counteract bullying. Those students who had been bullied were even less positive about their teachers' actions. Similarly, in a survey of high school students, two thirds of those who had been bullied believed that school personnel had responded poorly to bullying instances, and fewer than 1 in 10 believed that staff handled these problems very well (Hoover et al., 1992). Not only may some teachers fail to recognize or appropriately deal with bullying, but a small minority may also model inappropriate behavior for students. In their survey of school teachers, Holt and Keyes (2004) found that 26% had observed other teachers making fun of the way students talk, look, or act.

Only a handful of researchers have explored teacher characteristics that may be linked to more positive or negative attitudes toward bullying. Disturbingly, Boulton (1997) observed that teachers' sympathy toward victims of bullying decreased with their length of service. Kallestad and Olweus (2003) studied teacher characteristics that predicted teachers' use of bullying prevention strategies in the classroom. They observed that those teachers who viewed themselves, their colleagues, and their schools as important agents for change did more to prevent bullying in their classrooms. Moreover, those who perceived more bullying in their classrooms, who had been bullied themselves as children, or who reported feeling upset and uncomfortable about bullying were more likely to implement components of a bullying prevention program.

## COMMUNITY AND SOCIETAL INFLUENCES ON BULLYING

Just as a wide range of community and societal influences have been found to affect rates of violence among children and youth (e.g., exposure to community violence and media violence), so too may community and societal factors affect rates of bullying. To date, there has been little research on this topic. However, a recent study by Lee and Kim (2004) explored connections between media violence and bullying among a sample of 648 Korean junior high school students aged 12 to 16 years. These researchers found a direct, positive relationship between exposure to media violence and rates of bullying at school. The more media violence that students viewed, the more bullying the adolescents were involved in. They also found that two variables—anger and contact with delinquent friends—mediated these effects. They speculated that viewing violent scenes primes aggressive thoughts, which increases the probability that a child will respond aggressively to real or imagined provocation. Moreover, the more children are exposed to media violence, the more likely they are to take part in a delinquent group, which increases the likelihood of engaging in bullying.

## CONCLUSIONS

This chapter began with the recognition that bullying is a common yet complex phenomenon that affects millions of children each year, either directly or indirectly. Although much attention has focused on understanding individual characteristics of children involved in bullying, a growing research literature confirms that bullying is best understood within a social-ecological framework. Future research must further illuminate those aspects of the family, peer, and school environments that both contribute to and protect children from being involved in bullying. Evaluation and dissemination of bullying prevention and intervention strategies that address the multiple known risk and protective factors for bullying must be encouraged. And finally, an understanding of the broader societal or cultural influences on bullying behavior is needed. Although being bullied, harassed, and excluded are common experiences for many school children, we need not and should not accept that they are *inevitable* experiences.

## REFERENCES

Anderson, M., Kaufman, J., Simon, T. R., Barrios, L., Paulozzi, L., Ryan, G., et al., & the School-Associated Violent Deaths Study Group (2001). School-associated violent deaths in the United States, 1994–1999. *Journal of the American Medical Association, 286,* 2695–2702.

Baldry, A. C. (2003). Bullying in schools and exposure to domestic violence. *Child Abuse & Neglect, 27,* 713–732.

Baldry, A. C. (2004). "What about bullying?" An experimental field study to understand students' attitudes towards bullying and victimization in Italian middle schools. *British Journal of Educational Psychology, 74,* 583–598.

Boulton, M. J. (1994). Understanding and preventing bullying in the junior school playground. In P. K. Smith & S. Sharp (Eds.), *School bullying* (pp. 132–159). London: Routledge.

Boulton, M. J. (1997). Teachers' views on bullying: Definitions, attitudes, and ability to cope. *British Journal of Educational Psychology, 67,* 223–233.

Boulton, M. J., & Smith, P. K. (1994). Bully-victim problems in middle-school children: Stability, self-perceived competence, peer perceptions and peer acceptance. *British Journal of Developmental Psychology, 12,* 315–329.

Boulton, M. J., & Underwood, K. (1992). Bully victim problems among middle school children. *British Journal of Educational Psychology, 62,* 73–87.

Bowers, L., Smith, P. K., & Binney, V. (1994). Perceived family relationships of bullies, victims, and bully/victims in middle childhood. *Journal of Social and Personal Relationships, 11,* 215–232.

Byrne, B. J. (1994). Bullies and victims in school settings with reference to some Dublin schools. *Irish Journal of Psychology, 15,* 574–586.

Cairnes, R. B., Cairnes, B. D., Neckerman, H. J., Gest, S. D., & Gariepy, J. L. (1988). Social networks and aggressive behaviour: Peer support or peer rejection? *Developmental Psychology, 24,* 815–823.

Camodeca, M., & Goossens, F. A. (2005). Aggression, social cognitions, anger, and sadness in bullies and victims. *Journal of Child Psychology and Psychiatry, 46,* 186–197.

Charach, A., Pepler, D. J., & Ziegler, S. (1995). Bullying at school: A Canadian perspective. *Education Canada, 35,* 12–18.

Craig, W. M. (1998). The relationship among bullying, victimization, depression, anxiety, and aggression in elementary school children. *Personality and Individual Differences, 24,* 123–130.

Crick, N. R., & Grotpeter, J. K. (1995). Relational aggression, gender, and social-psychological adjustment. *Child Development, 66,* 710–722.

Cunningham, P. B., Henggeler, S. W., Limber, S. P., Melton, G. B., & Nation, M. A. (2000). Patterns and correlates of gun ownership among nonmetropolitan and rural middle school students. *Journal of Clinical Child Psychology, 29,* 432–442.

Dawkins, J. L. (1996). Bullying, physical disability, and the paediatric patient. *Developmental Medicine and Child Neurology, 38,* 603–612.

Duncan, R. D. (1999). Peer and sibling aggression: An investigation of intra- and extra-familial bullying. *Journal of Interpersonal Violence, 14,* 871–886.

Duncan, R. D. (2004). The impact of family relationships on school bullies and victims. In D. L. Espelage & S. M. Swearer (Eds.), *Bullying in American schools: A social-ecological perspective on prevention and intervention* (pp. 227–244). Mahwah, NJ: Lawrence Erlbaum.

Eagan, S. K., & Perry, D. G. (1998). Does low self-regard invite victimization? *Developmental Psychology, 34,* 299–309.

Eisenberg, M. E., & Aalsma, M. C. (2005). Bullying and peer victimization: Position paper of the Society for Adolescent Medicine. *Journal of Adolescent Health, 36,* 88–91.

Eisenberg, M. E., Neumark-Sztainer, D., & Perry, C. (2003). Peer harassment, school connectedness, and academic achievement. *Journal of School Health, 73,* 311–316.

Espelage, D. L., Bosworth, K., & Simon, T. R. (2000). Examining the social context of bullying behaviours in early adolescence. *Journal of Counseling and Development, 78,* 326–333.

Espelage, D. L., Holt, M. K., & Henkel, R. R. (2003). Examination of peer group contextual effects on aggressive behavior during early adolescence. *Child Development, 74,* 205–220.

Espelage, D. L., & Swearer, S. M. (2003). Research on school bullying and victimization: What have we learned and where do we go from here? *School Psychology Review, 32,* 365–383.

Espelage, D. L., & Swearer, S. M. (2004). *Bullying in American schools: An ecological perspective.* Mahwah, NJ: Lawrence Erlbaum.

Fein, R., Vossekuil, B., Pollack, W., Borum, R., Modzeleski, W., & Reddy, M. (2002). *Threat assessment in schools: A guide to managing threatening situations and to creating safe school climates.* U.S. Department of Education, Office of Elementary and Secondary Education, Safe and Drug-Free Schools Program and U.S. Secret Service, National Threat Assessment Center: Washington, DC.

Fekkes, M., Pijpers, F. I. M., & Verloove-Vanhorick, S. P. (2004). Bullying behavior and associations with psychosomatic complaints and depression in victims. *Journal of Pediatrics, 144,* 17–22.

Finkelhor, D., Ormonda, R., Turner, H., & Hamby, S. L. (2005). The victimization of children and youth. *Child Maltreatment, 10,* 5–25.

Fosse, G. K., & Holen, D. (2002). Childhood environment of adult psychiatric outpatients in Norway having been bullied in school. *Child Abuse & Neglect, 26,* 129–137.

Garofalo, R., Wolf, R. C., Kessel, S., Palfrey, S. J., & DuRant, R. H. (1998). The association between health risk behaviors and sexual orientation among a school-based sample of adolescents. *Pediatrics, 101,* 895–902.

Graham, S., & Juvonen, J. (2002). Ethnicity, peer harassment, and adjustment in middle school: An exploratory study. *Journal of Early Adolescence, 22,* 173–199.

Hanish, L. D., & Guerra, N. G. (2000). The roles of ethnicity and school context in predicting children's victimization by peers. *American Journal of Community Psychology, 28,* 201–223.

Hanish, L. D., Kochenderfer-Ladd, B., Fabes, R. A., Martin, C. L., & Denning, D. (2004). Bullying among young children: The influence of peers and teachers. In D. L. Espelage & S. M. Swearer (Eds.), *Bullying in American schools: A social-ecological perspective on prevention and intervention* (pp. 141–159). Mahwah, NJ: Lawrence Erlbaum.

Harris, S., Petrie, G., & Willoughby, W. (2002). Bullying among 9th graders: An exploratory study. *NASSP Bulletin, 86*(630).

Hawker, D. S. J., & Boulton, M. J. (2000). Twenty years' research on peer victimization and psychosocial maladjustment: A meta-analytic review of cross-sectional studies. *Journal of Child Psychology and Psychiatry, 41,* 441–455.

Haynie, D. L, Nansel, T., Eitel, P., Crump., A. D., Saylor, K., Yu, K., et al. (2001). Bullies, victims, and bully/victims: Distinct groups of at-risk youth. *Journal of Early Adolescence, 21,* 29–49.

Hazler, R. J. (1996). Bystanders: An overlooked factor in peer on peer abuse. *Journal for the Professional Counselor, 11*(2), 11–20.

Hodges, E. V. E., & Perry, D. G. (1996). Victims of peer abuse: An overview. *Journal of Emotional and Behavioral Problems, 5,* 23–28.

Holt, M. K., & Keyes, M. A. (2004). Teachers' attitudes toward bullying. In D. L. Espelage & S. M. Swearer (Eds.), *Bullying in American schools: A social-ecological perspective on prevention and intervention.* Mahwah, NJ: Lawrence Erlbaum.

Hoover, J. H., Oliver, R., & Hazler, R. J. (1992). Bullying: Perceptions of adolescent victims in the Midwestern USA. *School Psychology International, 13,* 5–16.

Janssen, I., Craig, W. M., Boyce, W. F., & Pickett, W. (2004). Associations between overweight and obesity within bullying behaviors in school-aged children. *Pediatrics, 113,* 1187–1194.

Juvonen, J., Graham, S., & Schuster, M. A. (2003). Bullying among young adolescents: The strong, the weak, and the troubled. *Pediatrics, 112,* 1231–1237.

Kallestad, J. H., & Olweus, D. (2003). Predicting teachers' and school's implementation of the Olweus Bullying Prevention Program: A multilevel study. *Prevention and Treatment, 6,* Article 21, posted October 1, 2003, http://journals.apa.org/prevention/volume6/pre0060021a.html

Kasen, S. Berenson, K., Cohen, P., & Johnson, J. G. (2004). The effects of school climate on changes in aggressive and other behaviors related to bullying. In D. L. Espelage & S. M. Swearer (Eds.), *Bullying in American schools: A social-ecological perspective on prevention and intervention* (pp. 187–210). Mahwah, NJ: Lawrence Erlbaum.

Kim, Y. S., Koh, Y., & Leventhal, B. (2005). School bullying and suicidal risk in Korean middle school students. *Pediatrics, 115,* 357–363.

Kochenderfer, B. J., & Ladd, G. W. (1996). Peer victimization: Cause or consequence of school maladjustment? *Child Develoment, 67,* 1305–1317.

Kumpulainen, K., & Rasanen, E. (2000). Children involved in bullying at elementary school age: Their psychiatric symptoms and deviance in adolescence. *Child Abuse & Neglect, 24,* 1567–1577.

Kumpulainen, K., Rasanen, E., & Puura, K. (2001). Psychiatric disorders and the use of mental health services among children involved in bullying. *Aggressive Behavior, 27,* 102–110.

Ladd, G. W., & Ladd, B. K. (1998). Parenting behaviors and parent-child relationships: Correlates of peer victimization in kindergarten. *Developmental Psychology, 34,* 1450–1458.

Lee, E., & Kim, M. (2004). Exposure to media violence and bullying at school: Mediating influences of anger and contact with delinquent friends. *Psychological Reports, 95,* 659–672.

Leff, S. S., Kupersmidt, J. B., Patterson, C. J., & Power, T. J. (1999). Factors influencing teacher identification of peer bullies and victims. *School Psychology Review, 28,* 505–517.

Limber, S. P. (2002). Addressing youth bullying behaviors. In M. Fleming & K. T. Owey (Eds.), *Proceedings of the Educational Forum on Adolescent Health: Youth Bullying* (pp. 5–16). Chicago: American Medical Association. Available online: http://www.ama-assn.org/ama1/pub/upload/mm/39/youthbullying.pdf

Limber, S. P. (2004). Implementation of the Olweus Bullying Prevention Program in American schools: Lessons learned from the field. In D. L. Espelage & S. M. Swearer (Eds.), *Bullying in American schools: An ecological perspective* (pp. 351–363). Mahwah, NJ: Lawrence Erlbaum.

Loeber, R., & Dishion, T. (1983). Early predictors of male delinquency: A review. *Psychological Bulletin, 94,* 69–99.

Martlew, M., & Hodson, J. (1991). Children with mild learning difficulties in an integrated and in a special school: Comparisons of behaviour, teasing, and teachers' attitudes. *British Journal of Educational Psychology, 61,* 355–372.

Maternal and Child Health Bureau, Health Resources and Services Administration (2005). *Take a stand. Lend a hand. Stop bullying now!* Retrieved from www.stopbullyingnow.hrsa.gov

Melton, G. B., Limber, S. P., Cunningham, P., Osgood, D. W., Chambers, J., Flerx, V., et al. (1998). *Violence among rural youth. Final report.* Washington, DC: U.S. Department of Justice, Office of Justice Programs, Office of Juvenile Justice and Delinquency Prevention.

Mishna, F. (2003). Learning disabilities and bullying: Double jeopardy. *Journal of Learning Disabilities, 36,* 1–15.

Nabuzoka, D., & Smith, P. K. (1993). Sociometric status and social behaviour of children with and without learning difficulties. *Journal of Child Psychology and Psychiatry, 34,* 1435–1448.

Nansel, T. R., Overpeck, M. D., Haynie, D. L., Ruan, W. J., & Scheidt, P. C. (2003). Relationships between bullying and violence among U. S. youth. *Archives of Pediatric Adolescent Medicine, 157,* 348–353.

Nansel, T. R., Overpeck, M. D., Pilla, R. S., Ruan, W. J., Simmons-Morton, B., & Scheidt, P. (2001). Bullying behavior among U.S. youth: Prevalence and association with psychosocial adjustment. *Journal of the American Medical Association, 285,* 2094–2100.

Olweus, D. (1978). *Aggression in the schools: Bullies and whipping boys.* Washington, DC: Wiley.

Olweus, D. (1991). Bully/victim problems among schoolchildren: Basic facts and effects of a school based intervention program (pp. 411–448). In D. J. Pepler & K. H. Rubin (Eds.), *The development and treatment of childhood aggression.* Hillsdale, NJ: Lawrence Erlbaum.

Olweus, D. (1993a). *Bullying at school: What we know and what we can do.* NY: Blackwell.

Olweus, D. (1993b). Victimization by peers: Antecedents and long-term outcomes. In K. H. Rubin & J. B. Asendorf (Eds.), *Social withdrawal, inhibition, and shyness* (pp. 315–341). Hillsdale, NJ: Lawrence Erlbaum.

Olweus, D. (1994). Annotation: Bullying at school: Basic facts and effects of a school-based intervention program. *Journal of Child Psychology and Psychiatry, 35,* 1171–1190.

Olweus, D. (2001). *Olweus' core program against bullying and antisocial behavior: A teacher handbook.* Bergen, Norway: Author.

Olweus, D., Limber, S. P., & Mihalic, S. (1999). *The bullying prevention program: Blueprints for violence prevention, Vol. 10.* Center for the Study and Prevention of Violence: Boulder, CO.

O'Moore, M. O. (2000). Critical issues for teacher training to counter bullying and victimization in Ireland. *Aggressive Behavior, 26,* 99–111.

Pellegrini, A. D. (2001). A longitudinal study of heterosexual relationships, aggression, and sexual harassment during the transition from primary school through middle school. *Journal of Applied Developmental Psychology, 22,* 1–15.

Pellegrini, A. D. (2002). Bullying, victimization, and sexual harassment during the transition to middle school. *Educational Psychologist, 37,* 151–163.

Pellegrini, A. D., & Bartini, M. (2000). An empirical comparison of methods of sampling aggression and victimization in school settings. *Journal of Educational Psychology, 92,* 360–366.

Pellegrini, A. D., & Long, J. D. (2004). Part of the solution and part of the problem: The role of peers in bullying, dominance, and victimization during the transition from primary school through secondary school. In D. L. Espelage & S. M. Swearer (Eds.), *Bullying in American schools: A social-ecological perspective on prevention and intervention* (pp. 107–117). Mahwah, NJ: Lawrence Erlbaum.

Perry, D. G., Kusel, S. J., & Perry, L. C. (1988). Victims of peer aggression. *Developmental Psychology, 24,* 807–814.

Rigby, K. (1993). School children's perceptions of their families and parents as a function of peer relations. *The Journal of Genetic Psychology, 154,* 501–513.

Rigby, K. (1994). Psychosocial functioning in families of Australian adolescent schoolchildren involved in bully/victim problems. *Journal of Family Therapy, 6,* 173–187.

Rigby, K. (1996). *Bullying in schools: And what to do about it.* Briston, PA: Jessica Kingsley Publishers.

Rigby, K., & Slee, P. T. (1991). Bullying among Australian school children: Reported behavior and attitudes towards victims. *Journal of Social Psychology, 133,* 33–42.

Rigby, K., & Slee, P. T. (1993). Dimensions of interpersonal relations among Australian school children and their implications for psychological well-being. *Journal of Social Psychology, 133,* 33–42.

Rivers, I. (2001). The bullying of sexual minorities at school: Its nature and long-term correlates. *Educational and Child Psychology, 18,* 32–46.

Rivers, I., & Smith, P. K. (1994). Types of bullying behavior and their correlates. *Aggressive Behavior, 20,* 359–368.

Roland, E. (2002). Bullying, depressive symptoms and suicidal thoughts. *Educational Research, 44,* 55–67.

Ronning, J. A., Handergaard, B. H., & Sourander, A. (2004). Self-perceived peer harassment in a community sample of Norwegian school children. *Child Abuse & Neglect, 28,* 1067–1079.

Roth, D. A., Coles, M. E., & Heimberg, R. G. (2002). The relationship between memories for childhood teasing and anxiety and depression in adulthood. *Journal of Anxiety Disorders, 16,* 149–164.

Rys, G. S., & Bear, G. G. (1997). Relational aggression and peer relations: Gender and developmental issues. *Merrill-Palmer Quarterly, 43,* 87–106.

Salmiavelli, C., Lagerspetz, K., Björkqvist, K., Österman, K., & Kaukianen, A. (1996). Bullying as a group process: Participant roles and their relations to social status within the group. *Aggressive Behavior, 22,* 1–15.

Seals, D., & Young, J. (2003). Bullying and victimization: Prevalence and relationship to gender, grade level, ethnicity, self-esteem, and depression.

Shields, A., & Cicchetti, D. (2001). Parental maltreatment and emotion dysregulation as risk factors for bullying and victimization in middle childhood. *Journal of Clinical Child Psychology, 30,* 349–363.

Slee, P. T. (1995). Peer victimization and its relationship to depression among Australian primary school students. *Personality and Individual Differences, 18,* 57–62.

Smith, P. K., & Sharp, S. (1994). *Bullying at school.* London: Routledge.

Smith, P. K., Talamelli, L., Cowie, H., Naylor, P., & Chauhan, P. (2004). Profiles of non-victims, escaped victims, continuing victims and new victims of school bullying (2004). *British Journal of Educational Psychology, 74,* 565–581.

Storch, E. A., Lewin, A. B., Silverstein, J. H., Heidgerken, A. D., Strawser, M. S., Baumeister, A., et al. (2004a). Peer victimization and psychosocial adjustment in children with type 1 diabetes. *Clinicial Pediatrics, 43,* 467–471.

Storch, E. A., Lewin, A. B., Silverstein, J. H., Heidgerken, A. D., Strawser, M. S., Baumeister, A., et al. (2004b). Social-psychological correlates of peer victimization in children with endocrine disorders. *Journal of Pediatrics, 145,* 784–784.

Sutton, J., Smith, P. K., & Swettenham, J. (1999a). Bullying and "theory of mind": A critique of the "social skills deficit" view of anti-social behaviour. *Social Development, 8,* 117–127.

Sutton, J. Smith, P. K., & Swettenham, J. (1999b). Social cognition and bullying: Social inadequacy or skilled manipulation? *British Journal of Developmental Psychology, 17,* 435–450.

Swearer, S. M., Grills, A. E., Haye, K. M., & Cary, P. T. (2004). Internalizing problems in students involved in bullying and victimization: Implications for intervention. In D. L. Espelage & S. M. Swearer (Eds.), *Bullying in American schools: A social-ecological perspective on prevention and intervention* (pp. 63–83). Mahwah, NJ: Lawrence Erlbaum.

Thompson, D., Whitney, I., & Smith, P. (1993). Bullying of children with special needs in mainstream schools. *Support for Learning, 9,* 103–106.

United States Department of Education. (1998). *Early warning, timely response.* Washington, DC: Author.

Unnever, J., D., & Cornell, D. G. (2003). The culture of bullying in middle school. *Journal of School Violence,* 2(2), 5–27.

van der Wal, M. F., de Wit, C. A. M., & Hirasing, R. A. (2003). Psychosocial health among young victims and offenders of direct and indirect bullying. *Pediatrics, 111,* 1312–1317.

Whitney, I., & Smith, P. K. (1993). A survey of the nature and extent of bullying in junior/middle and secondary schools. *Educational Research, 35,* 3–25.

Yude, C., Goodman, R., & McConachie, H. (1998). Peer problems of children with hemiplegia in mainstream primary schools. *Journal of Child Psychology & Psychiatry, 39,* 533–541.

CHAPTER 17

# *Bullying and Violence in American Schools*

ELLEN DELARA

*The attempt to trace the origin of violence to a single culprit is destined to cover up its complex origin; it is a sacrificial gesture par excellence. It is a matter of finding a scapegoat for a more generalized culpability, a more systemic participation.*

—Andrew J. McKenna, philosopher

Bullying, harassment, and emotional violence are prevalent in U.S. schools today (American Association of University Women, 2001; Devine & Lawson, 2004; Espelage & Swearer, 2004; Garbarino & deLara, 2002; Nansel, Overpeck, Pilla, Ruan, Simons-Morton, & Scheidt, 2001). Although bullying contributes to a socially toxic environment, American adults do not as yet have a good understanding of this pervasive phenomenon. While adults are enormously concerned about serious eruptions of violence, they still tend to take for granted that children are going to be bullied at school and they tend to blame the victim. The belief that if a child is bullied, he did something to bring it on himself is shared by the great majority of adults. Children, themselves, often reflect this sociocultural perspective, saying, in effect, "If you get hit at school, you probably deserve it" (deLara, 2000, 2002; Garbarino & deLara, 2002).

We have been slow to connect bullying with serious retaliatory actions among students in our schools. While adults were shocked after the tragedy at Columbine High School, when two students shot and killed classmates, a teacher, and themselves, other students across the country, though very upset, were not surprised (Garbarino & deLara, 2002; Gaughan, Cerio, & Myers, 2001). Research indicates that many children are afraid of "a Columbine" occurring in their school, or are concerned about other forms of school violence (Aronson, 2000; Garbarino & deLara, 2002; Gaughan et al., 2001; National Association of Attorneys General, 2000).

Why are our children afraid in school? In general, inclusion, dignity, and equality are not words that typically describe the climate of schools. There is no country that can say it is "a model of caring" in its public or private schools (Smith, 2003). This is a sad statement given the fact that school is considered by most adults to be the safest place for children. It is often the last refuge for many from a violent home or neighborhood.

School is our children's workplace, a workplace they must attend despite the conditions. They have no choice. Often these conditions would be both intolerable and illegal in the adult workplace. At the same time, children have far fewer legal protections from bullying and harassment than adults do. While we are still at the "blame the victim" stage about children bullied at school, the adult workplace jettisoned this attitude many years ago.

One way in which children are denied dignity, worth, equality, and inclusion is through the perpetuation of certain myths such as "Boys will be boys," "Kids are cruel," "Bullying is a part of life," and "Hazing is a just a rite of passage." Of course children can be cruel, just as adults can be. By believing in and holding onto powerful and age-old myths, however, we contribute to and perpetuate patterns that hurt children. Schools inadvertently enable bad behavior among children by believing in these myths. For true change, these fallacies must be challenged.

What is this phenomenon of bullying, harassment, and violence at school? Why is it that children seem to understand it while adults are puzzled? This chapter addresses bullying and school violence by answering several questions: What paradigm makes sense in trying to understand school violence? Who and what is involved in this ongoing and unhealthy behavior? Why does it happen? When and where does it occur during the school day? What can be done? Most importantly, this chapter offers creative solutions generated by *students* for curtailing the problem of bullying in our schools.

## A PARADIGM FOR UNDERSTANDING SCHOOL VIOLENCE

Currently, researchers are attempting to document the types, forms, perpetrators, victims, profiles, and numbers of incidents of school violence (DeVoe, Peter, Kaufman, Ruddy, Miller, et al., 2003; Vossekuil, Reddy, Fein, Borum, & Modzeleski, 2000). The theoretical frame of reference most often utilized in this research typically comes from the juvenile justice or adolescent development fields. Unfortunately, the intricacies of interactional patterns that result in violence at school are not fully investigated by the usual research paradigms. In contrast, if general system theory, as delineated by von Bertalanffy (1968) and others (Bowen, 2004; Sarason, 2001; Warren, Franklin, & Streeter, 1998), allows for a more holistic and accurate accounting of the experience of safety or violence for children. Moreover, the manner in which various members of the system contribute to or enable the persistence of a hostile environment is most readily understood from a systems perspective.

We need to ask, "Are schools inadvertently supporting or enabling a climate that allows bullying by not looking at the behaviors of everyone in the system?" A systems approach adheres to a holistic view that "the only hope of understanding any particular thing is by placing it in the appropriate system context and following the processes by which it acts" (Greenwood & Levin, 1998, p. 70). Systems seek homeostasis and balance. All systems maintain themselves through both overt and covert rules and norms. Systems will maintain even dysfunctional patterns, such as hostile environments, in the name of preserving homeostasis (Bowen, 2004; Steigelbauer, 1994; von Bertalanffy, 1968; Warren et al., 1998; Whitchurch & Constantine, 1993). Schools, as major functioning systems, are no different (Sarason, 2001). If dysfunctional behaviors or interactions have become habituated in the environment, the perceptions, behaviors, and interactions of everyone in the system need to be taken into consideration for significant change to occur. In our culture, we think in terms of cause and effect and in terms of individual responsibility. Most research on school bullying is aimed at individuals or the interactions of dyads, cliques, and small groups. However, schools, organizations, and communities operate as systems. Certain groups of kids at school are only one part of a system. The other parts are their peers and the adults. The system functions in certain, specific, and often predictable ways with norms and rules and behaviors, some of which are overt, and some covert. All of this makes up a school's own climate and culture (Rowan & Miskel, 1999; Sarason, 2001). Sometimes, in troubled systems, someone or some group will be scapegoated. The usual candidates are "those troubled kids"—children with emotional problems or special needs children.

Scapegoats and scapegoating are signals of dysfunctional systems. Where present, scapegoats serve a variety of purposes in any group or system. Two primary purposes are to facilitate group cohesion and to obscure group or collective responsibility. The original meaning of "scapegoat" harkens back to times when villagers literally pushed a goat out of town, over a cliff, or in some way sacrificed it as a figurative means of carrying away the blame for the villagers' troubles. Appointing a scapegoat allows individuals in an organization or system to evade responsibility for any actions they may have taken that contributed to the problems. Further, it allows everyone to continue to behave in the same tried and true ways. No one has to change. In this way, scapegoats and scapegoating are homeostatic mechanisms of dysfunctional systems (O'Hagan, 1993). This concept is especially prevalent in our culture, which is eager to blame someone, and not as eager to take personal responsibility when something goes wrong. The outcome, or "benefit," of scapegoating for any group is that the system does not need to change.

## DEFINITIONS OF BULLYING: WHO AND WHAT IS INVOLVED

Violence at school can take several forms and erupts on a continuum of seriousness. The continuum ranges from psychological intimidation (e.g., group exclusion, starting rumors, sexual gestures) to verbal abuse (name-calling) to physical abuse (hitting, kicking, inappropriate touching, sexual abuse) to life-threatening violence (threatening with a weapon, attempted homicide or suicide). Exclusion from the group and other similar behaviors are often referred to as relational aggression (Mullin-Rindler, 2003). Some regard relational aggression as primarily the territory of adolescent girls (Bonica, Arnold, Fisher, Zeljo, & Yershova, 2003; Crick, 1996; Crick & Grotpeter, 1995); however, there is growing evidence that boys are almost equally likely to engage in this form of bullying (Garbarino & deLara, 2002).

### *Cycle of Violence*

It is important to note that there is a cycle of violence. It is relatively rare to find someone who is exclusively a "bully." More typically, someone else has previously bullied a child who acts as a bully, at home or at school. Consequently, we see a bully-victim-bullying cycle (Widom, 1992). Sometimes, due to immaturity and their level of moral development, students believe that revenge is justified (Fatum & Hoyle, 1996). Unfortunately, the "bully" in most contexts is seen as the child who is physically aggressive, while the child or children who are verbal bullies slip under the notice of most adults.

### *Whose Definition Should We Use*

One of the shortcomings of current research in this area has been the use of adult definitions as well as adult-driven strategies and solutions for overcoming violence. Adults typically define bullying, and most interventions to prevent or curtail bullying are adult-determined (Garbarino & deLara, 2002; Harachi, Catalano & Hawkins, 1999; Olweus, 1993a). Students are left out of the process of program development. Their input is not solicited regarding what will be effective, yet many anti-bullying programs rest on student implementation (deLara & Garbarino, 2003). It is critical to understand what students mean by bullying and harassment, and it is crucial that they are involved in the determination of solutions for any program to succeed.

Alternative research efforts allow students, the primary stakeholders at school, to self-define violent situations, exchanges, and interactions in various parts of the school and among various subgroups, including teachers and other adults (Astor, Meyer, & Behre, 1999; deLara, 2000, 2002; Garbarino & deLara, 2002). Children's definitions and perceptions of violence at school are contextual. They are influenced by gender, age, grade level, ethnicity, geographic region, peer group associations, family factors, level of moral development, and individual attribution of cues in the environment (Alloy, Peterson, Abramson, & Seligman, 1984; deLara, 2000, 2002; Fatum & Hoyle, 1996; Garbarino & deLara, 2002; Hudley & Friday, 1996; Litke, 1996).

Children define bullying differently than adults do. Children tend to say such things as "He's picking on me" or "She started a rumor about me" or "He's following me." Their language about bullying is more understated than adults. Most surveys and anti-bullying programs use the definition of bullying developed by Olweus (1993a), which states that bullying must be chronic and perpetrated by one or more individuals with more power than the victim. This is simply not the case. Ask any young person who has been held upside down over a toilet bowl by four peers if he or she felt bullied. The answer, of course, is "Yes." That same child or teenager feels intimidated by those peers for a very long time, even though the incident happened one time and was, therefore, not chronic. Chronicity, or an adult attempt to figure out power differentials, should not be included as factors in any definition of bullying.

### *Specific Forms of Bullying*

#### *Sexual harassment*

Sexual harassment is a form of bullying. Sexual harassment can appear in many guises, from unwanted remarks to dating violence to stalking. In all of its forms, it interferes with healthy social development and academic success (Fineran & Bennett, 1998). Both girls and boys report high rates of being sexually harassed at school—83% of girls and 79% of boys (AAUW, 2001). Half of the students in the AAUW survey admitted to sexually harassing someone else. In the same sample of over 2,000 children, 38% said that teachers and other school employees sexually harass students.

The situation is worse for gay, lesbian, bisexual, transgender, and questioning (GLBTQ) students. GLBTQ adolescents are treated very badly in our schools (Elze, 2003). They are five times more likely to miss school for fear for their safety or to have been threatened with a weapon than are heterosexual kids (Garofalo, Wolf, Kessel, Palfrey, & DuRant, 1998). Human Rights Watch (2001) found that GLBTQ students spend much of their time trying to figure out how to be safe in school. As a result, nearly one-third of GLBTQ teens drop out of school due to bullying, harassment, and fear for their safety at school (Lambda Legal, 2002). Unfortunately, these children cannot always find refuge with the adults at school. Human Rights Watch (2001) found that adults often turn their backs, encourage, or participate in the abuse. This is a clear example of systemic shunning and shaming (Scott, 1995).

### *Hazing*

Hazing, with its full range of demeaning behaviors, has a long history in many societies. Hazing has been traditionally associated with entrance into fraternal organizations. Young men and women eager to join exclusive groups have allowed themselves to be subjected to all manner of treatment by members of the sought-after club. The inherently human need to belong promotes willingness to suffer whatever it takes to be accepted (Guynn & Aquila, 2004).

The extent to which tormentors and their victims would go in the name of traditional hazing was seen in 2003 at the so-called "Powder Puff Football" event in Illinois. During this activity, upper-class students kicked, punched, and tormented their blindfolded younger peers in the name of "tradition." The school and parents (even those who provided alcohol for the event) disclaimed any responsibility for the actions of those involved, especially since the younger students had "volunteered" to be part of the initiation (Napolitano, 2003).

### *Cyber-Bullying*

A relatively new form of bullying has developed along with advances in technology. Through cyber-bullying, children are able to torment one another in relative anonymity on cell phones and computers. Instant messaging (IM), personal Web sites, and Web logs (blogs) allow a new and pervasive form of nastiness by adolescents toward one another (Blair, 2003). Without having to see the devastation on the face of the other person, it is easier to deliver a psychological assault. According to some psychologists, children say things in these venues that they would never say face-to-face and often have no idea of the level of harm inflicted (Harmon, 2004). Out of the view of adults and with little chance of detection, adolescents are able to minimize any harm that might accrue from their behavior online. Further, they tend to "equate the legality of behavior with the ethics of behavior" (Berson, Berson, & Ferron, 2002, p. 66). In other words, for many teens, if it is legal, it is okay, regardless of any moral or ethical concerns.

## EXPOSURE TO BULLYING: HOW MANY ARE INVOLVED

It is difficult to make an absolute statement about the number of children exposed to bullying and violence in their schools as direct victims, bullies, or as bystanders. International research demonstrates that the problem of violence at school is a worldwide health concern (Eslea & Mukhtar, 2000; Smith, 2003; Smith, Morita, Junger-Tas, Olweus, et al., 1999). Virtually all children from kindergarten through high school are affected by bullying in some form each day at school as bystander, recipient, or perpetrator. Often, the bullying is "just" verbal or emotionally loaded exchanges. Frequently, it is meant as a psychological blow. Fried and Fried (1996) found that in a typical week, children receive over 200 insults from their peers at school. Recent comprehensive national studies place the rate of bullying at anywhere from 30–85% of all middle and high school students. In 2001, the *Journal of the American Medical Association* (JAMA) reported that 30% of U.S. students in the sixth through tenth grades were involved in moderate or frequent bullying activities, as perpetrator, victim, or both (Nansel et al., 2001). Another study found that 77% of junior high and high school students in small Midwest towns have been bullied at school (U.S. Department of Education, 1998). When bullying and violence take on the form of sexual harassment, the numbers of students involved can be staggering (AAUW, 2001).

### *Who Tends to Get Bullied*

The majority of students in U.S. schools are subjected to various forms of bullying. However, children who are different by virtue of appearance, disability, socioeconomic status, or other distinguishing characteristics are very likely subjects for bullying. Children with physical, emotional, or learning disabilities are among the most frequent targets (Eamon, 2001; Mishna, 2003). Students say those who look, act, or dress differently; are on the autism spectrum; or have mental health, alcohol, or other drug problems are the most likely to be excluded and abused at school (deLara, 2002; Garbarino & deLara, 2002). Ironically, more children than ever before with health and mental health problems are in the "mainstream" classroom. This change is due to shifts in educational philosophy, availability and prescribing of medications, and current public policy. In the United States, 21% of our children have a diagnosed mental disorder or addiction, 8% of secondary students suffer from clinical depression, and 20 to 25% of secondary students have seriously considered suicide (Commission on Children at Risk et al., 2003). Children and adolescents, with their limited maturity, are often not well equipped to interact appropriately with peers who display special needs. Most students respond and react to peers with special needs in benign or even helpful ways; however, this is not always the case. Education is compromised for children who are targets of bullying; sometimes, dropping out is a direct result (DeLuca & Rosenbaum, 2000; Rumberger, 2001). This complicates an already uncertain future, particularly for young people with disabilities (Balfanz & Letgers, 2001; Heubert, 1999).

Children do not really allow much room for their peers to be different or to express differences. When the shootings occurred at Columbine High School in April 1999, one young man, a Columbine athlete, summed up the opinions of some of his classmates toward the perpetrators:

> Columbine is a clean, good place except for those rejects [Klebold, Harris, and friends]. Most kids didn't want them here. They were into witchcraft. They were into voodoo dolls. Sure, we teased them. But what do you expect with kids who come to school with weird hairdos and horns on their hats? It's not just the jocks; the whole school's disgusted with them. They're a bunch of homos, grabbing each other's private parts. (Gibbs & Roche, 1999, pp. 50–51)

### *Who Does the Bullying*

#### *Problematic peers*

Research indicates a large portion of young people are involved in bullying others in the form of verbal abuse or sexual harassment (AAUW, 2001). While many students do not categorize their peers, others say trouble at school or on the bus is ignited by the "Goths," "kids who are different," "hicks and scrubs," "druggies," "athletes," or the "bullies" (deLara, 2002; Garbarino & deLara, 2002). Regarding drug use, students are concerned that school personnel and parents do not have adequate knowledge about drug use by other students. This lack of awareness of the extent of the problem makes students feel unsafe at school and taints their ability to trust adults (Garbarino & deLara, 2002; Gaughan et al., 2001).

*Teachers and other adults as bullies*

Teachers and other school personnel are among those who bully or harass children (AAUW, 2001; DeLuca & Rosenbaum, 2000; U.S. Department of Education, 2004). They make children feel insecure by virtue of some of their observable behaviors or due to a reputation for inappropriate student–teacher interactions (Human Rights Watch, 2001; Hyman & Snook, 1999; Kyle, 1999; U.S. Department of Education, 2004). The consequences of adult-to-child bullying or harassment can be devastating and include decreased interest in school, alienation from school, impact on academic achievement, and decisions to drop out (DeLuca & Rosenbaum, 2000; Orpinas, Horne, & Staniszewski, 2003).

### *The Role of Race and Ethnicity*

Students' cultural differences are expressed in styles of dress, behavior, eye contact, and verbal expression. Even when students and adults make good-faith attempts to figure out the meaning of such differences, the efforts can be anxiety producing. When students and school personnel fail to understand the meaning of cultural differences, needless conflict can be the result. Some teachers and other school personnel engage in disparaging remarks to students (DeLuca & Rosenbaum, 2000), perhaps to control or change behavior they find uncomfortable or unacceptable.

For example, teachers typically perceive Mexican American elementary students and Asian American students as cooperative and quiet, while they often see African American students as loud and aggressive (Cartledge & Johnson, 2004). Sociological studies reveal that African American students tend to be direct, confrontational, and highly energized in their arguing style, as well as in their playing style. Teachers and other adults can misinterpret this stylistic difference, leading to inappropriate responses or unnecessary discipline. To further complicate matters, minority students engage in derision within their own cultural groups toward peers who are academically inclined. Friends or peers who achieve academically or who dress like students from the mainstream culture are harassed and bullied for "acting White" (Cartledge & Johnson, 2004).

## WHY DOES IT HAPPEN

From an individual perspective, kids say picking on others can sometimes make you feel good because it gives you a sense of power. For a moment, "you're better than someone else." And sometimes you can impress your friends if you do it. But they express a sense of sadness that some kids get picked on every day, even though they are "so annoying" they "bring it on themselves" (deLara & Garbarino, 2003).

Bullying can become institutionalized and it is a form of institutional violence when this happens. In one example, a high school changed its policies to zero tolerance for bullying. When the new policies were implemented, school athletes were angry. They felt that the social hierarchy of the school culture had been disturbed. As seniors, they made comments like "Now it's our turn" and "Now [the freshmen] get away with whatever they want" (Leland, 2001, p. 6).

It may look like the purpose of bullying is to be mean, for retaliation, or for power over others. And while this may be a part of the truth, these are first-order purposes of bullying. The underlying purpose or function of bullying is as a form of social control and an attempt to force conformity with group norms (Pelligrini, Bartini, & Brooks, 1999). Another underlying function of bullying is to force conformity with certain very predictable societal norms. Bullying and harassment are means of enculturation and socialization particularly aimed at those outside of the norm—in dress, speech, general attitude, or behavior. School "superstars" are less likely to be reprimanded or censured for such behavior not only because they are prized by the school, but also because they are carrying out the work of adults and society. When older children do the work of adults in families, they are referred to as Parentified Children (Boszormenyi-Nagy & Sparks, 1973). In schools, those who bully with impunity may be the Parentified Children in the system. In effect, when teens bully others like Goths or GLBTQ, many adults agree with the overall goal of the bullying—enforcing conformity to social norms of behavior, dress, or attitude. This is a possible explanation for why they do not intervene to stop it (Duttweiler, 1997; Human Rights Watch, 2001). The school as an organization values conformity and considers it essential to its homeostasis (Rowan & Miskel, 1999) and mission (Sarason, 2001). The Parentified Children of the system will push, pull, and manipulate other children to coerce them into "proper" standards of dress, behavior, and attitude.

Conformity is an essential component of safety and security. Sameness promotes a sense of security. Uniformity is valued by adolescents (Lashbrook, 2000) and by society as a whole (Knafo, 2003), never more so than now. Consequently, the ability to predict the behavior of peers is valued. One way to facilitate "peer predictability" (deLara, 2002) is to bully people into specified modes of personal expression, personal behavior, and interpersonal interactions. Limiting the range of anyone's behavior enhances predictability, thereby enhancing a sense of safety for everyone. Meanness (physical, verbal, emotional, and psychological) does serve the purpose of establishing power over others, but power over another in and of itself is not the ultimate end. The end goal of most forms of bullying is in service to the "greater good" of conformity—leading to predictability and therefore a sense of safety (deLara, 2002).

Bullies are essentially fear-based people who respond aggressively when they no longer have control over a particular situation or relationship (Ehrensaft, Cohen, Brown, Smailes, Chen et al., 2003; McGuigan, Vuchinich, & Pratt, 2000). Fear is the underlying trigger for the response of violence. Similarly, school bullying at the secondary school level is fueled by fear as well—fear of the behavior of others who act different or have different values. The fear need not be for physical safety but may be experienced as a threat to the continuation of a particular group, lifestyle, or way of doing things. Bullying is an effective means of keeping things the same and acts as a homeostatic balancing mechanism.

Unfortunately, parents can be the first bullies in a child's life, inflicting abuse in a variety of forms from psychological to physical (Finkelhor & Ormrod, 2001; Straus & Field, 2003; Vorrasi, deLara, & Bradshaw, 2005). The research of Straus and Field (2003) indicates that fully 96% of all American children are subject to some form of verbal abuse by their parents. This may be part of the reason that children are unable to figure out how to deal with schoolyard bullying. At some level, they are used to it—but they are not encouraged to stand up to the parental bully.

## *Where and When Does Bullying Occur*

Students report that they feel unsafe at various times during the school day due to these general factors:

1. Bullying or harassing behaviors by some of their peers;
2. Unpredictable behavior of some specific groups of their peers;

3. Lack of adult awareness of the extent of verbal, sexual, and physical bullying;
4. Lack of adult awareness of alcohol or drug involvement of peers at school;
5. Lack of adult supervision and intervention.

(AAUW, 2001; deLara, 2002; deLara & Garbarino, 2003; Glover, Gough, Johnson, & Cartwright, 2000).

### *Unsupervised spaces*

Unsupervised or undersupervised spaces are unsettling for most students. They cite the hallways, locker rooms, restrooms, and school buses as problematic in terms of their potential for bullying and harassment (Astor, Meyer, & Behre, 1999; Doll, Murphy, & Song, 2003; Garbarino & deLara, 2002). Because restrooms are totally unsupervised areas, many avoid the restrooms all day. Others try to predict what their peers may do (deLara, 2002) while in the restrooms and locker rooms to enhance their sense of security. While a small high school allows for fewer unsafe or unowned spaces, it is not a guarantee to students that they will be safe from bullying or harassment (Astor et al., 1999; Garbarino & deLara, 2002). A small school theoretically allows for greater adult awareness, supervision, intervention, and caring than a student can expect at a large school. Researchers in this country as well as in Scandinavian countries are advocating for the creation of small schools to provide a better school climate and to reduce bullying in the school environment (Ancess, 2003; Coleman, 2002; Kelker, 1998; Smith, 2003).

### *The school bus*

There are a variety of problems associated with the daily school bus ride for children in Grades K through 12. The bus is a highly unsupervised part of the school day. Most districts cannot afford to provide an aide, so the driver is faced with the almost impossible expectation of driving safely and keeping order. Glover et al. (2000) notes that the school bus is a problem for children because "who you are and where you live is obvious to those who want to make your life difficult" (p. 147). Surveys indicate that the school bus is the most problematic part of the day for students (Richardson, 2002). It is an unpleasant and upsetting way to start and end the school day. Students are subject to harassment by their peers or to witnessing acts of varying degrees of bullying (Garbarino & deLara, 2002).

## IMPACT OF BULLYING

No child should be subjected to disrespectful treatment or a hostile school environment. In addition, there are many consequences of bullying for perpetrators, victims, and bystanders. We know that chronic victims experience more physical and psychological problems than other children (Coleman, 2002; Limber & Nation, 2004; Olweus, 1993b). Research has found that children who are victims of bullying may be at increased risk for depression, poor self-esteem, and other mental health problems as adults (Olweus, 1993b). Bullies, also, are at risk for poor short-term as well as long-term outcomes (Espelage & Swearer, 2003). Skipping school, dropping out of school, and vandalism are all great possibilities for this group of students (Olweus, 1993b). Several studies have documented that aggressive 8-year-olds are very likely to continue to be aggressive throughout school and to participate in criminal activity as young adults (Eron, Huesmann, Dubow, Romanoff, & Yarmel, 1987; Kellam, Xiange, Merisca, Brown, & Ialongo, 1998). Bystanders suffer in several ways. They experience considerable discomfort in witnessing the bullying, harassment, and victimization of their family, friends, or peers (Atlas & Pepler,

1998; Molnar, Buka, Brennan, Holton, & Earls, 2003). Bystanders often feel fearful at school and ashamed for not intervening (Garbarino & deLara, 2002).

Too many American students are afraid to go to school or fearful while they are there. Every day, 160,000 children skip school over fears for their safety (Jordan, McPartland, & Lara, 1999). The Centers for Disease Control (2003) surveyed more than 10,000 students in 2003 and found that more than one 1 of 20 high school students skip school due to safety concerns.

### *Bullying and Suicide*

Researchers and mental health practitioners contend that the impact of chronic bullying can be crushing and can have both immediate and life-long consequences (Ambert, 1994; Crothers & Kolbert, 2004; deLara, 2002; Fried & Fried, 1996; Hazler, Miller, & Green, 2001; Orpinas et al., 2003; Schuster, 1996). Perhaps as a result, a significant proportion of our young people are living with thoughts of suicide and despair. According to the 1998 Wisconsin Youth Risk Behavior Survey (Kadel, 1998), fully 50% of all high school students have "seriously considered" suicide before they graduate. Much of the despair they feel is not so-called "normal adolescent unhappiness." It is the result of the unrelenting, day-after-day emotional violence they experience in their schools (Garbarino & deLara, 2002). An important precedent to suicidal thinking and action frequently is depression. In a recent survey, 29%of all students in Grades 9 through 12 reported feeling persistent sadness or hopelessness almost every day for an extended period in the last year (Child Trends Data, 2003).

In systemic terms, when kids are suicidal it is a symptom. It is a symptom not only that they are in pain, but also that the system is malfunctioning. It is safe to conclude that this is another way that bullying is taking an unacceptable toll in the lives of children, their families, and their communities.

## STUDENT STRATEGIES TO TRY TO STAY SAFE

Individual and social protective factors such as temperament, cognitive-behavioral strategies, relationships with teachers, peer group supports, and connection with school and family heavily influence a child's ability to cope with bullying at school (Bowman, 2002; deLara, 2002; Lantieri & Patti, 1996; Naylor & Cowie, 1999; Smith, Hill, Evans, & Bandera, 2000). Students rely on their close friendships to protect them. Research indicates that the place of peer group support is essential as a buffer against bullying (Eamon, 2001; Hodges, Boivin, Vitaro, & Bukowski, 1999; Naylor & Cowie, 1999).

Students have specific strategies they use to get through the day. Some strategies are healthy ones such as joining a group with what they call a "worthy goal," e.g., a band, the track team, the student newspaper (Garbarino & deLara, 2002). Some strategies are less healthy. Children adopt a variety of ways to avoid the perpetrators of their victimization and to elude the sad and angry feelings that are generated in this environment. They may skip school, feel too "sick" to go to school, skip specific classes, drop out of school, use alcohol and other drugs, and in some instances resort to suicide as a means to escape the humiliation and intimidation they experience at school (DeLuca & Rosenbaum, 2000; Garbarino & deLara, 2002; Hazler et al., 2001; McPartland & Jordan, 2002).

### *Gangs*

Sadly, gangs provide protection at school and in the community, a sense of family, and a place of acceptance—elements that are missing for many young people in America (Goldstein & Kodluboy, 1998; Kodluboy, 2004). Gangs are not exclusive to urban area schools, although they are a common feature of most large urban schools (Juarez, 1996; Kodluboy, 2004). Research indicates that gangs and gang behavior are seen in suburban and rural areas as well (Barrow, VanZommeren, Young, & Holtman, 2001; Garbarino & deLara, 2002; Goldstein & Kodluboy, 1998; Kodluboy, 2004). It is important to point out that gangs are not the sole province of minority students as is often portrayed in the media. Rural and suburban areas also support gangs, many of them composed strictly of Caucasian students (Kodluboy, 2004). Though gangs can be found in many areas of the United States, schools administrators tend to deny the presence of gangs in their schools (Kodluboy, 2004). Adolescents, however, confirm the existence and impact of gangs, even in schools considered "safe" by the community (deLara, 2002; Garbarino & deLara, 2002).

### *Peer Predictability*

Another mechanism or strategy that adolescents develop to enhance their sense of safety is "peer predictability" (deLara, 2002). Effective peer predictability seems to have three basic components: small school size; familiarity or recognition of others by sight; and familiarity of behavioral range, patterns, and reactions. Many adolescents try to anticipate *where* on the campus bullying may occur and *who* may be a threat to them. Adolescents attempt to "size up" each other as potentially harmful or helpful (deLara, 2002).

## POSSIBLE SOLUTIONS

The solutions to the problems of bullying, harassment, and other forms of school violence can be found in implementing holistic, preventive programs; forming policies that incorporate input from students; and creating caring school climates.

### *Student Solutions for Safe Schools*

#### *Adult awareness*

Students have very important contributions to make in solving the problems of bullying and other forms of violence. They want to increase everyone's awareness of the problems in schools. Currently, they believe that adults are clueless about the realities of school life. Students suggest that schools should be small so everyone can get to know each other—teachers, students, and administrators (Garbarino & deLara, 2002). Many years of research on school size support the idea that keeping schools small (800 students or less) enhances academic achievement and decreases a student's sense of alienation (Barker & Gump, 1964; Garbarino, 1980; Martin, 2000; Raywid, 1998).

#### *Adult supervision*

Students want more adult supervision on school property and on buses. They are requesting more intervention and prevention efforts (Garbarino & deLara, 2002; deLara & Garbarino, 2003). Without adult supervision, they presume school personnel and parents do not really care about them as people. They conclude that adults are only interested in them as academic performers (deLara & Garbarino, 2003). Glover and colleagues (2000) found that fully 45% of the students they interviewed in 25 schools said their experience at school was not happy due to lack of adult supervision.

#### *A worthy goal*

Children say that if all students had the opportunity to pursue "a worthy goal" such as being part of a team or participating in a year-long service project, they would feel valued by their school. Studies indicate that adolescents in the United States believe one of the reasons the tragedy at Columbine High School occurred was because the perpetrators did not have anything worthy to work toward (Garbarino & deLara, 2002; Gaughan et al., 2001). Educational research has long supported the idea that students who are actively engaged in school activities are more likely to feel valued by their schools and thus are more likely to feel a positive attachment to the school (Calabrese & Schumer, 1986; Garbarino, 1980).

### *Character education*

Character education or "respect" classes are cited repeatedly by students as helpful because they believe some of their peers "need a second kind of parent" in school to help with good decision making (Garbarino & deLara, 2002). In an attempt to stem violence in schools, character education has been mandated in some areas of the country. In 2000, the New York State Legislature amended the education law to require instruction in civility, citizenship, and character education on the "principles of honesty, tolerance, personal responsibility, respect for others" through Project SAVE.

### *Student involvement in safety planning*

Adolescents believe that all students should be included in ongoing discussions of solutions to the problems in school culture. By this they mean that students from every level of achievement have something to offer and that without their inclusion, an important piece of the puzzle is missing. It is clear that students from the high-achieving groups have a very different school experience than the lower-achieving students in the same school. The middle-of-the-road achievers have yet another experience of the school and its climate. Thus it is important to heed the words of the students that to know what is going on, we need to ask students—all of them (deLara, 2000, 2002; Garbarino & deLara, 2002).

### *Change school design*

Students would like to see improvements in school design. They notice that hallways are not wide enough for the volume of students in the buildings. This facilitates physical bullying and sexual harassment (Astor et al., 1999). Overly close quarters and other undesirable design conditions make it more difficult for teachers to supervise and for students to escape trouble started by someone else in close proximity (deLara & Garbarino, 2003). Narrow, dark, unsupervised hallways should be eliminated in new school construction and better supervised in current older buildings. When classes change, all age groups are colliding in the halls at the same time. Adolescents believe it is not smart to put younger students in the hallways at the same time as the older ones. Further, they are mystified that adults cannot see this simple fact and figure out how to remedy it. According to students, changing this model would cut down on violence at school (Garbarino & deLara, 2002).

## LEGAL DECISIONS AND BULLYING

There have been groundbreaking legal decisions that hold schools accountable for bullying and harassment. Not only are families initiating legal action, they are winning decisions with considerable awards (Fineran, 2002; Garbarino & deLara, 2002; Guynn & Aquila, 2004). One avenue for the legal pursuit of schools is under Title IX, which provides federal funding to schools (Federal Title IX, 1972). Title IX prohibits sex discrimination in any educational facility receiving federal money. In *Davis v. Monroe Board of Education,* 1999 (Grube & Lens, 2003), the U.S. Supreme Court ruled that a school could face a sex-discrimination suit for failing to intervene when one student complains of sexual harassment by another. In another case, Jamie Nabozny's school district paid him over $900,000 after the court decided that his constitutional rights had been violated when school officials failed to stop other students in his junior and senior high school from bullying, taunting, and tormenting him once he acknowledged that he was gay (Logue, 1997).

## *Policy, Practice, and Programs*

Education policy makers have to reevaluate the current focus of teaching for testing and return to educating the whole child. If this goal is to be accomplished, policy makers have to understand the place of school safety in children's ability to concentrate and learn. There is a connection between children who feel unsafe at school and children who are "troublemakers" at school, children who are underachievers and children who drop out of school.

### *Technology*

The installation of high-tech equipment is utilized in school districts to provide some semblance of safety. In urban areas, children are accustomed to buildings equipped with metal detectors and other forms of technology meant to curtail violent incidents. Urban students often perceive their schools as a refuge from violent neighborhoods. As such they are tolerant toward technology used to keep their schools weapon free (American Civil Liberties Union, 2001). These same means are largely missing from most suburban and rural schools. Students in urban and rural areas perceive technological interventions differently. The majority say they do not want to attend a school where surveillance equipment is deemed necessary and believe other means for addressing safety concerns should be implemented (Garbarino & deLara, 2002). School districts should resist the wholesale deployment of technological quick fixes and instead do comprehensive surveying and problem solving with students as their partners.

### *Programs of promise*

There are programs that show promise for decreasing school violence. In general, these are approaches that take a holistic or systemic perspective (Astor, Benbenishty, & Marachi, 2004). One such program is Peace Power for Adolescents (Mattaini, 2001). This program is based on the concept that there are two types of power: coercive and adversarial, or constructive. Basis concepts of this model include four essential steps: (1) increase positive feedback to students from adults and their peers; (2) act with respect; (3) share power to build community; and (4) encourage a holistic understanding of how to resolve conflict.

### *First-order vs. second-order change*

Anti-bullying programs, anger management curricula, and dispute resolution mediation are all useful components of an effective safe school plan. However, used alone, they provide only first-order change. If incorporated into a holistic design, they are useful aspects for true second-order change. To expect any program to stand on its own, without a true systemic approach, is naïve and potentially dangerous. Currently, most schools implement some form of anti-bullying program without looking at evaluation studies or investigating the fit of the program for their particular school, grade levels, or mix of students and school personnel (Garbarino & deLara, 2004; Hazler, 1998; Orpinas et al., 2003). Further, most anti-bullying programs and curricula rest squarely on the shoulders of children to implement and require children to be responsible for providing the motivation for a respectful environment. This type of model is not developmentally appropriate.

Research recognizes the place of the bystander in the phenomenon of bullying. However, students say that attempting to interrupt bullying, in either a physical or psychological encounter, places them as the next target (Garbarino & deLara, 2002; O'Connell, Pepler, & Craig, 1999). When most adults are unable to interrupt sexist or racist interactions in their own workplaces, how can we expect more from children?

It is inappropriate to place the preponderance of responsibility for a safe school climate on programs that target intervention by bystander children. All models that demonstrate true second-order change involve adults as well as children in the program's realization and do not expect changes in school climate to come exclusively from the behavioral change of children.

In keeping with a systemic view of school violence and intervention, the U.S. Surgeon General's report (U.S. Department of Health and Human Services, 2001) addressing youth violence found that non-systemic or non-holistic approaches are ineffective. Successful programs use school-wide interventions.

## CONCLUSION

It is inaccurate to view the violence in today's schools as merely a statement of misunderstandings between one racial or ethnic group and another or one socioeconomic group and another. It is critical to consider the problems from a systemic perspective and to analyze the role of each member of the system, adults as well as children. Further, schools are a microcosm of society. On the national political front, we give a mixed message to our children about working together with others to try for a peaceful existence or for effective problem resolution. How do these ideas and behaviors compete with our local anti-bullying program messages? Children mimic what they see. Their greatest influences are not their peers, but the adults around them. All humans imitate those with power. Our children are witness through the media to an ethic, on a national scale, that says, "The strong survive" and "Might makes right." How can we be surprised if some of our children act this out?

The responsibility for the education of a community's children resides with everyone. All benefit or suffer from the local school district's successes or failures. Community stakeholders, including parents, teachers, bus drivers, business leaders, students, as well as school district administrators, should be engaged. However, in all communities, students *must* be included. Without the input of students from all levels of academic achievement, adults will be unsuccessful in program, practice, and policy development.

There are those who still cling to the belief that bullying will always exist at school and not much can be done about it. In the meantime, model schools across the nation dispel this myth. Children, themselves, are telling us that bullying and harassment are unacceptable to them. At the same time, they can affect only one part of the solution. It is the responsibility of adults to ensure a safe school environment and it is only in this climate that children can learn and teachers can teach. We must recognize this fact and move to provide school personnel with the resources to conduct the business of educating the whole child. School is our children's workplace, as well as their primary social environment. In endorsing this fact, we will accord children the protections under the law they deserve to grow and become the future well-prepared, contributing citizens our country needs.

## REFERENCES


Alloy, L., Peterson, C., Abramson, L., & Seligman, M. (1984). Attributional styles and the generality of learned helplessness. *Journal of Personality and Social Psychology, 46,* 681–687.

Ambert, A. M. (1994). A qualitative study of peer abuse and its effects: Theoretical and empirical implications. *Journal of Marriage and the Family, 56*(1), 119–130.

American Association of University Women (AAUW). (2001). *Hostile hallways: Bullying, teasing, and sexual harassment in school.* Washington, DC: Author.

American Civil Liberties Union (ACLU). (2001). *From words to weapons: The violence surrounding our schools.* Retrieved September 28, 2004, from http://www.aclu-sc.org/school.html

Ancess, J. (2003). *Beating the odds: High school as communities of commitment.* New York: Teachers' College Press.

Aronson, E. (2000). *No one left to hate: Teaching compassion after Columbine.* New York: W. H. Freeman.

Astor, R., Benbenishty, R., & Marachi, R. (2004). Violence in schools. In P. Allen-Meares (Ed.), *Social work services in schools* (4th ed., pp. 149–182). New York: Pearson.

Astor, R., Meyer, H., & Behre, W. (1999). Unowned places and times: Maps and interviews about violence in high schools. *American Educational Research Journal, 36*(1), 3–42.

Atlas, R. S., & Pepler, D. J. (1998). Observations of bullying in the classroom. *The Journal of Educational Research, 92*(2), 86–99.

Balfanz, R., & Letgers, N. (2001). How many central city high schools have a severe dropout problem, where are they located, and who attends them? Initial estimates using the common core of data. Presented at *Dropouts in America: How severe is the problem? What do we know about intervention and prevention? A forum convened by The Civil Rights Project* at Harvard University's Graduate School of Education and Achieve, Inc., on January 13, 2001, Cambridge, MA. Retrieved June 6, 2001, from http://www.law.harvard.edu/civilrights/publications/dropouts/dropout/balfanz.htm1

Barker, R., & Gump, P. (1964). *Big school, small school: High school size and student behavior.* Stanford, CA: Stanford University Press.

Barrow, R., VanZommeren, W., Young, C., & Holtman, P. (2001). School counselors' and principals' perceptions of violence: Guns, gangs, and drugs in rural schools. *The Rural Educator, 22*(2), 1–7.

Berson, I. R., Berson, M. J. & Ferron, J. M. (2002). Emerging risks of violence in the digital age: Lessons for educators from an online study of adolescent girls in the United States. *Journal of School Violence, 1*(2), 51–72.

Blair, J. (2003). New breed of bullies torment their peers on the internet. *Education Week, 22*(21), 6.

Bonica, C., Arnold, D., Fisher, P., Zeljo, A., & Yershova, K. (2003). Relational aggression, relational victimization, and language development in preschoolers. *Social Development, 12*(4), 552–562.

Boszormenyi-Nagy, I., & Sparks, G. (1973). *Invisible loyalties: Reciprocity in intergenerational family therapy.* Hagerstown, MD: Harper & Row.

Bowen, G. L. (2004). Social organizations and schools: A general systems theory perspective. In P. Allen-Meares (Ed.), *Social work services in schools* (4th ed., pp. 53–70). Boston: Pearson.

Bowman, D. H. (2002, April 24). School "connectedness" makes for healthier students, study suggests. *Education Week*. Retrieved May 23, 2002, from http://www.edweek.org/ew/ew_printstory.cfm?slug=32health.h21

Calabrese, R. L., & Schumer, H. (1986). The effects of service activities on adolescent alienation. *Adolescence, 21*(83), 675–687.

Cartledge, G., & Johnson, C. T. (2004). School violence and cultural sensitivity, In J. P. Conoley & A. P. Goldstein (Eds.), *School violence intervention: A practical handbook* (2nd ed., pp. 441–482). New York: The Guildford Press.

Centers for Disease Control (CDC). (2003). Youth risk behavior survey. 2003 National school-based YRBS: Public use data documentation. Retrieved August 27, 2004, from http://www.cdc.gov/HealthyYouth/YRBS/data2003/yrbs2003 codebook.pdf

Child Trends Data. (2003). Retrieved August 27, 2004, from http://childtrends databank.org/indicators/30FeelSadorHopeless.cfm

Coleman, D. L. (2002). *Fixing Columbine: The challenge to American liberalism.* Durham, NC: Carolina Academic Press.

Commission on Children at Risk. (2003). *Hardwired to connect: The new scientific case for authoritative communities: A report to the nation from the Commission on Children at Risk cosponsored by the YMCA of the USA, Dartmouth Medical College, and the Institute for American Values.* New York: Institute for American Values.

Crick, N. R. (1996). The role of overt aggression, relational aggression, and prosocial behavior in the prediction of children's future social adjustment. *Child Development, 67,* 2317–2327.

Crick, N. R., & Grotpeter, J. K. (1995). Relational aggression, gender, and social-psychological adjustment. *Child Development, 66,* 710–722.

Crothers, L. M., & Kolbert, J. B. (2004). Comparing middle school teachers' and students' views on bullying and anti-bullying interventions. *Journal of School Violence,* 3(1), 17–32.

deLara, E. (2000). *Adolescents' perceptions of safety at school and their solutions for enhancing safety and decreasing school violence: A rural case study.* Doctoral dissertation, Cornell University.

deLara, E. (2002). Peer predictability: An adolescent strategy for enhancing a sense of safety at school. *Journal of School Violence, 1*(3), 31–56.

deLara, E., & Garbarino, J. (2003). An educator's guide to school-based interventions In J. M. Cooper (Ed.), *Houghton Mifflin guide series.* Boston: Houghton Mifflin.

DeLuca, S., & Rosenbaum, J.E. (2000). Are dropout decisions related to safety concerns, social isolation, and teacher disparagement? *Harvard Law Review.* Retrieved September 4, 2004, from http://www.law.harvard.edu/civilrights/publications/dropouts/dropout/deluca.html

Devine, J., & Lawson, H.A. (2004). The complexity of school violence: Commentary from the US. In P. K. Smith (Ed.), *Violence in schools: The response in Europe* (pp. 332–350).

DeVoe, J. F., Peter, K., Kaufman, P., Ruddy, S. A., Miller, A. K., Planty, M., et al. (2003). *Indicators of school crime and safety:* 2003. (NCES 2004–004/NCJ 201257). Washington, DC: U.S. Departments of Education and Justice.

Doll, B., Murphy, P., & Song, S.Y. (2003). The relationship between children's self-reported recess problems, and peer acceptance and friendships. *Journal of School Psychology, 41*, 2, 113–130.

Duttweiler, P. C. (1997). Who's at risk? Gay and lesbian youth. *The Journal of At-Risk Issues, 3*(2). Retrieved September 28, 2004, from http://www.dropoutprevention.org/stats/whos_risk/gay_lesb.htm

Eamon, M. K. (2001). The effects of poverty on children's socioemotional development: An ecological systems analysis. *Social Work, 46*(3), 256–266.

Ehrensaft, M. K, Cohen, P., Brown, J., Smailes, E., Chen, H., & Johnson, J. G. (2003). Intergenerational transmission of partner violence: A 20 year prospective study. *Journal of Consulting and Clinical Psychology, 71*(4), 741–753.

Elze, D. E. (2003). Gay, lesbian, and bisexual youths' perceptions of their high school environments and comfort in school. *Children and School, 25*(4), 225–239.

Eron, L. D., Huesmann, L. R., Dubow, E., Romanoff, R., & Yarmel, P. W. (1987). Aggression and its correlates over 22 years. In D. H. Crowell, I. M. Evans, & C. R. O'Donnell (Eds.), *Childhood aggression and violence: Sources of influence, prevention, and control* (pp. 249–262). New York: Plenum.

Eslea, M., & Mukhtar, K. (2000). Bullying and racism among Asian schoolchildren in Britain. *Educational Research, 42*(2), 207–217.

Espelage, D. L., & Swearer, S. M. (2003). Research on school bullying and victimization: What have we learned and where do we go from here? *School Psychology Review, 32*(3), 365–383.

Espelage, D. L., & Swearer, S. M. (Eds.). (2004). *Bullying in American schools: A social-ecological perspective on prevention and intervention.* Mahwah, NJ: Lawrence Erlbaum.

Fatum, W. R., & Hoyle, J. C. (1996). Is it violence? School violence from the student perspective: Trends and interventions. *The School Counselor, 44*(1), 28–34.

Federal Title IX of the Education Amendments. (1972). *US Code, vol. 20,* § 1681 (P.L. 92–318).

Fineran, S. (2002). Sexual harassment between same-sex peers: Intersection of mental health, homophobia, and sexual violence in schools. *Social Work, 47*(1), 65–74.

Fineran, S., & Bennett, L. (1998). Teenage peer sexual harassment: Implications for social work practice in education. *Social Work, 43*(1), 55–64.

Finkelhor, D., & Ormrod, R. (2001). *Child abuse reported to the police.* Report by the U.S. Department of Justice, Office of Justice Programs, Office of Juvenile Justice and Delinquency Prevention (pp. 1–8). Washington, DC: U.S. Department of Justice.

Fried, S., & Fried, P. (1996). *Bullies and victims: Helping your child though the schoolyard battlefield.* New York: M. Evans.

Garbarino, J. (1980). Some thoughts on school size and its effects on adolescent development. *Journal of Youth and Adolescence, 9*(1), 19–31.

Garbarino, J., & deLara, E. (2002). *And words can hurt forever: How to protect adolescents from bullying, harassment, and emotional violence.* New York: Simon & Schuster/The Free Press.

Garbarino, J., & deLara, E. (2004). System-oriented interventions: Coping with the consequences of school violence. In J. P. Conoley & A. P. Goldstein (Eds.), *School violence intervention: A practical handbook* (2nd ed., pp. 400–415). New York: The Guildford Press.

Garofalo, R., Wolf, C., Kessel, S., Palfrey, J., & DuRant, R. H. (1998). The association between health risk behaviors and sexual orientation among a school-based sample of adolescents. *Pediatrics, 101*(5), 895–902.

Gaughan, E., Cerio, J. D., & Myers, R. A. (2001). *Lethal violence in schools: A national survey final report* (pp. 3–39). Alfred, NY: Alfred University.

Gibbs, N., & Roche, T. (1999, December 20). The Columbine tapes. *Time Magazine,* pp. 40–51.

Glover, D., Gough, G., & Johnson, M., with Netta Cartwright. (2000). Bullying in 25 secondary schools: Incidence, impact and intervention. *Educational Research, 42*(2), 141–156.

Goldstein, A. P., & Kodluboy, D. W. (1998). *Gangs in schools: Signs, symbols, and solutions.* Champaign, IL: Research Press.

Greenwood, D., & Levin, M. (1998). *Introduction to action research: Social research for social change.* Thousand Oaks, CA: Sage.

Grube, B., & Lens, V. (2003). Student-to-student harassment: The impact of Davis v. Monroe. *Children & Schools, 25,* 3, 173–185.

Guynn, K. L., & Aquila, F. D. (2004). *Hazing in high schools: Causes and consequences.* Bloomington, IN: Phi Delta Kappa Educational Foundation.

Harachi, T. W., Catalano, R. F., & Hawkins, J. D. (1999). United States. In P. K. Smith, Y. Morita, J. Junger-Tas, D. Olweus, R. Catalano, & P. Slee (Eds.), *The nature of school bullying: A cross-national perspective* (pp. 279–295). New York: Routledge.

Harmon, A. (2004). Internet gives teenage bullies weapons to wound from afar. *New York Times.* Retrieved August 26, 2004, from http://www.nytimes.com/2004/08/26/education/26bully.html?hp=&pagewanted=print&position

Hazler, R. J. (1998). Helping in the hallways: Advanced strategies for enhancing school relationships. In J. A. Kotler (Ed.), *Practical skills for counselors.* Thousand Oaks, CA: Corwin.

Hazler, R. J., Miller, D. L, & Green, S. (2001). Adult recognition of school bullying situations. *Educational Research, 43*(2), 133–146.

Heubert, J. (1999). High stakes testing: Opportunities and risks for students of color, English language learners, and students with disabilities. In M. Pines (Ed.), *The continuing challenge: Moving the youth agenda forward* (pp. 39–46). Baltimore: Sar Levitan Center for Social Policy Studies, Johns Hopkins University.

Hodges, E. V., Boivin, M., Vitaro, F., & Bukowski, W. M. (1999). The power of friendship: Protection against an escalating cycle of peer victimization. *Developmental Psychology, 35*(1), 94–101.

Hudley, C., & Friday, J. (1996). Attributional bias and reactive aggression. *American Journal of Preventive Medicine, 5,* Supplement to V. 12, # 5, 75–81.

Human Rights Watch (2001). *Hatred in the hallway: Violence and discrimination against lesbian, gay, bisexual and transgender students in US schools.* New York: Human Rights Watch.

Hyman, I. A., & Snook, P. A. (1999). *Dangerous schools: What we can do about the physical and emotional abuse of our children.* San Francisco: Jossey-Bass.

Jordan, W. J., McPartland, J. M., & Lara, J. (1999). Rethinking the causes of high school dropout. *The Prevention Researcher, 6*(3), 1–12.

Juarez, T. (1996). Where homeboys feel at home. *Educational Leadership, 53*(5) 30–33.

Kaufman, P., Chen, X., Choy, S. P., Peter, K., Ruddy, S. A., Miller, A. K., et al. (2001). Indicators of school crime and safety: 2001 (NCES 2002–113/NCJ-190075). Washington, DC: U.S. Department of Education.

Kadel, B. (1998). *Wisconsin Youth Risk Behavior Survey: Executive Summary and Report.* Madison, WI: Wisconsin Survey Research Laboratory for Wisconsin Department of Public Instruction.

Kelker, K. (1998). Resolving conflicts in rural schools. *Rural Special Education Quarterly, 17*(3–4), 18–26.

Kellam, S. G., Xiange, L., Merisca, R., Brown, C. H., & Ialongo, N. (1998). The effect of the level of aggression in the first grade classroom on the course and malleability of aggressive behavior into middle school. *Development and Psychopathology, 10,* 165–185.

Kovner-Kline, K. (2003). *Hardwired to Connect: The new scientific case for authoritative communities.* Washington, D.C.: Commission on Children at Risk; YMCA of the USA.; Dartmouth Medical School; Institute for American Values.

Knafo, A. (2003). Authoritarians, the next generation: Values and bullying among adolescent children of authoritarian fathers. *Analyses of Social Issues and Public Policy, 3*(1) 199–204.

Kodluboy, D. W. (2004). Gang-oriented interventions. In J. P. Conoley & A. P. Goldstein (Eds.), *School violence intervention: A practical handbook* (2nd ed., pp. 400–415). New York: The Guildford Press.

Kyle, P. (1999). Cooperative discipline to reduce classroom violence. In W. N. Bender, G. Clinton, & R. L. Bender (Eds.), *Violence prevention and reduction in schools* (pp. 15–30). Austin, TX: Pro Ed.

Lambda Legal. (2002). *Get the Facts 08/28/2002, Facts: Gay and lesbian youth in schools.* Retrieved August 3, 2004, from http://www.lambdalegal.org/cgi-bin/iowa/documents/record?record=1120

Lantieri, L., & Patti, J. (1996). *Waging peace in our schools.* Boston: Beacon Press.

Lashbrook, J. T. (2000). Fitting in: Exploring the emotional dimension of adolescent peer pressure. *Adolescence, 35*(140), 747–757.

Leland, J. (2001, April 8). Zero tolerance changes life at one school: Columbine makes a town get tough. *New York Times,* Section 9, p. 1.

Limber, S., & Nation, M. (2004). *Bullying among children and youth.* Retrieved March 9, 2004, from http://www.ojjdp.ncjrs.org/jjbulletin/9804/bullying2 .html

Litke, C.D. (1996). When violence came to our rural school. *Educational Leadership International, 54*(1), 77–80.

Logue, P. M. (1997). Update Articles 01/01/1997, Near $1 million settlement raises standard for protection of gay youth. *Lambda Legal.* Retrieved August 3, 2004, from http://www.lambdalegal.org/cgi-bin/iowa/documents/record? record=56

Martin, B. N. (2000). Meeting the challenge of a changing rural school/community cultural population. *The Rural Educator, 22*(1), 1–5.

Mattaini, M. (2001). *Peace power for adolescents: Strategies for a culture of nonviolence.* Washington, DC: NASW Press.

McGuigan, W. M., Vuchinich, S., & Pratt, C. C. (2000). Domestic violence, parents' view of their infant, and risk for child abuse. *Journal of Family Psychology, 14*(4), 613–624.

McPartland, J., & Jordan, W. (2002). Essential components of high school dropout prevention reforms. *Harvard Law Review.* Retrieved July 1, 2002, from http://www.law.harvard.edu/civilrights/publications/dropouts/dropout/mcpartland.html

Mishna, F. (2003). Learning disabilities and bullying: Double jeopardy. *Journal of Learning Disabilities, 36*(4), 336–347.

Molnar, B.E., Buka, S.L., Brennan, R.T., Holton, J.K., & Earls, F. (2003). A multilevel study of neighborhoods and parent-to-child physical aggression: Results from the Project on Human Development in Chicago Neighborhoods. *Child Maltreatment, 8* (2), 84–97.

Mullin-Rindler, N. (2003). Relational aggression and bullying: It's more than just a girl thing. *Wellesley Centers for Women Working Paper Series, 2003*. Working Paper # 408. Wellesley, MA: Center for Research on Women.

Nansel, T. R., Overpeck, M., Pilla, R. S., Ruan, W. J., Simons-Morton, B., & Scheidt, P. (2001). Bullying behaviors among US youth: Prevalence and association with psychosocial adjustment. *JAMA, 285*, 2094–2100.

Napolitano, J. (2003, May 8). National Briefing | Midwest: Illinois: Girls' game turns violent. *New York Times*. Retrieved September 5, 2004, from http://query.nytimes.com

National Association of Attorneys General. (2000). Bruised inside: What our children say about youth violence, what causes it and what we need to do about it. *Washington Attorney General Christine Gregoire's Presidential Initiative on Our Children in the New Millennium. A Special Report*. Olympia, WA: Sexual Assault Prevention Resource Center.

Naylor, P., & Cowie, H. (1999). The effectiveness of peer support systems in challenging school bullying: The perspectives and experiences of teachers and pupils. *Journal of Adolescence,* 22(4), 467–479.

O'Connell, P., Pepler, D., & Craig, W., (1999). Peer involvement in bullying: Insights and challenges for intervention. *Journal of Adolescence, 22*, 437–452.

O'Hagan, K. (1993). *Emotional and psychological abuse of children*. Buffalo, NY: University of Toronto Press.

Olweus, D. (1993a). *Bullying at school: What we know and what we can do*. Malden, MA: Blackwell.

Olweus, D. (1993b). Victimization by peers: Antecedents and long-term outcomes. In K. H. Rubin & J. B. Asendorf (Eds.), *Social withdrawal, inhibitions, and shyness* (pp. 315–341). Hillsdale, NJ: Erlbaum.

Orpinas, P., Horne, A. M., & Staniszewski, D. (2003). School bullying: Changing the problem by changing the school. *School Psychology Review, 32*(3), 431–444.

Pelligrini, A.D., Bartini, M., & Brooks, F. (1999). School bullies, victims, and aggressive victims: Factors relating top group affiliation and victimization in early adolescence. *Journal of Educational Psychology, 91*, 216–224.

Project SAVE, Safe Schools Against Violence in Education Act, NY CLS Education, Title II, Art 55, Sec. 2801 (2005).

Raywid, M. A. (1998). Small schools: A reform that works. *Educational Leadership, 55*(4), 34–39.

Richardson, L. (2002, September 22). A safer ride on the bus: Many high school students prefer to drive, at greater risk. *The Post Standard*, pp. B1–B2.

Rowan, B., & Miskel, C. (1999). Institutional theory and the study of educational organizations. In J. Murphy & K. Seashore-Louis (Eds.), *Handbook of research on educational administration* (2nd ed., pp. 359–383). San Francisco: Jossey-Bass.

Rumberger, R. W. (2001). Why students drop out of school and what can be done. Presented at *Dropouts in America: How severe is the problem? What do we know about intervention and prevention?* A forum convened by The Civil Rights Project at Harvard University's Graduate School of Education and Achieve, Inc., on January 13, 2001, Cambridge, MA. Retrieved June 6, 2001, from http://www.law.harvard.edu/civilrights/publications/dropouts/dropout/balfanz.htm

Sarason, S. B. (2001). *American psychology and schools: A critique.* New York: Teachers College Press and the American Psychological Association.

Schuster, B. (1996). Rejection, exclusion, and harassment at work and in schools. *European Psychologist,* 1(4), 293–317.

Scott, W. R. (1995). *Institutions and organizations.* Thousand Oaks, CA: Sage.

Smith, M., Hill, G. C., Evans, B., & Bandera, M. (2000). Perspectives and issues related to violence in a rural school. *The Rural Educator, 22*(1), 19–25.

Smith, P. K. (Ed.). (2003). *Violence in schools: The response in Europe.* New York: Routledge.

Smith, P. K., Morita, Y., Junger-Tas, J., Olweus, D., Catalano, R., & Slee, P. (Eds.). (1999). *The nature of school bullying: A cross-national perspective.* New York: Routledge.

Steigelbauer, S. M. (1994). Systemic reform: Perspectives on personalizing education. Washington, DC: U.S. Department of Education. Retrieved, February 1, 2005, from http://www.ed.gov/pubs/EdReformStudies/SysReforms/stiegel1.html

Straus, M. A., & Field, C. J. (2003). Psychological aggression by American parents: National data on prevalence, chronicity, and severity. *Journal of Marriage and Family, 65,* 795–808.

U.S. Department of Education. (1998). *Preventing bullying: A manual for schools and communities.* Washington, DC: U.S. Department of Education. Retrieved, November 3, 1998, from www.ldonline.org.Id_indepth/social_skills/preventing_bullying.html

U.S. Department of Education. (2004). *Educator sexual misconduct: A synthesis of existing literature by Carol Shakeshaft, Ph.D.* Washington, DC: Department of Education, Office of the Under Secretary, Policy and Program Studies Service. Available: www.ed.gov/rschstat/research/pubs/misconductreview/report.doc

U.S. Department of Health and Human Services (2001). *Youth Violence: A Report of the Surgeon General*, Rockville, MD: U.S. Department of Health and Human Services, Centers for Disease Control and Prevention, National Center for Injury Prevention and Control; Substance Abuse and Mental Health Services Administration, Center for Mental Health Services; and National Institutes of Health, National Institute of Mental Health.

von Bertalanffy, L. (1968). *General system theory: Foundations, development, applications* (Rev. ed.). New York: George Braziller.

Vorrasi, J. A., deLara, E., & Bradshaw, C. P. (2005). Psychological maltreatment. In A Giadino & R. Alexander (Eds.), *Childhood maltreatment: A clinical guide and reference* (3rd ed.). St. Louis, MO: GW Medical Publishing.

Vossekuil, B., Reddy, M., Fein, R., Borum, R., & Modzeleski, W. (2000). *USSS Safe School Initiative: An interim report on the prevention of targeted violence in schools.* Washington, DC: US Secret Service, National Threat Assessment Center.

Warren, K., Franklin, C., & Streeter, C. (1998). New directions in systems theory: Chaos and complexity. *Social Work, 43*(4), 357–372.

Whitchurch, G. G., & Constantine, L. L. (1993). Systems theory. In P. G. Boss, W. J. Doherty, R. LaRossa, et al. (Eds.), *Sourcebook of family theories and methods: A contextual approach* (pp. 325–352). New York: Plenum.

Widom, C. (1992). The cycle of violence. *National Institute of Justice: Research in brief* (pp. 1–4). Washington, DC: National Institute of Justice.

CHAPTER 18

# *Judging Juvenile Responsibility*

## *A Social Ecological Perspective*

MARK R. FONDACARO AND LAUREN G. FASIG

A separate system of juvenile justice emerged around the turn of the last century to provide child offenders with more humane treatment than they were receiving in the adult criminal justice system (Howell, 1997). Prior to this reform, the general assumption was that young children and early adolescents had not reached their full "developmental potential" for mature decision making. Accordingly, children under age 14 were generally considered too young to be held morally and legally accountable for their actions, whereas youngsters over age 14 were presumed to be competent, mature, and accountable (Tanenhaus, 2000). Thus, before the advent of the juvenile justice system, minors typically were exempted from criminal responsibility if they were under age 7, held fully accountable for their crimes if they were over age 14, and presumed exempted from criminal responsibility between the ages of 7 and 14, a presumption subject to rebuttal by contrary evidence (McCarty & Carr, 1980).

The influx of new immigrants at the beginning of the 20th century generated new pressures to extend the duration of adolescence so that these youngsters would not be exploited as a source of cheap labor and to provide them with some additional time to prepare for the assumption of adult roles and responsibilities (Grossberg, 2002). As youngsters in their later teens were increasingly seen as "works in progress," the dividing line between "youthful immaturity" and "adult maturity" was nudged forward to late adolescence or early adulthood by juvenile justice reformers (Scott & Grisso, 1997).

The juvenile justice system was designed to assist youth who had gone astray to return to the "right path." There was a belief that children and adolescents could be "helped" or reformed during their formative years in a way that would keep them from developing into career criminals (Howell, 1997). Blameworthiness was not at issue; a child's need for rehabilitation drove policy. This push toward rehabilitation in juvenile justice was born in optimism. Shifting away from a focus on criminal behavior and what the child did wrong, the goal instead was to focus on the personality and identity of the child (Mack, 1909). The hope was that if character flaws were caught early, they could be "mended" or "fixed." Presumably, rehabilitated youngsters would become better people and make morally sound choices in the future, ones that would keep them out of trouble with the law. The social sciences and mental health professions were enlisted to help develop and implement rehabilitative programs and interventions.

After nearly three-quarters of a century under this system, characterized by limited judicial oversight and little if any success at rehabilitation, observers of the juvenile justice system concluded that "nothing works" to rehabilitate juvenile offenders. (Martinson, 1974). Such pessimism among social scientists set the stage for the "due process" reforms in the juvenile justice system (*In re Gault,* 1967; *In re Winship,* 1970; *Kent v. United States,* 1966). Paradoxically, the push for more procedural safeguards, championed by those interested in children's rights, ultimately led to an erosion of distinctions between the adult and juvenile justice systems. At the same time, the public blamed lax treatment in the juvenile justice system for the danger from younger and younger children who were committing more adult-like crimes, but were escaping adult sanctions and being prematurely released back into society. Ensuing calls for punishment were rooted in the view that treatment was not working, that young criminals were being coddled, and that our juvenile justice system was actually encouraging and exacerbating youth crime by failing to impose justified punishment. There was the perception that the deterrent effects of the adult system were not being utilized by the juvenile justice system. Moreover, the approach to juvenile crime was viewed as contributing to moral failure among our youth, by failing to instill a sense of personal responsibility (Wilson & Herrnstein, 1985).

In response to this critique, the juvenile justice system has become more punitive over the past few decades. This policy shift has coincided with and indeed encouraged efforts to ensure that there are procedural safeguards in juvenile justice similar to those constitutionally mandated in adult criminal trials. The current trend in juvenile justice reform is toward adopting both the procedures and substantive policy goals of the adult criminal justice system (Ainsworth, 1991; Feld, 1999). An apparent rationale for this position is the assumption that due process and rehabilitation are somehow incompatible—they cannot be promoted simultaneously. Once social scientists began to conclude that rehabilitation "didn't work," legal reformers and the courts began to push for what were regarded as optimal procedural safeguards—adult criminal procedural safeguards, which were considered to be synonymous with due process itself (Fondacaro, 2001).

Public debate regarding considerations of due process and critiques of the efficacy of the juvenile courts continued to grow while a new concern surfaced in the 1990s: the perception that severe adolescent crime was on the rise (Redding & Howell, 2000). Graphic media accounts of homicides and other serious offenses, school shootings, and dire predictions of the emergence of a new class of juvenile super-predators fueled changes in juvenile justice policy. Concerns about the leniency and ineffectiveness of traditional juvenile courts brought about increases in waivers and transfers to adult criminal courts and increased acceptance of incapacitation and confinement of juveniles in the juvenile justice system in an effort to take youthful offenders off the streets and promote community safety (Grisso & Schwartz, 2000).

This shift in juvenile justice policy toward punishment and confinement versus rehabilitation led behavioral scientists to consider the role of human development in juvenile criminal activity. In an effort to protect children from severe consequences such as the death penalty and lengthy incarcerations, these researchers drew on basic scientific findings about cognitive development to argue that youth, especially those younger than age 15, generally lack the social cognitive skills and mature judgment to be held fully accountable under a culpability-based adult system rooted in a retributive rather than a rehabilitative justice philosophy. However, the behavioral scientists and legal scholars who advocated this position did not challenge the fundamental premise of the adult criminal justice system: that the legal consequences for crime should be based largely on a determination of the offender's "mental state" at the time of the crime. Instead, they argued that children and younger adolescents lacked full psychological capacity to form adult-like mental states. Their primary focus, however, remained on the internal, psychological functioning or "mental state" of the juvenile offender.

In this chapter, we will review behavioral science research suggesting that this relatively narrow focus on internal, psychological functioning as the basis for determining legal sanctions is incomplete and misguided, especially for juveniles. We will argue that there are both legal and empirical justifications for broadening the focus to include contextual influences on juvenile crime including family, peer, school, neighborhood, and media influences. We begin by reviewing the traditional model for judging criminal responsibility and the similarities and differences between the juvenile and adult criminal justice systems. We conclude by proposing and considering the implications of a more contextual, social ecological analysis of juvenile responsibility.

## THE TRADITIONAL MODEL FOR JUDGING CRIMINAL CULPABILITY

Although the adult and juvenile justice systems are still distinct in at least some respects, there is one sense in which both are, and always have been, similar: their underlying conception of human nature and behavior. Both are rooted in liberal philosophy regarding the capacity of individuals for free choice. In fact, it is this presumption of individual free choice that serves as the basis for holding people morally blameworthy for their intentional conduct, justifying a system of retribution and punishment. Although the criminal and juvenile justice systems do not consider children to have the same capacity for free choice as adults, juveniles are considered to be "works in progress," on their way to developing a mature capacity for free choice. Thus, our legal system presumes the capacity for free choice in adults and presumes that children gradually develop this capacity as they mature.

In the adult criminal justice system, the severity of criminal sanctions turns largely on a determination of the defendant's mental state at the time of the event. The law generally presumes that people make conscious choices about whether to engage in illegal behavior and it is the capacity, if not the exercise, of choice that provides the moral justification for retribution-based punishment. Whether or not a person has a "guilty mind" is generally based on a social judgment of the degree to which the person consciously chose to engage in criminal behavior or to ignore a substantial risk. Jurors and judges in a criminal proceeding are asked to engage in retrospective mind reading. However, the weight of behavioral science research contradicts the presumption that people act based on the exercise of consciously motivated rational and "free choice." Rather, human behavior is a function of both personal and situational influences (Bronfenbrenner, 1979; Moos, 1973).

As a matter of common sense and experience, people, including judges and jurors, attempt to understand human nature and to predict behavior based largely on judgments about a person's psychological attributes or personality characteristics. Here again, there is a very well-established body of behavioral science research that indicates that people tend to overestimate the importance of personal factors in guiding and directing behavior, a phenomenon referred to in the social psychological literature as the "fundamental attribution error" (Nisbett & Ross, 1980). When people are confronted by the unusual behavior of others, they tend to attribute that behavior to an aspect of the person's psychological disposition rather than objective aspects of the situation facing the person or the person's subjective appraisal of the situation (Nisbett & Ross, 1980). This fundamental attribution error is most pronounced when we are judging the behavior of others—criminal defendants, for example. In our adult criminal justice system, the assignment of the highest degree of criminal culpability is based on a retrospective and potentially erroneous social judgment that the person acted with intent, deliberation, and purpose.

Thus, the presumption of the human capacity for "rational choice," which provides the moral and legal justification for retribution-based punishment, is arguably flawed. Moreover, the retribution-based model of criminal justice does nothing to advance the well-being of the offender. It serves, at best, to satisfy the public's quest for retribution, revenge, and indirectly, incapacitation, by providing an apparent justification for incarcerating offenders.

## DUTY TO JUVENILES

Some may argue that society owes no greater duty to adult offenders than retribution-inspired criminal justice objectives. Even if one advocates the value of retributive justice principles (which we do not), there is still a strong argument that society and the state have duties to child offenders beyond those reflected in retributive criminal justice policy objectives. The state has some duty to educate and protect children (*Meyer v. Nebraska,* 1923; *Pierce v. Society of Sisters,* 1925; *Prince v. Massachusetts,* 1944). Moreover, in those cases where punishment is sought, there is some obligation to ensure that the punishment has a positive effect on the child, rather than serving only as an emotional release for the punisher. Historically, a juvenile justice system separate from the adult criminal system has been justified via the state's *parens patriae* power (*In re Gault,* 1967; *Schall v. Martin,* 1984). *Parens patriae* is the principle that the state must care for those who cannot care for themselves. It is the basis for many of the Supreme Court's rulings designed to promote the welfare of children (Tanenhaus, 2000). The state's authority to promote public welfare and safety under its police power also has served as a basis for protecting children's rights (*Prince v. Massachusetts,* 1944). Overall, the state's special duties to children suggest that the state must do more for children who break the law than simply "make them pay."

If juvenile justice policy must do more than feed the public's appetite for punishment, then our efforts to understand and address juvenile crime must do more than assign blame based on inadequate assumptions about the causes and consequences of human behavior. We need to draw on theory and research in the behavioral sciences that is aimed at educating, socializing, protecting, and effectively punishing children who break the law. Theory and research advanced by ecologically oriented behavioral scientists who study the influence of social contexts on human behavior hold considerable promise in advancing this wider range of juvenile justice policy objectives.

## BEHAVIORAL SCIENCE RESEARCH ON THE DETERMINANTS OF HUMAN BEHAVIOR

Conceiving of adult human beings as autonomous decision makers is grossly out of line with most of the systematic behavioral science research conducted over the past century. Early in the 20th century, social psychologists such as Kurt Lewin (1936) suggested that in order to fully understand human behavior, one needs to know something about personal characteristics and the social environment in which the individual is embedded. This ecological model of human behavior is also reflected in the work of interpersonally oriented psychiatrists such as Harry Stack Sullivan (1953) as well as behavioral scientists such as Rudolf Moos (1973) and Urie Bronfenbrenner (1979). Moreover, a long line of experimental studies clearly demonstrates that human behavior is strongly influenced by social and contextual factors (Ross & Nisbett, 1991).

Although we may have a natural tendency to view behavior as the result of free choice and illegal behavior in particular as the result of bad moral choices, the overwhelming weight of evidence suggests that contextual factors have a strong influence on the nature and meaning of human behavior. Under most circumstances, any human behavior, including that which is judged to be illegal, is influenced as much or more by contextual factors as by aspects of personal choice (Park, 1999). Unfortunately, people have difficulty understanding the importance of contextual influences on behavior, particularly when they are evaluating the behavior of others rather than their own conduct (Nisbett & Ross, 1980).

This is particularly salient in the area of juvenile justice reform because there is some evidence that children and adolescents are even more influenced by contextual factors than are adults (Woolard, Fondacaro, & Slobogin, 2001). A contextual understanding of human behavior clearly has important implications for juvenile justice reform. To the extent that behavior is seen as the result of both personal and environmental influences, it becomes questionable whether a moral judgment model of criminal responsibility is just, moral, or developmentally sound. For example, if the justification for punishment and retribution is based on the assumption that individuals freely choose to engage in illegal behavior, and this assumption is false, or only partly true, then the legitimacy, fairness, and morality of a backward-looking, punishment-oriented juvenile justice system is called into question.

## TREATING AND PREVENTING DELINQUENT BEHAVIOR

The inaugural and guiding philosophy of the juvenile justice system was to shift the focus toward who the child was as a person rather than what the child did that was wrong. This misguided focus and orientation to rehabilitation contributed in part to early failures to demonstrate that treatment interventions could be effective with juvenile offenders. Clinicians and case workers focused on trying to change the youngster's character or intrapsychic structure rather than focusing on changing behavior per se, or the situational and environmental factors that contributed to and maintained delinquent conduct. This approach was rooted in psychodynamic principles that have since been shown to be relatively ineffective in promoting behavior change, particularly among children who are acting out rather than holding in their anger and frustrations (Davison, Neale, & Kring, 2004).

The intrapsychic focus tied to individual psychotherapy proved to be a dismal failure with juveniles for several reasons. To begin with, this orientation was first developed as an approach for understanding and treating neuroses rather than conduct problems. In fact, psychodynamic therapy may not be particularly effective even with the target populations for which it was designed—young, attractive, verbal, intelligent, and successful or "YAVIS" clients. Many such clients tend to get better without professional help (Davison et al., 2004). Even if psychodynamic therapies were effective with such clients, the typical delinquent child does not fit the YAVIS profile, particularly with regard to verbal competence and the tendency toward introspection (Wrightsman, Greene, Nietzel, & Fortune, 2002). Moreover, to the extent that all human behavior is a function of personal and environmental factors, an intervention approach that focuses only on the personal side of the equation is doomed to fail. Even in those cases where some youngsters have been able to benefit from insight-oriented therapy while in institutional settings, these youngsters tend to recidivate once they return to the same social environments that contributed to the development of their initial delinquent conduct (Wiebush, McNulty, & Le, 2000). Therefore, it is no surprise that initial efforts to evaluate the efficacy of treatment and preventive interventions with juvenile offenders uniformly concluded that nothing seemed to help. Typically, recidivism rates were near 70% (Borduin, Mann, Cone, & Henggeler, 1995).

As ecological models of human development gained ascendancy in psychology and interventions began to focus on modifying maladaptive behaviors rather than restructuring personality, the treatment and prevention literature started to take on a more optimistic tone. In fact, intervention strategies have been improved to the point that modern multisystemic interventions aimed at risk management have reduced recidivism risk from around 70% to slightly above 20% (Borduin et al., 1995). In sum, a fair appraisal of "state-of-the-art intervention strategies" suggests that ecologically oriented, cognitive-behavioral interventions aimed at the multiple life contexts in which juveniles exist (family, peer, school, neighborhood) can be both clinically and cost-effective. Given the availability of some promising intervention strategies, the next task is to ensure that "state-of-the-art" interventions are adequately implemented and incorporated into the structure of juvenile justice administration (Soler, 1994). Along these lines, multisystemic interventions lend themselves nicely to a risk management model, where the emphasis is on changing dynamic risk factors in various life domains that are associated with delinquent behavior.

## BEHAVIORAL SCIENCE RESEARCH WITH ADOLESCENTS

As suggested, much of the early research on human behavior focused primarily on intrapersonal characteristics such as psychological attributes and personality factors. This approach advanced our understanding only so far, usually accounting for only about 10% of the variance in human behavior (Mischel, 1968). Increasingly, behavioral scientists began to recognize, and study, the importance of situational factors and the joint and interactive influences of both intrapersonal and social factors on human behavior. This shift in perspective resulted not only in explanatory models that accounted for a greater share of human behavior, but also more effective intervention strategies. Traditional models of criminal justice, however, dovetail with the emphasis on exclusively intrapersonal explanations of human behavior. In fact, many behavioral scientists continue to do valuable work that addresses primarily if not exclusively intrapersonal aspects of behavior, while recognizing that they are accounting for only a small percentage of variance in human behavior—an awareness that is lacking for most legal scholars and laypersons.

Many of the researchers seeking to inform analyses of juvenile responsibility have concentrated on intrapersonal aspects of adolescent decision making. This focus has been more or less dictated by the legal system's emphasis on the "guilty mind" of the presumed rational actor in choosing to engage in criminal conduct. With the recent shift in juvenile justice policy toward this "evil-doer" theory of crime, the degree to which a child's criminal actions are seen as the result of a rational and deliberate choice to do wrong has become the central factor in judging juvenile responsibility (Ainsworth, 1991; Grisso, 1996; Steinberg, 2003). Notwithstanding this focus on atomistic and intrapsychic explanations for complex human behavior, behavioral science research with this focus is relevant to discussions about why juvenile justice should maintain its distinct focus on rehabilitation and crime prevention rather than retribution.

Reviews of empirical research and developmental theory suggest, for example, that adolescent decision making may differ from adult decision making in ways that are relevant to judgments of responsibility. Adolescents, especially those under 15 years of age, have been shown to have a foreshortened time perspective, a greater proclivity for risk behavior, changing estimates of risk likelihood, a greater propensity to be influenced by peers, reduced social responsibility or "stake in life" (Woolard et al., 2001), attention to different aspects of information used in decision making, and different subjective values placed on perceived consequences (Scott, Reppucci, & Woolard, 1995). However, the research supporting this view includes ambiguous findings, especially in regard to adolescents older than age 14, in part due to the complex nature of the question under scrutiny (Scott et al., 1995). Not surprisingly, the failure of developmental researchers to identify systematic differences between adults and adolescents older than 15 on measures of various cognitive processes underlying decision making has fueled challenges to the view that adolescents should be regarded as less culpable than adults. In response, some proponents of the developmental perspective have shifted their attention to potential maturity differences in other capacities that impinge on decision making, namely, psychosocial factors or judgment factors (Steinberg & Scott, 2003).

Recent work examining comparative psychosocial maturity finds some differences between adolescents and adults. In one such study, adolescents were more likely than adults to express antisocial inclinations in response to hypothetical situations (Cauffman & Steinberg, 2000). The authors also found consistent age differences on measures of responsibility, perspective (future orientation), and temperance (impulsivity, situational evaluation). Finally, this research indicated that participants who demonstrated more psychosocial maturity were more likely to make socially responsible decisions in the hypothetical situations than were participants who demonstrated less psychosocial maturity. Further investigation of adolescent psychosocial development may provide additional support for the developmental differences position.

Scientists arguing the developmental perspective also have focused on neurobiological growth during adolescence. Studies utilizing recent advances in imaging technology are providing new information on brain development, suggesting that adolescent brains are less well-developed than previously believed. These studies focus on development of the brain via age comparisons and patterns of activation of the brain while the participant undertakes specific tasks. Results indicate that the frontal lobe undergoes significant change during adolescence, and is the last part of the brain to develop (Singer, 2005; Sowell, Thompson, Holems, Jernigan, & Toga, 1999). Frontal lobe maturation has been linked to the control of aggression and other impulses, and correlates with measures of cognitive functioning, such as long-term planning and abstract thinking (American Bar Association, 2004; Giedd, Blumenthal, Jeffries,

Castellanos, Lui, et al., 1999). Other neurobiological evidence indicates that changes in the limbic system around puberty correspond to novelty-seeking and risk-taking behavior (Dahl, 2001). However, several researchers caution that it is difficult for neuroscientists to bring imaging research into real-life contexts, and that no current research connects the specific brain activations of adolescents to behavioral problems (Bower, 2004).

Although these lines of developmental research provide useful insights into the process of adolescent decision making, knowledge regarding immaturity of decision-making abilities, judgment, and other psychosocial capacities provides an incomplete picture of juvenile offending. To fully understand the causes and consequences of any human behavior, we need to understand the dynamic interplay between the personal and situational factors associated with the behavior—a view captured by ecological models of human behavior.

## ECOLOGICAL MODELS OF HUMAN BEHAVIOR

Significant empirical research conducted over the past century demonstrates the powerful influences that situational factors have on guiding and directing individual behavior (e.g., Darley & Batson, 1973; Milgram, 1963; Mischel, 1968). A person does not act in a vacuum. Evidence demonstrates that factors extrinsic to the individual and embedded in multiple levels of context play a significant role in the actions of every actor. Theorists adopting this ecological view have focused on the dynamic interaction between the individual and aspects of his or her social environment. According to this view, understanding the ongoing relationship between the individual and aspects of his or her social environment is essential to understanding the actor's motivation and behavior on any particular occasion (Fondacaro, 2000). Bronfenbrenner (1979, 1989) applied this approach to human development, theorizing that the developing child is situated within structured, interconnected systems including family members, peers, the child's school environment and local community, as well as more macro-level influences such as the legal system and the national economy. Factors linked to any of these systems may influence the child's thoughts, feelings, and behaviors in a particular social context, even when the child is not in direct contact with these systems (Fondacaro & Jackson, 1999). The child and the child's conduct are embedded in many different contexts. Some of these relevant contexts, including families and peer groups, have been investigated more systematically than others. This has contributed to a growing body of evidence across the various domains that begins to inform a more comprehensive ecological analysis of juvenile responsibility in relation to delinquent behavior.

### *Individual Factors*

Behavioral science research traditionally has addressed the individual factors involved in delinquent behavior. Developmentally oriented investigators especially have focused on aspects of adolescent decision making, including cognitive processes, proclivity for risk taking, reasoning abilities, and impulsivity (Lynam, Caspi, Moffitt, Wilström, Loeber, et al., 2000; White, Moffitt, Caspi, Bartusch, Needles, et al., 1994). Most of this research has examined these factors in total or partial isolation from the other contexts bearing on the actor and from the situation in which the juvenile acts.

### *Family Factors*

Family factors are among the strongest predictors of risk for delinquent behavior (Gorman-Smith, Tolan, & Henry, 2000). Poor parental monitoring, including inadequate direct supervision and knowledge of the child's whereabouts and activities greatly increases the risk of delinquency (Laird, Petit, Bates, & Dodge, 2003). Moreover, Laird et al. (2003) found evidence for reciprocal influences between parental monitoring and delinquent behaviors.

Other parenting practices, including physical punishment and inconsistency of discipline, are related to increased risk for delinquency. Relational factors such as parent–child communication, emotional warmth, and parental involvement all have been found to have independent effects on the risk for delinquent behavior (Gorman-Smith et al., 2000; Loeber, Farrington, Stouthamer-Loeber, Moffitt, & Caspi, 2001; Scaramella, Conger, Spoth, & Simons, 2002; Wiesner & Windle, 2004). Personal characteristics of the parents themselves (e.g., antisocial behavior, substance abuse, psychopathology) also are related to increased risk for delinquency (Loeber, Farrington, & Petechuk, 2003).

### *Peer Influences*

Peer influences play an important role in adolescent crime (Reiss & Farrington, 1991). Peers may exert direct influence through pressures to conform, coercion (Berndt, 1979; Scaramella et al., 2002), modeling, and social comparison (Adler & Adler, 1998; Kiesner, Cadinu, Poulin, & Bucci, 2002). They also may exert more indirect influences through their impact on the approval-seeking motives of the at-risk child (Loeber et al., 2003; Scaramella et al., 2002).

Peer interactions occur in almost all of the contexts in which adolescents find themselves—schools, neighborhoods, and social activities. Through daily interaction in these contexts, peers form networks and create behavioral expectations within these networks and contexts. Social comparison and conformity pressures continually shape ongoing behavior (Fagan, 2000). Peers also serve as an audience in daily interactions. "Witnesses are part of the landscape of social interactions and they influence adolescents' decisions on how to conduct social relations and which behaviors to value" (Fagan, 2000, p. 373). Empirical evidence confirms that the majority of adolescent antisocial behavior occurs in groups (McCord & Conway, 2002), and that individuals take more chances when they are with peers than when they are alone (Steinberg, 2003).

### *Neighborhood*

Norms among peer groups and peer networks develop in neighborhoods (Bronfenbrenner, 1979). Opportunities and social controls in a neighborhood shape an individual's behaviors and, to some extent, circumscribe the possible range of behaviors. Over the last 20 years, sociological research has attempted to identify community characteristics that are most influential in the development of crime. Level of poverty and socioeconomic status has emerged as the neighborhood structural variable that best predicts a range of negative outcomes including low school achievement, psychopathology, and delinquent behavior (Leventhal & Brooks-Gunn, 2000). In general, living in a high-poverty or low-socioeconomic status neighborhood has consistently been linked to delinquency (Loeber et al., 2001; Sampson, Raudenbush, & Earls, 1997).

Several studies have examined the relationship between racial/ethnic diversity and adolescent offending and have found that greater ethnic diversity is positively related to criminal activity (Loeber et al., 2001; Sampson & Groves, 1989, as cited in Leventhal & Brooks-Gunn, 2000). This same research also found that high rates of residential instability are related to increases in juvenile crime. In addition, the Pittsburg Youth Study (Loeber et al., 2001) demonstrated that adolescents of an unemployed father were at increased risk for delinquency and violence.

### *Schools*

Poor academic performance is related to the prevalence, onset, and seriousness of delinquency (Brewer, Hawkins, Catalano, & Neckerman, 1995; Wiesner & Windle, 2004). In addition, low school commitment, low educational goals, and poor motivation place children at risk for offending (Hawkins, Herrenkohl, Farrington, Brewer, Catalano, et al., 1998). School characteristics that have been linked to antisocial behavior include low levels of teacher satisfaction, lack of teacher cooperation, poor student–teacher relations, the prevalence of norms that support antisocial behavior, poorly defined rules and expectations for conduct, and inadequate rule- enforcement behavior (Herrenkohl, Hawkins, Chung, Hill, & Battin-Pearson, 2001).

### *Social Controls*

Social controls on behavior include internalized restraints such as learned behavioral expectations and a continuum of external restraints ranging from informal social rules and regulatory processes to formal rules attached to specific locations (Duncan & Raudenbush, 1999; Fagan, 2000). "Social cohesion among individuals in the setting influences the strength of these regulatory processes" (Fagan, 2000, p. 375). Weak social controls and lack of community structure (disorganization) allow delinquent behavior to go on unchecked (Sampson et al., 1997). Adolescent problem behavior is negatively related to informal social controls (Elliot, Wilson, Huizinga, Sampson, Elliott, et al., 1996). Furthermore, strong social controls counter the impact on risk for delinquent behavior of negative neighborhood effects found in the poorest urban neighborhoods (Gorman-Smith et al., 2000).

### *Media*

Behavioral science data clearly demonstrate the influence of electronic visual media on viewers, both positive and negative. Over the past 40 years, research examining the relationship between viewing violent television and movies and the development of aggressive behavior has included experimental studies; observational studies; and more recently, longitudinal studies. Consortia of researchers, several different professional groups, and experts commissioned by the U.S. government have conducted numerous reviews of the literature dating as far back as the 1950s. The conclusions have been uniform, for the most part, and have only grown stronger as the breadth and depth of the research have increased. This literature base provides "unequivocal evidence that media violence increases the likelihood of aggressive and violent behavior in both immediate and long-term contexts" (Anderson, Berkowitz, Donnerstein, Huesmann, Johnson, et al., 2003, p. 81). Although theories regarding how this effect occurs and the differences between short-term effects and long-term effects are still developing, scientists investigating this topic agree on the following: Severe aggressive behavior usually occurs asa result of a convergence of multiple predisposing and precipitating factors, and exposure to media violence acts as one such factor (Huesmann, Moise-Titus, Podolski, & Eron, 2003).

Investigations in the field of media effects on child development recently have examined moderators of the influence of media violence on aggressive behavior. Such research demonstrates that viewer characteristics function as moderators. Specifically, highly aggressive individuals show greater effects of exposure to media violence than less aggressive individuals, although relatively nonaggressive children are also affected by violent media material (Bushman, 1995; Bushman & Geen, 1990, as cited in Anderson et al., 2003). Research also has shown that children's perceptions of the violence as "lifelike" or "real" and their identification with aggressive characters is positively related to aggressive behavior (Huesmann et al., 2003). Characteristics of the televised material, such as the traits of the aggressive perpetrator and the justifications and consequences of the aggression, moderate viewers' behavior (Anderson et al., 2003; Anderson and Gentile, 2005; Kunkel, 2005).

Unfortunately, little research has examined the social environment's ability to moderate the impact of media violence. Some studies show that parents' control of their children's viewing of violence, as well as what parents do when their children view violence, mitigates the effects of the televised violence (Anderson et al., 2003). Although researchers have begun to consider the influence of culture, neighborhood, socioeconomic status, and peers on the impact of media violence, the results are somewhat equivocal and the studies are too few to draw definitive conclusions (Anderson et al., 2003). However, the development of an integrated ecological approach to this issue is likely to provide insights useful in designing effective interventions aimed at reducing violent behavior.

### *Situational Influences*

Researchers have firmly established that people behave differently in different settings, even when experiencing similar motivations and emotions (Fagan, 2000). Features of the setting of antisocial acts interact with the actor to influence the outcome of the situation. Such features of the setting include the opportunities for crime; the people present; behavioral norms attached to specific aspects of the setting; provocations, such as alcohol or drug use; other criminal activity; and social controls (Fagan, 2000). The composition of a setting, such as the number and types of people present and the characteristics of those people (Stark, 1987); its physical location; and physical attributes such as lighting, noise, and décor (Felson, Baccagglini, & Gmelch, 1986) all influence behavior in that setting. Normative patterns of behavior within a setting, or beliefs about appropriate behavior in the setting, also influence current behavior—examples include beliefs about alcohol use in bars and at social gatherings (Fagan, 2000; Felson et al., 1986) compared to quiet, "mannerly" behavior in a courtroom or attentive behavior in a classroom.

### *Factor Integration*

In recognition of the importance of ecological context in the determination of behavior, a growing body of work brings two or more factors together to investigate multiple contexts of delinquency. A study by Lynam et al. (2000) examined how the individual characteristic of impulsivity and juvenile offending differed as a function of neighborhood variation. The authors found that impulsive boys were at great risk for offending in poor neighborhoods (as defined by the percentage of families below the poverty line, rates of male unemployment, number of single-parent households, median income, number of households utilizing public assistance, and the percentage of African Americans in the census track). However, impulsivity posed little risk for delinquency for boys in better-off neighborhoods.

Gorman-Smith et al. (2000) examined how patterns of delinquency related differently to various configurations of family risk in different types of neighborhoods. The researchers found that in families with consistent parenting and organization, and strong emotional cohesion and family orientation, the children were less likely to engage in delinquent behavior. These effects were greater in neighborhoods with greater resources. Other studies also indicate that differential parenting practices are more or less effective depending on the neighborhoods in which the families live (Leventhal & Brooks-Gunn, 2000).

Some researchers hypothesize that peers influence antisocial behavior because of a lack of community or neighborhood institutions (such as organized activities or adult supervision) to regulate behavior (Leventhal & Brooks-Gunn, 2000). Consistent with this argument, Dishion, Andrews, and Crosby (1995) found that close friends of antisocial boys live in the same neighborhood and they spend time together in unsupervised and unstructured activities.

At least one study has examined the influence, relating to delinquent behavior, of three contextual factors: parents, peers, and neighborhood. Scaramella et al. (2002) found that relationships with deviant peers predicted delinquency. Furthermore, parents influence the types of friends with whom their adolescents associate. Specifically, nurturing and involved parenting were related to less association of adolescents with deviant peers. Parents also influence their children's peer relationships by structuring their social environments. Parents select the schools their children attend, choose the neighborhoods in which they live, and influence the extracurricular and other activities in which their children engage (Bryant, 1985).

Taken as a whole, this research provides an emerging view of the adolescent offender that is more complex and differentiated than the image portrayed in recent juvenile justice policy. Considerations of multiple levels of influence are essential in addressing juvenile crime. As the empirical evidence suggests, an ecological approach requires an analysis of human problems in context and suggests a system based on more forward-looking solutions (Slobogin & Fondacaro, 2000).

## A SOCIAL ECOLOGICAL ANALYSIS OF RESPONSIBILITY

A social ecological analysis of juvenile responsibility would consider the personal and situational influences on the juvenile and the juvenile's behavior to make the determination of how best to prevent additional crime while meeting our social obligations to the child and the public at large. This perspective suggests that a rational thought process often is not the principal determinant of action (Slobogin & Fondacaro, 2000). Thus, if prevention of criminal behavior via deterrence is a goal of the system, punishment may have little impact, even assuming that the legal system is effective in detecting criminal behavior and that potential offenders are aware of this. Instead, deterrent effects will be linked to changing contextual factors that affect the well-being and behavior of adolescents. To promote general deterrence, laws passed primarily with a deterrent purpose need to focus at the aggregate level on those contextual factors that have been empirically linked to reduced risk for antisocial behavior. Although this perspective is based on a broader conception of deterrence than the one suggested by some scholars (Andenaes, 1966), we deliberately adopt the broader view because of the central role of general deterrence as a legitimate and popular criminal justice policy goal. To the extent that general deterrence continues to enjoy a privileged position in the law and wide popular support, future efforts to deter adolescent crime should broaden their focus beyond symbolic threats to include the promotion of environmental setting characteristics that are associated with reduced crime rates among adolescents.

Although recent policy shifts are moving the juvenile justice system further away from its original purpose, its goal has always been to prevent children from undertaking a life of antisocial behavior. This goal presumably benefits both society and the child. As noted above, the state has adopted a stance of societal obligation for the welfare of our children. In addition to processes aimed at general deterrence, a second approach to prevention is intervention to change individual behavior. A social ecological analysis dictates consideration of the youth's historical and current context as part of the development of individualized intervention plans aimed at preventing recidivism. Such individualized intervention plans utilize a variety of approaches, programs, and processes to enhance protective factors and reduce risk factors for antisocial behavior. While this approach may closely resemble the system's original goals, it would be a marked improvment because it would be based on empirical evidence of how best to effectively change human behavior. The adoption of a social ecological perspective would not mean that decision-making abilities and maturity of judgment, typically the primary focus of a "rational actor" analysis, would become irrelevant to judgments of juvenile responsibility. Such intrapersonal characteristics are important in the analysis of the individual's propensity to engage in antisocial behavior, and should be considered as one among many relevant personal and contextual factors. Overall, a juvenile justice system guided by a forward-looking social ecological perspective would be focused not only on protection of children and their future opportunities, but also on public safety and the prevention of future crimes and other harms to society (Slobogin, Fondacaro & Woolard, 1999).

The social ecological perspective suggests that sanctioning youth as rational actors who are making poor decisions neither accurately addresses the course of development of the behavior nor effectively serves to prevent future antisocial behavior. Thus, retribution-based legal policies are not likely to succeed either in preventing juvenile crime or in meeting our societal obligations to improve the welfare of children. Rather, sanctions should be informed by an understanding of how best to change behavior, including interventions aimed at rehabilitation, crime prevention, restitution, and even punishment when it is empirically linked to the constructive objectives of educating, socializing, and protecting juveniles. Such interventions serve the dual purpose of reducing criminal activity and meeting the state's special duties to children.

We believe the development and adoption of a risk management model similar to the one proposed by Slobogin and colleagues (1999) would begin to move us in this direction. A risk management model would not focus on assigning blame and meting out punishment that is deemed to be proportionate to culpability. Rather, the primary goal for dealing with juveniles who engage in illegal behavior would be to reduce the likelihood of recidivism in the future. As Slobogin et al. (1999) suggest, a risk management model of juvenile justice would be comprehensive and multisystemic, focusing on the various social systems that affect the child (family, peers, schools, neighborhood) and not just the child in isolation. What the child may or may not have been thinking at the time he or she offended loses its central importance and determinative influence under a risk management model.

Justice would be truly individualized, but not in the narrow sense that it would be tailored to the unique intrapsychic characteristics of the child. Rather, each juvenile offender would have an Individual Risk Management Plan (IRMP)—a plan that focuses on addressing dynamic (i.e., changeable) risk factors in the interconnected personal and social domains of the child's life (e.g., poor impulse control, social incompetence, parental deviance and incompetence, affiliation with deviant peers, academic and vocational underperformance). Each child's IRMP would be managed by a risk management team (RMT) headed by a caseworker who would seek input from the child and other relevant team members including school authorities, juvenile justice officials, mental health experts, vocational counseling professionals, and other interested parties. The RMT would oversee the implementation and ongoing evaluation of the IRMP, which would be subject to modification based on feedback and relevant empirical data on new and promising interventions that have been shown to work with juveniles with similar risk profiles. This would require the establishment of a juvenile justice record-keeping system capable of monitoring offender characteristics and risk profiles and tracking the efficacy of various intervention strategies to guide ongoing reform at the level of specific interventions and programs. Finally, the juvenile court or some organizational body with the competence to implement and evaluate juvenile justice policy should provide oversight of the risk management system and associated record keeping, which would provide important information to guide reform at the policy level.

## CONCLUSION

One of the key decisions facing policy makers and the American public in the 21st century is whether to maintain a separate juvenile justice system. Virtually everyone agrees that we must judge and address deviant behavior by very young children in a manner that is quite different from the way we presently judge and punish adult offenders. Even before the era of juvenile justice reform in the United States around the turn of the last century, children under age 14 were typically presumed not to be responsible for their criminal conduct. However, in the context of the prevailing political rhetoric that champions personal responsibility, we are willing to treat children in this age range who break the law even more harshly than they would have been treated before the creation of the original juvenile justice system. Now, children who are 12 years old and younger are being tried, convicted, and punished severely as murderers. This would not have happened even back in the frontier days.

Shortcomings over the last century in implementing the ideals of juvenile justice reform seem paradoxically to have brought us to a point where children are treated even less humanely than they were during periods of our history when child exploitation was widely ignored if not openly encouraged. The fact that we have reached this point should give us pause and signal to the general public that we are doing something seriously wrong. Punishing children harshly under the rhetorical banner of personal responsibility is not working, is not fair, and costs too much.

Some behavioral scientists have attempted to soften our harsh treatment of juveniles by arguing and marshalling some modest evidence that children "think differently" than adults and therefore should be held less accountable. One implication of this line of reasoning is that if children thought like adults, then it would be appropriate to treat them in the same way we currently treat adult criminals. Juveniles are considered "developmentally immature," on their way to adult-like autonomous decision making, but not yet there. We believe this premise itself is flawed but will leave to another day a full discussion of criminal responsibility across the entire lifespan. With respect to juveniles, we believe that focusing primarily on internal psychological characteristics of the child (i.e., mens rea) to judge criminal responsibility, as we do with adults, leads us to erroneous judgments. Arguably, at least from the standpoint of a moral judgment model, continuing to *knowingly* embrace the tenets of mens rea analysis in the face of compelling evidence that situational factors contribute as much or more to criminal behavior as conscious, albeit immature, decision making by juveniles is not only misguided—it is immoral.

Over time, juveniles are increasingly facing sanctions that look more and more like adult punishment. Apparently, we have gotten right back to where we started—some would say, we have even taken a step further back. Developmentalists and forensic psychologists working within the fundamental premises of a retributivist framework for criminal justice have provided some evidence that children and younger adolescents on average do not make decisions and exercise judgment in a manner that is as competent as decisions made by adults. They then suggest that this should lead to a presumption that children and younger adolescents who break the law should not be held fully responsible for their crimes and that a separate juvenile justice system is necessary for these youngsters. However, this approach abandons many older adolescents (and adults whose decision making and judgment may be indistinguishable from that of the typical younger adolescent) to an increasingly retributivist and punitive adult criminal justice system.

We believe that behavioral scientists and other informed citizens must challenge and change the narrow and outdated criteria for judging juvenile responsibility that presently tie harsh legal sanctions almost exclusively to what a judge or jury might believe the child was thinking at the moment he or she broke the law. The causes of human behavior are much more complex. This "immature evil-doer" theory of crime does not take full account of what we have learned over the past century about the interrelated social and personal causes and consequences of human behavior. We need a framework for judging and addressing juvenile crime that takes this complexity into account.

## REFERENCES


Adler, P. A., & Adler, P. (1998). *Peer power: Preadolescent culture and identity.* New Brunswick, NJ: Rutgers University Press.

Ainsworth, J. E. (1991). Re-imagining childhood and reconstructing the legal order: The case of abolishing the juvenile court. In S. Humm, B. A. Ort, M. M. Anbari, W. Lader, & W. S. Biel (Eds.), *Child, parent, and state: law and policy reader* (pp. 561–595). Philadelphia: Temple University Press.

American Bar Association. (2004). *Adolescence, brain development and legal culpability.* Washington, DC: Author. Retrieved from www.abanet.org/crimjust/juvjus.

Andenaes, J. (1966). The general preventive effects of punishment. *University of Pennsylvania Law Review, 114,* 949–983.

Anderson, C. A., Berkowitz, L., Donnerstein, E., Huesmann, L. R., Johnson, J. D., Linz, D., et al. (2003). The influence of media violence on youth. *Psychological science on the Public Interest, 4*(3), 81–110.

Anderson, C., & Gentile, D. (2005). Violent video games and the effects on youths and culture. In N. Dowd, D. G. Singer, & R. F. Wilson (Eds.), *Handbook of children, culture, and violence.* Thousand Oaks, CA: Sage.

Berndt, T. (1979). Developmental changes in conformity to peers and parents. *Developmental Psychology, 15,* 608–616.

Borduin, C. M., Mann, B. J., Cone, L. T., & Henggeler, S. W. (1995). Multisystemic treatment of serious juvenile offenders: Long-term prevention of criminality and violence. *Journal of Consulting and Clinical Psychology, 63,* 569–578.

Bower, B. (2004). Teen brains on trial: The science of neural development tangles with the juvenile death penalty. *Science News Online, 165*(19). Retrieved from http://www.sciencenews.org/articles/20040508/bob9.asp

Brewer, D. D., Hawkins, J. D., Catalano, R. F., & Neckerman, H. J. (1995). Preventing serious, violent, and chronic juvenile offending: A review of evaluations and selected strategies in childhood, adolescence, and the community. In J. C. Howell, B. Krisberg, J. D. Hawkins, & J. J. Wilson (Eds.), *Sourcebook on serious, violent, and chronic juvenile offenders* (pp. 61–141). Thousand Oaks, CA: Sage.

Bronfenbrenner, U. (1979). *The ecology of human development: Experiments by nature and design.* Cambridge, MA: Harvard University Press.

Bronfenbrenner, U. (1989). Ecological systems theory. In R. Vasta (Ed.), *Annals of Child Development, 6,* 187–249. Greenwich, CT: JAI Press.

Bryant, B. (1985). The neighborhood walk: A study of sources of support in middle childhood from the child's perspective. *Monographs of the Society for Research in Child Development, 50* (3 Serial No. 210).

Bushman, B. J. (1995). Moderating role of trait aggressiveness in the effects of violent media on aggression. *Journal of Personality and Social Psychology, 69,* 950–960.

Bushman, B. J., & Geen, R. G. (1990). Role of cognitive-emotional mediators and individual differences in the effects of media violence on aggression. *Journal of Personality and Social Psychology, 58,* 156–163.

Cauffman, E., & Steinberg, L. (2000). Researching adolescents' judgment and culpability. In T. Grisso & R. G. Schwartz (Eds.), *Youth on trial: A developmental perspective on juvenile justice* (pp. 325–345). Chicago and London: The University of Chicago Press.

Dahl, R. (2001). Affect regulation, brain development, and behavioral/emotional health in adolescence. *CNS Spectrum, 6,* 1–12.

Darley, J. M., & Batson, C. D. (1973). From Jerusalem to Jericho: A study of situational and dispositional variables in helping behavior. *Journal of Personality and Social Psychology, 27,* 100–119.

Davison, G. C., Neale, J. M., & Kring, A. M. (2004). *Abnormal psychology* (9th ed.). New York: Wiley.

Dishion, T. J., Andrews, D. W., & Crosby, L. (1995). Antisocial boys and their friends in early adolescence: Relationship characteristics, quality, and interactional process. *Child Development, 66,* 139–151.

Duncan, G., & Raudenbush, S. W. (1999). Assessing the effects of context in studies of child and youth development. *Educational Psychologist, 34*(1), 29–41.

Elliot, D. S., Wilson, W. J., Huizinga, D., Sampson, R. J., Elliot, A., & Rankin, B. (1996). The effects of neighborhood disadvantage on adolescent development. *Journal of Research in Crime and Delinquency, 33,* 389–426.

Fagan, J. (2000). Contexts of choice by adolescents in criminal events. In T. Grisso & R. G. Schwartz (Eds.), *Youth on trial: A developmental perspective on juvenile justice* (pp. 371–401). Chicago and London: The University of Chicago Press.

Feld, B. C. (1999). *Readings in juvenile justice administration.* New York: Oxford University Press.

Felson, R. B., Baccagglini, W., & Gmelch, G. (1986). Bar-room brawls: Aggression and violence in Irish and American bars. In A. Campbell and J. Gibbs (Eds.), *Violent transactions* (pp. 153–166). New York: Basil Blackwell.

Fondacaro, M. R. (2000). Toward an ecological jurisprudence rooted in concepts of justice and empirical research. *University of Missouri-Kansas City Law Review, 69*(1), 179–196.

Fondacaro, M. R. (2001). *Reconceptualizing due process in juvenile justice: Contributions from law and behavioral science.* Invited paper presented at the 1st Annual Conference of the Center on Children and the Law, University of Florida Levin College of Law, Gainesville.

Fondacaro, M. R. & Jackson, S. (1999). The legal and psychosocial context of family violence: Toward a social ecological analysis. *Law and Policy, 21,* 91–100.

Giedd, J., Blumenthal, J., Jeffries, N., Castellanos, F., Liu, H., & Zijdenbos, A. (1999). Brain development during childhood and adolescence: A longitudinal MRI study. *Nature Neuroscience, 2,* 861–863.

Gorman-Smith, D., Tolan, P. H., & Henry, D. B. (2000). A developmental-ecological model of the relation of family functioning to patterns of delinquency. *Journal of Quantitative Criminology, 16*(2), 169–198.

Grisso, T. (1996, June). Society's retributive response to juvenile violence: A developmental perspective. *Law and Human Behavior, 20*(3), 229–247.

Grisso, T., & Schwartz, R. G. (2000). *Youth on trial A developmental perspective on juvenile justice.* Chicago and London: The University of Chicago Press.

Grossberg, M. (2002). Changing conceptions of child welfare in the United States, 1820–1935. In M. K. Rosenheim, F. E. Zimring, D. S. Tanenhaus, & B. Dohrn (Eds.), *A century of juvenile justice* (pp. 3–41). Chicago: University of Chicago Press.

Hawkins, J. D., Herrenkohl, T., Farrington, D. P., Brewer, D., Catalano, R. F., & Harachi, T. W. (1998). A review of predictors of youth violence. In R. Loeber & D. P. Farrington (Eds.), *Serious and violent juvenile offenders: Risk factors and successful interventions* (pp. 106–146). Thousand Oaks, CA: Sage.

Herrenkohl, T. I., Hawkins, J. D., Chung, I. J., Hill, K. G., & Battin-Pearson, S. (2001). School and community risk factors and interventions. In R. Loeber, & D. P. Farrington (Eds.), *Child delinquents: Development, intervention, and service needs* (pp. 211–246). Thousand Oaks, CA: Sage.

Howell, J. C. (1997). *Juvenile justice and youth violence.* Thousand Oaks, CA: Sage.

Huesmann, L. R., Moise-Titus, J., Podolski, C., & Eron, L. D. (2003). Longitudinal relations between children's exposure to TV violence and their aggressive and violent behavior in young adulthood: 1977–1992. *Developmental Psychology, 39*(2), 201–221.

In re Gault, 387 U.S. 1 (1967).

In re Winship, 397 U.S. 358 (1970).

Kent v. United States, 383 U.S. 541(1966).

Kiesner, J., Cadinu, M., Poulin, F., & Bucci, M. (2002). Group identification in early adolescence: Its relation with peer adjustment and its moderator effect on peer influence. *Child Development, 73*(1), 196–208.

Kunkel, D. (2005). How real is the problem of media violence? The public health consequences of a violent media culture. In N. Dowd, D. G. Singer, & R. F. Wilson (Eds.), *Handbook of children, culture, and violence.* Thousand Oaks, CA: Sage.

Laird, R. D., Petit, G. S., Bates, J. E., & Dodge, K. E. (2003). Parents' monitoring-relevant knowledge and adolescents' delinquent behavior: Evidence of correlated developmental changes and reciprocal influences. *Child Development, 74*(3), 752–768.

Leventhal, T., & Brooks-Gunn, J. (2000). The neighborhoods they live in: The effects of neighborhood residence on child and adolescent outcomes. *Psychological Bulletin, 126*(2), 309–337.

Lewin, K. (1936). *Principles of topological psychology.* New York: McGraw-Hill.

Loeber, R., Farrington, D. P., & Petechuk, D. (2003, May). Child delinquency: Early intervention and prevention. *Child Delinquency Bulletin,* Office of Juvenile Justice and Delinquency Prevention. Retrieved from http://ncjrs.org/html/ojjdp/186162/contents.html

Loeber, R., Farrington, D. P., Stouthamer-Loeber, M., Moffitt, T. E., & Caspi, A. (2001). The development of male offending: Key findings from the first decade of the Pittsburgh Youth Study. In R. Bull (Ed.), *Children and the law: The essential readings* (pp. 336–380). Oxford, UK: Blackwell.

Lynam, D. R., Caspi, A., Moffitt, T. E., Wilström, P. H., Loeber, R., & Novak, S. (2000). The interaction between impulsivity and neighborhood context on offending: The effects of impulsivity are stronger in poorer neighborhoods. *Journal of Abnormal Psychology, 109*(4), 563–573.

Mack, J. (1909). The juvenile court. *Harvard Law Review, 23,* 104–122.

Martinson, R. (1974). What works? Questions and answers about prison reform. *Public Interest, 35,* 22–54.

McCarty, F. B., & Carr, J. G. (1980). *Juvenile law and its processes: Cases and materials.* New York: Bobbs-Merrill.

McCord, J., & Conway, K. P. (2002). Patterns of juvenile delinquency and co-offending. In E. Waring & D. Weisburd (Eds.), *Advances of Criminology Theory, Vol. 10: Crime and Social Organization* (pp. 15–30). New Brunswick, NJ: Transaction Publishers.

Meyer v. Nebraska, 262 U.S. 390 (1923).

Milgram, S. (1963). Behavioral study of obedience. *Journal of Abnormal Social Psychology, 67,* 371–378.

Mischel, W. (1968). *Personality and assessment.* New York: Wiley.

Moos, R. H. (1973). Conceptualizations of human environments. *American Psychologist, 28*(8), 652–665.

Nisbett, R. E., & Ross, L. (1980). *Human inference: Strategies and shortcomings of social judgment.* Engelwood Cliffs, NJ: Prentice Hall.

Park, D. C. (1999). Acts of will? *American Psychologist, 54,* 461.

PBS Frontline (1999). *Inside the teen brain.* Online at www.pbs.org/wgbh/pages/frontline/shows/teenbrain/

Pierce v. Society of Sisters of the Holy Names of Jesus and Mary, 268 U.S. 510 (1925).

Prince v. Massachusetts, 321 U.S. 158 (1944).

Redding, R. E., & Howell, J. C. (2000). Blended sentencing in American juvenile courts. In J. Fagan, & F. E. Zimring (Eds.), *The changing borders of juvenile justice: Transfers of adolescents to the criminal court* (pp. 148–180). Chicago and London: University of Chicago Press.

Reiss, A., Jr., & Farrington, D. (1991). Advance knowledge about co-offending: Results from a prospective longitudinal survey of London males. *Journal of Criminal Law and Criminology, 82,* 360–395.

Ross, L., & Nisbett, R.E. (1991). *The person and the situation: Perspectives of social psychology.* Philadelphia: Temple University Press.

Sampson, R. J., & Groves, W. B. (1989). Community structure and crime: Testing social-disorganization theory. *American Journal of Sociology, 94,* 774–780.

Sampson, R. J., Raudenbush, S. W., & Earls, F. (1997). Neighborhoods and violent crime: A multilevel study of collective efficacy. *Science, 277*(5328), 919–924.

Scaramella, L. V., Conger, R. D., Spoth, R., & Simons, R. L. (2002). Evaluation of a social contextual model of delinquency: A cross-cultural replication. *Child Development, 73*(1), 175–195.

Schall v. Martin, 467 U.S. 253 (1984).

Scott, E. S., & Grisso, T. (1997). The evolution of adolescence: A developmental perspective on juvenile justice reform. *Journal of Criminal Law and Criminology, 88,* 137–189.

Scott, E. S., Reppucci, N. D., & Woolard, J. L. (1995). Evaluating adolescent decision making in legal contexts. *Law and Human Behavior, 19*(3), 221–244.

Singer, D. G. (2005). Developmental differences among children and adolescents. In N. Dowd, D. G. Singer, & R. F. Wilson (Eds.), *Handbook of children, culture, and violence.* Thousand Oaks, CA: Sage.

Slobogin C., & Fondacaro, M. (2000). Rethinking deprivations of liberty: Possible contributions from therapeutic and ecological jurisprudence. *Behavioral Science and the Law, 18,* 499–516.

Slobogin, C. Fondacaro, M. R., & Woolard, J. (1999). A prevention model of juvenile justice: The promise of Kansas v. Hendricks for children. *Wisconsin Law Review, 1999,* 186–226.

Soler, M. I. (1994.). Re-imagining the juvenile court. In S. Humm, B.A. Ort, M. M. Anbari, W. Lader, & W. S. Biel (Eds.), *Child, parent, and state: Law and policy reader* (pp. 596–610). Philadelphia: Temple University Press.

Sowell, E. R., Thompson, P. M., Holems, C. J., Jernigan, T. L., & Toga, A. W. (1999). In vivo evidence for post-adolescent brain maturation in frontal and striatal regions. *Nature Neuroscience,* 2(10), 859–861.

Stark, R. (1987). Deviant place: A theory of the ecology of crime. *Criminology, 25,* 893–917.

Steinberg, L. (April, 2003). *Less guilty by reason of adolescence.* Invited Master Lecture, Biennial Meeting of the Society for Research in Child Development, Tampa, Florida.

Steinberg, L., & Cauffman, E. (1996, June). Maturity of judgment in adolescence: Psychosocial factors in adolescent decision making. *Law and Human Behavior, 20*(3), 249–272.

Steinberg, L., & Scott, E. S. (2003). Less guilty by reason of adolescence: Developmental immaturity, diminished responsibility, and the juvenile death penalty. *American Psychologist, 58*(12), 1009–1018.

Sullivan, H. S. (1953). *The interpersonal theory of psychiatry.* New York: Norton.

Tanenhaus, D.S. (2000). The evolution of transfer out of the juvenile court. In J. Fagan & F. Zimring (Eds.), *The changing borders of juvenile justice* (pp. 13–43). Chicago: University of Chicago Press.

White, J., Moffitt, T. E., Caspi, A., Bartusch, D. J., Needles, D., & Stouthamer-Loeber, M. (1994). The measurement of impulsivity and its relationship to delinquency. *Journal of Abnormal Psychology, 103,* 192–205.

Wiebush, R. G., McNulty, B., & Le, T. (2000). Implementation of the Intensive Community-Based Aftercare Program. *Juvenile Justice Bulletin.* Washington, DC: U.S. Department of Justice, Office of Justice Programs, Office of Juvenile Justice and Delinquency Prevention.

Wiesner, M., & Windle, M. (2004). Assessing covariates of adolescent delinquency trajectories: A latent growth mixture modeling approach. *Journal of Youth and Adolescence, 33*(5), 431–442.

Wilson, J.Q., & Herrnstein, R.J. (1985). *Crime and human nature.* New York: Simon & Schuster.

Woolard, J. L., Fondacaro, M. R., & Slobogin, C. (2001). Informing juvenile justice policy: directions for behavior science research. *Law and Human Behavior, 25*(1), 13–24.

Wrightsman, L.S., Greene, E., Nietzel, M. T., & Fortune, W. H. (2002). *Psychology and the legal system* (5th ed.). Belmont, CA: Wadsworth.

CHAPTER 19

# *Adult Punishment for Juvenile Offenders*

## *Does It Reduce Crime?*

RICHARD E. REDDING

The decade prior to 1994 saw a significant increase in violent juvenile crime, high-profile cases of serious and violent crimes committed by juveniles and young adults, and the resulting perception that America was experiencing a juvenile crime wave unlike anything in its history (Zimring, 1998). Based on the projected growth in the juvenile population during the early 21st century, some predicted a coming storm of youth violence (Welch, Fenwick, & Roberts, 1997) and the emergence of young "super-predators" (DiIulio, 1995).

The public, and perhaps even more so policy makers, demanded action. There was a rough consensus among legislators that the juvenile court was too lenient, that serious offenders were beyond rehabilitation and must be incarcerated to ensure public safety, and that juveniles were as culpable for their crimes as adults (Redding, 1997). Thus, states passed legal reforms designed to "get tough" on juvenile crime. The most significant change was states' revision of their transfer laws to expand the type of offenses and offenders eligible for transfer from the juvenile court to the adult court for trial and sentencing. Changes also occurred at the federal level with the passage of the Violent Crime Control and Law Enforcement Act of 1994, which allowed the transfer of 13-year-olds who committed crimes with firearms on federal property. Congressman Bill McCollum, a key sponsor of the federal legislation, said that "in America today, no population poses a greater threat to public safety than juvenile criminals" (Lacayo & Donnelly, 1997, p. 26).

This chapter discusses the research on the general and specific deterrent effects of transferring juveniles for trial in adult criminal court, identifies gaps in our knowledge base that require further research, discusses the circumstances under which effective deterrence may be achieved, and examines whether there are effective alternatives for achieving deterrence other than adult sanctions for serious juvenile offenders. As a backdrop to this analysis, this chapter first examines the role of public opinion in shaping the "get tough" policies, and how policy makers have misunderstood and perceived support for those policies.

## THE ROLE OF PUBLIC OPINION

During the 1980s and 1990s, the public appeared to support the new approach to juvenile crime. Voters passed state propositions allowing more juveniles to be tried as adults (Beresford, 2000). Consider California's Proposition 21, enacted by voter initiative, which lowered the age for transfer from 16 to 14 and shifted discretion for making transfer decisions from juvenile court judges to prosecutors (Gang Violence and Juvenile Crime Prevention Act of 1998). The 1993 Gallup Poll showed that 73% of respondents were in favor of trying violent juveniles as adults, and influential public officials like Los Angeles County District Attorney Gil Garcetti proclaimed, "we need to throw out our entire juvenile justice system" (Redding, 1997, p. 712). Alfred Regnery, administrator of the Office of Juvenile Justice and Delinquency Prevention in the Reagan administration, argued that juvenile offenders were "getting away with murder," that juvenile offenders "are criminals who happen to be young, not children who happen to commit crimes" (Regnery, 1985, p. 65).

Perhaps due in part to media hype, much of the public continues to believe that the juvenile crime rate remains high (Shepherd, 1999), reflecting an alarmist reaction to crime generally (Welch et al., 1997). But the public is misinformed about the juvenile crime problem. Since 1993, the decrease in juvenile crime has been three times greater than the decrease in adult crime (Snyder, 2004). Because of this decline, juvenile crime rates are now comparable to what they were in 1980 (Blumstein, 2001), before the policy shift toward increased transfer and other punitive responses to juvenile offenders. The juvenile arrest rate for violent crime, after peaking in 1994, has now reached its lowest level since 1980 and is 29% lower than it was in 1993. There has been a 64% decrease in the number of juveniles arrested for murder (Snyder, 2004), likely due to the declining crack cocaine market and tougher anti-firearms laws and policing programs (Butts & Travis, 2002; Zimring, 1998).

Despite erroneous public perceptions about juvenile crime rates, however, the public does not favor abandoning the rehabilitative ideal of juvenile justice in favor of wholesale punitive responses to juvenile offenders. While recent polls show that between 58 and 91% of Americans favor (depending on the type of crime and poll) trying violent juvenile offenders as adults (The American Enterprise, 2001; Schwartz, Guo, & Kerbs, 1993; Wu, 2000), there is far less support for imposing adult sentences (Schwartz et al., 1993). Most still believe in the efficacy of the juvenile justice system and want it strengthened, favor early intervention and prevention programs along with rehabilitation over punishment for juvenile offenders, would reserve incarceration only for the most serious and violent offenders, want juvenile offenders tried as adults to receive rehabilitative treatment, and strongly disagree with the confinement of juveniles in adult prisons (Moon, Sundt, Cullen, & Wright, 2000; Schiraldi & Soler, 1998). Polls that do report high public support for punitive policies typically ask omnibus questions about juvenile crime (e.g., asking whether respondents favor "punishing violent juvenile offenders as adults"). More nuanced survey questions that provide respondents with information about particular cases or sentencing options (e.g., the background of a particular offender, rehabilitative programs available) reveal considerably less support for punitive sentencing policies (Stalans & Henry, 1994). While the public favors incarceration for those serious and violent offenders who most threaten public safety, they do not favor the wholesale imprisonment of young, nonviolent, or first-time offenders (Sundt, 1999). But policy makers consistently overestimate the public's support for punitive policies (Latessa, 2004).

## LEGISLATIVE CHANGES IN TRANSFER LAWS AND THEIR IMPACT

Transfer laws (also called waiver or certification laws), which transfer juveniles from the juvenile court to adult criminal court for trial and sentencing, exist in every state (Griffin, 2003; Redding, 1997). During the last 20 years, states have revised their transfer laws to lower the minimum age for transfer, increase the number of transferable offenses, expand prosecutorial discretion while reducing judicial discretion in transfer decision making, and expand the reach of laws requiring that certain juvenile offenders be automatically tried as adults (Redding, 2003; see Fagan & Zimring, 2000). In 1979, for example, only 14 states had "automatic" transfer laws, but by 1995, twenty-one states had such statutes, with 31 states having these laws by 2003 (Steiner & Hemmens, 2003). In addition, 13 states lowered the age at which juvenile court jurisdiction ends, to age 15 or 16 (Sanborn, 2003).

As a result of the legislative changes, the number of youth convicted of felonies in criminal courts and incarcerated in adult facilities has increased (Redding, 2003). The number reached a peak in the mid-1990s and has declined since (Puzzanchera, 2003), due in part to the decrease in juvenile crime. Despite the legislative changes in transfer laws, transfer remains relatively uncommon; less than 1% of all juvenile court cases are transferred (Puzzanchera, 2003).

According to the most recent data available, an estimated 5,600 youth were committed to state adult prisons in 1999, representing 2% of all new prison commitments. These numbers reflect a 26% decrease in youth commitments since the peak year of 1995, but nonetheless an overall increase of 70% between 1985 and 2000 (Sickmund, 2004). These youth are overwhelmingly male (96%) and most were 17 years old at the time of their commitment; 36% were White and 57% were African American. Sixty-two percent were incarcerated for person offenses, 22% for property offenses, 5% for public orders offenses (e.g., weapons possession), and 1% for drug offenses (Sickmund, 2004). Seventy-eight percent were released before their 21st birthday and 95% were released before their 25th birthday, with an average of about 2 years, 8 months served.

Prior research (before about 1990) was inconclusive on whether juveniles sentenced in adult criminal court received more severe sentences than those sentenced in the juvenile court for similar crimes (Kupchik, Fagan, & Liberman, 2003). But several more methodologically sophisticated studies confirm that, in recent years, transferred juveniles do receive tougher sentences (Kupchik et al., 2003; Kurlychek & Johnson, 2004). Data from some states indicates that they may even receive more severe sentences than adults convicted of the same crime (Kurlychek & Johnson, 2004; Virginia Department of Criminal Justice Services, 1996). Indeed, the nationwide policy shift toward transferring juveniles to the criminal court is based partly on the assumption that more punitive, adult sentences will follow, and that these sentences will act as a general or specific deterrent to juvenile crime.

In terms of specific deterrence—that is, whether trying and sentencing juvenile offenders as adults decreases the likelihood that they will recidivate—seven recent large-scale studies in various jurisdictions have all found higher recidivism rates among juveniles convicted for violent offenses and sentenced as adults, when compared to similar juvenile offenders tried in the juvenile court. On the other hand, it is unclear whether transfer affects recidivism among nonviolent property offenders (Redding, 2003; Redding & Mrozoski, 2005). With respect to general deterrence—that is, whether transfer laws deter would-be juvenile offenders—the picture is considerably less clear, because there are only three systematic empirical studies, and the studies, which produced conflicting findings, were conducted 15 to 20 years ago (Redding, 2003; Redding & Mrozoski, 2005). The issues of general and specific deterrence are discussed in the following sections.

## GENERAL DETERRENCE: DO TRANSFER LAWS DETER AND PREVENT JUVENILE CRIME?

Two well-designed studies conducted in the 1980s found that transfer laws did not reduce juvenile crime. On the contrary, Jensen and Metsger's (1994) time-series analysis found a 13% increase in arrest rates for violent juvenile crime in Idaho after the state implemented its automatic transfer law. In a similar analysis, Singer and McDowall (1988) found that a New York state law that automatically sent violent juvenile offenders to criminal court (by lowering the age for criminal court jurisdiction) had no deterrent effect, even though the law was widely applied and publicized in the media. In addition, brochures were sent to public schools announcing the law and the risks juveniles faced, and juvenile court judges warned youth about the risks of committing violent offenses (S. Singer, 2004, personal communication). The limited evidence available at the time suggested that juveniles in New York were aware of the automatic transfer law (Singer & McDowall, 1988).

On the other hand, the results of a multistate economic analysis for the years 1978 to 1993 suggests that trying juveniles as adults may have moderate deterrent effects (Levitt, 1998). The study found a 25% decrease in violent juvenile crime and a 10 to 15% decrease in property crime committed by juveniles in states that lowered the jurisdictional age for criminal court from 18 to 17. The greatest decreases in crime were found in states having the greatest disparity in punishment severity between the criminal and juvenile courts. These data suggest the deterrent effect of criminal court sanctions. The researcher concluded that, "the estimated decrease in crime associated with incarcerating an additional juvenile is at least as large as the corresponding reduction in crime for adults" (Levitt, 1998, p. 1181). The same study, however, found no relationship between the punitiveness of juvenile court sanctions and later criminal offending in adulthood.

Levitt's (1998) aggregate analysis of crime rates across states differs substantially from the methodology used by Jensen and Metsger (1994) and Singer and McDowall (1988), which used careful offender case comparisons and quasi-experimental controls to study crime rates in a particular state. In addition, the Levitt study specifically examined the effects of criminal court jurisdiction (when youth reached the age of majority), rather than the effects of transfer laws per se. Unlike knowing that one could be tried as an adult for crimes committed while a juvenile, which most juveniles do not seem to realize (as discussed below), "it is probably well known that dramatically greater penalties for all offenses are imposed once a juvenile reaches the age of majority" (Robinson & Darley, 2004, p. 177).

Data from some communities also suggest that transfer laws deter juvenile crime. In Jacksonville, Florida, the juvenile arrest rate decreased 30% and the juvenile violent crime rate decreased 44% between 1993 and 1994, after the local prosecutor instituted aggressive policies to prosecute serious juvenile offenders in criminal court (Bennett, DiIulio, & Walters, 1996).

Only a few studies have interviewed juvenile offenders, however. Before the widespread expansion of transfer laws, Glassner, Ksander, Berg, and Johnson (1983) reported the results of interviews with a small number of juvenile offenders in New York, who said they had decided to stop offending once they reached the age at which they knew they could be tried as adults. A recent small-scale study interviewed 37 juvenile offenders who had been transferred to criminal court, for armed robbery or murder in Georgia. The study examined their knowledge and perceptions of transfer laws and criminal sanctions (Redding & Fuller, 2004). Georgia had undertaken a public awareness campaign to inform juveniles about the state's new automatic transfer law. Nonetheless, juveniles reported being unaware of the transfer law; only 30% knew that juveniles who committed serious crimes could be tried as adults. Even among those who knew about the law, none expected that it would be enforced against them for the serious crime they committed. On the contrary, many thought they would only get slap-on-the-wrist sentences from the juvenile court. These results are consistent with those in a recent Canadian study finding that many juvenile offenders did not think that they would receive a serious punishment if caught (Peterson-Badali, Ruck, & Koegl, 2001).

## HOW MIGHT TRANSFER LAWS HAVE DETERRENT EFFECTS ON JUVENILE CRIME?

There are likely two explanations for juvenile offenders' inaccurate perceptions about the risk of being tried as adults. First, juveniles' psychosocial immaturity (Beckman, 2004; Scott, Reppucci, & Woolard, 1995; Steinberg & Cauffman, 1996) may make them less likely to perceive accurately the likelihood of apprehension and serious punishment. Second, the relatively mild sanctions the juveniles had previously received from the juvenile court may have communicated the wrong message about the consequences of committing crimes as a juvenile. As one juvenile interviewed by Redding and Fuller (2004) explained, "[Being tried as an adult] showed me it's not a game anymore. Before, I thought that since I'm a juvenile I could do just about anything and just get six months if I got caught" (p. 39). The juvenile justice system may fail to provide meaningful sanctions until it is too late. "How is an offender supposed to judge which 'last chance to go straight' is really his last? He is likely to keep testing the system until it lands on him hard. . . . [Thus], every detected non-trivial violation of law ought to lead to some nontrivial deprivation of liberty" (Kleiman, 1999, p. 13). And as one Los Angeles Assistant District Attorney said, "You talk to youngsters . . . and they tell you, repeatedly, that they got away with so much—that they commit crimes, but aren't arrested, and if they are arrested, when they are brought into [juvenile] court, nothing happens" (Michaelis, 2001, p. 309).

An initial light sanction by the juvenile court followed by ever-increasing punishment severity for subsequent offenses, up to and including criminal sentences, may have counterproductive effects.

> . . . Judges often do not send youthful offenders to prison because the experience may increase their future likelihood of committing criminal offenses. . . . However, from the deterrence perspective, it may bring about the 'hardening to punishment' effect observed in animals, in which an escalating series of punishments, if it begins at a level that is ineffective in controlling the initial transgression, simply conditions the person to tolerate the increasing punishments, without reducing the rate of transgressions. (Robinson & Darley, 2004, p. 187)

If true, this offers an especially compelling rationale for ensuring that the initial sanctions applied by the juvenile court have enough bite. Nonetheless, the studies (e.g., Minor, Hartmann, & Terry, 1997; Wooldredge, 1988) are mixed on whether the initial actions by the juvenile court (diversion vs. adjudication and sentencing) impact recidivism, at least vis-à-vis first-time or relatively nonserious offenders.

The juvenile offenders interviewed by Redding and Fuller (2004) indicated that being tried as adults taught them, apparently for the first time, that their criminal behavior had real consequences. The challenge would be how to deliver this "wake-up call" without inflicting the permanently disfiguring (Zimring, 2000) and counter-rehabilitative effects of the criminal justice system. Scared straight programs, shock incarceration programs, and boot camps have all proved ineffective in reducing recidivism in juvenile offenders (Finckenauer & Gavin, 1999). But knowing they could be tried and sentenced as adults, juvenile offenders say, may have prevented them from committing the crime (Redding & Fuller, 2004). We cannot know whether their introspections are accurate. A recent study with serious juvenile offenders found a correlation between their self-reported likelihood of committing a future offense and the number of offenses they committed after their release (Corrado, Cohen, Glackman, & Odgers, 2003), mirroring a similar study with adult offenders (Burnett, 2000). The Redding and Fuller (2004) study, though conducted on a small sample in only one jurisdiction, provides some limited evidence that juvenile offenders may calibrate their behavior as a function of the perceived likelihood of receiving an adult punishment.

Some have argued that the recent decline in crime rates is due to "get tough" policies (see Bennett et al., 1996; Scheidegger & Rushford, 1999). There has been relatively little research on deterrence with respect to juveniles, and the results have been mixed, with some studies finding deterrence effects for certainty and severity of punishment and others finding no such effects or even negative effects (Corrado et al., 2003). Corrado et al.'s (2003) recent study with serious juvenile offenders incarcerated in a maximum-security facility found a negative relationship between intent to reoffend and sentence severity, with evidence that offenders made "some explicit calculations about the advantages and disadvantages of committing future crimes" (p. 197).

Given the paucity of research on juvenile crime deterrence, this chapter turns now to research with adults that is relevant to the question of whether we should expect transfer laws to deter juvenile crime. A comprehensive analysis of the extant research on criminal deterrence conducted in 1998 by the Institute of Criminology at Cambridge University concluded: "The studies plainly suggest that when potential offenders are made aware of substantial risks of being punished, many of them are induced to desist" (Von Hirsch, Bottoms, Burney, & Wikstrom, 1999, p. 47). The perceived certainty of punishment (e.g., being apprehended and tried as an adult) appears to affect crime rates. It is unclear, however, whether the severity of punishment (e.g., receiving a substantial adult sentence) affects crime rates, though the limited evidence available suggests that it does not. Von Hirsch et al. (1999) speculate that this is because potential offenders typically have much more information about certainty of apprehension than sentence severity; studies show that offenders and the public generally know little about potential sentences and tend to greatly underestimate their severity (Robinson & Darley, 2004; Von Hirsch et al., 1999). Moreover, punishment is an uncertain future event that offenders tend to discount (whereas the short-term rewards of crime are salient), and relatively small or large changes in penalties may not be calibrated to offenders' thresholds for offending. At the same time, "future contingent costs may be discounted less, if their magnitude is sufficiently great and their likelihood of being incurred increases. Severe sentencing policies thus might possibly have an impact if coupled with much higher probabilities of conviction" (Von Hirsch et al., 1999, p. 48). Thus, one might suppose that transfer laws would serve a deterrent function if would-be juvenile offenders are made aware of such laws and if the laws are widely implemented, with convictions resulting in significant adult sentences.

But in order for criminal sanctions to have deterrent effects, potential offenders must (1) believe that there is a reasonable likelihood of getting caught, (2) know that the likelihood of a conviction and receiving a substantial sentence is significant or has increased, (3) believe that the penalty will be applied to them if caught, and (4) consider the risk of the penalty when deciding whether to offend (Von Hirsch et al., 1999). Moreover, the perceived costs of obeying the law must outweigh the perceived benefits of offending. Robinson and Darley (2004) argue that, for a variety of reasons, such conditions rarely are present in the real world. Youths' psychosocial immaturity (e.g., impulsivity, risk-taking proclivity, short-term time perspective, limited ability to foresee future consequences, limited life experience and metacognitive skills) (Beckman, 2004; Scott, Reppucci, & Woolard, 1995; Steinberg & Cauffman, 1996) could make this rational-choice model of deterrence, which assumes that perceived consequences influence decisions about committing crime, less applicable to juvenile offenders (Schneider & Ervin, 1990). Consider each of these necessary preconditions for successful deterrence in the context of juvenile offending. A law cannot act as a deterrent if the targeted population is unaware that the law exists or does not believe it will be enforced. Recall Redding and Fuller's (2004) finding that few violent juvenile offenders knew they could be tried as adults, none thought it would happen to them, and few thought they would face serious punishment. Moreover, few reported thinking about the possibility of getting caught when they committed the offense. It seems that offenders generally underestimate the risk that they will be caught, thinking instead that they will avoid the mistakes that ensnarled others (Robinson & Darley, 2004). Juveniles' psychosocial immaturity makes it even less likely that they will perceive a significant risk of being convicted and sentenced as an adult.

Substantial further research is urgently needed to examine whether transfer laws have (or could have, given the appropriate conditions) the general deterrent effect of preventing juvenile crime. In particular, it is important to examine whether juveniles are aware of transfer laws, whether this awareness deters delinquent behavior, and whether they believe the laws will be enforced against them. In conjunction with such research, there is a need for better-designed and well-targeted public-awareness campaigns on the state and local levels designed to make would-be juvenile offenders aware of the consequences of serious and violent crime (Redding & Fuller, 2004), and for rigorous evaluations of their effectiveness. Such campaigns have proved effective in reducing adult crime in some contexts (e.g., Johnson & Bowers, 2003). Unfortunately, however, the few public-awareness campaigns instituted to inform juveniles about transfer laws have been of fairly limited scope and duration and of questionable effectiveness in targeting the population at risk (Redding & Fuller, 2004).

## SPECIFIC DETERRENCE: DO TRANSFER LAWS DECREASE OFFENDERS' RECIDIVISM?

Seven large-scale studies indicate that youth tried in adult criminal court for violent crimes have greater recidivism rates after release than those tried in juvenile court, though it is unclear whether transfer affects recidivism for property offenders.

Fagan (1996) examined the recidivism rates of 800 randomly selected 15- and 16-year-old juvenile offenders charged with robbery or burglary. Controlling for eight variables (prior offenses, offense severity, race, gender, age at first offense, case length, sentence length, and court), this natural experiment compared offenders charged in New Jersey's juvenile courts with offenders charged in New York's criminal courts under that state's automatic transfer law. Both geographical areas shared similar demographic, socioeconomic, sociolegal, and crime-indictor characteristics. Thus, the study provides a direct comparison of recidivism rates as a function of whether cases are processed in juvenile or criminal court, without many of the sample-selection problems inherent in studies comparing cases within a single jurisdiction where prosecutors or judges decide which cases to transfer. Youth who had committed robbery and were sentenced in adult criminal court had a higher post-release recidivism rate than those tried in juvenile court, but the recidivism rates for burglary offenders tried in criminal and juvenile courts were similar. The findings on robbery offenders suggest that criminal court processing, irrespective of whether youth are incarcerated in juvenile or adult facilities, produces a higher recidivism rate. This finding is emphasized by the parallel finding that youth sentenced to probation in criminal court had a substantially higher recidivism rate than those incarcerated in the juvenile justice system (see also Mason & Chang, 2001).

Bishop and colleagues (Bishop, Frazier, Lanza-Kaduce, & Winner, 1996) compared the one-year recidivism rate of 2,738 juvenile offenders transferred to criminal court in Florida with a matched sample of 2,738 juvenile offenders who had not been transferred. Florida relies almost exclusively on transfer by prosecutors, whose transfer decisions are largely offense driven and made soon after arrest, before gaining access to information about the youth's background. Therefore, it is less likely that the youth retained in the juvenile justice system had lower recidivism rates due to selection factors (Bishop & Frazier, 2000). Nonetheless, this study cannot completely rule out possible selection effects in some (and perhaps a significant number) of cases. The study, which controlled for seven variables (race, gender, age, most serious prior offense, number of referrals to juvenile court, number of charges, and most serious charge), found that the rearrest rates were higher (30 versus 19%) and the time until reoffending shorter (135 versus 227 days) for the transferred youth across seven offense types (ranging from violent felonies to minor misd meanors). Following the same Florida offenders 6 years after this initial study, Winner and colleagues (Winner, Lanza-Kaduce, Bishop, & Frazier, 1997) also found higher recidivism rates among those transferred to criminal courts, with the exception of property felons.

Controlling for demographic and offense-related variables (e.g., age of onset of offending, prior offenses, use of a firearm), Myers (2001) examined the recidivism rates of 557 violent juvenile offenders in Pennsylvania. Youth who were judicially transferred to criminal court were rearrested more quickly upon their return to the community than youth who were retained in the juvenile justice system during the same period. However, transferred youth who were incarcerated for longer periods had a lower recidivism rate upon release than those incarcerated for shorter periods. Similarly, Podkopacz and Feld (1996) compared transferred with non-transferred juvenile offenders in Minnesota, and found higher recidivism rates among those transferred.

The above five studies involved all three types of transfer laws (automatic, judicial, and prosecutorial), used fairly large sample sizes (557 to 5,476), employed different methodologies (natural experiment and matched groups), and were conducted in five different jurisdictions (Florida, New Jersey, New York, Minnesota, Pennsylvania). Yet they each had significant methodological limitations, primarily the inability to control completely for possible differential selection effects (vis-à-vis juveniles' amenability to treatment and recidivism risk) between those cases retained in the juvenile court versus those that were transferred.

But armed with two very recent large-scale studies that better control for possible selection effects, we can now conclude with much greater confidence that transfer generally does increase recidivism, though remaining methodological limitations still do not allow for definitive conclusions. Fagan, Kupchik and Liberman's (2003) recent finding of greater recidivism for transferred juveniles (charged with robbery, burglary, or assault) replicates Fagan's (1996) previous study but with a larger data set (2,400 juveniles) and methodology that better controls for important variables relating to possible selection effects. As in the previous study, by controlling for sentence lengths, the study showed that criminal court processing per se (rather than differential sentences between the juvenile and criminal courts) increased recidivism. Similarly, Lanza-Kaduce, Frazier, Lane, and Bishop's (2000) recent follow-up study to the Bishop et al. (1996) Florida recidivism study also replicated the previous findings of higher recidivism rates for transferred juveniles as a function of criminal court processing per se (rather than differential sentences), using better matching techniques to control for possible selection effects, more extensive recidivism data, and data drawn from six Florida judicial circuits in rural and urban jurisdictions.

## WHY DO JUVENILES TRIED AS ADULTS HAVE HIGHER RECIDIVISM RATES?

What explains the higher recidivism rates for violent juvenile offenders tried in criminal court? The stigmatization and other negative effects of labeling juveniles as convicted felons, the sense of resentment and injustice juveniles feel about being tried as adults, the decreased focus on rehabilitation and family support in the adult system, and the learning of criminal mores and behavior from adult criminals have all been singled out as possible reasons for the increased recidivism (see Bazemore & Umbriet, 1995; Thomas & Bishop, 1984; Winner et al., 1997). Moreover, a felony conviction also usually results in the loss of a number of civil rights and privileges (see Redding, 2003), further reducing the opportunities for employment and community reintegration.

Juveniles' sense of injustice at criminal court processing may cause them to react defiantly through reoffending and only harden their concept of themselves as "criminals" (see Thomas & Bishop, 1984; Winner et al., 1997). "The concept of fairness appears to be an important variable in an individual's perception of sentence severity and its subsequent relationship to future recidivism" (Corrado et al., 2003, p. 183). And, conduct-disordered adolescents, it seems, already have a sense of having been dealt an unfair hand by authority figures (Chamberlain, 1998). Bishop and Frazier (2000) interviewed 95 serious and chronic juvenile offenders in Florida who had been transferred to the criminal justice system and incarcerated in correctional facilities. Many of the juveniles felt a strong sense of injustice and resentment about being tried as adults:

> Many experience the court process not so much as a condemnation of their behavior as a condemnation of them. Unlike the

> juvenile court, the criminal court failed to communicate that young offenders retain some fundamental worth. What the youths generally heard was that they were being punished not only because their behavior was bad but also because they were personifications of their behavior. Far from viewing the criminal court and its officers as legitimate, the juvenile offenders we interviewed saw them more often as duplicitous and manipulative, malevolent in intent, and indifferent to their needs. It was common for them to experience a sense of injustice and, then, to condemn the condemners. (Bishop & Frazier, 2000, p. 263)

These findings are consistent with those of Redding and Fuller (2004) who found that juveniles tried as adults clearly did not perceive transfer laws as being fair and just. Many felt that their juvenile status and immaturity dictated that they should be tried as juveniles, despite the serious crime they had committed. They also did not understand what the law was attempting to accomplish by trying them as adults and felt that they were somehow being treated differently than other similarly situated juveniles. Both perceptions contributed to their sense of unfairness.

An especially compelling explanation for the increased recidivism is the greatly reduced opportunities for meaningful rehabilitation in the adult criminal justice system and the hardening of youth who serve time in adult prisons. Bishop and Frazier's (2000) recent study vividly portrays the differences between juvenile and adult correctional facilities. "Despite the punitive rhetoric" of juvenile justice in Florida (alongside Texas, the state having the highest per capita number of juveniles tried in criminal court), they found that the juvenile correctional institutions were treatment oriented and adhered to therapeutic models of rehabilitation (Bishop & Frazier, 2000, p. 255). Juveniles in these facilities had positive feelings about the staff, whom they felt cared about them and taught them appropriate behaviors. In contrast, Florida prisons were clearly custodial in nature (Annino, 2000), and the juveniles in adult prisons reported that much of their time was spent learning criminal behavior from the inmates and responding to pressure to prove how tough they were. They also were much more fearful of being victimized than they had been in juvenile facilities; more than 30% had been assaulted or had witnessed assaults by prison staff. Notably, most of the juveniles incarcerated in juvenile facilities felt confident that they would not reoffend after release, often crediting the staff with helping them make this positive change. But only a third of the juveniles in adult prisons said that they would not reoffend. In sum, "compared to the criminal justice system, the juvenile system seems to be more reintegrative in practice and effect" (Bishop & Frazier, 2000, p. 265). This is well described by Forst, Fagan, and Vivona's (1989) study, which found that unlike adult prisons, counseling in juvenile facilities was provided by line staff as part of their regular duties. Youth in juvenile facilities gave higher marks than youth in adult facilities to the available treatment and case management services, which youth in detention described as helpful in providing counseling, obtaining needed services, encouraging participation in programs, teaching the consequences of rule-breaking, and deepening their understanding of their problems.

Adult prisons are unlikely to provide an environment conducive to rehabilitation, for either adult or juvenile offenders. A prisoner's experience is "from the outset, an experience of being violently dominated, and it is colored from the beginning by the fear of being violently treated" (Cover, 1986, p. 1608). Force, intimidation, and threat from prison gangs are the norm, as are overcrowded and starkly inadequate living conditions and the significant physical and psychological stresses of prison life. As one federal court explained, modern prison life "may press the outer bounds of what most humans can psychologically tolerate" (*Madrid v. Gomez,* 1995, p. 1267). Beyer (1997) paints a bleak picture of life in adult prison for juveniles, who are at greater risk for suicide and physical and sexual abuse from older inmates. As compared with juvenile facilities, juveniles incarcerated in adult prison are 8 times more likely to commit suicide, 5 times more likely to be sexually assaulted, and almost twice as likely to be attacked with a weapon by inmates and beaten by staff (Beyer, 1997). One study found that 10% of youth held in adult prisons reported being raped or sexually assaulted, 10 times higher than the rate in juvenile facilities (Ziedenberg & Schiraldi, 1997). Because juveniles in adult prisons are exposed to a criminal culture in which inmates commit crimes against each other, these institutions may socialize delinquent juveniles into true career criminals. Violent juvenile offenders who were interviewed in an older study about their life in prison (Eisikovits & Baizerman, 1983) reported that their daily survival required finding ways to fit into the inmate culture, dealing with difficult and authoritarian relationships with adult inmates, and adjusting to the institution by accepting violence as a part of daily life and, thus, becoming even more violent.

Redding and Fuller (2004) found that juveniles whose jail or prison experiences were worse than they had expected, and those who reported witnessing or experiencing violence while incarcerated, were less likely to say that their incarceration would deter them from committing crimes in the future. This finding raises the possibility that incarceration in adult facilities may have brutalizing effects on juveniles, which may partly account for the increased recidivism among juveniles incarcerated in adult facilities. The term "brutalization effect" describes the finding that homicide rates in a state often increase after an execution (Bowers, 1998), perhaps because executions model and communicate that violence is an acceptable and psychologically cathartic alternative. Likewise, juveniles' brutal experiences in adult prison may teach the wrong lessons about the acceptability and psychological benefits of criminal conduct, particularly violent crime, while also contributing to their sense of being treated unfairly. Further research is needed on this important issue.

Psychological research and theory on the effects of punishment also suggest that harsher punishments for serious juvenile offenders, in the form of lengthy sentences in adult prisons, may have counter-deterrence effects. In what will surely become an important contribution to the deterrence literature, Robinson and Darley (2004) offer an intriguing analysis of the psychological literature on punishment, suggesting that lengthier prison sentences may have less of a specific deterrence effect than shorter sentences. Offenders gradually become desensitized to incarceration, which loses much of its initial aversive bite by the end of the lengthy prison term. Thus, a shorter sentence "will be experienced as much more aversive than a much longer sentence that is equally aversive at the beginning but less so at the end." The experience of the incarceration just before the offender is released is what matters most psychologically when the offender subsequently calculates whether to reoffend (Robinson & Darley, 2004, p.190). Moreover, because time passes much slower for juveniles than for adults, a juvenile will experience a prison term as lasting much longer, in psychological terms, than will an adult.

With increasing numbers of juveniles being incarcerated in adult facilities, research is urgently needed on the effects of such incarceration on juveniles' psychological and behavioral functioning and on effective, developmentally appropriate programming for juveniles in these facilities (Redding, 2003). Perhaps the most important challenge for future research is to determine what features of criminal court processing increase recidivism, an important question for policy making. For example, are there changes that could be made in the criminal court processing of juveniles to make it less detrimental? In what ways should the juvenile justice system be on guard against those features of the criminal justice system that serve to increase recidivism? How can states' blended sentencing systems, which allow the juvenile courts to impose adult sentences in certain cases (see Redding & Howell, 2000), incorporate the best features of both the juvenile and criminal justice systems while avoiding the inadvertent negative effects of criminal justice system processing?

## IMPLICATIONS FOR LEGAL POLICY AND PRACTICE

### *Effective Responses to Serious and Violent Juvenile Offenders*

It is important that the juvenile court's response to first-time juvenile offenders be calibrated so as to have sufficient bite without being too punitive. Overly punitive punishments, like trial and sentencing in the adult criminal court, may have the unintended effect of delaying desistence from crime and promoting life-course criminality (Scott, 2000). Yet in Florida, for example, 43% of the 1,100 juveniles incarcerated in adult prisons for offenses committed when they were 15 years old or younger had not previously been committed to a juvenile justice program (Annino, 2000). Thus, the juvenile justice system was never given a chance to rehabilitate these youth before they were transferred to the adult system. Consider also that many of these youth were accomplices (and not the primary perpetrator) to violent offenses committed by older juveniles or that they intended to commit a property crime but unintentionally committed a violent crime (Annino, 2000).

Florida is not unique in transferring first-time serious offenders to the criminal court. Transfer laws, particularly automatic transfer laws, target these offenders even though they do not pose the greatest recidivism risk or threat to community safety (Bishop, 2004; Redding, 1997). First-time offenders typically do not reoffend—"the probability of violence following violence is especially rare" (Bishop, 2004, p. 637). Rather, it is the chronicity of offending instead of the seriousness of the first offense that predicts recidivism and the offender's risk for committing another violent offense (Bishop, 2004; Piquero, 2000; Redding, 1997). Thus, transfer should be based primarily on the offender's characteristics and offending history, not the seriousness of the charged offense. (First-time offenders who commit particularly serious or violent crimes may, however, warrant transfer on retributive grounds.) Transfer should be discretionary, rather than automatic, with transfer decisions made by juvenile court judges based on statutory guidelines that direct the court to consider factors relating to the offender's psychosocial maturity, competence to stand trial in the criminal court, potential for rehabilitation, and recidivism risk (see Redding, 1997).

A small number of repeat offenders (about 8–10%) are responsible for most of the serious or violent offenses (between 60–80%) committed by juveniles, and are the offenders most likely to become the "career criminals" (Loeber, Farrington, & Waschbusch, 1998). The juveniles at risk for becoming chronic offenders can be reliably identified upon their first contact with the juvenile justice system because they have a unique constellation of risk factors that includes criminal involvement at a very early age and typically family problems, problems in school, substance abuse, and gang involvement or running away from home (Schumacher & Kurtz, 1999). Orange County, California, implemented a comprehensive early intervention program—called "the 8% solution"—for the 8 to 10% of offenders who are responsible for most of the serious juvenile crime, when they first come into contact with the juvenile justice system. The program provides an array of services that target the individual, family, school, and peer group risk factors that contribute to their offending. Initial evaluations have shown promising results in reducing recidivism (U.S. Department of Justice, 2001). An important agenda item for future research is the development of standardized risk assessment and classification instruments, such as the Structured Assessment of Violence Risk in Youth (SAVRY) (Borum, Barte, & Forth, 2002), that could be used to help to identify those few youth who should be transferred due to their high recidivism risk and relatively low rehabilitative potential. Unfortunately, however, a small percentage of offenders will require criminal sanctions. Since juvenile sanctions cannot be imposed past the age of 21, a criminal sentence is needed in some cases to ensure community safety, and this is the overriding reason for transfer (Redding, 1997). Such sentences may be achieved through transfer, or through the blended sentencing options now available in many states, which allow juvenile courts to impose limited adult sentences (see Redding & Howell, 2000).

## *The Role for Advocacy*

There is no out-of-control juvenile crime problem, an informed public does not support the widespread adjudication and sentencing of (even) serious and violent juvenile offenders as adults, the public still supports the rehabilitative goals of the juvenile justice system, and research does not support the efficacy of punitive juvenile justice policies. Convincing policy makers of these realities will require vigorous and sustained efforts by juvenile justice researchers and advocates. Importantly, policy makers must be persuaded that less punitive, rehabilitative responses to juvenile crime yield measurable benefits in terms of reduced crime and recidivism rates, as well as reduced justice system costs (Latessa, 2004). As a leading criminological researcher and advocate says, "I have found very few policy makers unwilling to at least listen to the empirical research when you frame it within the context of public protection" (Latessa, 2004, p. 549). Our knowledge about the "causes" (risk factors) of delinquency is strong, the effectiveness of evidence-based juvenile prevention and rehabilitative programs has been clearly demonstrated in rigorous evaluations, and evidence continues to mount on the counter-rehabilitative effects of adult sanctions (see Redding, Goldstein, & Heilbrun, 2005).

Sometimes policy makers do respond. For example, following hearings in 2003 on evidence-based correctional programs, the Oregon legislature passed legislation requiring that 75% of the spending of the Youth Authority and Commission on Children and Families be allocated to evidence-based programs by the year 2009 (Latessa, 2004)! In Florida, which has had some of the most punitive juvenile justice policies in the nation, the number of juveniles transferred decreased by two-thirds between 1996 and 2003 (while the total number of juvenile court cases decreased by only 9%), apparently due to research disseminated to policy makers showing the counter-deterrent effects of transfer (Bishop, 2004). In addition, Florida has undertaken vigorous efforts to promote and institute evidence-based programming (Latessa, 2004) and has expanded the number of placements within the juvenile justice system for serious offenders (Bishop,

2004). In the last several years, some states have even reduced the scope of transfer laws to make fewer juvenile offenders eligible for discretionary transfer (Bishop, 2004; Griffin, 2003).

But at other times it can be a hard sell. When it comes to crime control, "everyone is an expert" (Latessa, 2004, p. 551) with a strong intuitive sense of what works (e.g., tougher laws and punishment), even though their intuitions often run contrary to the findings of empirical research. In my experience working with juvenile justice policy makers and practitioners, I have found that they are fairly impressed by results from treatment programs such as Multisystemic Therapy (MST) showing sizeable reductions in recidivism for serious and violent juvenile offenders (Henggeler, Schoenwald, Borduin, Rowlands, & Cunningham, 1998), and by research showing the superior effectiveness of community-based treatment (Sheidow & Henggeler, 2005). It also is not difficult to persuade policy makers that incarcerating juveniles in adult prisons will fail to rehabilitate them.

Yet many policy makers still favor transfer laws on the theory that they will deter juveniles from committing crime in the first place or that such laws enhance public safety in the near term by incapacitating, through lengthier adult sentences, serious juvenile offenders. Many also are unpersuaded by studies showing the counter-deterrent effects of transfer, because of the studies' inherent methodological limitations (i.e., the inability to fully control for selection effects) and the somewhat counterintuitive nature of the findings (i.e., that tougher penalties have no deterrent effect). In addition, some policy makers are skeptical of research by social scientists, perceiving it to be shaped by a liberal political mindset (Redding, 2001) that is overly sympathetic to offenders. For example, in an analysis of the New York state legislature's debate on the death penalty during the years 1977 to 1995, Galliher and Galliher (2002) show how many legislators were unpersuaded by the social science research on deterrence because they relied instead on their own commonsense assumptions, distrusted statistical analysis or social science, or distrusted the social scientists. Consider the following statements made by state senators during the floor debates:

> It simply defies all common sense and all my knowledge of human nature to argue that a penalty of death does not act as a deterrent.
>
> These studies basically are the work of criminologists or social scientists; and why they are called scientists, I don't know.
>
> Almost all of the death penalty studies were done by people who started out opposing the death penalty and wanted in effect to find out how to oppose it through the deterrence argument. (Galliher & Galliher, 2002, p. 328)

It is a mistake to argue that transfer is never appropriate or that punishment is inconsistent with rehabilitation. Those who so advocate lose their credibility with policy makers and the public, who will never accept such propositions because of "the punitive necessity of transfer" (Zimring, 2000). A small number of chronic, juvenile offenders who have not responded to previous extensive efforts at rehabilitation in the juvenile justice system do warrant criminal sanctions.

Attorneys who represent juvenile offenders at risk for transfer also play a critical role. Good legal advocacy is one of the most practical and effective ways to improve the quality of justice and programming afforded to youthful offenders. Lawyers and juvenile justice professionals must be trained on the relevant juvenile mental health and forensic issues, and, most importantly, on the rehabilitative options available or potentially available. In arguing against transfer, lawyers must be equipped to provide the court with specific and detailed recommendations for effective dispositional alternatives that will ensure community safety while providing meaningful rehabilitation. Because juvenile court transfer recommendations may be influenced by the local availability of treatment options (Mulvey & Reppucci, 1988), the emphasis should be on whether the juvenile is amenable to rehabilitation and what kinds of programs could rehabilitate the youth, not whether the juvenile is amenable given locally available resources. "A finding of amenability places some pressure on the courts to provide adequate treatment to youth who are amenable to treatment" (Salekin, 2002, p. 67). Similarly, Shridharan et al. (2004) recommend that states require localities to have in place certain services before implementing a statewide transfer law.

On a systemwide level, it is important to educate local prosecutors and juvenile court judges about the counter-deterrent and counter-rehabilitative effects of transfer and about the effectiveness of community-based rehabilitation programs. There is evidence that programs aimed at educating judges and other juvenile justice professionals can have substantial positive effects in reducing the number of juveniles receiving adult sanctions. The Miami–Dade County Public Defender's Office developed the Juvenile Sentencing Advocacy Project (JSAP), a highly effective program that has produced a 350% increase in the number of transferred cases receiving a juvenile (rather than an adult) sanction (Mason, 2000).

## CONCLUSION

The juvenile justice system was created over 100 years ago "to save young people from the savagery of the criminal courts and prisons," by removing juveniles from the criminogenic influences of the criminal justice system while providing rehabilitative interventions (Zimring, 2000, p. 248). It appears that the founders of the juvenile court largely got it right. The available evidence, while not definitive, strongly suggests that transferring juveniles to the criminal court increases the recidivism rate. Moreover, although transfer has produced the intended effect of imposing lengthier sentences on serious juvenile offenders, the psychological literature on punishment suggests that shorter sentences may actually be experienced as more punitive (and thus, be a greater deterrent) than longer sentences. Policy makers must weigh the relatively short-term benefits of incapacitation resulting from transfer and imprisonment against the long-term costs of criminal justice system processing in terms of increased recidivism, which in turn would contribute to higher crime rates. If, however, transfer laws deter juvenile crime, then some of these offenders would not have offended in the first place. But based on current theorizing and the limited empirical research available, the weight of the evidence suggests that transfer laws, at least as currently implemented, likely have minimal general deterrent effects.

Thus, we can tentatively conclude that trying and sentencing juveniles as adults does not further the penal goals for which it was intended, particularly the goal of specific deterrence. Perhaps more importantly, however, most juvenile offenders are probably not deserving of adult punishment. As recently acknowledged by the U.S. Supreme Court in *Roper v. Simmons* (2005), which held that the death penalty for juveniles is unconstitutional, the limited life experience and psychosocial and brain immaturity of juveniles—particularly of juvenile offenders (see Redding, 1997)—lessens their culpability. Punishment that is proportional to the offender's culpability should be at the heart of the justice system.

## REFERENCES


The American Enterprise. (2001, June). Parents, juveniles, and justice. *The American Enterprise, 62.*

Annino, P. G. (2000). Children in adult prisons: A call for a moratorium. *Florida State University Law Review, 28,* 471–490.

Bazemore, G., & Umbriet, M. (1995). Rethinking the sanctioning function in juvenile court: Retributive or restorative responses to youth crime. *Crime & Delinquency, 41,* 296–316.

Beckman, M. (2004). Crime, culpability, and the adolescent brain. *Science, 305,* 596–599.

Bennett, W. J., DiIulio, J. J., & Walters, J. P. (1996). *Body count: Moral poverty and how to win America's war against crime and drugs.* New York: Simon & Schuster.

Beresford, L. (2000). Is lowering the age at which juveniles can be transferred to adult criminal court the answer to juvenile crime? A state-by-state assessment. *San Diego Law Review,* 37, 783–851.

Beyer, M. (1997). Experts for juveniles at risk of adult sentences. In P. Puritz, A. Capozello & W. Shang (Eds.), *More than meets the eye: Rethinking assessment, competency and sentencing for a harsher era of juvenile justice* (pp. 1–22). Washington, DC: American Bar Association, Juvenile Justice Center.

Bishop, D. M. (2004). Injustice and irrationality in contemporary youth policy. *Criminology & Public Policy, 3,* 633–644.

Bishop, D. M., & Frazier, C. E. (2000). Consequences of transfer. In J. Fagan & F. E. Zimring (Eds.), *The changing borders of juvenile justice: Transfer of adolescents to the criminal court* (pp. 227–276). Chicago: University of Chicago Press.

Bishop, D. M., Frazier, C. E., Lanza-Kaduce, L., & Winner, L. (1996). The transfer of juveniles to criminal court: Does it make a difference? *Crime and Delinquency, 42,* 171–191.

Blumstein, A. (2001). *Why is crime falling—or is it?* (NCJ 187007). Washington, DC: U.S. Department of Justice, National Institute of Justice.

Borum, R., Barte, P., & Forth, A. (2002). *Manual for the structured assessment of violence risk in youth.* Tampa: University of South Florida, Luis De La Parte Florida Mental Heath Institute.

Bowers, W. C. (1998). Deterrence, brutalization, and the death penalty: Another examination of Oklahoma's return to capital punishment. *Criminology, 36,* 711–733.

Burnett, R. (2000, March). Understanding criminal careers through a series of in-depth interviews. *Offender Programs Report, 4*(1), 1, 14–16.

Butts, J., & Travis, J. (2002, March). *The rise and fall of American youth violence: 1980 to 2000.* Washington, DC: Urban Institute, Justice Policy Center.

Chamberlain, P. (1998). *Family connections: A treatment foster care model for adolescents with delinquency.* Eugene, OR: Northwest Media.

Corrado, R. R., Cohen, I. M., Glackman, W., & Odgers, C. (2003). Serious and violent young offenders' decisions to recidivate: An assessment of five sentencing models. *Crime & Delinquency, 49,* 179–200.

Cover, R. M. (1986). Violence and the word. *Yale Law Journal, 95,* 1601–1629.

DiIulio, J. J. (1995, November 27). The coming of the super-predators. *The Weekly Standard,* 23–28.

Eisikovits, Z., & Baizerman, M. (1983). "Doin' time": Violent youth in a juvenile facility and in an adult prison. *Journal of Offender Counseling, Services, and Rehabilitation, 6*(3), 5–20.

Fagan, J. A. (1996). The comparative advantage of juvenile versus criminal court sanctions on recidivism among adolescent felony offenders. *Law & Policy, 18,* 77–113.

Fagan, J., Kupchik, A., & Liberman, A. (2003). *Be careful what you wish for: The comparative impacts of juvenile versus criminal court sanctions on recidivism among adolescent felony offenders* (Pub. Law Research Paper No. 03–61). New York: Columbia University Law School.

Fagan, J., & Zimring, F. E. (Eds.). (2000). *The changing borders of juvenile justice: Transfer of adolescents to the criminal court.* Chicago, IL: University of Chicago Press.

Finckenauer, J. O., & Gavin, P. W. (1999). *Scared straight: The panacea phenomenon revisited.* Prospect Heights, IL: Waveland.

Forst, M., Fagan, J., & Vivona, S. T. (1989). Youth in prisons and training schools: Perceptions and consequences of the treatment-custody dichotomy. *Juvenile and Family Court Journal, 40,* 1–14.

Galliher, J. M., & Galliher, J. F. (2002). A "commonsense" theory of deterrence and the "ideology" of science: The New York state death penalty debate. *Journal of Criminal Law & Criminology, 92,* 307–333.

Gang Violence and Juvenile Crime Prevention Act of 1998. (Cal. 2000). Retrieved December 1, 2004, from http://primary2000.ss.ca.gov/VoterGuide/propositons/2hext.htm

Glassner, B., Ksander, M., Berg, B., & Johnson, B. D. (1983). A note on the deterrent effect of juvenile versus adult jurisdiction. *Social Problems, 31,* 219–221.

Griffin, P. (2003). *Trying and sentencing juveniles as adults: An analysis of state transfer and blended sentencing laws.* Pittsburgh: National Center for Juvenile Justice.

Henggeler, S. W., Schoenwald, S. K., Borduin, C. M., Rowlands, M. D., & Cunningham, P. B. (1998). *Multisystemic treatment of antisocial behavior in children and adolescents.* New York: Guilford Press.

Jensen, E. L., & Metsger, L. K. (1994). A test of the deterrent effect of legislative waiver on violent juvenile crime. *Crime & Delinquency, 40,* 96–104.

Johnson, S. D., & Bowers, K. J. (2003). Opportunity is in the eye of the beholder: The role of publicity in crime prevention. *Criminology & Public Policy, 2,* 497–524.

Kleiman, M. (1999). Getting deterrence right: Applying tipping models and behavioral economics to the problems of crime control. In *Perspectives on crime and justice: 1998–1999 lecture series* (Vol. 3, pp. 1–29). Washington, DC: U.S. Department of Justice, Office of Justice Programs, National Institute of Justice.

Kupchik, A., Fagan, J., & Liberman, A. (2003). Punishment, proportionality, and jurisdictional transfer of adolescent offenders: A test of the leniency gap hypothesis. *Stanford Law & Policy Review, 14,* 57–83.

Kurlychek, M. C., & Johnson, B. D. (2004). The juvenile penalty: A comparison of juvenile and young adult sentencing outcomes in criminal court. *Criminology, 42,* 485–517.

Lacayo, R., & Donnelly, S. B. (1997, July 21). Teen crime: Congress wants to crack down on juvenile offenders. But is throwing teens into adult court—and adult prisons—the best way? *Time Magazine,* 26.

Lanza-Kaduce, L., Frazier, C. E., Lane, J., & Bishop, D. M. (2000). *Juvenile transfer to criminal court study: Final report.* Tallahassee: Florida Department of Juvenile Justice.

Latessa, E. J. (2004). The challenge of change: Correctional programs and evidence-based practices. *Criminology & Public Policy, 3,* 547–560.

Levitt, S. D (1998). Juvenile crime and punishment. *Journal of Political Economy, 106,* 1156–1185.

Loeber, R., Farrington, D. P., & Waschbusch, D. A. (1998). Serious and violent juvenile offenders. In R. Loeber & D. P. Farrington (Eds.), *Serious and violent juvenile offenders: Risk factors and successful interventions* (pp. 13–29) Thousand Oaks, CA: Sage.

Madrid v. Gomez, 889 F. Supp. 1146 (N.D. Cal. 1995).

Mason, C. A. (2000). *Juvenile sentencing advocacy project: Evaluation report.* Miami, FL: Miami–Dade County Public Defender's Office.

Mason, C. A., & Chang, S. (2001). *Re-arrest rates among youth incarcerated in adult court.* Miami, FL: Miami–Dade County Public Defender's Office.

Michaelis, K. L. (2001). School violence: The call for a critical theory of juvenile justice. *Brigham Young University Education & Law Journal,* 299–326.

Minor, K. I., Hartmann, D. J., & Terry, S. (1997). Predictors of juvenile court actions and recidivism. *Crime & Delinquency, 43,* 328–344.

Moon, M. M., Sundt, J. L., Cullen, F. T., & Wright, J. P. (2000). Is child saving dead? Public support for juvenile rehabilitation. *Crime & Delinquency, 46,* 38–60.

Mulvey, E. P., & Reppucci, N. D. (1988). The context of clinical judgment: The effect of resource availability on judgments of amenability to treatment in juvenile offenders. *American Journal of Community Psychology, 16,* 525–545.

Myers, D. L. (2001). *Excluding violent youths from juvenile court: The effectiveness of legislative waiver.* New York: LFB Scholarly.

Peterson-Badali, M., Ruck, M. D., & Koegl, C. J. (2001). Youth court dispositions: Perceptions of Canadian juvenile offenders. *International Journal of Offender Therapy & Comparative Criminology, 45,* 593–605.

Piquero, A. R. (2000). Frequency, specialization and violence in offending careers. *Journal of Research in Crime & Delinquency, 37,* 392–418.

Podkopacz, M. R., & Feld, B. C. (1996). The end of the line: An empirical study of judicial waiver. *Journal of Criminal Law & Criminology, 86,* 449–492.

Puzzanchera, C. (2003, September). *Delinquency cases waived to criminal court, 1990–1999* (Fact sheet). Washington, DC: U.S. Department of Justice, Office of Justice Programs, Office of Juvenile Justice and Delinquency Prevention.

Redding, R. E. (1997). Juveniles transferred to criminal court: Legal reform proposals based on social science research. *Utah Law Review, 1997,* 709–797.

Redding, R. E. (2001). Sociopolitical diversity in psychology: The case for pluralism. *American Psychologist, 56,* 205–215.

Redding, R. E. (2003). The effects of adjudicating and sentencing juveniles as adults: Research and policy implications. *Youth Violence & Juvenile Justice, 1,* 128–155.

Redding, R. E., & Fuller, E. J. (2004, Summer). What do juvenile offenders know about being tried as adults? Implications for deterrence. *Juvenile & Family Court Journal,* 35–45.

Redding, R. E., Goldstein, N. E., & Heilbrun, K. (2005). Juvenile delinquency: Past and present. In K. Heilbrun, N. E. Goldstein, & R. E. Redding (Eds.), *Juvenile delinquency: Assessment, prevention, and intervention* (pp. 1–18). New York: Oxford University Press.

Redding, R. E., & Howell, J. C. (2000). Blended sentencing in American juvenile courts. In J. Fagan & F. E. Zimring (Eds.), *The changing borders of juvenile justice: Transfer of adolescents to the criminal court* (pp. 145–179). Chicago: University of Chicago Press.

Redding, R. E., & Mrozoski, B. S. (2005). Adjudicatory and dispositional decision making in juvenile justice. In K. Heilbrun, N. Goldstein, & R. Redding (Eds.), *Juvenile delinquency: Prevention, assessment, and intervention* (pp. 232–256). New York: Oxford University Press.

Regnery, A. S. (1985). Getting away with murder: Why the juvenile justice system needs an overhaul. *Policy Review, 34,* 65–68.

Robinson, P. H., & Darley, J.M. (2004). Does criminal law deter? A behavioral science investigation. *Oxford Journal of Legal Studies, 24*(2), 173–205.

Roper v. Simmons, 125 S. Ct. 1183 (2005).

Salekin, R. T. (2002). Clinical evaluation of youth considered for transfer to adult criminal court: Refining practice and directions for science. *Journal of Forensic Psychology Practice, 2,* 55–72.

Sanborn, J.B. (2003). Hard choices or obvious ones: Developing policy for excluding youth from adult court. *Youth Violence & Juvenile Justice, 1,* 198–214.

Scheidegger, K., & Rushford, M. (1999). The social benefits of confining habitual criminals. *Stanford Law & Policy Review, 11,* 59–64.

Schiraldi, V., & Soler, M. (1998). The will of the people? The public's opinion of the violent and repeat juvenile offender act of 1997. *Crime & Delinquency, 44,* 590–601.

Schneider, A. L., & Ervin, L. (1990). Specific deterrence, rational choice, and decision heuristics: Applications in juvenile justice. *Social Science Quarterly, 71,* 585–601.

Schumacher, M., & Kurtz, G. A. (1999). *The 8% solution: Preventing serious, repeat juvenile crime.* Thousand Oaks, CA: Sage.

Schwartz, I., Guo, S., & Kerbs, J. (1993). The impact of demographic variables on public opinion regarding juvenile justice: Implications for public policy. *Crime & Delinquency, 39,* 5–28.

Scott, E. S. (2000). The legal construction of adolescence. *Hofstra Law Review, 29,* 547–598.

Scott, E. S., Reppucci, N. D., & Woolard, J. L. (1995). Evaluating adolescent decision making in legal contexts. *Law & Human Behavior, 19,* 221–244.

Sheidow, A. J., & Henggeler, S. W. (2005). Community based treatments. In K. Heilbrun, N. E. Goldstein, & R. E. Redding (Eds.), *Juvenile delinquency: Assessment, prevention, and intervention* (pp. 257–281). New York: Oxford University Press.

Shepherd, R. E. (1999). Film at eleven: The news media and juvenile crime. *Quinnipiac Law Review, 18,* 687–700.

Sickmund, M. (2004). Juveniles in corrections. *OJJDP Juvenile Justice Bulletin.* Washington, DC: U.S. Department of Justice, Office of Juvenile Justice and Delinquency Prevention.

Singer, S. I., & McDowall, D. (1988). Criminalizing delinquency: The deterrent effects of the New York juvenile offender law. *Law and Society Review, 22,* 521–535.

Snyder, H. N. (2004). Juvenile arrests 2002. *OJJDP Juvenile Justice Bulletin.* Washington, DC: U.S. Department of Justice, Office of Juvenile Justice and Delinquency Prevention.

Snyder, H. N., & Sickmund, M. (1999). *Juvenile offenders and victims: National report 1999* (Report). Washington, DC: U.S. Department of Justice, Office of Justice Programs, Office of Juvenile Justice and Delinquency Prevention.

Sridharan, S., Greenfield, L., & Blakley, B. (2004). A study of prosecutorial certification practice in Virginia. *Criminology & Public Policy, 3,* 605–632.

Stalans, L. J., & Henry, G. T. (1994). Societal views of justice for adolescents accused of murder. *Law & Human Behavior, 18,* 675–696.

Steinberg, L., & Cauffman, E. (1996). Maturity of judgment in adolescence: Psychosocial factors in adolescent decision making. *Law and Human Behavior, 20,* 249–272.

Steiner, B., & Hemmens, C. (2003, Spring). Juvenile waiver 2003: Where are we now? *Juvenile & Family Court Journal,* 1–24.

Sundt, J. L. (1999). Is there room for change? A review of public attitudes toward crime control and alternatives to incarceration. *Southern Illinois University Law Journal, 23,* 519–537.

Thomas, C. W., & Bishop, D. M. (1984). The impact of legal sanctions on delinquency: A longitudinal comparison of labeling and deterrence theories. *Journal of Criminal Law & Criminology, 75,* 1222–1245.

U.S. Department of Justice, Office of Juvenile Justice and Delinquency Prevention. (2001, November). The 8% solution. *OJJDP Fact Sheet # 39.* Washington, DC: Author.

Violent Crime Control and Law Enforcement Act. Pub. L. 103–332, § 108 Stat.1796 (1994).

Virginia Department of Criminal Justice Services. (1996). *Juvenile murder in Virginia: A study of arrests and convictions.* Richmond, VA: Author.

Von Hirsch, A., Bottoms, A. E., Burney, E., & Wikstrom, P.O. (1999). *Criminal deterrence and sentence severity: An analysis of recent research.* Oxford, UK: Hart.

Welch, M., Fenwick, M., & Roberts, M. (1997). Primary definitions of crime and moral panic: A content analysis of experts' quotes in feature newspaper articles on crime. *Journal of Research in Crime & Delinquency, 34,* 474–494.

Winner, L., Lanza-Kaduce, L., Bishop, D. M., & Frazier, C. E. (1997). The transfer of juveniles to criminal court: Reexamining recidivism over the long term. *Crime & Delinquency, 43,* 548–563.

Wooldredge, J. D. (1988). Differentiating the effects of juvenile court sentences on eliminating recidivism. *Journal of Research in Crime & Delinquency, 25,* 264–300.

Wu, B. (2000, Winter). Determinants of public opinion toward juvenile waiver decisions. *Juvenile & Family Court Journal,* 9–20.

Ziedenberg, J., & Schiraldi, V. (1997). *The risks juveniles face when they are incarcerated with adults.* Retrieved December 1, 2004, from http://www.cjcj.org/jpi/risks.html

Zimring, F. E. (1998). The youth violence epidemic: Myth or reality. *Wake Forest Law Review, 33,* 727–744.

Zimring, F. E. (2000). The punitive necessity of waiver. In J. Fagan & F. E. Zimring (Eds.), *The changing borders of juvenile justice: Transfer of adolescents to the criminal court* (pp. 207–226). Chicago: University of Chicago Press.

Zimring, F. E., & Fagan, J. (2000). Transfer policy and law reform. In J. Fagan & F. E. Zimring (Eds.), *The changing borders of juvenile justice: Transfer of adolescents to the criminal court* (pp. 407–424). Chicago: University of Chicago Press.

CHAPTER 20

# *Psychopathy Assessment and Juvenile Justice Mental Health Evaluations*

MATTHEW OWEN HOWARD, MICHAEL K. DAYTON, KIRK A. FOSTER, MICHAEL G. VAUGHN, AND JOHN L. ZELNER

Psychopathy has been recognized as a serious psychiatric malady for more than two centuries. Formal psychopathy assessments, however, have only recently been included in mental health evaluations of juvenile offenders. A small subpopulation of youth offenders—perhaps 5 to 8%—commits a majority of general and violent crimes. The notion that members of this group are psychiatrically disordered gained widespread currency with the publication of Dr. Terrie Moffitt's (1993) classic paper distinguishing "life-course persistent" and "adolescence-limited" delinquent subtypes. Moffitt observed the following:

> [L]ongitudinal research consistently points to a very small group of males who display high rates of antisocial behavior across time and in diverse situations. The professional nomenclature may change, but the forces remain the same as they drift through successive systems aimed at curbing their deviance: schools, juvenile-justice programs, psychiatric treatment centers, and prisons. The topography of their behavior may change with changing opportunities, but the *underlying disposition* persists throughout the life course. (p. 678) [italics added]

The disposition underlying persistent, life-course criminality was, Moffitt argued, rooted in early neuropsychological vulnerabilities and criminogenic environmental influences, which interact to produce the disorder.

As investigators have attempted to better account for the conspicuous heterogeneity among youth offenders (Loeber, Farrington, & Waschbusch, 1998; Tolan & Gorman-Smith, 1998; Wolfgang, Figlio, & Sellin, 1972; Wolfgang, Thornberry, & Figlio, 1987), other taxonomies of antisocial youth have emerged. Many of these taxonomies, including the distinction between psychopathic and non-psychopathic juvenile offenders, describe two primary offender subgroups: first, a relatively small group of early-onset, criminally versatile, chronic offenders who frequently have histories of violent behavior and comorbid attention-deficit/hyperactivity disorder (ADHD) and conduct disorder (CD); and second, a substantially larger group who offend later, have lower rates of interpersonal violence and psychopathology, and whose offending terminates in adolescence (Quay, 1993).

Implicit in many juvenile offender taxonomies is the notion that neurological or other biological factors play a key role in the development of the more serious youth offender subtype. The origins of the substantially more common and comparatively benign juvenile offender subtype, on the other hand, are considered primarily social in nature. While it is evident that valid schemes for subtyping juvenile offenders might lead to increased understanding and better treatment of early antisocial behavior, it is probable that such typologies would have seriously deleterious consequences for youth diagnosed with the more pernicious subtype. Many social service and legal practitioners regard "juvenile psychopaths" as untreatable, at least given currently available pharmacological, cognitive-behavioral, and social/criminological interventions (Young, Justice, Erdberg, & Gacano, 2000). There is some evidence (see Lyon & Ogloff, 2000) that adolescent offenders in the United States and Canada are increasingly subjected to assessments for psychopathy and that important determinations are made on the basis of these findings, including transfer decisions. Thus, it is critical that legal and social service practitioners be aware of key issues and recent findings vis-à-vis juvenile psychopathy research and practice.

Legal and social service practitioners in the adult criminal justice and juvenile justice systems likely will encounter the notion of psychopathy at some point in their professional careers. They should be aware of issues and research relevant to the construct. This chapter presents a comprehensive overview of the psychopathy research and clinical literature. The chapter reviews contemporary approaches to assessment, characteristics of youth diagnosed with psychopathy, potential applications of psychopathy evaluations, and possible effects of psychopathy diagnoses on legal proceedings.

## CONTEMPORARY PERSPECTIVES ON PSYCHOPATHY

One of the most significant events in psychopathy research was the publication of the *Psychopathy Checklist* (PCL) (1991), available currently in a revised format referred to as the PCL-R (Hare, 1996a, 1996b). The PCL-R operationalizes psychopathy in a manner generally consistent with Cleckley's (1941) clinical description. The PCL-R consists of 20 items reflecting a variety of personality and behavioral attributes that are each scored from 0 (not present) to 2 (definitely present) by a trained rater (Bodholt, Richards, & Gacono, 2000). Total PCL-R scores range from 0 to 40; scores of 30 or more are generally used to identify adult psychopaths. Ideally, ratings are based on semi-structured interviews with the target individual and family members or friends who have significant knowledge of the individual and a review of available criminal justice/mental health file records. On occasion, psychopathy diagnoses are based only on file records.

Factor analytic studies of the PCL-R have consistently identified two independent, though moderately positively correlated ($r$ = 0.5–0.6) factors (Bodholt et al., 2000). Factor 1—an interpersonal and affective dimension—incorporates items referring to dispositional glibness/superficial charm, a grandiose sense of self-worth, pathological lying, conning and manipulative behavior, lack of remorse or guilt, shallow affect, callousness/lack of empathy, and a failure to accept responsibility for his or her actions (Hare, 1996a, 1996b). Factor 2 includes items reflecting an unstable and antisocial lifestyle such as those assessing need for stimulation/proneness to boredom, parasitical lifestyle, poor behavioral controls, early-life problem behaviors, lack of realistic long-term goals, impulsivity, irresponsibility, a history of juvenile delinquency, and court-ordered revocation of conditional release. Factor 1 scores tend to correlate most highly with measures of narcissism and egocentrism, whereas Factor 2 scores correlate significantly positively with measures of substance abuse, criminal behavior, and antisocial personality disorder criteria (American Psychiatric Association, 2000). Although most research to date has employed the two-factor model of the PCL-R, several studies now support a three-factor model and a two-factor (4-facet subscale) model (Cooke & Michie, 2001; Falkenbach, Poythress, & Heide, 2003; Skeem, Mulvey, & Grisso, 2003).

Studies of the PCL-R indicate that the measure possesses good internal consistency, inter-rater, and test–retest reliability (Bodholdt et al., 2000). Validity assessments indicate that PCL-R scores predict general and violent recidivism (Salekin, Rogers, & Sewell, 1996), and institutional violence among forensic patients (Heilbrun, Hart, Hare, Gustafson, Nunez, et al., 1998). To date, hundreds of studies of adults have used the original PCL, PCL-R, or one of the other versions of the instrument such as the PCL:SV (Screening Version) (Sparrow & Gacono, 2000).

Only recently, however, have efforts been made to apply PCL-based and other psychopathy assessments to antisocial children, adolescent offenders, and members of the general adolescent population. Investigations of PCL-defined psychopathy in youth began with Forth, Hart, and Hare's (1990) study of adolescent offenders. PCL-R Items 9 (parasitical lifestyle) and 17 (many short-term relationships) were deleted and the scoring criteria for Items 18 (juvenile delinquency) and 20 (revocation of conditional release) were modified to reflect adolescent offenders' more limited opportunities for interaction with the justice system relative to adult offenders (Forth & Mailloux, 2000). This modification of the PCL-R was used in a number of studies of adolescents (Edens, Skeem, Cruise, & Cauffman, 2001; Seagrave & Grisso, 2002). However, several recent investigations have used the newer 20-item *Psychopathy Checklist: Youth Version* (PCL:YV), which is a modified version of the original PCL-R that was explicitly designed for adolescents (Forth & Mailloux, 2000).

As with the PCL-R, factor analytic studies of the PCL:YV have identified two factors—an affective/interpersonal dimension (Factor 1) and an antisocial lifestyle/behavior factor (Factor 2)—that underlie juvenile psychopathy (Brandt, Kennedy, Patrick, & Curtin, 1997). The alpha and inter-rater reliabilities of the PCL:YV appear to be acceptable for total scores, but more research evaluating the inter-rater reliability of the subscales is needed. A number of studies of adolescents have established the construct validity of the modified PCL-R and PCL:YV scales. However, no widely accepted cutpoints for the diagnosis of juvenile psychopathy have been established for PCL-based measures. Researchers have raised serious concerns regarding the developmental appropriateness of some PCL:YV items, such as those assessing parasitical lifestyle and many short-term relationships (Brandt et al., 1997). Edens et al. (2001) observed that "although the scoring criteria for several problematic items (e.g., impulsivity, irresponsibility, and need for stimulation/proneness to boredom) have been revised in an attempt to better tailor them to adolescent respondents, the stability of these items over significant time periods appears to be an open issue" (Edens et al., 2001, p. 61).

Several studies have recently examined the predictive validity of two- and three-factor versions of the PCL:YV. Corrado, Vincent,

Hart, and Cohen (2004) found that factor scales from both models predicted general and violent recidivism in 182 male adolescent offenders followed for approximately 1 year. Measures of antisocial behavior rather than psychopathic personality traits accounted for most of the instrument's explanatory power.

Other instruments designed to assess psychopathy in youth are discussed below (Frick, 2002; Frick, O'Brien, Wootton, & McBurnett, 1994; Lynam, 1997). Factor analyses of these scales also support a two-factor model of psychopathy similar to that assessed by the various PCL-based measures, although some support for three-factor models has also been adduced.

The relationship between the *DSM* conduct disorder diagnoses and juvenile psychopathy is asymmetrical. A majority of youth diagnosed as psychopathic meet the more behaviorally based conduct disorder criteria, but only a minority of youth who meet conduct disorder criteria also meet juvenile psychopathy criteria. Conduct disorder diagnoses are also far more prevalent than psychopathy diagnoses among adolescent offender populations across a variety of juvenile justice settings (Forth, 1995). According to the *Diagnostic and Statistical Manual of Mental Disorders* (*DSM*) (APA, 2000), youth meet conduct disorder criteria if they evidence "a repetitive and persistent pattern of behavior in which the basic rights of others or age-appropriate societal norms or rules are violated, as manifested by the presence of three (or more) . . . criteria in the past 12 months, with at least one criterion present in the last 6 months" (p. 98). A total of 15 criteria for conduct disorder are enumerated in the *DSM* (e.g., deliberately engaging in fire setting).

Despite all these PCL-based studies of youth, it remains unclear whether psychopathy is more appropriately regarded as a discrete disorder or a continuously distributed characteristic. One recent taxometric analysis supported the notion that persistently antisocial youth constitute a naturally occurring discrete class (i.e., a "taxon") of youth (Skilling, Quinsey, & Craig, 2001). Most studies of youth to date have used psychopathy measures as a continuous as well as categorical variable, implicitly embracing the notion that psychopathic traits may exist on a continuum among youth.

Studies to date suggest that PCL-R–based measures may eventually hold some utility vis-à-vis prediction of offending in youth; however, the use of these instruments in clinical or forensic settings at present would be premature. The developmental appropriateness and factor structure of these measures have not been clearly established, whereas the potentially adverse consequences of false-positive diagnoses with juvenile psychopathy are obvious.

In addition to the PCL-derived instruments, a number of other measures have been developed to assess juvenile psychopathy including the Antisocial Process Screening Device, Child Psychopathy Scale, and P-Scan (Edens et al., 2001; Seagrave & Grisso, 2002). To date, none of the juvenile psychopathy measures has been validated to the point necessary to justify its routine use in clinical or forensic settings. Each of the respective measurement approaches—structured interview versus self-report—has its drawbacks. Structured interviews are time consuming and expensive to conduct and require access to and a careful review of available clinical/forensic file data, whereas the validity of self-report psychopathy measures has been called seriously into question. Substantially more research is needed that addresses the reliability, validity, and utility of various approaches to juvenile psychopathy assessment before such measures can be considered for clinical and forensic uses.

## CHARACTERISTICS OF PSYCHOPATHIC YOUTH

Prior investigations assessing a range of additional variables have also helped to identify characteristics of psychopathic youth. Juvenile psychopathy has been evaluated in relation to demographic features such as age, ethnicity, and gender; sociodevelopmental experiences such as child abuse and neglect; psychiatric problems such as substance abuse and other co-occurring psychiatric disorders; and patterns of criminal offending including the age of onset, and the nature and frequency of antisocial conduct.

### *Demographic Factors*

Gender, ethnicity, and age have not been demonstrated as significant factors in psychopathy. Relatively few studies have examined gender differences in adolescent psychopathy. Three studies found that females had lower psychopathy scores, on average, than males: Gretton (1998); Rowe (1997); and Stanford, Ebner, Patton, and Williams (1994). However, only in one investigation (Stanford et al., 1994) was the difference statistically significant, perhaps due to the comparatively small number of subjects participating in these studies (Forth & Mailloux, 2000).

Five studies comparing Caucasian adolescents to Native Canadian, African American, and Hispanic youth reported nonsignificant differences with regard to psychopathy (Brandt et al., 1997; Hume, Kennedy, Patrick, & Partyka, 1996; McBride, 1998; Meyers, Burket, & Harris, 1995; Pan, 1998). Forth, Hart, and Hare (1990) found significantly lower psychopathy scores for native Canadian than Caucasian youth. Cross-sectional studies examining the relationship between age and psychopathy among adolescents have not generally identified significant associations (Forth & Burke, 1998).

### *Substance Abuse*

Clinical lore strongly supports an association between substance abuse and psychopathy (Cleckley, 1941). However, research investigating the link between the two in adults and adolescents is limited. Rutherford, Alterman, and Cacciola (2000) reviewed the adult psychopathy literature and concluded that, in general, there is a moderate association between measures of substance abuse and dependence and the PCL-R total and Factor 2 (antisocial lifestyle) subscale scores, respectively. For example, Hart and Hare (1989) reported correlations of $r = .31$ and $r = .40$, respectively, for PCL-R total and Factor 2 scores and a measure of drug abuse/dependence symptoms among 80 forensic psychiatric adult patients. Smith-Stevens and Newman (1990) found significantly higher rates of lifetime alcohol abuse/dependence and drug abuse/dependence among psychopathic Wisconsin adult inmates compared to their nonpsychopathic cohorts. PCL-R total and Factor 2 scores were significantly inversely associated with age at first intoxication and first arrest, whereas Factor 1 (core personality traits) scores were significantly inversely associated only with age at first arrest. Rutherford et al. (2000) concluded that, "Antisocial Lifestyle [i.e., Factor 2] consistently had a stronger relationship than Psychopathic Personality Traits [i.e., Factor 1] to alcohol and drug abuse/dependence among male offenders" (p. 354).

Studies of adolescent psychopathy and substance abuse report mixed findings. Mailloux, Forth, and Kroner (1997) examined the relationship between PCL:YV scores and measures of lifetime alcohol and drug problems. Total and Factor 2 (antisocial lifestyle) scores, respectively, were significantly related to Michigan Alcoholism Screening Test (MAST) ($r$'s = .46 and .41) and

Drug Abuse Screening Test (DAST) ($r$'s = .42 and .48) scores, age at drug use initiation ($r$'s = –.50 and –.50), and number of drugs tried ($r$'s = .56 and .54). Factor 1 (core personality traits) scores were not significantly correlated with MAST and DAST scores and had lower, although statistically significant, associations with age of onset of drug use ($r$ = –.39) and number of illicit drugs tried ($r$ = .46). Brandt et al. (1997) studied 130 adolescent offenders with multiple felony convictions and did not find PCL-R total, Factor 1 (core personality traits), or Factor 2 (antisocial lifestyle) scores to be significantly associated with a measure of substance abuse based on file records, although the assessment of substance abuse was relatively crude.

Forth (1995) also examined associations between PCL:YV scores and the MAST and DAST in a community youth sample (mean age = 17.2, *SD* = 1.6) and a sample of young offenders (mean age = 17.5, *SD* = .90). Total ($r$ = .48), Factor 1 (core personality traits) ($r$ = .33), and Factor 2 (antisocial lifestyle) ($r$ = .47) scores were significantly associated with MAST scores among community youth. Similar associations were observed between total ($r$ = .56), Factor 1 (core personality traits) ($r$ = .41), and Factor 2 (antisocial lifestyle) ($r$ = .52) scores and the DAST measure of lifetime drug-related problems among community youth. Only total and Factor 2 scores, respectively, were significantly associated with MAST ($r$'s = .23 and .28) and DAST scores ($r$'s = .28 and .36) among serious youth offenders and the observed correlations were lower for the offender group than the community sample.

In sum, findings with adolescent offenders approximate those obtained with adult offenders with regard to substance abuse measures (Rutherford et al., 2000). Antisocial lifestyle traits are more consistently and strongly associated with substance abuse than are the core personality traits of psychopathy. The causal nature of the relationship between Factor 2 (antisocial lifestyle) traits and substance abuse is unclear. It is possible that substance abuse is just one of many manifestations of an impulsive and risk-taking lifestyle, or that it plays an important independent role in the development of various antisocial outcomes. That is, early substance abuse might reflect a predisposition to antisocial behavior and contribute to further and more aberrant conduct by disinhibiting behavior and impairing judgment.

### *Moral Reasoning*

The conflation of psychopathy with moral turpitude can be traced back two centuries to the notion of moral insanity. Early studies of moral reasoning compared psychopathic youth, variously defined, to other delinquents (Fodor, 1973) or to non-incarcerated, non-delinquent youth (Campagna & Harter, 1975), and found more rudimentary levels of moral reasoning in psychopathic youth. Jurkovic and Prentice (1977) and Lee and Prentice (1988) found lower levels of moral development in psychopathic youth compared to normal youth, but had mixed results with regard to moral reasoning. Lee and Prentice (1988) identified nonsignificant differences between psychopathic and other delinquent youth, whereas Jurkovic and Prentice (1977) found the moral reasoning of psychopathic youth significantly less developed than that of other delinquent, but non-psychopathic, youth.

Trevethan and Walker (1989) compared the moral development and moral orientation of 14 psychopathic adolescents to 15 delinquent but non-psychopathic youth and 15 normal youth recruited from a local high school. Psychopathic youth were nearly 1 year older, on average, than youth in the delinquent and normal groups. Participants were asked to respond to hypothetical and real-life moral dilemmas during a lengthy interview. Psychopathic youth differed significantly from normal youth, but not from other delinquents, with regard to their stage of moral reasoning. Psychopathic youth did, however, display a significantly more "egoistic utilitarian" moral orientation than did normal youth or other delinquent youth in response to real-life moral dilemmas. Trevethan and Walker concluded that "although there were no differences across groups when discussing hypothetical dilemmas, when it was a situation in which they had actually been involved, psychopaths more frequently expressed the moral legitimacy of concerns for themselves" (1989, p. 100).

Blair (1997) compared the moral judgments of 16 psychopathic and 16 non-psychopathic residents of a school for behaviorally and emotionally disturbed youth. Blair presented each youth with a task story and assessed each participant's response to a transgression and the protagonist's emotions. Psychopathic youth were significantly more likely than non-psychopathic youth to consider moral transgressions acceptable if there were no formal rules prohibiting the transgression. Only 25% of the justifications provided by psychopathic youth for their judgments concerned the welfare of others, compared to 45% of the justifications provided by non-psychopathic youth ($p < .07$). Psychopathic youth were also less likely to attribute guilt to task story characters, suggesting that they were less sensitive to or aware of this potential emotional response.

Studies to date support the notion that psychopathic youth function at a less ethically developed level than non-psychopathic youth do, although findings of differences between psychopathic and other delinquent youth are less consistent. In general, the methodological limitations and mixed findings of the scant available research comparing moral reasoning in psychopathic and nonpsychopathic youth indicate a need for further research. Saltaris (2002) reviewed research suggesting that the capacity to feel empathy for others and to discern others' emotional states (i.e., "perspective taking") develops very early in life, varies greatly across individuals, and is potentially a key determinant of psychopathic (and altruistic) orientation. Longitudinal studies of perspective taking and empathy commencing very early in the lives of high-risk youth would contribute significantly to current knowledge regarding the developmental origins of the callousness and narcissism observed in adolescent and adult psychopaths.

## Child Abuse and Poor Parenting

Several investigators have examined the role of adverse early life experiences in the development of psychopathy. Forth and Tobin (1996) found that a history of child abuse was highly prevalent among 95 psychopathic and nonpsychopathic incarcerated male youth, although rates in the two groups did not differ significantly. Psychopathic and non-psychopathic offenders also did not differ significantly with regard to their histories of specific forms of abuse including physical, emotional, or sexual abuse or neglect. Experiencing or witnessing parental violence did not significantly predict PCL-R scores.

McBride (1998) found that parental antisocial characteristics and a history of physical abuse, but not other forms of abuse, were associated with psychopathy among 239 adolescent male sex offenders ages 12 to 18. A related investigation of 74 adolescent male offenders identified a significant association between a history of physical abuse and poor parenting, and adolescent psychopathy. McBride and Hare (1996) reported that PCL-SV scores were significantly positively correlated with a history of physical ($r = .33$) and sexual ($r = .16$) abuse. Together, a composite measure of parental deviance, a history of physical abuse, and a diagnosis of ADHD explained 22% of the variance in psychopathy scores, suggesting that these factors may play a role, but are not decisive, in the development of juvenile psychopathy. Burke and Forth (1996) found that a global index of family background variables, including sexual abuse or parental alcoholism, was significantly related to Factor 2 (antisocial lifestyle) psychopathy scores among a sample of 106 young male offenders, but not with PCL:YV total or Factor 1 (personality/interpersonal features) scores. None of the 10 family-background variables significantly predicted total, Factor 1, or Factor 2 scores among the young offender sample. Laroche and Toupin (1996) studied 60 adolescent male offenders and found that psychopathic youth participated in fewer family activities and were more poorly supervised than non-psychopathic offenders. Campbell, Porter, and Santor (2004) identified a significant association between a history of physical abuse and total PCL: YV scores in a sample of 226 male and female adolescent offenders. A history of non-parental living arrangements, such as living in foster care, predicted PCL:YV scores in multivariate analyses. Forth and Burke (1998) reviewed studies of developmental correlates of juvenile psychopathy, concluding that "relatively little research has examined whether psychopaths have dysfunctional family backgrounds. The research that has been done, though, has shown no decisive link between family history and the presence of psychopathy in adults" (p. 223). Gretton (1998) reported that psychopathic youth offenders were separated from their biological mothers and fathers at significantly younger ages, on average, than were non-psychopathic adolescent offenders, although no differences were found in the prevalence of childhood abuse.

Inconsistent findings about the role of parenting practices in the development of juvenile psychopathy may be due to failure to distinguish between correlates of the two factors thought to comprise the disorder. Wootten, Frick, Shelton, and Silverthorn (1997) predicted that youth high in callous-unemotional (CU) traits would not be substantially influenced by different parenting practices with regard to conduct disorder, whereas youth low in callous-unemotional traits would experience differential outcomes related to parenting practices. Wootten et al. found that "the association between ineffective parenting and conduct problems was moderated by the presence of C/U traits in the child . . . children with high CU traits exhibited high rates of conduct problems regardless of the quality of parenting they experienced . . . past studies may have ignored the important association between parenting practices and conduct problems by failing to distinguish between youth low and high in CU traits" (1997, p. 305). In a study of 136 adolescent Hispanic females, Vitacco, Neumann, Ramos, and Roberts (2003) found significant relationships between poor parental monitoring and inconsistent discipline, and the narcissism and impulsivity subscale of the Antisocial Process Screening Device (APSD), but nonsignificant associations with the C/U scale. Future studies should examine the effects of parenting on youth at the extreme ends of the callous-unemotional trait distribution.

### *Violent and Institutional Offending*

Current research supports a relatively robust association between psychopathy and violent offending for adult males (Bodholdt et al., 2000). Edens et al. (2001) reviewed 11 studies of adolescent offenders evaluating this relationship that used a variety of psychopathy measures, research designs, and violence outcomes. Overall, findings across studies were remarkably consistent, indicating that total psychopathy scores are moderately associated with violence, with most correlations ranging from .20 to .40. Brandt et al. (1997) and Forth et al. (1990) found that PCL-R total scores were significantly related to time-to-violent reoffending and number of charges/convictions for violent reoffenses, respectively, among incarcerated delinquents released into the community. Five studies assessed the relationship of the modified PCL-R to institutional misbehavior and infractions. Brandt et al. (1997) found moderate associations between PCL-R scores and verbal ($r$ = .31) and physical ($r$ = .28) misbehavior. Edens et al. (1999) found a significant correlation of .28 between PCL-R total scores and a combined measure of verbal and physical institutional misbehavior in a sample of 50 adolescent inmates. Significant associations were also identified between PCL-R scores and institutional charges for violent/aggressive behavior ($r$ = .46) (Forth et al., 1990), violent institutional infractions ($r$ = .39 for African American youth) (Hicks, 2000), and physically aggressive institutional infractions ($r$ = .28) (Rogers, Johansen, Chang, & Salekin, 1997).

The relationship of juvenile psychopathy to measures of verbal and physical aggression parallels that identified in the adult psychopathy literature in both direction and magnitude. The longitudinal stability of psychopathic characteristics identified early in life has not been established. For this reason, Edens et al. (2001) cautioned against the premature application of psychopathy measures for purposes of long-term prediction or decision making with long-term consequences. The respective independent and interactive roles of Factor 1 (core personality traits) and Factor 2 (antisocial lifestyle) (or Factor 3—narcissism) traits in violent offending remain to be elucidated by future investigations. Forth (1995) identified substantially stronger associations of Factor 2 traits with a variety of measures of criminal offending (e.g., age of onset of offending) compared to Factor 1 traits, although number ($r$ = .24) and variety ($r$ = .22) of offenses were significantly associated with Factor 1 (i.e., personality) traits. Future studies should explore qualitative assessments of differences in the nature of criminal offending by psychopathic and non-psychopathic youth. For instance, they should examine the interactive effects of factor traits on criminal behavior, particularly violence, and examine whether or not adolescent psychopaths commit more serious or instrumental violence than other youth offenders who engage in similar classes of crime.

### *Other Criminal Behavior*

Measures of juvenile psychopathy are associated with many aspects of juvenile offending. In a sample of 130 adolescent offenders, Brandt et al. (1997) found PCL-R total, Factor 1, and Factor 2 scores correlated significantly with younger age at first arrest and with the number of prior incarcerations and crime severity. Ridenour, Marchant, and Dean (2001) reported that PCL-R scores predicted future sentencing rates of a sample of adolescent offenders beyond baseline number of delinquency charges and a continuous measure of disruptive behavior, whereas conduct disorder diagnoses did not. Christian, Frick, Hill, Tyler, and Frazer (1997) found that a psychopathic group of children had higher rates of lifetime school suspensions (55%), police contacts (36%), and parental psychopathy (40%), than youth who had low scores on one or both scales. Vincent, Vitacco, Grisso, and Corrado (2003) performed a cluster analysis and identified a 3-factor model of the PCL:YV. The authors classified 259 male offenders ($M$ age = 17.0, $SD$ = 1.3) into 4 groups: those with low scores on all three scales, those with high scores on all three scales (i.e., the Psychopathy group), and those with predominantly impulsive or callous-deceitful traits. In general, the impulsive and psychopathic groups had the most severe offending histories. The psychopathic group had a substantially higher rate of violent recidivism (50%) than did the other 3 groups when followed an average of 14.5 months. The authors concluded that there is a subtype of adolescent offender with high impulsivity and callous-unemotional traits that is at particularly high risk for persistent and violent offending. Lynam (1997) reported that among community youth at high risk for delinquency, childhood psychopathy scale scores were positively related to seriousness of theft ($r = .26$) and seriousness of violence ($r = .32$), rates of general delinquency at age 10 ($r = .32$), and to the variety ($r = .19$) and seriousness ($r = .39$) of delinquency at age 13. Significant associations of CPS scores with measures of impulsivity and aggressiveness were also noted. Other studies indicate that psychopathic youth experience an earlier onset of criminal offending (McBride & Hare, 1996), engage in more frequent criminal behavior (Gretton, 1998), and are more likely to engage in intentional self-injurious behaviors (Gretton, 1998) than non-psychopathic adolescent offenders (Forth & Mailloux, 2000).

## *Comorbid Psychopathology*

Clinicians are understandably reluctant to diagnose children or adolescents with personality disorders given the many developmental transitions youth pass through that can produce disturbances mimicking personality disorder and the uncertain stability of any identified perturbations. Of course, it is often far from clear which signs and symptoms of personality disorder in youth are likely to reflect the presence of a relatively enduring personality dysfunction.

One of relatively few studies to examine comorbid personality disorders in relation to adolescent psychopathy is Meyers, Burket, and Harris's (1995) evaluation of 30 consecutive youth admitted to an adolescent inpatient psychiatric program (*M* age = 15.3, *SD* = .99). Each adolescent completed standardized semi-structured interviews for the assessment of *DSM-IV* Axis I and Axis II (i.e., personality) disorders (APA, 2000). Youth diagnosed with conduct ($N = 21$), narcissistic ($N = 4$), and sadistic ($N = 2$) personality disorders had the highest PCL-R scores—scores that were significantly higher than those of study participants without such diagnoses. Meyers et al. (1995) noted that adolescents diagnosed with narcissistic personality disorder had the highest PCL-R elevations, commenting that "psychopathy and narcissistic personality disorder share common ground in the areas of lack of empathy, exploitativeness, grandiose sense of self, feelings of entitlement, and a need for attention or stimulation" (p. 437).

Meyers and Blashfield (1997) examined 14 juvenile sexual homicide offenders, reporting that they averaged 2.3 major mental disorders and 1.9 personality disorders per person. substance use disorders (43%); attention-deficit/hyperactivity disorders (21%); and schizoid (38%), schizotypal (38%), and sadistic (31%) personality disorders predominated. PCL-R psychopathy scores were elevated (i.e., > 20) in 12 of the 14 youth. Contrary to expectation, Cluster A personality disorders such as schizoid and schizotypal personality disorder were more prevalent than Cluster B personality disorders in this sample. This was reflected in the paranoid ideation, odd beliefs, and social withdrawal exhibited by many of these youth. Few, if any, studies have examined the relationship of psychopathy factor subscales to personality disorders in youth offenders. Daderman and Kristiansson (2004) found no significant associations between a PCL-based measure of psychopathy and scores on the Karolinska Scales of Personality, although the sample was small and power was low to detect significant relationships.

Many theorists speculate that psychopaths have low levels of fear and anxiety that impair their ability to learn from aversive experiences (Lykken, 1995). Lynam (1997) found that psychopathy scores were significantly inversely associated with anxiety and internalizing disorders in a large sample of high-risk community youth. Frick (2002) also found an inverse association ($r = -.28$) between symptoms of negative affect (including anxiety) and scores on the APSD callous-unemotional factor subscale, when symptoms of conduct disorder were controlled for. The correlation between conduct disorder and anxiety symptoms was $r = .51$.

Moeller and Hell (2003) identified a significant positive correlation between PCL-R scores and number of prior traumatic events experienced; however, none of the psychopathic inmates they studied met *DSM-IV* criteria for posttraumatic stress disorder. These findings suggest that psychopathic offenders may be unlikely to develop posttraumatic stress disorder, despite life histories marked by repeated trauma. Moeller and Hell (2003) also found lower rates of affective disorders and suicide attempts in psychopathic offenders than in non-psychopathic offenders. Studies of the prevalence and etiology of posttraumatic stress disorder in adolescent psychopathic and non-psychopathic offenders are needed (Newman, 2002).

Ample evidence exists to support the association of comorbid attention-deficit/hyperactivity disorder and conduct disorder with juvenile psychopathy. McBride (1998) observed that "a pattern of HIA [hyperactivity-impulsivity-attentional deficits] and CP [conduct problems] is associated with an early onset of disruptive behavior, aggression, and an offending pattern marked by versatility and chronicity . . . the pattern of offending appears to be topographically similar to that uniquely associated with psychopathy" (p. 83). McBurnett and Pfiffner (1998) speculate that the arousal deficits and neuropsychological impairments observed in individuals with comorbid attention-deficit/hyperactivity disorder and conduct disorder both might play a role in antisocial behavior. Vitelli (1998) found that adult inmates with histories of both attention-deficit/hyperactivity disorder and conduct disorder were significantly more likely to be diagnosed with antisocial personality disorder and psychopathy as adults, and to have a history of committing violent acts in childhood, than inmates with only a conduct disorder. Recent findings provide further support for the notion that comorbid attention-deficit/hyperactivity disorder and conduct disorder is a particularly disabling syndrome associated with psychopathy-like features and far poorer outcomes than either disorder in isolation (Lynam, 1996, 1997, 1998, 2002).

Current findings are difficult to interpret with regard to comorbid personality disorders observed in psychopathic adolescents. There is some evidence for elevated rates of Cluster B (the impulsive or dramatic) personality disorders such as narcissistic personality disorder (Meyers et al., 1995), and Cluster A (the odd or eccentric) personality disorders such as schizoid and schizotypal personality disorders (Meyers & Blashfield, 1997) among juvenile psychopaths. Research supports an association between comorbid attention-deficit/hyperactivity disorder and conduct disorder and juvenile psychopathy. Comorbid anxiety disorders may be inversely associated with psychopathy, although findings are difficult to interpret given the widely varying definitions of anxiety and instruments for its assessment.

### *Reward Dependence*

A number of studies have examined antisocial adolescents' ability to modify previously rewarded behaviors when such behavior is no longer rewarded (Daughtery & Quay, 1991). Some theorists, using a neurobiological model of personality, have hypothesized that

> antisocial individuals would have a 'reward dominant' style in which their behavior is more dependent on appetitive drives than on avoidance of punishment. . . . [O]ne would predict that antisocial individuals would be more likely than nonantisocial individuals to persist in a previously rewarded response, even if the rate of punishment for this response increased. (O'Brien & Frick, 1996, p. 224)

Recent investigations lend credence to this notion. O'Brien and Frick (1996) asked 132 youths ages 6 to 13 (92 clinic children and 40 normal controls) to complete four computer games with three potential levels of prizes attainable based on cumulative point totals. Participants began each game with 50 points and had a point added or subtracted from their point total following each trial. Across the 100 possible trials, the rate of rewarded trials per 10 trials declined from 90% for the first 10 trials to 0% for the last 10 trials and was independent of subjects' actual responses. The total number of trials played served as the dependent measure.

Children with high scores on the APSD callous-unemotional subscale and no comorbid anxiety disorder displayed the most reward-dependent response orientations, compared to several other groups of clinic and community children with varying constellations of anxious conduct, and no symptoms. More anxious youths with conduct problems or psychopathy displayed a significantly less reward-dominant response style than did comparable non-anxious youth. Consequently, anxiety disorders were found to moderate the relationship between conduct problems/psychopathy and reward dominance. Psychopathic youth without anxiety disorders persisted in their efforts to obtain rewards despite being punished longer than did any other subgroup of youth offenders. Using a similar experimental paradigm, Lynam (1998) found that youths with both hyperactivity-impulsivity-attentional impairments and conduct problems displayed significantly more reward dominance than did youth with only one problem or neither problem. Lynam (1998) concluded,

> The present results are consistent with theories that identify deficits in response modulation . . . as the fundamental deficit in psychopathy. Although the response modulation hypothesis is a somewhat narrower conception than the reward dominance hypothesis, both suggest that the primary deficit in psychopathy involves dysregulation of behavior in the face of a strong set for reward. (p. 572)

At present, the origins of reward dependence/response modulation deficits are unknown. Dadds and Salmon (2003) noted that these dispositions are often seen as biologically based aspects of personality (i.e., temperamental traits). Their review of a substantial body of findings suggests that environmental factors can influence individual sensitivity to punishment.

Research over the past decade has supported earlier conceptions of juvenile psychopathy. In 1964, McCord and McCord contended that juvenile psychopaths are excitement seeking, impulsive, aggressive, and callous. Recent research presents a somewhat more refined portrait of "fledgling psychopaths," but substantially more investigation of their clinical characteristics is needed. Current findings indicate that psychopathic youth are substantially more likely to present with comorbid psychiatric disorders such as attention-deficit/hyperactivity disorder, conduct disorder, substance abuse/dependence, and other personality disorders, than are non-psychopathic youth offenders or adolescent nonoffenders. Psychopathic youth exhibit a moderately greater propensity to violence and institutional violence or misbehavior, and earlier and more persistent and varied criminal careers than do non-psychopathic delinquents. Psychopathic youth may evince more "egoistic" and less developed moral reasoning than do their general population counterparts, but it is currently unclear how, if at all, their ethical decision making differs from that of non-psychopathic youth offenders (Edens et al., 2001). Although there is some support for the relationship of early life experiences such as child abuse to the development of psychopathy, the respective roles of genetic and environmental factors remain to be elucidated. That is, although research characterizing the clinical features of juvenile psychopathy has produced some important findings to date, far less has been accomplished with regard to the development of a convincing etiological account of juvenile psychopathy.

## LABELING EFFECTS OF JUVENILE PSYCHOPATHY DIAGNOSES

Recent findings suggest that youth diagnosed with psychopathy may experience a variety of adverse outcomes. An analysis of 424 juvenile detention and probation officers' attitudes revealed that many (53.7% of juvenile probation officers and 37.9% of juvenile detention officers) believed that youth labeled psychopathic were unchangeable (Cruise, Colwell, Lyons, & Baker, 2003). More than three-quarters of these juvenile justice workers felt that incarceration was the best intervention for youth described as psychopathic.

Edens, Guy, and Fernandez (2003) presented 374 university undergraduates with one of two scenarios describing the case of a young man who was on death row for a murder committed when he was 16. Undergraduates presented with a case scenario including trait descriptions of the defendant consistent with psychopathy were significantly more likely (36.3% vs. 20.9%) to endorse the death penalty for the defendant than undergraduates presented an identical scenario describing non-psychopathic personality traits. Undergraduates who ascribed psychopathic traits to the defendant were also more likely to endorse the death penalty, irrespective of the scenario conditions they read.

Mock juror studies using case scenarios describing adult defendants have yielded findings consistent with those obtained using adolescent psychopath scenarios. For example, Guy and Edens (2003) found that female jurors participating in a mock civil commitment trial of a sexually violent predator who were presented with a defendant described as psychopathic were significantly more likely to support commitment than women who were presented with a case description in which the defendant was described as at "high risk" for reoffending but not psychopathic. Mock juror studies suggest that there are powerfully negative consequences for defendants when they are labeled or are otherwise described as psychopathic.

## FUTURE RESEARCH DIRECTIONS

The construct of psychopathy is a promising, though currently problematic, contribution to the study of serious, violent, and chronic youth offenders (Petrila & Skeem, 2003; Walters, 2004). More research is needed, particularly studies that examine the ethical, prevention, and rehabilitation implications of valid and false-positive diagnoses of juvenile psychopathy (Reed, 1996) and the nature, pervasiveness, and consequences of the stigma that characterizes public and professional perceptions of the disorder.

Future investigations should evaluate the temporal and cross-situational stability of behavioral and affective characteristics thought to comprise psychopathy and the concurrent/predictive validity of psychopathy measures designed for children and adolescents, including cutoff thresholds for psychopathy diagnoses and associated sensitivity and specificity rates (Seagrave &

Grisso, 2002). Studies should be undertaken to assess the interactive effects and temporal stability of the factor traits that together are thought to constitute psychopathy (Lilienfeld, 1998) and the similarity of adolescent and adult psychopaths with regard to psychophysiological, neuropsychological, psychiatric, autonomic, and affective characteristics (Forth & Burke, 1998).

Epidemiological studies should examine the nature, prevalence, and developmental manifestations of juvenile psychopathy and associated psychiatric disorders among girls and women (Lynam, 1996, 1997) and the relationship of ethnicity to psychopathy in a variety of adolescent offender and community samples (Seagrave & Grisso, 2002). Studies of the prevalence of psychopathic traits and frank psychopathy in large community samples of youth, might also offer new insights into the disorder and the factors that moderate its expression (Forth & Burke, 1998). Additional studies are needed that are similar to Frick, Kimonis, Dandreaux, and Farell's (2003) investigation evaluating the 4-year stability of psychopathy in youth and predictors of stability. Frick et al. (2003) found that parental ratings of juvenile psychopathy were highly stable across assessment intervals and noted that the factors that predict stability of psychopathic traits may differ from those that predict the initial development of the disorder. Genetic studies of long-term behavior are needed to describe factors associated with different trajectories to antisocial and violent behavior (Schaeffer, Petras, Ialongo, Poduska, & Kellam, 2003; Simonoff, Elander, Holmshaw, Pickles, Murry, et al., 2004).

Additional research pertinent to adolescent psychopathy assessment is vitally important to better identify and treat juvenile psychopaths. Studies examining the interpersonal behavior and validity of self-reports of psychopathic youth are especially needed. Investigations incorporating various psychophysiological and neuroimagining measures might also help to better distinguish psychopathic and non-psychopathic youth offenders (Lynam, 1996, 1997, 1998).

Studies should assess the long-term clinical and criminological outcomes of youth with various configurations of psychopathy factor traits (e.g., low Factor 1–low Factor 2, high Factor 1–high Factor 2, low Factor 1–high Factor 2, high Factor 1–low Factor 2). Investigations of the role of parenting practices and other experiential factors, particularly deficits in early attachment and factors that mediate affective bonding to parents and others, on long-term outcomes vis-à-vis psychopathy are particularly needed (Saltaris, 2002).

Policy analyses evaluating the extent to which measures of psychopathy are currently being used to make transfer, decertification, and sentencing decisions involving youth are critically important in determining to what extent the construct is being applied prematurely or inappropriately in the juvenile justice system (Steinberg, 2001).

Finally, clinical responses of psychopathic youth to a range of pharmacologic, psychosocial, and combined treatment/management interventions are needed to determine whether these efforts can be successful with this youth population given the current level of knowledge regarding the disorder (Steinberg, 2001). To some extent, the relative dearth of studies examining treatments for psychopathic youth may reflect the therapeutic pessimism that has traditionally accompanied the diagnosis of psychopathy.

## PROMISES AND PERILS OF A PSYCHOPATHY OF CRIME: THE TROUBLING CASE OF JUVENILE PSYCHOPATHY

Contemporary clinical, legal, and social service education and practice could profit substantially from greater appreciation of scientific research pertaining to mental disorders.

The promise of juvenile psychopathy research, specifically, is that it may eventually allow for effective early legal, psychological, and social intervention with youth who might otherwise proceed inexorably to adult psychopathy and to personally and socially costly criminal careers. However, given historical conceptualizations of the disorder and recent research findings, it is apparent that unbridled application of the construct within the juvenile justice system could result in the "writing off" of a significant number of youth. The most prudent course currently, given the uncertain state of scientific knowledge and highly stigmatized nature of the disorder, would seem to be to restrict application of the construct to research settings, pending additional studies that assess the stability of the disorder over a person's life and its amenability to a range of prevention, treatment, and management approaches.

## REFERENCES


American Psychiatric Association (APA) (2000). *Diagnostic and statistical manual of mental disorders* (4th ed.). Washington, DC: Author.

Blair, R. J. R. (1997). Moral reasoning and the child with psychopathic tendencies. *Personality and Individual Differences, 22,* 731–739.

Bodholdt, R. H., Richards, H. R., & Gacono, C. B. (2000). Assessing psychopathy in adults: The Psychopathy-Checklist-Revised and Screening Version. In C. B. Gacono (Ed.), *The clinical and forensic assessment of psychopathy: A practitioner's guide* (pp. 55–86). Mahwah, NJ: Lawrence Erlbaum.

Brandt, J. R., Kennedy, W. A., Patrick, C. J., & Curtin, J. J. (1997). Assessment of psychopathy in a population of incarcerated adolescent offenders. *Psychological Assessment, 9,* 429–435.

Burke, H. C., & Forth, A. E. (1996). *Psychopathy and familial experiences as antecedents to violence: A cross-sectional study of young offenders and nonoffending youth.* Unpublished manuscript, Carleton University, Ottawa, Ontario, Canada.

Campagna, A. F., & Harter, S. (1975). Moral judgment in sociopathic and normal children. *Journal of Personality and Social Psychology, 31,* 199–205.

Campbell, M. A., Porter, S., & Santor, D. (2004). Psychopathic traits in adolescent offenders: An evaluation of criminal history, clinical, and psychosocial correlates. *Behavioral Sciences and the Law, 22,* 23–47.

Christian, R. E., Frick, P. J., Hill, N. L., Tyler, L., & Frazer, D. R. (1997). Psychopathy and conduct problems in children. II. Implications for subtyping children with conduct problems. *Journal of the American Academy of Child and Adolescent Psychiatry, 26,* 233–241.

Cleckley, H. (1941). *The mask of sanity.* St. Louis, MO: C.V. Mosby.

Cooke, D. J., & Michie, C. (2001). Refining the construct of psychopathy: Towards a hierarchical model. *Psychological Assessment, 13,* 171–188.

Corrado, R. R., Vincent, G. M., Hart, S. D., & Cohen, I. M. (2004). Predictive validity of the Psychopathy Checklist: Youth Version for general and violent recidivism. *Behavioral Sciences and the Law, 22,* 5–22.

Cruise, K. R., Colwell, L. H., Lyons, P. M., & Baker, M. D. (2003). Prototypical analysis of adolescent psychopathy: Investigating the juvenile justice perspective. *Behavioral Sciences and the Law, 21,* 829–846.

Dadds, M. R., & Salmon, K. (2003). Punishment insensitivity and parenting: Temperament and learning as interacting risks for antisocial behavior. *Clinical Child and Family Psychology Review, 6,* 69–86.

Dåderman, A. M., & Kristiansson, M. (2004). Psychopathy-related personality traits in male juvenile delinquents: An application of a person-oriented approach. *International Journal of Law and Psychiatry, 27,* 45–64.

Daugherty, T. K., & Quay, H. C. (1991). Response perseveration and delayed responding in childhood behavior disorders. *Journal of Child Psychiatry and Psychology, 32,* 453–461.

Edens, J. F., Guy, L. S., & Fernandez, K. (2003). Psychopathic traits predict attitudes toward a juvenile capital murderer. *Behavioral Sciences and the Law, 21,* 807–828.

Edens, J. F., Poythress, N. G., & Lilienfeld, S. O. (1999). Identifying inmates at risk for disciplinary infractions. *Behavioral Sciences & The Law, 17*(4), 435–443.

Edens, J. F., Skeem, J. L., Cruise, K. R., & Cauffman, E. (2001). Assessment of "juvenile psychopathy" and its association with violence: A critical review. *Behavioral Sciences and the Law, 19,* 53–80.

Falkenbach, D. M., Poythress, N. G., & Heide, K. M. (2003). Psychopathic features in a juvenile diversion population: Reliability and predictive validity of two self-report measures. *Behavioral Sciences and the Law, 21,* 787–805.

Fodor, E. M. (1973). Moral development and parent behavior antecedents in adolescent psychopaths. *Journal of Genetic Psychology, 122,* 37–43.

Forth, A. E. (1995). *Psychopathy and young offenders: Prevalence, family background, and violence.* Unpublished report, Carelton University, Ottawa, Ontario, Canada.

Forth, A. E., & Burke, H. C. (1998). Psychopathy in adolescence: Assessment, violence, and developmental precursors. In D. J. Cooke et al. (Eds.), *Psychopathy: Theory, research, and implications for society* (pp. 205–229). Netherlands: Kluwer Academic Publishers.

Forth, A. E., Hart, S. D., & Hare, R. D. (1990). Assessment of psychopathy in male young offenders. *Psychological Assessment, 2,* 342–344.

Forth, A. E., & Tobin, F. (1996). Psychopathy and young offenders: Rates of childhood maltreatment. *Forum on Corrections Research, 7,* 20–24.

Forth, A. E., & Mailloux, D. L. (2000). Psychopathy in youth: What do we know? In C. B. Gacono (Ed.), *The clinical and forensic assessment of psychopathy: A practitioner's guide* (pp. 25–54). Mahwah, NJ: Lawrence Erlbaum.

Frick, P. J. (2002). Juvenile psychopathy from a developmental perspective: Implications of construct development and use in forensic assessments. *Law and Human Behavior, 26,* 247–253.

Frick, P. J., O'Brien, B., Wootton, J., & McBurnett, K. (1994). Psychopathy and conduct problems in children. *Journal of Abnormal Psychology, 103,* 700–707.

Frick, P. J., Kimonis, E. R., Dandreaux, D.M., & Farell, M. S. (2003). The four-year stability of psychopathic traits in non-referred youth. *Behavioral Sciences and the Law, 21,* 713–736.

Gretton, H. M. (1998). *Psychopathy and recidivism in adolescents: A ten-year retrospective follow-up.* Unpublished doctoral dissertation, University of British Columbia, Vancouver, Canada.

Guy, L. S., & Edens, J. F. (2003). Juror decision-making in a mock sexually violent predator trial: Gender differences in the impact of divergent types of expert testimony. *Behavioral Sciences and the Law, 21,* 215–237.

Hare, R. D. (1991). *The Hare Psychopathy Checklist Manual.* Toronto: Multi-Health Systems.

Hare, R. D. (1996a). Psychopathy and antisocial personality disorder: A case of diagnostic confusion. *Psychiatric Times, 13,* 39–40.

Hare, R. D. (1996b). Psychopathy: A clinical construct whose time has come. *Criminal Justice and Behavior, 23,* 25–54.

Hart, S. D., & Hare, R. D. (1989). Discriminant validity of the Psychopathy Checklist in a forensic psychiatric population. *Psychological Assessment, 1,* 211–218.

Heilbrun, K., Hart, S., Hare, R., Gustafson, D., Nunez, C., & White, A. (1998). Inpatient and postdischarge aggression in mentally disordered offenders: The role of psychopathy. *Journal of Interpersonal Violence, 13,* 514–527.

Hicks, M. M. (2000). Predictions of violent and total infractions among institutionalized male juvenile offenders. *Journal of the American Academy of Psychiatry and the Law,* 183.

Hume, M. P., Kennedy, W. A., Patrick, C. J., & Partyka, D. J. (1996). Examination of the MMPI-A for the assessment of psychopathy in incarcerated adolescent male offenders. *International Journal of Offender Therapy and Comparative Criminology, 40,* 224–233.

Jurkovic, G. J., & Prentice, N. M. (1977). Relation of moral and cognitive development to dimensions of juvenile delinquency. *Journal of Abnormal Psychology, 86,* 414–420.

Laroche, I., & Toupin, J. (1996). *Psychopathic delinquents: A family contribution?* Paper presented at the XXVI International Congress of Psychology, Montreal, Quebec, Canada.

Lee, M., & Prentice, N. M. (1988). Interrelations of empathy, cognition, and moral reasoning with dimensions of juvenile delinquency. *Journal of Abnormal Child Psychology, 16,* 127–139.

Lilienfeld, S. O. (1998). Methodological advances and developments in the assessment of psychopathy. *Behaviour Research and Therapy, 36,* 99–125.

Loeber, R., Farrington, D. P., & Waschbusch, D. A. (Eds.). (1998). Serious and violent juvenile offenders. In R. Loeber & D. P. Farrington (Eds.) (1998). *Serious and violent juvenile offenders: Risk factors and successful interventions* (pp. 13–29). Thousand Oaks, CA: Sage.

Lykken, D. T. (1995). The antisocial personalities. Hillsdale, NJ: Lawrence Erlbaum.

Lynam, D. R. (1996). Early identification of chronic offenders: Who is the fledgling psychopath? *Psychological Bulletin, 120,* 209–234.

Lynam, D. R. (1997). Pursuing the psychopath: Capturing the fledgling psychopath in a nomological net. *Journal of Abnormal Psychology, 106,* 425–438.

Lynam, D. R. (1998). Early identification of the fledgling psychopath: Locating the psychopathic child in the current nomenclature. *Journal of Abnormal Psychology, 107,* 566–575.

Lynam, D. R. (2002). Fledgling psychopathy: A view from personality theory. *Law and Human Behavior, 26,* 255–259.

Lyon, D. R., & Ogloff, J. R. P. (2000). Legal and ethical issues in psychopathy assessment. In C. B. Gacono (Ed.), *The clinical and forensic assessment of psychopathy: A practitioner's guide* (pp. 139–173). Mahwah, NJ: Lawrence Erlbaum.

Mailloux, D. L., Forth, A. E., & Kroner, D. G. (1997). Psychopathy and substance use in adolescent male offenders. *Psychological Reports, 80,* 529–530.

McBride, M. L. (1998). *Individual and familial risk factors for adolescent psychopathy.* Unpublished doctoral dissertation, University of British Columbia, Vancouver, Canada.

McBride, M., & Hare, R. D. (1996). *Precursors of psychopathy and recidivism.* Unpublished manuscript, University of British Columbia, Vancouver, British Columbia.

McBurnett, K., & Pfiffner, L. (1998). Comorbidities and biological correlates of conduct disorder. In D. J. Cooke et al. (Eds.), *Psychopathy: Theory, research, and implications for society* (pp. 189–203). Netherlands: Kluwer Academic Publishers.

McCord, W., & McCord, J. (1964). *The psychopath: An essay on the criminal mind.* Princeton, NJ: Van Nostrand.

Meyers, W. C., Burket, R. C., & Harris, H. E. (1995). Adolescent psychopathy in relation to delinquent behaviors, conduct disorder, and personality disorders. *Journal of Forensic Sciences, 40,* 436–440.

Meyers, W. C., & Blashfield, R. (1997). Psychopathology and personality in juvenile sexual homicide offenders. *Journal of the American Academy of Psychiatry and the Law, 25,* 497–508.

Moeller, A. A., & Hell, D. (2003). Affective disorder and "psychopathy" in a sample of younger male delinquents. *Acta Psychiatrica Scandinavica, 107,* 203–207.

Moffitt, T. (1993). Adolescence-limited and life-course persistent antisocial behavior: A developmental taxonomy. *Psychological Review, 4,* 674–701.

Newman, E. (2002). Posttraumatic stress disorder among criminally involved youth. *Archives of General Psychiatry, 60,* 849.

O'Brien, B. S., & Frick, P. J. (1996). Reward dominance: Association with anxiety, conduct problems, and psychopathy in children. *Journal of Abnormal Child Psychology, 24,* 223–240.

Pan, V. (1998). *Institutional behavior in psychopathic juvenile offenders.* Poster presented at the biennial conference of the American Psychology-Law Society, Redondo Beach, CA.

Petrila, J., & Skeem, J. L. (2003). Juvenile psychopathy: The debate. An introduction to the Special Issue on Juvenile Psychopathy and some reflections on the current debate. *Behavioral Sciences and the Law, 21,* 689–694.

Quay, H. C. (1993). The psychobiology of undersocialized aggressive conduct disorder: A theoretical perspective. *Development and Psychopathology, 5,* 165–180.

Reed, J. (1996). Psychopathy—A clinical and legal dilemma. *British Journal of Psychiatry, 168,* 4–9.

Ridenour, T. A., Marchant, G. J., & Dean, R. S. (2001). Is the revised Psychopathy Checklist clinically useful for adolescents? *Journal of Psychoeducational Assessment, 19,* 227–238.

Rogers, R., Johansen, J., Chang, J. J., & Salekin, R. T. (1997). Predictors of adolescent psychopathy: Oppositional and conduct-disordered symptoms. *Journal of the American Academy of Psychiatry and the Law, 25,* 261–271.

Rowe, R. (1997). *Psychopathy and female adolescents.* Unpublished raw data. Carleton University, Ottawa, Ontario, Canada.

Rutherford, M. J., Alterman, A. I., & Cacciola, J. S. (2000). Psychopathy and substance abuse: A bad mix. In C. B. Gacono (Ed.), *The clinical and forensic assessment of psychopathy: A practitioner's guide* (pp. 351–368). Mahwah, NJ: Lawrence Erlbaum.

Salekin, R.T., Rogers, R., & Sewell, K.W. (1996). A review and meta-analysis of the Psychopathy Checklist and Psychopathy Checklist-Revised: Predictive validity of dangerousness. *Clinical Psychology: Science & Practice, 3*(3), 203–215.

Saltaris, C. (2002). Psychopathy in juvenile offenders: Can temperament and attachment be considered as robust developmental precursors? *Clinical Psychology Review, 22,* 729–752.

Schaeffer, C. M., Petras, H., Ialongo, N., Poduska, J., & Kellam, S. (2003). Modeling growth in boys' aggressive behavior across elementary school: Links to later criminal involvement, conduct disorder, and antisocial personality disorder. *Developmental Psychology, 39,* 1020–1035.

Seagrave, D., & Grisso, T. (2002). Adolescent development and measurement of juvenile psychopathy. *Law and Human Behavior, 26,* 219–239.

Simonoff, E., Elander, J., Holmshaw, J., Pickles, A., Murray, R., & Rutter, M. (2004). Predictors of antisocial personality: Continuities from childhood to adult life. *British Journal of Psychiatry, 184,* 118–127.

Skeem, J. L., Mulvey, E. P., & Grisso, T. (2003). Applicability of traditional and revised models of psychopathy to the Psychopathy Checklist: Screening Version. *Psychological Assessment, 15,* 41–55.

Skilling, T. A., Quinsey, V. L., & Craig, W.M. (2001). Evidence of a taxon underlying serious antisocial behavior in boys. *Criminal Justice and Behavior, 28,* 450–470.

Smith-Stevens, S., & Newman, J. P. (1990). Alcohol and drug abuse-dependence disorders in psychopathic and nonpsychopathic criminal offenders. *Journal of Abnormal Psychology, 99,* 430–439.

Sparrow, B. J., & Gacono, C.B. (2000). Selected psychopathy bibliography by subject. In C. B. Gacono (Ed.), *The clinical and forensic assessment of psychopathy: A practitioner's guide* (pp. 455–482). Mahwah, NJ: Lawrence Erlbaum.

Stanford, M., Ebner, D., Patton, J., & Williams, J. (1994). Multi-impulsivity within an adolescent psychiatric population. *Personality and Individual Differences, 16,* 395–402.

Steinberg, L. (2001). The juvenile psychopath: Fads, fictions, and facts. Perspectives on Crime and Justice: 2000–2001 Lecture Series. *National Institute of Justice, Research Forum, Volume V,* 2002.

Tolan, P. H., & Gorman-Smith, D. (1998). Development of serious and violent offending careers. In R. Loeber, & D. P. Farrington (Eds.), *Serious and violent juvenile offenders: Risk factors and successful interventions* (pp. 68–85). Thousand Oaks, CA: Sage.

Trevethan, S. D., & Walker, L. J. (1989). Hypothetical versus real-life moral reasoning among psychopathic and delinquent youth. *Development and Psychopathology, 1,* 91–103.

Vincent, G. M., Vitacco, M. J., Grisso, T., & Corrado, R. R. (2003). Subtypes of adolescent offenders: Affective traits and antisocial behavior patterns. *Behavioral Sciences and the Law, 21,* 695–712.

Vitacco, M. J., Neumann, C. S., Ramos, V., & Roberts, M. K. (2003). Ineffective parenting: A precursor to psychopathic traits and delinquency in Hispanic females. *Annals of the New York Academy of Sciences, 1008,* 300–303.

Vitelli, R. (1998). Childhood disruptive behaviors and adult psychopathy. *American Journal of Forensic Psychology, 16,* 29–37.

Walters, G. D. (2004). The trouble with psychopathy as a general theory of crime. *International Journal of Offender Therapy and Comparative Criminology, 48,* 133–148.

Wolfgang, M. E., Figlio, R. M., & Sellin, T. (1972). *Delinquency in a birth cohort.* Chicago: University of Chicago Press.

Wolfgang, M. E., Thornberry, T. P., & Figlio, R. M. (1987). From boy to man, from delinquency to crime. Chicago: University of Chicago Press.

Wootten, J. M., Frick, P. J., Shelton, K. K., & Silverthorn, P. (1997). Ineffective parenting and childhood conduct problems: The moderating role of callous-unemotional traits. *Journal of Consulting and Clinical Psychology, 65,* 301–308.

Young, M. H., Justice, J. V., Erdberg, P. S., & Gacono, C. B. (2000). The incarcerated psychopath in psychiatric treatment: Management or treatment? In C. B. Gacono (Ed.), *The clinical and forensic assessment of psychopathy: A practitioner's guide* (pp. 313–331). Mahwah, NJ: Lawrence Erlbaum.

CHAPTER 21

# Cleaning Up Toxic Violence

## An EcoGenerist Paradigm

BARBARA BENNETT WOODHOUSE

Our children are growing up in a culture steeped in violence. Yet the presence of violence and children's exposure to violence is nothing new. Children in every nation and in every age have experienced violence. Killing of animals for food, killing of enemies in self-defense and for territorial conquest, beatings inflicted by the strong on the small and weak in order to gain control and exert power are common features of human societies. Nor are children always the helpless victims rather than the perpetrators of violence. Child soldiers are recruited because they are capable of inflicting senseless violence even more readily than adults (Anderson, 2000; Amnesty International, 2003). Children's encounters with violence can be beneficial and even transformative. Child freedom fighters in South Africa and in the American South have played a role in both violent and nonviolent struggles for justice (Halberstam, 1998; Woodhouse, 1999).

Even in societies that place a high value on sheltering children from violence, children will inevitably witness and engage in violence. It would be unwise as well as impossible to banish violence completely from children's environment. Violence plays a necessary role in children's play, allowing children to practice their survival skills and to confront their fears, both real and imaginary (James, 2004; Woodhouse, 2004). Understanding, controlling, and coping with violence, as a part of human cultural and physical reality, plays an important role in the socialization of children (Garbarino, Dubrow, Kostelny, & Pardo, 1992; Konner, 1991).

Our current reality, nevertheless, is qualitatively and quantitatively different. Today, as the research in this volume illustrates, we are reaching a saturation point of violence in our culture that has measurably altered the environment in which our children are born, grow up, and die. The statistics on children as victims, witnesses, and perpetrators of violence with which Nancy Dowd introduces this volume speak for themselves. As Dale Kunkel shows in this volume, actual physical violence in children's environment is compounded by the effect of violent words and images. Emotional abuse by caregivers, bullying, and hate speech can inflict severe and lasting harm, according to sources discussed by Naomi Cahn and Susan Limber in this volume. And as Robin Wilson explains, also in this volume, sexual exploitation and abuse, once treated as family secrets, are now understood as forms of violence.

For many decades, poor children of color in urban communities have suffered unconscionably high levels of violence in their streets, schools, and homes (Kotlowitz, 1991). Many would argue that poverty, and the ills that come with it, including unemployment, dislocation, parental stress and lack of family stability, are a form of cultural violence with especially pernicious effects on the young (Kozol, 1991). The culture of violence has now spread to children of all races and classes and every community. With TV, film, and the Internet, the market for violent images has exploded. Purveyors of a wide range of products have found creative ways to market their products to children using images of violence to exploit children's appetites for excitement and stimulation (Woodhouse, 2004). These products and the culture of violence that surrounds them pose special challenges to policy makers concerned with ensuring a healthy environment for children's growth. As Diana Russell shows in this volume, discussing pornographic images, new technologies have flooded American culture with representations of violence as never before experienced. Imagined violence can be more graphic than the real thing, made hyper-realistic through digital technologies (Putnam, 1997; Woodhouse, 2004). The nature of children's relationship with media has also changed, from that of a spectator to an interactive player. Children no longer play a passive role, as they did as consumers of violence in movies and television (Subrahmanyam, 2001). Modern children, playing with video games and Web-based interactive technologies, are able to participate directly in enacting violence.

Cultural critics have identified the growth of a post-modern hyperrealism, in which images can be more powerful than real experiences (Kincheloe, 1998; Woodhouse, 2003). In movies, videos, and games, on our streets and in our homes, image, myth, and reality seem to blend and merge. As Signorelli and Cantor discuss in this volume, myths about race and gender, and about class and religion, feed upon each other and produce more fear and more violence. These forces intersect in ways we do not fully understand. Images become more real than reality and produce a numbing sense of unreality in the face of actual and deadly violence. Many Americans, from researchers to parents to teachers, believe that the culture of violence is toxic to our children and to the society our children will inherit, but we cannot imagine how to begin to fix it.

This is hardly the first time we have been forced by new technologies and new research to confront the unforeseen effects of human activities on living organisms and their environment. And it is not the first time that scientists and citizens have turned to the law as a means to regulate and reform human activity in order to protect a precious, but not infinitely renewable, resource. In the last century, scientists allied with advocates for the environment aroused fellow citizens to the dangers of going blindly forward, spewing poisons into the air and water. In order to meet this challenge, reformers had to rethink and fundamentally reshape the legal framework for regulation of harmful human activities. Scientists and advocates for children have reached a similar crossroads. This chapter suggests a new paradigm for legal responses that draws from the environmental model, arguing for an ecological approach grounded in the principle of generism. Generism takes as its paramount social values the survival and nurturing of the next generation, hence an "ecogenerist" model. This chapter accepts as its predicate the empirical data of those chapters that precede it in this volume. Rather than exploring empirical issues, it focuses instead on critiquing the theoretical paradigm we use to inform legal problem solving and policy making.

First, there is a brief discussion of current legal approaches and their shortcomings, focusing in particular on barriers raised by the First Amendment. The second part is a description of the environmental paradigm that supports an ecological approach. Part III of this chapter discusses how ecological theories and concepts, including deep ecology, ecofeminism, sustainable development, and others, could be adapted to think about issues of children, culture, and violence. An ecological model requires a description or principle of the ecological "good" to be achieved, and this chapter argues for the child-centered principle of generism as a definition of "the good." Part IV articulates a new ecogenerist paradigm. In the last part of the chapter, suggestions are offered concerning how this paradigm might be applied to two specific issues of children and violence: regulation of violent images on the Internet, and dealing with the problem of youth violence.

## REGULATING HARMFUL CONDUCT AND TOXIC IMAGES: THE FIRST AMENDMENT SPEECH/CONDUCT DICHOTOMY

Traditionally, criminal laws deal with persons who intentionally hurt a child, while tort laws deal with the unintentional harms inflicted, for example, by a manufacturer who produces a dangerous toy or a toxic chemical. Elaborate child protective services systems have been designed to assist victims of family violence and parental neglect. The juvenile justice system evolved to protect immature children caught up in violence from the full force of criminal sanctions. These existing systems fail children in many ways. They allow children to fall into the cracks between the systems, they foster stigmatizing labeling (and mislabeling) of children, and they often ignore the larger social and cultural context, focusing narrowly on punishing the perpetrator rather than assisting the victim. However imperfect their functioning, these systems share one common feature: they recognize the central role of law in protecting children from conduct and substances that inflict both short-term and long-term harm.

Attempts to regulate production and dissemination of violent *images* present challenges of a different kind. As discussed by Craig Anderson in this volume, violent images can harm children by normalizing violence. Ironically, violent images can even make perpetrators out of child victims of overexposure to violence by increasing aggressive tendencies and reducing inhibitions.

But images have traditionally been shielded from regulation by the First Amendment (*Burstyn, Inc. v. Wilson,* 1952). While the First Amendment speaks of freedom of the press and of free speech, the Supreme Court of the United States has held that images as well are a protected form of speech, shielded by the First Amendment (Ross, this volume). The Supreme Court, in interpreting the free speech clause of the First Amendment, has drawn a distinction between conduct (which, if harmful, can be regulated) and speech (which presumptively is not harmful and therefore cannot be regulated) (*R.A.V. v. City of St. Paul,* 1992). The law generally distrusts regulation of speech as government censorship, inimical to values of free expression and healthy debate in a democratic society (*Brandenburg v. Ohio,* 1969). But the Supreme Court has recognized that children may need protection from speech that is appropriate to adults (*Ginsberg v. New York,* 1968). Shielding children from pornography, for example, is a compelling state purpose, and limitations on children's access that collaterally interfere with adults' access to pornographic materials may survive if narrowly tailored and necessary to the child-protective purpose (*Ashcroft v. American Civil Liberties Union,* 2004).

As John Cech (this volume) has noted, scary and violent images are an integral part of children's culture. Examples abound, from the Bible's Slaughter of the Innocents to the carnivorous wolf in *Little Red Riding Hood.* However, modern technologies of television, film, video games, and the Internet are changing every aspect of children's exposure to the culture of violence. The methods of delivery, the frequency of exposure, and the dosages of violent imagery are unprecedented in children's culture (Woodhouse, 2004). Modern children are also more likely to consume violent images without an adult present to act as a mediator or filter (Wilcox, 2004). Unlike the mass media, a live storyteller can actively interpret the meaning of violent images and calibrate the levels of violence to the child's ability to absorb them.

Efforts in the United States to regulate children's exposure to problematic images often seem to be motivated more by concerns about children and sex than about children and violence (Saunders, 1996). Nevertheless, film, CD, DVD, and videogame ratings systems; television V-chips; and computer filters have all included high levels of violence as an element in determining whether images are appropriate for consumption by children (Woodhouse, 2004). Congress has regulated the public airwaves of radio and television (Minow & Lamay, 1995). But most laws or systems of regulation operate primarily at the level of the individual child, rather than regulating violent images at their source. An underage child may be blocked from entering an X-rated film by the movie theater, but this is an exception to the general rule of parental control. It is left to the parent to decide whether to install a V-chip or computer filter and parents are expected to consult ratings to determine whether a given CD or electronic game is harmful to their child.

A look at First Amendment theory explains why this has been the preferred approach. The concept of "prior restraint" is anathema to First Amendment doctrine (*Near v. Minnesota,* 1931). Suppressing ideas before they can be expressed is far more dangerous to democracy than punishing a speaker if his or her speech actually produces a harmful and dangerous effect. Scholars and judges worry that punishing speech after the fact may have a "chilling effect" on free speech at its source, but the antidemocratic impact of censorship is obvious and direct (*New York Times, Co. v. U.S.,* 1971). Censorship allows government to block the free flow of information and ideas necessary to a robust democracy.

Reinforcing these First Amendment concerns about direct government intervention in speech is the strong American tradition of parental autonomy in deciding who and what the child will see and hear. Supreme Court cases establish that, absent a compelling reason, the family, not the state, should decide how children should be raised (*Meyer v. Nebraska,* 1923; *Pierce v. Society of Sisters,* 1925; *Troxel v. Granville,* 2000). Given this background, it is easy to see why we assume that informing parents of the potential harms from exposure to age-inappropriate speech is the method of choice for regulating children's exposure to harmful images. Yet parents may be unwilling or unable to monitor their children's media exposure (Woodhouse, 2004). Media violence is so pervasive that it defies efforts of even the most vigilant and affluent families to restrict children's exposure. Reliance on parental monitoring leaves too many children at risk. Moreover, children have a claim in their own right to our protection. While parents have both the right and the duty to protect their children from harm, the state also has a compelling interest in protection of children (*Prince v. Massachusetts,* 1944). Respect for family autonomy and for parental authority should not prevent state action to support parents in this endeavor, and even to override parental inaction if necessary to protect children from pervasive harms. Early laws prohibiting child labor foundered on concerns that such laws would impermissibly infringe on parents' authority, until it became clear that only a broad regulatory approach would be sufficient to protect children and their families from economic exploitation (Woodhouse, 1993). As the law has long recognized, society as a whole has a tremendous stake in seeing children grow into stable, healthy, and constructive adults. Instead of looking at the harm of cultural violence through the narrow lens of a classic First Amendment analysis, or reverting to notions of children as private property of their parents, we should draw upon our increasing knowledge of the interconnections between mind and body, as well as between individual, family, and community interests.

## AN ENVIRONMENTALIST PARADIGM

Legal scholars and scientists banded together in the 20th century to address pervasive problems caused by new technologies that seemed to evade effective regulation. The impetus for their actions was the realization that the impact of these seemingly discrete and previously unregulated acts posed a threat to the natural environment. They popularized the notion of ecological systems as a way of understanding the interconnections between zones of human and natural activity. Environmentalism focused social and legal attention on the preservation or destruction of conditions conducive to a healthy planet and, ultimately, to survival of the species (Abbey, 1988; Carson, 1962). In this section, I will draw upon environmentalist concepts and theories to shed light on how we might approach toxic violence.

### *An Ecological Model of Child Development*

The notion of studying children through the lens of ecology is far from new. Pioneers in child psychology long ago adopted this metaphor and it has become a mainstay of multisystemic theory, as Mark Fondacaro in this volume explains, teaching us to use a holistic approach for children and families in crisis. Scholars of legal theory can draw upon the ecological theory of child development expounded by social scientists such as Urie Bronfenbrenner (1979) and James Garbarino (1985, 1995). An ecological theory envisions children at the center of concentric circles of human and natural systems. Rather than proposing normative principles such as rights and duties, an ecological theory is descriptive of the world as the child knows and experiences it. It examines not the individuals in isolation from their environment, but the nature and quality of the relationships and environments (Garbarino, 1985).

In an ecological theory of child development, the focus of study is on "systems," in recognition of the importance of context and flux. "Microsystems" are those environments that directly touch and include the child. They range from the most intimate systems, such as the family, to larger environments such as the school, the peer group, and the neighborhood (Pearson, 2001). These microsystems can be supportive or destructive, and they may serve as the gateway to a larger world or they may fail to prepare the child to survive in that world (Pearson, 2001). The child's family as defined by law may be quite different from the child's family *system* as defined by ecological theory, as when a child lives with someone other than a parent and has no physical or emotional connection to his legal parents. An ecological approach teaches us to look at the world through the child's eyes, seeing as family those individuals whom the child knows as family.

Microsystems generally overlap. The overlaps between microsystems constitute a "mesosystem" (Pearson, 2001). For example, a mesosytem exists where school and family, and peer group and neighborhood, intersect.

In a very simple society, children's nurturing and socialization all occur within the extended family, and the political unit such as the tribe is seen as an extension of the family; in this instance, the child's school, family, and neighborhood microsystems might overlap almost completely, erasing the borders between micro- and mesosystems. Modern industrial societies are not so simple. Most children move back and forth between different microsystems during a typical day. If children are lucky, the relationships among microsystems are consistent and mutually supportive of the child's development, as when parents work closely and collaboratively with responsive community schools. Or microsystems may be in conflict, as when schools and families or parents and peer groups make inconsistent demands and promote inconsistent values. When this happens, children are caught in a double bind between expectations of family and school, peer group, and neighborhood (Pearson, 2001).

Encircling the micro- and mesosystems are the "exosystems." These are systems in which the child is not directly involved but which nonetheless affect the child's life (Pearson, 2001). For example, a child who has never ventured into the parent's workplace is nevertheless affected by whether the parent's employer offers flexible hours that promote quality time with the child and adequate health care benefits that include coverage for dependent children (Dowd, 2004). The child's relationship to various systems is not static but changes as the child's circumstances change. The child protective system (CPS), for example, may be an exosystem for most children—indirectly influencing but not directly touching their lives. But on the day a child is removed from his or her home and placed in shelter care, CPS becomes the dominant microsystem, entangled and forming mesosystems with the child's other microsytems of family, school, and community.

Perhaps the most important concept for purposes of this discussion is the macro system. In ecological theories of child development, all of the systems identified above— micro, meso and exo—are embedded in a cultural "macrosystem." A cultural macrosystem is described as the patterning by history, power, and ideas of the broader society in which the child lives (Pearson, 2001). All of our collective prejudices, politics, and ideologies, and our religious and moral values together create the cultural macrosystem (Pearson, 2001). The concept of the macrosystem allows us not only to place children in the context of the intimate systems that affect them, but also allows us to examine the pervasive influences of surrounding political, religious, and economic systems in children's lives.

In my paradigm of the child's ecosystem, the child is embedded in a system represented by concentric circles, sometimes overlapping, but all centered on the child. Some are circles that form part of the larger environment that surrounds the child (exosystems), and other circles represent places where children actually can be found interacting with others and the world (micosystems). Thus, no two-dimensional static drawing can capture the dynamic nature of the ecological approach. In contrast to the common wisdom that extols "the balance of nature," *flux* is actually the defining characteristic of a healthy ecosystem, as many environmentalists have concluded (Wiener, Botkin, Frampton, Norton, & Profeta 1996).

Where does law figure in this dynamic ecological system? It hardly seems like a distinct exosystem because it operates at all levels of social interaction. I have argued that "the law" provides an interface of the macrosystem and the other systems, and that its influence and action permeate throughout the ecosystem (Woodhouse, in press). Law is produced by the macrosystem and its function is to circulate the macrosystem's dominant values and power relations throughout the other systems, much as water systems carry elements and particulates from oceans to clouds to rain into rivers, creeks, and underground aquifers. There are many sources of law within the macrosystem, formal and informal. Together, they produce normative commands that translate values, ideology, and power into human action and restraint (Weyrauch, 2001).

## *An Ecological Approach to Issues of Children, Culture, and Violence*

How does an ecological approach differ from a more traditional approach for dealing with issues relating to children, and specifically, to issues generated by violence and children's well-being? An ecological model does not approach children, parents, and the government as separate autonomous actors, but rather as immersed together in a sea of culture and inevitably interconnected to each other (Woodhouse, 2004). An ecological model modulates the distinctions between private and public by recognizing that all systems are interrelated and all systems, including the family, affect the public good (Woodhouse, in press). Measuring the health of these systems involves measuring the well-being of individuals within these systems. Like the "miner's canary," children suffer first, and their distress provides an early warning of an environment that is toxic to human life (Guinier & Torres, 2002). How do we determine whether children's ecosystems are healthy or toxic? In law, we have tended to approach this question through the lens of individual responsibility, blaming or praising the family for the child's failure or success. Researchers in fields like public health and social welfare employ an ecological approach toward measuring child welfare. Data about infant mortality, immunization, and poverty rates in various geographic or political regions measure the environmental and social risks to children from *all* sources, not just from failures of personal responsibility (Guinier & Torres, 2002).

Internationally, legal advocates draw upon the principles of the United Nations Convention on the Rights of the Child (CRC) to measure both tangible and intangible aspects of children's well-being (United Nations [UN], 1989). The CRC represents an international consensus regarding the basic outlines of children's essential human rights. These include the rights to equality, dignity, and autonomy commensurate with the child's emerging capacities (UN, 1989). Social rights such as adequate food, health care, and education are identified as rights of children and as owed to children by adults and governments (UN, 1989). Children are viewed in context, with the realization that maternity and neonatal care, parental employment, housing, and access to education are all environmental factors that determine whether children do well or poorly. The international community uses this ecological approach in thinking about children's rights and governments' responsibilities toward children.

If adopted in the United States, this approach would require American law and policy makers to examine the state of the environment, specifically children's environment, and, if the environment is found to be toxic and unhealthy to children, would mandate a response. Such an examination would occur for all the systemic levels described above. From the microcosm of child custody laws to the macrosystem of child health policy, we would examine not only the conduct and condition of individual children and their parents, but also the ecological frameworks in which children and parents are embedded. Instead of treating children as private property of their parents, assigning to parents the duty to look after their welfare, we would treat children as a natural resource the protection of which is critical to the future of human societies and the responsibility for which is shared by all. Where the concept of children as private property implies that parents are responsible for the well-being of children, a natural resource perspective emphasizes that we all must be held accountable for our success or failure in caring for the next and future generations. This approach would focus on systemic prevention rather than on individualized punishment after harms have occurred.

### *Why the American Macrosystem Is So Toxic to Children*

Using an ecological paradigm would also begin to explain why children fare so poorly in one of the most affluent societies in world history. The dominant macrosystem in the United States is characterized by a number of mutually reinforcing values and ideologies. These include a belief in individual responsibility, the myth of individual autonomy, a belief in free market efficiency as the measure of good, and faith in consumption as the engine of the free market (Fineman, 2004; Woodhouse, in press). The American macrosystem is also characterized by deep-seated prejudices that divide people along lines of race, class, gender, and increasingly of religion (Guinier & Torres, 2002; Pew Research Center, 2005; Roberts, 2002). Americans embrace a success ethic, whether called survival of the fittest or a "meritocracy," that rejects as unworthy those who falter in climbing the ladder of success (McCord, 1997). This chapter uses the shorthand of "privatization" to describe the political, economic, and cultural directions in which these beliefs and ideologies have driven us. According to scholars as diverse as Martha Fineman (2004) and Amitai Etzioni (1999), Americans have developed a romanticized affair with the notion of the private and the individual, and have undervalued the public and the collective.

The autonomy myth and the focus on individual responsibility are deeply unfair to children. Very young children are clearly not autonomous nor can they be charged with responsibility for their condition in life (Singer, this volume). Children make no "choices" about whether to be born, about the families into which they are born, or about the caretaking resources available or unavailable to them. Whatever chance they may have at achieving autonomy depends on the emotional and material resources invested in them during their childhood. Yet the dominance within the American macrosystem of ideals such as the autonomy myth, market efficiency, and the value of consumption colors every aspect of the child's life. These ideals influence how family is defined, how childhood is defined, and how the good parent is defined, even by parents themselves (Woodhouse, 2004). Parents who work double shifts in order to provide their child with the largest house and the latest technological toys, are living out the myths of a macrosystem that measures the success of families by where they live and what they own, rather than by the quality of interactions *within* those homes and around those possessions. These same myths dictate how we respond to poor children and children who engage in or are victims of violence (Polakow, 2000).

To the extent we see victimization and violence as private failures of the family in raising and protecting the child, this viewpoint artificially confines us to solutions that ignore the systems in which children live. School shootings and sexual predators do not exist in isolation from the gun culture, the schoolyard bully, and the marketing and consumption of child pornography. Adopting an ecological approach, on the other hand, would require us to examine critically our individualist assumptions and confront the ways they affect the lives of children. Ecologists study habitats and the systems within them. Thus, ecology provides a very different way of looking at problems than the American legal paradigm of volition and choice, freedom and lack of freedom that characterizes our criminal, tort, contract, and even family law. An ecological approach poses questions that are more relevant to children's lives. It asks us to recognize the interaction of systems and the inevitable impact of systems on the organisms that inhabit them.

## ADAPTING THE LESSONS OF ENVIRONMENTALISM TO CHILDREN, CULTURE, AND VIOLENCE

Adopting an ecological model may draw attention to a toxic cultural macrosystem. However, it cannot, alone, transform the macrosystem. In order to affect the macrosystem, scientists and advocates for children need to articulate and promote an environmental ethics for children. This process will involve either rethinking and rejecting, or consciously reaffirming, ethical frameworks that pervade our laws and policies (Flournoy, 2003). The literature of environmentalism is rich with examples of ecological thinking that might inform that process.

First, environmentalists have utilized the notion of "deep ecology" to express the need for a seismic change in how we conceptualize problems. Deep ecology advocates dealing with environmental problems by diving into the depths rather than swimming on the surface (Naess, 1973, 1989). Deep ecology challenges the dominant Western paradigm of Newtonian science by approaching nature as something to be divided into parts and classified according to a set of rules based on mathematics and logic (Merchant, 1992). Deep ecology adopts instead a relational model that sees all organisms, including but not limited to man, as intrinsically interrelated. Deep ecology acknowledges the key roles of diversity and symbiosis. In addressing the natural environment, deep ecology looks at all the organisms, plants as well as animals, that share the environment and promotes the equal right to live and blossom of all organisms as a fundamental value (Merchant, 1992; Naess, 1973, 1989).

Deep ecology confronts the fallacy of a phenomenon environmentalists have labeled as "human exemptionalism" (Naess, 1973, 1989). Human exemptionalism is a form of environmental hubris that has characterized periods of abundance and expansion in human history. This paradigm assumes that human societies are exempt from the consequences of ecological principles and environmental constraints that threaten every other organism. Deep ecology recognizes that humans are subject to the same ecological laws and restraints as other organisms (Merchant, 1992). Ignoring the linkages and feedbacks that connect humans and the ecosystems in which they are embedded courts disaster. The same is true for ignoring changes to the ecosystems in which children are embedded.

Another strand of environmentalism that seems singularly relevant to children's environmentalism is "ecofeminism" (Merchant, 1992). The ecofeminist movement honors reproduction construed in its broadest sense to include the continued biological and social reproduction of human life and the continuance of all forms of life on Earth. A commitment to continuance of life on Earth makes explicit the linkages between what we do in the present and what happens in our children's future. It also emphasizes the connection between the actions and fates of individuals and the future of the relationships and ecological communities that are necessary for reproduction to occur and for the next generation to survive and thrive (Merchant, 1992). Both the values of ecofeminism and the fallacy of human exemptionalism should infuse our approach to issues of violence.

"Sustainable development" is a third strand of environmental thought that may prove relevant in thinking about our approach to children, culture, and violence. Sustainable development seeks to convert ecologically destructive development into environmentally sound and sustainable production and reproduction (Merchant, 1992). Its tactics are small in scale and intimate in design. For example, "biological control"—the use of native or natural organisms to fight invasive bacteria, plants, and animals—is presumed safer and more sustainable than insecticides or antibiotics (Merchant, 1992). This approach may have something to teach us about designing programs to prevent and respond to child abuse and neglect. Adherents of biological control, rather than attempting to eradicate a pest with powerful chemicals, will surround the field with undeveloped woods that harbor its natural enemies (Merchant, 1992). By the same token, offering quality preschools and other community-based services to at-risk children may be more effective and less costly, on an ecological scale over time, than incarcerating them for antisocial behavior when they reach adulthood (Yoshikawa, 1995).

Another concept, "restoration ecology," aims to restore the natural balance destroyed by human interventions. In designing remedies for past destruction, studying natural patterns and replicating them allows us to utilize the wisdom inherent in evolution (Merchant, 1992). The concept of restoration ecology mirrors the philosophy behind tested and successful approaches like community-based family systems therapy as an environmentally focused response to problems of delinquent youths, as described by Mark Fondacaro in Chapter 18 of this volume. "Bioregionalism" draws attention to the localized nature of ecological habitats and the importance of understanding their unique features and intrinsic diversity (Merchant, 1992). Bioregionalism in children's policy suggests a preference for policies that are culturally competent, and that recognize and build upon the uniqueness of the child's cultural, ethnic, or religious community.

Environmentalists also have much to teach advocates for children about avoiding paralysis in the face of scientific uncertainty and natural flux (Farber, 2003). The most common critique leveled at the "best interest" standard, which governs many legal decisions affecting children, is that it is too "indeterminate" and thus invites ideologically driven decisions. Many critics doubt whether we can separate scientific facts about children's welfare from subjective values (Woodhouse, 2004). Critics of regulation of media violence to protect children fear that we will be unable to distinguish toxic violence from speech that should be protected (Ashcroft, 2004). Environmentalists, rather than rejecting science as useless because it is inconclusive, would accept as a given that science is inherently value laden and incapable of precisely measuring or predicting the impacts of regulation on ecosystems. The "precautionary principle," made explicit in various environmental treaties and conventions, holds that we should not require scientific certainty about the precise effects of a course of conduct before regulating it, if the possible risks of leaving it unregulated may be serious or irreversible (United Nations Environment Programme, 1992). The precautionary principle when applied to issues of children, culture, and violence, suggests that we know enough about the harms of exposure to media and domestic violence and the corrosive effects of concentrated poverty to justify taking focused action to combat them. The precautionary principle would support action to reduce levels of cultural violence, despite scientific uncertainties about the costs and benefits, whenever the risks of inaction appear to be sufficiently high.

Tempering this principle are the related concepts of "ecological dynamics" and "adaptive management." Ecological dynamics recognizes that systems are not static or even, as commonly assumed, in balance. Ecological systems are in flux, because they are open systems and affected by complex outside influences. Policies that assume that existing conditions represent an immutable natural order lack the necessary resilience to respond to change and may eventually break down from stressors they previously appeared to tolerate or absorb (Bosselman, 2001; Holling & Sanderson, 1996). As applied to our responses to the culture of violence, the cautionary principle, an appreciation of ecological dynamics, and a commitment to adaptive management suggest we must be willing to make mistakes and willing to correct them. Our assumptions and intuitions about what works and what does not work can be tested and adjusted to reflect new realities. Policies and programs may be evaluated under widely accepted measures to determine their effectiveness (Brooks-Gunn and Duncan, 1997; Gomby, Larner, Stevenson, Lewit, & Behrman, 1995). Theories, like witnesses, can be cross-examined and impeached, and rejected if they lose their persuasive power or are overtaken by new scientific discoveries.

Not only the theories but also the successes and failures of environmentalists have much to teach us. The experiences of environmentalists provide a precedent for the sort of paradigm shift that will be needed to affect the macrosystem. Environmentalists' 20th-century challenge to an individualist model of regulation of the environment was at least partially successful, shifting the terms of debate away from a discourse of individual responsibility and individual liberty toward appropriate interventions to protect clean air and water and to preserve environments for the healthy growth of humans and other species (Tarlock, 2004). Advocates who propose an environmentalist approach to the culture of violence should be heartened by the knowledge that radical changes have occurred in other areas related to family law and policy. We have rejected laws that constructed relations between the sexes as a rigid, gendered hierarchy (*Orr v. Orr,* 1979). We have challenged traditional family law principles that treated children as the quasi-property of their parents (Woodhouse, 1992). A child-centered paradigm, the "best interest of the child" standard, is now the dominant principle of family law. This more child-centered and ecologically sound ideal provides a foundation for constructing a more effective and child-centered response to the culture of violence (American Law Institute, 1998).

## A CHILD-CENTERED ENVIRONMENTALIST PARADIGM: ECOGENERISM

Science measures outcomes. But it does not define what outcomes are valued or how. It does not define "the good" (Flournoy, 2003). In earlier writings, this author proposed a new "ism" called "generism" to express the paramount value we should place on nurturing the next generation (Woodhouse, 1993). A generist theory places children at the center of society and sees the highest goal of society as fostering the growth of the next generation. In making their case, generists adopt and adapt many of the concepts of feminism (Woodhouse, 1993). For example, they utilize practical reasoning to interrogate existing norms; they ask "the child question"—how have children's agency and interest been overlooked?—and they employ oppositional narrative, telling the stories of marginalized groups that challenge majority assumptions and stereotypes (Woodhouse, 1993).

In recent work, this author has begun to reframe the concept as "ecogenerism"—much as the notion of feminism inspired ecofeminism (Woodhouse, 2004). Ecogenerism is closely related to ecofeminism, which sees reproduction, rather than production, as the primary work of human society. Ecofeminism's woman-centered perspective moves the work of reproduction, done in large part by women, from the periphery to the center of society (Merchant, 1992). Ecofeminism challenges environmentalists and policy makers to examine the impact of policies with particular attention to their effects on the ecology of reproduction, in humans as well as plants and animals. In preserving habitats for the survival of wild salmon, for example, it is clearly not enough to count individual fish without paying attention to their role in the cycle of reproduction. The same is true of humans. A stark example of an ecofeminist natural disaster occurred in the tsunami that struck in the Indian Ocean in 2004. Because of their smaller size and lesser ability to resist the flood waters, far more women than men perished, leaving many affected communities bereft of not only wives and mothers but also of essential resources for reproduction and nurturing ("Report: Tsunami," 2005). Manmade disasters occur when societies fail to value the work of reproduction in their estimates of costs and benefits, as when a society fails to provide health care to pregnant women and infants or devalues the social worth of female babies ("Grim motives," 2003; "Report: Tsunami, 2005; Stark, 2003).

Ecogenerism, like ecofeminism, is a particular brand of environmental ethics. It is an ethics focusing on children's welfare and the future of children as the core definition of "the good," as opposed to other measures such as maximizing the greatest good for the greatest number or market efficiency. Ecogenerists, for example, might call for an environmental impact statement examining the impact of policies and conduct not only on existing children but also on future generations.

Ecogenerism, however, must borrow the insights of deep ecology and strive to dig deeper than generism. It must see "the good" in more natural and ecologically sensitive terms than a traditional legal standard of best interest of the child would encompass. Ecogenerism would examine policies toward the culture of violence with reference to communities as well as individuals, and with reference to mesosystems, microsystems, and exosystems, rather than with reference to narrow issues of parental success or failure (Woodhouse, 2004). Ecogenerists would identify not only the production of new generations, but also their flourishing and growth, as the most important outcome to be gained from fostering the stability, integrity, and beauty of the community (Flournoy, 2003). Of crucial importance, ecogenerism would take a child-centered perspective and would define "flourishing" through children's eyes and children's experiences. Rather than assuming that children serve as the passive objects of others' actions, ecogenerism would respect the ecology of childhood and the central role that children themselves play in their own development.

Empirical research would occupy a pivotal role. Imagine a regulatory scheme to preserve the environment for children's healthy development and flourishing that relied on established evidence-based benchmarks similar to those in various environmental laws (*American Forest and Paper Association, Inc. v. EPA*, 2002). For example, courts have invalidated government policies regarding endangered species such as grizzly bears and trumpeter swans that purported to adequately protect these species as required by environmental laws, but ignored the weight of the scientific evidence (*Carlton v. Babbit*, 1995; *Friends of the Wild Swan v. U.S. Fish & Wildlife Serv.*, 1997; *Fund for Animals v. Norton*, 2003; *Fund for Animals v. Williams*, 2003; *Moden v. U.S. Fish & Wildlife Serv.*, 2003;). Imagine a judge adjudicating child and family regulations who could strike down ideologically driven proposals (whether from the left or the right) as politically motivated and contrary to the weight of scientific evidence. Obviously, as scientists recognize, science itself is not value neutral or apolitical (Doremus, 2004). Nevertheless, science provides more objective benchmarks to the fact-finder than do opinion and ideology, which cannot be held accountable to empirical research standards.

## APPLYING ECOGENERIST THEORY TO ISSUES OF CHILDREN, CULTURE, AND VIOLENCE

How would ecogenerism work on specific issues? In this section, I will apply an ecogenerist analysis to explore two issues that present special challenges to legal attempts to protect American children from a culture of violence. One is the problem of toxic violence on the Internet. The second is the problem of youth violence as an adaptive response to a violent environment.

### *Cleaning Up Toxic Internet Sites*

As discussed earlier, while alarm has been expressed about the effects of violent media on children, the legal response has been limited by our assumptions that images that assault the senses, as opposed to physical assaults, are presumptively harmless. As we have seen, the legal response to regulation of violent images has been framed in terms of First Amendment freedoms of speech. Images are treated as a form of protected expression unless they are shown to be obscene—defined as materials appealing to the prurient interest and lacking any redeeming social value. The literature on the First Amendment is vast, and the cases relating to children have been discussed in depth by Catherine Ross in this volume. I agree with Ross that children are entitled to First Amendment protections of their access to information and culture on the Internet and elsewhere. I also see the danger that "protecting our children" can be invoked by a dominant political majority as a justification for ideological censorship of controversial but truthful and valuable ideas and information (UN, 1989).

But I disagree with the notion that, in order to protect free speech, we must accept our inability to regulate the current flood of violent images when we have solid evidence of their harmful effects on children's healthy development. While violence is an issue that cuts across all the media, the Internet poses special problems. The Internet is an ecological system and consequently evades an analysis based solely on individual responsibility. Control of the Internet is decentralized. Anyone can post an image. With the exception of obscene materials, including child pornography, there are few legal limits on what may be posted. Due to the ease of Internet transmission, there has been a surge in child pornography, especially of images involving violence, with 20,000 images of child pornography posted every week. (Malcolm, 2003). Purveyors of sex and sexual violence go to great lengths to reach out to consumers with pop-up ads and e-mails and employ techniques such as "mousetrapping" to prevent those who enter from exiting their sites (Malcolm, 2003). Parents are encouraged to install filtering software to block children's access to inappropriate sites. However, these filters only block 1 in 3 sites from accidental access. Computer-savvy children who want to defeat the filters are extremely adept at doing so, gaining access to 9 out of 10 blocked sites in one Kaiser Foundation study (*Ashcroft v. American Civil Liberties Union,* 2004).

Congress has enacted several different schemes to address children's access to objectionable materials, but all have come up against the barrier of First Amendment doctrines as interpreted by the U.S. Supreme Court. The most recent round of legislation to reach the Court was the Computer Online

Protection Act (COPA) (1998). COPA imposed a fine of up to $50,000 and a prison term of up to 6 months on operators of Web sites that allow children to access materials that are "harmful to minors." Web sites that established a credit card, pin number, or electronic verification system to verify a patron's age would be protected from liability. The Supreme Court, in *Ashcroft v. American Civil Liberties Union* (2004), held that this scheme was "overbroad" and violated the First Amendment. First Amendment doctrine requires the use of the least restrictive alternative. Since COPA's scheme of user verification impinged on adults' access to protected speech, its defenders would have to show that no less restrictive means existed to protect children. The Court remanded the case, asking the trial court to address whether filters provided a less restrictive and yet effective means to achieve congressional ends. According to the Court, filters posed a lesser free speech threat because they regulated speech at the receiving end, rather than at the source (*Ashcroft v. American Civil Liberties Union,* 2004).

Another First Amendment principle that leads to regulation at the receiving end rather than the source is a concern for pluralism and respect for the diversity of American cultural and social norms. Speech and other forms of expression are viewed, quite properly, through a cultural lens. Courts have measured whether a particular material was obscene with reference to the sensibilities of the community, rather than using more objective criteria such as evidence of harmful effects on the viewer (*Miller v. California,* 1973). The courts have looked to local community standards to determine whether an image merited First Amendment protection or could be suppressed as patently offensive and lacking redeeming social value. Time, place, and manner restrictions have also been upheld. Thus, an adult-themed film that could be shown in New York City near Times Square might be kept out of theaters in an Iowa City suburb (*City of Renton v. Playtime Theatres,* 1986). The Internet evades such localized regulation, since it crosses geographical and political boundaries and reaches consumers in their homes in every corner of the world.

In summary, under a First Amendment analysis, whether an image may be regulated may depend on whether it offends community values rather than whether it contains objective evidence of harmful effects. Even where an image is recognized as toxic to children, the First Amendment approach typically rejects regulation at the "source" and favors regulation by individual families downstream. Regulation is confined to the alternative that is least restrictive of individual rights of adults to view the images, rather than framed as a search for the most effective means, given the balance of individual rights and societal costs and benefits.

At least one critic of treating violent images as protected speech has argued that depictions of extreme violence are by their very nature obscene. Thus, regardless of the age or developmental stage of the viewer, violent images that are patently offensive and lack redeeming social value may be suppressed by government without infringing upon the First Amendment (Saunders, 1996). While this author agrees with many of the points made by those who argue that violent images should be subject to regulation as obscenity, the First Amendment framework seems inherently ill suited to addressing the seriousness and the complexity of the effects on children of growing up in a culture saturated with violence. Ultimately, a focus on First Amendment theory falls short of integrating all aspects of the culture of violence in a comprehensive analysis.

How would an ecogenerist theory using the tools of an environmentalist approach analyze the role of law in regulating the culture of violence and its effects on children?

As an initial matter, it would place children at the center of the analysis rather than at the periphery. First Amendment theory is predicated on free speech rights of an adult audience, and treats children as the marginalized exception to the rule. When considering violent images, we begin with the assumption that adults' access to such images is a constitutionally protected right. Defenders of free expression often warn that regulation to protect children will lead to a culture composed only of images that are fit for children (*Ashcroft v. American Civil Liberties Union,* 2004). Environmentalists take a different approach to environmental toxins. Toxins that pose a threat to living organisms are judged by their harmful effects on the most vulnerable of growing organisms, with special attention to regeneration of organic systems (Schon, 2004). The argument that some mature organisms can tolerate extreme doses and constant exposure to toxic images seems irrelevant when our focus is not on the adult's individual freedom to consume harmful substances, but rather on the survival of the young of our species. Why should we assume that a world made safe for children would be unfit for adults? The children of the world were drawing on a powerful environmentalist metaphor when they argued at the UN 2002 Special Summit on Children that "A World Fit for Children Is a World Fit for Everyone" (Woodhouse, 2003).

Environmentalists also favor regulating toxic emissions at their source, whenever feasible (Ratcliffe, 2004). Public education and industry self-regulation is encouraged but, if it fails in effectiveness, government regulation will be imposed. They understand that citizens are unable to avoid and control pervasive environmental toxins. They also understand that assigning to parents the right and responsibility to decide whether to expose their children to toxins places the children at serious risk. I have yet to hear a politician say, "Let them buy their children bottled water" when presented with a citizen complaint about the quality of the water flowing in the municipal drinking water systems. Neither do politicians respond with, "Let them keep their children indoors" when confronted by parents complaining about toxic levels of air pollution. Lead paint provides another example. One answer to the problem of children's exposure to lead paint is parent education. We warn parents not to rent or buy contaminated homes. But we do not stop there; we take additional steps such as banning manufacture of lead paint, requiring lead paint abatement by landlords, and providing chelation therapy for children exposed to lead (Souchuns, 1998).

The precautionary principle and the adaptive approach, when put together, promote a philosophy of taking cautious corrective action without demanding conclusive proof of its effectiveness in averting possible harms. As noted by Craig Anderson in this volume, regulators have discounted evidence that clearly establishes but falls short of conclusively proving a causal connection between harm to children and exposure to media violence. Similarly, the opposition to regulation of advertising junk foods to children is predicated on a lack of conclusive evidence of causation (Woodhouse, 2004). In choosing corrective actions, the adaptive approach suggests avoiding actions that are irreversible and set in stone. Operating assumptions must be open to reexamination. For example, the Supreme Court in *Ashcroft v. Free Speech Coalition* (2002) concluded that virtual child pornography (using digitized images rather than photographs of real children) is not covered by bans on child pornography. The Court reasoned that the harm at issue in child pornography is the harm inflicted on real children when they are made to participate in creation of pornographic images. Research on the effects on pedophiles of viewing and manipulating digitized images of children as objects of sexual gratification and sexual violence might suggest that the threat of child pornography to children as a group has been underestimated (Ladle, 2004). Concepts like bioregionalism and restoration ecology find their social work counterparts in cultural competency training and systems therapy (Fondacaro & Fesig, this volume). Viewing children in their ecological context also makes clear the futility of trying to deal with children in isolation from the systems that affect and surround them.

An environmentalist perspective would shift the analysis to measuring environmental harms to children and addressing them at their source rather than privatizing responsibility for protecting children's environment. An environmentalist analysis rejects the notion that the level of toxin we permit or prohibit in water supplies depends on subjective community values. We need not accept that the freedom of some to consume harmful quantities of a toxic substance trumps the protection of the many who are collaterally affected by a failure to address the toxins at their source.

Under this theory, I would ask lawmakers to challenge the assumption that expression is not harmful unless it leads to a direct physical assault or immediate injury—consider the examples of crying "fire!" in a crowded theater or calling for a rope at a lynching. However, I would place the burden on those seeking regulation to show that specific images delivered in a particular form and dosage are actually harmful to children and not just offensive to the regulator's eye. Drawing upon an environmental analogy, a tangled forest may seem offensive and unkempt but imposing order on the landscape may actually do more damage than good. We also need to address the most serious threats to the environment first. According to current research, while exposure to sexually explicit materials may have some adverse effects on children, violent materials including sexually explicit violence are far more damaging (Saunders, 1996).

In the context of legislation like COPA (1998), we might try approaching regulation of images in a more complex way. There are many other mechanisms besides criminal penalties that can be used to create disincentives for marketing images of obscene and senseless violence to children. We must utilize science rather than public opinion to determine which materials are, indeed, "harmful to children." If filters are shown to be an effective method of protection, we should promote their development and implementation through noncoercive financial incentives. But we cannot stop there, leaving the child's safety to parents who may lack the power or knowledge to ensure it. We must consider public alternatives, such as product safety legislation analogous to laws that require automakers to install safety devices on all their products so that a child-safe product is the norm rather than the exception. If the devices we have invented, like the V-Chip, fail in their protective function, we must find better alternatives for protecting children from the collateral effects of adult conduct. When it comes to extremely dangerous emissions that are concentrated in toxic levels emanating from identifiable sources, we must be able to regulate them at their source. If the most effective way to prevent harms to children is to prevent them from entering a dangerous environment, while preserving access for mature adults, then the First Amendment should not foreclose requiring sites hosting harmful materials (clearly and scientifically defined) to "card" or otherwise verify the ages of those who seek entrance.

### *Punishment Versus Prevention: Restoring Toxic Neighborhoods*

A second example of an ecological approach is considering the treatment of juveniles in the criminal justice system. The benefits of this approach can best be seen by considering the treatment of a first-time juvenile offender in our current system. Consider the case of a child we shall call X, who was the subject of one multidisciplinary case review in which this author participated. X was convicted of murder at age 14. Raised by a single mother in a violent inner-city neighborhood, he was bullied on the streets and in school from a young age. A skinny kid and an easy mark, he began to carry a gun. Confronted by a 21-year-old bully named Y, he fired a shot into Y's foot and, when Y kept coming, X shot him in the heart. Had X reasonably believed his life was in danger, this might have been excused as self-defense. But it was clear that X simply wanted the bullying to stop.

At the time of the crime, X was functionally illiterate. Of average intelligence, he had passed through each grade level without learning how to read. In ninth grade, he knew how to write only four words. A family history revealed that he had been abused by his father who abandoned the family years before. He was being raised by a timid mother, herself a victim of domestic violence who was isolated from community resources because she spoke very little English.

The justice system addresses the problem of X's violence against Y as a question of individual responsibility for intentionally harmful acts that resulted in Y's death. With X as the accused and Y as the victim, the state's role would ordinarily be limited to determining guilt and meting out punishment. However, in recognition that children are less culpable and more amenable to rehabilitation, we created the juvenile justice system (Redding, this volume). Juvenile law would have treated X as a resource needing restoration and placed him in a juvenile facility designed to rehabilitate, rather than simply to punish. His criminal record would be expunged and he would be freed at age 21 to succeed or fail in the adult world. But X's case was complicated by the more recent trend to give juveniles "adult time for adult crime" (Redding, this volume). X received a blended sentence of 30 years. He would be held in a juvenile facility until age 21, at which point he would be released if he could show that he had been rehabilitated. If not, he would serve the rest of his sentence in an adult prison.

Seven years later, when he turned 21, X's case was up for review. In the intervening years, X had completed his secondary education through a prison-based general equivalency degree (GED) program. He had also earned a number of college-level credits. He was a leader in his peer group, and his most serious infraction of rules had been pushing another kid on the basketball court. His teachers unanimously recommended he be released, with access to follow-up services. Nevertheless, the authorities decided he had not been rehabilitated and must serve his adult time. The risk that he might reoffend was unacceptable in a political climate that severely punishes officials who err on the side of clemency.

Our first instinct might be to complain that the system had failed X by mislabeling him. Once labeled a criminal, X was defined by a single act of violence. A common nostrum among children's lawyers holds that law tends to label children as "bad, sad, mad, or can't add." The bad child is a delinquent, the mad child is mentally ill, the sad child is abused or neglected, and the child who cannot add is learning disabled. Why, we might ask, had X not been identified earlier as a victim of abuse, which might have opened the door of the dependency system where the focus would have been on providing his family with services and support? Why had he not been diagnosed earlier as a child with a severe learning disability, and provided with a key to the special education system, where an Individualized Educational Plan may have opened the door to school success? Given the pattern of bullying by peers, why had he and his family not been identified as a child or family "in need of services," which might have opened the door of the systems tasked with providing community-based services to assist children and families at risk for delinquency? Given our current paradigm of individual responsibility and family autonomy, the system failure lies in our having failed to correctly label the "at-risk" child so that he can be provided with services. I believe the current paradigm leaves us searching for the right answers to the wrong questions.

If we place X and his situation in ecological context, our problem solving is entirely different. We can clearly see the relationship between the violence he inflicted and the violence he witnessed and experienced. The violence was not confined to his family but pervaded the environments of school, street, and peer group. Even a stable and authoritative two-parent family preaching nonviolence has difficulty overcoming the dissonant messages within mesosystems where the family overlaps with the other microsystems in which the child lives his life. As this volume shows, violence in children's lives is rarely an isolated episode; it is endemic, as described by Dowd in her introduction to this volume. In searching for the roots of environmental violence, social scientists have pointed to the relationship of violence and poverty or low socioeconomic status, exacerbated by effects of race, class, and gender (Polakow, 2000; Sampson, 1997).

One might argue that such vast societal problems are simply beyond the purview of the law. Law, one might argue, can only deal with individual failures, not with microsystems, mesosytems, or macrosystems. Individuals must be responsible for protecting themselves from environmental harms and must answer for their autonomous acts without using the culture of violence as an excuse. This is the same fallacious and short-sighted reasoning that might have prevented us from reforming our legal systems to address the ecological crisis we faced in the 20th century. In fact, law in the form of legislation *can* address environmental harms by focusing on prevention of environmental degradation and on restoration of healthy ecological systems.

Drawing on social science research, legal scholars have argued that relatively simple and straightforward policies and programs can produce significant measurable improvements in legal outcomes, whether measured in reductions in children's pain and suffering or in reduced expenditures for special education, criminal justice, and child protection (Garrison, in press; Minow, 1994). Quality early-childhood programs, such as maternal and infant care, Head Start, and others, as well as early delinquency–prevention programs and programs that reduce child poverty, show promise for reducing family violence, enhancing school readiness, improving children's mental and physical health, and insulating children from many environmental risks (Gomby et al., 1995; Mulvey, Arthur, & Reppucci, 1997; Solow, 1994; Yoshikawa, 1995). Designing a comprehensive, ecologically sensitive program for reducing violence in children's environment is beyond the scope of this chapter and beyond my skills as a lawyer. It requires a scientifically sophisticated, evidence-based approach. It may require ignoring myths and ideologies that conflict with the evidence. Certainly, as a first step, we must get beyond our current impasse of blaming the endangered species for their own endangerment and expecting them to rebalance an ecosystem that is out of their control.

However, none of this can be accomplished without major changes in the macrosystems that impose the myth of individual autonomy that fosters a paradigm of human exemptionalism and obscures the fact that we are linked in a fragile ecosystem characterized by interconnectedness.

## CONCLUSION

I have outlined the differences between an ecological approach and our current approach to children's issues. The data and observations confirm that, at present, we are miserably failing our children, and by extension, our species. We continue to build zoological and botanical gardens, such as foster care, where at-risk children can be removed from their environment for observation. We spend vast amounts of money on penal and leper colonies, the institutions where endangered children are isolated and confined. And those with options are creating private parks and palaces, those private schools and gated communities where the affluent believe they can shelter their own from the dangers posed by a pervasive culture of violence.

I have suggested that we must replace our current ideologies with a new ideology of ecogenerism. Our first line of action is to create a new macrosystem, shifting the power and ideology of individualism toward an ecogenerist ethic that meets the actual needs of children. Guided by the precautionary principle and adaptive approach, if we cannot instantly create a macrosystem that is safe for children, then we should find a way to isolate harmful images and activities in adult zones, or, at the very least, to create a system of child-safe spaces and refuges.

## REFERENCES


Abbey, E. (1988). *Desert solitaire.* Tucson: University of Arizona Press.

American Forest and Paper Association, Inc. v. EPA, 294 F.3d 113 (D.C. Cir. 2002).

American Law Institute. (1998). *Principles of the law of family dissolution: Analysis and recommendations, tentative draft no. 3.* Washington, DC: Author.

Amnesty International. (2003). *Democratic Republic of Congo: Children at war.* Retrieved March 25, 2005, from http://www.web.amnesty.org/library/index/engafr620342003

Anderson, K. (2000). War games. *Hunger Notes.* Retrieved March 25, 2005, from http://www.worldhunger.org/articles/fa11200/anderson.htm

Ashcroft v. American Civil Liberties Union, 124 S. Ct. 2783 (2004).

Ashcroft v. Free Speech Coalition, 535 U.S. 234 (2002).

Bosselman, F. (2001). A role for state planning: Intergenerational equity and adaptive management. *University of Florida Journal of Law and Public Policy, 12,* 311–333.

Brandenburg v. Ohio, 395 U.S. 444 (1969).

Bronfenbrenner, U. (1979). *The ecology of human development: Experiments by nature and design.* Cambridge, MA: Harvard University Press.

Brooks-Gunn, J., & Duncan, G. (1997). The effects of poverty on children. *The Future of the Children, 7(2)* 55–71.

Burstyn, Inc. v. Wilson, 343 U.S. 495 (1952).

Carlton v. Babbitt, 900 F. Supp. 526 (D.D.C. 1995).

Carson, R. (1962). *Silent spring.* Boston: Houghton Mifflin.

City of Renton v. Playtime Theatres, 475 U.S. 41 (1986).

Computer Online Protection Act (COPA), 47 U.S.C. § 231(c)(1) (1998).

Doremus, H. (2004). The purposes, effects, and future of the endangered species act's best available science mandate. *Environmental Law, 34*(2), 397–450.

Dowd, N. (2004). Bringing the margin to the center: Comprehensive strategies for work/family policies. *University of Cincinnati Law Review, 73,* 1–23.

Etzioni, A. (1999). *The limits of privacy.* New York: Basic Books.

Farber, D. A. (2003). Probabilities behaving badly: Complexity theory and environmental uncertainty. *University of California Davis Law Review, 37,* 145–172.

Fineman, M. A. (2004). *The autonomy myth: A theory of dependency.* New York: New Press.

Flournoy, A.C. (2003). In search of an environmental ethic. *Columbia Journal of Environmental Law, 28,* 63–118.

Friends of the Wild Swan v. U.S. Fish & Wildlife Serv., 12 F. Supp. 2d 1121 (D. Or. 1997).

Fund for Animals v. Norton, 294 F. Supp. 2d 92 (D.C.C. 2003).

Fund for Animals v. Williams, 246 F. Supp. 2d 27 (D.D.C. 2003).

Garbarino, J. (1985). *Adolescent development: An ecological perspective.* Columbus, OH: Merrill.

Garbarino, J. (1995). *Raising children in a socially toxic environment.* San Francisco: Jossey-Bass.

Garbarino, J., Dubrow, N., Kostelny, K., & Pardo, C. (1992). *Children in danger: Coping with the consequence of community violence.* San Francisco: Jossey-Bass.

Garrison, M. (in press). Reforming child protection: A public health perspective. *University of Virginia Journal of Social Policy and the Law.*

Ginsberg v. New York, 390 U.S. 629 (1968).

Gomby, D. S., Larner, M. B., Stevenson, C. S., Lewit, E. M., & Berhman, R. E. (1995). Long-term outcomes of early childhood programs: Analysis and recommendations. *The Future of the Children, 5*(3), 6–24.

*Grim motives behind infant killings.* (2003). Retrieved March 28, 2005, from http://www.cnn.com/2003/WORLD/asiapcf/south/07/07/india.infanticide.pt1/index.html

Guinier, L., & Torres, G. (2002). *Miner's canary: Enlisting race, resisting power, transforming democracy.* Cambridge, MA: Harvard University Press.

Halberstam, D. (1998). *The children.* New York: Random House.

Holling, C. S., & Sanderson, S. (1996). Dynamics of (dis)harmony in ecological and social systems. In S. Hanna, C. Folke, & K-G. Maler. (Eds.), *Rights to nature: Ecological, economic, cultural, and political principles of institutions for the environment.* Washington, DC: Island Press.

James, A. (2004). Understanding childhood from an interdisciplinary perspective: Problems and potentials. In P. Pufall & R. Unsworth (Eds.), *Rethinking childhood.* New Brunswick, NJ: Rutgers University Press.

Kincheloe, J. (1998). The new childhood: Home alone as a way of life. In H. Jenkins (Ed.), *The children's culture reader.* New York: New York University Press.

Konner, M. (1991). *Childhood.* Boston: Little, Brown.

Kotlowitz, A. (1991). *There are no children here: The story of two boys growing up in the other America.* New York: Doubleday.

Kozol, J. (1991). *Savage inequalities.* New York: Crown.

Ladle, J. (2004). Protecting pedophiles and valuing virtual child pornography: A critique of Ashcroft v. Free Speech Coalition. *Idaho Law Review, 40,* 457–507.

Malcolm, J. (2003). *Indecent exposure: Oversight of DOJ's efforts to protect pornography's victims.* Retrieved April 2, 2005, from http:/judiciary.senate.gov/testimony.cfm?id=961&wit_id=2559

McCord, J. (1997). Placing American urban violence in context. In J. McCord (Ed.), *Violence and childhood in the inner city*. Cambridge, UK: Cambridge University Press.

Merchant, C. (1992). *Radical ecology: The search for a livable world*. New York: Routledge.

Meyer v. Nebraska, 262 U.S. 390 (1923).

Miller v. California, 413 U.S. 15 (1973).

Minow, N. (1994). Learning from experience: the impact of research about family support programs on public policy. *Univ. of Pennsylvania Law Review 143*, 221–252.

Minow, N., & Lamay, C. (1995). *Abandoned in the wasteland: Children, television, and the First Amendment*. New York: Hill & Wang.

Moden v. U.S. Fish & Wildlife Serv., 281 F. Supp. 2d 1193 (D. Or. 2003).

Mulvey, E. P., Arthur, M. W., & Reppucci, N. D. (1997). The prevention of juvenile delinquency: A review of the research [Electronic version]. *The Prevention Researcher, 4*(2). Retrieved March 29, 2005, from http://www.tpronline.org/print.cfm?category=Articles&ID=22§ion=articles

Naess, A. (1973). The shallow and the deep, long-range ecology movements: A summary. *Inquiry, 16*, 95–100.

Naess, A. (1989). *Ecology, community, and lifestyle*. Cambridge, MA: Cambridge University Press.

Near v. Minnesota, 283 U.S. 697 (1931).

New York Times Co. v. U.S., 403 U.S. 713 (1971).

Orr v. Orr, 440 U.S. 268 (1979).

Pearson, L. (2001). *Creativity and inequity: An environmental scan of trends in the Americas affecting children's rights and development*. Retrieved May 14, 2004, from http://www.sen.parl.gc.ca/lpearson/hill/17_htm_files/Committee-e/ENV-SCAN-EN.pdf

Pew Research Center. (2005). Religion & public life: A faith-based partisan divide. In H. Morton (Ed.), *Trends 2005*. Washington, DC: Pew Forum on Religion & Public Life.

Pierce v. Society of Sisters, 268 U.S. 510 (1925).

Polakow, V. (2000). Savage policies: systemic violence and the lives of children. In V. Polakow (Ed.), *The public assault on America's Children: poverty, violence and injustice*. New York: Teacher's College Press.

Prince v. Massachusetts, 321 U.S. 158 (1944).

Putnam, F. (1997). *Dissociation in children and adolescents: A developmental perspective*. New York: Guilford Press.

Ratcliffe, J. (2004). Reenvisioning the risk bubble: Utilizing a system of intra-firm risk trading for environmental protection. *California Law Review, 92*, 1779–1823.

R.A.V. v. City of St. Paul, 505 U.S. 377 (1992).

*Report: Tsunami hit women hardest*. (2005). Retrieved March 28, 2005 from http://www.cnn.com/2005/WORLD/asiapcf/03/26/tsunami.women.ap./index.html

Roberts, D. (2002). *Shattered bonds: The color of child welfare*. New York: Basic Books.

Sampson, R. (1997). The embeddedness of child and adolescent development: A community-level perspective on urban violence. In J. McCord (Ed.), *Violence and childhood in the inner city*. Cambridge, UK: Cambridge University Press.

Saunders, K. (1996). *Violence as obscenity*. Durham, NC: Duke University Press.

Schon, M. (2004). Susceptible children: Why the EPA's new risk assessment guidelines for children fail to protect America's future. *Arizona State Law Journal, 36,* 701–723.

Solow, R. (1994). Wasting America's future. Boston: Beacon Press.

Souchuns, A. (1998). Old paint, new laws: Achieving effective compliance with the residential lead-based paint hazard reduction act. *Catholic University Law Review, 47,* 1411–1449.

Stark, B. (2003). Baby girls from China in New York: A thrice-told tale. *Utah Law Review, 2003,* 1231–1301.

Subrahmanyam, K. (2001). New forms of electronic media: The impact of interactive games and the internet on cognition, socialization, and behavior. In D. Singer & J. Singer (Eds.), *Handbook of children and the media.* Thousand Oaks, CA: Sage.

Tarlock, A. D. (2004). Is there a there there in environmental law? *Florida State University Journal of Land Use and Environmental Law, 19,* 213–254.

Troxel v. Granville, 530 U.S. 57 (2000).

United Nations (UN). (1989). *Convention on the rights of the child: General assembly resolution 25(XLIV) 44th session: Supplement no.49* (A/RES/44/25, reprinted in 28 I.L.M. 1448).

United Nations Environment Programme. (1992). *Rio declaration on environment and development, principle 15.* Retrieved April 29, 2004, from http://www.unep.org/Document/Default.asp?DocumentID=78&ArticleID=1163

Weyrauch, W. O. (Ed.). (2001). *Gypsy law: Romani legal traditions and culture.* Berkeley: University of California Press.

Wiener, J. B., Botkin, D. B., Frampton, G., Norton, B., Profeta, T. H., Flournoy, A. C., et al. (1996). Beyond the balance of nature: Environmental law faces a new ecology. *Duke Environmental Law and Policy Forum, 7,* 1–193.

Wilcox, B. (2004). *Report of the APA Task Force on advertising to children: Recommendations.* Retrieved April 4, 2004, from http://www.apa.org/ releases/ childrenads_recommendations.pdf

Woodhouse, B. B. (1992). "Who owns the child?" Meyer and Pierce and the child as property. *William and Mary Law Review, 33,* 95–1094.

Woodhouse, B. B. (1993). Hatching the egg: A child-centered perspective on parents' rights. *Cardozo Law Review, 14,* 1747–1865.

Woodhouse, B. B. (1999). The constitutionalization of children's rights: Incorporating emerging human rights into constitutional doctrine. *University of Pennsylvania Journal of Constitutional Law, 2,* 1–52.

Woodhouse, B. B. (2003). Enhancing children's participation in policy formation. *Arizona Law Review, 45,* 751–763.

Woodhouse, B. B. (2004). Reframing the debate about the socialization of children: An environmentalist paradigm. *The University of Chicago Legal Forum, 2004,* 85–165.

Woodhouse, B. B. (in press). Ecogenerism: An environmentalist approach to protecting endangered children. *University of Virginia Journal of Social Policy and the Law.*

Yoshikawa, H. (1995). Long term effects of early childhood programs on social outcomes and delinquency. *The Future of Children, 3*(5), 51–75.

# Author Index

# *Subject Index*

# *About the Editors*

**Nancy E. Dowd** is Chesterfield Smith Professor of Law at the Fredric G. Levin College of Law at the University of Florida, and Co-Director of the Center for Children and Families at UF. The author of *In Defense of Single-Parent Families* (1997) and *Redefining Fatherhood* (2001), and a reader on feminist legal theory, she has published extensively on nontraditional families, work/family issues, civil rights, and feminist theory.

**Dorothy G. Singer** is Senior Research Scientist, Department of Psychology, Yale University. She is also Co-Director, with Jerome L. Singer, of the Yale University Family Television Research and Consultation Center, and a Fellow of Morse College at Yale. She is also a Fellow of The American Psychology Association. Research interests include early childhood development, television effects on youth, and parent training in imaginative play. She has written 19 books (some of which have been translated into Japanese, Dutch, Turkish, Italian, and Thai), and over 160 articles. Her latest books with Jerome L. Singer are *Handbook of Children and the Media, Make-Believe: Games and Activities for Imaginative Play,* and *Imagination and Play in the Electronic Age.* A recent book, *Children's Play: Roots of Reading,* edited by E. Zigler, D. Singer, and S. Bishop-Josef, was selected for CHOICE's Outstanding Academic Title list. Dr. Singer received the Distinguished Scientific Contribution to the Media Award from Division 46 of the American Psychological Association in 2004.

**Robin Fretwell Wilson** is Associate Professor of Law at the University of Maryland School of Law. She has published articles on the risks of abuse to children in the *Cornell Law Review*, the *Emory Law Journal*, the *Journal of Child and Family Studies* (two featured articles, in press), and the *Child and Family Law Quarterly,* a British publication. She has testified on the use of social science in legal decision making before the Federal Trade Commission and Department of Justice Joint Hearings on Health Care. A member of the Executive Committee of the Family and Juvenile Law Section of the Association of American Law Schools, Professor Wilson frequently lectures on violence against children, including presentations at the Family Law Project hosted by Harvard University Law School; the National Society for the Prevention of Cruelty to Children in London, England; the Third International Conference on Child and Adolescent Mental Health in Brisbane, Australia; and the IXth Regional European Conference of the International Society for the Prevention of Child Abuse and Neglect, in Warsaw, Poland. Professor Wilson is the editor of a forthcoming volume with Cambridge University Press on child and family policy entitled *Reconceiving the Family: Critical Reflections on the American Law Institute's Principles of the Law of Family Dissolution.*

# *About the Contributors*

**Craig A. Anderson** is Professor and Chair of Psychology at Iowa State University. He is a Fellow of the American Psychological Society and the American Psychological Association. Anderson's 100+ publications span many areas, including judgment and decision making; depression, loneliness, and shyness; personality theory; and attribution theory. His recent work has focused on developing the General Aggression Model, integrating insights from cognitive, developmental, personality, and social psychology. His pioneering work on video game violence has led to consultations with educators, government officials, child advocates, and news organizations worldwide.

**Laura Braslow** is a New York City–based research consultant specializing in quantitative study design and the management of administrative data for policy applications. She has conducted numerous policy-relevant research projects in the areas of criminal justice, civil liberties, good government, health care, and social and environmental justice, and is currently working on another study with Ross Cheit focusing on motions to reduce criminal sentences.

**Naomi Cahn** is Professor of Law at the George Washington University Law School, where she teaches courses on family law and children and the law. Professor Cahn has written numerous articles in the areas of children's rights and feminist jurisprudence, and recently co-edited *Families by Law: An Adoption Reader* (NYU Press, 2004). She has held a variety of positions in both the private and public interest sectors, including as a staff attorney with Philadelphia's Community Legal Services. From 1988 to 1993, Professor Cahn was the assistant director of the Sex Discrimination Clinic at Georgetown University Law Center, supervising students who were litigating domestic violence cases. Professor Cahn's contribution to this volume was greatly aided by comments from Joan Meier and Jerry Silverman and by research assistance from Terra Nevitt and Lucy Cutolo.

**Joanne Cantor** is Professor Emerita at the University of Wisconsin–Madison. She has published more than 90 scholarly articles and chapters on the impact of the media, with an emphasis on children's emotional reactions to television and films. Her parenting book, *Mommy I'm Scared: How TV and Movies Frighten Children and What We Can Do to Protect Them,* translates her research findings for the general public. Her children's book, *Teddy's TV Troubles,* helps parents and young children work together to calm fears. Cantor's Web site, www.tvtroubles.com, keeps interested parties abreast of the latest developments in research and policy.

**John Cech** is Professor of English at the University of Florida, and the Director of the University's Center for Children's Literature and Culture. He is also the producer and host of *Recess!*—a daily public radio program about the cultures of childhood, past and present. He is the author of numerous works, both scholarly and creative, for both children and adults, including: *Angels and Wild Things, The Archetypal Poetics of Maurice Sendak* (1994) and the novel, *A Rush of Dreamers, Being the Remarkable Story of Norton I, Emperor of the United States and*

*Protector of Mexico* (1998). Cech is the editor of *American Writers for Children, 1900–1960* (1982), and is a contributor of essays, articles, and reviews to both scholarly and popular publications. His children's books include *My Grandmother's Journey* (1991); *First Snow, Magic Snow* (1992); *Boy With a Camera* (1994); and *The Southernmost Cat* (1995). Cech is a past president of the Children's Literature Association, and is a recipient of the Chandler Award for his contributions to the field of Children's Literature.

**Ross E. Cheit** is an associate professor of Political Science and Public Policy at Brown University. He teaches a seminar on the criminal justice system and a course on children and public policy. He is engaged in several research projects involving criminal courts, including another project with Laura Braslow, focusing on motions to reduce criminal sentences in Rhode Island. He is also working on a book on the law and politics of child sexual abuse in contemporary America.

**Ellen W. deLara** is an assistant professor in the School of Social Work at Syracuse University and a Visiting Fellow at the Family Life Development Center, Cornell University. She is the author of *And Words Can Hurt Forever: How to Protect Adolescents From Bullying, Harassment, and Emotional Violence* (2002) and *An Educator's Guide to School-Based Interventions* (2003), both written with Dr. James Garbarino. Her research interests focus on school violence and adolescent development. Dr. deLara presents nationally and internationally on the need for systemic and policy changes to improve school climate and reduce bullying.

**Lauren G. Fasig** is the former Director of Policy and Communications for the Society for Research in Child Development. She served as the James Marshall Public Policy Scholar of the Society for the Psychological Study of Social Issues and the American Psychological Association. Her research interests focus on policies designed to support families, juvenile justice reform, and alternative approaches to dispute resolution in family matters.

**David Finkelhor** is Director of the Crimes Against Children Research Center, Co-Director of the Family Research Laboratory, and Professor of Sociology at the University of New Hampshire. He has been studying the problems of child victimization, child maltreatment, and family violence since 1977. His work on the problem of child sexual abuse is reflected in publications such as *Sourcebook on Child Sexual Abuse* (Sage, 1986) and *Nursery Crimes* (Sage, 1988). In his recent work, he has tried to unify and integrate knowledge about all the diverse forms of child victimization in a field he has termed Developmental Victimology. He is editor and author of 11 books and over 100 journal articles and book chapters. In 1994, he was given the Distinguished Child Abuse Professional Award by the American Professional Society on the Abuse of Children.

**Mark R. Fondacaro** is Associate Professor of Psychology and Associate Director of the Levin College of Law Center on Children and Families at the University of Florida. He teaches law and social science, children's law, juvenile law, scientific evidence, criminal law, psychology and law, consultation and social intervention, and abnormal psychology. His core research interests focus on procedural and distributive justice and their relationship to family conflict resolution, juvenile justice reform, ecological jurisprudence, school violence prevention, and health care decision making.

**Douglas A. Gentile** is a developmental psychologist, and is an assistant professor of psychology at Iowa State University and the director of research for the National Institute on Media and the Family. Dr. Gentile has authored numerous studies and is the editor of the recent book, *Media Violence and Children: A Complete Guide for Parents and Professionals.* He directs the Media Research Lab at Iowa State University where he conducts research on media's impact on children and adults (both positive and negative). He received his doctorate in child psychology from the Institute of Child Development at the University of Minnesota.

**Matthew Owen Howard** is Professor of Social Work and Professor of Psychiatry at the University of Michigan where he teaches courses in psychiatric diagnosis and substance abuse treatment. His research interests include delinquency, personality disorders, and substance-induced neuropsychological impairments in adolescents. Prior to joining the faculty at the University of Michigan, Dr. Howard was a Research Assistant Professor in the Department of Psychiatry and Behavioral Sciences at the University of Washington, a Research Associate Professor in the Department of Psychiatry at Oregon Health Sciences University, and Associate Professor of Social Work at Washington University.

**Dale Kunkel** is Professor of Communication at the University of Arizona, where he studies children and media effects issues. In the 1990s, he was Co-Principal Investigator on the National Television Violence Study, one of the largest scientific studies of violent content.

**Susan P. Limber** is Associate Director of the Institute on Family and Neighborhood Life and Professor of Psychology at Clemson University. Dr. Limber's research and writing have focused on legal and psychological issues related to youth violence (particularly bullying among children), child protection, and children's rights. She directed the first widescale implementation and evaluation of the Olweus Bullying Prevention Program and co-authored the blueprint for the Bullying Prevention Program. Currently, she is providing consultation to the National Bullying Prevention Campaign. In 2004, Dr. Limber received the American Psychological Association's Early Career Award for Psychology in the Public Interest.

**Thomas D. Lyon** is Professor of Law and Psychology at the University of Southern California. His research interests include child abuse and neglect, child witnesses, and domestic violence. He is a past president of the American Psychological Association's section on Child Maltreatment and a former member of the Board of Directors of the American Professional Society on the Abuse of Children. He has published over 20 papers; has given over 30 research presentations at psychology conferences; and has conducted over 60 trainings with judges, attorneys, law professors, social workers, psychologists, and reporters. His work has been supported by the National Science Foundation, the United States Department of Justice, the National Center on Child Abuse and Neglect, the California Endowment, and the Haynes Foundation.

**Nicole Martins** is a doctoral student in the Department of Speech Communication at the University of Illinois at Urbana–Champaign. Her research interests include the social and psychological effects of mass media on children and adolescents. She is currently working on studies of the impact of media violence on children's emotions. She also is a research assistant on a longitudinal study that examines the role of the media on body image and disordered eating among elementary school children.

**Mindy B. Mechanic** is an assistant professor in the Department of Psychology at California State University, Fullerton. Her work focuses on the psychosocial consequences of trauma and interpersonal violence. Specific topics she has studied include intimate partner violence, stalking, domestic homicide, and the co-occurrence of child maltreatment and intimate partner violence She also works in the area of forensic psychology and has served as an expert witness in cases involving battered women charged with crimes and other legal cases involving victimization.

**Natalie J. Purcell** is early in her career at the University of California, San Francisco, where she has been researching obstetric exposures and neonatal/pediatric outcomes. In addition to her research in the medical field, Ms. Purcell is most interested in studying the role of commercial media in subcultural and mainstream America. Her first book, *Death Metal Music: The Passion and Politics of a Subculture,* was published by McFarland in 2003. In the future, she hopes to research the role of pornography and other media in gender role socialization.

**Charles Putnam** is Research Associate Professor of Political Science at the University of New Hampshire. He joined Justiceworks, a research and development institute at the University of New Hampshire specializing in criminal justice issues, in December, 2001. He was a member of the New Hampshire Attorney General's Office for 15 years before joining Justiceworks. His research interests include the prosecution of crimes against children, the impact of technology on criminal justice information systems, and the evolving issues of personal privacy versus public access to information held by government agencies. Putnam teaches a variety of courses, including Children and the Law, Mock Trial, and Introduction to Justice Studies.

**Richard E. Redding** is Professor of Law at Villanova University School of Law, Research Professor of Psychology at Drexel University, and Director of the J.D./Ph.D. Program in Law and Psychology at Villanova and Drexel Universities. His research interests include sentencing policy for serious juvenile offenders, the mental health needs of juvenile offenders, forensic mental health issues in juvenile justice, and trying and sentencing juveniles as adults. Professor Redding has served on state and national juvenile justice task forces; conducts forensic evaluation training programs for mental health professionals; and is a consultant to the U.S. Justice Department, Office of Juvenile Justice and Delinquency Prevention.

**Catherine J. Ross** is Professor of Law at George Washington University Law School. She has been a visiting professor at the law schools of Boston College and the University of Pennsylvania. She holds a PhD in History and was a post-doctoral fellow at the Yale Bush Center in Child Development and Social Policy. Before attending law school she was on the faculty of the Yale Child Study Center. A former chair of the American Bar Association's Steering Committee on the Unmet Legal Needs of Children, she currently chairs the Committee on the Rights of Children of the ABA Section of Individual Rights and Responsibilities. She has served on the editorial boards of the *Family Courts Review* and the *Family Law Quarterly.*

**Diana E. H. Russell** is Emerita Professor of Sociology at Mills College, Oakland, California. She has authored, co-authored, edited, or co-edited 17 books, mostly on sexual violence. Her book, *The Secret Trauma: Incest in the Lives of Girls and Women,* was co-recipient the C. Wright Mills Award for outstanding socially significant social science research. Her three books on pornography include an anthology entitled, *Making Violence Sexy: Feminist Views on Pornography, Against Pornography: The Evidence of Harm* and *Dangerous Relationships: Pornography, Misogyny, and Rape.* She is currently seeking a publisher for her manuscript entitled *Stolen Innocence: The Damaging Effects of Child Pornography—On and Off the Internet.* Her research interests continue to focus on sexual abuse and violence against girls and women.

**Nancy Signorielli** is Professor of Communication at the University of Delaware, Newark. Her primary research area focuses on television content and how media images are related to people's conceptions of social reality (cultivation theory). Her research examines gender roles, media messages about health and nutrition, and television violence. Her research has appeared in numerous journals and edited books including *Sex Roles,* the *Journal of Broadcasting & Electronic Media,* and the *Handbook of Children and the Media.*

**Laurie N. Taylor** researches and teaches on video games and digital media at the University of Florida. She has published articles in *Game Studies, Media/Culture, Computers and Composition Online,* and *ImageTexT: Interdisciplinary Comics Studies,* and has forthcoming articles in several collections on video games. She also writes newspaper and online gaming columns, and radio programs for the public radio program *Recess!* with the most recent program being about toy theaters.

**Brendesha Tynes** is an assistant professor of African American Studies and Educational Psychology at the University of Illinois, Urbana-Champaign where she teaches adolescent development and African American psychology. Her current research interests include race, identity, and intergroup communication online as well as the uses of multi-cultural curricula to reduce prejudice. She received a Ford Pre-doctoral Diversity Fellowship and was awarded a postdoctoral fellowship from the American Educational Researchers Association. Tynes has also published several articles and book chapters that explore adolescent online discourse.

**Barbara J. Wilson** is Professor and Head of the Department of Speech Communication at the University of Illinois at Urbana–Champaign. Her research focuses on developmental differences in how children and adolescents respond to the media. She is co-author of *Children, Adolescents, and the Media* (Sage, 2002) and three book volumes of the *National Television Violence Study* (Sage, 1997–1998). She has published over 50 articles and chapters on the impact of media on youth. Recent projects focus on children's attraction to cartoon violence, children's identification with media characters, and parents' and children's fight reactions to television news.

**Barbara Bennett Woodhouse** holds the David H. Levin Chair in Family Law at University of Florida's Levin College of Law. She is also Director of the Center on Children and Families and Co-Director of the Institute for Child and Adolescent Research and Evaluation at University of Florida. Before joining the Florida faculty, she was a co-founder of the Center for Children's Policy Practice and Research at University of Pennsylvania. Her area of specialty is children's rights and child law.

**Lara Zwarun** is an assistant professor of Communication at the University of Texas at Arlington, where she teaches advertising and communication law. Her research focuses on the effects and regulation of sensitive media messages.